PENGUIN BOOKS

FRANCE IN THE NEW

John Ardagh was born in Malawi, East Africa, the son of a British colonial civil servant. He was educated at Sherborne School and Worcester College, Oxford, where he took an honours degree in classics and philosophy. Between 1955 and 1959 he was a staff correspondent of *The Times* in Algeria and in Paris, where he began his long critical relationship with the French. Between 1960 and 1966 he was a staff writer on the *Observer*, and he has since been a freelance journalist and broadcaster, specializing in French, German and European affairs. His books include *Rural France*, *Germany and the Germans*, *Writers' France*, *Ireland and the Irish* and *France Today*. He is also continental editor of *The Good Hotel Guide* and a former member of the Franco-British Council. He remains a passionate believer in the battered old ideal of European unity. He lives in Kensington with his German wife, Katharina, and their two omnipresent Burmese cats, and he has one son by a previous marriage.

France in
the New Century

Portrait of a Changing Society

JOHN ARDAGH

PENGUIN BOOKS

To my wife
KATHARINA
and to my son
NICHOLAS

PENGUIN BOOKS

Published by the Penguin Group
Penguin Books Ltd, 27 Wrights Lane, London W8 5TZ, England
Penguin Putnam Inc., 375 Hudson Street, New York, New York 10014, USA
Penguin Books Australia Ltd, Ringwood, Victoria, Australia
Penguin Books Canada Ltd, 10 Alcorn Avenue, Toronto, Ontario, Canada M4V 3B2
Penguin Books (NZ) Ltd, Private Bag 102902, NSMC, Auckland, New Zealand

Penguin Books Ltd, Registered Offices: Harmondsworth, Middlesex, England

First published by Viking 1999
Published in Penguin Books with revisions 2000
1 3 5 7 9 10 8 6 4 2

Copyright © John Ardagh, 1999, 2000

CONTENTS

Contents

Contents

PREFACE

This book, written in 1998 and brought up to date in 1999 for this Penguin edition, is based on several months of recent field research in Paris and in the provinces, and gives a portrait of France as it moves into the new century. It also draws on material from my previous book, *France Today*, to present a broad picture of how France has changed since the war. It describes the anxious mood of the 1990s, but also looks forward to what may be a more cheerful future, as this basically very stable, prosperous and talented nation moves into the age of the euro.

There is rather more about politics than in my earlier book. I have looked at the Mitterrand years, the first Chirac years, the work of Lionel Jospin's Socialist Government, as well as at the recent corruption scandals, the rise and the current crisis of the Front National, and France's role in Europe. But primarily this is not a book about party politics, nor is it about foreign affairs. It is a study of economic, social and cultural change in France, with the accent on the provinces more than on Paris. And it is based on more than 1,000 recent interviews and informal talks, with people of every kind – technocrats and schoolgirls, farmers and factory workers, grocers and theatre directors, big-city mayors and ethnic immigrants.

I first lived in Paris in 1955–9 as a staff correspondent of *The Times*, and I have returned to France regularly ever since, sometimes staying for several months. During these decades I have seen the style and mood of the nation change radically, and more than once. Like other Francophiles, I have developed a lively love–hate relationship with this stimulating and exasperating people: but mainly it is love, and I feel as much involved in France as in my own country. So this book tries to look at France from within, more from a French than an English viewpoint. It is severely critical of many things in France, but much in the way that a reformist-minded Frenchman might be – and how the French do endlessly criticize their own country today! The book takes for granted all that is unique and lovable about French civilization. As the French say, *qui aime bien, châtie bien*.

Using the techniques of the serious analytical reporter, rather than the academic specialist, I have travelled again to nearly every corner of this land. In the late 1990s I have returned to many of my favourite cities and rural regions, to study their latest development – for example, to Grenoble, Toulouse and La Rochelle, to Brittany and the southern Massif Central. I have seen again many old friends. Everywhere, even in Paris, I have always met with courtesy, readiness to help, a high degree of Gallic articulateness, in every social class. The French can sometimes be tiresome: but if you go out to meet them on their own terms, rather than patronizing them in English, they can also be as charming and amusing as any people on earth.

This book examines the impact of the World Cup victory, of Disneyland and the Channel Tunnel – as well as of the euro, high unemployment, racist attitudes to immigrants, and fear of globalization. And indeed relations with British visitors and residents, and the latest admiration for many things English – from *The Full Monty* to the very full Tony.

My list of acknowledgements is on page 740.

NOTE: Europe – what's in a name? Quite a lot, for it can cause confusion. It was originally called the European Economic Community (EEC): 'Common Market' was never more than a nickname, often used pejoratively. Since the ratification of the Maastricht Treaty in 1993 it has become the European Union (EU). In this book, I use the term EU when referring to the present, EEC when referring to the past. The money figures are in French francs: the franc is fixed at 6.56 to the euro within that zone, while as I write, it is 10.0 to the £ sterling, 6.2 to the US dollar.

1

INTRODUCTION

At the end of the World Cup, in July 1998, when France exploded with joy and over a million people packed the Champs-Élysées, it was more than just the celebration of a triumph on the football field. Even the serious *Le Monde*, in its front-page editorial, wrote of 'something which could symbolize a change of epoch ... the idea that something has changed, or can change, in our collective consciousness ...' In part, it was the victory of a very multiracial team, in a nation prone to racism or feeling vaguely guilty about its racism. But it was more than this. The French seemed to be expressing a collective aspiration that somehow the Cup might break the evil spell of gloom, self-doubt and bad news that had coloured recent years. Of course it is absurd to suppose that a sporting success can change a nation's fortunes. But *Le Monde*'s editor was then not the only Frenchman who felt that the victory, symbolically, might mark a turning point, even provide a spur towards renewal of optimism. Had not President Chirac, in public, been repeatedly urging the French to snap out of their famous *morosité*?

During the 1990s the French have been through a bad period, due to multiple factors, some of them self-induced. The many corruption scandals in high places, the cynical leadership of Mitterrand, then the inept premiership of Alain Juppé, all served to fuel the public's disillusion with politics and politicians – dangerous in a democracy. Coupled with this has been the rise of the extreme-Right Front National (FN), worrying to many French; the growth of urban discontent, notably among young people from the ethnic minorities, who feel excluded; the high rate of unemployment, caused in part by France's rigid labour laws; and the new anxieties about 'globalization' and the place of France in this American-led world. Most French are still pro-European: but some pundits worry about France's 'national identity', not so much within Europe as in a broader sphere where French influence may have been waning. All these and other issues have led the French into a crisis of confidence about the future.

The problems are real. Yet, seen in perspective, it has to be asked whether they justify the degree of gloom. The French economy today is basically rather strong, its business leaders face the euro age with assurance, and most people enjoy a fair level of prosperity. After a poor patch, the economy boomed ahead again in 1997–8, as unemployment began to fall and Lionel Jospin's new Socialist Government was proving quite popular – all of which, along with the World Cup, served to brighten the mood a little. This may lend weight to the view that some of France's problems could prove temporary, or partially solvable, at least the political and micro-economic ones. And some of France's partners have been facing quite similar troubles and doubts: unemployment is as high or higher in Spain and Italy, while Germany still worries over its ill-digested eastern regions. The French, in fact, seem to have caught a dose of German angst. Ever mercurial, they have been going through one of their cyclical periods of crisis and self-doubt. And yet, if they think about it, they can reflect on their many assets and strengths in a modern prosperous society, after the amazing progress made in so many fields during the post-war decades.

France then went through a spectacular renewal, as the pre-war stagnant economy turned into one of Europe's most dynamic and successful. Material modernization proceeded at a hectic pace in the 1960s, as an agriculture-based society became mainly an urban and industrial one. Prosperity soared, bringing changes in lifestyles and throwing up some strange conflicts between rooted French habits and new modes. The French themselves seemed to be changing. Many grew fired with a new energy, a zealous faith in what seemed to be the technocratic cure-all of economic growth and technical progress. Long accused of living with their eyes fixed on the past, they suddenly opened them to living in the modern world – and it both thrilled and scared them.

Later, by around the 1970s, when the thrill had worn off, the French came to realize that rapid material expansion – unsurprisingly – had not cured all the ills of their rigid society. It was still beset with barriers and vested interests, still saddled with some outdated structures, notably the too powerful and too centralized State. Since then, various reforms have come, willy-nilly: the role of the State *has* been pushed back, in industry and finance and in local government. But its heavy bureaucracy still pervades much of daily and working life; and though the French complain about it, they are still unsure how to cope without it. Since the war, France has transformed itself remarkably: both mentally and physically, it has adapted in many ways to the modern world, without losing its own style. But in some other ways, its society and its structures are still not well adapted, and this underlies today's malaise. This book will try to trace that complex story.

If today's crisis is partly in the mind, so the roots of the first amazing post-war renewal are also psychological. They date from the wartime period, even earlier, and they relate to the birth rate, and the shock of the 1940 defeat and Occupation. France in the 1930s was an extreme example of the Western malaise of the time: industrial production was declining, the mood of the nation was sullen, defeatist and protectionist. The population, too, was slowly falling. For a developed nation such as France, a low birth rate can be dangerous; and today France is still underpopulated in relation to her neighbours and her size. As early as 1800 she had begun to fall behind her rivals in rate of growth, owing to social and political factors such as the Napoleonic laws of equal inheritance. In 1800 she had 28 million people, compared with Britain's 16 million and 22 million in what is now Germany: but by 1910 she had risen to only 41 million, overtaken both by Britain (45 million) and Germany (63 million). She then suffered worse than her rivals from the Great War, and after 1918 the demographic decline continued.

French politicians grew worried, and in 1932 a first attempt was made to check the decline, with the creation of family allowances. These brought results: in 1935–9 the birth rate crept up from 87 to 93 per thousand. Then the Pétain Government, disastrous in other ways, did at least promote a strong pro-family policy: so the birth rate under the Occupation was not as low as might have been expected. After 1944 the child allowances were extended, and have since been among Europe's highest. They were a cause of the demographic boom of the post-war years, but not the only one: it was due also to deeper psychological factors, to what the famous demographer Alfred Sauvy called 'a collective conscience', a survival instinct spurred by the shock of wartime defeat. According to him and others, this rising birth rate improved the nation's morale, thus spurring the new dynamism of the post-war era. In 1945–6 the rate jumped up to 126 per thousand, then stayed at roughly that high level until the 1960s, whereas in most of Europe it fell back sooner. The annual net increase of births over deaths stayed at between 250,000 and 300,000 right up until 1974; and owing to this and to immigration (including 800,000 repatriated settlers from Algeria in 1962–3), the population rose from 41 million in 1946 to 50 million by 1966. This rise, along with the rural exodus, provided a growing pool of labour, which helped enable industry to expand so fast until the mid-1970s. *Le bébé-boom* also brought with it a new cult of youth, as a symbol of national rejuvenation, in a land hitherto addicted to patriarchal values.

Since the mid-1960s the birth rate has fallen again, quite considerably, as in much of Europe. In France this has been due to the relatively late spread of birth control and legalized abortion, so that few children born today are unwanted. Also, many couples may hesitate to bring children into a country with high unemployment; or they have become more egotistical in wanting to lead their own free lives. But the fall has been less dramatic than in many countries: today the reproduction rate (i.e. the average number of children born to a woman) is 1.7 in France – behind Ireland and Sweden (both 1.9) and Britain (1.8), but well ahead of Germany (1.3) and Italy and Spain (both 1.2). Births in France still exceed deaths by around 200,000 a year. And the population is still rising: the 1998–9 census showed it to be just 60 million, slightly more than in Britain or Italy.

The second major factor behind the French post-war recovery was the effect of the defeat of 1940 and the Occupation. These humiliations, following the decadence of the 1930s, provided the French with a much-needed traumatic shock: it opened their eyes to the nature of their decline, and it stimulated some of the more forceful ones to take action to stop it happening again. The victorious British were spared this kind of shock: it may be one reason why we did not develop the same eager post-war energy as the French or the Germans.

Even the Vichy regime, though odious in many respects, contained a few incidental elements which helped pave the way for later recovery. In agriculture and regional development, Vichy's corporatist policies may have served to generate a new sense of local self-dependence. But more important than Vichy itself, the war gave the French a breathing space in which to rethink the future: under the enforced paralysis and inactivity of the Occupation, they had time to plan and regroup, while the British were too busy fighting. Many of France's post-war achievements and reforms can be traced back in inspiration to those years. Young farmers began to form the little groups that later took the lead in modernizing peasant agriculture; in the Church, priests and laymen were preparing for the new Catholic social activism that was to give so much to France. Even Sartrean existentialism had some roots in the Occupation. Elsewhere, little groups of *Résistants* and Free French were plotting how to renovate France's economy and structures: most important of these was the group formed around Jean Monnet in Washington, and out of it grew the 'Plan', that vital motor of the post-war revival.

After 1945, parts of industry and the upper civil service began to discover a belief in progress that was absent before the war. The innovating technocrat came to the fore. At first this new ethos was confined to some pioneers in key posts, like Monnet and his team, and to a few local leaders who sprang up around the country, like the Young Farmers. The rest of the nation stayed with its eyes on the past, protecting its *positions acquises*. But gradually, during the 1950s and '60s, the new spirit spread more widely. Before the war, the French had lived by a set of values based on stability, the golden ideal: now they moved to new values of growth and reform. Many people came to believe in progress and accept the need for change, however much some might still fight to defend their vested privileges when change presented itself. Today, in another age, the zestful faith in progress has waned: but this does not undo the contribution of France's remarkable transformation in the post-war decades.

It is often assumed that the French recovery was due essentially to de Gaulle and his decade of political stability, 1958–69. But the truth is more complex. His regime did achieve a good deal: but it also hindered much, or merely continued a process already in motion. In nearly every sector the transformations were under way by the time he returned to power, though overshadowed by colonial wars and weak, shifting Governments. The Plan had laid the foundations of industrial recovery, then a strong and stable civil service provided continuity of politics, despite the fluctuating leadership of the Fourth Republic. And it was this, not the Fifth, that prepared French opinion for the EEC and signed the Treaty of Rome, so vital for the new France. This is not to say that de Gaulle's record in the 1960s was negative. He was able to restore French self-confidence; and in many instances, his strong Government applied difficult key reforms where its weak predecessors had failed. But as many of the initial post-war changes took years to reach fruition, the Gaullists often managed to steal the credit for them, cleverly but unfairly.

The 1960s under de Gaulle were modernization's heyday, as France visibly put on a new coat of paint and the consumer society arrived like a whirlwind. It may all seem old hat today. But at the time the changes were strikingly dramatic – material changes, followed by social and psychological ones – as an old traditional society, in many ways backward, suddenly espoused the 'modern' world. To live through the process, as I did then in Paris, was exhilarating. Materially, for better or worse, picturesque squalor gave way to a new glitter, sometimes garish, sometimes elegantly French. Quiet old streets filled up with Renaults and Citroëns; new factories emerged in empty valleys; rows of badly needed apartment blocks appeared on the outskirts of every town. Along Paris boulevards, the grey house façades were scoured clean, while skyscrapers began to alter the city's familiar skyline, and odd novelties such as *le drugstore* made their début. It all led some to fear that France was losing her soul, selling out to an ill-digested Americanization. But most people welcomed this ritzy new world of affluence and technology. After all, the French have always been devoted materialists in their way; and after some initial reticence they threw themselves into the consumer society as eagerly as any people in Europe. The urge to make money and enjoy its fruits lent a potent motivation to their post-war work mania: like the Germans, they rebuilt and modernized their country through a mixture of technical flair, material ambition, and sustained hard work at all levels.

France seemed in some ways to be making a leap straight from the early nineteenth to the late twentieth century. The French, who do not do things by halves, moved in one sweep from the little corner shop to the largest hypermarkets in Europe; then from an antiquated telephone service to the pioneering Minitel. Under the momentum of economic advance, society shifted its balance, as agriculture's share of the active population fell from 35 per cent in 1945 to 9 per cent by 1980 (today it is 4.8 per cent). This mass exodus from the country to the towns, plus the high birth rate, caused France in the post-war period to undergo the kind of rapid urbanization that Britain knew in the previous century. Many cities tripled in size. The provinces, once derided as 'the French desert', shared even more than Paris in the economic upswing: towns such as Rennes or Dijon, quiet backwaters till the 1950s, became vibrant with new activity.

However, these and other changes were far from smooth. They created tensions, as small archaic firms were pushed out of business, or as the rural emigrants struggled to adjust to the alienation of suburban life. The new prosperity was unevenly shared, nor was it always accompanied by the needed reforms of bureaucratic public life. De Gaulle's Government did attempt a few measures to bring the fusty old formal structures into line with the new conditions and expectations. But they were not enough, and were often blocked by vested interests. And so the frustrations built up. They found their sharpest expression in the May '68 uprising, which was sparked off by a few Leftist students, then joined more widely by millions of French of all sorts. May '68 had complex causes, but above all it was a protest against the failure of economic change to be matched by social and structural change: it was the cry of a new-rich society discovering that expansion in itself was not enough. It was not an attempt to put the clock back, but to shift the direction of progress. The bourgeois students were in revolt against their stifling education system; then many others – workers, *cadres*, professional people – gave vent to their own, very different frustrations (see pp. 14, 163). The revolt soon fizzled out: it did not alter the political status quo, nor lead to big reforms, save in the universities. Yet its wider influence was to linger on. In working life, in education, even in families, it dealt a blow to the old French patterns of obedience to authoritarian rule, and it brought in a new spirit of freedom and initiative.

Despite these important shifts at grassroots level, the 1970s then saw the first signs of the kind of malaise that has developed recently – based on a weariness with politics plus economic anxiety. May '68 had not brought political change, nor any real social reform, and this disappointed many people. Under Georges Pompidou as President, then Valéry Giscard d'Estaing, they grew bored with having the same kind of centre-Right regime in power for so long. Yet many of those same people did not want to risk the adventure of a left-wing Government that would include the Communists. So France lacked the alternation of power that is normal and healthy, and the regime seemed to be growing stale and cynical. It led to a sullen public mood, made worse by the economic slow-down after the 1973 oil crisis. In France as elsewhere, this coloured daily life, as unemployment became a serious problem for the first time since the war. So the boom years were over, so it seemed – and this hit hard at the French psyche, since expansion had become so potent a creed. Maybe a god had failed? The French had grown so used to a steady 5 or 6 per cent annual growth that a drop now to 1 or 2 per cent seemed a calamity. You could say they were acting like spoiled children deprived of some luxury toy, for in fact real incomes continued to rise, if more slowly, and only a few jobless people were suffering real hardship. So *la crise* – the word on all lips – was less material than psychological: a fear of worse to come. The French had grown to expect an unending vista of ever larger cars, smarter flats, more lavish holidays. Now they were forced to reckon that this kind of happiness can be fragile. The technocrats' ardent gospel of growth began to ring hollow in their ears.

These diverse influences had led the French by 1981 into a strange phase, quiescent but not entirely negative. Beneath a rather grey public surface there were curious undercurrents, as people groped in disparate ways towards new outlets for their ideals and desires. In a word, they were shunning formal public life and turning back to private satisfactions both hedonistic and spiritual, to a renewal of links with the traditional past, and to a search for new kinds of community on a small and practical level. Oddly this entire trend seemed to be *both* a defence against the economic 'crisis' *and* a reaction against the earlier too-rapid material change. It also symptomized the backlash against politics. Ideologies were now out of fashion, as were institutions of all sorts. Various bodies saw their prestige or following decline, alike the left-wing unions, the Church, the universities and organs of State. Instead the French were engaged in *le repli sur soi*, a trend endlessly discussed by sociologists – a withdrawal into privacy, into greater dependence on personal resources, on small circles of family or friends, or local forms of community. For example, the churches were still emptying, yet more people were turning to informal groups of private prayer. And this nation of ex-peasants was nostalgically seeking some renewal of contact with its rural roots and with nature. It was turning against vast technocratic projects, the 'gigantism' in vogue in de Gaulle's or Pompidou's day, and was seeking out 'quality of life'.

It all added up to quite a striking change of mood, maybe marking a desire of the French to regain their balance after the era of hectic modernization. But they were not rejecting modernism or the consumer society: they wanted to have their cake and eat it, to find ways of reconciling new affluence with old traditions, so as to enjoy the best of both. One social analyst, Professor René Rémond, suggested to me in 1980, 'The pendulum has been swinging back. In the 1950s the French moved from the values of stability to those of growth and change. Now they shift back to stability. So we see the persistence of traditional values. But I do not regard this as reactionary.' These same trends are still strikingly evident today, twenty years later. There is the same flight from institutions, the same mix of a search for private satisfactions and new kinds of community.

Meantime, France in the 1980s had its first period of Socialist rule under the Fifth Republic. After the centre-Right had been in control for so long, this alternation of power was necessary and healthy, and it passed off smoothly. The Socialists did not produce nearly so radical a shake-up of society or the economy as they had planned – and this disappointed many of their supporters on the Left. On the other hand, they learned to come to terms with the market economy which many of their leaders had so much hated, and they proved able to govern moderately and efficiently. Some of the old demons of Left/Right manicheism in France were thus finally laid to rest, and a greater spirit of consensus emerged. Much was due to the strategy of President Mitterrand, who modernized his party, helped to guide it towards social democracy, and cleverly pushed his Communist 'allies' on their way to further decline. It was ironic that the positive record of his first years in power was followed, in the early 1990s, by his final period of weak, misjudged and even corrupt rule, which has contributed to the current French malaise.

The Socialists produced some valuable reforms in the early 1980s, notably their devolution of local government. This was a vital step in a land where the centralized power of the State, often a strength in the past, was becoming a liability under modern conditions, both for the economy and for democracy. Did not the old nanny-knows-best approach serve to discourage local initiative, or drive it into sullen opposition? The 1980s devolution has in practice had its problems: it has in turn created plenty of French-style feuding, and in some ways it has strengthened local centralized fiefdoms. But it is widely accepted as a move in the right direction. Later Governments, under Chirac, Balladur and Juppé, have since followed it up with massive reductions of centralized state control in the economic field – privatizations of banking and industry, and now deregulation, as decreed by Brussels. Even Socialists have generally accepted these moves as inevitable, if France is to compete in the new 'liberal' world which it cannot escape. However, some old-style Jacobins are still ranged against the doctrinaire 'liberals', so there has been repeated debate on what should be the proper role of the State today – at the national and economic levels, and in daily or local affairs.

The French have had a long love-hate relationship with the State. They resent it, yet cling to its apron-strings and expect it endlessly to provide. People grouse against state supervision, yet often they fail to circumvent it by making use of the scope they do have for improving their lot. Thus local citizens will sign angry petitions demanding government funds – or today maybe civic funds – for some new venture, say a crèche or youth club. It will seldom occur to them to group together, raise the money, then run it themselves. Happily, there have recently been some signs of change, as local people finally show more readiness to form ad hoc associations for this kind of self-help. But it is not easy to change rooted attitudes. In face of the contentious French temperament, the Jacobins still argue that if you give the French autonomy, they will often abuse it by splitting into warring factions (as happened with the post-1969 university reforms). State control has been falling out of fashion: but can there be a growth of new kinds of civic and community spirit? This has been one drama of France in recent years.

In private, family and social life, the French have evolved remarkably in the past three or four decades, as belatedly they have followed the British, Americans and others along the path of greater freedom and informality. Women have achieved more real equality. Sexual permissiveness developed hugely during the 1970s, though it has since been slowed by the rise of AIDS and other factors. Within the family, paternal authority weighs less heavily and parent/child relations are now more frank and equal. Even in schools, the old disciplinarian ethos has yielded since 1968 to an easier and more human teacher/pupil rapport. Some of the old guard regret these changes, and speak of a decline of moral values: certainly young people reject the old codes, yet they have been moving back towards the family for support, and today they are sceptical but serious, and not political rebels. In terms of lifestyles, the French are infinitely better housed than forty years ago; many have secondary country homes or take exotic foreign holidays (maybe with Club Med); and the waning of the old peasantry has brought big changes to rural life.

Some official reforms have been guiding French life along similar paths. Abortion was legalized in 1974, the death penalty was abolished by Mitterrand in 1981, television was freed at last from state control, and labour relations were modernized, giving stronger rights to unions and works councils. At the same time, management has become less authoritarian, generally more sympathetic to workers' aspirations. And yet, despite many moves of this kind, towards a more open and liberal society, France is still beset by varied obstacles, in official and in working life. Some are due to the heavy weight of state bureaucracy and its myriad regulations, which recent Governments have been trying to lighten, but slowly and half-heartedly. Others relate to vested interests not amenable to reform, or that Governments dare not reform. In many public firms, staff cling stubbornly to their rigidly stratified privileges, which can make modern flexible progress more difficult. And though social mobility may have increased a little, promotion in many careers can still depend on having the right contacts and diplomas: if you fail to acquire these in youth, then your advance can be blocked for ever.

This élitist system, epitomized by the Grandes Écoles, is today more than ever under question: but reform is slow. Some modern reformers argue that France, despite all the big changes, is still too much a 'blocked society'. According to this theory, economic change rendered out of date the old administrative and social structures, and only slowly and painfully have these been adapting. Lifestyles may have altered: but basic character-traits, built round individualism, social mistrust and desire for formalism and routine, have been slower to change. And so has the legal and official framework deriving from the French character. But more reform is now on the way. In 1998–9 Socialist plans were finally going ahead for making the judicial system independent of Government.

A last and crucial question: in modernizing, has France been losing her soul, the essential qualities of her unique civilization? French and foreigners alike are aware that much of what is best and best-loved about France, more maybe than in many countries, is bound up with a certain traditional civilized way of life and thought – in the arts and philosophy, in food, conversation and much else. And today? The performing arts are still lively, throughout France: but in the world of new creative culture, all is not so well. Paris, *ville lumière*, is no longer the world's art capital, and her theatres offer few new French plays. Where are the new front-rank French artists, writers or philosophers? Television, happily freed from state control, has relapsed into commercial mediocrity. This general malaise may be common in Europe today, but appears sharpest in France by contrast with her past glory. Or is it that the French have grown too seduced by their new material consumerism, or conversely too obsessed by new economic worries, to have so much time or concern for creative involvement in the arts or literature? At all events, our old image of France in the 1950s or earlier, fecund and original in culture and thought, but economically weak and politically unstable, has had to be revised.

Yet in many fields, not only artistic, the French have shown that they can bring a distinctive flavour to modern life, or can still innovate with a French flair and style. Three examples, maybe not to all tastes, are *nouvelle cuisine*, the inventive sensuous elegance of the Club Méditerranée, and the grand new monuments in Paris (often designed by foreign architects). And the French have been turning back to their cherished traditions, in folklore and the quality foods of the *terroir*, in a concern for local history and the restoration of old buildings. Tradition is not being lost. But what the French have lost a little, maybe, is their self-confidence about the role of their civilization in the world. They have become too defensively concerned with what they often describe, sometimes in self-mockery, as '*l'exception française*'. But are they so unique? They are good Europeans, with a strong and respected place in Europe. And despite recent doubts, most of them know that is the way of the future. They may however be emerging from a difficult period. Much will now depend on their political leadership.

In brief, these are some of the problems and challenges facing France in the new century. The following chapters will look at them more closely.

THE MITTERRAND YEARS:
FROM CRYPTO-MARXISM TO SOCIAL DEMOCRACY

Founded by Charles de Gaulle in 1958, the Fifth Republic has now lasted more than forty years, across five presidencies – his own (1959–69), Georges Pompidou's (1969–74), Valéry Giscard d'Estaing's (1974–81), François Mitterrand's (1981–95), and now Jacques Chirac's. During this time it has proved on the whole a success, and has provided stability – even during the periods of 'cohabitation', as today, when President and Government are of different political colours. The Presidents may have been of uneven quality, but several of their Prime Ministers have been excellent men of calibre – I would mention Jacques Chaban-Delmas, Raymond Barre, Pierre Mauroy, Michel Rocard, Édouard Balladur and today Lionel Jospin. Mitterrand was able to modernize his Socialist Party and help woo it away from its old crypto-Marxist leanings, towards a de facto social democracy. The Socialists then proved that normal alternation of power can work perfectly well, even in this once so polarized country. In the 1990s France's leadership may have faltered – but this is only one of the factors behind today's disillusion with politics.

There was disgust with politicians, too, in the years of the Fourth

Republic (1946–58), with its shifting, short-lived Governments. Then de Gaulle did much for France during his reign. He solved the Algerian problem, restored French self-confidence, and brought in a political stability which has endured. His technocratic Government showed far more vigour than its weak predecessors in pushing through valuable reforms in face of sectional opposition, for example in Paris town-planning. Yet in many cases the Gaullists' high-handed approach, their failure to consult those concerned, lost them much of the cooperation that the reforms needed to be fully effective. Towards the later 1960s their regime lost much of its earlier energy and idealism and veered towards classic conservatism in closer alliance with big business, even though de Gaulle was no lover of that milieu. He became ever more obsessed with national prestige, with costly projects such as Concorde, and less with the mundane needs of social progress. For these and other reasons, frustrations built up: yet the Left, weak and divided, offered no effective challenge. So France was in a political vacuum. The General's towering authority held the nation together, in a sense: but while many people found this reassuring, beneath the surface there were tensions.

This was the background to the May '68 uprising which shattered the calm. No one foresaw it; no one imagined that a revolt led by a handful of left-wing students in Paris would spread to infect the whole nation. There were various strands in the May movement – euphoric, revolution-ary, materialist and reformist, to put them in ascending order of import-ance. First was the element of national carnival. '*La France s'ennuie*' was the heading of a much-quoted article in *Le Monde* a few weeks earlier, and certainly the French were growing bored with years of papa-knows-best government. The barricades, the waving flags, the hitch-hiking across a strike-bound Paris, the jolly workers' picnics in the occupied factories: it is not to belittle the more serious aspects of the uprising to say that all this appealed to the theatrically minded French. Some observers even dismissed the whole affair as little more than a euphoric irresponsible holiday. But some rebels were revolutionaries in earnest, the Maoists, Trotskyists, anarchists and other little groups: for them, this was no carnival. Although many showed a vagueness about the kind of new society they wanted, they were patently sincere. 'Our society is rotten, I'm devoting my life to creating workers' communes,' said the educated daughter of a rich Parisian. Many of these *gauchistes* were rebelling against their own bourgeois milieu that put its stress on money values and competitive careerism. But, alas for them, their ideals were shared by few of the industrial workers whom they tried to rally to their cause. The rank and file went on strike because they wanted a larger share in the consumer society, not because they were sated with it. Hence the revolution's failure.

The most original aspect of the uprising was that these two groups were joined by large sections of the French artistic, scientific and executive intelligentsia, protesting against many of the real obstacles to the modernizing of public life. Their revolt was against over-centralization, failure to delegate power, clumsy bureaucracy and rooted privilege, in nearly all the professions as well as in industrial and office life. Doctors proclaimed the abolition of their old hospital hierarchies, while architects demanded of Malraux the liquidation of their 'evil' guild; even footballers occupied the HQ of their federation and hoisted a red flag. Maybe there was an element of carnival in all this too, a desire to show solidarity. But nearly all the protests were basically serious, a bid to achieve a more humane system, and to modernize old practices and structures which France's economic revolution had rendered out of date.

How far did the pioneers succeed? In the short term, there was no dramatic change. De Gaulle was able to put an end to the factory strikes by granting generous wage rises. Then fear of anarchy and Leftism provoked such a reaction among the conservative 'silent majority' that the Gaullists scored a landslide victory at the special general election in June. So politically the status quo was restored. A few reforms followed, but except in the universities they were hardly radical (see p. 553). And yet, as this book will suggest, May '68 was to leave a subtle and lasting impact on French life in many spheres: in schools and families, in ecology and consumer movements, in labour relations, regional affairs, justice and the role of women. It was a varied process. In some professions the mandarins soon reasserted their authority, the soviets dispersed and the brave resolutions added up to little. But in many other cases a more open spirit did emerge and has since survived, however confusedly, in firms and offices, in schools and colleges. Monsieur le Directeur is now readier to listen to the views of his juniors, and there is more human contact between the strata of the hierarchy – even if this has created new problems, in a nation with little aptitude for group decision and initiative.

De Gaulle stayed in power for another year. But he was now ageing, and he did little to answer the grievances expressed in the May revolt. After his resignation in April 1969, his former prime minister, Georges Pompidou, was elected president. This at first gave heart to reformists, for Pompidou chose as his own premier a man of known liberal intentions, Jacques Chaban-Delmas, who in turn named two radical civil servants as his chiefs of staff: Simon Nora, who had worked with Pierre Mendès-France, and Jacques Delors. They pledged themselves to unblock France's '*société bloquée*', and their Kennedyesque programme did have a few successes, notably in labour relations. But it soon became clear that Pompidou's own radicalism had strict limits. He believed that the priority for France was to become more wealthy, and most social problems would then solve themselves, for they sprang from a backward economy. He was a pragmatic conservative. Thus he allowed Delors's incomes policy deals to go through, as a way of keeping the unions quiet. But when it came to radical structural reforms that could impact on vested interests, he said no. His relations worsened with the excellent Chaban, whom he dismissed in 1972 and replaced with Pierre Messmer. Pompidou, a former banker, had close contacts with the business world, and he allowed various dubious property deals and town-planning abuses to go through almost unchecked. One radical said to me, 'De Gaulle may have been arrogant, with an outrageous foreign policy: but he had high integrity, and we felt that in his day the regime had a basic morality. Under Pompidou, we're not so sure.'

When he died in 1974, the French elected a more youthful president, on the non-Gaullist centre-Right, who brought with him a bolder vision of liberal reform – or so it seemed at first. He was to prove an enigmatic figure, this Valéry Giscard d'Estaing. He was an aloof super-technocrat, and a patrician élitist with a private social life of château weekends among the rich and titled. But he was equally a 'modernist' with an international outlook, anxious to move French society closer to the more open Anglo-Saxon model, which he admired. Once elected, he proclaimed a plan for wide-ranging humanist reforms, leading to his '*société libérale avancée*'. The results were to prove very uneven, and many critics were soon doubting his sincerity. Yet most probably he did genuinely set out wanting reform, but was then foiled by a mix of circumstances and his own failings.

He began well. In his first months, he reduced the age of majority and franchise from twenty-one to eighteen (a generous move, seeing that the young tend to vote Left); and he pushed through abortion reform (see p. 614) in face of hostility from most of his allies in Parliament. He also set in train the Haby reforms that aimed to bring more equality to education (see p. 535); and he gave a more liberal framework to state broadcasting. But other projects then fell foul of world recession, which forced him to switch his priorities. Worse, throughout his mandate he suffered harassment from his Gaullist partners, whose backing he needed for his majority in Parliament. The right wing of the Gaullist party upset his plans for a capital gains tax and blocked some other measures too, while his prime minister in 1974–6, Jacques Chirac, Gaullist leader, was personally jealous of him and openly critical of some of his policies. Giscard also had to face the rise of the united Left. The narrowness of Mitterrand's defeat in the 1974 election (he polled 49.2 per cent, against Giscard's 50.7) made the Socialist leaders feel that victory next time would be theirs: so they were in no mood to accept Giscard's efforts to woo them into collaboration. France remained polarized, and this did not favour Giscard's vision of promoting a more open society.

By the end of his seven-year mandate, he had made some progress with social reform, if much less than planned. He did more than his predecessors to reduce wage inequalities, to help the elderly and handi-capped, to check land speculation, and to promote new policies for the environment, in answer to new French aspirations for better 'quality of life'. But it also seemed that he steadily lost his reformist zeal: caught between opposing factions, he grew fatigued and cynical. For example, one major project for a new deal in labour relations was blocked by employers and unions alike. Many moderate Socialists were at heart sympathetic to his aims, but for tactical reasons they did not want to help him, and they hated his aloof style and snobbish milieu; on the other side, his own conservative electorate opposed much of his reformism. So this was the irony: he had come to power intending to change society, but millions who had voted for him wanted just the opposite. And he simply lost interest.

He was betrayed also by personal weaknesses. Initially at the Élysée he tried to show that he *was* capable of the common touch: in a bid to break through the stiff ceremonial around the President, he walked about in shirt-sleeves, gave breakfast to his dustmen, invited himself to dinner in ordinary homes. The public mostly approved: but many critics scoffed at it as PR gimmickry, or patronizing, or demeaning the dignity of his office. Soon he realized that this casual style did not come naturally, so he gradually swung to the opposite extreme. He became secretive, even monarchic, insisting on being served first at table in the presence of state guests, including Mrs Thatcher. His regime became more authoritarian, intolerant of criticism: he even began legal proceedings against *Le Monde*.

And then various scandals began to erupt: above all, he imprudently accepted a gift of diamonds from the hated African tyrant Bokassa, then acted evasively when pressed to reveal the facts.

By 1980–81 many French were simply growing bored with a centre-Right regime that had been around for too long – ever since de Gaulle's return in 1958. Giscard himself, when I visited him at the Élysée in 1979, spoke to me of the dangers to France if alternation of power were delayed too long: 'Sooner or later, the Socialists must share in government: that is the biggest single issue facing France. In Britain, the United States, West Germany, you have a normal alternation that is vital for democratic health. But in France, the strength of the Communists within the Left makes this harder to achieve without great risk. So my aim is to keep the door open to the Socialists.' For some years he wooed them, but without success. 'The French,' he once said, 'really want to be governed from the centre', and he felt that the artificial division of politics into Right and Left did not correspond to public opinion. But the Socialists did not want to be seen to consort with their enemies. For this, and for other reasons, they preferred to say no and bide their time.

'*Enfin, l'aventure!*' was the banner headline in one paper after the Left's victory in 1981. But what adventure was it to be? François Mitterrand, a successful minister under the Fourth Republic, was a late convert to Socialism: but in 1971 he had managed to win the leadership of this fractious and enfeebled party, and then used his immense authority and skill to build it up. He disliked the Communists, but electorally an alliance with them was essential: so a Joint Programme was signed, and it held. Even so, the Left's long march to power took another decade, for many middle-class floating voters, though fed up with the Right and ready to give the Socialists a chance, remained wary of an 'adventure' comprising the Communists, still so Stalinist. Even a mere five months before the presidential elections of May 1981, the opinion polls were giving Giscard a 60 to 40 lead over Mitterrand. But then the margin narrowed, and in the final vote Mitterrand polled 51.7 per cent to Giscard's 48.2. The swing continued in the National Assembly elections in June, when the combined Left scored 55 per cent, its highest vote ever. The Socialists and their allies won 289 seats and the Communists 44, while the Right *in toto* had only 155.

The alternation of power, routine in many countries, was quite a novelty for France: yet it passed off smoothly, and Mitterrand promised no crude acts of revenge against the old regime. His reign began in 'a state of grace', as he called it, a national mood of excitement that carried along even many sceptics and Giscard voters. 'Suddenly, everyone is a Socialist,' said one sceptic, 'just as after the Liberation everyone was a Gaullist or *Résistant*. I don't myself care for this French tendency to jump on the bandwagon, suck up to the victors. But the honeymoon will end, you'll see.' It did, finally: but at the start there was dancing in the streets, uncorking of champagne by teachers and students: in public offices the grim clerks behind counters suddenly seemed more friendly, and even the police were nicer. In the civil service, the transfer of power after twenty-three years went more smoothly than many had predicted. A few senior officials resigned or were asked to leave, including some university rectors, prefects, TV chiefs: but there was no general witch-hunt. France has never known the American 'spoils system'. When a minister changes even within the same Government, he takes his personal staff (*cabinet*) with him: but the permanent officials stay in their places (except in unusual times, such as at the Liberation), and they are ready to serve a new regime, out of public duty (or career interest). This happened in 1981, and has done so since, in 1993 and 1997.

Mitterrand was no Marxist: but by 1981 he had made it clear that his model was not the mild north European brand of social democracy. He and his Socialist colleagues wanted something more radical. And when they took office, their stated aim was to go beyond a point of no return: to make decisive changes in the balance of French society and the economy, which the Right would not be able to reverse if back in power later. In the Paris *beaux quartiers*, and in many a château, there was gloom and foreboding, even some attempts to take money or valuables out of the country. But Mitterrand, lover of French tradition, was at pains to be reassuring: all would proceed by gradual changes, without any revolution that would make France cease to be France. He placed moderates in the key positions: Pierre Mauroy as Prime Minister, Jacques Delors as Finance Minister, and so on. So the disquiet on the Right gradually abated: there was no brutal Marxist takeover as some had feared. However, the Socialists went ahead as planned with their programme of nationalizing key industries and banks (see p. 77), aiming to weaken decisively the grip of capitalism in France. For equally doctrinal reasons, they promoted a strong policy of reflation, as the best weapon against recession and unemployment: money was poured into higher minimum wages, welfare benefits, new public sector jobs, and so on. But this policy wrought havoc with the economy (see p. 70), thus forcing the Government by late 1982 into a tough fundamental choice: either to persist more radically down its left-wing path, with a dose of protection-ism, or else to switch over to austerity measures – at cost to Socialist ideals. Mitterrand himself was torn. But finally he was persuaded, by Delors and others, to take the latter path. His strong 'European' instinct guided his decision, since protectionism would have led to a serious breach with the EEC. But it put paid to the costly largesse launched in 1981.

This U-turn proved to be the most crucial turning-point in the thinking and behaviour of the Left in post-war France. Mitterrand's 'conversion to economic realism' (as many observers put it) meant that he now espoused the market economy and began even to praise free enterprise. And such was his authority that he pulled most of the Socialist Party with him towards the centre: its dogmatic left wing, hitherto so large, vocal and influential, became strangely silent. Indeed, one of the party's greatest achievements during its first years in office was its victory over itself. Without losing its unity, it loosened its old crypto-Marxist shackles and developed a more modern outlook. Mitterrand's secretary-general, Jean-Louis Bianco, told me: 'We have now discreetly done our Bad Godesberg, though without openly admitting it' (a reference to the German Socialist Party's more formalized switch to social democracy in 1959).

Despite their initial economic mistakes, the Socialists' overall record of reform during their first term, 1981–6, was positive. In the field of human rights, they gave better protection to coloured immigrants, they obliged the police to behave more gently and modernized the labour laws, while Mitterrand's abolition of the death penalty belatedly brought France into line with the rest of the EEC. He gave generous new support for the arts, under the popular young Culture Minister, Jack Lang; and he pleased ecologists by cancelling much-contested plans for a big new nuclear station in Brittany and a new Army firing range in the Cévennes. The regional devolution package (see p. 282), finally reducing the cen-tralized power of the State in local government, was perhaps the most important and far-reaching of all the Socialists' reforms.

And yet, though most of these measures were popular, troubles were piling up on other fronts. The austerity programme disturbed even many of those who accepted its necessity. It infuriated hard-Left Socialist voters, who turned against Mitterrand. And it destroyed his pact with the

Communists, who pulled out of his Government in 1984. Then the first of various political scandals began to break, sullying the Socialists' reputation for integrity and honesty. By now they had disappointed many on the Left for failing to deliver the promised utopia; and they were still mistrusted on the Right. Their popularity slumped. And in the general election of 1986, the Right won an overall majority of seventy seats.

This led to the novelty of France's first period of 'cohabitation', or shared power. Under the constitution devised by de Gaulle, the president has a seven-year mandate and the National Assembly a five-year one, so it was inevitable that one day the two would be of opposing political colours. When the Right won, Mitterrand's mandate still had two years to run: he had little choice but to appoint a Prime Minister acceptable to Parliament, and he took the most obvious one, Jacques Chirac, the leader of the neo-Gaullist party, the Rassemblement pour la République (RPR). These two men, so different but both so ambitious, then proceeded to work together fairly well. As they broadly agreed on foreign affairs and defence, Chirac was ready to let the President exercise his constitutional right to mastermind these matters: but Mitterrand could do little to prevent Chirac from making the running in domestic affairs. It was an uneasy balancing act between rival leaders, and it cut across all French political tradition: but it proved to be quite popular with the public. This 'cohabitation' would have been inconceivable even ten years earlier, and its relative success was evidence of the decline of the old polarization.

Mitterrand astutely stayed aloof from the daily fray, thus avoiding the odium for the Government's various failures which instead fell largely on Chirac – and this put him in the stronger position of the two for the next presidential contest, in 1988. Mitterrand was now over seventy, but he stood again, and he beat Chirac by an easy 8 per cent margin. Again he dissolved Parliament, enabling the Socialists once more to ride in on the crest of his own success, albeit with a smaller majority this time. As a mark of conciliation, he chose as premier his old Socialist rival and critic, Michel Rocard, a moderate and a man of consensus. Both leaders saw eye to eye on the need for subtle, gradual change, rather than the radical reformism of the early 1980s. Rocard thus disappointed many of his admirers by failing to carry through the major social reforms which he knew were needed, for example in education and the civil service. But he managed the economy well, and was quite popular.

Until about 1990, Mitterrand's reputation remained high, and he appeared in his best form both in France and abroad. But then he made a series of uncharacteristic errors of judgement. Seeming to misunderstand the changes in Eastern Europe, he made a clumsy attempt to stop German unification. At home, in May 1991 he dismissed Rocard although he was doing well, and appointed Édith Cresson (rumoured to be a former *amour*) as France's first woman premier. This lively but provocative lady made some tactless remarks in public about Anglo-Saxons and Japanese, and in more serious ways, too, she proved inadequate (see p. 599). Under pressure, Mitterrand went back on his choice, and in April 1992 he replaced Cresson with the reliable Pierre Bérégovoy, Finance Minister and his long-time friend. Yet the errors went on. Partly in an effort to bolster his own position, the President decided to seek a virtual plebiscite by putting ratification of the Maastricht Treaty to a referendum, though he need not have done so. The 'yesses' narrowly prevailed: but many people voted 'no' against Mitterrand personally. As his rash gamble almost failed, it did not help his position. At the same time, several Socialist leaders were by now caught up in a startling series of scandals, while growing recession and unemployment were also fuelling discontent. So in March 1993 a troubled nation again voted for change: in the National Assembly elections, the Socialists were victims of the biggest landslide in modern French history, as their number of deputies fell by over 200 seats. But the Right won more by default, through its opponents' failures, than thanks to its own merits and popularity.

During a decade in power, what had the Socialists achieved as a lasting legacy? Curiously, they may be remembered less for their specifically Socialist reforms than for others more general, less doctrinaire, which had more success. In the first category, they clearly did not manage the 'decisive change', in the economy and society, which they had planned. Their nationalizations were soon revoked by ensuing right-wing Governments; nor did they in practice do so very much to help the lowest-paid, to reduce the wealth gap or dismantle vested privileges. But they did put through a series of other reforms, aimed at modernizing and lightening the structures of French public life. Not in themselves left-wing, these could equally have been enacted by a good centre-Right Government; in fact, some of them marked a bid to carry through properly some changes that earlier regimes had vaguely attempted. Mostly long overdue, these measures were broadly popular with opinion of all shades, and later Governments did not try to rescind them. They included the regional devolution; the stronger democratic basis given to labour relations, which even the employers' milieu grudgingly approved; the greater support for the arts; a reduction of state interference in the media (but the go-ahead given to commercial television had dubious results); and the improvements in human rights. Also, in a less definable way, the Socialists helped to promote a rather more open, informal and humane spirit in public life – a projection of the mood of May '68.

Almost as important as these reforms, the Socialists were able to change themselves through the practice of power, and thus to provide France with the viable alternative Government that was badly needed. Out of office for so long, they arrived draped with outmoded dogmas: but their leaders then came to terms with realities. And so they could prove that, whatever their mistakes, they were fully capable of governing moderately and responsibly. Thus they killed the old myth that democratic *alternance* in France could never work: it has now worked several times. But although the basic economic policies of Left and Right moved closer together, this left many consciences uneasy. The Socialists had to face the dilemma of being a supposedly left-wing party following a 'liberal' market-geared path, and they did not always know how to explain this to themselves or their voters. The momentous U-turn of 1983 may have been a triumph for economic realism and modern social democracy. But it angered many on the left of the party who felt that its principles had been betrayed; they also felt disillusioned that a decade of rule by 'their' party had produced little but job losses and hand-outs. Some of them thus abstained or voted Green in 1993. And conservatives remained mistrustful of the Socialist Party: so it pleased neither side. The party failed to formalize its U-turn in a coherent manner. In face of its sharp internal divisions, its leaders lacked the courage to bury the old dogmas formally and create a new social-democratic programme, as the German SPD had done in 1959.

If these were some of the factors behind the 1993 débâcle, another was the rising tide of murky scandals, some involving corruption, but not all. The first, in 1985, was the affair of the *Rainbow Warrior*: this Greenpeace vessel, while preparing action against planned French nuclear tests in the South Pacific, was blown up and sunk by French secret agents in Auckland harbour, and a photographer on board was killed. As the truth leaked out, the Government at first tried a massive cover-up, but finally the Defence Minister, Charles Hernu, an old friend of Mitterrand, was forced to resign. The President's own responsibility remained darkly unclear. The French public agreed there had been a mighty bungle, humiliating for France: one poll found 78 per cent thinking that it had been wrong to blow up the ship. Yet a majority also believed that Greenpeace was being manipulated by Soviet or other foreign interests (even British ones), and they felt a sneaking sympathy for the two agents who were 'simply doing their patriotic duty' but were then imprisoned by New Zealand. Later they were transferred on parole to Tahiti, whence Chirac in 1987 managed to get them moved back to France. Altogether it was a shocking episode that harmed France's reputation and sullied Mitterrand's own image.

Then in the early 1990s came the equally shocking affair of the 'contaminated blood' (see p. 55) which again reflected on French under-hand nationalist policies: three Socialist Ministers were charged (but later acquitted). In other cases, bribery or embezzlement emerged – fraudulent fundraising for the Socialist Party, a few corrupt mayors. Only sometimes was personal gain involved: but the whole messy situation added to public cynicism. It was felt that too many Socialists had let themselves be seduced by a new world of money and power. And some scandals involved the Élysée itself: evidence later came out that a secret telephone-tapping unit had been set up under Mitterrand, which monitored the calls of some journalists, political opponents and others. One or two members of his own entourage became involved in corruption. He may not have been directly involved: but he may have known about some of it, and this the public sensed. Even Bérégovoy, when Prime Minister, was discovered to have accepted a personal loan from an insider trader on rather too favourable terms: it was this, as much as his shame at the Socialists' defeat, that led to his suicide soon after the elections. When *in extremis* he sought the support of Mitterrand, this former close friend would not even speak to him.

History may come to take a harsh view of this statesman who, ironically, cared so much for history and for his own future place in it. Today, even many of his former supporters regard him with mixed feelings. He had supreme dignity and brilliant political skills: but his wily, aloof and secretive style could be the enemy of his socialist humanism. Of his major achievements, one was to have forged ahead with an inte-grated Europe, based on close Franco-German entente (see p. 679). The other was to have built the Socialists into a modern and united party, when others had failed: he helped to loosen the old Left/Right polarization and thus to 'normalize' French politics. He had a readiness to adapt to new situations, and this was a strength: but in his critics' eyes he lacked consistency and was opportunistic, not to be trusted.

Reserved and very private, Mitterrand was always an enigma to the French: '*le Sphinx*' was one nickname. His dual nature seemed a mix of Machiavelli and Marcus Aurelius. On the one side, he was the astute and ambitious politician, self-confident and tenacious, a man of great natural authority who played his cards close to his chest, a constant manipulator behind the suave façade – '*le Florentin*' was another nickname. On the other side, he was the sensitive, withdrawn intellectual, a lover of nature and solitude, a gifted writer steeped in literature. Even in the hottest of battles he gave the impression that part of his mind was elsewhere – musing maybe about the flowers and trees of his beloved holiday home in the Landes. These inner resources, this detachment, added to his strength as a statesman. But they also made him aloof; and near the end of his reign he developed some of the monarchic imperiousness to which the French presidency lends itself – '*le nouveau Louis XIV*' became a third nickname. Like the French kings, he left his mark on Paris with some grandiose new architectural works (see p. 316).

In his relations with colleagues he could be authoritarian, and he was often hard on subordinates, or even unkind – as in the case of Bérégovoy. He was on '*tu*' terms with few people, and his wary attitudes towards those outside his own circle contrasted with his warm loyalty towards close friends, some of them businessmen; in return, he inspired great loyalty. At the end of his life, he fought stoically against cancer of the prostate. It was discovered that he had an illegitimate daughter, Mazarine, now adult, whom he had always greatly cared for. But if the public judged him at the end, it was not for this: a politician's private life is his own business, in France.

Far worse were the revelations about his post-war friendship with a former Vichy police chief, René Bousquet, and his efforts as President to block legal inquiries into the guilt of Vichy officials, notably Maurice Papon (see p. 243). Mitterrand finally went on television for ninety minutes, to admit all this and to claim that history would pardon him. But it left a very sour taste, notably among many Socialists, who felt betrayed, about this as so much else: Jospin today tries to avoid mentioning him in public. Mitterrand is judged by the French for staying in power too long, when he was so ill. And above all, for becoming apathetic and cynical, at a time when a troubled France so badly needed the firm moral leadership that he did not give.

*

The elections of March 1993 left the Socialists reduced to 67 seats in the National Assembly, against 242 for the RPR and 206 for its UDF (Union pour la Démocratie Française) allies. Despite this humiliation, Mitterrand chose not to resign but to stay on for the last two years of his mandate, even though it would involve further cohabitation, where he would now be more weakly placed against the Right than in 1986–8. Chirac could have again become Prime Minister: but he preferred to stay in the wings and wait for the presidential elections. So Mitterrand agreed to appoint Édouard Balladur, also of the RPR, a cautious, capable man who had previously done well as Finance Minister. He was a haughty patrician, snobbish in his tastes: yet during most of his two years in office he proved one of the most popular of recent French premiers.

After the Socialists' sleaze and bickering, he appeared upright and truthful; though pompous in manner, he managed to spread an aura of competence, and his very aloofness was seen as wisdom. He got on well with Mitterrand, and their avoidance of confrontation pleased the public. His Government now held the real power, and the weakened Mitterrand kept a lower profile than in 1986–8. But Balladur was careful to avoid humbling the President, and he deferred to him on many foreign policy issues. This gentlemanly dislike of conflict – 'Ballamou' (not *dur*) he was called – marked his domestic conduct too. In face of strikes and unrest, he frequently backed down, and though hard-line Gaullists rebuked him for it, he claimed that gentle action was best. On the economic front, as recession ended, his fine-tuning helped France back to recovery; and he resumed Chirac's 1986–8 policy of privatizing big firms. His greatest triumph was in the crisis over the GATT talks: he skilfully achieved a compromise with Washington that partially pacified French farmers and could even be sold to his own public as a French victory.

By early 1995 the opinion polls were showing Balladur as clear favourite for the presidential elections of April/May. He had upstaged his own party leader, Chirac, and relations between these old friends were now sour. The discredited Socialists had no strong candidate: in the European elections of 1994 they had polled only 14 per cent, which prompted the resignation of their once so popular leader, Michel Rocard. Their one hope was Delors, whose Brussels mandate was expiring, and the polls were putting him neck and neck with Balladur. But Delors then announced that he would not stand, mainly for personal reasons. So Balladur looked unstoppable. But then, dramatically, Chirac caught up with him in the opinion polls and even moved ahead. One reason: the staid Balladur proved a poor campaigner, whereas the dynamic and eloquent Chirac pulled out all the stops. He staged big rallies, made exuberant promises that he would find new ways of curing unemployment, and of giving a sullen nation the new deal that it needed. Many voters were sceptical, but others decided to give him a chance. Balladur, perhaps too honest, was more reticent. He had some senior politicians in his camp: but the powerful RPR machine swung behind Chirac. And Balladur's Government had also become involved in fraud scandals, with ministers resigning. The second surprise of this unusual campaign was that the candidate finally chosen by the Socialists, the mild Lionel Jospin, did far better in the end than anyone had expected. The percentage voting in the two rounds was as follows:

	first round	run-off
Lionel Jospin	23.2	47.4
Jacques Chirac	20.4	52.6
Édouard Balladur	18.5	
Jean-Marie Le Pen (Front National)	15.2	
Robert Hue (Communist Party)	8.7	
Arlette Laguiller (extreme Left)	5.3	
Philippe de Villiers (nationalist Right)	4.8	
Dominique Voynet (Greens)	3.3	

On the first round, 'extremist' candidates from outside the moderate parties thus took 38 per cent of the vote, more than ever before under the Fifth Republic. The combined vote for the far Right, including de Villiers, topped 20 per cent. Never before had the eventual winner scored so poorly on the first round: he won only by acquiring most of Balladur's first-round vote, and some of Le Pen's. So Chirac's victory was a modest one. And given the condition of the Socialist Party, Jospin did amazingly well. Though not a star performer, he waged a forceful campaign which he seemed to enjoy. His high vote also revealed the degree of scepticism about Chirac.

THE CHIRAC YEARS:
JUPPÉ'S BAD TACTICS, JOSPIN'S GOOD LUCK

So how has France fared, during the Chirac presidency – first with Alain Juppé of the RPR as Prime Minister, then with the Socialists under Lionel Jospin?

Jacques Chirac had been twice Prime Minister, and a powerful mayor of Paris for eighteen years. He was known as supremely ambitious: his goal had always been the Élysée Palace, which he had now achieved on a third attempt. Tall and handsome, he had terrific energy and a breezy informal charm; despite his élitist background he also had the common touch and was genuinely at ease with such people as the peasants of his Corrèze constituency. His warmth of heart and his 'social' concern were genuine too, as those close to him knew. But in his eagerness to be liked, he was frequently too glib in his promises. In his 1995 campaign he aimed his appeal at younger voters, promising '*le changement*': yet he was a conservative, over sixty. His real views on many issues were ambiguous, and he had often seemed too influenceable: 'His ideas are those of the last person he's talked to', it was said. Thus his support from the centre of politics was always limited. This time, enough floating voters gave him the benefit of the doubt, but others remained wary.

As his Prime Minister he chose Alain Juppé of the RPR, a cool technocratic figure but brilliantly capable, who had just done well as Foreign Minister. They formed a Government from the RPR/UDF coalition, as before. It would be wrong to call Chirac an old-style Gaullist nationalist, but some of his first measures were aimed at reasserting France's presence on the world stage. Maybe he felt this could bolster the flagging self-confidence of the French: but some of it was misjudged. He angered world opinion (and much French opinion too) by resuming nuclear tests in the Pacific; he annoyed his EU partners by delaying the Schengen measures for ending border controls. But he held to the key goal of EMU, saying he wanted the French to become 'more patriotic and also more European'. At home, he promised to scale down the 'monarchic' style of presidency, and to reduce bureaucracy and techno-cratic élitism: but it was not clear how this would be done. Above all, he promoted a 'one nation' vision of France that harked back to de Gaulle. He vowed to 'engage all my strength in restoring the cohesion of France', which had been damaged by loss of jobs and other ills; and he promised to put more public money and effort into fighting the 'gangrene' of unemployment. But he also planned to reduce the huge public deficit, in line with meeting the EMU criteria of a maximum 3 per cent of GDP – and many experts argued that the two aims were incompatible. However, Juppé produced a budget that aimed to reconcile the two: new subsidies for job creation were balanced by public spending cuts and tax increases.

Juppé soon ran into serious trouble. His austerity measures, plus his tactless and high-handed way of presenting them, both aroused massive opposition. And in November/December France was paralysed by a three-week general strike, led by all the main unions: trains and Métro did not run, people hitch-hiked to work, and anti-government rallies were held in several cities. It was the worst unrest since 1968. And once again it began in the universities, then spread to other sectors. But as commentators pointed out, it was all very different from May '68. The students were not promoting revolution: they and their teachers simply wanted better funding. And across France, this was no eager, forward-looking crusade to reform society: it was a scared attempt by various interest groups to hang on to their perks, jobs and privileges – especially among civil servants and railwaymen, who faced the biggest cuts. Compared with May '68, it was all very unidealistic, even selfish. Many strikers were expressing their distaste at having to make sacrifices for EMU and their growing fears about globalization; or they felt that Chirac was failing in his pledge to create jobs. So the great 1995 strike vividly illustrated the French *morosité* of the time.

Juppé managed to salvage the central aspects of his main reform, to reduce the deficit in the health service (see p. 153). But he made enough concessions on other fronts – over civil service pensions, cutbacks in the railways, etc. – for the unions to feel that they had won their case, so the strikes subsided. Yet the sour mood continued. And throughout 1996 and early 1997, opinion polls showed Chirac and especially Juppé as among the most unpopular of Fifth Republic leaders. In Juppé's case, it was a matter both of policies and of personality. He had been admired as Foreign Minister, alike by his foreign colleagues and his own ambassadors: but while good with diplomats, he lacked the common touch, despite coming from a fairly modest provincial background. He had then been through the French élitist training system, to become a proud *inspecteur des finances*, and this confirmed his arrogant technocratic streak, while his analytical mind earned him the nickname of 'Amstrad'. In 1995 he prepared his reforms with utmost thoroughness, and they were mostly sensible and much needed, in economic terms. But he set about imposing them with very little consultation: the more tactful Socialists, two years later, were to have far more success with some quite similar measures! He was a bad speaker, and he came to be seen as too sure of himself, too cold and uncaring. Sensing this, he made efforts to change his image: but it was not in his nature, and he failed. His reputation also suffered from his alleged involvement in the Paris housing scandals.

Whatever Juppé's own shortcomings, the French were in such a peevish, insecure mood that they might have taken it out on any Government. They remained generally hostile to his strategy of belt-tightening, despite his concessions. And many of them grew disillusioned at Chirac's failure to fulfil his campaign pledges. He had promised more jobs and lower taxes: but, as predicted, this proved incompatible with the state of the economy and the priority of cutting deficits. He had simply been very incautious. Equally, there was not much sign of his plans to simplify bureaucracy, or to heal the divisions in society and help *les exclus*. Had he been insincere all along? Or, more probably, did the reason lie in his choice of Juppé, effectively in charge, who was not very concerned, and nor were several of his key ministers, with such humanist priorities? Many young people who had accepted Chirac's campaign overtures now turned against him.

Chirac intervened very little in the strike crisis, and during 1996 he continued to keep aloof from the daily struggles, letting Juppé take the flak. Thus his own popularity did not suffer so much: many French when questioned said that they disliked his policies but still liked the man. As President, he managed quite well, personally. He used his natural charm and bonhomie to good effect, for example, on his state visit to Britain in May 1996; and while retaining the dignity of his office, he was more informal and jovial than Mitterrand. Like other French Presidents, he made defence his special preserve, and he took some major initiatives: a closer reintegration of France into NATO, and a decision to end compulsory military service (see p. 722). During this time, Juppé was becoming ever more criticized by the rank and file of his own party, the RPR, and several Gaullist barons were pressing for his dismissal.

Then in April 1997, Chirac suddenly dissolved the National Assembly and called a general election, though none was due for another year. He claimed to be acting 'in the name of Europe', so as to gain a new mandate for proceeding with EMU: but this was only part of the truth. In reality, he knew that further heavy and unpopular austerity measures would be necessary to meet that EMU goal: so he calculated that it would be wisest to have a snap poll first, before matters grew worse. He also saw the advantages of catching the Socialists unprepared, while they were still in disarray after their 1993 defeat. However, he reckoned without the canny French electorate, which did not like being manipulated and taken for granted to suit his own tactics.

The Socialists, it is true, were still mistrusted: so the Right was expected to win narrowly, despite Chirac's tactics. But Jospin quickly rallied his troops and once again he waged a very effective campaign. His patent honesty and warmth, his easy, likeable manner, made a contrast with Juppé, on all the hustings. The election was fought on the usual domestic issues such as employment and social services, rather than on EMU itself, which both centre-Right and Socialists saw as a risky vote-puller, best avoided (see p. 689). During the campaign, Jospin and his Green and Communist allies clearly edged ahead, and finally on 1 June they won by a margin of 62 seats. And so, a bemused electorate re-elected the same party that it had so roundly expelled only four years earlier. As then, the victors won more by default than on their own merits: there were a million spoiled ballot papers, and the turn-out was the lowest for forty years. Significantly, it was the fifth time running, since 1978, that voters for the National Assembly had thrown out the sitting majority – a fickleness that seemed to symptomize their disillusion with politicians. The results were as follows:

	percentage of votes (first round)	number of seats
Socialist Party	25.0	253
Communist Party	9.9	38
Greens	5.3	7
Various Left	5.3	21
(Total Left)		(319)
RPR	15.7	134
UDF and allies	14.2	108
Various Right	6.6	15
(Total Right)		(257)
Front National	15.0	1

Lionel Jospin, a former Education Minister and economics lecturer, got off to a brisk start. He formed a Government that included three Communists, a Green and several distinguished women. And he promised to govern with 'clarity and honesty'. His first problem was to deal with EMU before the EU's Amsterdam summit in late June. He and the bulk of his party were not nearly as opposed to EMU as British Eurosceptics wishfully thought: but they wanted to get its conditions modified to suit French needs, and this they largely achieved, in bargaining with the Germans (see p. 689). So the French still had a Government committed to EMU and its obligations: but it was Juppé's way of handling the issue that they had resented, more than EMU itself, and by now they had rallied to the single currency by about two to one.

For his domestic programme, Jospin was bound by the Socialists' election manifesto. But as they had not expected to win, this had not yet been fully thought out – and it led to some embarrassments. Notably, Jospin was saddled with a plan, which he had not expected to have to apply so soon, for reducing the legal working week to 35 hours – and it was promptly criticized by employers, economists, even a few of his own ministers, as likely to damage the economy yet do nothing for job creation (see p. 185). Apart from this, Jospin's programme was largely moderate, realistic, less 'ideological' than that of the party in 1981. He even carried on with much of Juppé's plan for reforming the Social Security, and with some aspects of privatization – quite a step for a Socialist. His Government set about tackling youth unemployment more directly than Chirac, through measures for creating 700,000 new jobs: again, sceptics wondered how this could be equated with reducing budget deficits.

Jospin's election pledges had included no more austerity, no extra taxes, and above all – Élysée, please note – a promise to keep his promises. But in practice he, too, did not quite succeed, during his first months. The EMU criteria forced him to impose new taxation and new spending cuts: however, the former went mainly on businesses and the latter on defence, so his own voters were not too directly affected. He also felt obliged, in face of reality, to slow down the time-scale of applying the 35-hour week and some other social measures. Growls about 'yet more broken promises' rose up on the left of his coalition. But Jospin's record was not as bad as Chirac's; and he was much more readily forgiven than Juppé by the public and the media. First, he was more likeably open and honest about it. Second, the economy was now improving fast, so the French had less to worry about.

This recovery was indeed the major development of Jospin's first year in office, and a wonderful piece of good luck and happy timing. The heavens shone on him, as did the dollar. The economic boom in America spread its influence into Europe, first to Britain, later to France, where unemployment began to fall – as did the budget deficit – and investment to grow. But this upturn was not just a foreign windfall: it was thanks also to the much-derided Juppé, whose dogged austerity policies were now starting to bear fruit under his successor, leaving the economy in a healthier state than for some years. Thus France, against the odds, was able to meet the EMU criteria. It was an ironic recompense for poor Juppé, after his brash courage – and for Chirac it was a personal disaster. He was publicly seen to have misjudged the timing of his election gamble. If he had waited the full term of Parliament, he might well have won.

After the election he was depressed for quite a while, according to his friends: 'He's eating a lot of charcuterie, drinking a lot of beer, and that's a sure sign,' said one. Isolated and pushed aside, he kept a low profile and it was Jospin who now had the whip hand: so Chirac seemed again to have lost out from *cohabitation*. Later he rallied, and began to snipe at the Government's 35-hour week project, also to interfere in a few policies outside the President's 'reserved domain' of foreign and defence affairs. So *cohabitation* today, though still liked by the public, has again been bringing some tensions. And this time it is set to last five years, not two: Chirac's and the Assembly's mandates will both end in 2002.

This has revived the old debate as to whether the system should not be changed, probably by revising the Constitution so that both mandates always coincide. The seven-year/five-year set-up, devised by de Gaulle to suit himself, was bound to lead sometimes to *cohabitation*. It has generally worked well, as a *tour de force* of French political maturity and pragmatism. And it is popular: it provides a balance of power which the French like, and it allows all main parties to have a say in government at the same time. But this can become clumsy and obstructive, and it leaves the role of the President ambiguous during these periods, more so than that of the American President in face of a hostile Congress. In France, he can no longer be a strong ruler as de Gaulle envisaged: but nor is he just a figurehead as in Germany. Since mid-1997, political leaders as diverse as Delors and Giscard d'Estaing have been calling for a rethink, and maybe a change. Such a reform today looks finally more probable.

During the Socialists' first year or so back in power, both leaders stayed quite popular in the opinion polls, Jospin more so than Chirac. After the

World Cup victory, their ratings shot up sharply, and both were being measured as among the most popular French leaders of recent years. Amazingly, one opinion survey in late July showed that even among Gaullist voters, 53 per cent were satisfied with Jospin's record; and even Front National supporters were more solidly in favour of him than against! Amid the euphoria of the World Cup, these figures should not perhaps be taken too seriously. But certainly the public mood is today much less morose than in early 1997; and Jospin since taking power has risen to fulfil his new role rather well. Even in July 1999, a Sofres survey was giving him 68 per cent and Chirac 55 per cent. And today many experts consider that he has a good chance of winning the presidential elections in 2002.

This upright Protestant, former first secretary of the Socialist Party, then an able Education Minister under Rocard, has always been seen as solid and reliable, if not charismatic. He is an *énarque* from the élitist education stream (see p. 90), but not technocratic like Juppé, more academic. His manner is precise and pedagogic, but he has humour, some warmth, and an engaging smile below his tousled white hair. Above all, he is seen as straightforward, honest, uncorrupted. And he carries most of his party with him, even though some on its left wing regret that he has shifted from doctrinaire Socialism towards a more pragmatic stance.

Europe itself has been shifting to the left: today, twelve of the fifteen EU states have Socialists in government, and the three most powerful of them are Socialist-led. By coincidence, Labour's victory in Britain was followed four weeks later by that of the French Left. Tony Blair is today admired in France (see p. 698), especially on the centre and moderate Right where his 'third way' is seen as more modern and enlightened than the French Socialists' approach. Some British observers like to compare Blair's New Labour with what they see as an unreconstructed 'Old Labour' in France. But this may not be quite fair. It is true that France remains more state-directed than Britain, but this is an old legacy, not the Socialists' doing. It is true also that in the 1980s their leaders never dared to convert formally to social democracy and bury the old doctrines. And today the change have yet to be made: there is still a desire to avoid conflict with the left wing of the party, and among moderates there remains some residual loyalty to the old Leftist ideals. But in practice – if less so than with New Labour – there has been tacitly quite a shift towards pragmatic market-geared policies. So Jospin's Socialists have no clear ideology. They do not care for the new post-Thatcherite 'liberal'

Europe, but they go along with it, and they try to soften it where they can. Blair's success has been influencing them, in a muddled way. 'The Left is doing well, but is it still socialist?' wrote the Socialist journalist Gilles Martinet with a hint of chagrin. 'In a world where capitalism seems triumphant, socialism's only ambition is to limit its all-powerfulness.' In 1999, when Michelin, despite its huge profits, announced sweeping job cuts, Jospin at first protested, then said resignedly, 'You can't expect the State to do everything.' The left of his party, and the Communists, saw this as another sign of his betrayal of Socialist values.

The Government installed in 1997 has been led mainly by moderates. Dominique Strauss-Kahn, who was Minister of Finance and Industry until 1999, was a realist and pro-European; he had crucial influence and was close to Jospin. Balancing him, and further to the left, was Jacques Delors's daughter Martine Aubry, deputy premier, Minister for Employment and 'Solidarity', and a believer in state intervention. Hubert Védrine at Foreign Affairs and Elisabeth Guigou at the Justice Ministry are former Mitterrand protégés from the Élysée, while Alain Richard at Defence is a Rocardian. The Interior Minister, Jean-Pierre Chevènement, a powerful figure with strong ideas of his own, is on the left of the party but a traditionalist.

As *Le Monde* wrote in June 1998, 'The marriage that Alain Juppé failed to achieve between the Séguin line [social Gaullism] and the Madelin line ['liberal'], Lionel Jospin has found between the Aubry line [social] and the Strauss-Kahn line [economy].' It was thus a heavy blow for Jospin when in November 1999 Strauss-Kahn felt obliged to resign. He was due to be questioned regarding fraud allegations – which he denied – dating back to 1994. He was replaced by Christian Sautter, who is continuing his policies but without the same authority.

Of Jospin's main reforms, only the 35-hour week, a project inherited from the past and demanded by the unions, can be said to be truly doctrinaire, maybe unrealistic. Other new measures, less ideological but humane, are aimed at improving social justice, helping the poor and jobless, and easing France's *fracture sociale* – precisely what Chirac claimed he wanted to do. These steps include the job-creation plan for youth, higher welfare charges for the well-to-do, and a revamping of the health service to benefit the really poor.

Jospin's team includes three Communists in the posts of Transport and Housing, Youth and Sports, and Tourism, while the Greens' leader, Dominique Voynet, is an active Environment Minister. The Socialists did not quite win an absolute majority in the elections: but even had they done so, Jospin might still have chosen a coalition, for he believes in balance and pluralism; he wants all trends represented and seems proud to preside over what is today called '*la gauche plurielle*'. They are a diverse bunch. But the coalition has remained largely under control, even though rank–and–file Communists and Greens have growled at some of its policies, such as the euro. In the European elections of 1999, the Greens, led by Daniel Cohn-Bendit from Germany, won 9.7 per cent of the vote and thus for the first time overtook the Communist Party (a mere 6.8 per cent). So the Greens proudly boasted of now being the second party of the Left, and they demanded a larger role in government. The Communists became ever more critical of Jospin's 'Blairist' policies, and his coalition has thus become more shaky. Even so, the situation is easier than it was under Mitterrand in the early 1980s, and would not have been possible without the remarkable recent changes within the Communist Party.

This party, for so long a major bugbear of the French public scene, has now at last broken out of its old Stalinist mould and has become more open and diverse – within limits. This may have helped to arrest its decline: its support has now held steady at about 10 per cent for more than ten years. But its post-war peak was 28 per cent, and it remained around 20 per cent until 1981 when its excitable leader, Georges Marchais, polled only 15 per cent. This fall reduced the Communist 'scare' and thus helped Mitterrand to victory, since many voters now felt that he would no longer be so much at the Communists' mercy. Although with his huge majority he had no need, he then chose four of them as ministers. He wanted to buy the party's goodwill and acquiescence, and that of its powerful allied union, the Confédération Génerale du Travail (CGT) – as Lyndon B. Johnson once said, when he allowed his sworn enemy Edgar J. Hoover to remain head of the FBI, 'I'd rather have that guy inside my train, pissing out of it, than outside, pissing in on me.' Mitterrand also hoped that the Communists, by sharing in the practical tasks of government, might eventually become tamed and integrated into society: his ambition was for the Parti Communiste Français (PCF) either to democratize itself or else wither away, and he saw more chance of this by welcoming it into power than by spurning it. It was a clever strategy, which has finally borne some fruit. It carried risks: but the Communists were given relatively harmless posts, such as Health and Transport, and they proved rather good ministers.

However, the PCF leaders remained wary of being overwhelmed by their rival party, now much the stronger: so they were unsure about the wisdom of being in government. After the Socialists moved to their austerity programme, the PCF became openly critical, and in July 1984 it walked out of the coalition and returned to its comfortable isolation. But this did not help it electorally: in 1986 its vote plummeted to 9.7 per cent. While its hard-line supporters may have applauded its rejection of 'Socialist capitalism', many others saw it as now more archaic and enclosed than ever, and they withdrew support. So although Mitterrand had not yet achieved his aim of liberalizing the party, he had succeeded in his alternative plan of hastening its decline. It was a notable achievement.

During those years, the PCF remained a puzzling anomaly within France's democratic society. It was no longer as subservient to Moscow as was often supposed: but it failed to shake off the classic Soviet model of 'democratic centralism', whereby decisions were taken in secret by a small oligarchy. It was something of a State-within-the-State. Many of its members as individuals have always been warm and accessible people, even idealistic, playing a useful part in the lives of colleges, factories, town councils and the arts. But the party at top level kept its ghetto mentality, and it seemed most at ease within that ghetto. So why did so many French go on supporting it? Among the diverse explanations, one was its patriotic Résistance record, not forgotten by older voters. Two, the effectiveness of the CGT in battling for better pay and conditions. Three, the party's sound record of administration in the various town councils it controlled (some big towns such as Le Havre and Calais, plus suburbs in the Paris 'red belt'). Here it could be ruthless in its systematic bid to take control of local life (see p. 212), but voters tolerated this. Four, it remained the expression of a certain old-style working-class solidarity. Five, it still benefited from the old French revolutionary tradition, which impelled so many intellectuals and students to vote on the far left (ignoring the party's ingrained conservatism).

Yet many other intellectual supporters gradually tired of its monolithic stance, its lack of real debate, its hypocrisy and condoning of Soviet abuses – and one by one they left, Sartre among them. After the fall of Communism in the east, and the centrewards shift of the Italian party, the PCF was increasingly isolated. Marchais made a few liberalizing gestures, but they added up to little. His histrionic manner in public, in television debates, with feigned rages and parading of brazen untruths, won him high ratings as a comic spectacle: but it also made him ridiculous. Many in the party came to see him as a liability: but he could not be dislodged, for he held it tightly with his clique of loyal apparatchiks. A few *réformateurs*, led by Charles Fiterman, tried to press for a more open and modern structure, but they were thwarted, and the party remained ossified and ostrich-like. Finally however, in 1994, Marchais was persuaded to stand down, aged seventy-four (he died three years later).

Robert Hue, his successor, aged about fifty, is a much easier man, warm, jovial and avuncular, a psychiatric nurse by training. He was chosen by Marchais as a safe pair of hands: but he has since diverged from his master's line and is presiding over significant changes, drawing on younger, more moderate elements whose voice is now heard. In a word, the party has become more diverse, less monolithic: 'We have no monopoly of truth,' says Hue, 'and we should admit that we made mistakes.' So the party now contains several tendencies, in open debate. First there is Hue, and his fellow leaders, followed by a majority who have more or less rallied to his line but do not want him to go too far. Then there are the old hard-liners, such as Maxime Gremetz, who try to resist change and are nostalgic for the old Marchais days: they number perhaps 10 per cent of activists. A third group, also 10 to 15 per cent, call themselves *refondateurs* and want to go further than Hue in transforming the PCF. One of their leaders, Lucien Sève, told me, 'We feel that the party should start again, rethink its role and its purpose. We should renew close contact with all those who have left the PCF, and with the rest of the Left, to build up a modern, democratic left-wing movement.' This minority group has some influence on Hue, who tries to navigate between the two extremes.

When I called on his senior adjutant, Pierre Blotin, in the party's vast concrete headquarters in eastern Paris, he said, 'We now talk much more with non-Communists. We listen to different opinions within the party, we try to find out what the workers really think, instead of imposing our views.' In a sense, this is true. The new pluralism is real: for instance, the big CGT union, though still linked to the party, it now less under its control than formerly. 'Another change,' said Sève, 'is that you can now oppose the official line and not be chucked out or treated as an enemy. Your views are tolerated. Yet the decision-making itself is still secretive: so the new *ouverture* has its limits.' The old doctrine of 'democratic centralism' has now been formally discarded, yet its practice lingers. For example, at a party congress or other meeting, various ideas can be presented and will be discussed: but there will be just one final text, prepared in secret, and not debated. Many former Communists remain sceptical about how far the party has really changed, and they do not think of returning. They include Charles Fiterman, who was so effective a Transport Minister in 1981–4.

In 1997 the PCF was divided on the wisdom of again joining a Government led by the Socialists. But Hue and most leaders were in favour, so he accepted Jospin's offer of three ministerial posts. Frictions ensued, for example, over the partial privatization of Air France (see p. 136). Jean-Claude Gayssot, the able new Transport Minister, a very moderate Communist, eloquently outlined his plans for opening up the capital of Air France; and Hue backed him, saying that nationalizations need no longer be considered essential for basic social change – quite a break with PCF dogma. But when Hue defended this policy at a party rally, he was roundly booed by hard-liners. He replied, 'The world is changing fast. We must change with it, or it will change without us' – echoing Gorbachev's fateful warning to Honecker before the Berlin Wall fell! Hue was also rebuked by the old guard for being too docile towards Jospin. But he spoke openly of his pride in belonging to this coalition of *la gauche plurielle*, and he manifestly gets on well with Socialist leaders. How times have changed. Yet the divisions within the party, and the disquiet of many older members, remain very real.

The PCF still differs from the Socialist Party on a number of issues, besides the EU. Notably, it wants a more radical redistribution of wealth and is more wary of a mixed economy. But it has also become more flexible and cooperative – witness the help it gave, in its fief of St-Denis, for the building of the World Cup stadium (see p. 329). Its membership, some 500,000 in 1975, is today estimated at 275,000. Its electoral support has ceased to fall and has even risen slightly since 1993, maybe linked to the departure of Marchais. But sales of its flagship daily paper *L'Humanité* are still declining, from 105,000 in 1988 to some 58,000 today, and it loses money. The party remains strongest in the Nord-Pas-de-Calais, the eastern Paris suburbs, parts of the Midi, and, surprisingly, in much of the Massif Central. It has lost many of its habitual 'protest' voters to the Front National, but has gained some others. In sum, it is now slowly merging into society, rather as Mitterrand planned, and has ceased to be a serious menace to French democracy.

★

It was Jean-Marie Le Pen's party that in March 1998, over the regional elections, provoked the worst political crisis on the French centre-Right for many years. Since its sudden rise in the mid-1980s, the Front National (see pp. 244–56) has been steadily scoring between 10 and 15 per cent of the vote, with a slight upward tendency. At parliamentary elections this is not translated into seats, for normally there is no proportional representation and the other parties refuse deals: thus in 1997, with a 15 per cent vote, it won only one seat. But for the regional assemblies, PR operates, enabling the Front to gain many more seats, unaided, and thus to hold the balance of power in some places. This happened in 1998, to disastrous effect. Until those elections, the centre-Right controlled 20 of the 22 assemblies set up under the regional reforms. As was inevitable, it now lost some of them to the Socialists, including Aquitaine, Ile-de-France and Provence-Alpes-Côte-d'Azur. The Front National, scoring 15.2 per cent, held the balance in several others.

In four of these, dramatically, the outgoing centre-Right presidents then began to negotiate deals with the Front, against the express orders of their parties in Paris, the RPR and UDF. Greedy to hold on to power, these local 'barons' were ready to make Faustian pacts with a devil that was eager to woo them into alliances. So they called on the Front to help them rebuild their ruling coalitions. Chirac then went on television to denounce any such deals with 'this racist party', and RPR and UDF national leaders were equally categoric: make pacts, and we expel you. Over 70 per cent of French public opinion supported this stance, according to the surveys. But locally the Right was in panic. In some regions, where the Front now held the balance, the outgoing presidents resigned rather than accept its support, so the Socialists won control. But in four others, all UDF-controlled, the alliances went ahead – the large Rhône-Alpes region around Lyon, under Charles Millon, former Defence Minister; Burgundy; Languedoc-Roussillon, led by a staunch Rightist; and Picardy, where the president pleaded an 'exception' as his opponent was a Communist. Everywhere, the Front had carefully posed tempting terms: it did not demand support for its racist policies, but simply proposed harmless joint goals such as lower taxes and fighting crime, which the UDF presidents found it easy to accept. But the parties in Paris saw it as a dangerous trap, and the four rebels were duly expelled. And before long the deals with the Front were creating serious conflicts in several regions (see p. 298). The crisis was moral as much as political.

The furore on the French centre-Right for the next few months was amazing. The ever witty John Lichfield, Paris correspondent of the *Independent*, wrote: 'A few of the President's men are trying to put Humpty Dumpty together again. Others are trying to tear him into even smaller pieces. The rest believe the only solution is to lay a new egg.' And he spoke of 'plot changes, betrayals, unbetrayals, back-stabbings, un-stabbings'. The UDF, always an uneasy coalition of centrist and rightist groupings, split in two: a moderate faction was formed around François Bayrou, former Education Minister, while the maverick Alain Madelin, Thatcherite 'liberal' and former Finance Minister, praised Millon and his fellow rebels. Then in April 1999 the RPR too erupted into crisis when its new president, Philippe Séguin, resigned, disagreeing with the pro-Europe and pro-NATO policies of Chirac. And in the EU elections of June, the decline of the classic Right was confirmed: its three lists won only 35 per cent of the votes. The Eurosceptics, led by Charles Pasqua, even came ahead of the more pro-European list of Nicolas Sarkozy. Badly demoralized, in December the RPR finally chose a new president, Michèle Alliot-Marie, a pro-European conservative. She was elected by the rank and file against the preferred candidate of Chirac, whose authority was thus further eroded. And Pasqua moved off to form his own party: so the RPR split in two.

Today the disarray of the centre-Right in opposition, and the relative success of the centre-Left after more than two years in power, present some parallels with the situation in Britain – though the reasons are different. By summer 1999, the centre-Right leaders had popularity quotients of around 25 to 35 per cent in the polls, while Jospin was riding high at around 65 per cent and his party was some 15 points ahead of the UDF or RPR. So William Hague and his Tories need not feel too lonely. Yet French democracy, in the longer term, clearly needs an effective non-Socialist opposition. For years politicians have been speaking of the need to rebuild the centre-Right, that amalgam of Gaullists left and right, and non-Gaullists of various shades. Today it is more than ever overdue, as Le Pen's army has acted as catalyst, proving how damagingly its power can upset the arithmetic of coalition. For too long the centre-Right has lacked new ideas or inspiring leadership. Now it is more seriously demoralized than at any time since the war. And this could be a handicap for parliamentary democracy. The Right is also paying the price for the mistakes of the Juppé period – and for the many corruption scandals of the 1990s. These implicated both Left and Right, but above all the Right.

CORRUPTION IN HIGH PLACES:
THE JUDGES' CRUSADES

The mayors of two big towns, Nice and Grenoble, have been sentenced and sent to prison. The former president of France's largest firm, Elf-Aquitaine, has been remanded in custody for some months in La Santé. Ministers facing charges have been forced to resign. A whole network of alleged sleaze has moved up on the mayor of Paris and his wife. And so on . . .

In short, France during the 1990s has presented the unhappy spectacle of widespread corruption in high places – bribery, embezzlement, or abuse of power, either for illegal political projects, or sometimes for personal gain. Ministers, mayors, business leaders and other household names have been involved. Over 500 political or economic leaders have been convicted, accused or put under investigation; and in 1993 some fifty-seven parliamentary deputies were facing charges. The Right above all has been involved, but the Socialists too. And former idols with glossy reputations, such as Bernard Tapie, inspiring entrepreneur, or Michel Noir and Alain Carignon, seemingly excellent mayors of Lyon and Grenoble, have been found with feet of clay. The whole messy morass includes scores of separate scandals. And the public has been left disgusted, not only by the sleaze itself, but by the efforts of those in power to protect their cronies, sometimes by deterring *juges d'instruction* (examining magistrates) from doing their job – in a land where *la justice* is not fully independent.

Political corruption, not at all new in France, began to grow worse after de Gaulle's upright reign. The 1980s were the so-called '*années fric*', when money was splashed around and companies' seduction of politicians, American-style, became more widespread. But if so many scandals have recently come to light, it is in part because far greater efforts have now been made to expose them. Inspired by the Italian example, the judiciary have grown more active, and so have newspapers: thus many *affaires* that might once have stayed hidden are nowadays ferreted out. The public, too, has grown less tolerant of abuses by those it elected, and it wants the truth. All agree that justice has become more open, more positive. But some of the crusading *juges* are today criticized for maybe going too far, and for failing to respect the '*présomption d'innocence*'. This whole matter of French justice, and its relations with politics, has become a major public issue, far more than before; and President Chirac and the Jospin Government alike have been promoting reforms, to include ways of making the judiciary more independent. A new law to this effect is now before Parliament. This chapter of my book examines first the recent scandals, then some relevant aspects of a French system of justice so different from Britain's.

It is often suggested that the Socialists' devolution in the early 1980s (see p. 290) has been one factor behind the rise in corruption – a downside of those otherwise positive reforms. Mayors and *conseils généraux* acquired much larger budgets and new responsibilities, while the prefects' controls over their spending were reduced. These local leaders were generally unused to handling such sums, so the power sometimes went to their heads and they yielded to temptation. It is true that new democratic checks on spending were set up inside councils: so devolution may also have helped bring to light some cases that in the past would have gone undetected. At any rate, some of the worst instances of corruption in recent years have been in civic affairs: in Grenoble, the mayor, Alain Carignon, a friend of Chirac and former minister, solicited large bribes from a water company and was given four years in prison (see p. 347). Michel Noir, in Lyon, was a dynamic and popular RPR mayor in the early 1990s who incautiously became involved in a sleaze affair and his career was ruined. And the scandals were not only on the Right. In Angoulême, a young Socialist teacher, Jean-Michel Boucheron, became mayor: he lost his head and overspent wildly, piling up 1.2 billion francs of debts, then fled to Argentina in 1992. But he was condemned *in absentia* to four years in prison, for fraud.

It is in Provence/Côte-d'Azur, however, with its Mediterranean habits and temperament, that scandals have been commonest. The glamorous image of Cannes was done no good by its *centriste* mayor, Michel Mouillot, who in 1996 was arrested on corruption charges. Allegedly he had received underhand money from a local British-run casino club to finance his political campaigns, and a suitcase full of banknotes changed hands in the Ritz Hotel, London. This bizarre thriller led to Mouillot staging a hunger strike in his prison, where in 1998 he was still awaiting trial. At Toulon, the record of sleaze and misspending by the former RPR mayor helped the Front National to win the *mairie* in 1995 on a 'let's be clean' ticket (see p. 251). Another murky local affair was the murder of Yann Piat, a deputy who had defected from the FN to join the UDF:

she was apparently investigating corrupt money-dealing on the Côte d'Azur when in 1994 she was shot in her car by a gunman. Later two journalists wrote a book claiming that Jean-Claude Gaudin, UDF mayor of Marseille, was behind the killing: he hit back, and they and their publisher were heavily fined by a local court. Today the truth behind the killing is still unknown: it may have been more to do with political revenge than corruption, and it caused a sensation in France. Even in the quiet Provençal hinterland, sleaze has also raised its head: in the spa town of Digne, the RPR mayor in the early 1990s, Pierre Rinaldi, was allegedly negotiating with Nice *mafiosi* to build a casino, and this involved some shady deals. The prefect at the time apparently knew, but took no action, for fear of annoying the RPR in Paris where Rinaldi had influence. But later, after Rinaldi lost office, the affair became known: he was charged, and the prefect, too, now faces sanctions. This whole mess of scandals has raised new doubts about the supervision of local finances.

Earlier, much the most notorious – and colourful – of the 'wicked' mayors was Jacques Médecin, in Nice. Since long before the 1980s reforms, he ruled his rich city in lurid Mafia style, and was later sent to prison for massive fraud and embezzlement. Yet in some other ways he had been an excellent, dynamic mayor, from 1965 to 1990, and was idolized locally. He took on a decadent resort living on its past, and through bold investment projects and skilful management he turned it into a booming, youthful business-cum-tourist metropolis, again Queen of the Riviera. He had 'inherited' Nice from his ex-Pétainist father, '*le roi Jean*', mayor in 1928–65. Médecin built Akropolis, a lavish business centre, he cleared up beach pollution, created urban expressways, renovated the *vieille ville*, rebuilt the opera house, founded the Musée Chagall, poured money into culture, and made Nice clean and tidy. Flamboyant and charismatic, with a breezy manner, a fast, glamorous lifestyle and a young blonde American wife, '*le grand Jacquou*' was a true Niçois, who ruled the city as a private fief, and was re-elected four times. 'In France,' it has been said, 'there's Paris, there's the provinces – and there's Nice', so very Italian, a kind of city-state.

Médecin himself did not belong to its powerful Mafia-like criminal milieu: but he felt the need to have links with it. In the 1970s his friends included the infamous Dominique Fratoni, implicated in the major corruption case of the Ruhl casino: it was the milieu of which Graham Greene, then living at Antibes, wrote in *J'Accuse* (1982), 'Avoid the region of Nice . . . reserve of some of the most criminal organizations in the South of France', and he spoke of 'the connivance of high authorities'. Médecin ran his city through a tight network of patronage and cronyism, centred on the *mairie*, which gave and received pay-offs: this provided the financing for his projects. But in the 1980s the city was piling up huge debts, reaching 600 million francs in some years. The fiscal authorities grew suspicious: Médecin had paid no income tax for some years, and it was thought that he had been laundering the city's turnover for personal gain. When the Right was in power in Paris, it delayed investigations: Chirac and others had been on friendly terms with Médecin (he had even been a junior minister for tourism in 1976–8) and they did not want awkward revelations. Nor did the Ministry of Justice have the courage to tackle the local judiciary, some of whom were thought to be in the pay of the Médecin network and were blocking inquiries.

But then the Socialists, back in office, sent special tax experts to Nice who uncovered plenty of evidence. In 1990, facing criminal charges and a claim for 20 million francs of unpaid tax, Médecin resigned, blaming a 'totalitarian Socialist plot', and flew by pre-arranged plan to Uruguay which had no extradition treaty with France. There he began a business selling T-shirts, and gave cheeky interviews to French TV. His son-in-law, a travel agent, organized tours to Uruguay, including '*trois jours de fête*' with Médecin. But the party ended when in 1994 Paris finally persuaded the Uruguay Government to arrest him, and he went on trial in Grenoble. There he was sentenced to two years in prison for 'passive corruption', plus another two years for embezzlement, and heavily fined. But as the sentences were to run concurrently, by the time the trial ended he had purged his term: so he slid back to Uruguay, as more serious charges were still pending. To many observers, his penalties seemed remarkably lenient. And though he had quarrelled with both RPR and UDF, he had clearly benefited, during his career, from high-level support in Paris – as Carignon and some others had done, too.

So how much, or how often, does the Government intervene to alter the course of justice or protect its friends? How independent is the judiciary? Today the system is under reform. But hitherto the Ministry of Justice has been able to give instructions to the *parquets* (local prosecutors' offices), or else to remove 'awkward' examining magistrates from a case by shifting them to other duties; or some *juges* have been afraid of offending the Government of the day, or have supported it politically.

Cases of direct pressure are not uncommon, notably when the careers of senior politicians seem at risk. By far the worst recent scandal has been in Paris and its *mairie*, since 1995. The alleged malpractices may have been less heinous than at Nice: but they have involved senior figures, possibly including Chirac himself. Indeed there is not just one scandal but several – a real can of worms – centring around Jean Tiberi of the RPR, who replaced Chirac as mayor in 1995. And the offences themselves have caused less furore than the crude official efforts to hush them up.

The first concerned Alain Juppé and the flats that he rented for himself and three members of his family, during the time that he was a Paris councillor in charge of the city's finances, before 1995. The flats belonged to the *mairie*, and Juppé was able to take them at rents far below the market rates; his own luxury apartment was refurbished at a cost to the council of over a million francs. He was Prime Minister when the judicial inquiries began, and it seemed that he might be prosecuted for 'exerting undue influence'. But the Justice Minister, Jacques Toubon, put pressure on the *parquet* and the case was dropped, in return for Juppé agreeing to move out of his flat, which he did. Much the same happened in the case of Tiberi, whose two adult children had been similarly lodged, at a time when he was in charge of the city's housing. His son Dominique's flat was rented at a third of the normal rate, and the *mairie* paid some 1.5 million francs for its renovation with marble flooring. There was an outcry: so the son gave up the flat, and the *parquet* shelved the case pending against his father. Even more peculiar was the affair of an alleged payment made to Jean Tiberi's wife, Xavière: after he became mayor, a magistrate raided their home, looking for details about a fraud scandal, and he found a document indicating that she had received 210,000 francs from a local council for writing what turned out to be a brief and banal report, apparently plagiarized, for a mayor who was a family friend. Again, the *juges* scented sleaze. But the Government, believe it or not, sent a helicopter into the Himalayas to seek out the senior *juge*, on holiday there, who alone could countermand the inquiry by his junior colleague. He refused to help, and later Xavière Tiberi was arrested for questioning.

Éric Halphen, in his mid-thirties, was the fearless young *juge d'instruction* charged with looking into the Tiberis' affairs, plus the related and far more serious matter of alleged illegal funding of the RPR by the city's housing agency. Halphen became a national celebrity, especially when the Juppé Government seemed to be using various tactics to 'destabilize' him. It made legal moves against his family; it sought to restrict his range of competence; and when in July 1996 he made his famous raid on the Tiberis' flat, the police refused to accompany him, as was their duty. Toubon, as Justice Minister, had come to office in 1995 with a promise to respect the independence of the judiciary: but he was an RPR loyalist, and he soon felt obliged to eat his words and to clamp down on them.

However, Halphen and other examining magistrates managed to go ahead with their inquiries; and over four years they amassed evidence that the HLM office of the Hauts-de-Seine *département*, plus the city's own housing development office, had allegedly been secretly involved in arranging for pay-offs from developers to be passed to RPR coffers – all this in the period before 1995 when Chirac was still mayor and Tiberi was his deputy in charge of housing! The former city personnel director also alleged that some 300 people had been on a 'fictitious' payroll at that time, at a cost to the *mairie* of 80 million francs a year. The 'phoney' report by Xavière Tiberi was thought to be an element in this network. At first the case against her was dropped on procedural grounds. But finally in October 1999 she went on trial – and Paris was agog with excitement. It was said that she hated Chirac, because he had failed to back up her husband earlier, and that if brought to trial she might well tell all about how the *mairie* was run in his time. So it seemed that the President himself could now be directly threatened and several senior magistrates were eager to question him. Since the change of government in 1997, the Tiberis and Juppé have had less protection. And the Minister of Justice, Elisabeth Guigou, has proclaimed that she was leaving the judiciary completely free. She said that a President, like any French citizen, could be brought before the courts if he were suspected of committing an offence. Alain Juppé himself was finally placed under judicial investigation, for his alleged part in the 'fictitious jobs' affair in the days when he was in charge of Paris finances. But the whole drama seemed likely to drag on for years to come.

So how does the curious French legal system work? 'The English have a judiciary of lawyers, the Germans of professors, and the French of civil servants,' wrote Max Weber a century ago. The French by tradition have looked to the State, more than to the system of justice, as the citizen's supreme guarantor: so the judiciary has tended to defer to the State and be coloured by it. The system is unlike that of Britain or

America. Notably, it is marked by a sharp distinction between the state prosecution service (the *parquet*) and the examining magistrates (*juges d'instruction*) – all of whom are known in popular parlance as '*les juges*' (the magistrature). The prosecutors (*procureurs*) are part of a hierarchy dependent on the Ministry of Justice, which can give them orders. The *juges d'instruction*, a species unique to France, are in many ways freer and more powerful. Their main role is to investigate cases, prior to making charges: they alone also have the right (until today's planned reforms) to remand suspects in custody, if they think it necessary. But they cannot open an inquiry without the authority of the *parquet*, which alone can open or close a case. In addition, there are various levels of tribunal, some involving a jury, appeal courts and a supreme quashing court. The distinction is sharper than in Britain between civil courts, dealing with private disputes, and administrative courts that handle those of a more public character. The whole system is archi-complex, and the process of law can be fearsomely slow.

'The French judiciary, since Napoleon, was installed in a culture of reverence, if not obedience, towards the political powers of the day,' says the lawyer Robert Badinter, Socialist Minister of Justice in 1981–6. Bonaparte set up a tight civil service structure, influential but docile; and from his day until recently the judiciary has been highly conservative. Its role under Vichy was shameful: only one *juge* refused to swear loyalty to Pétain and very few later joined the Résistance. Then after the war magistrates tended to be looked down on, even treated with suspicion, by politicians. Mitterrand himself, though he took law as a degree subject, shared these attitudes: he downgraded senior local magistrates in their privileges, and they took this very badly. The judiciary have always been rather poorly paid, and with their fixed salaries they earn far less than barristers (*avocats*), who are often rich. The two come from different worlds, and socially they mix little. The *juges* are trained mostly at a Grande École in Bordeaux, the École Nationale de la Magistrature: they form a closed little world, where '*ils se marient entre eux, et ils font des petits juges*', I was told.

However, in the past years a new wind has been blowing. In the 1970s a handful of magistrates of a new breed began to emerge – in the wake of May '68 and its ideas. Some young *juges d'instruction*, breaking with the old docility, started to make bolder use of their latent powers. One of them in the Nord secured the arrest of two senior industrialists – exceptional then, but quite normal today – following accidents caused by their alleged neglect of safety measures. Later, other *juges* began ferreting into the suspect financial dealings of large prestigious groups such as Elf-Aquitaine, or big city councils. And so, by the 1990s, new media stars were born, some of them today almost as famous as the politicians they have harried: besides Halphen, they included Éva Joly whose tough inquisitorial style with tycoons has become legendary. In some right-wing circles, the scare arose of '*les juges rouges de soixante-huit*', and a political plot was suspected. But none existed. In fact, the new *juges* have targeted Left as well as Right. One major scandal of the early 1990s concerned Urba, a front company set up by the Socialists to collect funds for the party. A zealous young *juge d'instruction*, Thierry Jean-Pierre, initiated inquiries which led to the discovery of illegal payments including slush-funding from contracts awarded by Socialist town councils. As a result the former party treasurer, Henri Emmanuelli, was indicted in 1992, by which time he had risen to the lofty post of president of the National Assembly. Finally he was given a suspended prison sentence, and lost his civic rights for two years. This further blackened the image of the Socialists at that time. But Jean-Pierre himself was widely felt to have been too partisan. Later he entered politics – on the extreme Right.

If no actual plot, there may have been an element of revenge in the *juges'* offensive. 'These politicians, Mitterrand included,' said one magistrate, 'they have stolen our honour and prestige, and they pay us badly. But now we'll show them! – we'll judge them, and put them in their place!' Some of the young *juges d'instruction* have been propelled by a Saint-Just-like fervour, a crusading desire to cleanse society, as in Italy. Most are fair and honest, and have been doing a valuable job in hunting down personal corruption. But just a few, so it is widely thought, have gone too far. Their new discovery of power has gone to their heads – just as it did with their foes, the corrupt mayors, after devolution. These *juges* have taken a savage pleasure in targeting power and wealth, in lashing out on all sides with their inquiries – and sometimes they have damaged the innocent. So politicians now fear them and try to protect themselves: 'We are living through a profound change in the relations between politics and the judiciary,' says Badinter. It is a struggle based on the odd paradox of a judiciary in some respects too dependent, in others maybe too powerful.

The right-wing intellectual Alain Minc analyses today's situation brilliantly in his book *Au nom de la loi* (1998). He says that, in the 1990s, France, almost unconsciously, had gone through her biggest revolution since the removal of the monarchy after 1789. Ever since then, French public life has been based not on law but on the sovereign power of the people, expressed most often, in practice, by élites ruling in the people's name. In this autocratic democracy, those who served the State, bureaucrats or politicians, came to see themselves as incarnating the people's sovereignty and being above the law. And *juges* were submissive to this system. As a result, says Minc, 'Like other Latin countries we have long functioned with an official law quite different from the applied law, a state of affairs which has always astonished the Anglo-Saxons . . . In this respect, France was more like India than the United States.' Minc quotes party funding as one example, or even drug taking on the Tour de France, long suspected and frowned on, but largely ignored until this year.

France, says Minc, has now 'surreptitiously' slipped towards 'an Anglo-Saxon situation' where laws are now applied more rigorously. Why has this change happened now, and not before? Minc quotes, first, the victory for the free market since the 1980s, which has pushed back the power of the State, enabling the law to fill the vacuum. Secondly, European law now often takes precedence over national law. Thirdly, new younger *juges* have arisen. Fourthly, *juges* and public alike were revolted by the hypocritical mix of idealistic talk and corrupt behaviour in the Mitterrand years. Fifthly, rising public anger against the élites made the politicians unable to curb the new zeal of the *juges*. Minc feels that the changes are basically for the good: but, like many others, he fears that the process might be getting out of hand. There is a danger, he writes, of an endless legal terror, in which all senior business figures or politicians might be at risk. Like the Starr–Lewinsky–Clinton case, this could at its worst turn into an irresponsible media conspiracy to destroy the powerful. One unaccountable élite might thus simply be replaced by another – and not for the first time in French history. Minc makes a plea for a refounding of French democracy, accepting the new Anglo-Saxon power of the law in French lives, but making all élites, both the political and the legal, more directly accountable to the people.*

There are some 550 *juges d'instruction*: but this is seen as too few for the amount of work to be done. Often a young, inexperienced magistrate is put on his own in a small town, and this can lead to errors. The most

---

* See John Lichfield's superb analysis of Minc's book in the *Independent* of 19 October 1998.

notorious recent case concerns the child Grégory, found drowned in a sack in rural Lorraine: the *juge*, aged twenty-eight, bungled his inquiry, lost some documents, so there was no proof of guilt, and the suspects stayed free. A *juge*, though responsible to a *parquet*, arguably has too much freedom, for example in initiating his own house searches. Even more controversial is his dual role: (a) primarily it is to conduct his investigation, but (b) he can also, if he thinks fit, have a suspect arrested by the police and remanded in custody (*détention provisoire*) for an indefinite period, while he continues to investigate. And it is the *juge*, not the *procureur*, who remands. The ostensible purpose is to prevent the suspect from escaping, or putting pressure on witnesses, or repeating his crime, and so on: but though intended mainly for common criminals, *détention provisoire* is sometimes used also against political or business people. And frequently it lasts unfairly long, or so it is felt: the current average is nearly four months, the longest in the EU. But *juges* claim that very often this cannot be helped, as it takes so long to prepare a trial.

By old tradition, *juges d'instruction* have another strong practical motive for detention: to put pressure on a suspect to make a confession. Either the threat of being locked up may make him confess, or else in his cell he can be pushed into it by tough interrogation – 'a modern form of torture, and it's shocking', one newspaper editor suggested to me. The brilliant barrister Patrick Devedjian has written in his book *Le Temps des juges* (1996):

This French passion for confession comes to us from the ecclesiastical justice of the Middle Ages. It has crossed the centuries, willy-nilly, and still seems to us the normal conclusion of any inquiry. Confession is still called 'the queen of proofs' . . . But it is a great weakness for justice to be obsessed with it . . .

The author adds that in 1254, by royal ordinance, the French monarchy adopted the ecclesiastical or 'inquisitorial' model, while England opted for the seigneurial or 'accusatory' model – and he suggests that after 750 years it might be time for France to learn something from its old rival. (But may not Britain's system lead to its own abuses? – witness the Guildford Four.)

Another point of controversy concerns '*la garde à vue*' (close watch) – the right of the police to hold a suspect initially for up to twenty-four hours, before any charge is made or an examining magistrate arrives. The period can be renewed once: then the person must be set free, or charged. He or she used to be forbidden even to speak to a lawyer: but a 1993 reform then permitted a lawyer to be present after twenty-four hours. And now the new Guigou reforms (see p. 59) will make immediate access to a lawyer a basic right for all. Hitherto the legal system has had little concept of *habeas corpus*, and this has sometimes encouraged police brutalities. These are now less frequent than in former days but still happen. In 1999 France became the first member of the EU to be indicted by the European Court of Human Rights for torture by the police. It was said that a drug trafficker, Ahmed Selmouni, had in 1992 suffered 'physical and mental acts of violence, grave and cruel' during his detention. And it is not only lowly 'common criminals' that can get cavalier treatment. In 1996, near Paris, after a disorder in a *lycée*, the headmaster was held by the police as responsible, questioned for nine hours, forced to take off his shoelaces (in case he strangled himself), and allowed to make no phone call: finally he managed to contact the Ministry of Education, which quickly got him released. 'The minister was furious,' I was told, 'but what could be do? – *les flics* are still a law unto themselves.'

Juges d'instruction are above all criticized today for their leaks to the press and their neglect of the 'presumption of innocence', in a country where the principle of *sub judice* hardly exists. *Juges* are supposedly bound by '*le secret d'instruction*': that is, during an investigation they should not give details about it, to the press or anyone else. But this rule is very frequently flouted. They will pass photocopies of their minutes to the newspapers or will connive at leaks provided by the police – and the papers will happily publish them, often assuming the suspect's guilt. *Juges* claim that they need this help from the press, in order to stave off official attempts to stifle a case, and they may sometimes be right (typically, Halphen arranged for reporters to follow him to Xavière Tiberi's doorstep). And editors claim, as in any country, that 'the public has a right to know', adding that they have a duty to help the bold *juges*.

Newspapers, which used to be rather tame, have now grown more assertive, just like the *juges*, and do far more of their own investigative reporting (see p. 510). They claim to be propelled by a public opinion that has become less tolerant of the malpractices of those in power. In many ways, this is positive: it is likely that fewer scandals are left unrevealed than in the old days. And the press is following an old if spasmodic tradition of campaigning for justice that dates from Zola and before. So *juges* and newspapers are today natural allies. But the press needs to sell its papers: often it will present news sensationally, unscrupulously, and this can bias opinion against a suspect who may well be innocent. Many lawyers and responsible journalists today feel that matters have gone too far: the legal requirement of 'presumption of innocence' is seriously infringed, and it can be the *juges*' fault for talking too much. Badinter has denounced 'this new media–judiciary union, as strong as it is irresponsible'. And the public agrees: in an opinion poll in *Le Monde*, 77 per cent of the sample thought it wrong for the press to abuse the '*secret d'instruction*'.

The British press may be worse in some respects: but at least, when legal proceedings are under way, a suspect in Britain is protected by the *sub judice* laws. Within the limits of the libel and privacy laws, the French press can say almost anything about a case while it is going on; often it will write about a suspect as if he were already proved guilty, especially if it makes a better story or if he is someone the paper does not like. So the press, with the help of *juge* or police, can conduct a virtual pre-trial. In 1973 the English tourist John Cartland was murdered in his caravan in Provence. His son Jeremy was arrested as a suspect; and the local papers, fed with details by the *juge d'instruction*, wrote articles under banner headlines, '*Jeremy, assassin de son père*'. It caused fury in Britain. Later the son was transferred to London and acquitted; robbers were thought to have killed his father, but they were never found. In the case of Maurice Papon, just before his final trial began in 1997, the TF1 channel staged its own television trial of the case, with evidence from lawyers and hostile witnesses, and a studio audience giving its views. In Britain, the TV producer would soon himself be in the dock.

The result is that some public figures have had their careers unfairly ruined. A suspect under examination gets on to the front pages, he is humiliated, perhaps forced to resign. Then, maybe years later, after the law has wound its way, the case is dropped or he is acquitted: but this merits a paragraph on an inside page and no one notices it, or they say, 'Yes, but there's no smoke without fire' – and he never recovers his earlier reputation. There have been several recent instances. Michel Roussin, *chef de cabinet* of Chirac at the Hôtel de Ville, was in 1994 investigated by Halphen over the illegal funding scandal: by then he was a minister under Balladur, who obliged him to resign. Later he was cleared: but he felt obsessively bitter, and gave up politics. Christian Pierret, Socialist deputy, was charged in 1986 over an affair of illegal financing, and not until 1995 did he get himself cleared: 'It took me nine years,' he wrote in *Le Monde*, 'to get a proper judgment in place of *un safari politico-médiatique*, during which I had to explain to my youngest daughter, "no, Daddy is not a thief." ' But Pierret has got his compensation: he is now a minister under Jospin.

These moral and legal issues are being rethought in France, as some people look to the British model for guidance. On the one hand, the laws protecting privacy are far stronger in France: it is one reason why the French press does not get filled up with details of the sex lives of politicians and pop stars (another is public lack of interest). On the other hand, though the principle of 'presumption of innocence' exists, it is less strongly enforced in legal cases than in Britain. Hence some people become deterred from taking up public duties, such as running for mayor: in the 1995 local elections, as many as 45 per cent of *élus* did not stand again. 'The law is so complicated and abstruse on many issues,' one barrister told me, 'that you just have to disobey it sometimes, in the public interest, or you never get anything done. But then these nosy little *juges* come and ferret it out, and they get you on some technical point, with the press at their heels. It's terrible.' And another added, 'Does investigative reporting, and tough inquiry by the *juges*, service the cause of true justice or not? It is the eternal dilemma of press freedom versus presumption of innocence. I personally think that the latter should now be given a higher priority than at present.'

Not only can the slowness of the law prevent the innocent from clearing their name: it can can also sometimes help the guilty, in a sense. A clever defence lawyer can find dodges to delay a trial for many years, by which time his client may have died peacefully on bail. Thus Papon evaded justice for fifteen years. In many other cases, seven or eight years have often elapsed between initial investigation and final appeal result. The French legal process grinds even more slowly than in most countries: first, because it is so complex, with over 35,000 different laws; and second, because magistrates generally lack the funding or the staff to go faster. Or so they repeatedly complain, as their offices pile up with vast files, and overwork threatens their health. It is especially the fat dossiers concerning corruption in large companies that can prove too much for their resources. Inquiry into the fraud aspects of the Crédit Lyonnais débâcle (see p. 83) had by 1998 been dragging on for five years, and was occupying twelve *juges d'instruction* full-time, in eight towns. Éva Joly, chief inquisitor, expressed her indignation.

Another spectacular recent financial scandal has concerned the huge oil company Elf-Aquitaine. In 1996 its former chairman, Loik Le Floch-Prigent, was arrested and cross-examined over money apparently given illegally to shore up an Elf textile subsidiary. Le Floch was by then chairman of French railways (SNCF), and was forced to resign: it was the first time that any head of a French state company had been sent to jail, and he spent the next six months in custody at La Santé prison, because of 'the risks of pressure being put on witnesses'. Then in March 1998, while Elf was still being investigated, the affair took a dramatic new turn as an even more senior public figure was placed under judicial scrutiny: Roland Dumas, former Foreign Minister and friend of Mitterrand, today chairman of the Constitutional Council. His mistress, Christine Deviers-Joncour, a society hostess, was arrested and allegedly admitted that she had taken 'commissions' of some 60 million francs from Elf to influence his decisions as minister, notably over the sale of six frigates to Taiwan. Dumas, examined for 'misuse of public funds', was suspected of taking kickbacks, including a 10,000-franc pair of shoes. This bizarre comedy dated from 1989–93, when Elf-Aquitaine was still a public company; and in 1998 these latest revelations of high-level sleaze under Mitterrand gave some solace to the much-battered Right. How on earth, they asked, could Dumas decently remain in his post as number one watchdog of public honesty? But he did so, even though under strong pressure to resign. By 1999 it was expected that he would be made to pay a large fine, but not be sentenced to prison.

The leading *juge* in charge of these Elf cases, and of Crédit Lyonnais and some other business investigations, has been the redoubtable Éva Joly, called '*la terreur des patrons*'. This Norwegian-born wife of a French doctor is known as a fiercely tough interrogator, a merciless avenging angel. One of her 'victims', and quite a match for her, has been the even more celebrated Bernard Tapie, the Marseillais who has upstaged Médecin as France's top charismatic rogue of recent years. In the 1980s he became an idol of yuppies as the showman entrepreneur who would take over small moribund firms, give them new life and make millions; he was also a star presenter on TV, a protégé of Mitterrand's, and Minister for Urban Affairs in 1992. But then clouds gathered. Unruly and outspoken, he was condemned several times for defamation, and once for hitting a policeman. In 1995–7 he was three times given prison sentences for fraud and suborning of witnesses, and spent a while in La Santé jail. One of these affairs concerned his luxury yacht, *Phocéa*, another the 'faked' finances of football matches played by Olympique de Marseille, the club of which he was president. Accused of embezzling 101 million francs of the club's money, he was finally in 1998, after an appeal, given a three-year suspended sentence, plus a fine of 300,000 francs and a five-year loss of civil rights.

Tapie was protected for some years by Mitterrand, who had been fascinated by his self-confident bravura and prevented inquiries. Then, after Joly and others got to work, Tapie and his clever lawyers played an amazing cat-and-mouse game with French justice, using every trick in the French legal book in order to try to avoid prison. He had to resign as minister, and finally also as deputy: but he went on hiding behind his immunity as member of the European Parliament, which in 1996 voted by a big majority to go on backing him. Then, just before going to prison in La Santé he played a starring role in a feature film by Claude Lelouch. In fact, the entire career of this epitome of chutzpah has been the purest cinema – and many French cannot help admiring him.

A far more serious scandal for the Socialists, involving not corruption but criminal negligence, was the famous affair of 'contaminated blood'. In 1991 it came to light that doctors at the National Centre for Blood Transfusion had in 1985 been using HIV-contaminated blood products as transfusions for haemophiliacs: some 1,300 patients were affected, and many later died. Four senior doctors were tried, and three were sent to prison for periods of two to four years. It emerged that although newer and safer American products were available, the French went on using their own less perfect ones – because they were cheaper, but also for nationalistic reasons. And they had the backing of the Health Ministry. By putting pressure on the state prosecutor, the Government had for years succeeded in hushing up any official responsibility. But at the doctors' trial it all came out: there was a public furore, and the Senate voted unanimously for three ministers to be tried, for 'complicity in poisoning', i.e. for having turned a blind eye – Laurent Fabius, Prime Minister at the time, and his Social Affairs and Health Ministers, Georgina Dufoix and Edmond Hervé. A special new court was created, made up of magistrates and politicians, with the role of judging ministers for offences committed while in office. And so the old debate erupted as to whether a minister should be held responsible for all that happens within his domain.* Had the politicians themselves sanctioned the use of these products? And if so, whose fault was it that their safety had not been verified? After a lengthy trial, the ministers were finally acquitted of the charge of 'complicity in poisoning' in 1998. But then the court, under strong pressure from the media, sent them for retrial on the lesser charge of 'involuntary homicide', which could still carry three years in prison. The trial was set for February 1999. It seemed unlikely that the three, if found guilty, would get more than a suspended sentence. But their careers, notably that of Fabius, had already been badly affected.

'What is the difference between Nelson Mandela and the French Government? Answer: Mandela went to jail before being elected.' So ran a joke in Paris in 1994 when several members of Balladur's cabinet were under judicial scrutiny or even in custody. The wave of recent corruption scandals has done untold harm to French morale. It has clearly been a factor behind *la morosité* and the success of the Front National. It may have contributed to the electoral defeat of the Right in 1997, since more scandals in the mid-1990s were on the Right than the Left. And the bad image it has given of politicians, and of big business, is unhealthy in a capitalist democracy.

The judiciary's efforts do seem to have produced some cleansing, at least partially, as in Italy. There may still be more scandals to come to light, but probably the worst is over: the most recent revelations, concerning Dumas and the *mairie de Paris* for instance, relate to events during the 'black period' of some years ago. As Henri Nallet, former Socialist Minister of Justice, told me, 'Anyone who would now try this kind of sleaze would be utterly mad. He must surely know that he'd be caught,

* Others, such as prefects of *départements* and headmasters, have been facing similar problems. In one *lycée*, a boy was killed in a sports accident and the headmaster was prosecuted for 'involuntary homicide', as it was alleged that the equipment might have been faulty: he was later acquitted, but his career suffered. After an accident in Brittany where a man was drowned, and another concerning a sports stadium in Corsica, prefects were similarly charged, on the grounds that security had not been fully checked. In these and other cases, there is generally an acquittal, but it leaves a nasty taste – and some excellent senior teachers have become deterred from accepting posts as heads of schools as a result. The law has now been eased, and the prosecution has to prove personal negligence by the accused or intent to harm. But it is still widely felt that those in authority are being asked to take too much legal responsibility.

and this will reduce the temptation. So the whole nasty episode has been a kind of victory, in the end, for justice and democracy. The body politic has been purified, and there's now more transparency, as in America. Public, press and judiciary are more alert to the dangers. We've all learned our lesson.' But although *juges* and investigative reporters have done a valuable job, their excesses have shown up the weaker sides of the French system of justice. So today the stress is on reform – to protect the blind goddess alike from power-hungry State, predatory press, vengeful *juges* and clumsy police. And recent years have already seen a few specific changes. The morally crucial abolition of the death penalty, by Mitterrand in 1981, has had the effect – as Devedjian puts it – of rescuing French justice from the medieval concept of retribution by suffering, in favour of the modern notion of 'a broken social contract that needs guarantees of reparation'.

One major practical reform in the 1990s has concerned the funding of political parties. Here legislation used hardly to exist, and there were many abuses. Parties would not only take big gifts from firms, but would solicit bribes from building or other contractors in awarding local contracts; and while the money went supposedly into party coffers, it was collected in so underhand a way that some of it was often syphoned off by those involved into their own pockets. Mayors and others profited. And all parties were up to these tricks, including the Communists with their *bureaux d'études* (Marchais and Hue were investigated by *juges* about this in 1996). Such practices were even connived at by tax inspectors. And several of the worst scandals of the 1980s and early 1990s involved such activity – the Socialists' Urba, Carignon in Grenoble, the *mairie de Paris*. A law passed under Rocard in 1990 sought to limit funding by firms, but was not very effective. Then Balladur, with Pierre Méhaignerie as his Justice Minister, promoted a stronger law, in 1994, that put a ban on all funding by companies, on the 'there's no free lunch' principle. It also placed strict limits on electoral spending (some Front National leaders have been penalized for this). Today party funding is allowed only from individuals, topped up by some state help. The 1994 law is regarded as fairly effective, and it adds to the confidence that the worst of the age of big scandals may now be over.

Even so, most French still feel cynically that a degree of corruption is inevitable in politics. And they judge their system of justice quite severely. A Sofres survey in January 1997 found 82 per cent of the sample seeing the judiciary as 'subject to the Government', and 79 per cent finding it 'too indulgent' to politicians; 66 per cent had a 'bad opinion' of French justice, and 76 per cent thought it essential to speed up its judgments. External bodies have been critical, too, notably the European Court of the Human Rights in Strasbourg. By 1996 it had condemned France thirty-two times since 1974 for violating the European Convention on human rights (Britain's tally was thirty-six times, often over Northern Ireland). Criticism by the Court led the Rocard Government to adopt tighter regulations over telephone-tappings.

Today the climate of opinion is all for change – alike for stricter measures against corruption and other abuses, *and* for an overhaul of the system of justice. But how? The reform debate centres on the anomaly of *procureurs* being too dependent on the State while *juges d'instruction* are too free. Their institution may be in many ways excellent, admired by the British and others: but many French have come to view it harshly. Governments over the years have made repeated efforts to reform it, but have always fallen foul of the *juges* themselves, a powerful lobby. In 1993 the Socialists, with Nallet as Justice Minister, did succeed in passing a law that would have remedied the most contentious aspect by removing from the *juges* their role of remanding in custody. But they replied with a strike, and the law was revoked under Balladur and never applied. Nallet, a gentle and cultivated man, was angry about this (and about the 'excessive' behaviour of *juge* Jean-Pierre in the Urba affair, when he was minister). He told me later, 'Our system of the examining magistrate has become very unfair, the British do it better. In my view, no compromise reform is possible. We have to scrap the system completely and move to something like the British or German model. Perhaps it will happen one day, as we build a new Europe together.'

Since early 1997 reform has moved faster. Chirac himself proposed that the *parquet* be made far more independent of the Government, and he set up a commission under a senior *juge*, Pierre Truche, to prepare proposals. This was generally welcomed – notably by Elisabeth Guigou who became Justice Minister in June, just when the Truche document was ready. She found it in line with the Socialists' own thinking, and she took it further: a 'global reform' was needed, she said, because public confidence in the system of justice was in crisis. Her project was in turn broadly accepted by Chirac, and, after many delays and modifications, it seemed to have a chance of being approved by Parliament during 2000. But it would require a small amendment to the Constitution. The centre-Right parties fought against the project, even though Chirac himself favoured it and in a sense had initiated it. *Le Monde* had a witty cartoon of Chirac and Guigou in fond embrace, talking of '*notre réforme*' as if it were 'our baby', while RPR leaders muttered, '*Y a pas de justice!*'

The new law takes up the two key themes of (a) reducing official pressures and (b) protecting suspects during inquiries. The ministry will still set broad policy lines, but can no longer give instructions to *procureurs* in individual cases; and if an inquiry is closed, magistrates will have to justify their decision, to show that they are not acting under pressure. A new independent commission will handle all complaints against magistrates, hitherto dealt with by the ministry. As for suspects, a defence lawyer can now be present from the first hour of custody and not the twenty-fourth (except in cases of drugs, terrorism and other crimes): this brings France into line with other EU countries, on the issue of *habeas corpus*. Limits will be placed on the length of detention, and photographs of suspects in chains or handcuffs will no longer be allowed. Steps will be taken to speed up the process of law. Most crucially, the decision to hold in custody will no longer be taken by the *juge d'instruction*, but by a separate judge sitting in court: this, it is hoped, will remove the temptation for *juges* to hold suspects in order to pressurize them. And newspapers will face fines if they infringe the 'presumption of innocence'. This could have quite an effect. But there will still be no *sub judice* role, so the press will still be free to conduct its own inquiries, before or during a trial. And sceptics doubt whether the new detention tribunals will be given the time and the funds to function properly.

The project was strongly opposed by conservative civil servants who feared losing some of their control, notably the Conseil Général de la Magistrature. Liberals, however, think that it does not go far enough in protecting suspects from the press and media – will the new fines have any effect? But in general, the reform is widely popular with the press and public, and does seem likely to serve a useful purpose in making French justice at last more fair, humane and independent. This can only benefit the bruised image of French political democracy.

2

PARADOXES OF THE ECONOMIC 'MIRACLE'

The French economy is a paradox of strengths and weaknesses. France has grown to be the world's fourth industrial power, with a superb record of exports, much technological prowess, and standards of living among Europe's highest. The Bourse today is booming, and most business leaders feel able to confront the euro with confidence. Yet many experts are still tearing their hair over the persistent remaining handicaps – the too high levels of public spending, the thousands of small outdated firms, the bureaucratic rigidities which can worsen unemployment. And they ask whether France is really so well placed to deal with the new global competition. Yet, viewed from another angle, the economy is amazingly strong and resilient.

The strength derives from the remarkable transformations of the post-war years, when this former inward-looking agriculture-based society became a modern industrial nation. Much was due at that time to intelligent central state planning; also to the rise of a new breed of dynamic private entrepreneur, less dependent on the State. Under the spur of entry into the EEC, the old protectionist attitudes gradually gave way to new concerns for competition, and for productivity, which today is 30 per cent higher than in Britain. Fine wines and farm produce may still be major French exports: but so are cars, aircraft and many other advanced hi-tech goods. Several of the larger industrial groups are world leaders in their fields.

During the first thirty years of post-war expansion, the so-called 'Trente Glorieuses', France's growth rate was among the fastest in Europe. Disguised at first by financial crises and political upheavals, the recovery began soon after the war, and industrial production tripled in 1952–73 – twice the British rate. The German economy grew even stronger: but the French 'miracle', in the context of French backwardness at the time, was just as remarkable. Today the Trente Glorieuses are over: France, like other countries, has faced periods of recession, and economic doubts have grown. Yet even since 1974, average annual growth has still been a respectable 2.3 per cent, just above the EU average. And time and again the French economy has responded to crises with astonishing buoyancy. As I write, at the end of 1999, the picture is bright. Industrialists, a breed often prone to gloom, are optimistic for once, with output and investment growing fast. The trade surplus for 1997 reached a record 173 billion francs: here the Asian and Russian crises are now the main shadows.

Long-term economic strategies were bedevilled for a while, rather as in Britain, by Left/Right doctrinal conflicts over the role of state ownership. But in practice the Socialists' wave of nationalizations in the 1980s proved short-lived: and ever since, there has been a tacit measure of agreement on ways to deal with basic economic problems. The Socialists today may be annoying the Patronat with their social plans for a shorter working week: but apart from this, Left and Right have displayed broad continuity over such crucial matters as monetary union and budget economies. The 'peace dividend' has made it possible to reduce military spending by some 20 billion francs a year. And these and other cuts enabled France, against the odds, to fulfil the 'Maastricht criteria' for joining EMU. The granting of semi-autonomy to the Banque de France has helped to lower interest rates; and the controversial policy of the 'strong franc' (*franc fort*), aligned on the Deutschmark, seems finally to have paid off.

Of France's famous old-rooted handicaps, some have finally been cured. High inflation, a scourge in the post-war period, has been remedied since the mid-1980s. The strong role of the State in the economy, possibly useful in the post-war years of renewal, then came to be seen as a liability in the new world of open frontiers; and it has now been much reduced. First, the practice of *dirigisme*, i.e. state control of finance and interference in private firms, has been lightened. Next, there has been a huge wave of privatizations, in industry, banking and insurance. These were initiated by the centre-Right, and the Socialists today have mostly continued them, not put them into reverse.

Yet the debate continues on whether the State should not retreat still further. Public spending accounts for 56 per cent of GDP in France: only in Scandinavia is it higher, while the percentage for Germany is 54, for Britain 45, for the United States 35. And total revenue from taxes and other compulsory levies accounts for 44 per cent of GDP, the highest level among advanced nations. Most experts, and not only the doctrinaire 'liberals', argue that these figures need to be reduced. The fiscal system, judged much too heavy, has now been simplified a little – and Jospin in 1999 announced huge tax cuts – but it still awaits a major overhaul. Despite improvements, liaison is still poor between pure and applied research. And the economy remains hampered by all kinds of complex bureaucratic rigidities, over matters such as the rules about the hiring and firing of staff. These, it is argued, add to costs and to unemployment, and will increasingly be a handicap in the new open 'liberal' world.

With some reluctance, France has signed up to the new EU rules on deregulation. But how will these affect the prized 'French model' of public services? And in a broader economic sense, can France keep some of the better aspects of her old state-led system, while adjusting to the new world of open competition? She has already come a long way. But the next years will be testing ones, in face of growing globalization, which Raymond Barre has called 'the true revelation of French weaknesses'. France is no longer protected behind her frontiers. Her old state technocracy, so long admired by foreign observers, is no longer such an asset, and it must adapt to new challenges. This will be a frequent theme of this and other chapters.

And now abideth privatization, deregulation, globalization, these three; but the greatest of these, as a worry for the French, is globalization.

RENEWAL AND GROWTH: FROM MONNET'S 'PLAN' TO THE EURO AGE

France in the eighteenth century was the world's strongest and richest power. But soon after 1800 she began to fall back, failing to keep pace with the fast industrialization of Britain and Germany. Later, she spent huge sums on her colonial empire but neglected the economy back home – despite the cultural richness of the Belle Époque. By the inter-war years, this was a pleasant and cheap country for expatriates, but not always such a happy country for the French, and in the 1930s industrial output was in decline. Then the Second World War brought less loss of life than the First but worse physical damage: by 1945 the railways were shattered, many factories, ports and northern towns were devastated. And yet, as in the case of Germany, the very scale of this destruction was a blessing in disguise, for it enabled a new start on modern lines. The British, who had the misfortune never to be defeated, lacked the same impetus.

.The opportunities might have been muffed, had not a number of French emerged from the war with a new determination. Some had used the enforced inactivity of wartime to think seriously about the future and explore new ideas: that is how the Plan was born. Then many of the older generation emerged publicly discredited for their part in the Vichy regime. This enabled new, younger ones to push them aside and fill some of the key posts in industry and the public service. A few key civil servants moved from a static to a more dynamic concept of their role: whereas before the war they had been the faceless executives of a smooth, unchanging regime, now they came to see themselves as reformers, apostles of economic progress, and some industrialists followed suit. This discarding of the economic pessimism of the 1930s was general in the West after the war: in France, it stood out most sharply, just because of the gravity of the earlier decline.

In 1946 Jean Monnet launched his first Plan, under the slogan 'Modernization or Downfall'. It was a long-sighted austerity plan that gave the immediate housing shortage a lower priority than the rebuilding of basic industries. In 1947 Marshall Aid began to arrive, providing the investments needed for the first Plan's success. And the traditional French flair for technology and engineering was given a new lease of life, as experts received the funding and encouragement to design and build new cars, aircraft and much else. The new industrial growth was helped also by the mass exodus from the farms, which gave factories a steady supply of new recruits. Yet the 1950s were not easy years for the economy. Parallel with the dynamic rebuilding of key industries went a series of financial crises due to the archaic structure of much of the rest of *la vieille France*, which stayed attached to its old ways, resisting change: in 1953 one expert described the pioneering new industries as 'just an isolated enclave of modernism inside old France'. The imbalance between the two structures was one cause of the alarming inflation rate, averaging 29 per cent a year in 1947–53: it was like putting too powerful an engine in a rickety car. Fourth Republic Governments patched over the budgetary cracks, but were too weak or short-lived to apply real remedies. Yet they did take one courageous decision in the mid-1950s: to go into the EEC despite the opposition of most private industry.

In France the State has traditionally played a more assertive role in the economy than in most Western countries. Not only have many big firms and banks been state-owned, but the Government has controlled most finance and has strongly influenced private industry. In today's 'liberal' age, this *dirigiste* system has come to be seen as a handicap, and for some years now it has been on the wane, amid numerous privatizations. But in the first post-war decades it was on the whole a source of strength, at a time when much of industry needed a lead.

It was in this *étatiste* context that the Commissariat Général du Plan was able to play so effective a role in guiding the post-war recovery. This was never a heavy state machine but a subtle think-tank and planning forum. And today France still owes a massive debt to the man who inspired and founded it, the great Jean Monnet. This warm idealist and international visionary was anything but a typical technocrat: his family were brandy distillers in Cognac, and his first knowledge of the world was in the humble role of salesman for their cognac firm. He came to know and admire the United States, and during the war he and some friends began to plot how to pull France up to its level – by novel, non-American methods. In 1945 he met de Gaulle in Washington and won him over to the idea of the Plan: a year later the first five-year plan was approved, and Monnet became Commissioner-General. Never a conformist, he broke with many of the habits and formalities of the French administration. Unlikely groups of people, old-style financiers and Communist union leaders, were shoved together at short notice, without form or ceremony. Instead of long memoranda, there might be little notes scribbled by Monnet on slips of yellow paper as he walked in the woods near his home. Rather than long business lunches, there were working meals of un-French simplicity at the Plan's offices in an elegant Left Bank mansion. Life was in some ways more monastic than bureaucratic. According to some accounts, there was even an air of revivalism about the inter-industry meetings of those early years, where the planners communicated their faith.

This helps to explain why a certain mystique grew up around the Plan, both in France and abroad. Many otherwise unexplained achievements were credited to it by public opinion. In fact, many economists have been dubious about just how valuable it has been in strictly *economic* terms. Some argue that much of the French recovery would have happened anyway, and they point to Germany's greater post-war progress with no planning. Yet few disagree about the Plan's psychological influence on industry. It tore some of the barriers of secrecy from private firms, helping to create a new climate of competition. It has always been voluntary rather than formally binding, without the executive powers of a ministry; and while ministries have listened to its forecasts and advice, neither they nor private firms have been formally obliged to do so.

The Plan's basic task was to set targets for growth, sector by sector. Monnet would convene round a table the heads of private firms, union leaders and civil servants, to thrash out in detail how to achieve their targets, say in textiles, aluminium or pig breeding. This flexible system was a working compromise between economic liberalism and French *dirigisme*. Gradually the Plan helped to instil in smaller firms a new awareness of the need to invest, to explore export markets, to group for shared research or sales; and it helped prepare them for the EEC. While the first two Plans concentrated on industry, the third and fourth (1958–65) widened the range to include social and welfare matters; parts of the Plan became regionalized, and each town was proud to have its own mini-Plan as a segment of the national one.

Under de Gaulle and then Giscard, the national importance of the Plan began to decline. First, political stability not only rendered it less valuable as a factor of continuity, but also caused it to be more identified with government than it was under the quick-changing prime ministers of the Fourth Republic. So anti-Gaullists grew less ready to cooperate, and the basis of Monnet's sacred non-party tryst was weakened. Next, as France's economy opened out to Europe and the world, so it became less amenable to purely domestic planning or the fixing of growth targets. The Plan, you could say, had served its purpose and was victim of its own success. In fact, there were no more formal five-year plans after that of 1973–7. The Socialists after 1981 restored the Plan to a more influential role: but more recent 'liberal' Governments have tended to neglect it, and so has Jospin. Today the Plan is still used as a think-tank for long-term analysis: thus Alain Minc directed a major forecast under its auspices in 1996. But it was not even consulted by Jospin over his employment policies, partly because the man still at its head was a right-winger appointed by Juppé – an example of the Plan's political vulnerability. None the less, in a wider sense, its ethos has had a lasting influence. Each ministry, state agency or private firm today does its own planning, inspired in some way by Monnet's original vision; even in Brussels, some of the forecasting routines of the European Commission are of French inspiration. France's economy is so integrated into a 'liberal' Europe that it clearly has no scope for its own Monnet-type plan. And yet, it was the Plan that helped prepare France for the European adventure in the 1950s.

*

When the Treaty of Rome was signed in 1957, it was thanks in part to the Plan that some industries were now well modernized and able to stand up to the new outside competition. One of the largest, steel, had already learned to face the German challenge under that valuable dress rehearsal for the Common Market, the European Coal and Steel Community, founded in 1951. The French employers' federation, the Patronat, had strongly opposed the creation of the ECSC, and was later surprised to find that French steel *was* able to compete. This helped to modify its later opposition to plans for the EEC: so finally Parliament accepted the Treaty of Rome, on the urging of Robert Schumann and a few other far-sighted politicians of the Left and centre. Many firms set about adapting to the new situation, after decades of protectionism – and again they discovered to their surprise that their fears of the German juggernaut had been exaggerated. So the EEC, too, helped shock French industry into modernizing. As in 1940–44, but this time without defeat or bloodshed, the German menace proved a catalyst.

As the tariff barriers came down by 10 per cent a year, so France's trade with the rest of the Six began to increase rapidly. Her sales there trebled in the period 1958–62 alone. The sectors that did best were those already well organized, such as luxury goods and cars: in 1958–77, annual French car exports to Germany rose from a mere 11,000 to 292,000, and to Italy from 2,000 to 271,000! By the normal process of give and take some other French industries were cut down by the new competition, for instance by refrigerators from Italy or office furniture from Germany. But the overall balance was positive; and whereas it was often said that France, by joining the EEC, expected to lose out on industrial exports but make up on agriculture, in fact her industry has done equally well. Many Frenchmen may be sceptical today about the workings of the EU, but it is unusual to find a businessman who does not feel that the whole European venture has been good for France and its economy (see pp. 678–91).

Yet adapting to the EEC was at first not easy. De Gaulle in 1958 inherited a situation where industrial output was rising rapidly but France's finances were in a fearful state: the franc was trailing along as one of Western Europe's weakest currencies. And with the first of the EEC tariff cuts due for January 1959, it seemed that France might have to suffer the ignominy of being the only member to invoke the escape clauses protecting her from competition. Such a prospect was intolerable for de Gaulle, so his experts prepared drastic remedies. The franc was devalued by 17.5 per cent, to the level it was to hold for the next ten years. As a boost for French morale, the decimal point was shifted and a New Franc born, worth a hundred old ones. And trade liberalization with OECD countries was pushed up to 90 per cent – a daring move for this land of protectionism. These were the greatest economic reforms of de Gaulle's regime, and the results were immediate, as gold and other reserves began to climb fast.

The Gaullist decade was one of rapid growth, often reaching 5 or 6 per cent a year. In 1968 the economy was in strong enough shape to survive with some ease the shocks of the May '68 crisis. And during the brief Pompidou years it again bounded ahead, with annual growth around Europe's highest level. But France, like other countries, was then badly hit by the first oil crisis of 1973: this revealed both the resilience of her new modern industries and the dangers of the old uncured weaknesses, notably inflation. In 1974–6 Giscard responded to the crisis with a succession of stop-go measures that inevitably brought erratic results. After the first austerity squeeze, growth in 1975 was −2 per cent, the first minus figure since the war: but by skilful reflation this was followed by 5 per cent growth in 1976. Yet the 'go' measures simply aggravated inflation, which was running at 11 per cent, twice the American or German figure.

It was thus a delicate situation that the sagacious Raymond Barre inherited as Prime Minister in August 1976, after Chirac resigned. Barre was an unusual man for the job, not a career politician but an academic with a wide experience of economic affairs, and a reputation for canny pragmatism. He told the French bluntly that they were living above their means and this must stop. And he set in motion two major lines of policy: (a) an austerity programme that included public spending cuts and other classic measures; (b) a longer-term structural overhaul, to make France's very uneven economy more effective. This 'liberal' economist was the first post-war leader to tackle seriously the issue of excessive government intervention in private industry. The time had come, he said, to modify the *dirigisme* that marked France for so long, and to oblige firms to stand on their own adult feet. So he began to lift industrial price controls in every sector except oil and pharmaceuticals: it would no longer be the role of the Ministry of Finance to fix the prices that industry could charge. This was a major break with French tradition, bringing France in line with 'liberal' States such as Germany. The aim was to induce more sense of competition. Of course it carried the risk of price rises, fuelling inflation – and there was a howl of 'we told you so' from Barre's critics when the price of a *baguette* of bread, that sacred commodity, rose overnight by some 22 per cent. But bread was just the kind of product that had hitherto been underpriced by state bureaucrats, anxious to keep down the retail index – and its quality had suffered.

In the public services, Barre pursued a policy of *la vérité des prix*, telling state concerns such as electricity that they must expect lower subsidies and should raise their prices nearer to the market level. But he was much less stringent than Thatcher in Britain, a few years later. With private industry, he stressed that public funds would now become less available for shoring up 'lame duck' firms, whatever the cost in jobs: so he insisted on big lay-offs in the struggling steel industry (see p. 110). His message was clear: companies must become efficient and pay their way, or perish. The Government would help the expansion of high-technology sectors where France was well placed in world markets: but in older sectors, such as textiles, where France was undercut by emerging countries, there would have to be large cutbacks. Probably this was a wise strategy for the longer term. But it was a painful one to apply in a time of recession, and it helped to provoke the first serious post-war rise in unemployment – from 0.5 to 1.5 million between 1974 and 1981.

Likewise, Barre's austerity programme failed to reduce inflation as planned: in 1980 this was running at 13 per cent, the worst level in France for twenty years. However, Barre was able to hold the franc steady, thus enabling France to keep her place in the new European Monetary System (trailblazer for today's euro). And a vigorous exports policy helped the trade balance to swing back into a huge surplus – at least until the second oil crisis in 1979. Barre fervently believed in his economic remedies and stubbornly refused to reflate. Once, when asked about the plight of the unemployed, he replied *à la* Norman Tebbitt, 'Let them start their own businesses.' His rough manner added to his unpopularity, and Giscard's. Yet after their defeat at the polls in 1981, within three years the public came to realize that Barre had been right all along – and he was revered as a lost saviour. What irony. By then the Socialists were in power, with policies at first very different.

The Socialists' shift away from crypto-Marxism towards the acceptance of a mixed economy was the great event of their first five years in office. They had come to power with an economic master-plan elaborated with the Communists under the Joint Programme of the Left. Reflation, redistribution of wealth and nationalizations – these were its three main planks, and to many critics they seemed like an uneasy blend of generous social idealism, outdated semi-Marxist dogmatism and ill-timed economic theory. Some of the men now in charge of the economy, such as Jacques Delors, the Finance Minister, were moderates who understood the real French problems: but they and Mitterrand were bound by their electoral promises. Their reflation programme not only marked a total break with the Barre policy of *rigueur*: it also cut right across the current wisdom in the West, where most nations were fighting recession with some monetarist austerity. But the Socialists, partly for doctrinal reasons, wanted to try their own solutions. In a bid to reduce unemployment, which had reached 1.8 million, they embarked on a Keynesian policy of massive public spending and easier credit. They created new jobs in public services, raised ministerial budgets and cut interest rates so as to help investment. The inevitable result was a big rise in the budget deficit. But inflation did not increase as much as feared; and reflation did stimulate growth a little. By early 1982 it was clear that the economy had not come crashing, as prophets of doom on the Right had predicted. But nor had there been any triumphant recovery, as many naïve Socialists had expected.

The nationalization of many banks and key industries (see below) did little for economic efficiency, but no great harm either. The Government swiftly imposed new taxes on the rich (see p. 195); it raised the minimum wage and welfare benefits, then extended the length of paid holidays and reduced the working week without loss of pay. In a country with such large material inequalities, these were valuable measures in terms of social justice. But the money thus taken from the rich was a fleabite compared with the sums now paid out by the State to the poor and by firms to their employees, and it hit their profits badly.

After Mitterrand's election the business world had at first reacted with alarm. There was panic selling on the Bourse where the share index dropped by 30 per cent; the franc came under heavy pressure, and Delors was able to keep it within the EMS only by hiking interest rates to a record 20 per cent and then devaluing. But then the panic subsided and the Patronat began to adjust to the need for a wary cooperation with France's new rulers. The brightest feature was the presence of Delors himself who emerged as a figure of great authority. He handled the economy with skill, convinced Mitterrand of the need to avoid excessive radicalism, and even won the confidence of the Patronat. But by mid-1982 it was clear to him and others that the reflation policy was going badly wrong. Unemployment and inflation, that unholy duo, were still both rising high; the rise in social costs had harmed firms' investment and competitiveness; and reflation had pushed France into heavy borrowing abroad, at a time of a strong dollar: so the franc was very weak, and the foreign debt rose alarmingly.

This led the Socialists into an agonizing reappraisal of their policies. An intensive debate ensued in government ranks, as Delors sought to persuade the President that basic changes were urgently necessary. On his side were some other 'realist' ministers such as Michel Rocard and the premier, Pierre Mauroy; on the other, Mitterrand's influential economic adviser, Jacques Attali, and doctrinaire Socialists such as Pierre Joxe. On the sidelines, the hard Socialist Left and the Communists were urging strong protectionist measures. But Delors was able to argue that a closed-frontier policy would be madness, reducing France to a kind of Cuba, and breaching all the EEC rules. At the same time the Socialists could not help noticing that the monetarist policies of Reagan and Thatcher were beginning to bear fruit in reducing inflation and ending recession: so Mitterrand and Attali steadily swung round to accepting the viewpoint of Delors, who was threatening to resign if his proposals were not adopted. So in two stages, in July 1982 and March 1983, the Government made significant semi-U-turns. It conceded that France, within the capitalist West, had no choice but to follow the trend and that market realism must come before dogma. It was the getting of wisdom – and for the Socialists, a key turning point.

Among other measures, Delors sharply reduced public spending, imposed higher taxes on rich and poor alike, and secured grudging union approval for a policy of wage restraint. As a result, after rising by 2.6 per cent in 1982, real spending power fell slightly in 1983–4: it was the first time for years that wage increases had thus been allowed to lag behind price rises. The inevitable effect of this austerity was to slow growth, which fell to around 1 per cent. But in other respects, Delors's medicine yielded dividends. Notably, inflation was at last brought under control: by 1985 it was under 5 per cent, around the EEC average. Thus one of the major weaknesses of the French post-war economy was finally cured – and it has remained so to this day. In addition, the gigantic foreign-trade deficit was reduced by three-quarters, to a 'mere' 20 billion francs a year by 1984 (it had been due in part to long-term failures to invest adequately, which had harmed competitiveness). Finally, the monetarist measures gave a new boost to industry, and the Bourse's share index rose to record heights. So by 1986 the economy was back in good shape, with a growth rate of 2.5 per cent. The Socialist leaders, Mitterrand included, had gone through an education in the realities of the market place and were no longer treating the business world with such suspicion. When Pierre Bérégovoy succeeded Delors as Finance Minister in 1984, he even resumed the Barre policy of price de-control. But many rank-and-file left-wing voters were disturbed by Delors's austerity policy, which some of them saw as a betrayal of Socialism and of electoral promises. So the Socialists in saving the economy lost much of their own popularity. It was one factor behind their defeat in the 1986 elections.

During their later period in power, 1988–93, they again managed the economy skilfully, and the general picture remained bright except on the jobs front. Inflation, the old enemy, was brought down to 2 per cent (for 1998 it was a mere 0.3 per cent, the lowest level since 1997), and annual growth was above the EEC average. When the world cycle of recession arrived, France warded it off for longer than many of her partners: then finally it bit hard, in late 1992, causing many firms to close or make heavy lay-offs. The Socialists, like Barre, had been urging companies to become more competitive, even if it meant shedding jobs: a firm in trouble was not baled out with public money but expected to restructure. This un-Socialist approach caused anger on the Left, where it was felt that social needs were being sacrificed to economic ones. Along with recession it added to unemployment, which rose from 1.8 to 3 million between 1988 and 1993.

In the eyes of many observers, France was also paying the price of its political choice of close attachment to Germany. Eager to maintain parity with the Deutschmark, the Government stuck to its policy of the *franc fort*, refusing to devalue or pull out of the Exchange Rate Mechanism when Britain and others had done so. Tied to the Bundesbank with its high interest rates, this *franc fort* came under severe strain (was it not symbolic that the French name for Frankfurt is in fact 'Francfort'?). The pressures caused France likewise to keep interest rates high, and this affected industry and jobs. The policy was then continued under Balladur and Juppé, and it caused a drain on France's reserves. Economists have endlessly argued whether the *franc fort* has been healthy for the economy or not. It may well have harmed growth and employment. But it did not prevent France from keeping a healthy trade balance. And it was valuable in helping to prepare for monetary union.

In 1993–5 Balladur's RPR-led Government helped France back to some recovery as recession eased, and growth in 1994 was 2.7 per cent. Balladur had no magic cure for unemployment, but at least it was stabilized. In order to prepare for the European Monetary Union, he gave semi-independence to the Banque de France. And he relaunched the massive privatization programme (see p. 78) which Chirac had begun and the Socialists had then halted but not put into reverse. Apart from this, his policies were not so different from Bérégovoy's. Whereas economic strategy used to divide Left and Right so sharply, ever since the 1983 U-turn it has become a matter of some consensus and continuity, across changes of government. The divergences are more of rhetoric than substance, in face of tacit recognition that often there is only one realistic way of tackling a problem, within an international free market. With exceptions on the social front, this remains the picture today under Jospin.

When they came to power in May 1995, Chirac and Juppé faced two opposing challenges: to tackle high unemployment, and to reduce the huge budget deficit so as to meet the criteria for EMU by 1999. They set about trying to do both at once, despite what many critics saw as a basic contradiction. At first their main emphasis went on growth and job creation, with special grants and tax concessions for firms hiring more staff. But when this failed to reduce the jobless total of some 12.5 per cent, they shifted to the other priority, of austerity measures to lower the deficit – and it landed them in the strikes of the following December. The policy would anyway have been unpopular, as Chirac publicly admitted: worse, it was clumsily applied. But in economic terms it was probably the wisest path, and courageous, and it came to bear fruit later. Helped by various cuts in public spending, the deficit of over 5 per cent of GDP was steadily reduced to under 4 per cent. At the same time, the *franc fort* strategy was continued, helped by low inflation and fairly high interest rates; and growth was kept going by the continued huge export surplus, generated by France's modern industries and by agriculture. Juppé went ahead with the deregulation of some public services required by the new EU rules (see p. 84). And he continued Balladur's programme of privatizations, which brought in some funds to help limit the deficit. His 'liberal' strategy, though mild compared with Thatcher's, marked a continuation of the anti-*étatiste* trend that had started in the 1970s.

The economic upturn began to show in the spring of 1997. It was helped by Juppé's austerity measures, and more so by the world recovery, American-led. So Jospin's Government was able to benefit. During his first two years in office, unemployment at last began to fall, from 12.5 to about 11.3 per cent of the workforce. Spurred by a fall in interest rates, industrial investment revived, and by mid-1998 it was growing at a rate of 9 per cent a year, while production as a whole was rising at 8 per cent, and the Paris Bourse broke all records. Business optimism rose, too, as did domestic consumption – a sign that even the public was stirring from its gloom. The rise of the pound and dollar against the franc helped the French trade surplus to reach yet dizzier heights of 173 billion francs for 1997. It fell back to 138 million for 1998, due partly to the crisis in Asia. But French overall growth for 1998 was over 3 per cent, and likely to be 2.4 per cent for 1999. This is a better level than Britain's. France today has been creating new jobs at a faster rate than any other large advanced country except the USA. And the economy is in its healthiest state since 1992.

This recovery made it easier for Jospin and his astute Finance Minister, Dominique Strauss-Kahn, to get the finances in shape for the crucial decisions on monetary union in 1998. This was their immediate priority on taking office, once they had agreed to try to meet the EMU timetable. Jospin had promised 'no austerity': like Chirac, he was then forced by the EMU criteria to eat some of his words: but he managed it more skilfully and tactfully. In order to reduce the deficit further, he produced an array of measures, some aimed at the rich, others requiring wider sacrifices. He made big cuts in infrastructure projects, such as new motorways and the planned Rhône–Rhine canal: these saved money but affected jobs. He put a new means test on family allowances and emergency taxes on companies and higher incomes. And he raised welfare contributions, which hit his own voters as well as the rich. He was thus able, against expectations, to bring the deficit down to a bare 3.1 per cent, just low enough to satisfy the fateful EMU criterion laid down at Maastricht in 1991. It was quite an achievement, part good luck, part good management; and he was spurred on by Jean-Claude Trichet, the all-powerful governor of the Banque de France, who was adamant that France should join EMU. Jospin managed to persuade Chancellor Kohl to accept a 'gentler euro', including Italy, with the aim of thus cushioning France against its rigours (see p. 689). Today it remains to be seen whether this will make for a less effective EMU, as the sceptics predict.

On the domestic front, the new Government pursued a mix of doctrinaire Socialist measures and modern market-geared policies. A real effort to reduce youth unemployment was marked by Aubry's creation of over 100,000 new jobs in the public sector; and private firms were urged to provide a similar number. This was applauded, despite the strain it might put on the budget. But there was still no plan to ease unemployment by making the labour market more flexible, *à l'anglaise*. And the project for a shorter 35-hour working week (see p. 185) was roundly criticized, notably by the Patronat. But they were much less worried by other aspects of the new Government's policies. The privatization programme was allowed to go ahead, offering the strange spectacle of a Communist Transport Minister presiding over the partial sell-off of Air France. This, plus the relinquishing of Aerospatiale, are the latest moves in the steady waning of state control – one of the major trends in France in recent years.

THE WANING ROLE OF THE MIGHTY STATE: PRIVATIZATIONS, AND THE CRISIS OF THE 'FRENCH MODEL'

The role of the State in the French economy used to be so very strong. Now it has been relaxed considerably in some sectors, but less in others. Since about the mid-1980s, France has belatedly followed the Western 'liberal' trend: nearly all of banking and insurance has been privatized, plus most of the state-run manufacturing industries. This has all meant quite a change. Even the Banque de France has been given a new semi-autonomy, on the lines of the Bundesbank, and can now set interest rates itself.

In the public services, however, the power of the State remains great. It is true that many have lost their monopoly, as France hesitantly follows the deregulation laid down by Brussels and competition arrives; and minority private shareholding is now allowed in Air France and France Télécom. But the main public services, including railways and electricity, are not yet privatized as in Britain. The hold of the State also remains powerful in the welfare system, education and some aspects of culture. As we have seen, public spending comprises a higher percentage of GDP than in nearly all other countries; and most economists are convinced that the figure should be lowered. Moreover, the European Commission has expressed disquiet at the huge sums of money spent recently by French Governments on aid to public enterprises in trouble: the figure of 190 billion francs has been given for the 1992–7 period, including some 20 billion for Air France and around 100 billion to rescue the state bank, Crédit Lyonnais.

This nation remains proud of its specific 'French model' of public services, generous if costly. And recently a debate has raged on whether these should resist deregulation, or else adapt to it and modernize while trying to preserve some of the essential 'French' qualities. Another debate, wider and more profound, has centred for some years on the changing role of the French State: does it remain a strength for the economy, or has it become a handicap? – and how far are the French capable of adapting to a new 'liberal' ethos, so far from their tradition? Most experts would argue that the *dirigiste* French system was an asset in the post-war years, when private industry was still weak and dynamic state leadership was able to do much for development, with the help of the élitist network of the Grandes Écoles and Grands Corps (see pp. 90–100). In the regions, the State often took the lead in associating public, private and local interests, to promote such ventures as the giant tourist resorts along the Languedoc coast: it pushed ahead with Europe's most ambitious nuclear programme, with modern state-led industries in aerospace and telecommunications, with the architectural '*grands projets*' in Paris, and with the high-speed rail network for the Train à Grande Vitesse (TGV), while coaxing Britain into building the Channel Tunnel – in all, a tremendous record. Even private companies were sometimes grateful for the regular guidance and loans they received from the State.

However, the counter-argument voiced loudly since the mid-1980s by the 'liberal' lobby – led by the Thatcherite former Finance Minister, Alain Madelin – is that this system was costly and not always so efficient, and had become a liability under the new global trade conditions of open frontiers and multinational groupings. If the French economy is now to prosper in this world, then it must become more market-geared, and firms must cease to rely so much on the State with its political considerations. The big state operations were often directed more with an eye to prestige and political kudos than economic usefulness: 'Firms under state tutelage,' Madelin told me, 'whether in public or private ownership, have been ruled by a *marché politique* and not by the real market.' He has even suggested, with some truth, that France's vaunted telecommunications industry, though technically brilliant, was a burden on the taxpayer.

Today opinions on this whole issue still vary greatly. Few politicians want to go as far as the dogmatic Madelin. But it is generally agreed – save by some on the extremes of Left and Right – that if France is to play its part in Europe, then the old *étatiste* system must change radically, however valuable it may have been in earlier years. There are plenty of voices pleading for compromises; and many compromise measures there indeed have been, often under union pressure. But today even the new Socialist Government has accepted deregulation, and is making no attempt to renationalize the world of industry or finance. It is just putting the brakes on a little, here and there. Jospin has pleaded publicly for this middle course. And one Socialist told me, 'Today ideological dogmatism has changed camp. It is we ex-Marxists who are now the pragmatists, while the liberals like Madelin are the Thatcherite ideologues.'

And yet, in a France with such an ancient and powerful tradition of *étatisme*, how well can the new order succeed? 'France is not a blank page,' said one economist; 'you can't just graft an alien system on to our old structure with its ingrained habits and methods.' In the civil service, and in some firms, plenty of bureaucrats are still resisting the change, either out of genuine belief in state control, or more often to protect their own influence and vested interests; and the mandarins in the Ministry of Finance still have strong reserve powers. On the whole, in the privatized industries and finance bodies, the adaptation has gone quite well (many, like Renault, were already being run on sound commercial lines). In the public services, it is too early to tell, for mostly deregulation has only begun to be applied since 1997–8. In electricity and telecommunications, it will be a tough challenge; and in the railways, that odd bastion of union-backed state control, the battle has hardly begun.

French *étatisme* is not new. The oldest nationalization, that of the tobacco industry, dates from Louis XIV: so do the first ventures in centralized economic planning. Then in the nineteenth century the mines, railways, banks and heavy industry, though in private hands, were all built up with the help of public capital. So when large-scale nationalization began in the 1930s, it did not mark such a turning point as in Britain. The Popular Front Government took over most armaments factories and the railways, and it set up state aircraft firms. The post-1944 Governments then acted more sweepingly – a task aided by capitalism's taint of Nazi collaboration. They swiftly nationalized Renault, the coal mines, electricity, gas, and the main insurance companies and clearing banks. Much of this was done in an anti-capitalist spirit, with de Gaulle's backing. Later, powerful state oil concerns were built up, such as Elf-Aquitaine, in the interests of defending French independence. During the post-war decades, the State's influence over much of private industry and business remained strong, along with its dominant control of the finance markets. The State owned most of the big insurance companies, and the larger credit bodies such as the Caisse des Dépôts: so firms depended on it for many of the loans they needed. And a company required the formal authorization of the Ministry of Finance over a far wider range of matters than in Britain.

The Socialists after 1981 then extended state ownership much further. For them it had long been a key dogma, and it was in their election programme. Acting fast after taking power, their Government pushed through a bill that nationalized thirty-six private banks and five French multinational industries, including Rhône-Poulenc (chemicals) St-Gobain (glass), Péchiney (aluminium, chemicals) and Thomson (electronics); it also took majority holdings in Dassault (aircraft) and the dynamic Matra group, strong in armaments and electronics. This was no random list: the takeovers brought a number of advanced or 'strategic' sectors, notably in defence, under full or substantial public ownership. It was a drastic move for a nation within the capitalist world, and it put up the State's share of industrial production from 15 to over 30 per cent. Several moderate Socialist leaders, including Mauroy, Delors and Rocard, were doubtful of its wisdom, and some urged delay. But they were overruled. Not only was Mitterand committed to the programme, electorally, but he believed in it. One of his aides at the Élysée told me, 'He feels that he must strike an irreversible blow at the power base of capitalism, if an effective new order is to be created in France.'

His defenders pointed out, not unfairly, that nationalized industries had so far worked better in France than in most countries. They cited Renault; and they claimed that as public ownership lay deep in the French tradition, the Socialists were merely extending a process developed by de Gaulle. The aim was to create 'a fleet of new Renaults' that could act as pace-setters for their private competitors. But many other Frenchmen saw the policy as rash, gratuitous and too expensive (the cost to the exchequer was some 40 billion francs). Public opinion was largely indifferent. And was it wise to tamper with firms that were doing well and making a profit, such as St-Gobain and Dassault? Might not the take-overs reduce effective competition?

In the short term, these fears mostly proved excessive. The Government appointed capable non-partisan technocrats to manage the firms. Rhône-Poulenc and Péchiney in particular, which had been making losses, were nursed back to health by intelligent restructuring and good leadership – helped, it is true, by large injections of state funding. In general, the Government refrained from direct interference. But sometimes it did seek to bend a company to its own national strategy: thus St-Gobain was obliged to abandon its move into electronics because the Government wanted to reserve that domain to Thomson. Worse, the state-owned firms now found it harder to change their capital structure or form foreign alliances: they became less flexible, more inward-looking. In the longer term, the Left's policy of mass state ownership might have become damaging to French industry, in a world of growing open competition. But, maybe fortunately on this score, the Right soon came back to power; and when the Socialists returned to office later, they had learned wisdom.

With Chirac as Prime Minister in 1986–8, and Madelin his Minister of Industry, the Right rapidly embarked on a more concerted effort than ever before in France to reduce state ownership and influence in all kinds of fields. In part this was a gut reaction to Socialism, an 'ideological revenge'. But the Right was also latching on to 'liberal' ideas by then dominant in the West, in Thatcher's Britain and elsewhere ('So the French have succumbed to *le vice anglais*,' quipped one cartoonist); and it saw itself as trying to adapt France's economy at last to the new conditions of world competition. The keystone of the policy was privatization: sixty-five companies worth over 200 billion francs were to be sold, a programme twice the size of Thatcher's. A successful start was made with St-Gobain, whose share offer was oversubcribed fourteenfold! There followed several large banks, and companies as diverse as the main television channel, TF1 (see p. 490), Havas, the advertising giant, and Matra. It was not just a question of denationalizing what the Socialists had acquired: major banks in state hands since the 1940s were to go too, and much else: but not utilities such as the railways. The programme was making progress when it was stymied by the Wall Street crash of October 1987 – and then postponed, for the next five years, by the Left's return to power in 1988.

One aspect of the anti-state drive under Chirac was to complete the freeing of prices begun by Barre. This was quickly achieved for most industrial goods except pharmaceuticals, books and tobacco – and the Patronat was delighted, for the controls had been irksome, typical of the worst side of *dirigisme*. This is how they worked. If an electrical firm, say, wanted to increase the price of some model, it had to arrange with its competitors to prepare a joint dossier showing how production costs and other factors had affected business. It took this to the Ministry of Finance which then weighed the economic and social implications, and after much haggling the decision on a new price – to be applied to all firms – was taken by the bureaucrats. The system distorted competition and often made it harder for a firm to plan its production: it is argued that the steel industry might not have got into such a plight if it had been able to raise its prices as it wished at the right time. The controls were not always applied too rigidly, and some clever firms found ways round them: but *patrons* thought the system time-consuming and humiliating. Worse, it tended to encourage ententes, notably among smaller firms who would share out the market between them as they could not compete on prices. All that has now gone.

The Socialists, back in office in 1988, had by now accepted the market economy, so they did not try to renationalize: but nor did they want to continue the privatizations. So Mitterrand announced a policy of '*ni . . . ni*', 'We'll do neither one nor the other', and for the next five years the status quo was kept. But then Balladur, after March 1993, assertively took up Chirac's half-finished programme, and earned over 100 billion francs from sales of prosperous firms that easily found buyers, including more banks, the revived Rhône-Poulenc, and the oil giants Elf-Aquitaine and Total. Juppé in 1995–7 had more difficulty, for most of the 'easy' sales had by now been made, and many of the firms left on the list either were heavily in debt or had an uncertain future. The fragile steel group Usinor/Sacilor was re-privatized; so was Péchiney, but for a 'mere' 6 billion francs. Renault, by now losing money, moved back into majority private control, and there were plans for selling Air France, Aerospatiale and the troubled Crédit Lyonnais (see below).

Juppé's Government was glad of the extra money from the sell-offs, in order to help it subsidize job creation and reduce the state budget deficit. However, the net revenue from the programme had always been less than expected: some 240 billion francs had been made from the sales since 1986, but nearly as much had been spent, according to official estimates, on special aid to state-owned firms in trouble, notably Air France and Crédit Lyonnais. The buyers of the privatized firms were in most cases the French banks plus individual shareholders, or other industrial firms that took holdings. Under EU rules the sales were equally open to European buyers, and to non-Europeans, too, within limits, and many American pension funds began to acquire holdings (see p. 711). The Government did not want this process to go too far. In Balladur's day, it tried in some cases to retain part control of a newly privatized firm, through the notorious so-called '*noyaux durs*': that is, it would arrange for its own trusted allies in industry or finance to acquire a 'hard nucleus' of the shares, often in a sensitive sector such as armaments. This blatant exploitation by the RPR of its links with the banks and Patronat attracted heavy criticism, and later the practice was mostly dropped. But in a sense it re-emerged dramatically late in 1996, when the tycoon Jean-Luc Lagardère was chosen by Juppé – with Korean help – as a *noyau dur* for the huge defence electronics group, Thomson.

This Thomson saga has been the most amazing of the planned privatizations of recent years, and it shed some light on the devious methods of the Juppé Government. The group consisted of Thomson CSF, main supplier of electronics and telecommunications equipment to the armed forces; and Thomson Multimédia (TMM), a giant producer of TV sets and videos, with a worldwide staff of 50,000. Both were nationalized in 1982, TMM totally, Thomson CSF by 58 per cent. Juppé then set about selling them off, secretively, by private treaty. He was widely expected to choose Alcatel, the reputed telecommunications firm, an eager candidate. But finally he and Chirac opted for Lagardère, political ally of the RPR, affable playboy, thrusting financier, and brilliantly successful boss of Matra and its media affiliate, Hachette. Lagardère badly wanted Thomson CSF, but not TMM, which despite its expertise had been piling up a large debt. So Juppé agreed to the sale of TMM to the Korean electrical group Daewoo, keen to increase its presence in Europe. This provoked a storm among the public and especially the unions. 'Will Daewoo really honour its promise to protect French jobs and create new ones? – what of its poor social record at its existing factory in France? – is not its own output too downmarket? – and is it right to sell such a proud French firm to Asians?' Such questions were asked, some openly xenophobic.

There was also anger that Juppé was planning to sell off TMM for 1 symbolic franc, i.e. for nothing, because of its debt and the need to recapitalize first. The EU Commission, too, expressed doubts. And then, astoundingly, in December 1996, France's own Privatization Commission came out against the entire planned sale to Lagardère and Daewoo, as being 'not in the national interest'. This government-backed semi-autonomous body of seven 'wise men' had generally been a rubber stamp in the past, but now showed its muscle. Juppé had little choice but to cancel the whole project, and was left looking very foolish. So next the Government decided to postpone any sale of TMM until it was refinanced, and to start again with offering Thomson CSF to new bidders. This had not yet been done when the Socialists came to power. They were expectedly wary of privatizing so crucial a defence supplier, but they wanted to bring in new capital. So they announced a complex plan whereby Thomson CSF would go into partnership with Alcatel and Dassault: these firms would have 25 per cent of the capital, 30 per cent would be put on the open market, while the State with 40 per cent would keep some control. This would form part of a basic restructuring of the French defence industry, which had begun under Juppé; European alliances would be sought later. It seemed a realistic compromise solution to a tormented drama. As for TMM, its huge debt would first be reduced by restructuring, before any new buyer was sought; by 1998 it was starting to show a profit and the Government began to sell part of its capital to Alcatel, Microsoft and others. So why did Jospin switch from Matra to Alcatel? Partly because its industrial profile on defence was closer to Thomson's. Or was it just because Juppé had preferred Lagardère?

Jospin, in many ways a traditional French Socialist, had come to power very wary of further privatizations. But he was persuaded by his Finance Minister, Dominique Strauss-Kahn, a pragmatic social democrat, that if France was to join EMU, and keep abreast of world competition, then she must adapt. So the new Government went well beyond Mitterrand's cautious *ni . . . ni*: it allowed some enterprises to open their capital widely to the market, while keeping majority state control. This was true of Air France, as of France Télécom. Jospin carefully avoided using the word 'privatization', but spoke of 'involving the private sector': he knew that he had to keep a careful balance between market realities and the views of his own rank and file and of the unions and his Communist partners. It was helpful that even the PCF had now relaxed its classic abhorrence of any kind of privatization, and was accepting that Air France could put shares on the market (see p. 136). Remarkably, Jospin in 1998 agreed that the mighty Aerospatiale, which makes military equipment as well as civil aircraft, should be largely privatized, in the context of plans for a new European aerospace merger. It was the most striking example of how far he had moved from his earlier stance, in just a year. Today, apart from a few other firms in the defence field, such as Snecma (engines) and GIAT (tanks), there are hardly any manufacturing industries still left wholly in state hands. And the same applies to banking and insurance.

*

The French upper bourgeoisie, or a large part of it, has long been suspicious of the world of private banking and finance. This was true of Mitterrand, and earlier of de Gaulle, who in 1945 nationalized the three biggest clearing banks and the main insurance companies. So the French economic 'miracle' of the boom years was achieved at a time when 70 per cent of banking was in state hands. In those days, this worked fairly well, for the State had its own dynamism. But it meant that the banks were slow to modernize. Some, such as Société Générale, were among the largest in the world: but they remained cautious about risk financing, and this sometimes inhibited industrial ventures. The few big private banks, led by Paribas and Suez, were a little more adventurous. But state control of the big banks impeded the growth of the Bourse and limited the capital for investment. The Socialists then made matters worse: they spared the mutualist banks and a few tiny local ones, but they took over thirty-six other private banks. The State thereafter used its near-monopoly of finance with some discretion, and there were few reported cases of direct pressure, e.g. of loans being refused to a firm hostile to the Government; banks were left free in their day-to-day policies. But there was an inherent lack of flexibility and true competition. 'It was a crazy policy, just when the rest of the West was liberalizing,' a Banque de France director told me.

Chirac after 1986, and later Balladur, not only freed the banks taken over by the Left but went on to privatize almost all the big ones, and the insurance firms, that had been in state hands since 1945. Today this process is nearly complete, save for Crédit Lyonnais. As in the case of industry, Governments have been motivated not just by ideology, but by the belief that France's financial world has no choice but to align with other countries, in the new context leading to EMU. Even on the moderate Left, state control of banking today has few supporters, and the Jospin Government has no plans to renationalize. The banking world itself has modernized considerably in recent years. It has become more enterprising, more helpful to clients and less enmeshed in red tape.

This has been helped by the semi-autonomy given to the Banque de France since 1994. Balladur wanted to bring it in line with the Bundesbank, in preparation for monetary union. It is now free to set French interest rates itself, rather than follow government dictates; and so far it has been able to do this without undue pressure. The recent banking changes have also helped to strengthen the Bourse de Paris and to make it more lively and modern. The total of individual French shareholders tripled during Chirac's privatization drive of 1986–8, to reach 4.5 million: but ordinary Frenchmen are still less used than *les Anglo-Saxons* to putting their money into shares, and they have been deterred by some nasty failures, such as that of Eurotunnel (see p. 145). Mergers have grown recently both in banking and in insurance, where AXA joined up with GAN in 1997 to form one of the world's largest groups in its field. The Indosuez bank has been acquired by the remarkable Crédit Agricole, the world's fourth largest bank, a highly successful mutualist operation that began as a service to farmers and in 1997 made a profit of 9.9 billion francs. Now most experts believe that French banks are still too numerous, too undercapitalized, and that more regrouping must come as France enters the world of the euro.

In 1999 the attempt by the big Banque Nationale de Paris to buy Société Générale caused a mighty stir. Finally the authorities forbade this hostile take-over, and BNP had to content itself with acquiring just Paribas. The crisis showed how much French habits have been evolving under the pressure of an open global economy. Instead of the usual secrecy, the battle was fought out in broad daylight, in an Anglo–American manner. But the Government still played a role. And one major objective, that of preventing these banks from being sold abroad, was achieved.

Today banking is mostly a stable and successful world, despite one huge and spectacular disaster in the early 1990s. Jean-Yves Haberer, a clever and ambitious *inspecteur des finances*, became chairman in 1988 of Crédit Lyonnais, one of the leading state-owned banks. Planning to build it into the world's largest bank, he invested massively abroad and expanded recklessly, speculating that the franc would re-enter inflation and devalue, and that he could exploit this. He was encouraged by Bérégovoy's Government. But the strategy failed, the franc did not devalue, and by 1992–3 Crédit Lyonnais was piling up gigantic losses. Haberer left, and succeeding Governments were obliged to shore up the bank's liabilities at a cost of over 100 billion francs. It was the biggest banking crash in French history. The Government began to take action against Haberer for gross imprudence, and in 1998 he was under judicial investigation for 'complicity in bankruptcy by ruinous methods'. The EU Commission in 1998 finally agreed *post hoc* to the Government's massive special aid, in breach of the competition rules. But it posed strict conditions. The bank must pull in its horns radically, closing seventy branches in France (it has already sold its British and Italian subsidiaries) and it must be privatized by late 1999. The whole affair has lent fuel to the 'liberal' argument against state-controlled banking, seen as either too cautious or, in this untypical case, too rash. The head of a private bank, responsible to his shareholders, might have been more easily restrained from such adventures.

While the sell-offs in industry and banking are now largely settled, another issue – the deregulation of public services – has been causing heated discussion. Here the French are torn. On the one hand, their Government has subscribed in principle to the new EU policy: it accepts that more open competition may be needed, in terms of cost and efficiency. On the other, the French remain proud of their own model of state monopoly services, mainly in electricity, telephones, post and railways. They feel that this prized *modèle français* has served the public well and provides equality of access. Ideally, they would like to keep some elements of this model, while deregulating. But can they have it both ways? No other recent issue has underlined more sharply the dilemma in France between *étatisme* and liberalism.

The French know that in some other countries such as Britain, where state services have previously worked less well, deregulation has already brought benefits – for example, to British Telecom. And in France the 'liberal' lobby argues that its public services may have become an expensive luxury. These have high technical quality and are fair to all, rich and poor: but, lacking competition, they suffer from overstaffing and rigidity, and are allowed to make operating losses. Yet the public is generally satisfied, and there has been little grassroots move for change. And the French system has had its virtues, as one defender, Jacques Dondoux, former head of France Télécom, suggested to me in 1996: 'I come from a remote district in the Massif Central, where electricity and telephones cost no more than anywhere else; there are plenty of public cabins, and the services are kept in good repair. Yet in these rural areas they run at a loss, inevitably. Our grave worry is that, despite the legal assurances, if competition arrives the effort will go to the towns, and country folk will either have to pay much more, or the services there will steadily decline.' There are signs today that he might be proved right.

Meanwhile the staff of these services have grown anxious that deregulation could lead to loss of jobs, or it could mean the end of their privileged status as state employees, even if their service is not privatized. The unions, far stronger in this sector than in industry, have several times called strikes. So the Juppé Government, in a period of unrest in

1995–6, proceeded warily with a deregulation that in fact it wanted. It negotiated hard in Brussels to be allowed to keep some aspects of the 'French model': in the end, it did win some concessions, and agreements were reached. And the Socialist Government has gone along with this, for although it is ideologically attached to the public-service tradition, it is also pro-Europe. In fact, nearly all parties, except the Communists, now accept deregulation. An influential lobby in the upper civil service fought long and hard to prevent it. Many were idealistic believers in the 'French model', as their leader, Christian Stoffaës, told me: 'We have the best public services in the world, it would be crazy to spoil them.' But basically he did not get his way.

Deregulation has been going ahead at various speeds in the different services. It makes best sense in an internationally competitive area such as air flights, and here the Government has accepted the new European rules and obliged Air France to follow (see p. 135). But there is no question yet of deregulating the railways (see p. 140), nor the postal services. The main disputes have been over telecommunications, and over Électricité de France (EDF), a proud body with a statute dating from 1946 and a monopoly since then in public supply. EDF is technically advanced, but sometimes wasteful. In face of deregulation, it has fought to retain its monopoly as far as possible: it has argued, first, that it is a vital national utility like the post, not a mere commercial enterprise like an airline; and secondly, that as 75 per cent of French electricity is nuclear by origin, EDF plays a role in French independence and must keep its special status.

Yet, in Europe, pressures for open competition have been growing. Germany and Britain have led the way, wanting total deregulation; Italy and Spain have held a middle position, while France and some other countries have been reticent. The Government has accepted in principle a degree of deregulation, but has fought for it to be limited. After long negotiations, France in 1996 finally reached a compromise with the European Commission, whereby it would open about a third of its market to free competition and free prices, in stages, from 1999. The major consumers, mostly the big firms, will then be able to choose their supplier freely, while EDF will keep a monopoly for its myriad small customers. And about 30 per cent of production will be freed too, enabling a foreign company to produce and sell electricity in France, under the new EU rules. But EDF is not to be privatized (quite another matter), nor will the status of its staff be changed.

Telecommunications are a different story. Here there has been no compromise, and France Télécom has had to face the full impact of open competition, since deregulation came into force in 1998. Though losing its monopoly, it remains a public service, under state majority ownership: but it is being forced to adapt radically to the challenge of a new era. Though heavily bureaucratic, it has long been technically brilliant, with its fully automated network and its pioneering Minitel; and in recent years it has even shown an operating profit. It has been in far better shape than British Telecom used to be. Yet big changes have been needed.

In 1995 France Télécom was lucky to acquire a new chairman, Michel Bon, who had been head of the dynamic hypermarket chain Carrefour – a vigorous man with commercial attitudes and experience, who enjoyed the task of adapting the venerable public service to its new role. He faced the hostility of the staff to the changes, which included a new statute. But he managed to negotiate a deal, whereby overstaffing would be resolved by early retirement, not dismissals; and the existing staff would keep their prized status as *fonctionnaires*, while new ones would be hired on a different basis. It all involved a long tussle with the unions. And Bon in various ways modernized France Télécom. In 1996–7, so as to prepare for competition, he reduced telephone charges considerably, as in other countries. Technical advances made this feasible. There remains the problem of how to pay for the upkeep of uneconomic lines in rural areas. A new law provides subsidies for this, and makes it obligatory. Even so in 1998 France Télécom was planning to close down thousands of phone boxes, claiming that their use had been much reduced by the spread of mobiles and their upkeep was too costly. Local people and regional groups reacted with fury.

While in some other European countries, not only Britain, privatization has been complete, in France it was decided that the State would keep majority control of France Télécom but would open out its capital – and the Socialists, at first wary, came to accept this policy. So 1997 saw the historic spectacle of a Socialist Government presiding over the sale, on the Bourse, of part of a public service. Some 20 per cent of shares were sold, with great success, for 42 billion francs, mostly to about 4 million small buyers. Then in 1998 more were sold, and Michel Bon said that the State's share would be reduced to 63 per cent. Today domestic competition is finally growing. The market for mobiles in France has been free since 1987, and after a slow start it is now expanding fast: it rose sharply in the summer of 1998, to reach a total of over 8 million subscribers. For fixed lines, a new private company, Cegetel, allied to Britain's BT, started up in 1998 as the main rival to the public service. Private or foreign firms have now taken 13 per cent of the market, and as in Britain this new competition has cut tariffs by some 30 per cent. Some experts remain doubtful as to how far France Télécom, with its rooted non-commercial habits, will be able to succeed in this new cut-throat world. But Michel Bon is determined to prove that a French public service can adjust from *étatisme* to the free market.

The French telephone service has succeeded once before in making a dramatic change. Until about 1970, as a daily tool, it suffered from startling neglect. This was not through any lack of technical flair, where France has always excelled, but simply from underinvestment. Governments showed a curious tendency to regard the telephone as a private bourgeois luxury rather than a business and social necessity; and the first 'Plans' ignored it. In 1970 France still had fewer lines per capita than Greece, and the saying went, 'Half the nation is waiting for a phone to be installed, and the other half for a dialling tone.' There was very few trunk lines, and the long queues waiting to make calls in many a post office were a disgrace for a nation calling itself modern. Many new firms in the provinces had to survive for months with just one or two lines: this wasted thousands of business man-hours a day, and even dissuaded some companies from moving their plant. Finally the Government woke up and sanctioned huge investment by the Ministry of Post and Telecommunications (P. et T.), whose budget for it rose from 2.5 billion to 245 billion between 1969 and 1979! So today France is fully abreast of other countries: some 96 per cent of homes now have a telephone, and the number of lines has risen since 1970 from 4.2 to 33 million. Even in remote areas, public cabins have become plentiful, mostly taking phone cards. Yet thirty years ago a local village exchange would shut down totally outside office hours, lunchtime included. And the waiting list for getting a phone, for a private subscriber, has been cut since 1975 from an average sixteen months to about a week.

Yet while millions were still waiting for a phone in their home, the brilliantly inventive engineers of the ministry were in the vanguard of world progress. Soon after the war, France pioneered the first experiment in long-distance automatic dialling. Then in the 1970s the P. et T. excitedly set up a prototype videophone link between Paris and West Africa. And the previous long backlog in France has at least meant that the network finally developed is super-modern: for some years it has been totally automatic and totally digital, ahead of Britain. Much of the new equipment has been developed and made by French firms, notably Alcatel. And today the officials of France Télécom are bursting with national pride in their achievements.

The famous Minitel was pioneered by France Télécom in 1984, well ahead of Internet. It is a small screen with keyboard, which serves as an electronic telephone directory and is also linked to the central databanks, thus becoming an instant newspaper, mail-order service, booking office, encyclopaedia and so on. Not easy to operate at first, it is far less cumbersome than piles of paper directories: if, for example, you type a name on to the screen, Minitel will at once come up with the details of all those in France with that name. It has also become used as a lonely-hearts dating service, even as a plaything for *risqué* erotic exchanges between strangers. France Télécom at first offered Minitel free to any subscriber, hoping to recoup the costs from the extra telephone usage, and from not having to issue printed directories. And today the simpler Minitels are still supplied free, though you have to pay a small rent for the newer, more sophisticated models. Today there are some 6.5 million terminals, 80 per cent of them in private homes. The operation has been considered a success, far more so than the British equivalent, Prestel, which flopped. And the French are proud of their Minitel, as a home-grown invention.

It has however now delayed the penetration of Internet in France, for obvious reasons. Rather than switch to Internet, many French households and even offices prefer to stick with Minitel, which has the advantage of not needing a PC and modem. National pride is involved too, the cult of French genius: 'Minitel is better than Internet in some ways,' a France Télécom engineer told me, 'so we have less need to import a foreign invention.' But this arrogant short-sighted attitude means that France has been doing less than many of its rivals to link into the new 'information highways' – and this could be harmful.

The Socialist Government is aware of it, and Jospin in 1997 pledged an 'action programme' for Internet and personal computers. This is needed, for the French have also been slow to take part in the PC revolution: many schools do not even have one, and the conservative French teaching world has been reluctant to put computer training into the curriculum. Private purchases are now at last growing fast, and the hypermarkets are full of PCs with modems: but still only some 16 per cent of French households have a PC, compared with 20 to 25 per cent in Britain and Germany, 40 per cent in America. With Internet, the gap is far greater: some 500,000 offices or homes are linked to it in France, against 4 million in Britain and 40 million in the US. However, under government impulse, more schools are now getting PCs, more public offices are taking Internet – and it is tacitly accepted that Minitel will slowly fade away. It is even argued that the French, having the 'keyboard culture' in their bones thanks to Minitel, will now find it easier than most to adapt to the Internet world, if they try. Meanwhile Internet is posing the same legal problems of control and censorship as in other countries: a book banned in France, about Mitterrand's last illness, was cheekily put on Internet by a café in Besançon, and the judiciary had no idea how to deal with it.

As far as the larger private firms are concerned, the old issue of *étatisme* today seems largely solved. They have much the same normal relations with the Government as in other countries, and can carry out their own policies without undue pressure. Most today are doing rather well, in the new cross-frontier world of open competition; and they will agree that the old state *tutelle* has lightened considerably. The new EU rules on fair competition have played their part, making it harder for a government to play the old game of bribing a firm with loans in return for political obedience. When two big companies today want to proceed with a joint venture or a merger, they will go ahead and fix it up themselves, without undue reference to the Élysée or Matignon. Even in the case of the still partly nationalized Renault, the State was unable in 1997 to prevent it from closing down a factory in Belgium, despite the uproar. If any strong *tutelle* survives today, it is primarily in the social field, where the State still supervises a firm's staffing policies (see p. 176), with a mountain of bureaucratic regulations that govern not only dismissals but hiring of staff: for each new recruit, this can involve filling in ten to twelve different forms. The larger or more modern firms know how to cope. But for smaller ones, the weight of bureaucracy can add to their reluctance to expand or take risks.

It is in the public services, inevitably, that the old *étatiste* rules and attitudes persist most strongly. Change has been coming, but slowly. The arrival of deregulation and of more competition will make a difference, but it will take time. Meanwhile the job security of public employees, plus overstaffing, have served to produce ingrained rigidities: the Banque de France, for instance, has a staff of 16,000, compared with the Bank of England's 6,000 for a comparable work load, and slimming can be done only slowly, by agreement with the unions, as older staff retire. Most foreign analysts of France stress that staff resistance to change, above all in the public sector, is greater than in comparable countries; and it contrasts with the dynamism of many of the technical élites, and of *cadres* in private firms. The director of one American consultancy firm in Paris told me, 'The blockages are considerable. Usually the people at the top know exactly what needs to be done to remedy matters, but they fail to apply it. They dare not go against their lower management, who do not want to lose their *positions acquises* or change their working methods' (see p. 721). 'There is always this gulf in France between the élitist few at the top and the rest. It has something to do with education, and having the right diplomas.' That is one key to the problem. France still has this distinctive élitist structure, based on a few colleges and exclusive state corps. Have their clever alumni been a major factor behind French post-war success, as is commonly supposed? Or are they now an obstacle?

THE ÉLITIST TECHNOCRATS OF 'X' AND ENA: STILL A STRENGTH, OR NOW A HANDICAP?

A former women's prison in Strasbourg is today the principal home of by far the most influential college in Europe. Its alumni include Chirac, Jospin, Aubry, Rocard, Giscard, Balladur, Juppé . . . over half of the big names in recent French politics. This is the École Nationale d'Administration (ENA), created by de Gaulle in 1946 to train senior civil servants, though today in practice it has gone well beyond that brief: ENA's products, nicknamed *les énarques* (a term with a ring of Grecian wisdom?), have acquired much of the real influence in France, in diverse fields, and their disciplined rule is loosely dubbed *l'énarchie* – the opposite of *l'anarchie*. Their postgraduate college has been steadily gaining ground over its older rival, École Polytechnique ('X'), a Napoleonic creation, breeder of high-level engineers and grandest of the Grandes Écoles.

This self-perpetuating élitist system is peculiar to France, with little equivalent elsewhere: it is not at all the same as Oxbridge. And for years it has been much criticized. Is it still a strength, or has it become a liability? On the positive side, it has supplied the State and the economy with a pool of high-level technocratic talent, able to push through bold schemes (such as the TGV) or to govern strongly. But, socially, it has served to add to French inequalities. The two rival schools may each have a fairly wide intake: but then they create narrow privileged élites with too much power. Or so it is argued, and it leads to grievances: those without the right diploma, however gifted, can find their careers blocked for life. And today the rigidities of the structure might even be breeding some economic inefficiencies. Criticisms have come alike from Left and Right – from the Socialists and recently from Chirac. Yet Left and Right equally tend to find the system useful, once they are in power. Many key politicians are themselves alumni, thus wary of reform.

Technocracy, in its dictionary definition, means 'the government or control of society or industry by technical experts' – the domain of Polytechnique. But ENA too, though its training is more general, tends to foster a technocratic spirit. This has flourished in France since Colbert's day; and under the Fifth Republic it took a big step forward. De Gaulle, who despised the old career politicians, put civil servants with a technocratic bent into many key ministerial posts: Edgard Pisani, Olivier Guichard and others. In that heady period of post-war economic renewal, many technocrats were idealistic crusaders, bound by a faith in technical progress as a key to human happiness. One archetype was Louis Armand, a *polytechnicien* who reorganized French railways, led the state search for mineral wealth in the Sahara in the 1950s, pioneered Euratom, then rounded off a fabulous career by heading the Channel Tunnel study group (which the British sabotaged). It is hard to imagine a 'mere' engineer in Britain enjoying the same status as visionary sage and Grand Old Man. But his kind of inspired ethos has today waned. Many technocrats have abused their power; or they are seen as remote, impersonal figures, arrogantly imposing their decisions in the belief that they, with their special expertise, are bound to know best.

The revulsion against this was one factor in Mitterrand's 1981 victory. He was not a technocrat, while Giscard before him was an arch-technocrat, a supreme product of the élitist system, wearing all three of its proudest badges, 'X', ENA, IF – that is, one of the very few Frenchmen to have passed through *both* Polytechnique *and* ENA, and then to have joined the Inspection des Finances, most influential and exclusive of the so-called Grands Corps. These dozen or so state collegiate bodies, recruited mostly from 'X' and ENA, and operating parallel to the ministries, are the key to the French élitist apparatus. Some of their mandarins, with their tight old-boy networks, have been able to move into senior posts in politics, and Giscard's years in power were the apotheosis of this trend. Mitterrand failed to reverse it, even though he and some of his key ministers, such as Delors, were not products of the system.

The structure itself is not new: some Grands Corps date back to before Napoleon. Their mechanism is highly complex, and there is nothing like them in Britain. Each corps has a specific technical role – for instance, the Cour des Comptes audits state accounts – but their more significant function, by tradition, is to provide State and industry with an invaluable reservoir of top-level talent, mobile and polyvalent. The corps are in two rival camps: technical ones (such as the Corps des Mines), led by engineers recruited mainly from Polytechnique; and 'administrative' ones (e.g. the Conseil d'État, Inspection des Finances), whose members come mainly from ENA and are today the more influential. Each school and corps has its active old-boy loyalties, notably strong among *les X*, as *polytechniciens* are nicknamed. Some other leading Grandes Écoles, too, have potent networks, such as the École des Hautes Études Commerciales (HEC).

All this may bear some relation to the days when the British Cabinet and Whitehall were dominated by Etonians, Wykehamists and Balliol men: but whereas in Britain these old-school-tie mafias have today weakened and become largely social, in France they have grown stronger since the war and closer to politics. And the prestige of the great Écoles and the grander corps, and the golden careers they offer, inevitably tempt much of France's best young talent to join them. Conversely, such fields as the media, the universities or merchant banks offer lower prestige and fewer lofty outlets than in Britain: so the kind of brilliant graduate who might aim for the BBC or the City is more likely in France to go into public service or industry, via a wide range of state agencies or private firms which seek their leaders from the Grands Corps. This system may have brought various advantages for the economy, but it also has drawbacks. And it is constantly under criticism for its rigidity and 'unfair' élitism – especially from its own ex-alumni, stricken maybe with conscience at their own privileges. Sometimes they turn out books with such titles as *La Mafia polytechnicienne*.

ENA, not itself a Grande École, is entirely postgraduate or in-service. It was founded in Paris in 1946: but today half of the teaching is done in Strasbourg, in a former women's prison. It might have been just the place to put Édith Cresson, according to the many people who reacted with alarm and fury to her decision as Prime Minister, in 1992, to transfer ENA *en bloc* to Strasbourg. She had Mitterrand's backing (both were non-*énarques*, disliked ENA, and wanted to reduce its influence): but she consulted no one else, and her bombshell provoked near-disbelief and bitter protests from most of the French establishment, including some of her own ministers. But she pushed ahead, pointing out that the move was in line with the long-established state policy of decentralizing some key bodies from Paris to the regions (see p. 265). The rebuilding of the ex-prison began; and when Balladur, a devoted *énarque*, became premier, he found it too late to scrap a project which he, too, hated. So he came up with a Solomonic compromise: the school would be split in equal halves; its headquarters would be in Strasbourg, but half of a student's studies would still be done in its handsome older building near St-Germain-des-Prés. And that remains the situation today, much resented for its expense and inconvenience. The Cour des Comptes has worked out that the split costs an extra 16 million francs a year. Few of ENA's lecturers are on the staff, so they have to come specially from Paris each time. As for the staff, 'We are constantly to-ing and fro-ing, staying in hotels, it's a fearful waste of time,' said one executive, while students feel much the same. And though Strasbourg is a delightful city, its European political role does not benefit the school much, for MEPs are there only about three days a month.

ENA has often been accused of having a narrow élitist recruitment: but this is not quite true. Matters were worse in pre-ENA days, when the Inspection des Finances recruited its members via an oral test where candidates wore white gloves and had to prove their high social status. ENA was created partly to counter this snobbery and to widen the intake to the Grands Corps. It has had some success, if limited. About half its intake today consists of students in their twenties who come direct from higher education. Their ultra-competitive entrance exam, though fair in itself, is passed mostly by those who have enjoyed the right specialized teaching at a handful of élite colleges, led by the mighty 'Sciences-Po' in Paris. This has always recruited largely from the better Paris *lycées*, heavily upper-bourgeois. Today its intake, and thus ENA's too, has become a little more provincial and socially diverse: but it is still true that over 75 per cent of ENA's student entrants come from the families of senior *cadres*, teachers or other professional classes.

However, ENA does also operate a parallel late-entrant system, the *concours interne*, for civil servants in their thirties or early forties who have proved their ability; and they are of more varied social origin. This stream has expanded since the 1970s and today accounts for as many ENA entrants (*c.* 45 per cent) as come direct from higher education; a further 8 to 10 per cent are recruited from the professions, local politics, trade unions, etc. So the élite, though still super-competitive, has widened its gates. ENA has also grown much more international: as well as the 100 French entrants each year, some thirty-five others are foreign, from a range of countries. Many are from the EU: at one time, *twelve* of the members of Chancellor Kohl's staff were *énarques*, including his chief diplomatic adviser, Joachim Bitterlich, a true Francophile. So ENA has become less *hexagonal*, more open, more like the London School of Economics.★

Today ENA does not so much recruit from a privileged caste as create one: it is still open to the charge of élitism, in the attitudes it moulds and the career doors it opens. Take the case of Alain Juppé himself, son of a modest farmer in Gascony: he did superbly at his local *lycée*, went to the École Normale Supérieure (ENS), then to ENA, became an *inspecteur des finances*, and by the time he was Prime Minister he was a byword for a certain cool technocratic arrogance – due not entirely to his own personality, for ENA's training is thought to encourage such traits. During their 27-month course, its French entrants first spend a year away on a *stage*, often in a *préfecture* or a French embassy abroad, or even in a foreign organization (e.g. a Whitehall ministry). This usefully broadens the horizons of those who have come straight from education. And it is popular with the students: I met a group who had worked at embassies in Lagos, Lisbon and Buenos Aires, at *préfectures* in the Jura, St-Étienne and Tahiti. Then fourteen months are spent inside ENA, where the course today includes a stress on languages and European matters, but is primarily concerned with inculcating the techniques and correct attitudes of the upper civil service. It produces a breed who are brilliant, very self-assured, and mostly conformist in ideas – '*l'école de la pensée unique*', it has been called. If you ask an *énarque* a question, he will snap back, '*Il*

★ It has also become more like another renowned French post-war creation, INSEAD, at Fontainebleau. This Institut Européen d'Administration des Affaires, Europe's premier international business school, gives expensive postgraduate training to future managerial leaders, helping them to develop a 'European' outlook. It did not succeed in making a keen Europhile of its best-known British alumnus: William Hague.

y a quatre points, ici', and then proceed to ad lib them. In the Brussels corridors of power, only British Eurocrats have an equal reputation for mental dexterity.

Above all, the final exam classifies *énarques* in rigid order of merit, enabling the top ones to choose, in order, the thirty or so places offered each year by the Grands Corps. The rest of the annual output must then settle for more ordinary jobs in ministries or other public bodies: but even this ensures them a decent career for life, with far better status and promotion prospects than *non-énarques*. Some 20 per cent today go into the private sector: but if they do so within ten years, they must refund the cost of their studies (ENA otherwise is free to the French entrants). Of the five Grands Corps served by ENA, the Inspection des Finances remains the most sought after by those high on the pass-out list, followed by the Conseil d'État, the Cour des Comptes, the Corps Diplomatique and then the Corps Préfectoral. So why does the prospect of becoming an ambassador or prefect have less appeal than joining a corps whose work might seem relatively dull and anonymous? – the Corps des Comptes, like IF, has the job of verifying public accounts, while the Conseil d'État advises on legal disputes between State and citizen. In practice, the Quai d'Orsay, like the Foreign Office, has seen its appeal decline in an age when diplomatic work is done by jet-setting Clintons and ambassadors are 'post-boxes'. The prefectoral corps hoisted its prestige during the Gaullist era, but has lost some of it again since the Socialists' devolution of power to local bodies. Nor has it ever been able to compete, in the eyes of ambitious young *énarques*, with those three corps that offer the greatest freedom and scope and are often the best springboards for a political career, whether of Right or Left: Chirac is a member of the Cour des Comptes, Balladur of the Conseil d'État, and Rocard of the Inspection des Finances.

Consider the Conseil d'État: with its elegant premises in the Palais Royal, it is almost a political club, and to join it is a little like becoming a Prize Fellow of All Souls', save that it is *far* closer to the seats of power. A young *conseiller* may have to spend some of his time there on routine work, but with initiative he can soon pick up more interesting part-time jobs too – say, advising a minister on Eastern Europe. Nor is the high pay any disincentive. And the right contacts may lead him to a position of some power in a minister's *cabinet*.

Once a member of a corps, you remain so for life and are salaried by it. So, if your political or business career comes unstuck for a while, you can always make a tactical retreat to the security of the corps, and from there plan some new venture. Many less ambitious souls do in fact remain in their corps, using it as a sinecure. But it also provides a flexibility that can enable a brilliant and energetic man to make full and diverse use of his gifts in the State's service. And this reservoir of talent has been valuable to France. It is the *inspecteurs des finances* who have best exploited the system. Their corps is attached to the Ministry of Finances, and its junior members spend their time – as under the monarchy – touring France to check that state funds are not being misspent. But the more senior ones have manoeuvred their way into many corners of real power. Jean-Claude Trichet, governor of the Bank of France, is an *inspecteur*; so are Michel Bon, head of France Télécom, and Roger Fauroux, former head of St-Gobain. By unwritten custom, a minister is expected to have in his *cabinet* at least one *inspecteur*, chosen by the corps and acting almost as a spy for *les Finances*. The Inspection is a real mafia, maintaining its hold not only through intellectual prowess but by fostering a calculated mystique: 'Do not allow the politicians you serve to understand you too well,' its secretary-general once advised some new members; 'preserve the mystery of your economic intuition and they will respect you the more.'

These hierarchies, based on ENA's final exam, are criticized for perpetuating a dual élitism: the average privileged *énarques*, and then above them, the super-élite of a few hundred in the three main Grands Corps, wielding such power. Many *énarques* themselves are critical. In 1972, in the wake of May '68, a whole 'year' of them bravely decided, on passing out, to boycott the grander corps in favour of mere ministries: one was Martine Aubry, who passed out high but opted for the Ministry of Social Affairs, with its lower prestige. Their gesture had no sequel.

The *inspecteurs* are often resented by the *polytechniciens* in the rival camp, whose fiefs – such as French railways – they have been invading. *Les X* form a larger mafia than the *énarques*, with a stronger solidarity, and are even more conservative. After a two-year technical course at their college, many of them go on to more specialized postgraduate *écoles d'application*, such as the École des Mines. And each school breeds its own old-boy corps of haughty exclusivity. They are less close to the political scene than the ENA corps: but in technical ministries such as Transport or Industry, and in the state bodies running electricity, postal services and so on, *les X* have long enjoyed a near monopoly of power. Rivalries are intense even between different clans of the *les X*, notably the Corps des Mines and the Corps des Ponts et Chaussées. But they will always drop the feud and close ranks in face of their common foe, the non-'X'. Any 'X' will usually try to fill a vacancy on his staff with another 'X', and will prefer to do business with another 'X', or help him out. It can cause bitterness to those who do not belong.

This virtual closed shop can lead to conservatism as often as to dynamism. Many 'X' develop a *rentier* spirit: their status protects them with a cushy job for life, and they feel little sympathy with innovation: the former failings of the French telephone service were often laid at the door of the 'X' who ran it. Trained as engineers, not executives, many *polytechniciens* have found themselves in a competitive world of modern management to which they are not well suited. Change is now coming, for a number of 'X' have been on courses to such places as the Harvard Business School and have returned with new ideas: but they are still a minority. A bigger change is that today up to 75 per cent of 'X' buy themselves out of state service, after a few years, and move into private industry or commerce where they can command huge salaries. Many firms welcome these élitist recruits with open arms, maybe less for their actual abilities than for their precious contacts. If you have an 'X' on your staff, or an *énarque*, he may be able to ring up just the right pal in the ministry that is blocking the crucial permit that you need. The French branch of Sony was once in dispute with the Ministry of Finance on some issue, and getting nowhere: so Sony in Tokyo astutely appointed an 'X' as its director for France, and he quickly settled matters with another 'X' in the minister's *cabinet*. It happens all the time.

So these and other networks have created an intricate mesh of personal links between public and private sector, including banks. This has brought advantages in a France notorious for its rigid barriers: a few men at the top, on the same wavelength, have been able to short-circuit the bureaucratic *lenteurs* of contact between rival administrations and get things moving. The Plan benefited from this. And yet, though the élites are a means of bypassing some blockages in society, they can create others. So it is not easy to draw up a balance sheet. One virtue of the system is its relative integrity: in all the recent corruption scandals, 'X' or *énarques* were involved far less often than politicians or businessmen. By paying them highly and treating them well, the State over the centuries has built up a body of senior servants who are generally honest and unbribable. And many do retain a sense of vocation and public service.

Yet time and again one is struck by the contrast between the dynamism of some individuals and the rigidity of the system enclosing them: it is as if initiative thrives on the challenge thus created.

The most damaging aspect of this rigidity is that people tend to be judged on the diplomas they possess, more than on their true merits. Hence the gulf that exists, in many a public body, between the élite stream and the rest. If by ill chance you failed to acquire the right diplomas in your youth, from ENA or some Grande École, you have little means of moving far up the hierarchy, however able you can prove yourself. The closed shops prevent it. This is especially true in the technical bodies, also in the Ministry of Finance where by custom the key posts are reserved for *inspecteurs* and other *énarques*. Inevitably, this leads to frustration and lack of initiative in the middle ranks, where so much regular work is done. ENA's late-entrant system now provides a way round this blockage, for some lucky ones: but you still need that ENA diploma to get proper promotion. In private industry, however, the barriers have now loosened, more than in state service: in most firms it has become much easier than thirty years ago for a gifted technician or *cadre* to move up the hierarchy without formal diplomas.

Another, if less formidable, barrier exists between the public service and other professions: people seldom move from one to the other, except via party politics. University professors, in their proud ghetto, would rarely deign, or be invited, to take up other public duties. Raymond Barre, who alternated for years between university and civil-service duties before going into politics, was an exception. Similarly, a clever businessman or industrialist would seldom be co-opted into state service as happens in the United States or even Britain: he would not be accepted without the right pedigree. A reverse process does happen often enough, as state technocrats become managers of private firms: but *les corps* will not allow the process to be two-way. It is partly a matter of family custom, in a land where the bourgeoisie has its own barriers: some leading families are producers of civil servants, others of academics, and others own factories. This has been changing slowly with a new generation, but many experts would like the trend to go faster.

Simon Nora, an eminent liberal *inspecteur* and former head of ENA, told me, 'Our élite system was a great asset in the post-war period when France was modernizing fast. The technocrats then were a dedicated *clergé*, the secular priests of progress, pulling France forward with autocratic zeal. But France is now largely modernized, and a more open and flexible system is needed.' On paper, Polytechnique and ENA are entirely democratic: anyone can go there, the entry and final exams are impartial, and nepotism only comes later. Both colleges may be still heavily middle class, but both have been widening their intake: 'X' has many entrants from worker and peasant families. Yet once inside the system, the élites are secluded by privilege, and this is a factor behind the citizen's regular sense of grievance against the State. Not that this is new: read Balzac, and you will find the same criticisms of *les X* as are made today of *les énarques*.

Recent Governments, both of Right and Left, have made only modest attempts to reform the system. They may denounce it while in opposition, but once in power they find they depend on it. Thus Chirac, campaigning for President in 1995, railed against his fellow *énarques* as 'an omnipotent caste divorced from reality, more talented in flattery than decision-making', and he promised reform – but then did little. Mitterrand himself, from a classic university stream, was no lover of the system. But many of his key ministers were among its products – Fabius, Rocard, Joxe, etc. – and the *cabinets ministériels* were as full of young Socialist *énarques* as they had been earlier of Rightist ones. *Plus ça change. . .* The Socialists, when nationalizing, needed to depend on the authority and stability of the system. And today they find they need it still, in the delicate tasks of deregulation. Lionel Jospin (Corps Diplomatique) has a team that includes Hubert Védrine (Conseil d'État), Jean-Pierre Chevènement (*énarque*) and Martine Aubry who, despite her earlier gesture, did later join the Conseil d'État. Their Government has promised, or attempted, a few reforms. It has asked Jacques Attali to propose crucial changes in the Grandes Écoles (see p. 570). And it is trying to persuade young *énarques* to start with junior jobs in the provinces, or to accept greater career mobility. But any such efforts to reduce the gulf will always meet with opposition. And the Socialists have no major blueprint for reform.

However, even if the élitist structure does not itself change, some recent developments have been tending to curtail its power. First, the regional devolution of the 1980s has not only reduced the role of the prefectoral corps, but diluted the influence of some major Paris-based technical corps, such as the Ponts et Chaussées: instead of working for a central authority, many of their members are now responsible to regional or local bodies, and this weakens their mafia. Secondly, the recent privatizations of many big firms, together with deregulation, have likewise tended to loosen the grip of the technocrats over the levers of power. Thirdly, and most importantly, as the French business world becomes more international, so the value of a French élite diploma begins to lessen: 'Until recently,' said one economist, 'a big firm might feel it wise to have an "X" as its boss. But now, with so many foreign contacts, it may feel that someone, say, with a Harvard degree can do the job better.' The brilliantly successful L'Oréal is headed by Welshman Lindsay Owen-Jones, from Oxford and INSEAD. And while French companies still hire some *énarques* or 'X', for their most senior posts they now increasingly want those who have had a broader training, too – for example, have gone on to the Harvard Business School or the Massachusetts Institute of Technology, or on some American postgraduate course. The growth of this super-élite within the élites is a major trend. Inside the civil service and politics, the Grands Corps may still hold sway: but in terms of real power, they are now yielding ground to the ascendant world of international business. With globalization, the bright *énarque* or *polytechnicien* thus faces a challenge that will require all his Grecian wisdom in the new climate of industry.

MODERN INDUSTRY'S SUCCESS STORY – AS LAME DUCKS ARE LEFT TO DROWN

France's larger industrial firms are today, nearly all of them, a big success story – whether it be Alcatel/Alsthom in engineering, L'Oréal making cosmetics, Danone in food products, Aerospatiale with Airbus, or others. They have weathered the recession of the 1993–5 period, and many have now restructured and raised their productivity. They may still complain about the rigid labour laws and high social charges: but they have now escaped from many of the more negative aspects of old-style *dirigisme*. The better ones have benefited from the spur of competition on world markets and have greatly increased their exports or their foreign assets. Many are still weakly capitalized. And during the uneasy 1990s, most were reluctant to invest: but this suddenly changed with the recovery of 1997–8, as new investment soared. Today most leading *patrons* are optimistic – about the euro and much else, if not about the impact of the proposed 35-hour week.

The Gaullist era of the 1960s was one of rapid modernization but also of some costly prestige ventures – such as the liner *France* – which may have added to national glory but did not always make good economic sense. This policy was then reduced under Giscard: he preferred that France should move ahead in high technology or luxury fields where she could do well on world markets. He and Barre also reduced the money and effort spent on shoring up older industries that had little competitive future. 'We must move towards a specialized economy,' said Giscard; 'we must steadily give up the production of mass goods at low prices: that is not our speciality.' One of his aides added, 'The hallmark of French exports, in the new technologies as in our traditional goods, must be high quality and sophistication — it's no use trying to compete with T-shirts made in Malaysia.' Ever since, even under the Socialists, this has broadly been the strategy that manufacturing firms have been encouraged to pursue.

On the whole, private companies have been doing better than the few that are still wholly or partly nationalized. With some ups and downs, the large concerns with the best recent record include St-Gobain and Air Liquide (both in chemicals); Alsthom, maker of the T G V locomotives, in the same group as Alcatel (telecommunications and other electronics); Michelin, pioneer of the radial tyre, now the world's largest tyre producer; and L'Oréal (cosmetics), also brilliantly multinational. Péchiney (metals, chemicals) and Rhône-Poulenc (chemicals) are now doing well after a hard period. The two big car firms, Peugeot-Citroën and Renault, have both run into trouble recently (see pp. 125–7). But Aerospatiale has been excelling with missiles and helicopters and in the Airbus (see p. 128–31). And the two oil firms, Elf-Aquitaine and Total, both make good profits.

These and other successes have been due in part to the rise in France of a new style of manager over the past forty years. For various reasons, industry enjoys higher prestige than in Britain as a career open to the talents: so it attracts graduate recruits of a higher calibre, which in turn lifts its prestige further. Some are the brighter alumni of ENA or the Grandes Écoles, and may have been trained also in America. Some try to marry French habits and attitudes with the best of American methods, and they may even get their firms reorganized by American consultancies. These new modern-minded managers have been gaining ground at the expense of the older-style family *patrons*, usually more wary of innovation or expansion: many an owner, worried by modern competition, has retired to a chairman's desk and handed over the daily running of the firm to a new-style executive. But a few of the older family empires survive, such as Michelin and Peugeot.

Parallel to the growth of the big corporations, recent decades have also seen the rise of a new style of independent entrepreneur; and a few have built up their own firms with dazzling results. Many have been self-made men without élite training: either they have inherited small family concerns and expanded them, or they have come in from outside, or even started from the shop floor. And the French 'miracle' has owed much to these *fonceurs* (whizz-kids) who have disproved the rule that in France you get nowhere without the right diplomas. Inside a hierarchy, that may be true, but not if you start on your own and have the right guts. In the boom years, these men included Paul Ricard, the king of pastis, in Provence; Laurent Bois-Vives, who built up Rossignol, near Grenoble, into the world's leading producer of skis; Pierre Fabre, a chemist near Toulouse who forged a pharmaceuticals empire (see p. 361); and in the services and leisure sectors, figures such as Marcel Fournier of Carrefour hypermarkets and Gilbert Trigano of Club Méditerranée. Most of these firms are today still doing well: but a few have been forced to cut back, such as Moulinex, the household electrical firm created with panache by Jean Mantelet. In today's tougher economic climate, new examples of whizz-kid private entrepreneurs are fewer, though one could cite the pastry-making Pasquiers and Jean-Luc Lagardère of Matra. France has not recently produced the equivalent of a Branson or a Bill Gates. But the legacy of the earlier mavericks remains: they have been almost as vital a French phenomenon as the Grande École smoothie.

In the post-war decades, the small size of the average firm and the paucity of really big ones were seen as among the main weaknesses of French industry, in face of the growing world competition; and much effort went into trying to improve this. In 1964 one much-quoted survey showed that of the world's 64 largest companies, 49 were American and *none* was French. But in the 1970s came a spate of mergers, regroupings, diversifications and setting up of joint subsidiaries – all encouraged by the Governments of the day. Among larger firms, the Peugeot/Citroën merger was one example, St-Gobain (glass) with Pont-à-Mousson (engineering) was another. In some cases the trend went too far: some larger groups were encouraged to expand too fast without being properly capitalized, and they made losses. But greater wisdom has now been learned, and the regrouping still goes ahead relentlessly, as in other countries. In industry, Alcatel has joined up with Alsthom, and Aerospatiale with Matra; in insurance, AXA has taken over UAP; in services, the big Vivendi group (formerly Compagnie Générale des Eaux) now controls the advertising giant Havas; and so on. Vast new meshes of cross-financing have been spreading, for good or ill. Other firms have expanded simply by buying up smaller ones or developing abroad. Today, in terms of turnover, five French companies are among the world's top 45: Elf-Aquitaine, Électricité de France, Renault, Alcatel/Alsthom and Peugeot. There may still be too many really small firms in France: but among the larger ones, their size is no longer seen as such a problem when it comes to competing with the US-based multinationals.

In EEC's earlier years, some people believed that one answer could be to create 'European' firms of American scale, through cross-frontier mergers or ententes; and Governments encouraged this. But it seldom happened, at least where France was involved: differing national habits, differing legal and fiscal systems, differing languages proved too dissuasive, and many companies found it more useful to form links with American expertise than with each other. The failure of the merger plan between Renault and Volvo has been one instance. However, following the success of the multinational Airbus Industrie, the union of Aerospatiale/Matra with DASA (Germany) in 1999 may have set a more positive trend. Meanwhile, Britain's General Electric Company is successfully associated with Alcatel/Alsthom. And now the arrival of the euro may give new incentives for the creation of truly 'European' companies. A more striking development, since the 1970s, is that many European countries have been developing their own multinationals, not through inter-EU mergers but by the worldwide expansion of some big national firms. Daimler-Benz, Unilever and others have long been in the field. So have French groups such as St-Gobain, L'Oréal, Michelin and Renault (see p. 709).

At the same time, foreign investment in France has been encouraged (see p. 710), not only for the jobs it creates, but in some sectors for the new technology that it can bring in. Even today this can be needed, for the state of scientific research remains uneven in France, and it leads to some dependence on imported know-how. This is a thorny subject. It is true that some major firms have made brilliant progress with their own research – Thomson, Alcatel/Alsthom, St-Gobain and others – and this lies behind the recent French successes with some advanced technologies. The State, too, has spent sizeable sums, much of it for military purposes. Its overall budget for research, some 2.3 per cent of GNP, compares adequately with that of other advanced countries. But too much of the effort has gone into major projects in a few key modern sectors, such as nuclear energy, telecommunications and aerospace, while the more humdrum yet important worlds of pharmaceuticals, consumer goods and food-processing have been – hitherto – rather neglected. And too few private firms have been doing enough to keep abreast of their world rivals. Hence France's 'balance of patents' is heavily adverse: she sells only one patent to the US for every three she buys in return.

France has a fine historical record of scientific invention: but her weakness has been a failure to marry the three strands of pure academic research, practical innovation and industrial application. While Pasteur and later the Curies were at work in their laboratories, the French were also among the leading world pioneers of photography, cinematography, and some aspects of aeronautics. But industry and pure science inhabited two separate worlds; and if French industry fell behind that of Britain and Germany in those days, a major cause was French firms' neglect of the inventions of the time – many of them French. More recently, France did much to pioneer the micro-computer, but left its application to the Americans and Japanese. In fact, French opinion has long tended to regard discovery as its own reward: as one Frenchman once told an American, 'No, we don't have pasteurized milk in France, but we *have* Pasteur!'

Today at last these attitudes are changing, as the French start trying to solve their old problem, in part political, of the gulf between industry and academia. The State gives plentiful funds to some universities and to the Centre National pour la Recherche Scientifique (CNRS), said to be the world's largest body of its kind: but the 'pure' scientists in these ivory towers, nearly all on the Left, have long been suspicious and ignorant of private industry and its needs, unwilling to defile themselves by helping to shore up capitalism. 'Our research is for the glory of humanity: to bother with its application is dishonourable', has been a common attitude. One example: when Giscard's Government persuaded the Institut National pour la Recherche Agronomique (INRA) to sign contracts with food-processing firms for mutual benefit, it was met with a four-month protest strike by staff. The result of this situation is that many firms, denied the benefits of France's own research, and unable to afford much of their own, have been forced to seek help abroad. De Gaulle, scornful of the CNRS, once quipped, '*Je vois beaucoup de chercheurs, mais où sont les trouveurs?*'

Over the past ten years, a growing number of these *chercheurs* have become readier to collaborate. Their sense of public duty, it seems, has shifted: the rise in unemployment has made some of them more aware that their research could lead to the creation of jobs in firms; problems of environment and health have had a similar impact for those working in those fields. So these Leftists have come to accept that humanity needs something more urgent from them than just the abstract glory of their science – even if it means working for the hated Patronat. The mutual mistrust has waned as the volume of annual contracts between CNRS and private industry has risen sharply. One leader of the new trend is Pierre-Gilles de Gennes, Nobel prize-winner and director of the Paris School of Chemistry, who is now a consultant with Rhône-Poulenc. His research with yoghurt, for example, has helped firms to create paints that do not dry out too fast.

Governments since 1993 have been trying to stimulate this *rapprochement*. Older traditionalist boffins at the CNRS are being eased into early retirement, as younger, more open-minded ones are recruited. Researchers at the CNRS or other official bodies are given new financial bonuses if they also act as consultants to firms, or if they patent and market their inventions. Many have responded. Scientists are even being encouraged to set up their own small firms – a trend set in the late 1970s by the large CNRS centre in Toulouse, the Laboratoire d'Automatique et d'Analyse des Systèmes. Its 400 researchers were urged either to collaborate closely with local companies or even to create their own: one recent venture has been the creation of robots for cleaning Paris buses and Métro carriages. There are said to be some fifty little firms of this kind in Toulouse today, where LAAS also has research contracts with local industries such as Alcatel/Alsthom and Motorola, for micro-electronics and biotechnologies. And its initiatives have now been copied in some other towns. At one hi-tech Grande École in Poitiers, I found that half of the research budget was paid by firms. Such development might seem normal in many countries: in France, for the CNRS and other bodies, it is quite a break with tradition. But not all its *chercheurs* are yet so keen to be *trouveurs* too. In 1994–6 there were protests that a Government eager to make economies was simply trying to get industry to help with the burden, and that fundamental research would suffer. Even so, a strike such as INRA's in the 1970s would be hard to imagine today.

The State's own budget has fluctuated. It went up fast under the

Socialists in the early 1980s, when the powerful Jean-Pierre Chevènement was Minister for Research: then it was cut back under the Right. Recently, it has remained stable, as Governments have urged private industry to do more research, with modest success: in 1995 the share of the private sector in the national effort rose above 50 per cent for the first time. The major recent shift is towards the 'human' sciences such as biology, and away from the less obviously 'human' ones such as aerospace. France is no longer such a leader in telecommunications or space research; and the military research budget, paid mainly by the State, has been reduced by 30 per cent – an aspect of the 'peace dividend'. Instead the stress today is on pharmaceuticals, food-processing, medicine, DNA, and environment technologies such as recycling – a return, you might say, to the humane tradition of Pasteur. In 1983 a French professor at the Institut Pasteur was one of the first to identify the AIDS virus: but then the Americans got ahead faster in applying his work (see p. 616). Despite the progress since then, an official report in 1998 warned that the French still lagged in the application of their fundamental research, especially in biotechnologies and computer sciences.

In industry as a whole, while many large firms do so well, there are still too many that are too small – in manufacturing, as in farming or retailing. France entered the EEC with the albatross of some 600,000 small industries employing fewer than twenty people each. Some goods, that in Japan or Germany were made in factories, were still being produced on a cottage-industry basis – a system that ensured high craftsmanship in some cases, but in marketing and other techniques was generally too inefficient to be economic. Happily, as in farming, this milieu threw up some post-war leaders who urged on it the need to adapt. One powerful French figure of that time was Léon Gingembre, a needle-maker from Normandy who founded and led the federation of Petites et Moyennes Entreprises (PME). Until the late 1950s he and his friends were allies of the reactionary grocer-demagogue Pierre Poujade, who preached that society had a duty to subsidize helpless small businesses. But then Gingembre, like the Patronat, saw the light: he dropped his hostility to the EEC, accepted the inevitable, and threw his vast influence into persuading his million PME members to modernize and regroup, or perish. So his federation set up services helping small firms to export or make use of new technologies. In Normandy, for instance, seven makers of farm tools formed a joint supplies and sales service, and were able to break into foreign markets. Slowly there was a shift of attitudes within the archaic world of tiny self-centred firms, hitherto suspicious alike of each other and of progress.

Since that time, many small firms have gone out of business; others have expanded, or have merged of their own accord. Since the mid-1960s, the proportion of employees in firms with fewer than 200 staff has fallen from two-thirds to less than one-third. This inevitable process of regrouping has been painful in many cases, and often very hard. The little town of Thiers in Auvergne calls itself 'the French Sheffield', but only quite recently has it emerged from medievalism. On my first visits in the 1970s I found its side-streets still lined with hundreds of cutlery workshops producing thousands of models – a tradition dating from the thirteenth century. I met old men who had spent their working lives lying on their bellies on wooden planks, polishing knives: some suffered from chronic rheumatism. Then finally this artisan work died out in face of foreign competition, and today modern factories account for nearly all the local cutlery output. For a while, ironically, these mass-produced knives were of lower quality than the old ones. But now the Thiers industry has been largely taken over by the high-quality new cutlery venture at Laguiole, way to the south (see p. 414) – a fine example of the dynamic reassertion of tradition, in a modern guise.

A few other PME firms have shown similar flair in moving with the times and developing their markets. A case often cited is that of Rossignol, near Grenoble: this old family workshop, producing a few pairs of skis, acquired a new manager, Laurent Bois-Vives, who steadily built it into the world's largest ski maker, with factories in five countries and 22 per cent of the global market. Not that size and growth are everything: with the right specialization, some firms are able to export brilliantly and make good profits, while remaining small. And yet, while today far more PME firms have become export- and investment-minded, they are still a minority. Many others remain backward, anxious about the future, complaining that Paris and Brussels neglect them, compared with the endless help given to small farmers. Though much less than they used to be, these tiny industries can still be a burden. And, compared with Germany, France still has too few go-ahead medium-sized enterprises.

Even some very large firms have closed down or been forced to cut right back under today's conditions – especially in older industries such as textiles, steel and shipbuilding. Since the time of Raymond Barre, the policy has been to encourage modern or luxury products, but not throw public money at shoring up less effective firms. Some 'lame ducks' judged incurable have been left to die; others, thought to be salvageable, have been given grants for radical overhauls; and in some cases, such as the Lorraine steel belt, the Government has sought to bring in new modern firms to replace the stricken ones. The anti-lame-duck strategy was at its toughest under Barre, then was modified for a while by the Socialists, but has generally been continued by all recent Governments: they judge, wisely or not, that it is better to pay for unemployment than for artificial aid to uncompetitive firms. This is the policy over manufacturing firms: however, in the state service sectors, such as railways, where the unions are stronger, Governments have to be far more cautious.

A scenic tour of France's lame-duck-pond could begin with the once-mighty textile empire of Marcel Boussac. He used to personify the old-style family *patron*: his racing stables were second only to the Aga Khan's, and in his seven châteaux he entertained princes and premiers in lordly style. But then he failed to adapt to Third World competition. Amid stories of gross mismanagement, his firm by 1978 was losing 10 million francs a month: but Barre refused to underwrite his survival plan. One minister even insulted the tottering tycoon in Parliament: 'We have no intention of throwing public money at a group that has not the slightest notion of basic accounting methods.' So Boussac, then aged over ninety, was obliged to sell out cheaply to another big textile group, Agache Willot, more downmarket. Whereas Boussac's prestigious cloth used to be styled into *haute couture* dresses by Dior and Saint-Laurent, under Willot the firm moved into synthetic nappies and plastic bags. *Sic transit . . .*

France's large textile industry has overall been suffering worse than most in the EU: in fifteen years its workforce has fallen from some 800,000 to under 200,000. Hundreds of firms large and small have closed, mostly in the Nord and the Vosges. A worried Government in 1996 broke its own lame-duck rules and offered special fiscal relief, to the annoyance of Brussels; and this began to have some effect. But, saddled with the high French social charges, most firms find it hard to compete. And yet, there are some success stories. At Quimper, Brittany, in 1996, I found that the bright modern Armor-Lux firm had increased sales by 50 per cent in ten years. It does a busy trade in women's knitted clothes, notably sailor-style Breton striped jerseys. 'That's our secret,' I was told:

'the *cachet* of Brittany, and local loyalty.' It might be less easy to emulate in the Vosges.

Down the coast from Quimper, the big shipyards at St-Nazaire have been in trouble for some years. In the days of Gaullien grandeur, the mighty 63,000-ton liner *France* was launched at St-Nazaire in 1962: but she soon made heavy losses and was taken out of service after only twelve years and sold to the Saudis. Today this costly prestige policy is largely out of favour: the shipyards still receive some government aid, but far less than in former days, and those at Dunkerque and near Marseille have closed. The yards have faced growing competition from Japan, Korea and China, also from Germany, Italy and Finland, all of them today more successful at building and selling ships than France, despite its greater maritime tradition.

Another mighty crash, as great as Boussac's, was that of Manufrance, a venerable old firm with a staff of 4,000 in the depressed industrial city of St-Étienne. Known as '*la vieille dame*', it consisted of a hotchpotch of activities: it made shotguns, bicycles and sewing-machines, it ran a large mail-order business and a chain of general stores across France, and it published a big-selling magazine, *Le Chasseur français*. It used to be a glory of French industry: but its management, smug and incompetent, saw no reason to invest in new equipment, so rooted were they in the myth of the grand old lady. Yet their goods were being undercut by modern rivals, their shops were outflanked by the new hypermarkets. As huge losses piled up, the Communist-led town council made a series of bizarre attempts to save the firm, on which so many jobs and so much local prestige depended. But no outside firm would buy up so risky a venture. Here clearly was a lame duck deserving to die: but Giscard for a long time wavered, not wanting to provoke a left-wing revolt, and he put in some aid. Then finally Manufrance went bankrupt and a tribunal closed it down. The *mairie* and CGT promptly occupied the plant and declared a cooperative. But this failed to work. The lucrative parts, such as the magazine, were sold off, and the rest of the old lady's corpse was left to decompose. The famous shotguns, used by so many *chasseurs*, became fading memories.

Of all the lame-duck sagas, the most dramatic was in the Lorraine steel town of Longwy, in 1979, where the explosion of industrial unrest was the worst of the past thirty years. France's steel industry had long been a lame duck of diplodocus size, and was thus badly hit by the world steel recession of the late 1970s. So Barre applied his medicine, pushing the private firms to contract drastically – and the workers of Lorraine hit back hard. Here the veteran steelworks were set close to old iron-ore mines, with other plant in the Nord near Valenciennes. Under Monnet's impetus, the industry had been well modernized in the post-war years, and output doubled in 1950–66. The old family firms merged to form two major groups, Sacilor and Usinor. But – a familiar story – they failed to invest adequately in new equipment. And Lorraine, with its own iron mines wearing thin, found itself ill placed geographically for receiving imported ore: so new steel mills were built on the coast, at Dunkerque and at Fos near Marseille. But French productivity was far below that of Germany and Japan, due in part to serious overstaffing, especially in Lorraine with its 80,000 steelworkers. Here the firms made losses of over 4 billion francs in 1977. So Barre agreed to bail out the two steel giants with what amounted to semi-nationalization, alien to his philosophy but the only pragmatic solution. The State took over their debts by acquiring 67 per cent of their shares. And Barre promoted an urgent plan for 22,000 lay-offs, mostly in Lorraine, with the closure of several mills. The moment of truth had arrived.

The Lorrains were aghast. This land of Verdun, homeland of Joan of Arc, had long been a citadel of French patriotism, reinforced by its annexation to Germany in 1871–1918. And now it felt betrayed. Not that its economic crisis was new: along with the Nord, this was one of two French regions where the problem had been that of reconverting an archaic industrial tissue, rather than enticing new factories to rural zones as in the west (see pp. 263–5). For some years, the State and local bodies had strained their sinews to work the miracle of diversification – and with some success in the coal belt near the Saar, and in the Vosges. Scores of small firms moved in, many of them German, drawn by Lorraine's central position in the EEC and its excellent labour force; and by 1978 the old declining industries (coal, steel, textiles) accounted for only one-third of productive jobs, against two-thirds in the 1960s. But further west, in the sad valleys between Thionville and Longwy, where steel for centuries had been a way of life, industrial decay was setting in.

However, Lorrains are a tough people, and they do not take adversity lying down. Barre's plan was a sane one, economically: but he presented it tactlessly, in his usual take-it-or-leave-it manner; and he gave little assurance that replacement jobs would be sought or proper compensation given. Soon 50,000 workers were marching through the streets of Metz, demanding a better deal from Paris. One local journalist, Charles Bourdier, later gave me his own emotional account: 'We became aware that people in the steel towns felt utterly abandoned. Reports were coming to us of suicides, delinquency, a rising collective anguish. The unions warned us that they could no longer control their rank and file and sabotage was imminent. The local steel bosses had abdicated, the prefect had lost credibility, the Church meant nothing, and the CGT was too narrowly political. In this void, there was a real danger that there would be uncontrolled explosions. Or Longwy would set up its own République Populaire in the French romantic revolutionary tradition. And then the riot police would move in . . .'

It all but happened. Longwy, an ugly one-industry town in a deep valley by the Luxembourg frontier, was the centre most threatened by Barre's plan. It had already suffered from earlier cuts, and was now due to lose half of its remaining workforce of 12,700. So the reaction began. Groups of young workers held their managers prisoner, attacked a police station, halted trains, occupied government offices and threw files from the windows. Finally, the CGT managed to take control of the revolt, in this Communist bastion of a town, which for the next few weeks was virtually run by union and party. Their aim was to force Barre to climb down, but without the odium of provoking violence. However, the Élysée was growing scared that Longwy might indeed spark off a new May '68 in France, so Giscard made conciliatory noises. And his staff intensified their urgent search for replacement firms, not easy in a time of recession. The *deus ex machina* was Ford Motors, then planning to set up a new assembly plant somewhere in Europe. Giscard ceremoniously received Henry Ford, who even expressed interest in Longwy, and soon his prospectors were buzzing around the doomed steel town. As Giscard hoped, France's own car firms were panic-stricken by this new threat to their home markets, so the Government was able to twist their arms, as *dirigisme* thundered into action: 'If you don't agree *now* to invest in Lorraine, we'll sign up with Ford', was the message spelt out to Renault and Peugeot-Citroën. And it worked. Today it remains unclear whether the Government was bluffing about inviting Ford. Probably it was almost as keen as the French car firms to find a 'French solution', and that is what happened. Ford dropped out, and the French car giants plus some other firms agreed to invest in a new plant creating 6,000 or so new jobs by 1983, in Longwy and nearby steel towns. The episode could be seen as an example of the positive side of *dirigisme*: the ability of the French State to dictate its measures to industry for social reasons. Admittedly, Renault was state-owned, but in theory master of its own investment policies.

The workers were encouraged but anxious, aware there would still be a big shortfall of jobs. So the Government offered generous indemnities: some 12,000 steelworkers in France were given early retirement, with pensions of up to 90 per cent of wages, while others got golden handshakes. All this was worked out voluntarily, with no enforced sackings, at a cost to the State of 7 billion francs. Next Paris enforced rationalization on the steel firms: uneconomic blast furnaces were closed, and productivity rose by some 30 per cent, moving ahead of British levels. Then the Socialists completed the takeover of Usinor and Sacilor, and promised to raise steel output again. But as Europe's steel crisis worsened, this proved impossible, and more lay-offs were inevitable. There were renewed strikes, though brief. 'One advantage of having a period of left-wing government,' a free-market economist commented to me shrewdly, 'is that the workers now realize that plant closures are inevitable. They used to think it was all a wicked capitalist plot.'

Usinor and Sacilor were reprivatized by Balladur in 1995. Their fortunes have since varied with changes in the world steel market, but mostly they have been doing well. And the area around Longwy, together with the steel zones just across the border in Belgium and Luxembourg, have been turned into a 'European development pole', with special EU aid. This has attracted some new jobs, but not enough to restore Longwy to its former vitality: in 1999 three new Daiwoo factories closed, victims of the Asian recession. You can see groups of early-retired steelworkers listlessly playing boules in the squares; or at night they visit the imposing new casino and leisure centre, built atop a former slagheap near Thionville with European aid. All around is a landscape of industrial decay, as on Tyneside. Rail tracks to closed factories are lost in weeds. Grimy canals stagnate in disuse. Derelict mineshafts crown the hills, above valleys where a few steel furnaces still belch their black, pink and orange fumes over the ugly terraced houses. The steel towns have names like Hayange, Uckange, Gandrange – but these are angels with dirty faces. Some younger workers have moved off to other regions, but remarkably few. In France peasants will leave the land and move to cities, but industrial workers expect new jobs to be brought to *them* (see p. 265). Lorrains are specially attached to their homeland. Some of them did agree in the

1970s to move to the new steelworks at Fos: but they saw this more as exile than as a move to the sunny paradise of Provence.

Further east, in the old coal belt near the Saar border, the picture is brighter. Here the Coal Board has had quite a success in attracting new investment to the former mining towns such as Forbach, where scores of German and Japanese firms are active, making TV sets, plastics, etc. Near Sarreguimines, beside the *autoroute*, there now stands the large new factory making the Smart, the tiny two-seater car produced jointly by Mercedes and the Swiss firm Swatch. Despite initial production delays, it is due to create some 2,000 new jobs locally. This will be a useful boost for Lorraine, where the last coal mines are due to close in 2005 – virtually the end of the road for France's once-powerful coal-mining industry. So does this mean that she will turn more than ever to nuclear power? Quite possibly not.

ENERGY RESOURCES: NO OIL, NOT MUCH COAL – AND NEW DOUBTS ABOUT THE GREAT NUCLEAR EFFORT

France is endowed with few natural energy resources of its own: hydro-electricity, a little oil, coal mines now largely exhausted – that is about all. So in the boom years of industrial growth it relied more and more on imports, notably of oil, which rose fast from 27 to 116 million tons between 1960 and 1973. But this was bearable, as oil was still cheap. Then the explosion in the price of crude hit France especially hard, for it was importing over 75 per cent of its energy needs, against an EEC average of 55 per cent. This situation was alarming, politically as well as economically. So Giscard's Government reacted vigorously to the energy crisis with a three-point strategy: strong conservation measures; a search for new energies, such as solar; and above all, nuclear expansion.

This last has been the controversial trademark of French energy policy ever since. From a mere 1 per cent in 1973, the share of nuclear power in electricity output rose to 30 per cent by 1981, and in recent years has run at about 75 per cent – the highest proportion in the world. Within its own terms, the policy has indeed brought results. Thanks to it and to other factors, dependence on imported energy has fallen from 78 to 47 per cent, while oil imports have fallen from 119 to 84 million tons a year. However, oil today has become cheaper again, relatively, than it was in the crisis years; also, the French public's acquiescence in the nuclear policy has begun to fray, as ecological ideas gain ground.

Of the country's own natural energy resources, the coal mines were nationalized just after the war, and then modernized so well that productivity for a while was the highest in Europe. Output reached 60 million tons a year. But today it is down to 9 million, coming mainly from Lorraine, also the Massif Central. The famous mines of the Nord, described by Zola in *Germinal*, are now exhausted and have closed. French coal, on the whole hard to extract and of middling quality, today works out more expensive than foreign coal: so France imports some 13 million tons a year, mostly from the United States, Australia and Poland. After the Second World War Électricité de France, also nationalized, set about exploiting every drop of power from a country rich in hydroelectric possibilities: some thirty new dams were built in mountainous areas. A third domestic source of raw energy was, for a while, natural gas, after a large deposit was found in 1951 near Pau. For years this was meeting nearly a third of French gas consumption: but it has now run dry, and France imports its natural gas, mainly from Algeria, Norway and the ex-Soviet Union.

Oil is still the major energy import. This has long been a complex political issue, tied up with sovereignty. Since the 1920s France has been trying to gain more control over its imports by securing for its industry a degree of independence from the Seven Sisters – and with some success. The Government in the 1970s was able to create one mammoth state company, Elf-Aquitaine, which made oil-prospecting deals with Middle East countries, thus breaking the American and Anglo-Dutch monopolies there. Elf-Aquitaine was privatized in 1994. Its main French rival, also privatized, was TotalFina, and the two controlled about half of French importing and refining. They made good profits recently (Total's in 1997 was 7.6 billion francs). Then in July 1999 Total made a 'hostile' bid for Elf in the form of a public offer of exchange of shares. After beating off Elf's counter-bid, Total finally won, and the merger of these two firms was set to create the world's fourth largest oil firm. The Government was satisfied with this 'French solution' which, it felt, protected national interests from foreign interference. But France's oil is almost all imported. Until 1971 the French drew 40 per cent from the Algerian Sahara, where they had joyfully discovered it themselves in colonial days; but Algeria then nationalized the remaining French assets. Today the main French supplier is Saudi Arabia, followed by Britain, Norway, Nigeria and other Middle East countries. Meanwhile French companies have been involved in the search for oil around the world's oceans. They have been drilling off their own coasts, too, but with little success, and few experts expect any North Sea-style bonanza there. However, some oil has now been found inside France, in the Paris basin, of all places, and this accounts for 3 per cent of France's needs.

After the panic of the oil crisis, Giscard's Government stepped up not only its nuclear effort but also an energy-saving campaign, with a range of measures mixing persuasion and compulsion. The car industry was encouraged to devise less fuel-greedy vehicles; double-glazing and other forms of insulation were promoted; for a while it was made illegal to heat homes or offices above 19°C, even on a freezing day. Some of the measures have since been relaxed, now that oil imports are again cheaper and more secure. But the public response at the time was good: according to EU figures, intelligently thrifty use of fuel has enabled France to cut overall energy consumption by the equivalent of 28 million tons of petrol – a record exceeded only by Denmark. This was achieved without harming either industrial output or living standards, and the policy has been a good example of the more effective side of French *dirigisme*.

In the search for alternative forms of energy – solar, geothermal and wind power – France has been much less successful, despite great efforts. These 'new' energies are still supplying only 1.8 per cent of overall French needs, no great advance on the 1.1 per cent of 1973. In the 1970s the French were placing some hopes on solar energy, where their programme was the most advanced in Europe. In the Pyrénées-Orientales, France's sunniest *département*, they built a huge experimental solar furnace, whose sixty-three mirrors reflect the sun on to a tower-shaped boiler, backed by a gigantic concave prism of more mirrors. Today this spectacular apparatus is still used for the study of the reactions of materials to high temperatures (3,500°C), and it even produces some token electricity, just to show that the sun *can* do so. But a solar-power plant built nearby has never been put into operation, for it was judged to have no commercial future. In fact, even in sunny southern France, the use of solar heat to make electricity may have only a limited practical future – as compared with some Third World areas where the sun is hotter and normal electric power is more costly. The French instead have been trying out the use of solar panels for central heating, but here, too, there are problems: no effective storage system has been found, and the panels make house façades look ugly. Solar water-heaters are simpler, and have a more viable future: some 100,000 French homes, fewer per head than in Japan or Israel, make use of a device placed on the roof, to harness sunlight. All in all, progress in the field of new energies has been disappointing. But, with the future of oil supplies and of nuclear power both uncertain, it may be wise to encourage scientists to work on long-term research; and France here remains ahead of others in Europe.

France remains ahead, too, in nuclear development. Today doubts about its future may finally be growing, even in Paris. But it is not hard to see why French Governments for so long have put such an emphasis on the nuclear. Since exploding its first atomic bomb in 1960, France has belonged to the military club of nuclear powers (and its tests in the Pacific in 1995 made enemies, see p. 665). De Gaulle pursued a nationalist go-it-alone policy, spurning American technology and relying on home-produced uranium gas-cooled reactors. This was barely viable. But then in 1969 Pompidou made an historic turn-about, switching to an American light-water system based on enriched uranium: he saw it as the only sane economic choice, albeit at the price of some dependence on US technology. So a French firm, Framatome, began to build pressurized water reactors under licence from Westinghouse.

This left France well placed, when the energy crisis came, to push ahead with a civil nuclear programme, which soon became far bigger than the military one. By 1981 France was completing five or six new reactors a year, and was building as much nuclear plant in two years as Britain had done in thirty. France was helped by having large uranium deposits of her own. Above all, without relying on American technology, the French became among the pioneers of the fast-breeder reactors. In 1977 work began on Superphénix, a multinational French-led project for a 1,200 MW fast-breeder using uranium and plutonium, that took shape beside the Rhône near Geneva. This has since had fearful problems: but it did initially help to put France in the forefront of nuclear technology. For some years, firms such as Framatome have supplied developing countries and others with reactors and with know-how, and this has become a lucrative French export.

The nuclear programme came under expected attack from ecologists: but they made less impact than in many countries. After the accident at Three Mile Island, Pennsylvania, in 1979, EDF officials tried to claim that French reactors had a different design, so a similar incident was less likely. And the public, in those days, broadly believed it. So Giscard ordered a speed-up of nuclear construction – an action politically unthinkable then in almost any other free country. Officialdom reiterated the view that France had no alternative to nuclear power, if national independence *and* living standards were to be kept up (Britain had far more oil of its own, Germany far more coal). But the Socialists, alone of the major parties, were becoming reticent, and this put the Left in a dilemma when it took power in 1981. The party, with its strong anti-nuclear element, had put into its manifesto a pledge to cancel all future nuclear projects. But Mitterrand himself was more equivocal; and he and his Government, faced with economic realities, were soon having doubts about the wisdom of too drastic a cutback. They knew that to halt nuclear expansion could put at risk many of the 100,000 or so jobs in that industry. So they decreed less of a slow-down than had been expected, halting work on only five new sites out of fourteen. The Left, as today, was divided on the whole issue, with the Communists being pro-nuclear. During its time in office, the Left did slow the programme. Yet nuclear capacity doubled between 1981 and 1985; and ultimately the slow-down was due less to any anti-nuclear dogmatism than to a realization that the previous Government had overestimated future energy needs.

Within weeks of the Right regaining power in 1986, there came Chernobyl. Characteristically, reactions from the public and from official sources alike were more muted than in many countries. The Government and EDF were quick to stress that French technical and security standards were far higher than in the Soviet Union: there was no question, they said, of modifying France's nuclear programme – and it went on as before. Today it remains clear that this, along with the conservation measures, has done much to reduce dependence on imported energy, as figures can show. Oil imports as a share of total energy consumption fell from 69 per cent in 1973 to 41 per cent by 1985; in the same period, France's level of self-sufficiency in energy rose from 22 to 53 per cent. Today there are 57 nuclear power stations in operation, producing some 350 billion kWh a year, or over 75 per cent of France's electricity. In Western Europe, only Belgium (56 per cent) comes anywhere near this figure. Some other percentage figures are: Japan 33, Britain 32, Germany 30, United States 19. France's nuclear equipment has been costly to install: but the electricity can now be produced quite cheaply on a large scale, and some 16 per cent of French output is exported – some of it to Britain, in return for oil, you might say.

Today the picture is beginning to change, as the rest of Europe increasingly turns against nuclear power. Some countries, including Britain and Germany, have ceased to build new stations, either because of the cost or through public fears about safety and health hazards. And finally France, too, is now shifting. There is no question yet of phasing out the nuclear effort, in which some 1,000 billion francs have been invested: but the building of new stations, to replace the earlier ageing ones, has been postponed, and doubts about the nuclear future have grown. The shift, latent under Juppé, became more marked when the Left returned to power and Jospin appointed a leading Green, Dominique Voynet, as his Environment Minister. She played an influential role in two key decisions. First, plans were cancelled for a large new power plant in the Loire estuary, which had aroused local opposition. Next, the decision was finally taken to close down the Superphénix fast-breeder reactor. This had been posing grave technical problems for years, with leaks of its sodium-cooling fluid, and had been in active operation for only three of its eleven years. It had become a costly white elephant, and the decision to put it to sleep was taken more on budgetary than safety grounds. A third controversy concerned the large reprocessing plant at La Hague on the coast near Cherbourg, which had long caused local worries. In January 1997 a report had been published by a French doctor suggesting that children using local beaches, or eating local shellfish, were prone to leukemia. The plant's operators, Cogema, a state-owned body, issued fierce denials. But Voynet stepped in: she banned fishing and boating in the canal beside the plant, and accused Cogema of bungling its repairs. Cogema was even alleged to have sent divers down to confiscate material used by Greenpeace for checking flaws in the plant's handling of nuclear wastage – shades of *Rainbow Warrior*.

Basically, the new pattern means that EDF no longer has such a free hand in its day-to-day running of nuclear power. Hitherto governments would let it assess the risks, take its decisions, then make its explanations to the public – and only rarely, as in the case of one project in Brittany in 1981 (see p. 281), was it thwarted. Today, '*We* now take the decisions over major risks,' one of Voynet's aides told me, 'and EDF does what we decide.' And Jospin in 1998 was preparing a new law to make EDF more accountable and to strengthen safety in the nuclear industry. He has said, 'Though this industry may be an important asset, it cannot be exempted from the rules of democracy, nor left to pursue projects which are too costly.' But his ruling coalition remains deeply divided over nuclear power, as it was under Mitterrand. The Communists have always been strongly pro-nuclear, for patriotic and for employment reasons, and their union, the CGT, has even demonstrated against cutbacks. Marc Blondel, the new leader of the pro-Socialist union, Force Ouvrière, has spoken in similar terms: 'I'm pro-nuclear; I know what it is for miners to end up at forty-five with silicosis.' But some other unions back the Greens, and so does a part of the Socialist rank and file. And the French public? Surveys show that a large majority are still in favour of nuclear power: but there have been growing signs of wariness about the health hazards involved, and the costs.

In ten or so years' time, the older generation of reactors will begin to need replacement, and this will be expensive. Other countries have now been moving back to greater use of oil, gas or coal for their electricity; and France may feel the need to follow this logic, for nuclear power may no longer be the most cost-effective choice, quite apart from safety problems. But the change would involve a return to greater dependence on imports, for France has far less coal of her own than Germany, less gas than Holland, much less oil than Britain. This will be her great dilemma, in part political, and the choice may be harder than it was in Giscard's day – unless, by some miracle, there comes a breakthrough in the use of the 'new energies'. Meanwhile Jospin pursues his balancing act: greater democratic openness about nuclear ventures, plus a bid to diversify, but basically still a huge reliance on a nuclear industry almost as valuable to France as building cars and aeroplanes.

RENAULT, PEUGEOT, AIRBUS:
TECHNICAL TRIUMPHS, BUT TOUGH WORLD MARKETS

The dependable robustness of Peugeots, the flair and ingenuity of Citroëns, the dexterity and economy of Renaults – today the French remain immensely proud of their achievements as car-makers; and ever since the pioneering days of Panhard and Louis Renault in the 1890s, the automobile industry has held a place of honour in this land of creative engineers. For much of the time since the war, it has been a major success story of the French economy; and France today is still the world's third car exporter, after Japan and Germany. Its firms have also built factories and assembly plants around the globe, from Peugeot in Egypt and Argentina to the big new Renault venture in Brazil and another now starting in Moscow. But there have been failures, too; and today, in a Europe facing overcapacity, the French industry with its high costs has been losing ground a little to its main rivals. Both the major groups have made heavy trading losses in recent years, though in this mercurial market the picture keeps changing. Global competition has toughened, and the French car-makers need to show even more flair and resilience than in the easier post-war decades of euphoric expansion.

After 1945 the shattered industry rebuilt itself, and in the 1960s its growth was second only to Japan's. This was achieved through a mix of flair for technical innovation, concern for quality and enterprising investment. Today, after some mergers, concentration is more advanced than in any other industrial sector: annual production of around 3 million cars plus 400,000 commercial vehicles – twice the British output – comes from just two giant groups, the private Peugeot-Citroën, and Renault, long state-owned but now 52-per-cent privatized. These are two of the five major European-owned groups, behind Volkswagen, roughly equal with Fiat, and ahead of BMW–Rover in terms of market share. The French public's passion for cars helps to keep the home market buoyant: but the major effort has gone into exports, which amount to more than half of output. And although imports have been steadily increasing, they are still only half the volume of exports. Britain, by contrast, buys from abroad four times as many cars as it sells.

Louis Renault founded his firm in 1899. He was a young self-taught mechanic who, in the manner of Ford or Nuffield, built his firm up steadily into a leading car company. In 1944 he was charged with Nazi collaboration: the State confiscated his empire and, this being the era of nationalizations, decided to hold on to it. Some inspired technocrats were put in to run it on commercial lines, and they made it into a torch-bearer for all French industry. Its main factory, at Billancourt, in the Paris suburbs, was in 1946 the first in Europe to use automation, and it began to produce a remarkable baby car, the *quatre chevaux* (i.e. 4 hp). This became a symbol of the social philosophy which was then to guide the Régie Renault under its remarkable chairman, Louis Dreyfus, a humanist who argued that every family had the right to own a car – a novel idea in those austerity days. So he stressed the mass turn-out of small, cheap cars, the models growing in size only as living standards rose: thus the 4CV in the mid-1950s gave place to the brilliant Dauphine.

Another feature of the Dreyfus philosophy, rare in those days, was that a firm owed its workers more than just good wages. With state backing, Renault in the 1950s led the field in labour relations, often to the annoyance of more staid firms. Not only did it spend generous sums on housing, welfare and other schemes for its staff, but in 1954 it pioneered a labour charter that committed it to regular annual wage increases, in return for guarantees by the unions not to strike. This was by then common practice in Germany, but novel for France, and it was later copied by many other firms. For years it worked well at Renault: yet it did not prevent the May '68 uprising, when it came, from being fiercer and lasting longer there than in most other factories. One possible reason was that *les métallos de chez Renault*, well paid and politically sophisticated, were critical of the firm's benevolent paternalism. Renault by then had diversified intelligently into lorries, tractors and machine tools; and for many years, despite its ups and downs, it was seen as the best example in Europe of a nationalized firm run commercially and able to compete dynamically.

Of its two French competitors, Citroën has a history of quirky individuality. Until its takeover by Peugeot in 1974, it was controlled by the Michelin tyre company, which had bought it in 1934 when its founder, André Citroën, went bankrupt. The Michelin family empire had long been the most arrogant and secretive in French industry, and Citroën took its colouring from that. It would scorn publicity, take little trouble with exports and treat unions with a chilly disdain. It believed in making cars that could be kept in production for twenty years or more, like the tin-can 2CV; and such was the firm's mechanical genius that it could get away with these methods. In the booming 1960s it made the best progress of any French car firm. Since then, under Peugeot, the approach has steadily changed and Citroën has become more 'normal'. But it keeps its reputation for advanced design, and its newer models, such as the Xantia, are still noted for their hydro-pneumatic suspension which makes them flop gently when they stop, like tired elephants. They have been the official ministerial car in many countries, including France. De Gaulle loved his fleet of big frog-nosed DSs, and twice he owed his life to their excellent handling and brakes: once, when he was shot at by the OAS, his chauffeur had to make a fast getaway on bullet-punctured tyres. Today Chirac too prefers Citroëns. But Mitterrand was loyal to his big Renault 25s.

Peugeot, with its head factory at Sochaux in the Jura, was created by a wealthy and clannish Protestant dynasty. Today the Peugeot/Citroën group, known as PSA (Peugeot Société Anonyme), is still controlled by the Peugeot family, who sit on its board and own 80 per cent of its capital. If less so than at Michelin, the accent here, too, is on aloofness and discretion: the head office in Paris does not even have the group's name outside; total staff loyalty is expected and union membership is discouraged. Managers are chosen to suit this ethos: Jacques Calvet, the powerful chairman in 1984–97, was a byword for the old French style of tough, arrogant right-wing *patron*. Peugeot's cars, like their prudent Protestant makers, are thorough and reliable, with qualities seemingly more German than French. Their toughness has been proven by regular victories in safari rallies.

By the mid-1960s the French were aware that to have four rival firms was a wasteful extravagance (the fourth was Simca, controlled by Chrysler since 1963). They must group together. So Renault and Peugeot announced a tie-up for some joint production. This left Citroën looking isolated: but finally it accepted that in the new age of battles between giants it might need to modify its splendid idiosyncracy. So it reached for an entente, and Agnelli of Fiat offered one. But de Gaulle said no: he knew it would lead to Citroën being swallowed up by its more dynamic Italian partner. Citroën, losing money, then turned to an obvious domestic saviour, Peugeot, with its fine record of expansion. This time the Michelin family sank its pride, selling over 90 per cent of its interest in Citroën to Peugeot in 1974. The merger has since worked well: 'Our success has been due to the marriage of two very different firms, each keeping its own image and personality,' a Peugeot chief told me. The PSA group then set its sights on the top world league, and in 1978 was able to buy up the European factories of the ailing Chrysler. French national pride was satisfied that Simca had thus been recovered from the Americans. But PSA found it hard to digest its catch (renamed Talbot) and was obliged to close the factory near Glasgow, to Scottish fury. Talbot today has vanished as a brand name: its factories have been closed or sold, or they just produce Peugeot or Citroën cars. And the PSA/Renault joint ventures continue, for some gear-boxes and engines, so that rival cars – the Peugeot 605 and Renault Laguna – actually have the same V6 engine.

The French car industry has had varying fortunes since the 1970s, as the quality of its product has not always been equalled by the effectiveness of its marketing or cost-cutting, in competition with the Germans and

Japanese. It did superbly in the late 1970s, raising annual output of vehicles from 2.5 to 3.6 million. There were many big new factories, notably the Citroën plant in Rennes, Renault works in Le Mans and the Nord, Peugeot in Mulhouse. But in the early 1980s the industry slumped, as both Renault and PSA made heavy losses, and Volkswagen and Fiat were able to move far ahead. Then, in this fast-changing car-making world, French fortunes were partially restored by two brilliant chairmen, Calvet at PSA and Georges Besse at Renault: both were able to increase sales and reduce debts, while trimming their excess staff. Besse, the best kind of state technocrat, had almost completed his programme when he was murdered by terrorists outside his Paris home in 1986.

By the 1970s, both PSA and Renault were well established as major worldwide internationals. PSA formed a joint venture with Fiat for making commercial vehicles, and this still works well today, with factories in the Nord and southern Italy. But Renault fared less well with its project in the early 1990s for a full merger with Volvo: 'Our arrogance and slowness were at fault,' a Renault executive admitted to me. 'Volvo was keen at first, but we mishandled the talks, and the Swedes ended up feeling that they would be swallowed up by our larger firm, so they backed out. A pity.' In the field of exports, Renault has long had more success, especially inside Europe: but it has failed to break into the US market on any scale. Back in the 1950s, its little Dauphine at first appealed hugely to Americans: they had never seen a car so cute and they bought 200,000 in three years, often as playthings for wife or kids. But then the mighty VW invaded the scene, and Renault was eclipsed by a swarm of Beetles. Worldwide, however, more than 50 per cent of its domestic product now goes for export, while PSA with 62 per cent does even better. Britain is PSA's top customer; Renault is strong in Spain. Both firms see Europe as part of their home market: but they are too dependent on it, since only 15 per cent of their exports go further afield. PSA, like Renault, has had little success in the United States.

The French companies have also met with setbacks in their policies of building their own factories abroad or of starting joint ventures. Renault today has successful operations in Portugal, Spain, Slovenia and Turkey. But after failing to import much into the United States, it then failed equally in its bid to build cars within that country. In 1979 it bought a 46-per-cent stake in American Motors, fourth largest US motor-maker: but despite heavy investment it piled up losses, and then sold its venture to Chrysler which thus took a sweet revenge on France. PSA, meanwhile, has also burnt its fingers abroad. It opened a factory near Canton, but then ran into such troubles on the Chinese market that in 1997 it backed right out. Earlier, Peugeot had launched a joint venture with the Nigerian government for a big assembly plant in Kaduna. For a while all went well, but today the African market has contracted, and the venture is struggling. However, both the French groups are now expanding fast on the growing South American market. PSA has factories in Argentina and Uruguay, and in 1998 it started one in Brazil. Renault also opened a plant in Brazil at the end of 1998, which is due to assemble some 120,000 Méganes a year. Other Méganes are to be built at a factory in Moscow, under a joint venture which began operations in 1998. In 1999 Renault acquired 37 per cent of the Japanese firm Nissan, thus becoming the world's fourth largest automobile maker. But it was a risky gamble, for Nissan was heavily in debt.

At home, Renault and PSA have for years been level-pegging for first place on the French market. Renault was often just ahead: but recently PSA has moved forward, with a 28 per cent share in 1997 (Peugeot 16, Citroën 12), against its rival's 27. More important, both firms have been steadily losing ground to foreign imports, which in 1978 won only 22 per cent of the market share, but then rose fast and today run at 40 to 45 per cent, with Germans well in the lead. Taste, as in Britain, has become more international. Japanese imports, with a bare 4 per cent of the market, are no great threat: but Germany today sells far more cars to France than vice versa, especially in the upper prestige range where Porsche and the bigger BMWs and Mercedes have no true French equivalents in performance.

French firms have always put more stress on smaller models, even if their average size and comfort have naturally increased since the early days of the tiny 2CV and 4CV. All companies now have a decent range of models. For years, they oddly preferred to call them by numbers or initials – the Renaults 4, 6, 10, 12, and on up to 30; the Peugeots 305, 309, etc.; the Citroëns AX, ZM, etc. (and the DS, which by a clever pun also meant 'goddess'). Today Peugeot remains faithful to numbers (the older 205 and new larger 406 and 605 are successful): but Renault has moved from the R5 to the excellent little Clio and the quaint bubble-like Twingo, a big seller, while the Laguna and big Safran hold the top of the range. Citroën's newer models include the little Saxo, the medium-sized Xsara and the larger Xantia.* The French public in the main still looks for fairly small, inexpensive and economical cars, but it will as readily opt for a Golf or a Mini Minor as one of its own models. And for a few richer people, there is still nothing like an imported Jaguar, Rolls-Royce or Porsche – or indeed a Mercedes, whose prestige was hardly dented by the most famous motoring accident in world history in a Paris tunnel in August 1997. It was not the car's fault.

In this age of privatizations, Renault today is 52 per cent in private hands. It had always been run commercially, with little more state interference than was usual in French industry. Yet the feeling arose recently that the anomaly of public ownership was now doing it more harm than good. It might still make sense for a service company such as railways, but not for an industrial firm in today's world. The old juggernaut had grown too bureaucratic, too ready to rely on state loans, too cautious about making lay-offs in hard times – or so the argument ran. Chirac made a bid to privatize in 1987 but was stopped by Mitterrand, believer in the State. Balladur then had more success and sold 46 per cent of the capital, mostly to a few big shareholders such as Elf, Matra and Swiss banks. The staff were not as worried by these changes as in the case, say, of France Télécom, and two-thirds of them bought shares. Juppé then sold another 6 per cent, allowing the State to lose majority control. But Renault was now making heavy losses again, for the first time for ten years, and the value of shares fell badly for a while. They picked up when the new chairman, Louis Schweitzer, announced a much-needed overhaul, including some lay-offs in the 140,000 staff and the possible closure of some factories. In March 1997 his hatchet fell, not in France, but on the plant at Vilvorde, outside Brussels: it must close totally, he said, along with its staff of 3,100, making the Clio and Mégane. This provoked a remarkable outcry, not only in Belgium but among the French unions and others, showing Euro-solidarity with their Belgian brothers. Jospin came to power, promising to do something: but he was soon convinced by Renault, and by his own advisers, that the decision could not be reversed without jeopardizing the firm's wider new strategy.

---

* On a personal note, over the forty-three years of my motoring life, I have owned only French cars. First, a succession of eleven Renaults, starting with a wee 4CV in Paris in 1955, then graduating via the Dauphine, the excellent R16, R20 and other models to the Laguna, which I liked less. In 1997 I divorced Renault to marry Citroën, whose Xantia pleases me a lot.

So the State's 46 per cent of shares counted for nothing. Renault had fully proved its independence.

PSA has likewise seen a fall in its profits recently. If it has sometimes fared a little better than Renault, this has been due in part to the restructuring efforts of Jacques Calvet in 1986–97. He reduced staff in that period from 165,000 to 139,000, and he set about integrating Citroën more tightly with its larger sister company: both brands now have the same engines and gear-boxes. 'We find that the public no longer wants non-serious cars, so we've made the Citroëns less idiosyncratic, less technically innovative,' one veteran Peugeot executive told me smugly – but some devotees regret this trend away from endearing quirkiness. PSA has also been facing up to the problems of urban pollution (see p. 276). It has been criticized for putting too much stress on diesel-engine cars – one reason why it is now pioneering the electric car, ahead of other European firms. But it still finds it hard to sell these to individual customers. In line with the cleaner-fuel drive, the Government in 1994–6 offered a subsidy of some 6,000 francs to any buyer ready to trade in a car more than eight years old for a new one. Some 180,000 vehicles were thus sold, nicknamed 'Balladurettes', then 'Jupettes'. The aim was partly to boost sales of the flagging French car industry: but this flagrant breach of EU competition rules was sanctioned by Brussels for its ecological content, as the new cars could use lead-free petrol.

France still produces cars of high quality, but has recently not been as effective as some of its rivals in cutting production costs and pushing sales. In terms of cars sold as a share of the European market, PSA by 1995 had slipped to fourth place behind Ford: first came the Volkswagen group (17.1 per cent), then General Motors (Opel, Vauxhall, etc., 12.6), followed by Ford (12), PSA (11.9), Fiat (11.4), Renault (9.9), BMW-Rover (6.2), Mercedes (3.6). In terms of turnover the picture is different, for the luxury firms can earn more while selling fewer cars. But here France's lag is even greater, according to figures given by the Institut National de la Statistique et des Études Économiques (INSEE) for world sales in 1995, in billions of francs: Mercedes 356, VW 274, Fiat 226, Renault 179, PSA 166. Amid general alarm, overall sales of French cars fell slightly in 1995–6: but they have since been picking up, both at home and for exports. In 1998 sales rose by 11 per cent, a sign of the French economic recovery. Renault that year even moved ahead of VW to become the market leader in Europe with 2.13 million vehicles sold worldwide.

Manufacturers are now trying to cut costs and sale prices by reducing frills on cars. But many foreign firms can sell more cheaply, and the French remain handicapped by high labour costs and overcapacity. The Germans, with similar problems, have been more flexible in adapting to the market. And so today the heirs to the brilliant traditions of Louis Renault, and of André Citroën, require all their flair and ingenuity to survive healthily in a sector where *la mondialisation* has gone so far.

France's aerospace industry has also shown enterprise and brilliance since the war. Its one big commercial failure, Concorde, was less its own fault than due to Anglo-French governmental mistakes. Today France has Europe's largest aerospace industry, pace-setter in the very successful Airbus joint venture which has taken some 40 per cent of the world market in larger civil aircraft, in the face of Boeing. But even this industry has now been totally restructured on a European scale: in 1999 Aerospatiale merged with Matra, then this big new group formed a union with DASA of Germany (see below).

National pride is much involved in aviation: were not the French pioneers from the days when Blériot was the first man to fly the Channel, in 1909? The French aircraft industry then led the world: but by 1945, after working perforce for the Germans, it was nearly derelict. Its main firm, Sud-Est Aviation of Toulouse (later called Sud-Aviation and today Aerospatiale), was reduced to making refrigerators. But then came a spectacular renaissance. The state-owned Sud-Est was entrusted to a gifted young technocrat, Georges Héreil, who rebuilt the workshops and then took a gamble on making the Caravelle. With over 90 per cent of the free world's construction in American hands, he needed to probe their weak point, and this fast medium-range twin-jet seemed the answer. In order to get in ahead of the rival jet that Boeing was planning, Héreil persuaded the State to invest large sums in an initial batch of forty Caravelles, to be ready by 1959, before any airline, even Air France, had placed orders. For three years engineers and designers worked round the clock in Toulouse on a project that was entirely French save for its Rolls-Royce engines – and the gamble paid off. Air France, then Alitalia, SAS and others, quickly bought a plane whose speed (500 mph), silence, comfort and resistance to fatigue put it ahead of other aircraft in its class. This was the measure of the French triumph, a mix of daring and brilliant inventiveness, at a time when the British and Americans with their wartime experience were still far ahead in expertise.

With 286 sold to thirty-four airlines by 1972, Caravelle was by far the most successful European plane of its day. But Héreil failed in his ambition of breaking into the American market. And Aerospatiale then made the mistake, not since repeated with Airbus, of failing to follow up Caravelle with a family of related models. Instead, the firm fell victim to a misguided Franco-British governmental fancy that the long-distance market was about to go supersonic. This led to the great winged white elephant of Concorde, which Héreil's successors in Toulouse had argued against from the start, but they were shouted down by prestige-hungry politicians. Probably Concorde could never have paid its way: but the delays caused by Whitehall's repeated shilly-shallying greatly added to its final cost. But though a commercial disaster, the aircraft was technologically a triumph. In the end the 'captive' Air France and British Airways were the only airlines that took the fourteen Concordes built for sale, and they got five of them as presents in 1979, after no other takers had emerged. Today they are doing well commercially, but this does not make up for the earlier money misspent.

The failures did not prove that such joint projects are impossible: simply that they should be tackled differently. No European country can today make a major civil aircraft on its own, but the technical cooperation needs the minimum of state interference: that was the lesson bequeathed by Concorde to Airbus from the start, in 1970. The four-nation Airbus Industrie has always been a consortium of individual firms, even if Aerospatiale until today has been state-owned. Of the partners, Aerospatiale and Daimler-Benz Aerospace Airbus (known as DASA) each have 38 per cent, British Aerospace owns 20 per cent and the small Spanish CASA 4 per cent (there are also Belgian and Italian associates). And with some ups and downs it has all worked well. The French make the 'brains' of the machine, i.e. the cockpit and the middle fuselage; the British make the wings and the Spanish the tail, while the Germans make 'the boring bits', i.e. most of the fuselage. The plane is assembled mainly in Toulouse, and fitted partly in Hamburg.

The French still tend to regard Airbus as their 'baby'. They were initially the driving force behind the operation, and they still provide much of the technical expertise. But the Germans today have a prime managerial role, while the British supply much of the sharp financial wizardry; and both these private firms claim to be more efficient than Aerospatiale. 'We French are in this for the glory, the Germans for the power, the British for the money,' said one *polytechnicien* I met in

Toulouse. Yet despite the inevitable frictions and jealousies, the team operate as an above-average example of European cooperation, and have now sold over 2,000 Airbuses to 167 airlines since the first A300 flew in 1972. This wide-bodied 250-seater, ideal for medium-range routes, was followed by the slimmer 200-seat A310, then the popular A320 and larger A340 which can seat over 350 and is a rival to the bigger Boeings. The triumph of Airbus is that it has carved out some 40 per cent of the world market in larger civil aircraft, in face of Boeing which has the other 60 per cent (having swallowed up McDonnell-Douglas); and these two giants are alone in the field. Airbus has even sold well inside the American market: in 1997 US Airways signed up to buy 124 models.

Today Airbus is being transformed from a consortium into a normal company, jointly owned. It is also preparing its own jumbo, the A3XX, a 500- or 600-seater, aimed to compete with the Boeing 747 and to enter service maybe by 2004. Abroad, Airbus's main concern is that its lucrative Far Eastern market could become affected by the economic crisis in that region. But nearer home, it has won an important victory. British Airways, long hostile to Europe, had for years been one of the few major European airlines to stay just with Boeing alone and buy no Airbuses. But in 1998 it finally agreed to buy 59 of them, with options on a further 129. This was not due to sentiment: Airbus had offered more favourable terms than Boeing.

Aerospatiale has always been highly diversified. Airbus has made up the major part of its civil aircraft effort: but it has also made a successful smaller plane, the ATR, together with the Italians. And it has been the world's leading exporter of civil helicopters (see p. 166). Military production has included the Tiger helicopter, Franco-German, and missiles such as Exocet, which Argentina used in the Falklands war. In the space industry Aerospatiale has been a major player, making satellites for both civil and military purposes, and parts of Ariane 4. The group has large aircraft factories at Nantes and St-Nazaire, as well as Toulouse.

France's other major aircraft producer, Dassault, was for long one of the most successful firms in post-war France. Much was due to its founder, the legendary Marcel Dassault, who began by designing planes himself in 1918, became reputedly the richest man in France, and died in 1986 aged ninety-four. His company's speciality has been military aircraft, notably the Mirages and Mystères: he exported over 1,000 Mirage III multi-role fighters, many of them to Israel, Libya and pre-democratic South Africa. He also shone in the civil field with a small executive jet, the Falcon, which American and other tycoons bought in hundreds. The Socialists after 1981 semi-nationalized Dassault, taking a 51 per cent stake: today the Aerospatiale group and Marcel's son Serge each own some 47 per cent. But the ageing Marcel made some mistakes at the end. He had always despised international cooperation, preferring to go it alone: but he could not accept that this had ceased to be realistic. Thus he backed out of the four-nation European fighter project, and instead banked on its French rival, Rafale: but under today's changing conditions, this has not proved nearly such a success as his previous warplanes. By 1998 no Rafales had yet been sold abroad, and the French Air Force had bought only thirteen. Dassault's great firm seems to have lost some of its old dynamism and creativity.

Today huge changes are under way. Airbus is ceasing to be a mere consortium, and is due to become one single company owned by its partners: this should make decision-making easier. DASA initially sought to join up with British Aerospace to create a new group equal to Boeing. But BAe preferred to keep its independence, so DASA then looked instead to Aerospatiale. However, the latter's state-owned character was going to make a union hard, so the Juppé Government planned its privatization. Then Jospin, arriving on the scene with a pre-election promise that Aerospatiale would stay in state hands, was put under pressure by France's partners to shift position, and in 1998 allowed Aerospatiale to merge with Matra, a private firm: the State would keep a 47 per cent share, Matra hold 33 per cent, and its chairman, J.-L. Lagardère, would become the effective boss of this new semi-privatized group. Then, in October 1999, came the supreme *coup de théâtre*: Aerospatiale/Matra was set to merge with DASA, to become EADS (European Aeronautic Defence and Space Company), the world's third biggest group after Boeing and Lockheed Martin. The French State would own only 15 per cent of EADS, which would then have 80 per cent control of Airbus. Dassault was invited to join EADS. The aim, clearly, was to build up a giant European group that would rival the American titans. One Aerospatiale executive told me, 'Only a Socialist Government could have done all this, persuading the unions and Communists that there's no other choice but privatization if our aircraft industry is to survive.' Once again, the French Left and the French State have been forced to bend to *la mondialisation*.

France is also the leader of Europe's space and satellite programme, with its Ariane rockets. When de Gaulle in 1960 initiated France's own space policy, the results at first were meagre and he was accused of costly prestige hunting. But the venture has since borne fruit: France has enlisted eleven other nations to join her in the European Space Agency's (ESA) launching of Ariane rockets, under French technical management, from a base in French Guiana. The programme has had its setbacks: sometimes the rockets fail at take-off and have to be destroyed, with loss of expensive equipment, as happened at the initial launch of Ariane 5 in 1996; and elaborate plans for a European-manned spatial aircraft, Hermes, were abandoned by ESA in 1992. But apart from this, ESA has been more successful than its larger American rival, NASA, in developing rockets at reasonable cost and doing good business with them. ESA in fact has secured nearly 60 per cent of the world's commercial market in satellite launching, mainly for telecommunications; and Ariane usually has a full order book. This is far from mere prestige hunting. It could be seen as part of France's highly ambitious recent efforts in transport and communications. Leading the way with Airbus and Ariane is one aspect. The TGV and Eurotunnel are another.

A BRILLIANT TRANSPORT NETWORK, AND DAMN THE COST — AS THE TGVS HURTLE THROUGH THE TUNNEL

France has developed a brilliant modern transport system – at a price. In the post-war years the railways were effectively modernized, and today they include the vaunted high-speed TGV. French railways generally put British Rail to shame, while the main initiative and eagerness for building the Channel Tunnel has come from the French side. France has one of Europe's most elaborate networks of domestic air flights, plus excellent modern roads and *autoroutes*, which make this an easy and delightful country for the motoring tourist (if expensive).

Yet the flair and enthusiasm of engineers and planners have not always been matched by hard-headed work on costs. The Société Nationale des Chemins de Fer Français (SNCF) remains a public monopoly, while the major airlines too are still under majority state ownership. And these firms have long tended to be run bureaucratically, with overstaffing, heavy central administration and big deficits. Projects were often planned with one eye on national prestige, or on political needs. This mattered less in the boom years, when cash was plentiful and the building of a super-modern infrastructure was seen as a major priority. But today attitudes have changed. SNCF's mounting losses have prompted plans for drastic reform; even the building of new TGV lines is now queried, while French shareholders in Eurotunnel have been aghast at its financial bungles (more often than not due to the British?). Air France, also in heavy deficit until recently, has now undergone a major overhaul, to prepare it for the new open competition in the deregulated skies of Europe. So the entire French transport system – even the role of the truculent lorry drivers – has come under reappraisal.

Two state-owned airlines were developed after the war: Air France for international flights, and the smaller Air Inter which at first had a monopoly of French domestic flights. Air Inter was owned partly by Air France, and partly by SNCF, which was also its main competitor. Of these two state-owned rivals, initially the Government strongly favoured SNCF, because of the big sums invested in it; and so it held back the expansion of Air Inter. By the 1960s this short-sighted policy was discouraging foreign investors in France, thus harming the State's own industrial policy for the regions: one firm, for example, chose Savoie for its plant, simply because it was near the Geneva airport with links to Paris. So Air Inter was given the green light to expand; some small private airlines were sanctioned, too, such as Touraine Air Transport (TAT), founded at Tours in 1968; and by the 1980s France was claiming to have Europe's most elaborate domestic air network. The initial tendency was to radiate flights from Paris, in the French centralized tradition: Lyon, Toulouse and Bordeaux had no links with each other until 1965. But then inter-city regional flights were encouraged, and others between those cities and the outside world. This policy had much success in the boom years. Limoges, for instance, even started direct Air Inter flights to Lyon two years *sooner* than to Paris, then began a daily run to the little Massif Central town of Aurillac. Direct scheduled flights multiplied between London and various smaller towns in France, such as Colmar. Some of these lesser flights, internal or foreign, have often made a loss: but the State or local bodies have helped to keep them going for other reasons, political, economic or regional. Or at least, until today.

Air France had also expanded in the boom years. But by the early 1990s it was piling up heavy losses, reaching 7.5 billion francs for 1993. Nearly all world airlines were then doing badly for a time, during the recession, but Air France was worse hit than most: in 1990–94, the turnover of British Airways, KLM and Lufthansa rose respectively by

27, 25 and 13 per cent, while that of Air France fell by 13 per cent. Those companies and others had started much sooner to prepare for the agreed EU deregulation whereby, from 1997, any airline would be free to fly to or from any EU airport without the strict national controls that had long operated, especially in France. British Airways had been privatized in the 1980s, then restructured, and Lufthansa a little later. Air France was far behind, and was still saddled – in the eyes of its critics – by a system of state control that maybe had advantages in earlier post-war years but was now a liability in the new 'free market' Europe. The State had failed to invest adequately in the company at crucial periods; it also had the legacy of a heavy state-style bureaucratic management, ill-geared to profits; and it suffered from the overstaffing chronic in the French public services, plus the usual high French social costs, more than twice those at BA. Pilots and some other staff had exorbitant salaries, exacted by their tough unions. As deregulation loomed, Air France was not going to be competitive, and EU rules would forbid special subsidies.

Fully aware of these dangers, Balladur in 1993 encouraged Air France's chairman, Bernard Attali (twin brother of Jacques), to put forward a restructuring plan that *inter alia* would have killed 4,000 jobs. He was met by massive strikes; and Balladur, typically, had the plan withdrawn rather than face trouble. Attali then resigned – to be replaced by Christian Blanc, who soon proved himself to be one of the greatest French *hauts fonctionnaires* of recent decades. Brilliant pragmatist, superb negotiator, man of vision, this 'saviour' of Air France was an ex-prefect (but not an *énarque*) and a mild Rocardian pro-Socialist who came also to believe warmly in the virtues of private enterprise, at least for a service firm such as Air France. Whereas Attali had imposed his plan tactlessly, Blanc first talked carefully to all the staff and their unions, and explained bluntly, in effect, 'We must all make sacrifices, or this firm simply goes bust, and in the long run the State cannot save us.' He won the support of twelve of the sixteen unions, then held a referendum in 1994 that secured him the backing of 81 per cent of the staff for a radical plan not so different from Attali's but far more astutely presented. 'I made my staff the partners of change, not its enemies,' he said later – 'a way of proceeding rather unusual for France, but normal in northern Europe, for example.'

Crucially, to help him to restructure and to deal with Air France's huge debt, Blanc was granted a 20 billion franc special government subsidy. This was contrary to EU competition rules and was strongly contested by the British Government and others. But Brussels allowed it, as a one-off concession. So Blanc was able to set about a three-year rescue campaign on three main lines: staff cuts; the future of Air Inter; flight strategy. First, he negotiated a reduction in the staff of Air France from 40,000 to 35,000 over the following five years without compulsory sackings: this was to be done by early retirement at fifty-four (instead of the usual sixty) and by not replacing all those who left. All won golden handshakes. Blanc was able to persuade some 1,200 cabin stewards and hostesses to leave early, and he then took on younger ones at lower wages. He tried to do the same with the pilots. Their salaries could reach 650,000 francs a year, and even a co-pilot earned some 330,000 francs, whereas British Airways hired at the sterling equivalent of 170,000 francs, and Lufthansa salaries were 40 per cent below Air France's. Blanc wanted to hire at 220,000 francs plus, roughly the European average. The unions were hostile: but many of the pilots and crews did provisionally agree to reductions in salaries in return for shares in the company.★ Blanc also persuaded them to accept longer hours – 670 hours a year, in place of the total of 540 which they had won through a long and hard strike in 1971.

Christian Blanc had to deal with Air Inter which was also making losses. Since SNCF had sold its share, this company was now largely owned by Air France, which in 1990 also bought up the long-haul French airline UTA, part-owner of Air Inter. The domestic line was still being expected to keep up a number of loss-making local flights, as a matter of duty, something not expected of smaller private airlines. Yet in January 1996 the first internal phase of EU deregulation was due to start, as each nation's skies became free to its own airlines (and TAT, though now controlled by the dynamic British Airways, counted as French). To prepare for this, Blanc proposed first to integrate Air Inter with Air France, aligning staff conditions. But Air Inter pilots and crews, curiously, were paid even higher than those of the big airline, so they refused and went on strike. Blanc flung ultimatums at them, without success, and finally had no choice but to merge Air Inter totally into the new semi-decentralized Air France. The unions could not prevent him.

★ The issue then dragged on for years, and in June 1998, long after Blanc had left, the 3,200 pilots staged a strike against the plan, grounding aircraft just before the start of the World Cup. They were finally persuaded into a compromise, whereby they agreed to a 15 per cent drop in salary in return for shares, or else to a seven-year pay freeze, if they preferred.

Blanc reorganized Air France's flight schedules. Gone was the policy of keeping some minor lines open for political reasons: commercial profit would now be the sole criterion. Thus he closed Paris–Quito (Ecuador), to the annoyance of the Quai d'Orsay; he pulled out of Australia; and he cut some minor links with Britain, such as Paris–Cardiff, but other airlines took these over. Within France he caused a stir by killing the Paris–Perpignan line, though another airline stepped in. Blanc hired the expertise of the American-Indian, Rakesh Gangwall, known as the 'pope' of flight scheduling, who had saved a number of airlines. He preached the doctrine of the 'hub', which Blanc followed: that is, he built up Charles de Gaulle airport as a rival to Heathrow, Frankfurt and Schiphol, a hub from which world routes would radiate, offering a vast choice of connections with short waits. And he introduced a shuttle service every thirty to sixty minutes on the routes from Paris to Nice, Marseille and Toulouse. This was quite successful. Blanc claimed in 1997 that with the flight changes, staff cuts and other economies, he had increased Air France's overall productivity by 32 per cent. He needed it, for under the EU's new 'open skies' regime, he faced growing competition from British Airways' subsidiaries on some domestic French routes. BA had merged Air Liberté and TAT into a dynamic company which now controlled some 20 per cent of the traffic in and out of Orly.

Blanc took the new-style British Airways as his role model, his ideal of what a big modern airline should be. But whereas BA had been privatized for some years, Air France was still wholly state-owned, under the tutelage of the Ministry of Transport. Blanc, however, won the tacit support of Balladur for running it on fully commercial lines, with minimal subservience to the State – and he had the personal authority and panache to carry this through. This civil servant used amazingly bold language to criticize the French system, as in one talk he gave in 1996: 'Our Jacobin country has been carrying out a catastrophic policy. In the Netherlands, Germany and Britain, air transport generates profits; *chez nous*, it's been piling up losses and destroying jobs. Our concept of industrial policy has grown twenty years out of date, in face of the new economic realities ... I note the incapacity of the State to understand deregulation.' In other words, as Blanc saw it, if Europe chooses the free market, then a state firm has no option but to follow profit and efficiency, ahead of the old ideals of public service if needs be. This was the brief he had been given – and he succeeded brilliantly. He reduced Air France's 7.5 billion loss of 1993 to 1.2 billion for 1995–6: then for 1997–8 the airline made an operating profit of 1.8 billion francs.

Blanc saw the privatization of Air France as the natural outcome of his efforts, and was assured by Juppé that this would happen. But Jospin, with other commitments, suspended the project when he came to power; and as Minister of Transport he chose a Communist, Jean-Claude Gayssot, who said, 'I shall not be the minister of privatizations.' Blanc, furious, resigned. He claimed that the change was a 'breach of contract', for Brussels had sanctioned the 20-billion-franc loan on condition that the firm would be privatized. And he argued that Air France, to prosper, would need to form alliances with foreign companies, as British Airways had just done with American Airlines, and this would be less feasible if the firm stayed in state hands. However, Ministry of Finance experts argued in return that Air France was just not ready yet for privatization, if it was to attract a good price. There followed much debate about this, and the wider issue of the state ownership of competitive companies; and it cut across lines of Left and Right, with Michel Rocard springing to the defence of Blanc against the Communists.

Jospin soon made it clear that he was ready for compromise: he intended the State to keep majority control, but he was quite ready to open out Air France's capital to the market, as had been done with Renault. When Jean-Cyrille Spinetta, former head of Air Inter, took over from Blanc, Air France prepared to sell some shares on the Bourse and others to its staff. In 1998 the State was set to relinquish over 45 per cent of the capital: so the issue of privatization is no longer black-and-white. In a deregulated world, the deeper issue is how far such a company can follow the dictates of the market *and* remain a public service. If some lonely town is to lose its flight because of the implacable dictates of profit, what is the answer? Despite Blanc's brilliant performance in rescuing Air France, the debate goes on.

The building of modern motorways has been much less controversial. Like the air services, this got off to a slow post-war start: in 1967 France still had fewer kilometres of motorway than little Holland, and not until 1970 was the central Paris–Lyon–Marseille *autoroute* laboriously completed. One reason for the lag was that this spread-out country enjoys the legacy of about the best network in Europe of older main and secondary roads: they run straight across plains, or are finely engineered in hilly areas, and are a delight compared with most roads in Britain. So motorways at first seemed less urgent: but then this changed as traffic grew. Initially, this being France, all *autoroutes* were built and run by the State, and it led to endless budgetary delays. But from 1969 the Government allowed private operators to take part, with private capital, and this changed the picture. France soon overtook Britain in total length, and today she has some 9,000 kilometres of motorway, compared with 11,000 in Germany, 7,000 in Italy, 3,000 in Britain; and almost all are now built and run by private firms. Eight of them radiate from Paris, as far as Nice, Perpignan, Strasbourg, etc.; and just a few transversal ones have been built, for example from Bordeaux via Toulouse to Avignon. But there is still no motorway across the Massif Central from Clermont-Ferrand to Bordeaux.

Motorists feel aggrieved that France, along with Italy, is one of the few European countries to exact tolls on motorways, except on short sections outside cities. These are quite high, averaging 40 francs per 100 kilometres. As a result, many drivers prefer to go on clogging up the old roads, thus lessening the usefulness of the new investment: it is reckoned that motorway traffic might rise by 30 per cent if there were no tolls. The authorities argue that the cost of upkeep of the traditional network is such that they could not pay for the *autoroutes*, too, without an exorbitant rise in other motoring taxes. The transport lobbies are unconvinced. But at least French motorways are elegantly landscaped, and not disfigured by hoardings as in Italy. They even – a typical imaginative French touch – carry attractive pictorial signs every few kilometres, informing you that on your left is some medieval abbey, on your right some famous beauty spot, and so on. Perhaps it makes the tolls more bearable.

Recently, the emphasis has been also on the widening of older main roads into fast dual carriageways, with urban ringways. Brittany now has a good network of these. They cost less to build than *autoroutes*, and no tolls are exacted. It seems a sensible compromise. But under Balladur and Juppé, the motorway programme went ahead too, as some 280 kilometres a year were added. Then Jospin's Government decided to rethink; and with a Green as minister for regional development, work has now been postponed on several new projects, including a planned *autoroute* through the Alps from Grenoble to Sisteron. Jospin also cancelled outright a major scheme that had been lying around for years for an industrial canal from the Rhine near Mulhouse to the Saône near Dole, leading to the Rhône. This had been planned in the 1970s, then repeatedly delayed, as local opposition grew as well as doubts about its commercial viability, in a time of waning use of water transport in Europe. The mayors of Lyon and Marseille were furious with the decision, but ecologists were delighted. It seemed that another blow had been dealt against the policy of *grands travaux* which had guided France for so long.

The most belligerent users of French motorways can be the long-distance lorry drivers, whose notorious strikes and road blockages have infuriated visitors, notably British truck drivers and tourists caught in their mammoth jams. Four times at least in recent years, *les routiers* have staged this kind of nationwide strike to press for better pay or conditions. And they have found that militancy generally pays off, for such is the disruption caused that the Government backs down and sees they get what they want. Thus in 1996 the drivers blocked the roads for twelve days, pressing for shorter working hours and earlier retirement; a year later they did the same, demanding higher guaranteed wages; and both times they basically won. Their employers are a chaotic, fragmented industry of private haulage contractors, including a few big firms and a mass of tiny ones, perhaps 38,000: many of these claim that they cannot afford to give the truckers more, so they tend to ignore the rules that the Government sets. And this simply leads to further strikes. Often the drivers' grievances are legitimate; and their strikes even win the sympathy of the French public, which enjoys a touch of anarchy and street drama – unless caught up in it directly. Today hauliers and drivers alike are worried at the approach of EU deregulation: this could put many smaller firms out of business and so lead to loss of jobs, as more efficient foreign contractors move freely into France.

Paradoxically, the haulage industry has in other respects been doing well against its main rival, railway freight. Since 1960 the railways' overall share of freight has fallen from 58 to 25 per cent, while that of lorries has risen from 30 to 60 per cent (the remaining 15 per cent of tonnage goes by waterways and pipelines). More and more firms have been finding it easier and quicker to send their goods door to door along modern highways, rather than by rail. The trend seems regrettable in many ways, for lorries are the more likely to pollute and to cause traffic jams or accidents; and so much public money has been poured into modernizing French railways, yet their freight capacity is today hugely and wastefully underused. Despite SNCF's bid to develop modern containers, usable alike on road and rail, the decline in its freight traffic has slowly continued. This is a major cause of its huge deficit.

The story of the Société Nationale des Chemins de Fer Français has been a typical French mix of technical triumphs and commercial failures. Nationalized in 1937, French railways ended the war with four-fifths of their engines and coaches destroyed and much of their track and rolling stock also out of action. But this, as with some other industries, proved a blessing in disguise. Louis Armand, France's greatest post-war technocrat, modernized the railways brilliantly as head of SNCF after 1946. He closed many small branch lines, and he gave generous budgets to research technicians to prepare new designs: this tradition has continued, and today France remains a major exporter of electric and diesel locomotives. SNCF trains are reputed for their efficiency, speed and comfort: the French-built Corail carriages are rather like the first-class sections of an airliner. Only 45 per cent of the total track is electric, but this carries more than 80 per cent of all traffic, including the fast inter-city lines such as Lyon–Strasbourg. These have vastly improved since the pre-war centralized days, when it was quicker to go from Toulouse to Lyon via Paris (1,092 km) than direct (544 km). SNCF's punctuality is good. In a cold winter spell, its trains are more likely to go on running smoothly than those in Britain. As for accidents, after several disasters in 1985–91 which cost 136 lives, SNCF introduced an ultra-modern automatic signalling system, costly but effective, which has virtually eliminated the factor of human error. Thanks to this, French railways have since enjoyed one of Europe's lowest fatal accident rates: the Paddington disaster would have been 'almost impossible' in France, it is claimed.

The other side of this bright coin is that SNCF for many years has been making a deficit of anything between 8 and 16 billion francs a year; and if other charges are included, the net cost to the State has been higher still. There are multiple reasons. While freight has been deserting rail for road, some passengers have been doing the same, preferring to go by car or by air: passenger traffic fell by 7 per cent in 1984–94, and in the same period SNCF's turnover dropped by 13 per cent in real terms. As it is a public service, Governments have been reluctant to allow it to recoup by making radical fare increases. What is more, this state monopoly is run in a heavy bureaucratic style with a huge and costly administrative staff. The unions are unusually strong, especially the CGT; and officialdom has tended to yield to their demands, so that the *cheminots* have steadily been allowed to build up exceptional privileges, hard to dismantle: these include retirement at fifty for engine drivers, on something close to full pay. Another factor in the deficit: Governments have always invested heavily in SNCF's development, partly for reasons of national prestige, without worrying too much about costs: the TGV is the prime example. But attitudes are now beginning to change.

For some years SNCF has been trying to reduce its high salary costs by slimming down its staff – not via redundancies, but by replacing only about a third of those who retire. Thus the total personnel was cut from 200,000 to 175,000 in 1991–7. But Juppé in 1995 decided that this process was not enough: so in the context of his general budget-cutting policy, he proposed a major overhaul of SNCF. This would include the closure of some 6,000 kilometres of branch lines, to be replaced by buses, thus shedding many jobs; and major economies in the railwaymen's lavish pension schemes. It was this above all that pushed the *cheminots* into the lengthy and successful strikes of November/December 1995. The pension reform was dropped, the branch closures were postponed *sine die*. Instead, Juppé in 1996 put forward a very different plan for SNCF, which the unions accepted. Quite simply, he split it in two, rather as had happened in Britain, but without losing state ownership. A new public body was formed, the Réseau Ferré de France, which would look after the railtrack and infrastructure, and inherit some two-thirds of the accumulated debt of over 200 billion francs. SNCF would still run the trains, but would be cleared of most of its debt. This, you could say, was little more than shuffle of accountancy. But the aim was to help SNCF to make a new start, on a more profit-geared basis, with a new slimmer regionalized framework. The scheme went ahead, and was then endorsed by the Jospin Government. SNCF's operating loss for 1997 was reduced to some 800,000 francs for 1998.

The *cheminots* in 1995 were also worried that Juppé's 'liberal' Government might be planning to activate a much-ignored EU directive of 1991, whereby a nation's railtrack – somewhat like its roads – should be open to use by any railway vehicles, including foreign ones. This ultra-deregulatory measure would in practice destroy state rail monopolies. Britain and Sweden were in favour, but other countries were opposed, and notably France – so the *cheminots* need hardly have worried, though they boldly went on strike, 'to defend a French public service against the awful threat of competition', as their union leaders put it. In fact, unlike the airlines with their broader vocation, Europe's national railway companies, frontier-bound, have remained relatively inward-looking: they have not taken easily even to the cooperation required by Eurotunnel or other new cross-border express links. Thus rivalries between the French and German networks were such that for a while

SNCF put up technical barriers against German freight trains using the Tunnel. However, in 1997 the two sides finally reached an agreement on coordination.

The pioneering technology at SNCF has not always served the best practical interests either of its European partners or even of its own customers. The best recent example is Socrates, a new computerized reservation system introduced in 1993, which at first proved completely unworkable. It was not compatible with other countries' systems, so it drove their travel agents mad; and even the French found it impossible to operate – 'It was a typical example,' said one British critic, 'of the crazy French belief that technocracy must always be right, so they won't admit its faults.' Finally, however, the blatant unwisdom of Socrates was corrected, and it was made to work as intended. Other aspects of the booking system were modified, too: for example, it is now no longer necessary to book in advance for the TGV. This has formed part of the campaign of SNCF's dynamic new president, Louis Gallois, to try to woo back its waning public and restore its image after a difficult recent period. Passenger traffic did indeed rise by 9.9 per cent in 1997–8.

The Government and SNCF are also having to reassess the future of the TGV, which has been a brilliant success in itself, but the building of new track for it is fearfully expensive. This sleek orange-and-white 'bullet train' is a product of French engineering, built by Alsthom, and is the world's fastest train: on one trial run in 1990 it reached 515 kmph, beating the German and Japanese records. Even for its normal top cruising speed of 280 kmph, it requires special new lines. The first of these, on the 456 km from Paris to Lyon, was opened in 1981, and it cut the normal four-hour journey to two hours (see p. 355): some 200 high-speed trains now use this busy route each day, and between city centres they are much faster than the airlines, whose share of traffic has gone down to 10 per cent. The TGV line was extended to Valence, and is now being built on to Marseille. A second line goes to Tours, with a branch to Le Mans, and these trains at slower speeds can continue to Bordeaux and Brittany. A third line now runs to Lille and on to Calais and the Tunnel, whence the TGV rumbles quaintly through Kent to London. The Belgians and Dutch, unlike the British, have also done their bit to build new high-speed links, and many of the TGVs to Lille now go on to Amsterdam. They link in also with the fast new German network.

The TGV has been popular with the public, and is justly admired abroad as a brilliant contribution to railway technology in this 'age of the train'. So it is more than just a matter of prestige. But its track construction has added greatly to SNCF's deficit: the cost per kilometre was 25 million francs for the Paris–Lyon line, then 41 million for Paris–Calais, and will now be 55 million for Paris–Strasbourg. Compensation to landowners forms a large part. In 1992 Mitterrand gave the go-ahead for a big expansion of the network: he was especially proud of the TGV. But Juppé's Government, worried about meeting the 'Maastricht criteria', began to re-examine costs and talked of cutbacks on building of new lines. Today a Left is back in power that is more devoted to trains than to air or road: a Green Environment Minister finds them less polluting, while a Communist Transport Minister is traditionally sympathetic to SNCF as a bastion of the CGT. Yet the budget-cutting pressures remain strong, too. Several new TGV lines are projected, in theory: from Tours on to Bordeaux and Toulouse; from Le Mans to Nantes and Rennes; from Avignon (on the Paris–Marseille line) to Perpignan; from the Paris–Lyon line near Dijon to Mulhouse. Most important is the 'TGV Est' from Paris to Strasbourg, seen as crucial because of the latter's special European role. And in 1998 this line was definitely given the go-ahead, while it seemed that the others might be delayed.

Today a great debate continues about the value and the basic cost-effectiveness of the TGV. There are those who argue that, while it helps major inter-city contacts, it does not do much for the regional development that the French still hold so dear: its speed means there are few stops, so it ignores the smaller towns and rural areas and may even be reinforcing economic centralism. Another argument is that there does exist a cheaper alternative to the TGV: this is the new 'pendular' train, which goes less fast but can use existing lines and is thus less costly to develop. It is already in service in Italy, Sweden and Canada. So the debate about the TGV will go on. Until now at least, big-town mayors and regional leaders have lobbied hard to obtain their TGV lines, while local environmental opposition, from those along the route, has mostly been muted. How different from the picture in Britain – as witness the notorious contrasts in the two nations' attitudes to building that Tunnel.

This grandest of *grands projets* has had its teething troubles, heaven knows. But it remains a great positive venture. Its Eurostar trains have become popular; and in the long run it may even make money, despite the initial financial blunders. Significantly, the enthusiasm and ideas for the Tunnel have always come mainly from the French, even though Britain as an island has stood to gain more from it, whereas for France it is just one more land link among many. This may say something about British wariness of the Continent, or British scepticism about adventurous *grands projets*, so loved by the French.

The first idea for a tunnel under the Channel was launched in 1802 by an engineer of Napoleon, then planning to invade England. The notion was revived seriously in the 1870s and '80s, by which time tunnelling on this scale was fully feasible technically, as witness the big tunnels under the Alps. But plans were vetoed by the British Army, on security grounds – and this was to remain the obstacle for many years to come. Then, in the 1960s and '70s, British and French interests united for a scheme that began to find some acceptance politically, even on the British side; and experimental boring actually began. But the Wilson Government dropped the plan in 1975, on cost grounds. Then in 1984 Thatcher suddenly became converted to the idea of a fixed Channel link, to demonstrate the virility of the private sector. So serious talks with the French began.

Thatcher favoured a suspension bridge; Mitterrand preferred a tunnel, which could be used to promote French railway prowess with the TGV. A more serious disagreement was over money: the French typically wanted public financing, but Thatcher said No No Never, and Mitterrand had no option but to bend to her will. However, compromise was allowed on the French side, as state-owned banks put up some money. On this basis, tenders were invited. Of the four main ones, one was for a multi-span suspension bridge, one for a combined road/rail system with floating islands, one for a broad road-and-rail tunnel, and one for a rail tunnel alone, to carry freight, a car shuttle and passenger trains. All were technically feasible. The last of the four was accepted, as being the cheapest and the safest, presenting no dangers to shipping in the busy Channel. So in January 1986, Thatcher and Mitterrand met at Canterbury, to sign a solemn treaty for building the Tunnel. The National Assembly then ratified it in two days, while the British Parliament took fifteen months.

The Eurotunnel private company was formed to manage the project, together with a consortium, Transmanche Link (TML), of five British and five French building contractors. They began tunnelling at both ends, on a 50-kilometre route from just west of Calais to just east of Folkestone. The French used mainly local workers, whom they trained and disciplined well. The British gathered an international team of veteran construction workers – and the result at first was chaos. As Eurotunnel officials told me later, the British firms failed to manage their workers properly: there were eight fatal accidents on the British side, against only one on the French side, and by the end of 1988 only 7 kilometres had been tunnelled, most of it on the French side although the terrain there was harder. Finally, Eurotunnel insisted that TML get rid of the separate British management and install a new joint one which restored better control.

This issue was soon dwarfed by the escalating financial problems of the Tunnel – an oft-told saga. In a word, Eurotunnel was subsidized by a number of large banks, mainly British and French, and all wanted the Tunnel to be completed as fast as possible, so as to minimize interest costs. So Eurotunnel pressured TML to get ahead. But TML began to suffer unforeseen problems with equipment deliveries, safety standards and the tunnelling itself, and delays piled up; TML also underestimated its costs. So relations between Eurotunnel and TML were sour for a long time, as each suspected the other of cheating and of trying to cut corners. But this was never a Franco-British quarrel as such: executives from the two sides mostly got on well, notably André Bernard, Eurotunnel's first chairman, and Sir Alistair Morton, the forceful South African banker who became co-chairman and who very skilfully did all he could to limit the growing financial disaster. But it was not until spring 1994 that Eurotunnel and TML finally resolved their dispute over costs. By then, the project was over a year behind schedule, and the initial estimated £4.8 billion cost had spiralled to some £10.5 billion, with interest charges running at £2 million a day. In the post mortem that followed, most experts agreed that grave miscalculations had been made at the start. The construction work should not have been launched so rapidly: TML should have been given more time to get its costs and its technical programme right. Its contractors had been seriously imprudent, even greedy. But the banks and Eurotunnel, too, had made mistakes.

Among the losers have been the many small shareholders, most of them French. When the marketing of shares in Eurotunnel began, the response could not have been more different on the two sides – typically. Market research showed that the British public was indifferent (this was the era of 'hop off, you frogs', and 'do we want French rabies?'), so little sales effort was made. But the French were treated to a massive PR campaign on television, with surreal space flights, triumphal music, and slogans about '*un pas de géant!*' And the public reacted eagerly, thinking they were buying a slice of France's future; many humble people acquired shares for the first time, and some even thought this was a purely French project, with no British involvement. About 600,000 French bought shares, against 130,000 British. On both sides, the big institutions were more wary, so there was no *noyau dur* of major shareholders – unusual for such a project – but many little ones. The shares were first quoted at £3.50 each; then in the early euphoria this rose to the unrealistic height of £11. But as the Tunnel's problems grew, the price collapsed to 60p by early 1996, then settling at around 80p. Angry action committees were formed, as the French media ran sob stories of simple families who feared they were ruined. Eurotunnel managed to pacify the furore. And today it seems that the shareholders may in the end earn some money. But they will have to be very patient.

The two tunnels met under the sea in 1990, with much popping of champagne corks. Then finally, more than a year behind schedule, the Tunnel opened for business in May 1994, and the Queen came by TGV to the terminal near Calais, for a celebratory lunch with President Mitterrand. Freight services began then, while the car shuttles and the passenger trains, called Eurostar, started six months later. They are operated by a company owned jointly by French and Belgian state railways and a British firm, paying a handsome rent to Eurotunnel. Eurostar initially ran two TGVs a day each way between London and Paris, and today it runs about twelve, with others to Brussels.

Apart from one fortuitous accident in 1996, the services have been running smoothly. But one aspect of the sorry financial drama is that Eurotunnel, just as it underestimated the building costs, also much overestimated the likely volume of traffic – and so it may take longer than expected for debts to be repaid. Some 10 million passengers a year by 1996 were at first predicted for the Eurostar trains: but the actual figure today, though rising, is still only 6 million. Less traffic than anticipated has been taken from the airlines, which have managed to retain some 40 per cent on the Paris–London routes. Bad initial marketing has been blamed, also the Socrates fiasco, though this was later corrected and traffic picked up in 1997–8. Trains are now running at 60 per cent capacity on the Paris route (35 per cent to Brussels). But the dismal British failure to build their high-speed rail link across Kent for the TGVs has meant that it is still slightly quicker to go by air between Paris and London city centres – a three-hour train journey, compared with two hours Paris–Lyon for an only slightly shorter distance. This may have deterred many people from switching to Eurostar.

The freight shuttles have done better, often running at near capacity. But the service for motorists, at first quaintly called 'Le Shuttle' and now known as Eurotunnel, suffered fiercer competition than expected from the ferries, which hit back by introducing new, larger ships with enticingly cheap return fares, and by playing the duty-free card for all it was worth. Eurotunnel was never able to offer duty-free shopping on its trains, passengers having to remain in their cars during the 35-minute journey; although duty-free goods could always be bought prior to departure, this added time on to the journey. On the much longer ferry crossings, on the other hand, shopping could be done at leisure, and passengers were able to enjoy lavish duty-free bargains laid on as part of the ferries' desperate campaign to keep their custom – a ploy which proved successful as they were initially able to hold on to 60 per cent of the cross-Channel motorized tourist traffic. Eurotunnel considered their competition methods grossly unfair and it welcomed the European Commission's plan to abolish, in July 1999, the gross anomaly of duty-free goods within what was now a customs-free union. Access to such goods was an undoubtedly pleasant perk for the tourist, but it could not be justified. However, duty-free goods provided the ferries with much of their profits, and now that these privileges have ended, Eurotunnel has been able to take some trade away from them.

As a frequent traveller to France, and a Euro-freak living in Kensington, I confess to being torn about the virtues of the Tunnel. Like most people, I find the Eurostar trains comfortable, and less hassle than those tedious airports: it is pleasant to settle down for three hours of quiet reading, or chatting, and I put up with the feeble catering. Pricewise the two services work out much the same (but this can vary), and timewise they are comparable, too, each just about four hours from my home to the Gare du Nord. The air flights can suffer delays, notably in bad weather: but so sometimes can the trains. And the absurd archaic trundling through Kentish fields and suburbs brings out my latent Anglophobia, after the smooth lightning spurt from Paris to Folkestone, where you hardly notice going through the Tunnel itself. In sum, I now go by Eurostar, not air. When I take my car, however, I remain loyal to P&O, whose shareholder I have been for many years: thus I get half-price on all tickets, whereas I failed – maybe wisely? – to subscribe at the time to Eurotunnel's *pas de géant* and so collect its freebies. What's more, I enjoy the ferry's taste of sea travel, its comfort and food: the one time I took Le Shuttle it was late, and I found it ugly and claustrophobic. The time difference, 25 minutes against 75, is in practice less, if you want to shop duty-free before descending to the depths.

Down in those depths, a nasty accident occurred in November 1996 – just what Eurotunnel's bruised image needed least. A fire broke out in a lorry aboard a shuttle, and several drivers were affected by fumes. It happened by pure chance and did not indicate anything wrong with the Tunnel's design or security system. But it was a miracle that no one was worse hurt; and the damage took more than three months to repair, disrupting regular services. At about the same time, Eurotunnel managed to negotiate with its banks a restructuring of its £7 billion debt, whereby the banks would take shares and gain some 45 per cent control, in return for a lessening of the debt and lengthening of the period of concession. The company was thus able to breathe more easily. But today, in both London and Paris, the debate continues as to whether the system of private financing imposed by Thatcher was a wise one. Many French experts argue, 'We told you so': they hold the French traditional view that financing purely by banks and shareholders is not right for so vast a public infrastructure, with all the risks involved, and that state money should have been involved. Even in Britain, not so many people today would support Thatcher's dogma, 'not one penny of public money!' Probably a way should have been found of welding the public and private sectors. In the darkest days of completing the Tunnel, there was even some talk of cancelling the project. But this would never have been allowed: too much European prestige was involved, as well as investment. Doubtless, if Eurotunnel had finally failed in its dealings with the banks and contractors, then Governments would have had to step in, or the EU itself, and the venture would have been 'Europeanized'. For many people, it has become one symbol of a united Europe.

The passenger trains and the shuttles have now been showing operating profits since 1997. Their trade is increasing; and the Tunnel's long-term commercial and practical future seems assured, despite the mistakes. Its impact on Franco-British relations is hard to assess. But it is a boost for the Nord–Pas-de-Calais region of France, with its declining older industries yet superb central position at the heart of Europe's 'Golden Triangle'. Pierre Mauroy, the region's former president and still the mayor of its capital, Lille, lobbied hard from the start for the Tunnel, and for its TGVs to pass through his city (see p. 370). The population backed him, and today they still look with some pride and fascination at a venture that has brought them plenty of new investment (much of it British) and will bring more. Some of them still look with bewilderment, even contempt, at reactions on the British side, where Kent is such a different place – a county full of pretty orchards and retired middle-class people, with little industry. Here opposition to the Tunnel focused on hatred of the plan for a new high-speed rail link – and this became compounded with the failure of British planners and backers to get this link organized.

Today prospects seem a little brighter for this rail link through Kent finally being built, one day. But the French remain scornful: as *Le Monde* commented sourly, '*Les Anglais* are the Tunnel's foremost users, but it continues to wound their insular fibre.' This may not be quite fair. But the contrast between national attitudes will remain. As one senior SNCF manager said, 'It's not easy to work with British Rail. They're never exactly *against* anything, but they're never in favour of anything either.' Probably, the British will never emulate the French enthusiasm for building costly TGVs and other *grands projets*. But can Air France ever emulate British skill in running a modern airline so effectively?

3

SOCIAL PROGRESS, BUT SCARES ABOUT WELFARE, JOBS, RACISM

The Germans and British may have invented the Welfare State, thanks to Bismarck and later Beveridge. But France has caught up, and today has a welfare system that is one of Europe's most elaborate and generous, including lavish old-age pensions and plentiful modern hospitals. It is very expensive, and recent necessary efforts to reduce its costs – by Jospin, as well as Juppé – have made progress, despite strong opposition from doctors and others.

One aspect of the structure is France's high level of social costs, and the tight official rules on staffing – allegedly major causes of the high unemployment of recent years. And one weakness of the system is that the dole allowances, though generous for some, do not adequately cover many others, especially the young and the long-term jobless. This aggravates the division between 'haves' and 'have-nots', in a mostly very prosperous society where great wealth and privilege are balanced by the spread of real poverty. This so-called '*fracture sociale*', and the problems of '*les exclus*' (those unable to share in the prosperity), have become a key political issue; and Martine Aubry in 1998 presented a new 50-billion-franc package for fighting *l'exclusion*.

The problems are at their worst in some of the poorer high-rise suburbs that have sprung up since the 1960s on the edge of many French towns. Here frustration, violence and delinquency have grown in recent years, and unemployment is up to 50 per cent among young people of immigrant origin, mostly North African. They often feel rejected by the native French, who have been called 'Europe's most racist nation'. Today, paradoxically, with the World Cup victory, footballers from the ethnic minorities have become major national heroes: so the climate may improve. But meantime the racist feeling has been one of the obvious factors behind the ominous rise since the mid-1980s of the Front National. All of this, we shall now explore.

SOCIAL SECURITY:
CUTTING THE COSTS OF THE CRAZE FOR HEALTH

Doctors on strike, unions furious, drugs firms accused – the crisis in the French health service has been one of the major dramas and talking points in France during the late 1990s – more so than in Britain. It is a complex service, mostly of high quality, and specific to France in many ways. But it has become very costly, and was piling up a huge annual deficit, along with the rest of the welfare system of which it is part. The growing cost of pensions and the dole, as more people are elderly, or out of work, has added to the budgetary problems. Recent Governments, first Juppé's and now Jospin's, have been making serious efforts to reduce overspending, and to check abuses in hospitals and surgeries. They have finally made some progress. But they have had to face the anger of the medical profession, plus the doubts of a French public that expects, as ever, a high level of state cosseting, and feels little shame at being the world's top consumers of medicines, notably tranquillizers.

Earlier this century, France made a slower start than many of her neighbours in developing a proper welfare system. The health service began just after the war, as in Britain: but for years it remained very far from adequate. Many hospitals were overcrowded and fearfully old-fashioned, and few new ones were built to serve the growing suburbs. Then a well-funded crash programme began in the 1960s; and today, with their 470,000 beds in the public sector and some 200,000 private ones, French hospitals are if anything too large and numerous for the country's needs, and some are overstaffed. It makes a contrast with the NHS in Britain: some London hospitals have seemed to me cramped and understaffed, compared to, say, the bright, spacious two-bed ward I had just seen in a small public hospital in Brittany. Waiting lists in France, for beds or for operations, are now few. Another sign of the improvements, in the medical service and in hygiene, is that the infant mortality rate has dropped since 1950 from 53 to 6.8 deaths per 1,000 births: here France has moved ahead of Britain and Germany and is close behind Sweden. As for doctors, their numbers have increased since 1970 from 68,000 to some 160,000, and France today has 3.2 per 1,000 inhabitants, above the Western average (Germany has 3.2 and Spain, remarkably, 4.1: but the US figure is 2.3 and Britain's 1.5).

These and other dry statistics underline the point that the French, as individuals and as a society, have freely chosen to spend a great deal on health. Since 1950, spending has risen from 3 to 9.7 per cent of GDP; and given the rise in GDP, this means that the French are today devoting about eight times as much to their health care as forty years ago, in real terms. They are the world's biggest health spenders per head after the Americans (14 per cent), ahead of the Germans (8.6) and the British (7.1). But whether the French service actually offers better value for money than the super-efficient German system is another matter.

In France it is supervised by the State, but liberal in the freedom it allows to doctors and their relations with patients. A GP can move around as he wishes, and he and his patients can choose each other freely; the Sécurité Sociale ('*la Sécu*', as the French call it) intervenes purely as a kind of insurance service, repaying the bills. Doctors are highly attached to this system, which, as they see it, safeguards the independence of their profession and prevents them from becoming 'mere civil servants' like British NHS doctors; and the public likes it, too. Another difference from Britain is that the patient pays his doctor direct for each consultation, and must then apply to the Social Security for a refund, which involves delay and much form-filling. And the refund is not total: it is some 75 per cent of the 115-franc fee that most GPs today are allowed to charge (specialists get more, and some GPs are in a higher bracket where the fees are not restricted). So the service is not entirely free. But some very poor or elderly people are on a special regime where they pay nothing. And many families subscribe to a *mutuelle*, a semi-private insurance body often related to their job, which tops up the 25 per cent. In hospitals, where the house physicians are public servants, the reimbursement is at 70 to 90 per cent, while for serious illnesses it can be 100 per cent.

If health spending has been rising so fast, one factor, as in other countries, is that hospitals are using more expensive and sophisticated equipment, for transplants and the like. Another factor, less justifiable and more specific to France, is that many doctors overprescribe expensive drugs, sometimes in tacit conspiracy with the pharmaceutical industry from which they may get pay-offs of a kind: GPs are repeatedly solicited by commercial visitors from the big drugs firms, offering what can amount to bribes. And as the reimbursement rate for prescriptions, some 35 to 70 per cent for most medicines, can reach 100 per cent for the costlier ones, the State foots much of the bill. But this drug boom is partly the patients' own fault. One trend of the new France is that the French have become far more fussy about their health – maybe an aspect of their recently growing anxiety or concern for ecology. The consumption of medicines has risen by 60 per cent in volume since 1970, and France holds the world record: the level is more than twice that of Britain, while for tranquillizers it is *three* times the British or German level. So much for the image of French hedonistic *joie de vivre*. 'We've become a nation of hypochondriacs,' said one doctor. So the public forks out readily for its own share of the costs, and the Ministry of Finance tears its hair. The overuse of tranquillizers was strongly condemned in an official report in 1996, and doctors were blamed for prescribing them too readily.

One special problem is that generic medicines – i.e. the simpler and commoner kinds not patented by the drugs firms – are still very little used in France, accounting for only 5 per cent of medicines sold, against over 30 per cent in Britain, Germany and America. They are some 30 to 50 per cent cheaper than the patented brands, and in 1996 it was officially reckoned that 34 billion francs a year could be saved if just eight common generic drugs were substituted for similar patented ones. One explanation for the bias in France may be the conservatism of doctors and their ententes with the pharmaceutical firms: but another is certainly the behaviour of chemists' shops which cling to an old privilege legally forbidding the sale of medicines in other stores. This monopoly helps the pharmacies to keep prices high and, in league with the doctors, to discriminate against the cheaper brands which would earn them less. Despite the recent inroads made by the hypermarkets in selling some paramedical goods such as vitamin pills (see p. 639), there is still a wide range of simple medicines that in other countries can be sold anywhere without prescription but in France remain the preserve of the pharmacies.

Governments in France, as in some other countries, were generous for years in allowing the Social Security budget to rise faster than national income. During the boom years this posed little problem, and was even valuable as a means of remedying some injustices in the service, such as the low old-age pensions. But as the service grew generous it also grew more wasteful; and to this day it has been complicated by a vast array of different semi-autonomous insurance funds and *caisses* that manage the state reimbursements, and by a complex system of work-related contri- butions paid by employees and firms on a sliding scale. The scheme has come under rival political pressures from unions, employers and doctors, and has been hard to control or reform. Already by the mid-1970s the Social Security budget was making a big annual deficit. Barre was the first to take serious action: in 1978 he enforced a large rise in contributions and managed to get public hospitals to trim their spending a little. But when he asked the doctors to accept a plan that would penalize those who over-subscribed, he was met by a year-long wrangle and three strikes, and his project foundered. Later, other Governments of both Right and Left made their own repeated efforts to redress the accounts of *la Sécu*, but without much success.

Then enter Alain Juppé. By 1995 the annual deficit had reached a gigantic 67 billion francs (40 billion of this was for health alone). So Juppé, with the backing of Chirac, took urgent action. His top priority was to reduce the State's overall budget deficit in line with the EMU criteria: but he wanted also to give the Social Security a drastic and much-needed overhaul, for its own sake. He was met by a three-week national strike which had various motives, and a desire to wreck his welfare plan was maybe not the strongest. In fact, though he made concessions on other fronts, he managed to keep his Social Security reforms intact; and when the strike ended, he was able to push most of them through Parliament. Whatever his other failures, this was the major achievement of his two years in office. It was courageous, for the reforms, though not perfect, were crucially needed.

The central measure was to transfer to Parliament the annual task of setting a ceiling for Social Security spending, thus removing this role from a body drawn from unions and employers. The militant unions were furious. But the main advantage of the change was that Parliament, generally of the same colour as the Government, was much more likely to keep a tight rein on spending – and in 1996 this began to bring results. Another complex measure was to shift the method of financing Social Security from the usual wage-based contributions to a broader 'social' tax, the *contribution sociale généralisée* (CSG): this meant that some people would pay more, notably the better-off, and the overall welfare revenue would increase. A new special tax was imposed, to help reduce *la Sécu*'s accumulated debt. And taxes on tobacco and spirits were put up. These and various other steps began to help reduce the deficit a little in 1996, if more slowly than the Government had forecast. Although Juppé himself was unpopular, and his Government too, his shake-up of *la Sécu* was grudgingly accepted by a public that saw its necessity. But it ran into heavy opposition from the medical profession – and this more than anything put limits on its success.

One key element was a plan to reorganize the public hospitals and reduce their cost. These are under state *tutelle* but internally autonomous: many are lavish and impressive but have been wastefully run. By late 1996, varied ad hoc reforms were in progress, when I visited a 500-bed hospital in the small Burgundy town of Tonnerre. Part of it is in a majestic thirteenth-century *hôtel-Dieu*, most is in a fine big modern building. The maternity ward had just been closed by the prefect, as too few babies were now being born in the area. Then a scandal erupted when it was found that a twenty-bed clinic in the hospital was being illicitly used by some doctors for their private practices (an abuse common to several towns). There were fears that the whole hospital might be closed down by the authorities: but Tonnerre's influential mayor, Henri Nallet, a former Socialist Health Minister, was able to negotiate a plan whereby it would make some cutbacks in staff and equipment, sharing some services with nearby hospitals, and so it was saved. Its new director told me that hospitals could certainly do much more to share equipment and cut costs, without any loss in quality of service. This the Juppé plan proposed, and some hospitals followed suit; a few small ones even closed or merged. Juppé also aimed to set up new regional boards, which could keep a tighter check on budgets. And he began to take steps to reduce overstaffing. At this point, in March 1997, as a mood of dour austerity settled over many hospitals, their house physicians went on a nationwide strike, angry about the staff cuts. After four weeks the strike ended, but by 1998 the whole issue was still unresolved.

Juppé's efforts to reduce overspending by individual GPs and specialists ran into equal trouble. He began to urge them to make more use of generic medicines; and he promoted a new scheme to deter patients from consulting a range of doctors or going straight to a specialist, as in theory they had a right to do. Above all, doctors would now be penalized, collectively or individually, if they went above the new ceilings on spending. The aim was to punish those who overprescribed – and it provoked a furore from nearly all the various doctors' unions, leading to sporadic strikes and work to rule in 1996. Doctors in France form a militant lobby; and, like the hospitals, they have been split on the Juppé reforms. Many privately accepted the need for change: but collectively they were hostile, save for the large moderate MG-France union which finally signed an agreement with *la Sécu*. Many doctors were undoubtedly sincere in wanting to defend their patients, and the quality of the service, from what they saw as Juppé's 'rationing of health care'. But they were also protecting their own interests, and I heard this remarkable view from one small-town GP: 'The health service is so precious, it would be crazy to spoil it. Politicians call us wastrels, but it's just not true. And the cost of medicines is a false problem: if *la Sécu* has got so expensive, it's simply because there are more elderly people, who need more drugs. Yes, I agree that too many patients demand tranquillizers, but that's because life has grown so stressful, and I can't refuse them. As for the "generics", I'm not interested: I'd rather help little French laboratories to survive than give custom to the big international firms with their generic medicines. Is taxpayers' money wasted? *Yes*: we should spend less on foreigners who visit France!'

Doctors are trained to cure sickness, not to take account of costs; and they are ill at ease with this aspect of the free market. In opposing the Juppé reforms, many have been giving vent also to a wider sense of anxiety. So popular did their profession become, in the boom years, that they are now too numerous in many places; and despite the *numerus clausus* in medical faculties (see p. 559), their numbers have continued to grow. So, in their open market, many a GP has been having to fight harder to make a good living. It is a profession with a wide income range: while a surgeon or GP in private practice can easily reach 600,000 francs a year, an average GP might earn some 300,000, comparable to a *cadre* in industry. But some GPs in industrial or rural areas exist on 150,000 or so, which is low for a French liberal profession. Many doctors work up to sixty hours a week, or have to take on extra part-time jobs to keep up their living standards. And they complain that the statutory health service fee, now 115 francs (the one aspect of their job that is not at all 'free market'), has not risen in line with their real costs.

In 1997–8 the Jospin Government, to its credit, broadly continued the various Juppé reforms. 'He applied them clumsily, but basically they were sound and we support them,' I was told by an aide to Martine Aubry, now in charge of Social Security. It was a remarkable example of non-partisan continuity. Jospin even intensified the moves to reduce the deficit: he increased the CSG tax, despite some union opposition; and he set a means test on child allowances. This was a neat Socialist way of getting the well-to-do to pay for some economies in the welfare system. But it provoked angry dissent, not only from the Catholic lobbies and the middle classes, but also from some unions, who argued that it infringed on the basic principle of equality. So in 1999 the means test was dropped. Instead, well-off families will be penalized by new changes in levels of income-tax relief for parents with children. Martine Aubry, like Juppé, was still facing protests from the doctors as she tried to press ahead with the measures to reform hospitals and reduce spending. Some doctors at first began to cut on costly prescriptions, rather than face the new system of fines. But in June 1998 the Conseil d'État came to the doctors' aid by ruling that these fines were unconstitutional, as they were to be imposed globally by region and might be unfair on individuals. So Aubry had to find another way of curbing the expenses of the health service; and in July she produced a plan for 3 billion francs of economies that would fall mainly on dentists, radiologists and the pharmaceutical companies. She also imposed cuts on the refunds for specialist doctors. And she stepped up the efforts to induce doctors and drugs firms to make more use of generic medicines. Today surveys show that more doctors, perhaps 40 per cent, are at last becoming readier to prescribe them.

The overall Social Security deficit fell from 67 billion francs in 1995 to 35 billion for 1997 and 13 billion for 1998; and the health service's share from 14 to 5 billion in that period. But for 1999 the health insurance deficit seems set to rise again, to some 18 billion. Today this is the only Social Security sector which remains in deficit: prescription costs are still rising, for doctors and patients have not properly followed the ministry's edicts. If the overall deficit of *la Sécu* has none the less fallen, this has not been due to health economies but to some other aspects of Juppé's reforms, and in part to other factors too, notably the upturn in employment since 1997, which has rapidly produced more income and fewer expenses. Rising unemployment had been a major cause of the deficit, since the welfare contributions are job-related, while another cause was the growing cost of old-age pensions. With longer life expectancy, plus earlier retirement, there are now more elderly people taking pensions on the welfare budget, and usually needing more medical care than the young. Some experts even argue that old-age pensions, once unjustly low in France, are now too high (see p. 196). Of the total Social Security budget, normally about one-quarter relates to pensions, and another quarter to family allowances. These are relatively less costly to the State than formerly, since there are now fewer children: but they are still quite generous. In a nation anxious to keep up its birth rate, allowances are nil for the first child but start with the second and soar from the third one on. In the case of dependent teenagers with no jobs, the grants continue till eighteen. And a mother with two or more children gets an extra monthly grant of some 3,000 francs if she wants to give up her work and devote herself to the family. The recent new tax levels imposed onthe better-off families will help to reduce the deficit.

In 1998 Martine Aubry put forward yet another health service reform, this time within the context of a wider plan to help the poorer unemployed and *les exclus*. Her aim was to create a system that would give the same protection to everyone, whether or not they paid contributions. It was a move towards the British model, though the French system of *post hoc* reimbursements was to be kept. At the time of writing, however, this reform has been shelved.

So the Socialist Government is pursuing a tricky balancing act: it tries to make the health service fairer for all, while cutting down its costs and wastages. Of course, there will always be private doctors and clinics in France for the well-to-do: but the French are anxious to avoid moving towards the American model, where the poor can ill afford to pay for good treatment. They are proud of their health service, and with reason: the issue today is how to reduce its expense without spoiling its quality, and doctors are right to be concerned. But they will have to make sacrifices, and so will the public. One clear need is to rationalize the hospitals; another, to curb the privileges of the pharmacies. And the public? A prosperous society has chosen freely to spend lavishly on health. But has not its passion for medicines become itself a kind of sickness?

While this habit has grown, another bad one, quite the opposite and far more lethal, has declined: the excess drinking of alcohol. Fine wine may be one of France's great glories: yet alcoholism, due mainly to overconsumption of cheap wine, has often been described as 'the worst of French social scourges', ruining the lives of millions. Today the scourge has been much reduced, thanks to an official anti-alcohol campaign and above all to spontaneous social change. Overall wine consumption has dropped by half since 1960. Inveterate alcoholic café-going has declined, as many younger people have turned against their parents' style of heavy drinking and sales of soft drinks have soared. Deaths from cirrhosis of the liver or alcoholic excess have dropped since the 1970s from some 20,000 a year to around 11,000: but this is still a high figure for Western Europe. As in other countries, alcoholic consumption per head has been falling quite sharply: yet the French remain the world's heaviest drinkers, after Luxembourgers: in 1994, they consumed 11.9 litres of 'pure' alcohol a year, per head, compared with Germany's 10.4, Britain's 7.3, the United States' 6.8. As for wine drinking, France comes third after Italy and Portugal. However, prosperity has brought big improvements in the quality of what is drunk: consumption of champagne, whisky and good wines has risen fast, while that of the old liver-rotting strong coarse wines and eaux-de-vie has dropped sharply.

Pierre Mendès-France, as Prime Minister in 1954, first gave official status to the anti-alcohol campaign, and won himself some derision for his milk-drinking image. He also fought against the *bouilleurs de cru* or home-distillers – the millions of farmers who had the right to produce ten litres of eau-de-vie from their own fruit or grapes, and who often illicitly distilled and sold a great deal more. A tough new law then limited the privilege; and with this and the decline of the peasantry, large-scale illegal distilling has been slowly fading away. It is no longer a serious cause of alcoholism.

Mendès-France set up an official commission, still active today, for fighting alcoholism. At first its campaign produced riots in some wine-producing areas. But over the years it has done something to wean young people away from traditional French ideas that not to drink is unmanly, even bad for health. And various statutory measures have followed. One of these forbids cafés and restaurants to serve alcoholic drinks to minors: it is often winked at, in the case of wine or beer with meals, but it does limit the kind of practice that used to horrify me in France in the 1950s – the sight of babes of two or three in cafés being given full glasses of undiluted wine. A law presented in 1991 by the Socialists' Health Minister, Claude Évin, then went further: it banned most advertising of alcoholic drinks, notably on radio and TV. The law was contested by the wine and spirits lobbies, which secured some concessions: advertisements can show a bottle, but not people drinking! In a land where some 3 million people, including farmers, earn their living from the booze trades, reforms are inevitably hard to carry through.

It was mainly in older slum districts and backward rural areas that the problem of alcoholism was worst. You see few merry drunkards on the streets in France, for wine and eau-de-vie do not have that effect, they strike deeper; and French heavy drinking comes not so much from neurosis or unhappiness, as with many Anglo-Saxons, as from ancestral habit. The picture may be improving, but it is reckoned that over a million French still drink more than the litre of wine a day that doctors consider the safe maximum for a manual worker. According to official figures, some 1.3 million sick people are classified as alcohol-dependent; some 50 per cent of road deaths and 25 per cent of suicides are due to excess drinking or alcoholism; in hospitals, about 30 per cent of the men and 5 to 10 per cent of the women are alcoholic. Curiously, the scourge remains worst not in the vinegrowing regions of the Midi, but in Brittany and the Nord where cheap red plonk fills the hypermarkets. In poorer districts, much social and even economic life has traditionally revolved round the habit of drinking *gros rouge* together in a café, as business is transacted. A litre bottle can still be bought for only six or seven francs; and wine (unlike spirits) carries no special tax, for it is still regarded as a staple commodity like bread.

In these poorer areas, it is mainly older people who drink so much; younger ones now do so less. Education, rehousing, the rural exodus and other factors have all been helping to reduce the problem. And in the 'smarter' classes, excessive drinking of spirits through stress or neurosis is less common than in many countries. In bourgeois homes, the old convention that no meal is complete without wine has been losing much of its force; and at lunchtime in restaurants, many people simply drink mineral water. In the early 1950s, amazingly, this was sold mainly in pharmacies and was considered a medical product. Since then, with sales up a hundredfold, it has grown *à la mode* as a symbol of purity and vitality. Some restaurants offer a *carte* of mineral waters, along with their wine list; and in Paris there is even a fashionable water-bar whose sixty brands include 'exotic' ones such as Ballygowan.

The French today are the world's leading drinkers of mineral water per capita. As they are also one of the top three nations for wine consumption, does this mean that they imbibe more fluid than others, and hence all the *pissoirs*? No, for they drink less tap water than some people: although *l'eau du robinet* in France is generally good and clean, this health-conscious nation has grown worried about water pollution – and with good reason, in some regions (see p. 398). Also, the French still drink much less beer, fruit juice and cola than many peoples, even though sales here, too, have been rising. Consumption of beer doubled in 1955–75, but has since fallen off and is only 37 litres per head per year, far less than that of wine: the French are not great beer drinkers and have few really good beers. Sales of fruit juice have multiplied sixfold since 1980, but are still no more than 13 litres a year per head: juices are twice as expensive as cheap wine, and this limits their sale among poorer people, though it can lend them a prestige appeal among the better-off. Sales of many *digestifs* and *apéritifs* have fallen back, except for *anis* drinks which have made a comeback thanks to the dynamism of the Ricard/ Pernod firm. And the 'smart' drinks, champagne and Scotch whisky, have made huge advances. Whisky is now the commonest *apéritif* in the middle classes, where many people are far more knowledgeable about it, and keep a better range in their homes, than the average Sassenach.

The sum of these trends shows that the French are drinking far more discerningly, and more healthily, than in the old days. While overall consumption of wine per head has fallen since 1960 from 127 to 64 litres a year, the sales of quality *appellation* wines, generally much better for health, have almost trebled in the same period (see p. 403). But though alcoholism is a waning problem, it may never be solved completely. While younger people on average drink less than their elders, a sizeable minority of them, boys more than girls, have recently been turning back to heavier drinking, mostly of strong beers and spirits. Many are students facing exams, or the unemployed, who drink as a solace and escape. 'If you want to get stoned, at least it's less damaging than taking drugs' (see pp. 575–6) is a common remark.

Drinking is probably more damaging than smoking. But this, too, has now become a controversial issue, due to a recent law which has attempted to ban it in public places. Intellectuals such as Jean-Paul Sartre, chain-smoking his Gitanes in Left Bank cafés, may have given the world an image of a nervous people addicted to nicotine. But in fact the French today are less-than-average smokers, well behind the Americans and Japanese, just behind the Germans, Italians and British. Smoking has been falling by about 2 per cent a year: today some 44 per cent of men smoke, against 60 per cent in 1976, while the proportion of women smokers has stayed stable at about 29 per cent. In general, heavy smokers persist, while occasional ones are more and more likely to give it up. One reason given is that tobacco prices have recently risen faster than inflation. And yet, in a nation which does not care to penalize private pleasure, taxes on tobacco remain among the lowest in Europe: cigarettes are little more than half their British prices.

Governments have chosen other weapons than high taxation. Tobacco advertising has long been outlawed from radio and television, and the ban was later extended to other media. Most important, the Évin law of 1991 made it an offence to smoke in any enclosed public space, except in certain reserved areas (i.e. parts of cafés). This seemingly strict measure answered a growing public anxiety about pollution, and according to one poll was welcomed by some 84 per cent of people, including 66 per cent of smokers. It has since been fairly well respected on public transport, at airports and in shops. But of course it has been harder to apply inside cafés and restaurants, or in factories and offices. Here employers are expected to arrange for segregated areas where staff can take smoking breaks, and a few have been fined for failing to do so; a *cadre* can smoke in his office on his own, but not if he shares it with a secretary who does not like it. This can lead to disputes and protests, but generally a compromise is worked out between staff delegates and management. 'More important than any legal change, there's been a general shift in attitudes, a move towards the US situation,' said one executive I know. 'The rights of smokers are now far better respected.' In just a few cases, a dispute has come to court: when one bank employee died of lung cancer, her sister sued the bank for letting the staff create noxious fumes. The bank was found guilty, but not fined.

Cafés, bars and restaurants are supposed to provide separate areas or rooms for smokers. Most restaurants have done so: in the spacious luxury ones, the *patron* will usually allow smoking, discreetly, at some tables. But many bars and cafés are too small, and have taken less notice of the new law. In some, their owners and smoking *habitués* reacted at first with outrage to a law they saw as an affront to their freedom. They have now gone ahead with their old habits, and their anti-smoking customers have moved elsewhere. But the police have turned a blind eye to small places of this kind that break the law: their priority is to see that it is properly observed in public buildings and on transport. Here the quality of air has improved. And the Évin law has at least legalized the rights of non-smokers: in public, the lowliest worker now has the right to insist that the loftiest tycoon must put out his cigar, or go elsewhere. You could even call it an aspect of the changes in French labour relations.

In June 1999 the Government announced that it would bring smoking and excessive drinking within the orbit of the anti-drugs campaign: that is, use of these two 'legal drugs' would be tackled with the same kind of propaganda as that of illegal drugs like cannabis. Health experts approved, but the tobacco and drink industries were angry.

LABOUR RELATIONS:
EMPLOYERS GROW MORE LIBERAL, BUT UNIONS
STAY WEAK

Labour relations in France have become much more open and human in the past thirty years, thanks above all to changes of heart within French management. This used to be seen as one of the most authoritarian in Europe: ideas like job-enrichment were scarcely known, and many firms would not even permit unions. Then in the wake of May '68 the old rigidity ended, and the Patronat began to experiment with new liberal ideas. Many *patrons* became more responsive to their employees' aspirations; some even embarked on worker-participation schemes. At the same time, labour legislation itself was modernized – a field where France had been seriously backward. The rights of workers and unions within firms were strengthened, under some laws passed after 1968 and others enacted later by the Socialists.

Today a Patronat grown worried by high labour costs, rising world competition and government plans to shorten the working week has become more wary of trying out new schemes. But it has not returned to the old authoritarianism. Employees, for their part, have been made insecure by high unemployment, and in some public services by plans for deregulation. Their discontent has been expressed by the one major strike of 1995, and by rumbling smaller stoppages in some branches – the railways, the banks and defence arsenals, even hospitals and television. Sometimes they will cynically try to hold the nation to ransom by going on strike at an awkward moment, as Air France pilots did, and railwaymen and others threatened to do, just before the World Cup began in 1998. Yet classic strikes in productive industry remain extremely few. This relates to the most remarkable feature of labour relations in France: the weakness of trade unions, their low membership and lack of unity.

A foreign visitor to Paris, seeing the boulevards sometimes filled with demonstrating workers and their angry banners, might conclude that the unions are powerful and poised for insurrection. He would be wrong. The protest marches can be little more than a ritual, a way of showing the flag and masking the unions' inability to take more effective action. They are strong in some public services, but in the private sector they are amazingly weak, and numbers have been falling. In 1978 some 25 per cent of all French employees were unionized, but today it is under 10 per cent, the lowest figure in the West.

One of the many explanations could be that workers have been wearied by the feuding between unions, which in France are divided on lines of politics, rather than by craft as in Britain. The Confédération Générale du Travail (CGT), whose numbers have dropped to some 620,000, is less directly controlled by the Communist Party than in the old days, but the links are still close. Of its main rivals, Force Ouvrière (FO), formerly moderate, today more pugnacious, has Socialist sympathies and is strong in the public services (around 450,000 members). The Confédération Française Démocratique du Travail (CFDT) (*c.* 600,000), also pro-Socialist, blends anti-capitalist ideals with a cool pragmatism. Other unions include the Confédération Générale des Cadres (CGC) (180,000). The political divisions on the Left in France have been mirrored by the conflicts between these unions, making joint action often difficult – one reason why the recent French strike level has been fairly low. In 1983 some 1.5 million working days were lost through strikes, but this has since dropped to an average of 500,000 a year (it was 800,000 in 1995 because of the December strike). Official figures for days lost per 1,000 workers in 1996 were 58 for both France and Britain, 53 for Germany, 51 for the United States. In France strikes in some public services can be severe, but they rarely last long. In private industry they are very few, though in some special sectors they can get nasty – as the truculent lorry drivers showed once again in 1996–7.

The rise of a more open and modern spirit in French labour relations, and the decline of the old authoritarianism, can be traced back to the May '68 uprising and the new ideas it brought forward. The revolt was sparked off by students, but millions of workers soon joined in without waiting for their unions' orders. They occupied their factories, hoisting red flags on the roof and in many cases locking their bosses in their offices. Nine million took part in the strike, the largest in Europe since the war. Motives were very mixed (see pp. 13–14). Some aspirations were the usual material ones: but the strike was also an explosion of long frustration – an outburst against employers' aloofness and secretiveness, against the repetitiveness of much modern factory work, against the rigid and bureaucratic chains of command, the fear of delegating authority and the lack of group discussion, which characterized French industry at all levels. In some firms, the *cadres* were the ones who led the revolt against a system of which they, like the workers, were victims. This was novel in modern France: rarely before in this stratified society had two social classes, *cadres* and workers, taken action together.

Finally, the union leaders gained control of the movement and pressed for the immediate aim of higher pay: so the Government and Patronat were able to bring the strikes to an end by offering large all-round wage increases and promising a fairer deal in labour relations. But what kind of deal? It seemed to demand a change of heart, more than of texts. De Gaulle proceeded to talk about 'participation', an ideal of labour/management partnership which he had nourished for many years. But little was to come of this in practice. The unions had other objectives, and May '68 did bring them one important gain: a law passed later that year accorded them at last the kind of legal status inside a firm that had long been usual in Britain and many other countries. Shop stewards now had the right to do union work in the firm's time, and to have their own offices and do their own canvassing inside factories. The unions saw this as the ending of a serious anomaly and the major achievement of the strikes.

The wider legacy of May '68 lay in its effect on work relations inside firms. This varied immensely. In some cases, contacts across the hierarchical divides became less formal, and white- and blue-collar workers emerged with more sympathy for each other's problems. In others, the barriers went up again, and some older family firms even made last-ditch attempts to hold on to authority. But most employers did accept that a change at least of style was now necessary. The wiser ones took note that the strike had often been bitterest in the autocratic old-style firms such as Citroën, whereas those with a more open labour policy had less trouble. Many firms began to take staff relations more seriously: their personnel manager, previously an ignored junior executive, now had a big desk and sizeable staff. Overall, May '68 brought a new questioning of the old assumptions about authority: it sounded the death knell of a certain rigid autocratic French style of command.

The post-May '68 mood soon began to influence the thinking of the Conseil National du Patronat Français (CNPF), the federation of almost all French employers. This body had hitherto been stuffily old-fashioned. It had shown in the case of EEC entry that it was capable of adjustment to change: yet until the early 1970s it remained an incarnation of the more stolid aspects of French management. However, a liberal pressure group within its ranks, the Centre des Jeunes Patrons (CJP), had since the 1950s been promoting a philosophy novel in France, that a *patron* has a moral duty to his workers, he must associate them with his policies, and see profit as a means for the wealth of them all. The CJP's inspiration, as with many of the more dynamic forces of the France of that period, was rooted in new-style Catholicism (see p. 582). At first the Patronat rejected its ideas: but after the jolt of May '68, it began to look at them more sympathetically.

A new liberal-minded figure of some charisma then came to the fore in the Patronat: François Ceyrac, its president from 1973 to 1982. Tall and craggy-faced, an expert on dealing with the unions, Ceyrac managed gradually to persuade most of his own senior colleagues of the need for a new strategy. Inevitably, many employers stayed in the old mould, but among the rest a consensus grew that it was in their own economic interests to meet the workers' new aspirations. So a number of themes came into vogue within the Patronat, hard to imagine before 1968: job enrichment, group work, the right of staff to take part in some daily internal decisions (but *not* in formulating wider company policy). With its new benevolent image, the Patronat embarked on 'social marketing', by challenging the unions on their own ground for the right to defend workers' interests, and for staff loyalty. And the unions began to hit back: 'Like a girl with two suitors, the employee stands to benefit from this competition,' said one *patron*. This remains broadly the pattern today, save that worries over jobs have created new tensions.

In the heady days of social innovation in the 1970s, a few pioneering managers and *patrons* took the lead. Curiously, the most striking example was in a state-owned firm: Aerospatiale's big helicopter factory at Marignane, near Marseille. Here Fernand Carayon, one of the most impressive Frenchmen I have ever met, was put in as manager to rescue a plant in disarray, plagued by CGT-led strikes. He had a Grande École background but was no aloof technocrat, more a maverick with the common touch, speaking fast and excitedly in a Midi accent. First he talked on the shop floor to the 6,500 staff, at all levels: 'Let's install industrial democracy together.' 'What's that?' 'I don't know, but let's work it out together.' The CGT opposed him, but he won the backing of the more moderate unions; and so popular were his radical changes in work methods that over the next ten years those unions' share of the works vote rose from 25 to 65 per cent, while the CGT's fell accordingly. His central innovation was to divide the factory into semi-autonomous groups, each dealing with a wide range of the assembly process – a little like the job-enrichment ventures then at Volvo and Fiat. Each Écureuil helicopter was assembled almost *in toto* by a small team who would agree to a certain output of work per week and then do it in their own time, knocking off when they had finished. 'It's a return to the medieval craftsman, and it adds to motivation,' said Carayon. Productivity gains were enormous, and output soared. Aerospatiale's Paris head office had qualms at first: but when his methods brought such results, they were accepted, and even applied in part in the group's other factories. But when the Left came to power in Paris, the CGT got its revenge and secured Carayon's removal. Today some of his measures survive, notably the very flexible hours: but the group system, hard to operate except under his own inspired leadership, has been modified.

An even more spectacular venture of the 1970s, much publicized at the time, took place in the unlikely setting of a Paris luxury hotel, the Plaza-Athénée. It was the work of the astonishing Paul Bougenaux, who began as a washer-up, rose to be head porter, and was then spotted and made manager by the owner, none other than Sir Charles Forte. This flagship of his group was losing money; and when Bougenaux proposed a staff-participation system, Sir Charles curiously said yes. Bougenaux, rather like Carayon, regrouped the staff into small semi-autonomous units, and set about inspiring them with his own humanist ideals. At the monthly meetings, the most junior bellboy could put his views on how the hotel should be run. 'For example,' Bougenaux told me, 'when the hotel's silver was to be expensively replaced, we collected ten samples and the staff gave their choice. Most of us opted for the same elegant set – save for one young commis who said, "Look at the milk-pot, the handle's too heavy, every waiter will be spilling the milk." None of us had noticed it. That commis saved us a costly mistake.' Bougenaux improved morale, hence work quality, and thus the hotel's fortunes. He became a national figure, lecturing on his methods, rewarded by Giscard with the Légion d'honneur. But then the Italian–Scottish tycoon suddenly dismissed him – was he jealous? Did he fear that the thirst for participation would prove too infectious, elsewhere in his empire? Bougenaux is now dead. But today some aspects of his scheme are still in force at *le Plaza*. As at Marignane, the messiah may have been victimized but his influence lives on.

Slowly these ideas have spread more widely. Only a few cases attract the limelight, but some hundreds of little firms have been modestly carrying out their own ventures, often discreetly for fear of stirring up union reprisals. Some companies have introduced Japanese-style 'quality circles', where staff meet in small groups to discuss how to improve their work. The Faiveley electronics firm, in Touraine, went a stage further, dividing the staff into small units which took some internal decisions democratically. So popular was the scheme that union branches at Faiveley disappeared through lack of support. The CNPF was suspicious at first of these various innovations, but Ceyrac then lent his support. Of course, there are limitations to the trend, which usually depends on some persuasive leader, and they are not easy to replace. Nearly always, too, the impetus has come from management rather than from the rank-and-file pressure more common, for instance, in Sweden. But if a manager applies his plan tactfully, the staff generally end up welcoming it – maybe a sign that the French will still respond to the lead of benevolent paternalism, while remaining weak at their own collective initiatives (save those of protest).

The major unions reacted warily to these various initiatives, which they tended to see as part of a Patronat campaign to limit their own role by dealing with staff directly. In some firms, CGT militants at first opposed measures such as flexible hours, but then backed down, seeing they were so popular. The CGT also opposed management-inspired autonomous work groups. At the Berliet lorry plant in Lyon, when a scheme of this kind was introduced, the CGT adopted the tactic of cooperating to the point of trying to take control of the groups and run them in its own way – at which point the employers got scared and dropped the project. Generally, the other unions have been more open to the innovations than the CGT. Sometimes they have been tempted to respond to the Patronat with another solution, that of forming their own industrial cooperatives. But this has not proved easy, despite a long tradition in France of worker cooperatives. In the 1970s, when the Swiss-owned Lip watchmaking plant at Besançon went bankrupt, its thousand employees made a bid to keep it going as a cooperative: but although they won their legal battle over the right to do so, they were defeated economically by the cheap watches flooding into France. Today the Lip venture survives on a small scale, making other goods, and is one of a number of small worker cooperatives that struggle along, with an average of 70 workers each. But the movement is marginal – unlike the large cooperatives that flourish in agriculture.

So the initiative for new workplace ventures seems to remain with employers. But the 1970s heyday of innovation is past: both sides today are far too preoccupied with job preservation.

One of the major formal roles of a French trade union is that of collective bargaining with employers, on wages and on the length of the working week. This statutory system of *conventions collectives* dates from 1910, and has since been revised. The negotiations are bilateral, either per industrial branch or within each firm: the State itself is not directly involved. This very active system leads to some 4,000 wage agreements each year; and despite their low membership, the unions are able to wield power. By contrast, for other matters that concern the internal running of a firm, unions may have less influence than two other worker delegate bodies, the *comités d'entreprise* (works councils) and *délégués du personnel*. The former, dating from the late 1940s, are obligatory in all firms with over fifty employees. A council is elected by the staff and has regular meetings with management. Its main role is social, to organize outings, parties, welfare schemes, and so on, with the help of a sizeable budget: but it is also intended to be consultative. How this works varies greatly. In some firms, a common jibe is 'All the *comités* do is organize the *fêtes de Noël*': but in others, management uses the council to keep staff informed of its policies, and to invite discussion. The obligatory *délégués du personnel* have the job of feeding management with any grievances about working conditions or fears about lay-offs: with this down-to-earth role, they are often more effective than the *comités*. In the case of both bodies, the members do not always belong to unions, nor are they chosen by the unions.

Profit-sharing is also statutory in France. De Gaulle, no lover of old-style capitalism, believed in it strongly; and in 1967 he initiated a law obliging all firms with a staff of over fifty to distribute a portion of their profits in the form of shares. The Patronat was not thrilled; and even the unions were lukewarm, tending to regard profit-sharing as a capitalist lure to weaken worker solidarity. But the scheme went ahead and is still in force today. Parallel plans, first put forward under Giscard, to increase worker involvement through some kind of co-management on the German model, have never got far at least in the private sector. The Patronat has long been opposed; most unions have seen it as a trap; and even pressure from the shop floor has been limited. French workers are less interested than German ones in this kind of boardroom representation.

However, many Socialist leaders have long favoured co-management;

and after 1981 they proceeded to introduce it in the state sector. In all state-owned manufacturing firms, one-third of board members, with full voting rights, are now elected by the staff from candidates designated by the unions. This system has worked out fairly smoothly, and has been retained by law in the state firms recently privatized. One *patron*, himself no left-winger, spoke to me quite warmly: 'Our staff delegates are conscientious and constructive, and they seem loyal to the firm, even the CGT ones. They do their homework thoroughly, obliging us to do the same.' On the other hand, some union delegates feel that they have too little influence: 'The management takes the decisions and uses the board as a rubber-stamp,' said one.

This co-management measure was part of a wider package, the so-called *lois Auroux*, introduced after 1981 by the Minister of Labour Jean Auroux. His laws were wide-ranging but mostly quite mild. They did little more than continue the process of providing French workers with the kind of rights that Swedes or Germans, for instance, had long enjoyed. One law reinforced the *conventions collectives* system. Another removed some archaisms in the complex Code du Travail, such as one that put a limit on how often an employee could go to the toilet! A third, more controversial, sought to formalize the workers' right to 'self-expression' at shop-floor level: staff should be split into small groups to make proposals to management on work improvements and conditions. This was a *post hoc* legal recognition of what some firms had been doing anyway – and the Patronat objected strongly to this bid to make it compulsory. Many *patrons* refused to cooperate; and the CNPF lobbied to get the measure repealed, which is just what happened when the Right returned to power in 1986. However, most of the other Auroux laws today remain in force, and are generally accepted by employers as positive. *Les lois Auroux* are no longer much of a live issue, superseded by other more urgent priorities in the ongoing struggle between unions and Patronat.

Even during the recent periods of friendly left-wing rule, the unions have seldom been able to regain the initiative from the Patronat. Their membership has continued to fall; and they are so diverse, in their make-up, tactics and ideology, that they still find it hard to unite for joint action, save during major exceptional strikes. And this disarray adds to their weakness and lack of popular support. Their main leaders contrive a façade of comradely unity when they meet in public, but when apart they denounce each other's policies. However, there are signs today, at local level, that more rank-and-file members are tiring of this rivalry and are looking for greater cooperation. This has been one outcome of the December 1995 strikes.

Of the three larger unions, the CGT is the oldest, founded in 1895, and has long tended to reflect the twists and turns in Communist Party strategy. In the post-war decades it did well by pressing harder than the other unions for immediate practical gains such as higher wages: hence it has long appealed to many workers who are not themselves Communist. Today it seeks to keep this broad base, for example by including Socialists or Catholics on its governing body: but much power has remained in the hands of PCF loyalists, under its secretary-general (Bernard Thibault). The main change is that, with the PCF itself now milder and more diverse, the CGT has likewise grown less authoritarian, and is now less closely tied to the party. At its congress in 1999, it formally adopted a policy of 'autonomy'; then in October it refused to take part in a big PCF-led rally for employment, asserting that this was 'too political'. Some veteran shop-stewards are idealists of the old school, warm-hearted believers in human brotherhood, men of honour who bargain toughly and keep their word – 'You know where you are with them,' said one *patron*. Within firms, officials are often ready to reach sensible shop-floor compromises with employers in order to keep factories going and thus preserve jobs (so long as the CGT's own role is preserved too). Nationally, the CGT remains anxious to uphold its 'responsible' image, parading as the champion of order, opposing wildcat strikes. And yet, if a grassroots movement emerges that seems to have popular backing, the CGT may step in and try to take control and win the kudos – as happened during the anti-Jospin protests by the unemployed in 1998.

So the CGT deftly doses principle and opportunism. Its leaders indulge in nationalist talk, not only anti-globalization and anti-Maastricht, but often protectionist, too: 'In order to preserve jobs in the textile industry, France should close its frontiers to cheap Third World imports' – so much for human brotherhood. The CGT line can be more polemically ideological than is popular in today's apolitical climate: with slogans and posters it carries *la lutte ouvrière* on to factory floors. And this does not always go down too well with its rank and file. This, plus the general decline of the PCF, the contraction of the working class and the waning of old bastions like the steel industry, have all been factors in the union's steady fall in membership – from about 1.6 million in 1976 to an estimated 620,000 today (it claims rather more).

Of the CGT's main rivals, Force Ouvrière has always been pro-Socialist, yet readier than most unions to cooperate with management, in the German manner. Its main strength lies in the public services, not in industry. The CFDT, Liberal-Catholic by origin, has had a curious history: it was quite moderate until May '68 when many of its militants caught the *gauchiste* virus, and for a while it was more truly radical than the CGT, and toying with utopian versions of co-management. Its leader in 1971–88, Edmond Maire, was a highly respected figure, gentle and pensive, a far cry from the usual trade-union demagogue – 'the Jean-Jacques Rousseau of French unionism', he was called. But he was also a pragmatist, able to charm Raymond Barre's Government into making real social improvements; and later he had influence in shaping Socialist reforms. His union and FO have both seen their membership fall much less heavily than the CGT since the early 1980s; both are international-minded and 'European' in outlook, even if critical of some specific policies. In the 1995 strikes, the unions were able to improve their image a little. They exacted concessions from the Juppé Government, which they could present as a kind of victory. As a result, rather more inter-union cooperation began to emerge locally during 1996. But at leadership level, the unions were still locked in conflict.

One remarkable development since the mid-1990s is that the CFDT and FO have both changed their characters, in some ways reversing roles. And they have grown tougher, under the impact of economic events, also of their new abrasive leaders. While the CGT's management remains more collegiate and secretive, both FO and CFDT prefer strong, personalized leadership in the French style – and under Marc Blondel and Nicole Notat, sharp enemies, they today have it in full measure. For years FO was led by the moderate André Bergeron: but he has now given place to the bombastic Blondel, from a Nord mining background, who has driven his tanks on to the CGT's lawn and is trying to win over its members with his new harder line. 'It is the economic situation and the Patronat that have changed, more than our own policies,' I was told in 1997 by his right-hand man, Jean-Claude Mailly: 'so we have to fight and bargain more toughly. Yes, indeed we have now gone beyond the CFDT in our radical questioning of capitalism, and are now closer to the CGT in our analysis of the present crisis of society. We see it as not just a routine economic crisis, but a deeper one of the whole system. And it demands a radical rethink.' This rejection of Bergeron's gentler social-democratic line has spread dismay among many FO veterans, causing Blondel to be contested within his own ranks.

Similarly, at the head of the CFDT, the visionary Maire approach has given way to that of Nicole Notat, an abrasive pragmatist, dubbed '*la Tsarine*' or 'the Iron Lady of French unionism'. She believes in winning power and influence by cooperating with authority: hers was the only union to support Juppé's plans for Social Security reform, and it came to be seen as the 'privileged partner' of his Government. She has even cooperated with the Patronat: with its help, she was able to extend her empire by winning for herself and the CFDT the presidency of the two key bodies that administer the dole and sickness insurance. Jean Gandois, head of the Patronat, praised her as a 'modern' unionist. But her relations with Jospin and Aubry were never warm, and when they came to power, the CFDT was no longer 'privileged'. Moreover, like Blondel but in reverse, Notat has come to be contested by part of her own rank and file – notably by those Leftists who had followed the CFDT's utopian ideals in the 1970s.

Her CDFT, and FO, have also been finding themselves opposed by the rise of small militant autonomous groups outside the main unions. The most important, SUD, had been expelled from the CFDT in 1989 for *gauchisme*, and is today quite strong in France Télécom and SNCF. It has taken over some of the older CFDT ideas, such as the utopian vision of worker-run factories. Other autonomous groups, known as '*coordinations*', are found among nurses, teachers or truck drivers. They fight for their own precise objectives, and their rise has worried the Patronat, which finds them harder to handle than the big confederations. They are a clear symptom of employees' disaffection with classic unionism and of their desire to find new styles of action.

Even the bigger unions are so ill-funded that they can seldom afford decent premises. In Lyon I found the headquarters of the CFDT to be a shabby little office in a drab backyard – what a contrast it made to the lavish modern premises of many a German union, or the sleek provincial offices of the powerful French farmers' union, the Fédération Nationale des Syndicats des Exploitants Agricoles (FNSEA). This poverty reflects the declining subscription dues: overall membership has been falling steadily since the mid-1970s, and was down to 15 per cent of all employees by 1986 and under 10 per cent today. This compares with 39 per cent in Britain and Italy, 33 in Germany, 25 in Japan, 15.5 in the United States. In France, the average in the public services is 20 per cent, and it rises much higher in some sectors such as the railways and the post office. But in private industry it is only 6 per cent.

The historical weakness of worker unionism in France can be explained by various factors – the relative lateness of industrialization, the rural roots of so many workers, the French lack of clubbiness, and the refusal of some autocratic employers (at least till recently) to permit unions at all. This last is today illegal: but there are still some firms, such as Michelin, which will find subtle ways of refusing promotion to union activists, or of putting them first among redundancies – and this can deter new members. The recent decline in numbers has other causes too, such as the rise of unemployment and part-timing in labour-intensive industries. And the French tendency since the 1980s to reject formal institutions affects the unions as well as the Church and other bodies. Many employees today feel that unions serve little purpose, or they do not want to pay the fees – 'Far from promoting solidarity, unemployment makes people selfish,' one FO official lamented to me.

In addition, the mistakes and failures of the Left have discouraged some workers: the sharpest fall in union membership was in 1983–5. And the CGT's political crusading is often held to blame. One skilled worker told me, 'It has tried to politicize the *comité d'entreprise* meetings here. So instead of dealing with welfare matters or work improvements, as we should, our time is taken up with angry political debates, say on Marxism or the evils of the Bundesbank.' The minority liberal wing of the CGT is aware of this handicap, as one of its leaders, Gérard Alezard, told me in 1997: 'The CGT is stuck in its old discourse about *lutte ouvrière* and *lutte des classes*, and has failed to realize that workers have changed, with the rise of a new class of skilled technicians and *cadres* who have other aspirations. So there's a gulf between union claptrap and workers' real needs and anxieties. No wonder we lose members. Our harping on *la lutte* is too negative. We need to rethink, basically – about this, and our relations with the Patronat. The German model may be out of date: but we need to be much more constructive in our battle with employers, and to put forward our own projects for job creation instead of just complaining.' For his sensible ideas, Alezard was pushed off the confederal board of the CGT in 1995.

For some years now the unions have also found it hard to rouse the workers out on strike. The rank and file may often be discontented: but when times are tough, they hesitate to risk their jobs by downing tools. And the industrial unions lack the funds to support lengthy strikes. A visitor to Paris may form a different impression from the repeated short-term strikes in the public services – the Métro stops for a day, traffic controllers halt air flights, postal workers stage a go-slow. But these are usually short-term protests: longer, more serious action is less common. Often this is started by the railwaymen, whose three-week strike in 1986, joined by Électricité de France staff, was in protest at Chirac's policy of wage restraint. Similarly, the big strikes of 1995 were launched by the *cheminots*, and again they showed the power of the public service unions.

Major strikes in the private sector are fewer, and the more dramatic tend to be in services such as transport, rather than in factories: in 1996, and again in 1997, lorry drivers disrupted ports and main roads with stoppages in support of wage and other claims, in their archaic branch of industry (see p. 138). In factories, during the 1970s, one aggressive tactic that the unions used in place of strikes was the sit-in: if a firm threatened to close or make lay-offs, then militants would occupy its offices, haul up the red flag, maybe even kidnap the owner or manager. At one time, there were reckoned to be over a hundred of these sit-ins in progress, mostly in small firms. They were easier to organize than a big strike, for they needed only a handful of activists: so they were another sign of union weakness, in a way. The Patronat did not take them too seriously, and by the early 1980s the vogue had died away.

The Patronat today is made up of diverse trends, and its stance can vary from year to year. It has certainly not gone back to the old pre-Ceyrac authoritarian days, and most *patrons* remain alert to their staff's needs. But the idealistic Carayon-type experiments are out of fashion, for the context has changed. The fall of Communism in Europe, the spread of 'liberal' economic ideas, plus French Socialism's new acceptance of the vital role of private enterprise – all this has served to give many *patrons* a renewed confidence in their own values, even a sense of triumph. At the same time, today's tough economic climate forces them also to be tough. They have to worry about being competitive on world markets, so it makes them angry about high French labour costs. They feel the need to raise productivity, yet are also being urged constantly to create new jobs. It is a hard dilemma that makes the shop-floor issues of the 1970s look out of date. And staff feel the same. For a worker, self-expression is a less urgent matter than simply keeping his employment.

THE STRUGGLE AGAINST HIGH UNEMPLOYMENT

For some years, high unemployment has been the Achilles' heel of the French economy. Even when exports are booming, growth is steady and inflation almost zero, the jobless total has remained among the highest in Europe. This has been seen as the major factor behind the French *morosité*, creating a climate of insecurity and in some cases hardship and despair – especially for the many long-term unemployed. Among the various reasons for the high figure, one is usually thought to be the rigid labour regulations, which deter firms from taking on more staff: but the French do not wish to move to a less secure system, even if they have to pay a price. At all events, with economic recovery since mid-1997, matters may at last be improving: the unemployment total fell by almost 5 per cent in the year to August 1998, and possibly this did as much as the World Cup victory to lighten the gloom in France. It has to be seen whether the trend can prove durable.

In a free and prosperous society, some degree of unemployment is healthy and normal – maybe up to 3 or 4 per cent. It shows that people have choice, they can afford to take time off between jobs, while the flexibility of labour adds to growth. That used to be the position in France, and it is the ideal in America today. But French unemployment has been steadily rising to much higher levels: it reached its peak in 1997 at some 12.5 per cent, then fell to 11.3 per cent by August 1999, or just 2.7 million people. But this remains a much higher proportion than in Britain or even in Germany, beset with similar problems.

Governments for years have tried various remedies, hitherto without great success. Today, the Socialists have embarked on an expensive new job-creation scheme for youth, with better results: if the number of under-25s seeking work fell by 12 per cent in 1997–8, this was a main cause, along with the economic upturn. Jospin's Government is also preparing its much-contested plan for a move to a 35-hour week, though without any certainty that this tacit job-sharing will produce many new posts. The Patronat claim that the answer must lie in fewer rigidities and lower social costs: but the French as a whole, not only their union leaders, remain opposed to any move towards what they see as an American model that maybe creates jobs but leads also to social injustices and poverty. The French remain attached to their rigid systems of protection and relative job security, their generous benefits – even if these tend to create overstaffing and structural unemployment. It is a vicious circle not easy to break.

The proportion of unemployed has risen elevenfold since 1960. In Pompidou's day the total began to nose above 500,000, and a million was then regarded as the limit of the politically acceptable. But by 1981 it had reached 2 million – without any popular explosion, for most workers were too scared of redundancies to go on strike. Giscard poured money into job-creation schemes for the young, with modest results. Mitterrand then promised to reduce unemployment through reflation, and in a TV debate with Giscard before the election he warned, 'If your austerity policies continue, we'll have 2.5 million out of work by 1985.' Ironically, that was precisely the figure reached in 1985 under his *own* regime. France's unemployment was then around the Western average, well below Britain's, just above Germany's. Since then, her position has worsened, due in part to cutbacks in the manufacturing industry caused by improved productivity. Matters improved under Balladur in 1994, but then grew worse again as the economy slowed down: Chirac came to power with eloquent promises, but he and Juppé achieved little. Today, according to latest OECD figures, France (11.8) has the highest percentage of unemployment in Europe after Spain (22.3) and Finland (15.7): she is equal with Italy and well ahead of Germany (9.0), Britain (8.2), the United States (5.4) and Japan (3.4).

Why does France manage so badly, even at times when economic growth is good? The reasons most often given are the high labour costs and the rigidity of the labour laws – or at least this is what employers complain about most bitterly. But there may be other factors, too. The working population is still growing, due to the fairly high birth rate of the 1970s. There is still some exodus from the farms. Improved technology may be adding to productivity faster than in some countries. And the Front National blames immigration – but this is debatable (see p. 224).

In a country where benefits are unusually generous, the labour costs may be a real issue. The social charges that an employer pays, for health, pensions, family allowances and the rest, add 41 per cent to his wage bill, against 18 per cent in Britain, where charges are unusually low. Overall costs are even greater in Germany, where social charges may be slightly lower than in France but wage levels are higher. According to INSEE, the average cost of staff is highest in Germany, while France is on a level with Belgium and the Netherlands, and both Britain and the US are some way behind. Employers allege that another deterrent from hiring staff is what they see as the unreasonably high level of the French legal national minimum wage (SMIC, see p. 193), currently about 6,200 francs a month. But employees generally do not want France to move to a lower-cost, less protective work system, even if the price they pay is a higher unemployment. Some experts claim that the real total may be much higher than the official figure of just 3 million, which comprises only those registered as seeking a full-time job.

While those in work are quite well looked after, many of the unemployed find life especially hard because of the inequities of France's complex dole system. This is not as unfair as it used to be: but even after a reform by the Socialists in 1992, it remains related to earnings and insurance payments, in a manner that benefits most the higher-paid or those who have been in jobs for some years. The very young, and the long-term unemployed, get much less, or nothing. In a word, benefits start at around 57 per cent of a person's last salary, then drop by 17 per cent every three months, so that before long they almost vanish. And those who have not yet made social-security payments, i.e. the young, are not eligible. There is no equivalent of the British long-term flat-rate benefit: yet a middle-aged man with a good past salary will at first do far better than in Britain, and may have little incentive to find another job. Hence the common criticism that the French system makes some people lazy and others into paupers. An official report in 1996 found that some 1 per cent of beneficiaries were receiving over 15,000 francs a month, while 48 per cent were getting less than 3,000 francs and nearly one-third of all job-seekers were entitled to nothing. They have to survive on the RMI or social assistance (see pp. 197–9).

Single women, immigrants and the very young are among those worst affected by unemployment. Some 14 per cent of women are registered as looking for work, against 10 per cent of men. However, as many of the women have husbands with jobs, their plight is not always so bad. Prospects can be bleaker for young school or university leavers, boys or girls: among 16- to 24-year-olds, some 23 per cent are unemployed. But matters are not necessarily worse than in some other European countries, since so many French in this age group are still students. In fact some of the hardest cases, psychologically, are people in their forties or fifties who suddenly find themselves axed. They may be cushioned at first by their dole benefits: but after years devoted to their job, and with little prospect at that age of getting another one, they find it hard to adjust to being 'useless'. 'I'll never forgive the way I've been fucked up,' said one middle-aged *cadre*. 'Some bright young *énarque* bastard came to "reorganize" our firm, and he threw me out, just like that, after all my years of loyal effort. I feel shattered, in my pride and identity, and ashamed in front of my kids.' Factory workers were at first the worst hit by rising unemployment, but today *cadres* and professional people are almost equally affected. In all classes, long-term unemployment is one of the gravest aspects of the problem: of the 3 million seeking jobs, 1,150,000 have been out of work for a year or more. Those most affected are not only older people, whose benefits have eroded, but the less qualified or less enterprising among the young. After endless applications, they become demoralized, and the weaker ones even stop looking for work. Some of them sink into chronic depression or even suicide, or drugs, or delinquency in *la banlieue*.

Some leading Frenchmen have come to believe, rightly or wrongly, that much of the unemployment is due to laziness or lack of motivation – either among young people supported by their parents, or older ones who prefer to live on their dole benefits or RMI, plus family allowances: 'They find it cheaper not to work,' said one senior Patronat figure. It is hard to tell how many *chômeurs* might be of this kind, perhaps not many. But welfare allowances can be generous in some cases: I know a girl whose doctor has put her on heavy medication, but her sickness benefit plus another insurance sum from her previous employer add up to more than her previous salary, so she has little incentive to try to end her treatment and look for a new job. Pierre Méhaignerie, an open-minded *centriste* and former minister, told me, 'You can have larger family allowances if you give up work, and many people sign on as unemployed so as to get these. I reckon that of the 3 million registered job-seekers, about a third are truly motivated, another third are maladapted and unemployable, while a further million are not really looking for work and they register for other reasons.' Most experts would see this as an exaggeration. But even one FO trade-union official echoed Méhaignerie's view to me: 'Many of the younger people here are lazy, they prefer to live on the dole or RMI, and get out of bed late. And the Government should ban all the *travail en noir* [moonlighting] by retired people who go on doing jobs while drawing their pension. They should be obliged to choose; it's not fair on the real unemployed.' This is quite a common view.

Over a third of the adult population are reckoned either to have been out of work recently, or to have a close relative who is or has been unemployed. So the *mal* is widely spread. Many parents with secure jobs live in fear that their educated children will fail to find work; and according to one official survey, unemployment today comes ahead of serious illness, pollution, poverty, drugs or law and order, as the principal daily anxiety. In Catholic France, the work ethic may never have been quite as strong as in some countries: even so, the generally hard-working French have tended to put a moral value on work and thus attach a stigma to not working. Today, however, so many people are out of work that the stigma has waned. There may still be plenty of hard-working careerists or money-makers: yet the feeling has grown, not only that leisure has its own moral values too, but that attitudes to work must change.

Many people have come to believe that the employment crisis can never be solved by traditional means. Technological change, plus competition from developing countries, plus tight rules on job security, all mean that total salaried employment is gone for ever. So new patterns must be found – either of shared work or part-time work, or else a new concept of work, a blurring of the old distinctions between regular work and other activities. '*Le plein emploi est mort, vive la pleine activité!*' wrote one sociologist, while even from a hardened industrialist I heard the view: 'Our society is too structured on the idea of work versus no work: we should end the idea that work is essential for all. Instead of the dole, every citizen should have a basic fixed state income, and on top of that, wages would fluctuate. I could then take on more staff. I know other *patrons* who share my view.' This may sound fanciful. But even the Commissariat au Plan has been at work on similar ideas, whereby a regular wage contract might be replaced by some wider 'contract of activity' between an individual and several employers, public or private. Everyone would be expected to do some work and receive an income: but gone would be the dichotomy between having no job and a full-time salaried job for one firm. To some *patrons*, this sounds horribly like Karl Marx's dogma, 'From each according to his abilities, to each according to his needs.' Yet ideas of this kind are now in the air in France.

The hundreds of local job centres of the Agence Nationale pour l'Emploi (ANPE), backed by the Ministry of Labour, try to help people find work. Most towns also have a Mission Locale that aims to provide young people with training, advice or job contacts. And over the years, governments have subsidized various job-creation schemes: Juppé's in 1995–6 were said to have yielded some 100,000. But generally the ventures have been expensive and poorly targeted, and have done little more than prevent the total jobless numbers from rising even faster.

One lively private initiative came in 1993 from Martine Aubry herself. Back in opposition after being Minister of Social Affairs, she founded the Fondation Agir contre l'Exclusion (FACE), using her own name and contacts, and her father's, to persuade a number of big firms to join her in a scheme to help create jobs in the 'difficult' suburbs: Péchiney, Renault and others signed up. So FACE attracted much media attention. Aubry may have had one eye on her political future, but her crusade was also genuine. She set up FACE projects in the grimmer parts of Lille, Lyon and other towns, and these are still active today. There have been failures, and the total of permanent jobs created has not been high. But in the northern industrial suburbs of Marseille, around l'Estaque, success has been better. Here in 1997 I visited FACE's office in a high-rise HLM block, where Hanifa Taguelmint, the vital young Algerian-born woman in charge, said: 'We have managed to create 400 jobs in various fields. We have helped to found a little firm that cleans and repairs telephone booths (often needed in Marseille); and another that acts as a home-help service, providing part-time chars and so on. We send local *chômeurs* to firms that agree to work with us. Thus McDonald's, the FNAC bookshop and Continent hypermarkets have all provided jobs. Many young unemployed here are well-qualified graduates, grown desperate, and we have helped to change their lives. We are friendly with Serge Trigano of Club Med, and he has taken on sixty of our *chômeurs*, mostly Maghrebis, and has trained them as GOs [*gentils organisateurs* – see p. 657]. One Maghrebi girl even won the Club's "Best GO of the Year" award.' From the Marseille slums to the Club's paradise – a heartening story.

The rigidity of the French labour laws is often cited as one reason for high employment. It seems a paradox, for many of these laws are aimed at providing job security against dismissal: but employers claim that this simply deters them from taking on extra staff, because of the difficulty of getting rid of them again in harder times. So the laws can have a perverse effect, it is said. As there are no data about how many potential jobs are thus lost, or preserved, it is hard to judge the argument. But certainly the labour regulations are of horrifying complexity, enshrined in a vast tome, the Code du Travail, which by a kind of Parkinsonism is constantly being added to by zealous bureaucrats, despite the intentions to simplify it: for one European Commission inquiry on labour, the British submitted a working paper of six pages, while the French document was 1,000 pages. And one clerk in a private firm told me that his monthly pay slip had grown in the past few years from sixteen to thirty lines, because of a series of new regulations: this is a typical case. Large firms with good accountants can manage to cope with the added paperwork: but many small ones become reluctant to take on more staff.

Many of the myriad rules are about safety, hygiene, holidays, maternity leave, working conditions, and so on. Those most affecting employment are either on job security or on working hours. Until recently, many *conventions collectives* laid down precisely the total and the timing of the hours to be worked in each firm, and it was not easy for an employer to alter this, even if staff, too, wanted it – for example, to allow some people to start early, others to work late or at the weekend. But under an agreement between unions and Patronat in October 1995, hours can now be more flexible. 'I can even negotiate an annual rather than a weekly total,' one factory owner told me, 'so that my staff work a longer week at some periods, at others a shorter one, depending on my workload. This in fact gives them greater security, for I need to rely less on temporary labour.' In the banks, a decree dating from the Front Populaire made it illegal for a bank to work more than a five-day-week: but this was repealed in 1997 by the Juppé Government, under pressure from the banks, and many are now open on Saturdays.

The more important rules concern dismissals. The Auroux laws of 1981–2 had made it harder to enforce redundancies: a firm would have to apply to the Ministry of Labour, then go through complicated procedures lasting up to six months. If the economic case was reasonable, permission was usually granted. But the complexity of the red tape seemingly scared many smaller firms: they grew more hesitant to recruit, not wanting to risk being left with surplus staff later on. Then the Right under Chirac modified this picture, to help employers. Today a firm wanting to make more than ten 'economic' lay-offs must still consult the ministry and its own *délégués du personnel*, and present a detailed plan of restructuring. To dismiss a smaller number, it has to negotiate case by case with the local *conseil des prud'hommes*, a conciliation board, which tends to allow the redundancy in about half of all cases. In general, larger firms with the experience and resources find that they can in practice make the redundancies they need, so long as they are patient. But many smaller ones still find it hard to cope with the complex rules; or they complain that it is too difficult to sack an employee who is lazy or incompetent. And compulsory severance pay is two months' salary or more. For all these reasons, many firms nowadays prefer to hire staff on short-term contracts.

Urged on by the Patronat, Giscard in 1979 produced a law making it easier to take on temporary staff: this is still in force today, and is widely used. The Left have never liked it, but as it clearly creates extra work, they have not rescinded it. The contracts can last up to a year, after which the firm must either part with the employee or offer a permanent job. So the *patron* can do his own weeding out, retaining the good recruits and getting rid of the duds. The unions complain, with some reason, that this creates a climate of insecurity among the many short-term workers, most of them young: they are not fully covered by Social Security and the like, so a discriminatory wedge exists between them and the regular staff. Unions have failed to rally strikes against the law, for most short-term workers are glad to have any job rather than none. Near Orléans in 1996 I met the owner of a small building firm: 'I used to have a staff of fourteen, but times are hard and now we are eight. If I get extra orders, I go to a little local agency that deals with *chômeurs*, and I hire them by the week, on the minimum wage, with social charges at below half the normal level. It's not a good system, too precarious for them and for us – but what else can I do? If charges were lower and sacking was easier, I'd gladly take on more regular staff. But we don't want to get like America. It is right that workers should have some protection.'

Various ways of sharing out the burden of unemployment more fairly have been tried or suggested. One is to have more part-time work, a field where France has hitherto lagged: despite a recent increase, only 16 per cent of all French jobs are part-time, against 28 per cent in Britain. Men are outnumbered six to one by women, many of them cleaners or other lower-paid workers. But some major firms including Renault have now introduced part-time work, and the Patronat would like to see more of it. The unions are more wary, claiming that employees of this kind are more open to exploitation. However, unions have been keener than the Patronat on another possible remedy for mass unemployment: earlier retirement. Most unions, and staff, too, would like to see the legal age brought down from sixty to fifty-five. But it would be politically impossible to reduce the level of pensions: so for this reason all recent

Governments have decided that a general measure on earlier retirement would be far too expensive.

Instead, the main emphasis recently has gone on reducing the length of the working week, as the best way of sharing out work more equally – and of enriching quality of life for employees bored with routine jobs. This has been a major talking point in France since the mid-1990s. In theory, to shorten working hours should lead to mass job creation: but will it in practice, given the steady advances in productivity? No wonder that the major innovation of the Jospin Government's first year in office, the proposal for a 35-hour week, has led to such controversy.

France, with its long holidays (see p. 653), already has a shorter tally of hours worked annually than most countries. According to OECD figures, the French work on average 1,645 hours a year, more than the Germans (1,578), but less than the British (1,732) and much less than those strange Americans (1,951), who are so prosperous yet rarely take long holidays. The French legal working week was reduced in 1982 by the Socialists from 42 to 39 hours: but overtime is allowed (usually at 25 per cent extra pay), and INSEE has found that the real average total is 41 hours per week. Since the early 1990s the feeling has grown, among a public worried about unemployment, that to reduce working hours per head, thus hopefully creating more jobs, would be the most logical and effective way to proceed. The Germans and the Dutch have done just this, with some success. Balladur in 1993 began to suggest a four-day week, then Chirac as President urged the Patronat to 'show imagination' about shorter hours. The unions, save maybe for the CGT, had long been in favour; the Patronat was at first more wary, but has since come round to the idea. It is legal, so long as an agreement is reached voluntarily by negotiation between employers, unions and staff delegates, within each firm or sector. The big issue, of course, is whether shorter hours is also to mean lower weekly wages, and this has generally been the sticking point.

After an agreement of principle in 1995 between the Patronat and all the main unions except the CGT, the number of firms adopting shorter working time grew steadily during 1996. Those involved included Usinor, Bull and Alsthom, all reducing their weekly hours to 36 or less. At one big Bordeaux bank that was planning lay-offs, the staff accepted some salary cuts in return for an assurance that nearly a hundred jobs would be saved. Most remarkably, Électricité de France reached an agreement for the week to be shortened gradually to 32 hours, paid at the rate of 35 hours, and promised in return not to lay off staff. Three main unions accepted this de facto wage cut: but the CGT refused, always opposed on principle to any fall in salaries. However, in some other instances the CGT broke its own principles and agreed to collaborate. Some firms have accepted to shorten the working week without any cut in wages, believing that better productivity can make up the shortfall. Others have managed to persuade their staff to make sacrifices in return for the creation of jobs for others. Staff altruism here may have been evolving, but how much is not clear. According to one survey in 1966, some 86 per cent of wage-earners felt a shorter working week to be necessary, but only 37 per cent were prepared to accept a cut in wages. Several other surveys, however, have found up to 70 per cent of staff today ready to earn a little less and work less, so long as they are sure that this can create new jobs.

In 1996 a public-spirited UDF deputy, Count Gilles de Robien, put forward a private bill whereby the Government would subsidize firms to create or save jobs. In a word, a company would have its social charges reduced by 30 to 40 per cent, if by shortening its working hours it was able to take on extra staff or avoid planned redundancies. Juppé, under pressure, accepted this plan, even though it was clearly going to be very expensive – and at once the *loi Robien* proved widely popular, as hundreds of firms applied. The hard-hit Crédit Lyonnais was thus able to save 1,100 of some 5,000 planned lay-offs. The Patronat itself was divided about the law. Many employers feared that the extra cost to the State of many billions of francs a year would oblige the Government to put up taxes in other ways. But Robien's scheme did succeed better than most previous ones in preserving thousands of jobs.

The Socialists in the early 1980s had put forward a plan for a general 35-hour week. This was shelved for economic reasons, but in 1997 was again in their manifesto. Jospin was not really expecting to win that election: so when he did, he was mildly put out at finding himself obliged to fulfil a crucial promise that was bound to cause huge controversy. But he went ahead, and Martine Aubry prepared a bill for a legal working week of a maximum of 35 hours, to be applied in 2000 to all firms and public services with over twenty employees, and extended to smaller ones in 2002, in both cases without reduction in pay. And a great debate at once began as to whether this would really create more jobs. It is true that some firms had just done so by reducing hours: but there was surely a difference between doing this as part of one firm's restructuring, and applying it right across the board. Even the unions did not greet Jospin's plan as a top priority.

As for the Patronat, it was aghast. It was happy for individual firms to reduce to 35 hours or even less, if they wished: but it was flatly opposed to any overall statutory measure. It argued that many firms simply could not afford it without a corresponding cut in pay. And the Patronat's president, the moderate Jean Gandois, angrily resigned, claiming that he had not been properly consulted. His successor, Ernest-Antoine Seillière, was a tougher man; and under his flag the Patronat pledged itself to fight the 35-hour week all the way. According to one survey, some 90 per cent of *patrons* felt that the plan would not create more jobs, and they feared that it would make French firms less competitive.

Even within Jospin's own ranks, all was not unity. Martine Aubry, a determined Socialist, was committed to the project. But Dominique Strauss-Kahn, a moderate realist, was more dubious and he said so in public. But Jospin and Aubry went ahead, and the bill passed through the National Assembly in 1998. Jospin sought to reassure critics, stressing that 35 hours would be the 'legal' week and a firm could in fact work longer, on overtime rates, if the staff agreed. But as the *raison d'être* of the project was to reduce unemployment, he needed to carry conviction. He received support in January 1998 from a remarkable Banque de France report, which forecast that the measure could create up to 700,000 new jobs within three years, so long as the economy was doing well. However, a few months later, when the first voluntary agreements were reached within industrial branches on the application of the measure, *patrons* and some main unions preferred to go for extended overtime as the best way of making up for the shorter hours. It was costly for employers, but it meant that new jobs would not be created – and so the main purpose of the new law was in danger of being subverted. In some cases job creation has fared better: notably at EDF where the tough CGT in January 1999 reached an agreement with management on shorter hours that was expected to yield 4,000 new jobs. In October Aubry claimed that shorter hours had already created some 120,000 jobs. Then Parliament began the ratification of the second 35-hour law, which would make the measure compulsory in all firms except the smallest. Today it seems that if economic growth continues then the 35-hour project may produce jobs. Otherwise, it could add to the burden on firms, and employment could suffer.

Another proposal by the new Government was better received and seemed more realistic. This was Aubry's plan to put state money into creating some 350,000 new short-term jobs for young people in the public sector, and if possible a further 350,000 in the private sector – at a time when youth unemployment had reached 27 per cent. Aubry wanted schools, cultural and welfare bodies, local authorities, and so on, to take part in creating fairly simple 'social' jobs of new kinds – maybe helping with sport or *animation*, protecting children or the elderly, keeping public places tidy, helping to prevent violence, introducing new technologies, and much else. Young people under twenty-six, or in some cases under thirty, would be given five-year contracts and be paid roughly at minimum-wage level, from a special new fund of 35 billion francs. The Ministry of Education took on some 16,000 young people, and its schools gave them such tasks as aiding backward pupils with their homework, or organizing outings. Other ministries joined in, also some town councils, though many others were wary. Aubry hoped that many private firms would take part, too. After a slow start, by August 1999 some 186,000 youth jobs had been created in the public sector, with others to come. Right-wing politicians criticized the scheme on some practical grounds but applauded its intentions – 'It is not easy to shoot Father Christmas when he comes bringing gifts,' said Alain Madelin. Aubry's plan was to short-circuit the usual laborious long-term job-creation schemes with a more immediate, concrete package that might do something to assuage the growing frustration, even hopelessness, of so many younger people. And the plan soon had some success. It was certainly one of the factors between the 12 per cent fall in youth unemployment by mid-1998.

However, neither this nor the 35-hour project did much to raise the hopes of the long-term adult unemployed, whose patience suddenly snapped at the end of 1997. The out-of-work, like the elderly, the sick, even the immigrants, had never formed a coherent political lobby in France; and as their numbers grew over the years, they had stayed curiously passive, not giving vent publicly to their growing despair. But then in December groups of them started to 'occupy' some dozen unemployment offices across France, demanding special bonuses. After Christmas, others barricaded railway lines at Marseille, while groups of homeless people invaded a Paris luxury hotel and a famous restaurant, Fouquet's, whose manager placated them with forty free meals. In Strasbourg there was rioting. Jospin, embarrassed, made a few concessions, including a new 1-billion-franc fund for those in acute need. Under police pressure the sit-ins at public offices ended. The protests had been fuelled by the CGT and so became in part political. But they were also an expression of real grievance, and were met with wide public sympathy. Significantly, the protesters were not demanding work but larger benefits – as if they knew that real jobs might never come their way. Martine Aubry promised regular talks with the associations of unemployed – and this was new.

According to official figures, the total of youth unemployed fell substantially in 1997–8, from 28 to 25 per cent of the age-bracket. This was thanks in large part to Aubry's scheme. The overall 2-per-cent drop in that period was also due to this, but equally to the upturn in the economy. And it lightened the mood a little. If economic growth holds steady, the fall may continue. Yet the French do not expect miracles, and broadly they accept that high unemployment is a price they pay for their chosen social system. Repeatedly one hears, 'No, we do not want to move towards the American model,' with its easy hiring-and-firing, low welfare protection, very low wages for the poor. There is always remarkably little popular demand for a reduction of overstaffing in the public services: the French would rather keep their rigidities and their generous welfare system that protects nearly everyone. The result is a continuing high level of unemployment, bearable for most people, awful for a few. The French have learned to live with it – just as they live with the inequalities of class, wealth and income.

THE AFFLUENT CLASS SOCIETY:
ITS PRIVILEGED, ITS *EXCLUS*

The land of civic *égalité* still has plenty of other kinds of *inégalité* and vested privilege – despite post-war change. The old class structure has been loosening a little: peasants, for example, are now much less of a society apart. And all classes have shared in the huge growth of prosperity since 1945, if not very evenly: workers' salaries have continued to rise, but not as fast as the unearned incomes of the rich, from property and investment. Differences of wealth are far less than in America, slightly less than in Britain, but above the average for northern Europe. And though education is supposedly free and the same for all, it can produce some social inequalities almost as striking as in the nation of Eton and Harrow.

Today the old division between rich and poor is being accompanied by a new one, between those in work and the long-term unemployed, many of them very young. This, plus other factors, has led to a growth of real poverty and of social alienation. And it has become a major talking point, this so-called 'fracture sociale' or 'exclusion' of parts of society. In earlier years, first de Gaulle's regime, then especially Giscard's, did make efforts to reduce poverty by raising pensions and the minimum legal wage. Mitterrand continued the process, imposing some new taxes on the rich: but he never really fulfilled his pledge to create a more equal society. He made the poor a little less poor, but his measures had no great impact on the narrow élite of wealth and privilege that still has so much influence in France. In exploring these complex issues, let us look first at social-class divisions, then at wealth and income inequalities, then at the new poverty and les exclus.

The United States may have far greater extremes of wealth and poverty than France. But it also has more social mobility, and thus more freedom of opportunity than France's older society where many class divisions today remain quite rigid, behind the shifts in lifestyle. This can be more a matter of attitudes than of economics. For example, while the British may remain more class-conscious than the French, they are now less class-divided, to my mind. In Britain, the enforced mucking together of wartime helped to produce a post-war social fluidity; the French, being split up and paralysed under the Occupation, did not have this experience. In Britain, the classes are fascinatedly aware of each other on a personal everyday level, making it seem a class-ridden society; in France, class divisions are taken more for granted, and are seldom discussed with the same gossipy concern. Certainly there is more social mobility than before the war, but not much sense of classless meritocracy. The bourgeoisie retains much of its aloofness, its ignorance of the lives of workers. They in turn, even when well salaried, remain reticent about thrusting forward to share in the bourgeoisie's own world of smart cafés and theatres; and their lives and ideas are less featured on television, which is less populist than in Britain. There is no French EastEnders, just as there have been no French Beatles.

The causes of these rigidities lie deep in French history and character. The desire to avoid open conflicts has led to a protective formalization, whereby each class stays in its fixed place. Conflicts take the form of political demands, prises de position, mass rallies, the taking of pot-shots from behind barricades, rather than the British hand-to-hand jousting.

This has its positive side. A French worker may resent the alien bourgeois world, but when he meets one of the species he is likely to treat him naturally as a fellow citizen, without the chip-on-the-shoulder awkwardness common in Britain. For, paradoxically, the tradition of civic *égalité* remains real and strong, and it leads to a mutual respect between all individuals when regarded as citizens rather than as members of a class. This produces a kind of legal fiction that the gross inequalities of income and opportunity do not exist.

Class patterns have been changing, but less through a merging of classes than a blurring of their outward distinctions. Under modern conditions, their interests and habits have grown closer. A skilled worker may own much the same kind of car as a bourgeois, and off duty he may dress in much the same way; the working class has long given up its old class 'uniform' and is dressing more like the middle class, so it has become harder to tell them apart. But real barriers remain: the bourgeoisie retains control of certain professions, which the lower classes still find it hard to enter via the supposed equality of education. A man's accent places him socially less than in Britain (only regionally), but his family background clings to him more closely. And while a worker's son may enter the white-collar lower middle class by training to be a teacher or *fonctionnaire*, he will rarely aspire to be a banker or doctor. Upward mobility comes more often from the peasantry than the working class, and often it takes two generations: Jacques Delors, for example, is the son of a simple usher at the Banque de France whose own parents were peasants in the Massif Central.

Within these divisions the character of each class has been changing, and nowhere so much as in the aristocracy. In pre-1914 days the French nobility set the tone in all of Europe for taste and gallantry. More recently it has been pushed on to the sidelines of national life: but it survives. Many of the great families, the de Rohan-Chabots and the rest, have managed to keep their identity and their solvency by coming to terms with the modern economy. In the nineteenth century their lordly code of values led them to scorn business, so the new empires of banking and industry fell into the hands of the bourgeoisie. Today, late but not too late, they have been taking up essential salaried posts in these milieux. Economically the nobility has thus been merging into the upper bourgeoisie, just as in the last century many bourgeois families managed to merge into the aristocracy, prefixing the lordly 'de' to their names.

With their landed fortunes eroded by inflation, taxes and social changes, aristocrats may have to devote part of their new industrial incomes to the upkeep of their cherished châteaux, if they want these to remain habitable (many have fallen into ruin or been sold). A family may spend part of the summer in its château, and most of the year in its Paris flat, maybe in a dignified older quarter such as the Faubourg St-Germain. Here the great families live for the most part discreetly, clinging together in their exclusive social world, inviting each other to formal cocktail parties or an occasional banquet with echoes of past glories. And the rest of France ignores them. For although the French public adores foreign royalty or the idea of an English *milord*, it cares not a jot for its own nobility, whose doings find little place in French gossip columns. It is one facet of the stratified privacy of French society. Snobbishness exists, but not in the national limelight. And this seclusion may have helped the aristocrats' own true qualities to have endured. Many are cultured and gentle people, often politically liberal, less grasping than the bourgeoisie. Today a count or baron will seldom use his title in public or professional life, but is simply 'Monsieur'. He will, however, keep it in private social life, and his pride in his family name remains deep.

This nobility forms part of a milieu today known as '*BCBG*' (*bon chic bon genre*), roughly the equivalent of 'Sloane Ranger' or, in America, 'Preppy'. It is a world that works hard, does not flaunt its wealth, and has impeccable, rather formal, manners; and it includes the well-connected *bonnes familles* that form the upper bracket of the bourgeoisie. The equivalent of the English upper middle class is divided between this *grande bourgeoisie* and, just below it, the *bonne bourgeoisie*. De Gaulle was a product of the former, as Mitterrand, son of a businessman, was of the latter. These professional and money-making strata retain much of their power, even if the bourgeoisie has been changing with the times. Traditionally its strength was based on property, passed on through family hands and so requiring close family loyalties and careful marriages. Today the bourgeois family firm has been yielding to the managerial corporation, so these families now rely more on income from senior salaried positions. But many of these jobs, plus much of the real influence in France, still remain within their grasp, via the élitist upper rungs of higher education (see pp. 566–70).

At the same time a new middle-middle class has been growing fast in numbers and grassroots commercial influence. Economic growth of tertiary services has thrown up from the ranks of the lower bourgeoisie a group that has achieved some affluence: advertising executives, specialist technicians, *cadres* in modern firms, and those tradesmen or small industrialists who have marched with the times – men like the master-butcher whose lavish party I attended in a small town. From one modest shop he had moved to owning a chain of large stores, and he was living in high *nouveau riche* style in a new country house with swimming pool. This assertive status-seeking world, upwardly mobile, is more than half in love with American or German material values. But elsewhere in the *petite bourgeoisie* the rise of prosperity has been far more uneven. In the days of high inflation, many older people saw their savings eroded, and they relapsed into genteel poverty; many small traders also slumped into decline. And today this continues, as so many little businesses have gone bankrupt and their owners have not found other work. They form a new fringe of middle-class poor.

In country areas, one positive change in class structures is that medium-sized farmers are now largely integrated into the commercial middle class (see p. 384). So the former sharp gulf between *paysan* and *citadin* has been waning, as the two grow closer in lifestyles. And as many middle-class town-dwellers now have rural weekend or holiday homes, they are getting to know country folk as they have never known the alien urban working class on their doorstep. Indeed the other sharp gulf, between *ouvrier* and *bourgeois*, has proved more resistant to change. Workers in their new flats may be acquiring some bourgeois habits and property-owning aspirations; they may watch the same TV programmes, and the young may frequent the same discos. But, with exceptions, the broad mass of the working class still lives in a social world of its own, especially in the older industrial areas. It seldom attends theatres or classical concerts. Yet the old emotional class solidarity, born of hard times, declined during the boom years, as in Britain. Today high unemployment has revived a little of that feeling. And thanks in part to periods of Socialist rule, the working class tends to feel less alienated from the French mainstream than in former days. But it has lost much of its faith in the Communist Party and has found no other obvious focus. Moreover, industrial change has made this class less homogenous. Its better-paid workers, such as the envied *métallos de chez Renault*, have formed new proletarian élites who can find that their interests are closer to those of the junior *cadres* than those of lower-paid workers in more backward firms, such as women in old textile factories.

Maybe I have drawn too severe a picture of French class divisions. A new social fluidity has certainly been growing, as farmers, tradesmen, junior *cadres* and others mix more than before. The rural exodus and mass rehousing have played their part, as the suburban estates now provide the various groups with new social contacts they never knew in their old homes. Schooling, at junior levels at least, is less class-divided than in Britain: most children attend the same primary schools, and under the Haby reforms of 1977 (see p. 535), more of them are now likely to follow the same general courses in secondary schools. But at higher levels of education, the picture is different, and this, more than anything, serves to perpetuate class differences. The proportion of students from working-class backgrounds has been growing but is still only about 13 per cent, less than in Britain. And although education in France is in theory free and equally open to all, in practice the bourgeoisie has managed to retain its dominance over some of the élite colleges that lead to the best careers (see pp. 566–70). To obtain the right diplomas in youth is still crucial; and despite improvements it remains harder than in many countries for an able person to win promotion from the shop floor or the clerical desk. These hidden barriers are notorious in France, and are more serious than the purely social divisions. They help to explain why this affluent nation is not more equal in opportunity or in lifestyles.

How great are the inequalities of wealth and of income? Of course, all classes have shared in the post-war prosperity boom, in a country where for years the rise in living standards was among the fastest in Western Europe, during the '*Trente Glorieuses*'. According to statistics from INSEE, OECD and other sources, average real spending power more than trebled between the late 1940s and the mid-1980s. After this, the rise slowed right down: but even during the 1990s, real wages have continued to go up slightly, while average living standards, too, have still been rising, especially among the better-off. The difference is that the growth is now unfairly shared in a new way. Those in jobs are doing all right: but more people are getting poorer, because of the growth of long-term unemployment. This is hitting the very young much more than older retired people.

So how does this place France internationally? The latest figures available from OECD are surprising: in 1993, in terms of 'purchasing-power parities', private consumption per capita was $11,395 in France, less than in the United States ($16,444), Switzerland ($13,730), Japan ($11,791) and Canada ($11,863), but ahead of Italy ($11,029), the United Kingdom ($10,942), Germany ($10,733) and Spain ($8,412). These figures can be misleading as a guide to living standards, for they reflect also the strength of shifting currencies at a given moment (sterling was then much lower than by 1998); and the German figure would be much higher if the east were excluded. We must also take into account the differing proportions of national production ploughed into investment (then higher in France and Germany than in Britain), plus the differences in the cost of living, which were then highest in Germany and lowest in Britain, by perhaps 10 to 15 per cent. So it might be fair to say that Britain until about 1960 was the richest of these three countries, but is now slightly behind France, while the West Germans remain ahead. Living standards, however, depend also on factors inherited from the past, such as housing: despite the huge improvements in France since the 1960s, the British still have a better legacy of older housing, so they often live more comfortably. But at least at the upper-bourgeois level they have less spending money than their French equivalents, who choose to live in greater style (if not comfort) and can afford it. Not only are their salaries higher (and their income tax lower), but they rarely inflict on themselves the same burden of private-school bills. Hence their long, lavish holidays, smart clothes and dining out. In short, it is not easy to make summary comparisons.

As for income differentials, the new wealth is shared a little less unevenly in France than in Britain, taking all social classes together. According to an OECD report, the ratio between the top 10 per cent and bottom 10 per cent of incomes is 3.48 in France, compared with 3.79 in Britain, just 3 in Germany, and 5.94 in the United States. Wage differentials are greater in France than in Britain: but as welfare benefits are larger, too, the gap between the net income of a top manager and that of an unskilled worker may not be so different in the two countries.

The size of the gulf between rich and poor in France has fluctuated curiously. During the rapid expansion of the Gaullist years, senior *cadres* were getting richer much faster than unskilled workers. Then after 1968 the gap steadily narrowed: according to official figures, the differential fell from 4.6 in 1967 to 3.2 by the mid-1980s. The reasons? First, workers won big pay increases from the May '68 strikes, and union pressures then helped them to extend their incomes faster than *cadres*, who complained of being squeezed. Secondly, France's legal minimum wage, the *salaire minimum interprofessionnel de croissance* (SMIC), created in 1950, had for years been lagging behind inflation: but in 1970 it was reformed and indexed properly on prices, and for a while was even pushed up faster than ordinary wages. Today some 8 per cent of all wage-earners are on the SMIC, including 33 per cent of catering and hotel workers, 16 per cent of shop workers, but few in industry. The SMIC, some 6,000 francs a month in 1996, is reckoned to be about half an average wage, and it guarantees a manual worker at least a subsistence living.

The main reductions in differentials took place in the 1970s. Then the Socialists in the 1980s were criticized for not doing more to reduce them further. And now in the 1990s the gap in real wealth has tended again to increase. Wage differentials between *cadre* and unskilled worker may have remained steady at about 3.2 per cent: but the gulf in actual living standards has grown. According to an official report in January 1997, in 1984–94 the standard of living of an unskilled worker's family fell by 5 per cent, while that of clerical staff remained stable and that of *cadres* rose by 13 per cent: on average a *cadre* had been 2.5 times better off than a worker, and was now 3 times so. This paradox – stable wage structures versus growing wealth gap – has three explanations. First, the rise in unemployment falls more frequently on lower-income families. Secondly, the SMIC was allowed to lag, and not until 1995 was it raised again, by Chirac. Thirdly, and most importantly, the recent rises in gross income have come more from property and investments than from earnings, and this benefits most the well-to-do. Wages may have continued to go up slightly in the 1990s, but income from property has risen faster, by some 4 per cent a year.

The ultra-complex statistics on income give only part of the picture. The oddities of the taxation system, too, tend to favour the well-to-do and the self-employed, who can most easily indulge in the old French pastime of tax evasion. Partly because of the difficulty of getting the French to pay direct taxes, the State has long put its main emphasis on indirect taxation, such as high VAT. But this can be socially unjust, for consumer taxes hit rich and poor alike, and a progressive income tax does not. This latter equals only 6 per cent of GDP in France, against 10 per cent in Britain. It is certainly progressive, for some 48 per cent of households pay none at all, essentially those with low incomes or several children, while the top bracket rises to 55 per cent. By contrast, VAT, at between 15 and 20 per cent for most goods and services (food excluded), brings the treasury twice as much as income tax, and was twice increased in the mid-1990s. In September 1999 Jospin and Strauss-Kahn judged the economy to be sound enough for them to make 'the biggest tax cuts in ten years' – some 39 billion francs, consisting mainly of varied cuts in VAT levels. But there was still no concerted attempt to reform the income tax system.

As for tax evasion, an official report in 1996 estimated its cost at between 175 and 235 billion francs a year, equal to two-thirds of the revenue from income tax! Of this sum, about 32 billion was reckoned to come from non-payment of VAT, some 15 billion from income-tax evasion, and anything between 100 and 160 billion from undeclared *travail au noir*. This is where professional people have their field day, as well as farmers, tradesmen and other self-employed workers. Successful lawyers, actors, private doctors and others can make huge sums and declare only part for tax – and this has long been connived at by tax inspectors, who lack the staff or machinery for making proper checks. It all goes some way to explain the big inequalities of real income between the richer self-employed and salaried staff on pay-as-you-earn.

What's more, death duties and wealth taxes have generally been lower than in many advanced countries. Giscard in 1976 managed to introduce a modest capital gains tax, despite strong opposition from his own Gaullist allies, in a land where *liberté* includes the freedom to show very little *fraternité* when it comes to promoting material *égalité*. Then the Socialists did increase the maximum rate on death duties, from a mere 20 per cent to 40 per cent: but this remains lower than in Britain, and is often dodged. Mitterrand also introduced a new wealth tax, which was abolished by Chirac in 1987 but brought back a year later, and was then extended by Jospin in 1998. The tax is paid by some 170,000 families: but even its upper rates are quite modest, in a land where inequalities of fortune are much greater than those of income. The top 1 per cent of families own 20 per cent of the wealth the lower 50 per cent own 7 per cent.

The Socialists came to power in 1981 with a programme of redistribution; and to show they meant business, they brought in some measures right away. They raised old-age pensions, the SMIC and family allowances all quite generously; they remodelled income tax to ease the burden on the lower paid; and they even slapped a new luxury tax on expense accounts, yachts and luxury hotels, in addition to the wealth tax and higher death duties. But after this energetic start, they did little further to reduce inequalities. Their switch in 1982–3 to a policy of austerity made it hard for them to do much more to help the lower incomes. The new wealth tax was bringing in only about 4 billion francs a year, less than 1 per cent of income tax plus VAT: it may have been a useful symbolic gesture, but the Government came to accept that it was not a practical weapon for the true redistribution of wealth, for the rich are so few. Politically, Mitterrand lacked the means, and maybe the will, to undermine the power of the more opulent families. So he ended up disappointing many on the Left.

One curious feature of the situation today is that the old on average have been getting richer while the young get poorer. Old-age pensions used to be wretchedly low in France: then Giscard raised them sharply, and retired people saw their real incomes go up by 58 per cent in the 1970s. Mitterrand continued the process, and today pensioners are actually better off than those still in active life by an average 8 per cent, whereas in 1970 they were 20 per cent poorer. State pensions, work-related, average some 6,000 francs a month, but can be three times this for senior *cadres*; in addition, many people have separate retirement funds, often also linked to their jobs. While many of the elderly live in genteel poverty, others enjoy themselves handsomely so long as their health lasts – and they fill out the restaurants and resorts. It is widely felt that pensions have risen *too* high, and Martine Aubry in 1998 was preparing a reform that would reduce some of the privileges.

For young people, the overall picture is so very different: their average standard of living fell by 15 per cent between 1989 and 1994, says INSEE. In the 18–25 age group, unemployment is 25 per cent: but the dole is minimal for those who have not worked before, nor can they claim the RMI subsistence benefit until they are twenty-five (see below). So they eke out a living as best they can. Many are supported by their families: but others have been flung on to the street by parents who have no legal obligation to look after them once they are eighteen. Many enrol as students and subsist on tiny grants. They face a prospect of graduate unemployment, at 20 per cent; and they know that most jobs for young people are poorly paid, except for a small élite. Inevitably many become depressed, apathetic, even suicidal, and their parents worry anxiously – 'It's a major aspect of today's *morosité*,' said one sociologist I met, 'and of today's problems of poverty' (see pp. 573–4).

'*L'exclusion*', '*la fracture sociale*' – the phrases today are on every politician's lips, in many a newspaper's editorial. Real poverty may not be nearly as bad as it was, say, in the 1930s, let alone in Zola's day. But expectations are now so much higher. And after a time when poverty seemed to be slowly disappearing from the new prosperous France, it has now grown worse again, through unemployment, the break-up of family, and other factors. The notion has grown of a society deeply fractured between haves and have-nots; and of various sections who are excluded or feel excluded: either their welfare aid is inadequate, or they are homeless, or they have struggled too long to find work and are pathological cases; or they are immigrants feeling rejected. This is a wider problem than poverty alone. And increasingly it has caught public concern in recent years, either from genuine compassion, or a vague sense of guilt, or else a personal fear that the *mal* may spread. Chirac on becoming President tried to rally the nation against *l'exclusion*, but has not done much since. More revealingly, donations to charities dealing with the poor have tripled in the past few years.

Some 5 million people are estimated to be in real poverty and another 6 or 7 million to be living 'precariously', including most of the poorer unemployed and their families. Many are immigrants, or the very young, or what is left of the poorer peasantry; some are single parents, or drug addicts. In the old days destitute people were often looked after by their families: but less so nowadays, as family cohesion wanes. Instead various official bodies make efforts, and so do some private charities, church-backed or other, such as Médecins sans Frontières, which won fame in Bosnia under the charismatic Bernard Kouchner and is today more active in France than abroad. But there are simply not the funds for solving so vast and disparate a problem.

Some half a million people, *les SDF* (*sans domicile fixe*), are reckoned to be without a proper home. Just a few of these are the old-style *clochards*, shaggy oddballs who prefer life *à la belle étoile* and resent well-meaning attempts to domesticate them. But the vast majority of the homeless today are people who cannot even find low-cost social housing (see p. 204). You see them in the Métro, where their desolate begging may irritate some passengers but is tolerated by the authorities. They distribute their own magazines, similar to the *Big Issue* in Britain, but the principal one closed in 1996 for lack of funds. It was called *La Rue* – 'And life on the street, say for a young *chômeur* on his own,' a social worker told me, 'can turn him into a mental case after a few months – the cold, the thefts, the fights, the drugs.' A few of them manage to squat, or otherwise survive. I met an ex-gardener of thirty-four, living on the RMI benefit plus a few odd jobs: but no hostel would take him in because he refused to be separated from his black dog.

Since the dole in France is of limited duration and is linked to previous employment, many *chômeurs* are not eligible. This was causing such hardship that Rocard's Government in 1988 created the famous *revenu minimum d'insertion*, a fixed-rate benefit for those without the dole and out of work, aged twenty-five or more. Running today at some 2,400 francs a month, this RMI is less than half the SMIC and barely a subsistence wage: but it has done something to alleviate the worst poverty. However, it has had less success in its other aim which, as its name implies, is to 'insert' people into active life by helping them to get jobs. Few *RMIstes* have found work, so their numbers have swelled, reaching over a million – and the public cost has led some politicians on the Right to denounce the RMI, claiming that it can dissuade people from looking for jobs. Juppé's own minister in charge of 'the fight against exclusion', Éric Raoult, even spoke of 'an RMI culture of inactivity'. Others have argued that many beneficiaries simply cheat, by drawing the RMI when they are happily moonlighting from odd jobs. This may sometimes be true. But the RMI is so low that it can rarely be a real deterrent from finding a proper job. Matters are worst for those under twenty-five who are not eligible. For them, the only refuge is a modest public assistance fund.

In 1995, with matters growing worse, Chirac began his election campaign with a ringing appeal. Denouncing *la fracture sociale*, he promised an urgent new law that would 'commit the entire nation to conquer *l'exclusion*', and he spoke of 'a wounded and vulnerable France that, through unemployment and *exclusion*, pays the cost of our conservatism'. This became a major theme of the campaign: Chirac struck a chord, and his evident concern and sincerity was one factor that led to his defeat of Balladur. But then his Government proceeded to do very little, very slowly. An official report was commissioned, its proposals were then rejected as too ambitious and expensive. Finally the promised new draft law was published, in October 1996: it added up to little, causing wide disappointment, and was still under debate when the Government fell in May 1997. So much for Chirac's urgency. No doubt he meant well: but his Government, in a period of economy cuts, lacked the will to find the funds needed to tackle so vast a problem as poverty. Few ministers were really interested.

Jospin and Aubry in 1997–8 then relaunched the efforts, on a larger scale, and with more conviction. Aubry's much-heralded 'solidarity' programme, with a 50-billion-franc budget spread over three years, is aimed at the creation of youth jobs and the extension of the health service (as we have seen), also at giving more help to the homeless and destitute.

A special tax will be levied on empty flats in the Paris area. And a new law on *l'exclusion* aims to reduce the abuses of the RMI system by giving *RMIstes* more incentive to look for jobs, and bosses more means to provide them. It is a campaign 'without precedent', said Aubry. But as usual it is slow work.

Before this, all recent Governments have at least been making some efforts to provide emergency housing for desperate families. A few squats have been more or less legalized: one is in an empty railway carriage at the Gare de l'Est, aided by the Salvation Army. A Socialist law of 1990 reinforced the basic right of every family to obtain decent housing, and to stay there: guided by this, the courts were several times able to pass judgments in favour of *de facto* tenants, in disputes over squats or attempted expulsions. And so the Juppé Government laid plans for requisitioning up to 10,000 flats in the Paris area, many of them in empty blocks belonging to banks or insurance companies. This had a modest success: but it ran into legal obstructions, or a lack of funds for basic renovation, or even opposition by local mayors whose middle-class voters might like to see *les exclus* reincluded somehow, but not in *their* own street, thank you. Some Paris districts flatly rejected the plan. In the overall campaign to help the homeless and the poor, all town councils are expected to play their part and make some housing available. Many do what they can. But often it is the richer ones in right-wing hands (such as Neuilly) that make least effort, while the poorer ones, where matters are worst, can least afford it.

And so, amid a flurry of acronyms – '*Ah, ces pauvres SDF! – ces tristes RMIstes!*' – the battle against poverty goes on, in a land where some poorer people are still excluded from decent housing. But for nearly all other French, housing has improved radically since the 1950s.

HOUSING: VAST IMPROVEMENTS, BUT THE HLMS ARE STILL TOO FEW

It is more in housing than in any other field that French living standards have improved since the war. Even in the 1960s, the shortage was still being called 'national disgrace number one'. Many people lived in overcrowded, even squalid conditions, without bath or shower. But at least it was all very cheap: so, unable to find better homes, they spent their money on other things.

Today the shortage is largely solved, and homes are far more modern and comfortable. But prices have rocketed. And the average share of family income devoted to housing – rents or mortgages, plus heating and other charges – has risen since 1945 from the amazingly low figure of 3.4 per cent to 21.8 per cent, higher than in Britain. The French have even become house-proud. But the new costs are unevenly shared. While many working people are helped by a system of direct grants for subsidized housing, some of the poorest are excluded if they have no regular job; and many in the middle class find it hard to afford their modern flats or suburban villas on the free market. State housing policy, with its mesh of bureaucratic controls, has repeatedly been altered, relieving some injustices only to create others.

In the mid-1950s the housing situation was disastrous, following decades of neglect. Much of the problem dated back to August 1914, when the Government froze all rents in order to protect soldiers' families from profiteering landlords. This was a fair wartime measure, but it was never revoked. So between the wars developers had little incentive to build, and in that period France completed only 1.8 million new homes, a quarter of them the rebuilding of wartime losses, compared with 4 million in both Britain and Germany. The low rents also gave landlords an excuse for making no repairs, so that many houses fell into premature decay. Then after 1945 the Government gave priority to industrial recovery, whereas Britain and Germany began massive rehousing right away: in 1952 France was still completing only about 75,000 new homes a year, one-sixth of the German figure. Yet the population was rising, and the rural exodus to the cities was under way. Poorer families lived huddled in one room, Moscow style; and archaism was such that, in 1954, only 10 per cent of French homes had a bath or shower, only 27 per cent had flushing lavatories. Surveys frequently cited poor housing as the prime cause of divorce, crime, suicide, mental illness, infant mortality and the high rate of illegal abortions.

In face of a growing public outcry, the Government in the mid-'50s finally began to pump much more money into new social housing (equivalent of Britain's council housing). This in France takes various complex forms, the commonest being the *habitations à loyer modéré* (HLMs) which are built by private or public agencies, supervised and subsidized by the State from long-term low-interest loans. Under their crash programme, the rate of new building soared to reach about 400,000 units a year in the 1960s, and to peak at 550,000 in 1975. So in quantity the problem was largely, if not completely, solved, helped by a boom in the private sector, too, as rents were freed. By 1990 new homes had been built for half the population, and every town was ringed with post-war blocks of flats.

The earlier HLMs were of basic utility standard, with tiny rooms, minimal sound-proofing, and often no bathroom. But then the norms steadily improved, and for some years now all new flats have been built with baths and showers. Newer HLM blocks will often have balconies, cheerful façades and decent sound insulation. So French housing has been pulled up radically from its very low level. According to INSEE, between 1954 and 1992 the proportion of homes without running water fell from 42 to 3 per cent; without bath or shower from 90 to 6.2 per cent; without indoor flushing lavatories from 7.3 to 4.9 per cent; and most of the dwellings still without such amenities are old farmsteads. Even so, France has not quite yet reached the standards of some other north European countries. Not only are rooms on average of smaller size, but the ratio of people to rooms is one-third higher than in Germany. Nearly every home is full of modern electronic gadgetry, but space is often so cramped that there is hardly room to install it all.

At least the sheer quantity of housing is now such that most people are freer to pick and choose what they really want – and this has led to some striking changes. Whereas in the 1960s only 30 per cent of new building was of individual houses, in the 1980s this figure rose to 80 per cent, against only 20 per cent for flats. In the crisis years, the French had submitted to new blocks of flats as the quickest way of solving the shortage: but at heart the French as much as the English would rather have their own little house, and developers and even public agencies have been helping to give them just this. On the suburban estates, efforts have been made to group the houses pleasantly into 'hamlets', thus avoiding either the monotony of ribbon development or the anarchy of unplanned villas that scarred outer Paris between the wars. But in rural areas, too many commuter or weekend houses have been built at random. In today's stricter times, the proportion of new flats built as opposed to houses has risen again: but it is still only 45 per cent.

In all classes, the trend until recently was towards buying rather than renting. Before the war, most urban flats were rented: but the proportion of homes that are owner-occupied then rose steadily from 36 per cent in 1954 to 54 per cent by 1990 (in Britain it is about 66 per cent). Many French have thus been satisfying their property-owning instincts, and the trend has been encouraged by Rightist Governments for political reasons. Even about one-third of HLMs are now owned by their occupants, some of them helped by a generous state mortgage system that works out cheaper than paying rent. In the private sector, however, mortgages are more of a problem. Building societies on the British model are underdeveloped in France; and although banks will operate a kind of mortgage system to help young couples without capital, this usually involves some initial savings-bank deposits. So a couple may have to wait years to take possession, or else find down-payments from a bank at up to 17 per cent interest. Many middle-class couples spend up to 30 per cent of their income on mortgage repayments. Hence the 1990s have seen a slight trend back towards renting. With jobs now more precarious, and fewer, many young people hesitate to take the risk of having a mortgage; or if they lack a secure job, they will find it harder to get one.

Matters were made worse in the 1980s by the boom in the property market. Prices were pushed up by building costs, by the growing scarcity of good urban land, and by speculation. Since the early 1990s this rise has stopped, unlike in Britain, and prices in Paris are now back to their 1988 level. But they are still high, if not by absurd London standards. A four-room flat can cost 3 to 4 million francs in central Paris, and 1.5 to 2 million in the suburbs or provincial towns. Private rents are affected, too. They vary by area, but on average a four-room flat might cost 10,000 francs a month in the Paris *seizième*, 8,000 in Nice or a better Paris suburb such as St-Cloud, and 3,500 in a cheaper suburb or in Lyon. These high prices, whether for rental or for buying, hit above all the lower-middle-income groups who are earning just too much to qualify for an HLM.

Land speculation is now less serious than in the boom years: but it still limits the number and quality of new HLMs, since so large a part of their funds has to be spent on the initial buying of land. Governments for some years have made efforts to check speculation in development zones, by setting up entities known as *zones d'aménagement concerté* (ZACs), with the power to forbid sales of land or to pre-empt them. This has worked quite well for some housing schemes, for example in the *villes nouvelles* (see p. 208): but in other cases it has failed to control the vagaries of the office-building market. Giscard's Government in 1975 made a useful move against speculation in city centres, where prices had risen so high that promoters felt obliged to build to a high density. His new law imposed density limits of one storey in town centres (1.5 in

Paris): that is, a new two-storey building could cover only half the site, and so on. But the law, although useful in principle, was in practice not very effective. It may have thwarted some ugly high-rise schemes: but in others it simply deterred owners from selling, thus making less land available.

In rented housing, one flagrantly unjust anomaly from the post-war period has finally been cured. Under a law of 1948, private-sector rents became entirely unrestricted on housing built since that date, but earlier flats were subject to strictly controlled increases, far below inflation. This produced differentials of up to one-in-three on flats of similar quality. And pre-1948 tenants had security of tenure even on expiry of their lease. If most of them had been poorer people, this might have been less unjust: but many were prosperous bourgeois families in the homes they had occupied for generations. So in central Paris in the 1980s you could still find senior *cadres* living in six-room flats for 2,000 francs a month, the rental of a two-room flat in the suburbs. These privileges gave rise to various rackets: for example, a family in a large flat might sublet one room furnished for as much as their entire rent. Today nearly all the older flats in this category have been pulled down; or the ending of inflation has *de facto* put their rent increases nearer to those of newer ones; or they have been renovated, which has freed their rents. Very few homes still benefit much from the old anomaly.

The problems remaining are very different. They relate to whether the right people are getting access to HLMs, and whether the poorest ones can afford their rents. This issue first became acute in the mid-1970s, when HLM rents were being allowed to rise fast, yet there was almost no means test for applicants. As a result, many HLMs were going to middle-income people such as skilled technicians or young *cadres*, rather than to the poorer workers for whom they were intended, but who now found it hard to afford them. This was both socially unjust and a waste of public money – as was pointed out vigorously by a government commission headed by Raymond Barre, soon before he became Prime Minister. He proposed that the method of financing should be inverted: instead of going just to the HLM agencies ('*aide à la pierre*'), subsidies should go mainly to the occupants ('*aide à la personne*'). Rents and prices could thus be put at an economic level, but families would be helped to pay for them according to their means. This plan became law in 1977, and it remains the basic system today. It has helped many poorer families with top-up grants for their rents. But it has often forced the HLM agencies to reduce their building programmes. Nor has it prevented abuses in the allocation of HLMs.

Some HLM agencies are owned jointly by the State and local authorities; others are private but depend on state subsidies and regulations. They account for some 16 per cent of all French housing – over 50 per cent in some poorer areas – and they are of various categories, some cheaper than others. The system of allocation is crucial: on average, some 40 per cent of applicants are selected by local employers (their taxes fund HLM costs), mostly for their own staff; 20 per cent are chosen by the local *mairie*; 30 per cent by the *préfecture*; and some 10 per cent by the HLM agencies. It is the *mairie*'s quota that has become so controversial: in the case of the better-class HLMs, there is evidence that numerous mayors or councillors have allotted them to cronies or relatives, and even accepted bribes. This has been true in some wealthy cities such as Paris (where it has caused a major scandal, see p. 45), more so than in towns where HLMs are less sought after by the middle classes. The extent of this nepotism is not clear: but in 1996 it did prompt the Government to look at ways of making the allocations more transparent. A lesser injustice is that, despite the 1977 law, there are still some middle-income people in social housing not intended for them. There is a means test for entry: but this is not verified later, so you can stay even if you get richer. And as some newer HLMs are well built and well sited, they make decent middle-class homes for those who prefer to save their money for other things. I know an *énarque* managing director living in one Paris HLM. And the HLM agencies themselves often prefer to keep their middle-class tenants: they judge them less likely than others to be behind with the rent or charges, or to cause other trouble.

Fewer HLMs are thus available for the poor. They face the further setback that the total sum of state aid has been cut back in recent years, for economy reasons, while the categories eligible for it have been extended beyond families with children, to include students, the elderly and single parents. So the butter is spread more thinly: the average family now receives less *aide à la personne*, and the poorest ones may find it hard to pay the rent, which for a simple HLM could average 2,000 francs a month for a three-room flat, 2,600 for a four-room one, plus some 700 francs for heating and charges. Sometimes the agency has to step in and pay the charges. Agencies are wary of having too many tenants who default, so they set a criterion whereby the rent must not exceed 30 per cent of a family's income. And they demand guarantees. Many very poor people, including the jobless, and the *RMIstes*, are thus excluded from getting an HLM. So they remain with their parents; or they try to squat; or the prefect has somehow to bale them out, maybe paying part of their rent. This help for *les exclus* (see p. 196) is a sizeable part of a *préfecture*'s job these days.

A larger supply of HLMs is badly needed. For one reason, many of the older blocks are now being pulled down. Thrown up hurriedly in the 1950s and '60s, they have often developed leaks or cracks, or are judged too ugly or primitive by today's standards. Or in some cases they have become ghettos for crime, drugs or disease. One notorious fourteen-storey block of 260 flats at St-Denis, near Paris, was dynamited in 1995. It had 31 per cent of immigrants, high youth unemployment, and a rising rate of mental illness, even of tuberculosis – 'But it was like a village, we were all friendly, we shall miss it,' said one Muslim resident. One housing official at the *préfecture* then told me, 'As technocrats, we regret this government policy of pulling down HLMs to avoid ghettos. It would be better to renovate them. In this *département* of Seine-St-Denis we demolish about 200 each year, and we improve up to 7,000 others.' He added, 'But I agree that we are creating not enough cheaper HLMs for today's needs, and too many high-quality ones that fewer people can afford.' All over France, and for all kinds of older housing, the policy today has moved towards rehabilitating where possible, rather than demolishing, especially in city centres. It can help the environment, and is often cheaper. But although many flats are thus upgraded, *de facto* this has tended to reduce the number of very cheap ones, for the old *chambres de bonne* and tiny tenements disappear in the internal renovation. This simply worsens today's major problem: shortage of housing for the really poor.

The tempo of new building has slowed since its peak of 550,000 in 1975. Since the mid-1980s, the total of dwellings completed annually has been running at between 250,000 and 300,000. This decline may seem normal, now that the main needs have been met and urban growth has been falling. But the building industry is in something of a slump, as banks have grown tighter about loans and Governments, too, have become less generous. There is still not enough new housing on the free market at the lower middle range, nor enough HLMs for the truly poor. And yet, how matters have improved since those early post-war days! Some sad cases apart, most French are now decently housed. They no longer tolerate the old overcrowding. In the working classes, a newly wed couple no longer expects to have to remain living with their parents for years before getting a home of their own. With more choice available, some French seek to live in restored flats in city centres, in the Latin tradition; others opt for individual houses amid greenery on the outskirts. Many more live on the new suburban estates. But even these have improved hugely since the first sad high-rise dormitories were built in the crash-programme years. Town-planning in France, like housing, has come a long way.

THE DRAMA OF *LA BANLIEUE*: FROM NEW-TOWN BLUES TO NEW-TOWN 'REDS'. AND NOW, NEW-TOWN BLACKS AND BLACKSHIRTS

In English, 'suburbia' implies cosy comfort, maybe dull, but contented. In French, '*la banlieue*' has today come to evoke something very different – a term for social tensions on the poorer HLM estates, racked by listless delinquency, high jobless rates, frustration, maybe racial conflict. This 1990s stereotype has often been exaggerated by the media, and most *banlieues* are peaceful: yet the problems are real. More than half the urban population lives in these new suburbs, some of them neat and cheerful, others ugly, ill-planned and depressing.

The first were thrown up in the 1950s and '60s, during the worst of the housing shortage; and for years their new residents, often migrants from the farms or urban slums, found it peculiarly hard to adapt to new styles of suburban living. The planners were at first heavily at fault, failing to provide these austere dormitories with social or leisure amenities; and this led to epidemics of 'new-town blues', aggravated by the temperament of the French, wary of new neighbours and community self-help. But the newer suburbs were then better built, and the older ones finally won their needed equipment. Gradually, through time and habit, the new towns have been finding their soul. Some have been groping towards a new community life, under the impulse of worthy pioneers or even of municipal action – as on one HLM estate in Grenoble, where a bid was made to develop a 'utopian' society. But such attempts to create a more lively and caring life can easily fall victim, in France, either to public apathy and family-geared privacy, or else, conversely, to the political extremism of those who see the creation of clubs or even crèches as weapons in the class struggle. Today this is less evident, but other social issues have come to the fore: notably, the malaise of unemployment, fomenting violence between racist French and ethnic youth. To put it crudely, some suburbs have thrown off their new-town blues only to catch a new virus, new-town Reds, and now a third, new-town blackshirts (in conflict with new-town Blacks).

The complex suburban saga speaks volumes about the French character, their society, their attitudes to each other, to authority, to outsiders. We can begin at Sarcelles, largest and most notorious of the earlier HLM estates outside Paris. Most initial post-war housing in France was thrown up piecemeal: but then the policy was launched of the *grands ensembles*, each to be self-sufficient with its own schools, shops, and so on. They were higher-rise than the first new towns in Britain, and less coherently planned. Sarcelles, the archetype, near St-Denis, today housing 40,000 people, was started in 1956: yet for the first fifteen years there was no *lycée* and no proper shopping centre. The criss-cross streets were given such names as Allée Marcel Proust and Avenue Paul Valéry, but there was no poetry in the flat utility façades of their HLM blocks. Sarcelles and other *ensembles* almost as ugly were built in the flurry of the crash housing campaign and little care was given to their architecture. It is true that, for the slum evacuees, Sarcelles was in some ways a paradise of modern plumbing and fresh air. It was granted a fair amount of space, with trees and playgrounds, in contrast to the high density of most of central Paris: but this hardly atoned for the rectilinear concept, the austere gridiron of grey blocks, up to seventeen storeys high. Foreign experts were horrified: one denounced 'the intellectual arrogance and paucity of invention of this loveless, pre-cast concrete desert'. Sarcelles, in fact, sprang from a clumsy attempt to apply some of Le Corbusier's ideas without properly understanding them.

These aesthetic failings were matched by the administrative troubles of the earlier *grands ensembles*. They were entrusted to development bodies, but these were not given adequate funds for matters other than the housing, nor did they have proper powers of coordination as in Britain. They provided roads and basic utilities, but had no means of coercing ministries or state agencies into producing other needed equipment: so the *ensembles* went for years with a grave lack of schools, clinics, post offices, public transport, and the like. This was due to sheer lack of liaison, worsened by inter-ministerial rivalries and parsimony over funds. Nor was much thought given to attracting new employment locally, so the working population had to face lengthy commuting. Moreover, the towns were often 'parachuted' on to the territory of semi-rural communes, without proper consultation, and this led to endless conflicts. At Massy-Antony, south of Paris, the local farmers and traders began systematic opposition to a new suburb, and building could start only when the State made use of its ultimate right to overrule a commune's veto, and sent bulldozers into the cornfields during harvesting. The mayor retaliated by blocking the dossiers of some useful projects that needed his signature, such as a sports centre.

These practical problems were compounded by the French difficulties in adapting their lifestyles. Sarcelles gave its name to a new disease, 'Sarcellitis' (new-town blues), as stories emerged of nervous breakdowns, delinquency and bored housewives resorting to part-time prostitution. Reporters went hurrying in droves to Sarcelles and other places, as the French in the 1960s suddenly woke up to the social problems of modern mass suburbia, and were fascinated and disturbed. The *grands ensembles* were analysed in a stream of books, conferences and sensational articles: the conservative French found the new-town experience more traumatic than the British, and life there was scrutinized as if it were the planet Mars. However, the planners finally learned from their early mistakes. By the 1970s, if a new suburb was built, its amenities arrived sooner, its administration was more coherent and its architecture less grim. At Sarcelles today the newer blocks are not linear but harmoniously grouped, and their façades are less austere. Throughout France, after the horrors of the earlier period, many of the newer estates show quite a pleasing sense of landscaping, detail and design.

In the Pompidou era, the previously ignored British model of large new towns coherently planned and managed was finally accepted: one new town, Cergy-Pontoise, even hired British consultants. There are nine of these *villes nouvelles*, five in the Paris region (see p. 327), others outside Marseille, Lyon, Lille and Rouen; they are all now nearing completion, and compared with Sarcelles they are a big success. They have been criticized for being too ambitious (most have over 100,000 inhabitants): but their scale has made it easier to provide them with full amenities. They are more spacious and less high-rise than Sarcelles or other early *grands ensembles*: yet the buildings are grouped to provide the ambience of a real town, far better than in a too-dispersed new town like Milton Keynes.

Their management system was designed to obviate the feuding and lack of liaison that had bedevilled the *grands ensembles*. Each town was given its own state agency – rather like a New Town Corporation in Britain – to take charge of planning and building, with legal powers to ensure coordination between ministries. The communes were also brought into the process democratically. This being France, it was not politically possible to create a new commune for each *ville nouvelle*; and as each, being so large, straddled several communes, the latter were obliged to form a syndicate to cooperate with the state agency on such matters as new equipment. This complex system provided a balance between technocratic and citizen needs, and in most cases it has worked quite well. The new towns really *did* get their factories, schools and other amenities at the same time as the housing instead of years later. Some even have a new university, and in the Paris region most are served by the RER express Métro. Each town has developed its own visual style. L'Ile-d'Abeau, south-east of Lyon, set along a hillside in the form of a series of villages, is most attractive; so is Évry, south of Paris, with its cheerful multicoloured flats. Here the largest multi-purpose centre in France, the Agora, has three theatres, a skating rink and dance halls, while new factories have opened nearby. Marne-la-Vallée has some striking buildings designed by Ricardo Bofill in his monumental style. The new towns' population tends to be youthful, and unemployment is not too high: while many people find jobs locally, others commute to the nearest big city. One opinion poll found that 88 per cent of people were happy with their new homes and the shops, while some 75 per cent were satisfied with the school and leisure facilities. 'Sarcellitis, like malaria, can be stamped out,' said one jubilant technocrat.

Cergy-Pontoise, north-west of Paris, has taken shape on a spacious site above a loop in the river Oise. The city centre includes some strikingly original public buildings in blue-and-green glass and steel, with one dramatic skyscraper. By the river is a delightful Mediterranean-style marina designed by the architect of Port-Grimaud, near St-Tropez; above, on a hill by the river, lies an elegant white-columned terrace. It is all most impressive. Not only does the town have its own theatres and a new university, but the housing is pleasingly sited over a wide area, with some unusually attractive HLM blocks. Cergy-Pontoise now has some 185,000 inhabitants, including the 40,000 who originally lived in its eleven communes. And some 80,000 jobs now exist locally, thanks to the pre-planned creation of offices and industrial zones. Other inhabitants are *cadres* who work in Paris: they choose to live at Cergy where house prices are relatively low and deep countryside is nearby. With about 1,000 clubs and societies, Cergy today has the feel of a real town. It has its problems, as anywhere: but it shows what French planners can do when they try.

The French took time to adapt to their new surroundings, in these and many other new towns and suburbs. The new-town problem may be common to many countries, but it has been special among the French, with their traditional wariness about making new friends or pooling resources with strangers, or sharing in self-help activities. The new arrivals generally enjoyed their new homes – a little flat with all mod cons where the family could bolt the door and build its nest, a playground outside for *les gosses*. But they were wary of contact with the world outside. In their old villages or slums, for all the discomfort, people were close to friends and shops they had known for years. In a new setting, their instinct was to draw in their horns, and cling to what was familiar: the family cell. Friendly calls by neighbours were even resented, or thought to have some ulterior motive. Of course, within each new suburb there was always a small minority who reacted differently, trying to create little cells of animation. These pioneers, far from drawing in their horns, were inspired by the challenge of turning the concrete deserts into spiritual gardens. Many were educated people, maybe Catholics or Leftists, or social workers. They busily created clubs of all kinds, but their brave efforts seldom found a wide response. This was very much the pattern in Sarcelles in the 1960s.

Then, by the late 1970s, a new style of spontaneous citizen initiative began to spread more widely in France, even in the new towns, where people were now adjusting. It was a period when the French – as today – were turning against public institutions, both state and non-state, and were looking for more informal kinds of community. Many would talk eagerly about a strange new growth industry, *la vie associative*, by which they meant the local life of clubs and other spontaneous associations that the Anglo-Saxon world has long taken for granted. For the French, it was something rather new. Today such associations are for leisure, sport or culture; some are privately created welfare bodies for citizen self-help or aid to the weak; and a few, sometimes politicized, are environmental. The number of *associations* has more than trebled since 1972, and is now put at about 700,000 – as many as in Britain, it is said, though French ones tend to be much more dependent on official support.

What does it all add up to? The French believe there has been a real change. At Orgeval, a big commuter village west of Paris, a middle-class Socialist told me, 'Associations here are booming. They used to be the privilege of the rich, meeting to dispense charity to the poor, but now anyone takes part. We had no sports ground, and neither the State nor the council would give us the money, so some of us grouped together, dug into our own pockets, and now we have various new sports clubs, plus a committee for welcoming new inhabitants. An Englishman like you must find all this very obvious, but in this country it hardly existed before.'

It is in welfare and self-help that the French have found it hardest to adapt to today's more informal needs. In a nation with little tradition of voluntary non-partisan public service, most welfare work had long been institutionalized, provided either by the Church and its *bonnes sœurs*, or else by official bodies in juridical style. And in this *étatiste* land any private initiative is looked on with mistrust unless it gains an official stamp of approval by adhering to the complex legal statutes of the famous 'law of 1901' that governs non-profit-making bodies. This can be inhibiting for anyone wanting to start up anything as simple as a crèche or old folks' club. Yet, with the Church's role in decline, the need for more voluntary work has clearly been growing, especially in the new suburbs. And a new generation of pioneering do-gooders has been spreading: some journalists have written lyrically about 'these new T-shirt missionaries' who spend their free time visiting the old and sick, helping immigrants with their schoolwork in French, preparing street festivals, trying to recreate in the HLM milieux some of the lost warmth of the old village societies. This trend has even grown during the 1990s, as many people out of work find they have not only the leisure but also the emotional need to show solidarity and give themselves a new sense of purpose in life.

And yet, in a confused and varied situation, there is still a long way to go, in terms of citizen self-help. At Cergy, I met a civic employee who knows the United States well: 'In our Maryland twin-town, the associations do their own fundraising and virtually run the community: their role is more active than the town council's. But here, citizens are still not used to helping themselves. When they form an association, it sits on its backside and demands that every franc come from the State and the communes. For our big spring festival, its committee made no effort to raise money from the inhabitants, it expected us to pay, *and* to take the main decisions. The French are still way behind the Americans in this kind of community action.'

Some town councils, in the wake of Grenoble under Hubert Dubedout (see p. 345), have themselves made efforts to encourage *comités de quartier* (neighbourhood associations) as a form of active citizen participation. These now work well in a few towns, mostly Socialist-led, such as Nantes, and they enable citizens to put their case to the *mairie* on local issues. In some other towns, *comités* have arisen spontaneously, often for environmental defence, and some have had success in putting a stop to brash new projects. However, in the years after May '68, so much of French local life became highly politicized that this frequently cast a shadow over disinterested community action. Either the Communist Party, or else groups of far-Left activists, pursued a policy of exploiting local issues, or welfare or cultural activities, for their own political ends. It might even become hard to run an arts club without finding it infiltrated by *gauchistes* wanting to use it as a forum for the overthrow of society.

Today, as ideological Leftism has declined and the PCF has grown milder, so this whole problem has become less acute. But it can still exist, and until about ten years ago, examples of it were everywhere. In Toulouse, with its centre-Right council, the twenty-five *comités de quartier* fell mostly into the hands of left-wingers who would issue tracts denouncing the *mairie*'s schemes: 'Its town plan is tailor-made to swell the speculators' profits while exiling the working class to the far suburbs', etc. The mayor threw the weight of his civic apparatus into fighting back: so community action in the city degenerated into a running political dog fight – and the inhabitants were the losers. In Grenoble it was the Communist Party, ironically, that sabotaged Dubedout's plan to set up ward councils on the model pioneered by Communist-run Bologna! He wanted his *mairie* to delegate some regular responsibilities to the *comités de quartier*, thus bringing democracy closer to the people, *alla bolognese*. But his PCF partners in the *mairie* were aghast at such a departure from 'democratic centralism' and forced him to drop the plan. What better example of the difference in those days between PCF and PCI?

The Communist Party may have a sound record of civic administration in towns it has ruled for some years (see p. 36). But in others, where it was trying to increase its grip, in its heyday it could be ferocious. Sarcelles itself, by the 1970s, was at last feeling like a proper town and had lost much of its new-town blues: but then, behold, the new-town Reds! Its PCF mayor in 1965–83, Henri Canacos, a dour technical worker, was under orders to add Sarcelles to the party's ring of bastions in the Paris Red Belt. But only 32 per cent of voters were Communist, leaving the party uncomfortably dependent on its Socialist partners in the *mairie*. So it set out systematically to take over the town's community life – and the non-Communists, as so often, were too easy-going and divided to stop it. Of the hundred or so associations, the party got control of two-thirds, including most of those for sport and culture. The gymnastics club split in two, like Berlin. And as the council controlled the sports centres, it sometimes denied their use to clubs not of its colour. Many voluntary workers left the town, for without a party card they were victimized. A Protestant pastor managed to run a successful youth and culture centre inside his church, but it was only after the *mairie* had tried every dodge to stop him, including a lawsuit, which it lost. Most Sarcellois showed little taste for these power battles raging around them. The polarization left them feeling uneasy and irritated – until in the 1983 municipal elections the Communists were swept out of power.

There is more than one side to the argument about bringing politics into community action. Many left-wing activists, Communist or other, are of course warm-hearted people who are not just bent on revolution but care about humane causes. Yet too often they confuse ends and means. At Sarcelles I met one young militant who told me he was active in promoting crèches, arts clubs, visits to the sick, and so on. Splendid, I said. 'Yes,' he explained, 'we see these activities as an essential means of arousing the public's awareness of the evils of this capitalist Government, so it can be mobilized for *la lutte des classes*.' I gulped, and replied that I thought a crèche was for helping young mothers, an arts club was for those keen on art, and visiting the sick was a matter of human compassion, not a ploy in a political crusade. My friend saw the two levels of action as equally important and interdependent. But I would argue that the baby goes out with the Marxist bathwater if non-political activity is constantly harnessed for political ends. It creates endless conflict over matters where humane consensus should be possible. But the two visions of society are fundamentally different. By the 1990s it seemed that many ordinary French people had become sickened and revolted by the constant dragging of politics into non-political areas: it was one reason why many of them withdrew into their own circles of privacy, and community activity in all its forms did not win wider support in France. But then, as the 1990s wore on, not only did dogmatic Leftism wane, but the rise of other problems, from jobs to racism and corruption, and much else, made the old Left/Right local dog fights take second place.

Returning to Sarcelles in 1997, I found that it had clearly come of age; it was not beautiful but lively. People were even proud of it, indignant at any talk of 'Sarcellitis'. Gleaming white in the sunlight, the older HLM towers had been pleasantly renovated; the newer ones had coloured façades and balconies. There were avenues with modern sculptures, swimming pools, a synagogue, factories and music schools. Old men were playing boules in the park, as in the Midi. The *mairie* was won back by the Left in 1995, and the Communists were now junior partners in a coalition run by the excellent Socialist mayor Dominique Strauss-Kahn, soon to move on to be Minister of Finance. 'Sarcelles has found its soul,' he told me. 'We're into the second generation, people have put down roots, they feel some loyalty. The geometric grid of streets may not be ideal: but at least the housing, shops and other amenities are mixed together, so it's not just a dormitory – and that's a plus for Le Corbusier's ideas. Our *vie associative* is active. But too much of it is centred on individual ethnic communities: we try to encourage more social mingling, but it's not easy.'

With its vivid cosmopolitanism, much of it Caribbean and Sephardic Jewish, the town has something of a southerly street life; clubs flourish, the old wary isolation has declined. But if Sarcelles has overcome some of its initial problems, it has acquired others, typical of *la banlieue* today. Racial tension is not acute, but there is high unemployment, some delinquency, and rivalry between ethnic groups. These are of every kind. A big colony of Chaldeans has recently settled, Christian refugees from eastern Turkey and Iraq: I found the Église Paul XXIII full of them, dressed in Turkish peasant clothes, chanting hymns, men on one side, women on the other. 'It's terrible,' said one elderly conservative Sarcellois, 'the Reds have seized back the *mairie*, and the Turks have seized the church!'

La banlieue! There are many places today worse than Sarcelles, in terms of poverty, vandalism or discontent. Social deprivation and unrest do exist in some inner-city areas in America, even Britain: but in France, it is the high-rise suburbs that are affected. These are much smaller than the big American ghettos, and their violence is far less. In fact, the media sometimes overdramatizes the issue in France: but it does exist, and has become a focus of public attention, as '*la banlieue*' and '*les quartiers difficiles*' get used as catchwords, as often as '*l'exclusion*'. Riots began in the early 1990s in some Paris outer suburbs, in the poorer parts of Marseille and at Vaulx-en-Velin outside Lyon. In the following years the violence continued sporadically in various towns, then exploded on New Year's Eve 1997 in prosperous well-ordered Strasbourg, where youths went on the rampage, burning over fifty cars and throwing bombs in schools. Yet this model Socialist-led city had been making special efforts for its *banlieues* (see p. 367). In May 1998, after a teenager had been lynched by a gang in one Paris suburb, the tough Interior Minister, Jean-Pierre Chevènement, reflected the views of many on both Right and Left when he told Parliament, 'Such acts are symptoms of a profound crisis . . . Conflicts between rival gangs have their roots in a culture of hatred . . . Our suburbs suffer from ghettoization, and a complete loss of value references.'

The unrest is frequently seen in terms of racial tension, but this is not the prime factor. It is true that young Maghrebis are often involved, and there can be scuffles between them and the police. But there is not much interracial gang warfare of the American kind; and the Front National's vote (see p. 247) is seldom high in these mixed suburbs, where the different ethnic groups may not love each other but rarely fight. Almost all the experts agree that the basic factor is high youth unemployment, which leads to fear, frustration, anger at school failure, compounded often by bad housing, family tensions, or drugs. The persistent petty thieving and vandalism are seldom the work of organized criminals, but simply an expression of this malaise – the broken shop windows, burned cars, endless thefts from cars, often part of the desperate search to get money for drugs. In Toulouse in 1997, I visited the notorious *quartier difficile* of Bellefontaine to talk to a headmaster, who told me that local unemployment was at 40 per cent (see p. 548). I put my Citroën in the school's outdoor staff cark park, and stupidly left my mac and typewriter visible on the back seat. Two hours later, I found the window smashed and they were gone.

Vandalism of this kind, common in many a country, probably worse in Italy, does not quite justify the bad reputation of some *banlieues*. I visited Vaulx-en-Velin, a grim suburb of Lyon with 45,000 people. Its HLM towers looked dour in the November rain, its 1960s concrete *mairie* was hideous: but there was a lively modern theatre, a handsome new planetarium, and the young Blacks in the street shouted at me amiably, 'Hello, Mister!' as they saw my English numberplate. Vaulx in the 1990s has become the prime symbol in France of suburban horror, like Sarcelles in the 1960s, but with the accent this time more on social malaise than bad planning. It was the home town of a famous Algerian 'terrorist', Khaled Kelkal (see p. 233), and in riots in 1990 a commercial centre was burned down and cars destroyed. More recently, it has grown fairly quiet, but its bad name has survived – to the fury of its go-ahead mayor, Maurice Charrier, a former Communist, still full of militant Leftist zeal. He had just received a visit from President Chirac, who had praised his efforts for *les exclus*. 'Chirac may be sincere,' he told me, 'but I hate the way that his Government, and the French as a whole, look down on our *banlieues* as haunts of barbarity and patronize us with their special "aid". In fact, we are haunts of suffering, victims of a cruel capitalist system that kills our jobs. Vaulx is full of creativity, it gives a lot to France, it should not be treated by the media as some horror spot. This simply adds psychologically to our bruising *fracture sociale*. To call Vaulx a "sensitive zone" is downright *in*sensitive.'

Government efforts to help *les banlieues* began under the Socialists in the 1980s and were continued under Balladur. Some 200 local councils were persuaded to sign '*contrats de ville*', whereby they received special state aid for their social policies. Then Chirac promised a '*plan Marshall*' for the *banlieues*, and Juppé followed it up with a scheme creating some 38 '*zones franches*' in the *quartiers difficiles*. They were to be given varied aid for improving equipment and services, creating local jobs, and so on. It was all well meant: but, as with the law on *les exclus*, this mighty Marshall Plan proved a bit of a damp squib. In fact, the flurry of measures since the 1980s seemed to typify the French love of elaborate administrative blueprints as a way of trying to solve human problems. Then the Socialists, back in power, pledged more strenuous efforts. In 1998 their official inquiry found a serious lack of essential services, such as public transport and post offices, in some of the worst-affected *banlieues*, and it urged they be given more help. But would the money be made available? – and the staff? One disturbing revelation is that more than half the police and schoolteachers in the *quartiers difficiles* near Paris have asked to be transferred somewhere else.

There are two aspects of the earlier policies that could prove more permanent. One is cultural – to encourage local creativity by sending professional artists to the *banlieues* (see p. 440). An actor/producer may help young people to write and stage their own play; or a painter may open a local workshop; or a group of girls from an ethnic minority may be helped to form a dance troupe. Directors of the stature of Armand

Gatti (in Sarcelles) have been doing such work. It might seem paternalistic, and it can never do much more than scratch the surface: but, as with sport, it is seen as a way of giving jobless young people some new sense of purpose and self-expression. Another policy, in some Socialist-run towns, is that of trying to develop mixed housing as a way of averting the ghettos that have grown so vast in America. In Montpellier, Nantes and Strasbourg, councils have built some new HLM blocks inside bourgeois residential districts, rather than grouping them on their own. Of course this meets opposition – 'I'm selling out and moving to a village,' said one indignant Strasbourg lawyer – but for the long term it seems a valuable policy.

One famous bid to create a new utopian mixed society was made at Grenoble, back in the 1970s, by its idealistic mayor Hubert Dubedout and his Socialist-led council (see pp. 345–7). These pioneers developed the high-rise HLM district of L'Arlequin as social laboratory: with the help of special architecture, and an army of social workers, they tried to break down the usual barriers of race and class, and to woo the inhabitants into a new kind of caring, integrated community. It was controversial, and it drew from all over France and Europe a stream of sociologists, town-planners, reporters, TV crews, professors and politicians. Today L'Arlequin still stands, with its Maghrebi street-market, its philosophical café, its cheek-by-jowl fraternity and petty vandalism – not quite what its authors intended, but not a total failure.

Seen from outside, this concrete Eden may look monstrous – a phalanx of multicoloured twelve-storey blocks, in neo-brutalist style, housing 7,000 people. But *côté jardin* L'Arlequin is more attractive, beside its park with a backdrop of snowy Alps. Its main physical innovation is a long central walkway or covered arcade, curving gently below the tower blocks, while all traffic is sited outside the area. The high density, in most towns today regarded as a fault, was here chosen deliberately to promote a womb-like feeling of animated human contact, medieval style. The flats, too, of good quality by HLM standards, were conceived to facilitate contact, being built on a deck-access pattern, with passageways. This was intended to help integration, the key word at L'Arlequin – integration of different kinds of people, and of activities normally kept separate. In each block, the flats were of differing prices and categories, to encourage a social mix; special efforts were made to welcome Maghrebi families; and amid the flats the planners placed old people's homes, a student hostel and a foyer for the handicapped. France had lagged behind Anglo-Saxon or Nordic countries in efforts to integrate weaker minorities into the community, so these moves caused a stir. '*A nous les Arabes, à nous les vieillards, à nous les fous,*' wrote one admirer of Dubedout's aims.

In L'Arlequin's early years, in the afterglow of May '68, many idealists flocked to live there, fired by the challenge of building this new Jerusalem, which won the local nickname of 'Chicàgauche', a clever double pun. One priest deserted holy orders to start a shop. Eight city councillors took flats there, followed by many of Grenoble's *cadres*, intellectuals and professional people: one survey in 1977 found that 54 per cent of inhabitants were in this category. And this gave a somewhat artificial hot-house quality to the whole experiment: the élites dominated social life, enjoying their roles of radical chic, while other classes kept a lower profile. Then in the 1980s worse setbacks arose. Dubedout's right-wing successor as mayor, Alain Carignon, was no lover of L'Arlequin and he dismissed most of its army of paid social workers. The 'open' school experiment did at first survive: one major innovation from the start had been that the local state secondary *collège* was integrated into the *maison de quartier* within the main shopping area, and the school's library and canteen were equally for the public, while parents were free to visit classes. This was revolutionary for France, and it caused quite a rumpus in the conservative teaching world. The Education Ministry went along with the experiment for some years, but then suspended it in the 1990s (see p. 548).

Today many of the middle-class pioneers have left, and L'Arlequin is not quite the same. But seven councillors still live there, by choice, and the place remains a little special. In the 1980s it had been allowed to grow tatty, for the HLM agencies said they lacked the funds for new paint or repairs; and it seemed not to occur to the idealistic residents to band together and do this job themselves. On a visit in 1986, I found the concrete walkway shabby with torn posters and graffiti, its op-art colour schemes faded and dismal. But ten years later it had been tidied up, the broken lifts had been replaced, the arcades were bright with new African-style murals. Muslim women were shopping in an outdoor market, beside a new 'philosophical' café holding a debate on tolerance! Two teachers, living in a duplex flat with Alpine views, summed up for me the pros and cons of sharing the Arlequin adventure: 'We belonged to a group of ten couples, all friends, who moved into this block when it first opened. At first it was all "utopian", we even thought of pooling our salaries! But slowly individualism reasserted itself. The more bourgeois couples moved off to little houses with gardens, and today's arrivals tend to come because it's cheap, more than through any idealism. So L'Arlequin has become "normalized". Yet it *is* still different: maybe this architecture helps to bring a sense of togetherness. There's more neighbourliness, more casual dropping in, than in most new suburbs. People are always ready to baby-sit for free, or to lend things. And the old and handicapped are not made to feel left out: they are housed right here beside us. So Dubedout's ideals *have* left their mark. L'Arlequin may be far from a total success: but it's a failure only in the sense that people's hopes for it were pitched absurdly high.'

One of the hopes was for a social integration of the ethnic minorities who today make up some 30 per cent of L'Arlequin's population, most of them Maghrebis. Residents were at first housed pell-mell together: but gradually a tacit apartheid developed as white families moved out of blocks dominated by Muslims. Despite the persistent efforts of social workers and others to help the immigrants, some of the younger ones formed into unruly gangs and much of the hooliganism at L'Arlequin was blamed on them. Today matters have improved a little. There is still some petty vandalism: but the Front National's presence is remarkably weak, and racist incidents are few. Many young Muslims would like to integrate more closely, but are not always easily accepted by other residents. At least, more is done for them officially, by local councillors and others, than in many a French *banlieue* – and this again is a positive legacy of Dubedout. Integration in a multi-ethnic society is a crucial issue in France today.

TROUBLED ETHNIC MINORITIES: THE DILEMMA OF BEING BOTH FRENCH AND ARAB. BUT NOW, '*VIVE ZIDANE!*'

'I am a French citizen, born in France. I'm also an Arab, with a Muslim culture. I have a right to be both, to feel both. But these bloody French constantly make me feel rejected' – a young man of Algerian origin was summing up a common dilemma. Today, so the surveys tell us, some 40 per cent of French admit to being 'very' or 'rather' racist. And there are endless reports of discrimination against non-whites, in jobs or housing, or of rough police treatment, or of counter-violence by frustrated youngsters wounded in their dignity. Yet paradoxically, all the evidence shows that racist feeling is worst in areas where there are *not* so many immigrants: in suburbs where communities mix more closely, the preju- dice is less. Fear and ignorance are thus a big part of the problem. And happily a great many French are not racist: they even make valiant efforts to show solidarity with the minorities.

This at least has been the picture in recent years. In July 1998 an official survey found the French, along with the Belgians, 'the most racist society in Europe'. But then, a week later, it was a multiracial team that won the World Cup for France, with star players who had their origins in Algeria, Senegal, Guadeloupe and elsewhere; they became national heroes, as the French crowds in Paris shouted '*Zidane, Président!*' (he has Algerian roots). And many serious experts were predicting that this could perhaps mark a turning point, bringing the French at last to accept and admire the spurned ethnic minorities. As I write, six months later, it is too soon to tell whether the impact will be lasting. But there is new hope.

It is only in the past twenty or so years that the place of immigrants in post-war society has become a serious problem – due to rising unemployment and other factors. The French used not to be thought of as so colour-conscious, maybe they appear less so than the British. But the recent growing resentment is directed above all at those with darker skins or of non-European cultures. They form the majority of the 3.6 million foreign nationals in France, and of the 4 or so million others of immigrant origin who are now French. Terminology can be invidious, or 'politically incorrect': but in this chapter I shall speak of 'ethnic minorities' or 'ethnic immigrants', terms loosely used to include all those of African, Asian or Caribbean origin, whether or not born in France, and whether or not they are now French citizens. The French tend to describe all such people as '*les immigrés*'.

State policies, though generously intended, do not always make matters easier. The Government pursues a traditional French doctrine of expecting immigrants to integrate fully, once they have become French citizens; it grants them all the same rights and does not encourage multiculturalism on the British model. But this fine policy of equality of citizenship does not work so well in practice, if France's own people fail to accept the immigrants as their equals (see p. 225). And so, as problems have worsened, Governments have swung awkwardly between trying to help immigrants more humanely and seeking to control their numbers more toughly. Many peoples are involved: but much the largest group are the Muslims from the countries of the Maghreb, across the Mediterranean – France's former colony of Algeria, and its former protectorates of Morocco and Tunisia. These Maghrebis are mostly Arab, but many are Berber. While some are middle class and educated, most come from simple backgrounds, and they find themselves parked in grim HLM *banlieues* on the edge of Paris or other cities. People of Algerian origin, many of them now French citizens, number well over a million. Surveys show them to be the least popular of all the ethnic minorities: partly this is a legacy of France's colonization and the war of independence, which is now aggravated by Algeria's own civil war and French horror of Islamic extremism there. Algerians, too, hate that extremism, and many of the younger French-born ones would like nothing more than to integrate into France. In most ways, they feel they belong to it more than to Algeria, an alien land that maybe they have never visited. But as French people will not accept them, they feel stranded between two cultures. Hence, in fury, some of them turn to crime.

Ironically, the French State has a strong and successful history of accepting immigrants of all kinds: in 1930 she had even more foreigners proportionately than the United States. She also enjoys a decent reputation for granting political asylum. White Russian exiles were welcomed after 1917, then Jewish and other fugitives from Nazism, then countless post-war refugees from Communism, including 5,000 'boat people' from Vietnam. Others came escaping dictatorships of the Right in Latin America. But while Governments have followed this human rights policy, most French as individuals used to be wary, until quite recently, of accepting even other Europeans as fully part of their society. Before the Second World War, xenophobia was common: the many Poles, Italians and Portuguese who had settled in France, looking for work, were treated with suspicion, even hostility. But this has changed: Europeans, with some exceptions, are now easily accepted and can integrate as fully as they wish (see p. 692). Instead, the feeling has increased against Maghrebis, black Africans and Caribbeans. As one French liberal put it to me, 'Generalized xenophobia has narrowed to racism – are we to call that progress?'

These ethnic minorities were relatively well tolerated until about the 1970s. They arrived in large numbers during the boom years of fast expansion, and were appreciated for the extra cheap labour they brought.

Even during the colonial war in Algeria, there was relatively little trouble. Most of the Maghrebis were single men, living together in hostels or shanties, working hard at drab jobs, sending money home to their families. But then came two changes. First, when the immigrants realized that for economic reasons they would not be returning to their homelands, many decided to bring their families to join them. So they moved into HLMs or slum areas alongside the French, and thus the social problems began. Secondly, when unemployment began to rise, many French felt that the immigrants were taking their jobs, and resentment grew. This remains the basis of the problem today, and it has helped the Front National.

Many French are fearful that immigrant numbers have been growing fast: but in fact this is not true. The total has remained roughly stable for the past twenty-five years, ever since the Giscard Government put severe curbs on new non-EEC immigrant labour in 1974. The total of foreign nationals living in France rose merely from 3.4 million in 1975 to 3.6 million in the last census of 1990, and will have altered little since then. The total of immigrants, i.e. those born abroad as foreigners, is also fairly static, at 4.2 million. Of course there has been the usual population flow of births, deaths and new arrivals. Furthermore, about 100,000 people each year obtain French nationality. Of the foreign nationals, Portuguese (649,000), Algerians (614,000), Moroccans (572,000), Italians (252,000), Spanish (216,000) Tunisians (206,000) and Turks (197,000) were the main groups in 1990. The number of Europeans in the total has fallen since 1975 from 61 to 41 per cent, while other nationalities have increased, notably Turks and West Africans. In addition, about 5 million other people are the children of immigrants but French citizens. Many of these, the Poles and others, have merged into the landscape: but the Maghrebis and other ethnic minorities still stand out, often for reasons of culture and religion, as well as obvious visibility. They are still perceived by many ordinary French as being 'different' and not fully French; and on average they have more children than the Europeans. Today, of the people of Maghrebi origin in France, those who are French citizens may have fuller rights and better job security than those still foreigners: but the racist feelings against them, and their general sense of insecurity and resentment, can be as great.

Many organizations try to combat racism, and they do good work in supporting the ethnic populations. The well-educated young French, too, are more tolerant than their elders: some have joined the nationwide 'SOS Racisme' campaign that seeks to promote solidarity with young

Blacks and Beurs – as young Arabs are known in their own slang; and in 1995 they flocked to see the film *La Haine* see p. 481), which celebrated interracial friendship in a Paris suburb. Racial violence is well below American levels. In fact, in some *banlieues* such as Grenoble's L'Arlequin, tensions are relatively slight whenever the different communities live closely together; as I have suggested, racist bigotry tends to be strongest in areas such as rural Alsace, where there are few immigrants yet the Front National vote is high. All analyses bear this out (see below).

However, several towns have seen occasional race riots or other violence, much reported in the media. For example, in 1998 three Front National supporters were jailed for murdering a Muslim teenager in Marseille; one of them got fifteen years. 'Racism has been getting worse,' I was told by a woman social worker of Berber origin, in the Marseille slums: 'my brother was murdered by a Frenchman. I can tell you, it's not easy in France today to be Maghrebi, French and a woman.' And in Lyon, the wife of a senior professor did not hide to me her scorn for Africans of all sorts – '*ces abrutis*' ('stupid clots'). She could hardly believe it when I spoke of the civilized Togolese and Tunisian girls I had just met at a local *lycée*. Many French complain of the immigrants' role in crime and drug-trafficking, and of their alien customs in the HLMs. All in all, in a disparate situation, Maghrebis today have a much harder time than their equivalents in Britain – harder, too, than the Turks in former West Germany.

Racist insults, and discrimination in such matters as jobs or housing, are illegal under a law of 1972. Thus a café or dance-hall owner who refuses entry to an Arab, as often happens, could be prosecuted. But generally proof is difficult; and though several cases are brought to court each year, few lead to convictions. In 1996, after a spate of racist utterances by Le Pen and his friends, the Ministry of Justice prepared a law to strengthen the vague rules against 'inciting racial hatred': but the project was then dropped under opposition from pro-government deputies who, as so often, feared losing votes to the Front National.

Discrimination over jobs is frequent, whether the immigrant has French citizenship or not. An employer may in private plead, 'Yes, I'd be glad to take on immigrants myself, but, you see, the rest of my staff wouldn't like it' – and so those with darker faces get left out, or if they write in for a job, their names give them away. Compared with the French average of 12 per cent, unemployment is over 30 per cent among Maghrebis; in the 15–24 age bracket, it is around 50 cent, against the

French average of 23 per cent. And of course the frustration can fuel violence. Many immigrants with low skills take casual jobs on building sites, or the women work as cleaners, at hourly rates well below the SMIC. It used to be said that immigrants were welcomed for doing the most menial tasks that the French would not do: but this is less true now that many French are desperate to find work of any kind. And yet, immigrants who do get steady jobs are generally well accepted and their efficient hard work is appreciated. At professional levels, say among doctors, lawyers or media people, the discrimination drops sharply, and it hardly exists among university students. In fact, experts often claim that the whole problem is more one of social class than of race.

Discrimination by the police is the worst. *Les flics* can still be quite often heavy-handed, and many are openly racist in outlook. Recent Governments, mainly Socialist, have several times issued orders for them to be gentler in their check-ups: but this has seldom had effect for very long. Since a large part of the petty crime and drug-peddling does involve ethnic minorities, and likewise the illegal immigration, so the police simply find it easier to select the darker faces when they make their repeated random check-ups of suspects: 'I'm pissed off with being end-lessly picked on, when I go out,' said one Beur student. Police can be gratuitously rude, even violent, beyond the bounds of what is legal – or so many Maghrebis feel. It is a worse problem than in Britain. In some *banlieues*, a state of semi-war rages between the two sides, as Maghrebi fury leads to more vandalism, and so to more police repression – a vicious circle. Added to this, ethnic minorities can face gratuitous rudeness from petty officials in public offices.

There is some discrimination over housing, too. After 1975 the Giscard and Mitterrand Governments organized special funding for immigrants' housing; and this enabled many to be settled adequately in HLM blocks. But the scheme was then dropped. And today, among those who find it hard to get an HLM as they lack a regular job or secure income, a high proportion are immigrants. Many town councils and HLM agencies try to be helpful: but there are cases of mayors, even on the Left, practising political discrimination. At one town near Versailles, the PCF mayor found means of preventing Maghrebis from taking HLMs, since very few vote Communist and he did not want them in his commune. But far more widespread than this is the *de facto* discrimination practised by white residents of HLMs, who will try to move out of a block if it becomes too full of immigrants. This has tended sometimes to create

Maghrebi or black ghettos, which the official French policy of integration expressly seeks to avoid. Rightly or wrongly, the whites allege that immigrants cause damage, such as broken lifts; or they complain about untidiness, rowdy kids, cooking smells, alien customs. And if the local school fills up with dark faces, some families will try to move elsewhere. The French often speak of their fear of a growing tide of immigrant children. In truth, the average birth rate among Maghrebi and black parents in France has fallen by some 30 per cent since 1980, but it is still nearly twice the native French level. All in all, while immigrant numbers have in reality risen little in this period, the prejudices have worsened, or at least they have polarized. According to some surveys, about three-quarters of French – five times as many as vote for Le Pen – fear that immigrants pose 'a threat to national identity'. But another survey in 1998 found that a growing majority of French are opposed to discrimination against legal immigrants in jobs, welfare or housing. In other words, while a large minority of French are openly racist, the majority want immigrant numbers restricted but feel that individuals legally resident in France should be treated fairly.

The State promotes an integration which the public then obstructs; the public stresses cultural differences which the State refuses to recognize. That, in a word, is the basic dilemma of immigration today in a France that officially does not accept multiculturalism or ethnic communities. On the one hand the State regards all citizens as equal, with the same full rights, and turns a blind eye to any distinctions between them of race or culture. But the French public, in its mass, does *not* regard immigrants as fully or equally French, and will constantly remind them of their otherness. The State expects those who become French citizens to integrate fully, and many immigrants would themselves like this: but the French people make it hard. Conversely, many immigrants would like to retain something of their own culture and identity: but the French State in turn makes this hard. It is a terrible paradox. A Breton, for example, is easily accepted as Breton yet also fully French: but the many Beurs who see themselves as French Arabs, and would like to be respected as such, find it much more difficult. Although they may hate the American model, they sometimes envy its acceptance of diversity. The dilemma is mainly for those who become French citizens: but even those who do not seek French nationality can suffer, if they want to feel at home in France yet remain 'ethnic'. For some years, a debate has been raging on these issues. Some politicians and others plead for more open recognition of multiculturalism: but they are still a minority.

The official French doctrine, derived from the ideals of the Revolution, then of the *état laïque*, is that since all citizens are equal in rights, so their racial origins, or their culture or religion, are purely a private matter. From this it follows, first, that official research and statistics about origins are not allowed: you cannot, for instance, find out how many French are of Moroccan extraction, or indeed Polish, and in an individual's official records, such details are expunged when he is naturalized. Secondly, and more to the point, it follows that although ethnic cultural associations are tolerated, ethnic communities are not encouraged as in Britain, nor can their representatives enjoy any public status. One noble aim may be to ensure that all citizens have equal benefits from being French, and equal protection. But there are other motives, too. One has always been to ensure the unity of the French State, by limiting the dangerous threat of competing loyalties. Another, a hangover from the colonial period, is a belief in the innate superiority of French culture and its *mission civilisatrice*. This is no longer part of official doctrine: but it lingers, for instance, in the attitudes of some teachers in face of a class of immigrant children whom they seek to 'civilize'.

The so-called '*modèle anglo-saxon*' is firmly rejected. But frequently it is misunderstood by those who do not realize how different the British and American 'models' are from each other. There is an understandable horror of the American ghettos, with their violence and their lack of protection for the very poor. The British model may not be ideal, but to me it seems a viable middle way between the others: communities do not swell into vast ghettos, but they and their leaders are recognized, and this can help the ethnic minorities to feel more secure while also sharing in British life. At all events, Maghrebis who know both countries generally say that ethnic minorities get a better deal in Britain, where they are treated with *le fair play*, that great British virtue. But French officials claim that the community system could not work in France: it would breed endless conflicts, and go against the republican tradition of equality.

'I spent a while in Britain, where it was all much easier,' said a young worker I met on an HLM estate in Montpellier. 'I'm a French national, born here of Moroccan parents, and I feel totally bicultural. I speak French at my job, Arabic with my family, where we keep our Moroccan festivals and customs. I'd like to walk proudly as a French Arab, but it's not so simple. Most French round here just can't accept that you can be a Frenchman in France with a non-French culture. And on the opposite side are the awful pressures of Islamic integrism, making it harder to create an easy multicultural climate.' He put his finger on one controversial point – the difficulty of the French in coming to terms with a religion that to many of them seems so alien and intolerant.

Hitherto the policy of integration may have had many strengths. Education in state schools has been a powerful force, helping the second generation of immigrants to adapt to French norms. And many liberal politicians see legal civic integration as an essential protection for immigrants in face of French racism. But could this now have become counter-productive? In the past, when most newcomers were other Europeans, integration helped to break down the prejudices, to the point where second-generation Portuguese, for instance, now feel fully French and easily accepted in France, yet can keep their national culture if they wish. But today most immigrants are from further away, and from cultures more alien. In an ideal world, it could be that one day they will be fully accepted, as Europeans now are. But many French experts today argue that this will not happen, and that therefore the whole concept of integration must be modified. In a word, the French State should openly accept multiculturalism, and stop pretending that it does not exist.

Mitterrand himself in 1981 spoke of '*le droit à la différence*', and his new Government removed legal restrictions on foreigners' rights of association: immigrants can now, for instance, form a local sports club or charity on an ethnic basis, if they wish. But since then, under pressure from the Right and from public opinion, it has politically not seemed possible to move further towards concrete multiculturalism. All recent opinion polls indicate that three French in four think immigrants should adapt to French cultural norms rather than keep their original traditions. And the debate cuts across party lines. Even many on the Left defend the republican status quo – for instance, on the issue of Muslim girls wearing headscarves in state schools (see below). The Haut Conseil à l'Intégration, a venerable body of sages created in 1990 by Michel Rocard partly to fight racism, warned in 1997 of the growing dangers of *communautarisation*, implying that integration remained the best shield against a drift towards the dreaded American model. It is a fundamental debate: is full integration, or multiculturalism, the best weapon against racism and the ideas of the Front National? – or can some balance be found, whereby immigrants can keep the warmth of their own cultures and communities, while also being fully French? Recent Governments,

notably Socialist, have in practice been moving towards greater acceptance of cultural diversity, but without daring to say so, and thus with no
clear policy. It is a muddled and fluid situation.

The State does give some funding to the ethnic associations; it also
pays for some children of immigrants to have school classes in their own
languages. A few town councils, too, encourage minorities to keep up
their own culture: at Hérouville, near Caen, I found the Socialist-led
mairie holding an annual *fête des communautés*, with singing, dancing and
theatre. And in Paris the many concerts by ethnic singers or musicians
are popular. But in practice, in daily life, a great many ordinary immigrants
simply forget their original culture, or are reticent about displaying it
openly. The North African Muslims have no public tradition of joyous
festivals: their very private culture is related to prayer, the mosque and
the family foyer; and apart from raï music, pastry shops and couscous
restaurants (mostly run by *pieds-noirs*),★ little of it appears outwardly.

Blacks, from West Africa or the French Caribbean, are generally more
exuberant and extrovert. They have borrowed rap music from America
and reinvented it in their own style: some have even become major
French pop stars (see p. 454), with their often serious and angry songs
about *la banlieue*, thus making a big contribution to the popular music
scene in France today. Yet it would be hard to imagine French *Noirs*
mounting in Paris any equivalent of the Notting Hill Carnival, even on
a lesser scale. It would not be accepted, certainly not in a city so firmly
led by the Right. Juppé's Minister for Integration, Éric Raoult, told me,
'What shocks the French is people wearing ethnic clothes like djellabas
or African *boubous* [long tunics]. We are a jacket-and-tie nation, and
immigrants must adapt. No, we don't want your Birmingham-style
"rainbow" communities here, thank you!' I gulped. It was a revealing
insight into the creed of integration.

One aspect of it is that immigrants' representatives cannot have the
same status as in Britain. The associations can elect their own leaders or
officials, but the Government does not recognize them formally, nor
negotiate with them. This is all part of the policy of republican unity:
but it can leave ethnic groups feeling a little isolated. Informally,
the picture is different, and there is nothing to prevent a mayor or
other politician from consulting immigrant bodies: some towns, mostly

★ When the first settlers arrived in Algeria in the nineteenth century, the barefoot
Muslims called them after their black shoes, and the nickname stuck.

Socialist-led, have set up advisory councils of immigrants, drawn from the associations. They can discuss housing, jobs, culture or other matters. But these local efforts to encourage informal representatives have not made wide progress, and often it seems due to many immigrants' own reticence to come forward: Europeans or Asians will do so, but the Maghrebis with their different traditions are more reserved. In some towns, political parties, again usually Socialist, have taken individual citizens of ethnic origin on to their election lists, so that a few are now civic councillors: in Sarcelles there are five, three of them Maghrebis. In all elections, minority groups have the right to put up their own election lists on that basis, if they wish: sometimes they do so, but they never score many votes.

There is nothing in theory to prevent an immigrant, if a French citizen, from rising to a high post in any field. Not many yet do: but the pattern has been improving. A growing number are now doctors, lawyers, professors, actors, even senior civil servants: a few *énarques* are now of Maghrebi origin, unthinkable twenty years ago. And athletes who won gold medals in the 1996 Olympics included a Beur, a girl from Guadeloupe, and others. But in sectors where public opinion is involved, the picture is less bright. Few ethnic immigrants are in key visible positions in the media – when will France have its Trevor McDonald? And very few have yet become notable politicians, save for those representing France's overseas *départements*. A Togolese-born Catholic, Kofi Yamgnane, very Frenchified, was appointed Minister for Integration by Édith Cresson, and he is also mayor of a Breton village: but this is quite exceptional: never has an ethnic immigrant been mayor of a town. This tacit discrimination may partly explain why the voting turn-out at elections, local or national, is so low among citizens of ethnic origin, Beurs especially, and above all in the *banlieues*. 'They feel that it doesn't concern them, they're outside the system,' I was told; 'they don't even bother to put their names on the electoral register.' But it can be a vicious circle, adding to the sense of isolation in the *banlieues* – for example, at notorious Montfermeil, a small town I visited just east of Paris.

Staring out from the back of London buses in recent years has been the forlorn childish face of Hugo's heroine, Cosette, who lived at Montfermeil with her cruel foster-parents. Today's *misérables* are almost as badly off – those 2,000 immigrants, mostly Maghrebis, who inhabit the horrific HLM ghetto of Les Bosquets, in one corner of this neat *petit bourgeois* town. The hard-Right municipality, part RPR, part Front

National, sees Les Bosquets as a thorn in its flesh, and does as little as possible to help it. Its population, all the poorest kind of immigrant, was once dumped in this grim sanctuary, whose high-rise 1950s tenement blocks are shabby and neglected. Repeated vandalism has caused its post office and some shops to close; the mayor, Pierre Bernard, even tried to exclude immigrant children from local primary schools, and was fined for racial discrimination. The State has sent in social workers and I talked to some, including a young Moroccan woman, who was also an anthropologist. I asked her, 'These unfortunate people, mostly without jobs – who do they have to represent them?' 'No one. Hardly any of them vote. They feel lost. We and the teachers alone try to help them.' Yet she went on to defend the French model of integration: 'If they had their own community leaders, it could lead to conflicts, and dangerous pockets of opposition.' So I spoke up for the British community model, arguing that if immigrants were better encouraged to organize their own lives in their own way, then, whatever the risks, it could provide them with more sense of identity and security, and it might reduce delinquency. My friend agreed that I had a point. But Les Bosquets is not entirely typical. In some other *banlieues*, a few younger immigrants are now doing more to create their own activities.

French pressures to integrate can be in conflict with Muslim family structures, or with the special position of women in Islam. Nothing has spotlighted this more sharply than the running crisis over the wearing of headscarves in schools: is the French system a bright gateway towards female emancipation, or an unwarranted intrusion into Islamic custom? The debate has been endless. Under a French law which dates from the anticlerical movement of the nineteenth century, religious proselytism is forbidden in state schools, though symbols such as the crucifix or yarmulka are allowed if worn discreetly. The general aim, a worthy one, has been to keep schools free of religious disputes. The headscarf was also tolerated, and was worn by some Muslim girls – and this caused no problem until the 1980s, when the rise of Islamic extremism led some teachers to take fright, and to fear that girls were being 'manipulated'. One headmaster near Paris took matters into his own hands in 1989, claiming that the scarf *was* proselytic: he expelled three girls, and some other schools followed suit. The Minister of Education, Lionel Jospin, backed by Mitterrand, then ruled in favour of tolerance, and the scarf was more or less accepted again. But a great debate had opened within the Left, and many teachers openly called for a ban. In a sense it was a clash between French law and Koranic teaching on female dress: but neither was very explicit.

The affair died down, only to re-emerge in 1994 when the new centre-Right Education Minister, François Bayrou, took a tougher line, decreeing that 'ostentatious' symbols should be banned, and implying that he meant the scarf, not the crucifix or yarmulka. As a result, over eighty girls were expelled. But the Conseil d'État then came up with a milder ruling, that the wearing of the scarf 'need not necessarily be considered an act of proselytism', whereupon tribunals reinstated some girls. And this, broadly, remains the situation today – confusing, almost absurd, and still unresolved. In order to forbid the scarf, a headteacher should be able to prove that it is being worn provocatively. Otherwise, schools must allow it: but few girls do in fact wear it.

Mostly though, the pressure from Muslim families has been fairly limited, and the whole conflict has been not so much between France and Islam as between two opposing French viewpoints: while the Right is against scarves, the Left and radicals are split down the middle. Some argue the multicultural case, saying it is insensitive of the ministry to ban a simple ethnic custom, and that to do so could only strengthen the hand of integrists. Others retort that French education has a solemn duty to help emancipate Muslim girls – and many teachers feel this strongly ('We must rescue them from the slavery of Islam,' one told me). It is true that many girls wear the scarf only under pressure from their parents, or from some imams, while the vast majority of Muslim families have understood French *laïcité* and do not insist: probably fewer than 10,000 girls have been involved, among the 350,000 in state schools, and according to one poll only 22 per cent of Muslims favour scarves being worn in class. So, although a few families are militant, the issue is not really widespread. Yet it illustrates clearly the French dilemma over integration: if ethnic minorities are to be encouraged to keep their cultures, does this include aspects of those cultures abhorrent to Western values, such as the subservient position of women in Islam? It is a debate fiercer in France than in some countries such as Britain, where scarves are easily allowed.

Other problems have been over Muslim girls taking part in sport. The stricter families will not let their daughters go to the *piscine* or the gym, or on school excursions where they might get mixed up with boys, or attend biology classes that include sex education. But these pressures have been waning, and at Les Bosquets I was told that most Muslim girls do now use the *piscine*. In general, influenced by their French context, more and more members of the younger generation of *Maghrebines* have been standing up against the old traditions: they refuse arranged marriages, for example, or they insist on taking jobs when they leave school. But according to sociologists the rise in unemployment has produced a setback to this process of emancipation, as more girls now choose to remain within the security of their family or accept early marriages. And the forces of Islamic tradition can still be strong among adult women: some are prevented from attending literacy classes by husbands who expect them to stay inside the home.

For Muslim boys, it is all very different. Some are macho, finding it hard to accept the authority of a woman teacher; and those with a difficult home background can be unruly in class. While many immigrant pupils are keen to pass their exams and compete on the French market, some others reject the school system and its hard work. I met teachers from a town near Lille who spoke of repeated fisticuffs, even scuffles with knives, between rival Maghrebi gangs, or between Maghrebis and Blacks or Europeans (the Asians usually stay quiet). It is today's growing problem of violence in schools, not due just to immigrants, that the Ministry of Education has been trying to fight (see p. 548).

A gulf has been growing between these young Muslims and their parents' generation, in a culture where family solidarity has hitherto been so strong. Maghrebi relatives cling tight together and will succour those in trouble: hence there are few homeless drop-outs among the many destitute out-of-work Muslims, for mostly they are sheltered by family. But this model could be in danger. Young Maghrebis generally speak French among themselves and have little Arabic: yet their parents often talk Arabic at home and keep some Muslim culture. So the young tend to reject their elders with their alien set of values: it is a sharp generation gap, and I met one Maghrebi teacher who bitterly criticized the French integrationist model of education for 'destroying Muslim families, setting children against parents'. Yet the young feel rejected in turn by French society, and adrift between two cultures – it is the hub of the immigration drama. After their schooldays, while some turn to vandalism as a blind revenge, some others have been moving back towards Islam, not so much for religious reasons as to find an identity. Just a few even move to Islamic terrorism.

The best-known case is that of Khaled Kelkal, Algerian-born, from the Lyon area, who was shot dead by the police in October 1995, on suspicion of involvement in the Paris bomb outrages. In an interview given earlier, he had spoken of his life of anguish – of his schooling at a *lycée* where he 'never felt comfortable'; of the 'huge wall' that separated Lyon from the *banlieue* of Vaulx-en-Velin where he grew up; of his failure later to find a job. On a 'trumped-up' charge he was sent to prison, where he turned back to the Islam of his boyhood. Whether he had really been a terrorist can never be known. But he became a martyr in the eyes of much of the Muslim population of the Vaulx-en-Velin area, where for a while there was a backlash against French values: Beurs gave up the pursuit of an integration which many had wanted, and turned back towards their parents' religion. As one observer wrote, 'The racist gulf that pushes some young whites towards Le Pen pushes young Muslims to Islam.' But this has to be seen in perspective. Just as only a handful become terrorists, so very few really embrace the harsh dogmas of fundamentalism. They move to Islam for comfort, or in a spirit of revenge against a France that has deeply wounded their dignity.

In reality, how strong is Islam in France? Many French regard it with extreme distaste, and some fear it as a political threat, when bombs go off in the Métro. But in fact the fundamentalist movement in France is small, probably accounting for only 1 or 2 per cent of imams and their faithful: the imam recently deported for declaring, 'Allah's law takes precedence over French law', was quite untypical. And Islam as a whole is weakly organized and split into rival groups. It lacks a clear hierarchy, which makes it harder for the French authorities to consult with Muslim leaders, even when they want to. 'The imams here keep such a low profile,' said the mayor of Vaulx-en-Velin; 'I do not know who they really are, nor what they represent.' And in 1990, when Pierre Joxe, Interior Minister under Mitterrand, urged Islamic organizations to set up a consultative council (as exists for Jews and Protestants) which could advise the Government, he was thwarted by the disputes between the rival bodies. Nor is religious belief a very strong force among France's 3 million Muslims. The older ones may still practise their faith, and families will observe the rituals of Ramadan: but few younger ones have any powerful sense of devotion. Their loyalty to Islam is more for reasons of racial solidarity in face of French xenophobia: some Beurs call themselves 'Muslim atheists'. Perhaps more might be drawn to keep up their faith if France had a better array of mosques. Until recently these were few and hidden away: many were just a room in a building. But more proper ones are now being built, and some mayors are even giving help to Muslims for this.

Attitudes to countries of origin are also ambiguous. Algerians now suffer the spectacle of a second major conflict in their homeland within fifty years; and today's civil war has sometimes spilled over into France itself, though more in the form of individual terrorist attacks than of battles between the two sides. In 1994 terrorists tried to hijack an Air France plane in Marseille; then in 1995 a bomb in an RER underground train in Paris killed seven people – one of a wave of attacks.* These were generally thought to be the work of Islamic extremists: but there is evidence that they may in fact have been planted by Algerian government secret agents in a bid to stir up French opinion against the extremist cause. In the same period, several French Catholic priests, monks and nuns were murdered inside Algeria. All these events, plus the many massacres in Algeria, not only horrified the French; they also deeply disturbed Muslims in France, and contributed to the malaise in the *banlieues*.

The earlier waves of post-war immigrants expected their stay to be temporary. But Maghrebis have since come to accept that they are unlikely ever to return to live in their homelands. Few could find work there; and the younger ones brought up in France would feel out of place, above all in today's Algeria. Yet those who remember North Africa retain a certain nostalgia for it. They like to watch Arab TV, generally Egyptian: so on the roof of many an HLM block you can see their satellite dishes turned towards Cairo, as for prayer they turn to Mecca. Many of those born in the Maghreb keep *de facto* dual nationality, with a certain pride. The saddest case is that of the *harkis*, the Algerians who fought alongside the French army in the earlier war, and then had to escape to France. They have since been shunned as traitors by many fellow Algerians. With their descendants, they number maybe 500,000, and the Government has given them some special aid.

Other races, too, are caught up in France's dramas of immigration. The Maghrebis, being the largest group, may attract the most attention. But

---

* In May 1998, just before the World Cup, France arrested 53 suspected Islamic militants, and her neighbours held 27 others as a precaution against possible terrorist attacks.

Turks, West Africans and others have roughly similar problems. In many suburbs, scores of different nationalities coexist: they tend to keep to their separate groups, and though there are clashes between rival teenage gangs, these are less common than in some countries. The Turks number some 200,000: many have arrived fairly recently, via Germany, and have settled above all in eastern France. Most are from the poorer Anatolian regions. They suffer from some of the same anti-Muslim prejudices as the Maghrebis; and, coming from a country outside French influence, they tend to speak little French and have found integration quite hard. Kurds have arrived too, from Turkey and Iraq. At first they were greeted with some sympathy for their struggle against those severe regimes: but when it emerged that many were armed PKK rebels, eager to fight the Turks in France, support waned. A third group from that part of the world are the Chaldeans, Christian and entirely peaceful, who have settled above all in Sarcelles and are well accepted. As for peoples from further east, Indians are few in France and not very well known; the Chinese and Vietnamese are more numerous. They have generally been welcomed as refugees from Communism. They retain something of their own cultures, and they keep to their own social circles: yet they readily obtain French citizenship, and economically they are well integrated. Like Chinese everywhere, many of them successfully run their own small firms, shops and restaurants; and their children tend to be model pupils, bright, disciplined and hard-working. Their success seems to indicate that a positive balance between integration and ethnic vitality is entirely feasible.

Blacks, too, have often been better accepted than Maghrebis – but even they have today found life getting harder. Of the 600,000 or so Blacks living in France, 40 per cent are from the former French colonies in West Africa; almost all the rest, some 350,000, are from the so-called DOM-TOMs (*départements d'outre-mer, territoires d'outre-mer*). The TOMs, such as Tahiti, are mainly in Polynesia. The DOMs are the four overseas *départements* of La Réunion (in the Indian Ocean), and Guadeloupe, Martinique and French Guyana (all in the Caribbean): they are 100 per cent part of France, as much as the Seine-et-Marne, and their people (*les Antillais*) are French citizens, able to come to *la métropole* as they please, and making up most of its DOM-TOM population. It has been an entirely opposite colonial solution to the British one of granting independence to Caribbean islands. And mostly it is liked by the inhabitants who, with their French welfare services, enjoy better living standards than their Anglophone neighbours. On my visit, I was intrigued to see *mairies* precisely like any in France, with the same notices posted up outside. And to meet groups of Caribbean schoolkids gaily singing 'Sur le pont d'Avignon', which most of them will never see.

Those who do come to live in France have generally been well liked. Many are middle class, and with their French education they often get jobs in the civil service. The French have tended to find them more lively and friendly than Maghrebis, and their treatment of women so different; *antillaise* ladies are often active in social and leisure centres. And yet, today, even the Antillais have not escaped the whiplash of French prejudice. 'My father and grandfather fought for France in two wars, but this is now forgotten,' said one, bitterly. It was Harlem Désir, student son of a Martiniquais, who in 1984 founded SOS Racisme, the movement that rallied so many young French people to fight the racist cancer. He wrote, 'We have forced a part of French society to look at what it really is: sick from old age and fear . . . This kind of racism is the expression of a retreat, a reflex of fear in face of others and of a style of living . . . that is different.'

Brave words, and his campaign has been of value. Yet it has not stopped prejudice from spreading, against not only the *Antillais* but even more the black Africans: their numbers in France swelled from 82,000 to 240,000 between 1975 and 1990, and most are not French citizens. They are feared for their high birth rate, almost three times the French level. And they present two other social problems. One is polygamy: while this is sharply on the wane in the Maghreb, among Muslims in Senegal and Mali it is still common, and the French Government does permit those nationals to live polygamously in France. There are several thousand such families. Secondly, though circumcision of young girls is strictly illegal in France, it is still widely practised by African parents. They are sometimes prosecuted, but will plead that it is an essential part of their culture (an uncircumcized girl, in some parts of Africa, may find it hard to get a husband). So this cruel practice remains one sharp symbol of the moral conflict between integration and multiculturalism.

French official policies over immigration have fluctuated ever since the mid-1970s. It used not to be a great political issue, but has now become one of the major recurrent themes of parliamentary debates and government blueprints. In a word, the Socialists have put the stress on humane measures to help families, while the centre-Right, fearful of losing votes to the Front National, has repeatedly tried to clamp down. But the pattern is really more complex. Even the Socialists have taken some tough steps against illegal entrants.

Giscard's Government, in 1974–5, was the first to take serious action, as unemployment began to rise fast. Like others in Western Europe, it put a virtual ban on new non-EEC immigrant labour. And it offered bribes of 10,000 francs to any foreign workers agreeing to go home: but this met with little success. The Socialists, with their anti-racist ideals, then set about applying a more humane policy. They instructed the police to use gentler methods in their regular checks on suspects. And they offered an amnesty to illegal immigrants: some 130,000 responded. But even Mitterrand felt obliged to limit his generosity, as the worsening job situation fuelled popular resentment, and more clandestine immigrants flocked in, many from countries such as Iran. Some 12,000 illegal entrants were expelled in 1984 alone, and new discriminatory checks were imposed at frontiers: thus, for example, visitors from Britain on no-passport day excursions found that Blacks and Asians were sometimes turned back, while whites went through. This was partly a bid to control terrorism: but it left a sour taste, and did nothing for the Socialists' image abroad. In some other respects, however, they did manage to fulfil their election pledge to make daily life a little easier for legal immigrants: *inter alia*, these were granted full welfare rights, and it was made simpler for their families to join them. Overall, the Socialists' record in office was very positive. But they lacked the political courage to be more liberal.

When the Right returned to power in 1993, with unemployment and the FN vote both still rising, Balladur felt that stronger measures were needed. He gave the job of Interior Minister to Charles Pasqua, a tough nationalist and son of a Corsican policeman. Calling for 'zero illegal immigration', Pasqua was the driving force behind a package of laws that came to bear his name, though some were prepared by other ministries. He imposed tougher police checks, he stepped up the fight against illegal immigrants, and he put new restrictions on visas, residence permits and family regroupings. These measures horrified the radical Left, but they seemed to please most voters, and in terms of numbers they had some short-term effect: the total of visas issued to Algerians fell from 380,000 in 1992 to 40,000 by 1996. At the same time the Minister of Justice, Pierre Méhaignerie, a mild *centriste*, was drawn into putting through a controversial law that deprived children born in France to foreign

nationals of their automatic right to citizenship: in future, they would
have to apply for it specially between the ages of sixteen and eighteen.
This was much criticized as being invidious and contrary to the French
tradition of *jus soli*. One of its aims was to make it possible to expel
young people judged undesirable (i.e. in trouble with the police), and
this indeed was done. No official figures have been given as to how
many of those affected by the law have in fact applied since 1993, but it
may be little more than half. Even though citizenship would improve
their rights, many young Maghrebis have not asked for it, either from
ignorance or apathy, or maybe through anti-French feeling.

The law proved short-lived, for the Jospin Government rapidly
rescinded it, as part of a package of measures passed by Parliament in
December 1997. The *jus soli* was reinstated: any child of a foreigner
born in France would now automatically acquire French citizenship at
eighteen. The Jospin measures, rather like those of the 1980s, aimed at
drawing a balance between being more humane to families and taking
firm steps against clandestine immigration. Asylum, family reunions and
residence permits were again made easier. But some of the Pasqua rules
concerning unwanted immigrants were kept, even tightened. So the
package came under criticism alike from the Right and the human
rights lobbies. But in the quagmire of immigration politics it probably
represented a fair and realistic compromise.

The high total of illegal immigrants, estimated at some 300,000 to
400,000, has worried nearly all of French opinion. Some arrive on
short-term visas, then quietly 'disappear', maybe sheltered by relatives;
others cross over the borders, easy enough in the new frontier-free
Europe. Most are not from the Maghreb but from sub-Saharan Africa,
Eastern Europe or Asia. Some, from poor countries like Mali, are 'economic refugees'. Others, maybe from Turkey, Sri Lanka or Romania,
come hoping to find political asylum – Germany, with its liberal laws,
has faced the same problem on a larger scale. France in Pasqua's day, like
Germany, cut down on the granting of asylum. He also gave orders to
the police to be tougher in ferreting out *les clandestins*; and he embarked
on a campaign of evictions. About one charter plane a week was soon
taking the hapless migrants back to their homeland – for example, a
group of fifty-one Romanian gypsies. Over 10,000 a year were expelled
from 1994 onwards. This well-publicized policy did reduce the total of
illegal immigrants, and may have succeeded in one of its key aims – to
win some voters back from Le Pen. But the League of the Rights of

Man, among others, protested that the aim was achieved only by copying the Front's ideas. Moreover, the policy was random in its effects, and far from efficient: in 1996, for example, only 27 per cent of expulsion orders were actually carried through, thanks very often to the cleverness of the victims or their lawyers in exploiting the vagaries of French law. Many managed to go into hiding, or to destroy their papers, making it hard for the police to bring evidence. Some liberals saw it as a *de facto* victory for legal clemency, in this homeland of the *droits de l'homme*. But it did not clear up a messy situation. Some immigrants, it was felt, should be treated more humanely, others properly evicted after a fair trial.

Matters came to a head in August 1996, in the mighty drama of the Church of St Bernard, in Paris. Some 300 Africans, mostly families from Mali, staged a sit-in of several weeks there, demanding to have their papers regularized as they feared expulsion from France. Ten of them went on hunger strike. Juppé's Interior Minister, Jean-Louis Debré, said at first he would evict them from the church: 'It would be tragic to yield to blackmail.' But the Archbishop of Paris took their side, and the public seemed mostly sympathetic to their human plight. After much prevarication, with 1,100 gendarmes and riot police involved, *les flics* finally moved in, on Chirac's orders: they cleared the church, under the glare of the world's media, as the bells tolled and France was transfixed with emotion. But then what happened? Only eight of the Africans were expelled from France right away. Some eighty others were promised that their situation would be legalized, while the rest were released back into a precarious illegality. It appeared that the magistrates trying the cases were furious at being unable to treat them fairly, faced with a mass of police dossiers badly prepared, full of false evidence, drawn up with the aim of swelling the expulsion statistics – echoes of the Guildford Four? *Le Monde* wrote, 'The tribunal sensed a disproportion between the aims of the decision to expel them and the right to a normal family life, protected by the European Convention on the Rights of Man ... The French system of dealing with illegal immigration has displayed its inefficiency.' And the public, too, however hostile to clandestine immigration, felt that France should have found a better way of dealing with a mass of African women and children, in their bright clothes, seeking sanctuary in a Christian church.

The Juppé Government reacted by tightening the rules yet further. Debré tabled a remarkable bill that required citizens to report the arrival and departure of foreigners staying in their homes. This provoked outrage from intellectuals and media stars, who said they would never obey, and hoped to be prosecuted: 'It's like Vichy,' said one. The measure had barely been applied when the Socialists came to power, and it was dropped. Their Government then put forward a law aimed at making the campaign against *les clandestins* more efficient but also more humane, after the débâcle at St Bernard's. Rules on deportations were slightly strengthened, to the annoyance of human rights groups. But the right of asylum was extended, to cover those – such as refugees from Algeria – who could prove that their life was in danger. And an amnesty was offered to a large number of immigrants who were not in France legally but had family living there. They would now be granted proper residence – and some 150,000 came forward to apply, and by June 1998 over half of these had been granted the amnesty. The Socialists were being as generous as they dared. But politically they still had to strike a balance – between a concern for human rights and the public's demands for stronger controls.

Today in day-to-day life there are two opposing trends. On the one hand, more ethnic immigrants are *de facto* adapting to French life, and at educated levels more of them are slowly rising to better jobs and becoming more accepted. On the other, grassroots racist feeling has been growing worse, or so the French believe and many surveys show – but not all. An encouraging opinion poll by Sofres, in June 1998, suggested that a growing majority of French were opposed to the Front National doctrine of giving 'national preference' to French over immigrants, in jobs, housing and welfare. The numbers thinking that legal immigrants should have the same treatment as the French in these matters rose from about 50 to about 67 per cent between 1991 and 1998. Yet in some poorer areas, feeling against *les immigrés* has hardened.

In a confusing situation, it is hard to tell which of the rival trends will dominate. This will depend in part on the economic situation and maybe on the lead that Governments can give. Officially, the doctrine of full integration remains. But in practice, Governments and local bodies have become a little readier to accept a degree of multiculturalism: witness the help for associations. Yet in official minds there still lurks the fear of communities whose claims to loyalty could compete with those of the State. And that is what could happen, if immigrants continue feeling such hostility against them. Most of them do want to integrate into French life, while retaining their ethnic personalities and having these recognized and respected. It should not be impossible to find that balance. But it requires a clearer lead on the part of Government and informed opinion to discard the fiction of the unity of French culture, and to accept that different models can coexist. Yet this needs both courage and clarity. Meanwhile, the muddled debate goes on. And now, a new shaft of light.

In July 1998, France's victorious World Cup team was one of the most multiracial in the tournament, chosen from the best talent in France (see p. 676). Zinedine Zidane, who scored two of the goals against Brazil in the final, was of Kabyle Algerian origin, born in Marseille; Lilian Thuram, whose two goals were crucial in winning the semi-final against Croatia, was born in Guadeloupe. Some other players were also from Guadeloupe, while yet others had origins in Senegal, Ghana, Armenia, Argentina and New Caledonia. The crowds on the Chámps-Élysées chanted '*Zidane, Président!*', '*Thuram, Président!*', and so did some of the elegant guests at President Chirac's Élysée garden party on 14 July (he took it in good part). Blacks and Maghrebis from the grim suburbs invaded central Paris in their thousands, some of them claiming that at last they felt able to identify fully with France. One West African said, 'A black Frenchman has won the game for a rainbow French team, what a wonderful day.' And the French everywhere cheered 'their' French heroes, leading one Arab to say wryly, 'If a child of immigrants helps France to win, he's French. If he goes to prison, he's an immigrant.' That reminded me of the time when the Irishman Richard Harris was named Best Actor at Cannes and the London press rejoiced, 'British actor wins award'; when he got drunk a month later, the headlines ran 'Irish actor arrested in bar'. Typical.

Just after the Cup, some seasoned observers were suggesting that the victory might prove to be a catalyst in race relations, creating a change in the French collective conscience. Ordinary Frenchmen, they said, might at last become readier to accept immigrants as truly French, to accept their differences, to treat them with more respect, to reject the evil propaganda of Le Pen; and immigrants in turn might at last feel able to identify fully with France. As I write, it is much too soon to tell what real change there will be, on the grim HLM estates, in the hearts and minds of policemen, Beurs and others. But though the euphoria will fade, something may endure.

If there are any racist feelings today against fellow whites, they are directed above all at France's 600,000 Jews, the largest Jewish community in Western Europe. Anti-semitism in France has a sorry history: witness

Dreyfus. Later, some French took advantage of the Occupation to carry out their own private vendettas, while few did much to prevent 76,000 French Jews being deported to the Nazi death camps. This left a sour taste, even a sense of guilt, and after the war anti-semitism died down. But today it still sometimes lingers, mainly among older people.

French Jews in turn have become more assertive in recent years, more concerned with retaining their identity: this has been due in part to the militant Sephardim who arrived from North Africa in the 1960s. They are more exuberant than the Ashkenazim from Alsace and Central Europe who had previously made up the greater part of French Jewry. They are proud to flaunt their Jewishness and have revitalized the Jewish community: thanks mainly to them, there are now twenty kosher restaurants in Paris, against none in 1950. In Sarcelles a large colony of strict orthodox Sephardim, with their beards and yarmulkas, now occupy parts of the town centre, enforcing tight rules about Sabbath observance. Many less religious-minded Jews have moved away.

In the 1980s the Jewish scene was affected by the menace of Palestinian violence. Terrorists bombed a synagogue in a smart part of Paris, killing four; and in 1982 they fired on a crowded kosher restaurant in the Marais, the main Jewish quarter of Paris, killing six. These and other incidents roused the French conscience: big public rallies, of people from all parties save Le Pen's, claimed solidarity with French Jews. More recently, trouble has come from a very different quarter, as a few French neo-Nazi terror groups have shown their ugly heads. In 1990 five skinheads attacked a Jewish cemetery at Carpentras, in Provence, digging up bodies and desecrating thirty-seven tombs. They later confessed and were tried and sent to prison: they claimed that they adored the Third Reich and its values and had wanted to 'celebrate Hitler's birthday'. These loonies were apparently unconnected with the Front National, despite being right in its heartland, near Orange. Le Pen expressed his outrage, and was clearly embarrassed: he has his own anti-semitism, but it is not so blatant (see below). The affair was the tenth vandalization of a Jewish cemetery in France in ten years, and it horrified French opinion. Today decent Frenchmen want Jews to be left in peace. Yet they do not always treat them quite like other citizens: Jews find there can still be subtle pressures against them in their careers, for day-to-day anti-semitism is not entirely dead.

The trial of Maurice Papon in 1997–8 reawoke the issue of wartime guilt. He had been a senior Vichy official in Bordeaux, then after the war had a respectable career, being at one time Paris prefect of police, then Budget Minister under Giscard. Not until 1981 did evidence begin to come out that in Bordeaux he was involved in the deportation of Jews. Judicial inquiries were then blocked under Mitterrand (who had himself worked for Vichy) and it was sixteen years before the trial began: Papon was given a ten-year sentence for 'complicity in crimes against humanity' after it was proved that he had helped organize the transfer to the death camps of some 1,560 Jews in Bordeaux. Behind this tragedy of one man misguidedly 'doing his duty' lay the saga of French post-war attitudes to Vichy. All leaders, from de Gaulle on, had tried to hush up the nasty episode and turn the page, in the cause of national reconciliation: de Gaulle declared Vichy 'null and void'; and Mitterrand admitted that he had held up Papon's prosecution to 'preserve civil peace' – 'One cannot go on living with bitter memories and resentment for ever.' Chirac was then the first President to admit publicly the State's responsibility for deporting Jews; the Church, too, 'repented' formally, fifty years late (see p. 581). Opinion surveys showed that some 75 per cent of French were in favour of the trial being held, and most Jewish leaders expressed satisfaction with the result. Amid the torrent of books, articles and broadcasts on the subject, the impression emerged that the public admissions of guilt had finally helped lay to rest an uneasy national conscience – but long after most of those involved were dead. In a sense, France may have now formally apologized at last to its Jewish community. Yet, according to surveys, some 10 per cent of French still admit to being anti-semitic, while less than 25 per cent think Jews are people 'like anyone else'. It is one of the strains in the bigotry of the Front National.

THE FASCISTIC FRONT AND ITS APPEAL TO ANGRY VOTERS

Jean-Marie Le Pen, at a Front National rally in his native Brittany, 1995: 'We French are being diminished in our own country, in face of this frightful internationalist ideology!' Wild cheers from the big crowd waving tricolors. 'This glorious *patrie*, this cradle of liberty, blessed by God, we are in danger of losing it! This land of great poets and artists, of Racine, Ronsard . . . Better than rap, isn't it? – yet rap is now killing our own culture!' More cheers. With his heavy ox-like frame and his big round face, he strides around the stage – a magnetic orator, sometimes pugnacious, but tonight full of seductive charm, as he woos his faithful. Though a Breton with a Breton audience, he says not a word about Brittany but enthuses with endless lyrical passion about *la France*, and how *all* foreigners must be spurned. At the end, giant flags wave across the stage, floodlights play, spangles and flaming torches shine, with echoes of Nazi rallies. Then music blares – and it's that great French tune 'Land of Hope and Glory', by that great Frenchman, Elgar. I was transfixed.

Shorn of their all-devouring xenophobia, some of Le Pen's cultural ideas might even make a certain sense; or at least it is sad to see lyric fervour and passionate purpose harnessed to such a cause. If only honest politicians like Lionel Jospin could speak half as well. Today Le Pen has turned seventy. His hated rival, Bruno Mégret, a younger and less bombastic figure, left the Front in 1999 to create his own movement: but this so far has had little success. So Le Pen is still the master, with a platform that remains: anti-immigrant, anti-Europe and almost anything international; anti-high spending and high taxes; and sharply critical of the recent failures of the centre-Right parties and the corruption of some of their leaders. And it is easy to see why this mishmash of a recipe has had a certain appeal for many French voters, in their recent scared mood: 'Le Pen,' said one Socialist, 'does ask some of the right questions, even if he gives the wrong answers.' Many French have been rightly worried. But in 1999 the schism between Mégret's and Le Pen's supporters provoked a clear decline in the party's fortunes. So, has the Front National now ceased to be a serious threat?

Former brawling student, paratrooper, Poujadist deputy and publisher of Nazi songs, Le Pen founded his party in 1972. For a decade it made hardly any impact. Then in the 1984 European elections, with unemployment rising, it leapt to 11 per cent, and until 1999 it held between 10 and 15 per cent, tending to do best in presidential elections, where Le Pen's personal appeal counts. He scored 14.4 per cent in 1988, 15.2 per cent in 1995; his party won 12.5 per cent in the parliamentary contest of 1993, 14.9 per cent in that of 1997, and 15.2 per cent in the regional elections of 1998. So, up until then, there had been a slight but steady rise. But in the elections of June 1999, the total of Le Pen and Mégret votes was only 9 per cent. Back in 1986–8, when Mitterrand moved to proportional representation, the Front had thirty-three deputies in the National Assembly. But then the electoral law was reversed; and as other parties initially refused to make deals, the Front won only one seat in 1988, none in 1993, and one (briefly) in 1997. However it holds numerous seats on local councils, where a kind of PR still exists. In 1995–7 it won control of four town councils in Provence; and in 1998 some centre-Right leaders finally agreed to deals.

The Front's essential doctrine (and that of Mégret's movement, which has much the same policies) is what it calls '*la préférence nationale*': French citizens should get priority, in jobs, housing, education, and so on, to the exclusion of all foreigners. Legally, the Front cannot make distinctions between citizens of different ethnic origins, though its implication is that whites are those preferred. Although Le Pen has spoken of 'the inequality of races', the Front is usually careful not to parade its racist tenets too blatantly: but, were it in power, its programme would include the repatriation of 3 million non-Europeans, the removal of welfare rights from non-nationals, and the tightening of rules on gaining citizenship. It has fought against European integration; and although its leaders claim not to be anti-European, they would favour a very loose '*Europe des patries*'. Le Pen's own European vision has been to try to link Rightist groups – such as Jörg Haider's in Austria and the Italian neo-fascists – within an organization called Euronat. Globalization in all its forms is denounced as an 'American plot'; and the Front if in power would try to promote commercial protectionism. It has ultra-Friedmanite views on the need to cut public spending, and it urges the ending of all income and business taxes, with reliance just on VAT. Arguing that most crime comes from the immigrants, it seeks tougher law-and-order measures. And it wants the death penalty restored.

This utopia was expounded to me by the Front's director of public relations, an eager young intellectual with the amazing name of Martial Bild (his grandfather was German): 'We are the only party to defend France patriotically against *l'Europe maastrichtienne*. And the State, corrupt and laxist, prevents freedom of expression. For instance, any real debate on the death penalty is taboo, in Parliament or the media, even though surveys show that most people want its return. It is also taboo to discuss immigration, or real tax reform. On the EU, we think the European Parliament is a farce and that Brussels makes life impossible. Unlike America, France is not a country meant for immigrants: our social welfare system discriminates positively in their favour, so they flood in – this above all explains the Front's success. We *must* avoid becoming a multi-ethnic society.' We were talking at the Front's headquarters, a former factory by the Seine in St-Cloud with the tricolor flying. Up the hill behind, I visited Le Pen's own bizarre late-Victorian mansion, bought with a lavish inheritance from a rich friend who died of drink. Its iron gates were opened by a negress (*sic*), as a camera eyed me and two huge Dobermanns barked. Inside the big brick villa was a clutter of *second Empire* décor like a stage set, with gilded chairs, brocaded sofas, pianos – and Le Pen's personal press officer (he was away), a tall, blonde *grande bourgeoise* proffering friendliness and video cassettes.

So the Front National has presented this double image. On the one hand, in its language, it is often provocative, tough and threatening. Yet it also seeks to parade as reasonable, respectable and humane – even as the democratically elected victim of an undemocratic persecution: '*On nous diabolise, c'est pas juste.*' On some issues, some of its leaders are quite reasonable, as well as being open and friendly. One consistent policy is to go to the succour of those 'poor whites' in trouble who form a large part of its electorate, by helping them with jobs or housing, even setting up soup kitchens for the homeless. This may sometimes be genuine, not just demagoguery: Front militants who do such work remind me of those old PCF Stalinists who went along with the Gulag and Soviet dictatorship, yet could also be sincerely kind and warm-hearted in local activities. Leaving aside its bizarre blind spot about foreigners, the Front even seems to hark back to old-fashioned Christian values. Love thy neighbour – so long as his skin is the right colour.

But of course there is more to it than this. Like the old Communist Party, the Front has always been tightly organized and has a policy, wherever possible, of systematic infiltration. It has formed cells inside the big trade unions, and has set up its own parallel unions, too, notably in the prison service and the police, where it is expectedly strong. This campaign was orchestrated with zeal by strongman Bruno Mégret, who promised that the FN would be actively present 'wherever things are going badly'. He would go into factories himself, like a shop steward: 'Workers of Moulinex, you are victims of *mondialisme*, only the Front is fighting for you!' And many workers responded. With its 'liberal' views on taxation and public spending, and its dislike of the welfare state, the Front *a priori* might not seem to have much appeal to the working man. Yet in the 1990s it moved ahead of the PCF to become the foremost working-class party of France, with some 30 per cent of the worker vote and 25 per cent among all unemployed. Some voters transferred directly from the Communist Party; others, having lost faith in the old Left, would otherwise have abstained. Many are workers in the old declining industries who feel deeply insecure and turn to the Front for its strong lead and promise of renewal. Other voters are tradesmen and small farmers who feel threatened by economic change – the kind who voted Poujadist in the 1950s. Yet others are *pieds-noirs* who have brought from North Africa their contempt for '*les bicots*' ('wogs'). So the FN vote has covered a wide spectrum, across the age groups – from elderly conservative ex-Vichyists to scared out-of-work skinheads who go Beur-bashing in *la banlieue*.

Its vote has been highest in Provence and Alsace, then in parts of the Ile-de-France and eastern France generally; it is lowest in the west, where immigrants are fewer. Yet there is a crucial and curious paradox in the FN's vote. It is highest *near* to areas with a dense immigrant population, but lower *inside* those areas – and many surveys have confirmed this. It is true that Front supporters tend to cite immigration as a main factor: in one survey in 1993, 72 per cent of them gave this reason for voting for it. And yet, in another revealing inquiry, in communes with less than 1 per cent of ethnic minorities, 47 per cent of the sample called themselves racist, whereas this figure fell to 29 per cent in places where the ethnic minorities population was over 10 per cent. And I found the same pattern on my own visits. It is true in Alsace (see below); in Vaulx-en-Velin, where the Front's vote is highest in wards with fewest immigrants; and in Grenoble, where the Front in 1997 scored 14 per cent overall but only 6 per cent in the Arlequin quarter where Maghrebis and 'poor whites' rub shoulders. In these and other suburbs, there may well be scuffles between rival youth gangs: but the adults mostly tolerate each other, because they have got to know and have de-demonized each other. The conclusion is ringingly clear: anti-immigrant hatred in France is above all a matter of ignorance and fear of the unknown. And the same is true in Germany. This is mildly encouraging, for it makes a solution to the racist problem more conceivable. And it makes the biggest nonsense of the Front's demands for mass repatriation.

Other motives for voting for the Front may have been just as strong as fear of immigration. Some are linked with unemployment, for instance the worry that globalization is killing French jobs (see p. 712). The Front has played astutely on this, as on fears of the EU's threats to French national identity. It has won votes from its stress on tougher law-and-order measures in face of the rise in crime. And especially popular has been its crusade against the older centre-Right parties, condemned for 'betraying France' and for overspending or misspending. This has drawn in many regular RPR and UDF voters. Above all, the

Front won immense credit for parading as the anti-corruption party, clean and honest, after a period when so many politicians have been caught up in scandals. The victory at Toulon was won more on this ticket than on the immigration issue. Some FN leaders are old-style purists who genuinely loathe corruption and easy money. The Front has not yet had much chance to prove its own honesty in practice. But already there are signs of nepotism on the local councils, plus reports of illicit party funding from business interests. Its 'virtuous' image may not survive long.

One illustration of the pattern of FN voting comes from Alsace (see p. 365). Here in 1995 its vote of 25 per cent, the highest of any French region, was greater in many rural areas with hardly any immigrants than in city suburbs with mixed populations. The villagers were alarmed by tales of the spread of violence in the 'alien' *banlieues*. And Alsatians, with their Germanic concern for order and decency, grew horrified by the corruption in Paris and the failures of a weak Government. This was fertile ground for the Front, which held its annual rally in Strasbourg in 1997. The popular Socialist mayor, Catherine Trautmann, could not prevent it: but she hit back with a massive counter-demonstration, a big success. 'The way to deal with the Front,' she told me, 'is not to ignore them, nor try to ban them, for that allows them to parade as victims. We need to arouse people to fight them actively, and to propound solutions which show up the stupidity of theirs. So I organized this *riposte citoyenne*. Another good tactic is to tease and mock them. They hate that, they just can't cope.'

In 1997 it was Provence-Alpes-Côte d'Azur, not Alsace, that produced the highest FN vote of any French region: 23 per cent. With its large *pied-noir* population and its record of Rightist extremism in Nice and other towns, this is more predictable Front terrain. And in the 1995 municipal elections all three of the councils won by the Front in France were in south-western Provence – the naval port of Toulon, the Roman city of Orange, and industrial Marignane, north of Marseille. A fourth, Vitrolles, near Marignane, was captured in a notorious election in 1997. So what has now changed, in those towns? There has been no reign of terror, nor could there be. A mayor in France has only limited powers for imposing such doctrines such as *la préférence française*; and immigrants have been persecuted relatively little. But in others ways, FN mayors have been doing their best to curb civic spending, to withdraw subsidies from 'useless' welfare associations, and to tighten law and order. Much of their action has been aimed against culture which they see as a natural enemy. They may sometimes have promoted concerts by crypto-fascist skinhead rock groups, or recitals by elderly Vichyist actors. But mainly they have tried to clamp down on 'wasteful' or 'hostile' culture, in festivals, arts centres and libraries. This has led to some highly publicized battles – as the national media focuses with horrified intensity on every action of these four mayors.

At Orange, in his *mairie* below the majestic Roman theatre, Jacques Bompard, a dentist, rules in rigid praetorian style. I attended a press meeting he gave, flanked by thuggish-looking vigilantes. He is seen locally as a mix of the vulgarly abusive and the sycophantic, and he spoke in a manic, tight-lipped, anal-retentive manner. 'Yes, I'm called an economic fanatic, but I'm proud of having cut the civic budget by 15 million francs. And I got rid of useless staff. The previous Socialist council had overspent disgustingly: they copied Mitterrand's pharaonic projects by building a big new cultural centre, quite pointless. But it was too late for me to stop it.' The Front's victory had been narrow and unexpected, and it left many Orangeois traumatized: few people would at first admit to having voted for it, but it was clear that many disgruntled workers and tradesmen had done so. Bompard set about a policy of tidying up the town, improving traffic, and won some kudos for it. Two anti-Front associations have now been formed, with some 600 members, and they distribute leaflets. Bompard tried to ban this, but the prefect overruled him.

Bompard has removed subsidies from voluntary bodies that try to help immigrants and other *exclus*. He has expelled African traders from the outdoor market. But overall he has not been able to do much against immigrants, and few have left town. 'Of course we feel uneasy,' said one Algerian, 'but for the moment we're OK. The prefect gives us protection.' However, Bompard has stepped up the activities of his municipal police, which operate parallel to the national gendarmerie, as in all towns: 'We now send them on night patrols, so the streets are safer. The rough youth bands have disappeared – it's magic! Even the prefect's statistics show that petty crime in Orange has dropped sharply and is now one of the lowest rates in the area. Perhaps it is the publicity we get in the media that deters criminals from coming here. And we've been able to prove that local Orangeois do after all have equal rights to those of tramps and foreigners!'

The campaign against culture has meant, first, that the *mairie* withdrew support from the town's official arts centre. So its leaders set up a rival one in a nearby commune. As for Orange's distinguished annual opera festival, the Chorégies, held in the Roman theatre, the Ministry of Culture in 1995 was able to prevent the new mayor from remaining as its president: so Bompard hit back by cutting off all subsidy, and the ministry had to take over the *mairie*'s share. This dog fighting provoked a debate in Paris on how to treat the Front National culturally. If its towns were boycotted, as many politicians wanted, then festivals such as the Chorégies might have to close down. The Culture Minister, Philippe Douste-Blazy, argued convincingly that isolation might simply make the Front tougher, and it would be better to give support to local populations in their struggle (the same old argument as over apartheid). He was probably right. Even so, many singers and other *artistes* have preferred to keep away.

The major issue in Orange has been over the municipal library (Bompard: 'Such a silly luxury'). When the Front arrived, it sacked the head librarian, excised some pages from a hostile book, and removed from the shelves a volume of African tales and others by 'foreign' writers. Instead, it bought works by fascist thinkers and FN leaders. There was an outcry, and the ministry conducted an inquiry, which it had the right to do as it gave the library a subsidy. Legally, it could not dictate to the *mairie* on its choice of books, but it published a critical report – and this had an impact, for the missing books were suddenly 'found' and replaced. Bompard's publicity director, A. Y. Beck, a bright, plausible young history teacher, gave me his view: 'It's not true that we censored books. In any town, most library staff are on the Left and they buy left-wing books. But surely the elected mayor of a town has a right that his views, too, be represented. So our aim is balanced pluralism, Trotsky alongside Le Pen – isn't that democracy?' Much the same happened at Marignane, where unaccompanied pupils under nine were banned from the 'dangerous' library, and the *mairie* took over the acquisition of many books from the Front's own bookstore in Paris.

Toulon is a very different case. In its deep bay, ringed by mountains, it has a glorious setting: but its tourist trade is minimal, its naval port is in decline, and today it is a rather sad, run-down place, ashamed of its history, jealous of its larger neighbour, Marseille. Many inhabitants are retired sailors and naval staff, nostalgic for past French glories – fertile soil for the Front. What's more, Toulon in the early 1990s had a fearful record of civic misspending and corruption, almost as bad as Nice: its

RPR mayor, Maurice Arreckx, spent time in custody and was allegedly close to the local mafia. This above all explains the victory in 1995 of the Front and of its mayor today, Jean-Marie Le Chevallier, who campaigned as 'Mr Clean'. Mild and courteous, an elderly old-fashioned Vichyist type, not an ideologue, he is very unlike Bompard. The real power behind him is his Evita-like wife, Cendrine, from a rich, reactionary family. Since taking office, he has done little and spent little, knowing that inaction is the best way of staying popular. In fact, in the 1997 parliamentary elections he won the Front's only seat in France. But six months later this was invalidated by the Constitutional Council, which found him guilty of breaking the rules on campaign funding. And other hints of nepotism and sleaze began to emerge, so his 'clean' image came under test.

Le Chevallier's 1995 victory had little to do with the immigrant issue: he is said to be not racist himself, and has even helped some Maghrebis to find jobs and housing. But his adjutants, more militant, have been busily infiltrating local bodies and have set up a large well-funded youth organization, feeding the young with Front propaganda. On the cultural front, there has been conflict over Toulon's annual book fair. When its directors decided to invite some left-wing authors, the *mairie* objected, took the fair over, and proceeded to hold it as a shop window for Front writers – such as exist. So local booksellers staged their own rival fair, in a nearby Communist-run town.

This typical drama was small beer compared with the amazing affair of Châteauvallon, which made the national headlines for months on end. This multi-purpose cultural centre was created back in 1965 by a young local man, Gérard Paquet, in a handsome seventeenth-century *bastide* up in the lovely hills just outside Toulon, in the commune of Ollioules. He began on a fairly popular level, with jazz and Yves Montand: then he extended into more highbrow activities too, with lots of modern dance, plus modern theatre, seminars on science and ecology, and the like. It was a superb venture, which drew audiences from Paris and all over Provence, and it won support and subsidy from the Ministry of Culture, the Ville de Toulon, and other local authorities. But then came the Front's victory whereupon Paquet, still director, broke off relations with the *mairie* and forewent his municipal subsidy. It was a risky, provocative step, for although his centre was outside Toulon, the city council was in effect its landlord and part owner, under a complex convention. So Le Chevallier began a campaign to take full control and get Paquet removed.

And he hit back by organizing anti-racist seminars, attended by Socialist leaders such as Jack Lang, and by Minister Douste-Blazy himself who laudably pursued his anti-FN policy. Finally, in early 1997, the mayor managed to get a tribunal to pronounce Paquet's dismissal for 'serious administrative failure', i.e. for damaging the centre's finances by giving up his civic subsidy.

I visited Châteauvallon just after this – a magical domain, complete with Roman-style outdoor theatre, spreading over a lyrical pine-wooded landscape – and I found a euphorically defiant atmosphere among its young staff, as if they were at the barricades. 'This is *the* major symbolic fight against the Front,' said one – and the Paris media were saying the same. But, as one local journalist suggested to me, maybe the symbol was not ideal: the intelligentsia might love Paquet's cultural programmes, but ordinary Toulonnais, whether pro-FN or not, found them too highbrow, and had not attended the centre very much. They by far preferred the diet of Provençal folkloric culture that Le Chevallier has astutely fed them within his borders.

A complicating factor in the drama was the curious role of the prefect of the local Var *département*, Jean-Charles Marchiani. This Corsican, an RPR stalwart and friend of Pasqua, was posted to Toulon to keep a watch over the Front. In fact he shared many of its views and methods: but the Government initially felt that a more liberal prefect might be less effective. His first clash, in 1996, was with the abrasive rap group Nique Ta Mère ('fuck your mother'), which had sung at Châteauvallon, then played its song, '*Je pisse sur la police*', at another local concert. Marchiani declared that 'as a Christian' he found NTM disgraceful, and he stirred up the local pissed-on police to launch a civil prosecution: as a result, a right-wing judge sent two members of the group to prison for six months. Marchiani later tried to ban NTM from revisiting Châteauvallon. And he openly sided with Le Chevallier in his crusade against Paquet. French prefects, though servants of the Government of the day, are supposed to be objective and apolitical: but here was a blatant example of a breach of this rule. So France faced the unique spectacle of a prefect backing a Front mayor *against* the Minister of Culture. Later, when the Socialists came to power, they transferred Marchiani. Then in 1998 they appointed a new director at Châteauvallon and relaunched it on a new basis, while the Toulon council backed out and gave up its subsidy. So Le Chevallier lost his battle, in the end.

Earlier in 1997, some 200 artists and intellectuals had come to Toulon from all over France to demonstrate in favour of Paquet and the Left's book fair. This was just after Paquet had been fired, NTM had been jailed, and the Front had won its victory at Vitrolles: so it was feeling triumphant. The forceful Cendrine Le Chevallier, champagne glass in hand, raised the victory toast as she stood Evita-like on the balcony of her town hall, and the anti-Front protesters marched below her, shouting slogans. Don't cry for her, Châteauvallon. Then in 1999 Le Chevallier himself quit the Front in disgust; and his majority on the town council collapsed amid strife between Le Pen and Mégret factions. 'Perhaps we are incapable of running such a big town,' said one FN councillor.

At Vitrolles, a dreary Marseille suburb with 20 per cent unemployment, Bruno Mégret had wanted to stand himself in the 1997 local by-election, but was debarred by his earlier campaign overspending: so his wife Catherine took his place, and was narrowly elected mayor. She dismissed eighty staff, cut aid to welfare bodies by 50 per cent, and sacked the manageress of the civic cinema for showing a film about homosexuals. She also doubled the strength of the municipal police force, claiming that the national police were too lax in enforcing order on the HLM estates with their immigrant youth.

Madame Mégret has seemed more openly racist than the other Front mayors. She closed down one musical café which presented rap singers, and her team have organized lectures and other events on what the Nazis called 'Aryan' culture. She tried to apply *la préférence française* by offering couples with French citizenship a cash grant for every child born: but this was judged illegal by the courts. She also took up the theme of the 'inequality of the races', and spoke scathingly in public about the immigrants in her town: for this she was given a three-month suspended sentence and a 50,000-franc fine, for 'complicity in public provocation towards racial hatred'. But behind the scenes her husband is the real ruler at the *mairie*, using it as a testing ground for his doctrines and a base for his national offensive. Before he left the Front he had emerged as one of a new brand of younger leader, less blustering and more plausible than Le Pen.

Another, Yvan Blot, I found fascinating. Leader of the Front in Alsace, and an MEP, he was put there by Le Pen to charm and convince the European Parliament. He is an *énarque* and former *sous-préfet*, a clever, civilized man who was on Chirac's staff in the 1980s, but left after failing to persuade the RPR to form an alliance with the Front against immigration, his nightmare. I drank wine with him and his sweet wife in their Strasbourg home, kitschily overdecorated but cosy, with oriental rugs, a harp in one corner, an imitation Greek sculpture, a fine grey Persian cat. Despite *la préférence française*, they have an Italian son-in-law, and a son about to marry an English girl: Blot said he was keen on France having close relations with Germany, so long as they were not Euro-institutional. The Blots complained at being more or less ostracized, socially, by Strasbourg's large diplomatic set, notably the French delegations. Madame struck me as being wistful about this, and lonely. After all, this civilized upper-crust couple would hardly find much in common culturally with local Front militants: yet they had excluded themselves, by choice from their own kind. It seemed an affecting case of a no doubt sincere sacrifice for a doubtful ideal.

Another Front leader has been Bruno Gollnisch, a university professor of Japanese at Lyon, a stylish, popular lecturer with a Japanese wife ('So how can I be racist?'). As for the remarkable Bruno Mégret, this élitist in his late forties, with a Polytechnique and Berkeley (California) education is like Blot a defector from Gaullism in the 1980s. Slight and dark, with a ferret-like face, Mégret is no great orator but has a quick wit and a smooth charm, and is known as a very subtle operator, a clever strategist, and a tough ideologue with views maybe even harsher than Le Pen's. Before he left the Front, he was trying to strengthen its appeal to younger middle-class voters and to workers. He played its anti-Brussels, anti-American card very strongly, but was finding its anti-welfare and anti-public spending tenets a bit of a liability with workers.

Le Pen, son of a Breton fisherman, took a law degree at the prestigious 'Sciences Po' in Paris, and later volunteered to fight for '*l'Algérie française*' where he played his part in army brutalities. His racism includes a brash anti-Semitism, as when on the radio in 1987 he spoke of the Holocaust as a 'mere detail' of the Second World War. Then later, with typical cheek, he compared the French 'persecution' of the Front to the Nazi persecution of the Jews! Though rough by nature (in one political brawl in Paris, he lost an eye), he has generally been careful not to be *too* aggressive – but with lapses. During the 1997 election campaign, in a small town near Paris, he was seen on television grabbing at the clothes of the local woman Socialist candidate and screaming at her. For this, a local court later found him guilty of 'riotous and insulting behaviour, unworthy of a political leader', and banned him from public office for two years: after the verdicts against Le Chevallier and both Mégrets, this was the fourth time that the courts, with a severity widely admired, had awarded penalties against Front leaders. The incident added to the growing feeling within the party that Le Pen had become more of a liability than an asset, and should step down.

In its strenuous efforts to appear respectable, the Front has sometimes succeeded. Le Pen has had his excesses: but the party's stance against corruption, its fairly good civic record, its help for poorer white people, have made it seem virtuous in some eyes. Even a few celebrities have come to support it: Brigitte Bardot's autobiography eulogizes Le Pen as well as cuddly baby seals. And at some bourgeois Paris dinner parties it was for a time acceptable to say, 'Well, the Front does have some good ideas, you know. It gets its vote democratically, so it's wrong to treat it as the devil.' The classic centre-Right parties have been facing this dilemma. They lost some voters to the Front: so how can they win them back? – should they fight against its ideas? – or, conversely, discreetly adopt parts of its programme? – or even do electoral deals with it? Since the mid-1980s, they have hesitated between these choices. The RPR and UDF leaders in Paris have been against all deals: but locally several mayors have drawn on tacit support from the Front, so as to retain power. This came to a head in the regional elections of March 1998 (see pp. 39–40 and 298). And the ensuing crisis showed more vividly than ever before the power of a strong Front to influence and disrupt.

The French remain unsure of how much of a threat this diverse movement poses to democracy. While some of its ideas seem in themselves reasonable, others are wildly unrealistic in economic terms (e.g. those on taxation); and yet others, the xenophobic and hyper-nationalist ones, appear viciously dangerous to many people. Yet the parallel with Germany in 1932, though easy to make, is excessive. Much will probably now depend on whether the euro is a success; on whether the negative aspects of globalization can be contained; on whether the wave of political corruption is seen to be over; on what Governments can do to reduce unemployment and illegal immigration; and of course on Bruno Mégret.

The French have been forced to ask themselves: why is it that France, Belgium and Austria now much more so, are the only EU countries to have a far-Right movement of this strength? In a Germany wary of neo-Nazism it is confined to pockets in the east. One reason sometimes given is that the French, Austrians and Belgians, all once permeated by Nazism, were never properly denazified like the Germans: but this does not seem quite convincing. There are other, more obvious factors. Meanwhile, a great many decent French citizens are left shamed by the tarnished image of the land of hope and glory that Jean-Marie Le Pen and the like are giving to the world.

The Le Pen/Mégret conflict has always been less one of ideology than of personalities and political style. And in December 1998 it erupted into open crisis. Le Pen dismissed his enemy from the post of deputy leader (*délégué général*) and sacked many of his main supporters too from key posts. Mégret hit back by holding a special congress in January – boycotted by Le Pen – where he created a new rival party, the Mouvement National. As his support among militants was greater than Le Pen's, it seemed that his new party might push the old Front on to the sidelines. And yet, at the European elections in June 1999, Le Pen's list scored 5.7 per cent and Mégret's only 3.3. The total, just 9 per cent, was well below the FN's usual score. And all local French elections later in 1999 confirmed this trend: the Front ahead of Mégret by two or three times as many votes, while the far Right total has been much reduced.

So Mégret seems to have lost his gamble. And the departure of this dynamic entrepreneur is a blow for the Front, for the ageing Le Pen has no other *dauphin* of this calibre. More importantly, the spectacle of its schism has seriously weakened the Front, as recent elections show. And French democracy could be the winner.

4

THE REGIONS AGAINST PARIS:
RENEWAL AND REFORM

Proud historic Brittany, or Provence, or Burgundy, all of them just did not exist, politically or administratively, from the Revolution until quite recently. But now they are real entities again. And if a small town wants to build a swimming pool, or change a street name, or hire extra staff, it no longer has to go cap-in-hand to the local Paris-appointed prefect, or wait years for the approval of some unknown bureaucrat in a far-off Paris ministry. It can actually decide for itself.

In this hitherto most centralized of nations, the Socialists have granted devolution at last. In the 1980s they gave a degree of autonomy to France's twenty-two regions and to other levels of local government; and they cut back the powers of the prefects, who had long ruled them so tightly in the name of the State. Politically, this has marked quite a change; and with many ups and downs the reform has been going fairly well. It has been the belated sequel to other important changes, too, economic, cultural, psychological, that since the war have been tilting the balance away from Paris and towards the provinces.

As in many other parts of Europe, a new regional awareness grew in the 1960s and '70s. This was stronger in some regions, those with a true historic identity such as Brittany, than in others; and it took various forms. Some people sought to revive local languages and folk cultures; others began to press for more autonomy; and tiny separatist groups resorted to violence, in Corsica and a few other places. But above all it was the economic renewal of post-war France that provided the motor for the remarkable revitalization of the provinces, bringing a surge of new activity to sleepy towns long eclipsed by Paris. *La France profonde* asserted itself; and finally the State had to loosen the reins of centralization.

The French provinces used to be second to none in Europe for lethargy and bourgeois narrowness. Bourges, Tours, Dijon and a score of other

towns, with their soaring cathedrals, graceful old streets and calm reflection of history – how delightful they were to visit, and how tedious to
live in. In no other country was the contrast more striking between the
dazzling capital and the rest, '*le désert français*' as it was often called.
Nowhere was 'provincial' quite such a term of contempt as in Paris:
even the Larousse dictionary defined it as 'gauche, undistinguished'.
French literature is rich in examples of Parisian writers' love-hatred of
their home towns, from Flaubert's Rouen to Mauriac's Bordeaux: for
the dullness of the provinces went hand in hand with strong local
attachments, and many a Parisian would proudly proclaim, '*Moi, je suis
angevin*', or *auvergnat*, or *charentais*, but would never dream of going back
to make a career there. Paris over the centuries sucked the blood from
her provinces, appropriating their intellectual life, their talent and initiative, their powers of decision.

This picture started to change soon after the war. The rural exodus,
the new industry, wealth and mobility began to give a new liveliness and
confidence to many towns and regions. And Paris was no longer able to
hog all the progress and prosperity as she had done in the last century.
In fact, by about the 1970s some smart Parisians were dropping their old
scorn and moving to the provinces. The cultural revival of many towns
has been striking: new theatres, concert halls, art galleries and research
centres have helped to make life more exciting, and the influx of populations has created a more open and varied society.

Since the 1950s regional development has been a major French obsession, a pillar of official policy under all Presidents. But we need to
distinguish between economic or cultural decentralization on the one
hand, and political devolution on the other. Of the former there was
plenty; of the latter there was little sign under the centre-Right Governments of the 1958–81 period. They eagerly poured money into aiding
the provinces, but they kept control of how most of it was spent; and
they gave up little real sovereignty. Politicians would preach the need
for devolution: but French tradition, and the power of the central civil
service, proved stubborn obstacles.

After 1982 the Socialists then carried through a more extensive reform,
which later centre-Right Governments basically have not altered. Greater
scope for initiative has now passed to locally elected bodies at the three
levels of region, *département* and commune; and economic development
is now less centralized. But the State keeps many powers: this is not a
federal solution, nor even as radical as the devolution now on the way

for Scotland. However, it means that France has finally fallen into step with other recent European moves to regionalize and to strengthen local democracy. The reform is far from perfect and has had many teething troubles: the French have not been finding it easy to change their Jacobin habits and mentalities and to adapt to a looser system. But it is generally seen as a step in the right direction. We shall look to begin with at the great economic changes that came first.

DATAR'S VICTORIES FOR REGIONAL DEVELOPMENT

The origins of French centralization go back to the Capetian monarchs, who welded one nation out of the diverse peoples living in what is now France. In more modern times, the great centralizer was Napoleon: he carved up the old provinces, which under the *ancien régime* had enjoyed some autonomy, and replaced them with ninety artificial *départements*, mostly named after rivers. Thus Brittany no longer existed legally: Rennes, its chief town, became the capital of Ile-et-Vilaine. And in charge of each *département* Napoleon put a prefect, a strong ruler answerable to Paris. Through the next century, the political dominance of Paris encouraged other forms of centralization, too. When the railways were built, for political and strategic reasons their network was traced radially round Paris with few good cross-country lines, so that even in 1938 it was still quicker to go from Toulouse to Lyon via Paris (1,092 km) than direct (545 km). When heavy industry grew, some of it settled near the coal and iron-ore mines of the north-east or the upper Loire, but much of it went to Paris, to be near the sources of finance and the key ministries. Yet at this time new techniques and transport systems were, in other countries, encouraging *de*centralization.

The big banks gradually became centred in Paris, while the snobberies of the literary salons joined with the hold of the Sorbonne over the state university network to deprive the provinces of much of their intellectual resources. And the masses arrived, too, hungry for work. The great building programmes of Baron Haussmann in the 1860s saw little counter-part in the provinces, and this helped to draw to the capital hundreds of thousands of poor peasants. The statistics are astonishing. From 1851 to 1931 greater Paris went up by 4.4 million in population, the Nord and the Lyon-St-Étienne area by 1.8 million, while the rest of France dropped by 1.2 million. Paris's share of France's population rose in this period from 5 to 15 per cent, while by the 1931 census many lesser provincial towns were smaller than they had been in 1800. In Britain, Germany and Italy, the nineteenth-century growth was shared much more widely.

Until 1939 France had been investing eagerly in countries like Morocco and Senegal, where the legacy of the colonial growth still catches the eye today. But she neglected her own provinces, notably in the south and west. The notion grew of 'two Frances', divided by a diagonal line from Caen to Marseille. To the east, Paris and 85 per cent of the industry, the big modern farms and the rich Riviera playgrounds; to the west, a territory more thinly populated than Spain (except in Brittany), with poor farms, and towns without industry. Only after 1945 did this imbalance catch public attention. But already before that the pendulum had begun to swing back a little. The pre-war strategic decentralization of a few aircraft factories, mainly to Toulouse, was a harbinger. Then came those familiar blessings in disguise, Vichy and the Occupation. Some dynamic individuals withdrew from Paris to the 'free' Vichy zone where the southerly areas, cut off from the capital, were forced to act for themselves.

After 1945 a wider movement gathered pace, due to government action and some spontaneous factors. The sudden upswing in the birth rate was not confined to Paris, and curiously it gave a psychological boost to stagnating towns. The growing rural exodus was still directed first towards Paris, but less exclusively: between 1945 and 1968, greater Paris grew from 6 to 8 million, while some other towns doubled or even trebled in size. Today this provincial growth has slowed right down, and there have been popular reactions against too much urbanization. But after the war France had little other choice. It can be argued that Paris is still the only town to have passed its optimum size: its congestion, high costs and commuting problems have led to an undercurrent of neurosis. From the 1970s a trend *against* Paris began to take shape in the middle classes: some engineers, *cadres*, professors and others came to see that life in other towns, in the warm south or near the sea or mountains, could be more human and pleasant, even if less intellectually stimulating. A new and amazing anti-Parisian snobbery even emerged alongside the age-old anti-provincial snobbery. Even today, more such people move to new jobs in the provinces than follow the classic route of Julien Sorel, to seek fame and fortune in the capital; it is almost *more* chic to say that you live and work in Annecy or Avignon than in Montparnasse – an odd reversal.

According to census results, for the first time in history the net migration since the mid-1970s has been *away* from Paris. The net flow into the Paris region (Ile-de-France) fell from 700,000 in the census period 1954–62 to 377,000 in 1962–8 and then 87,000 in 1968–75. In 1975–82 there was a net emigration of 273,000, and this trend has since increased, with 70,000 more people leaving the region each year than settling in it, during the 1990s (see p. 329). Today its overall population is still increasing: but this is due mainly to the high birth rate, as there are so many immigrants and younger families.

Many of those who leave the Paris region, in all social classes, return to their native provinces, to work or to retire. Few of them regret the move. The rhythm of life is calmer than in Paris, the children can have more fun, often there are good theatres and concerts. It is true that some big towns, such as Toulouse or Lyon, are now in danger of catching the same big-city disease as Paris: they have sprawling, ill-planned suburbs, and serious rush-hour traffic jams. But many others, not so large, still offer a happy balance between new-style animation and old-style *douceur de vivre*. It is possible to find a villa with a garden only ten minutes' drive from one's place of work, and to fit in a swim or a game of tennis on a summer evening after work, something Parisians can rarely do. The growth of air services, motorways and the T G V has helped to make life away from Paris seem less like exile to a cultured family used to its stimulus. This new mobility has livened staid provincial towns. Some of the keenest local pride comes from young citizens who have put down new roots there.

These spontaneous changes of the past forty years have been lent added stimulus by government policies. *L'aménagement du territoire* (regional development in the widest sense) was almost unheard of before the war, but it then became a key priority of Monnet and his planners. In 1947 Jean-François Gravier, a young geographer attached to the Plan, published his famous book, *Paris et le désert français*, which brilliantly analysed the dangers. He showed how the neglect of the west wasted the country's resources, while the concentration on Paris and other key areas led to high costs. If France was to become a modern country, he said, this must change. His warnings alarmed official milieux, and many of his proposals soon became government policy. In 1950 it started the first subsidies and tax concessions for firms willing to create new plant in the provinces or transfer from Paris. This met with a few successes, for example a big new Citroën factory at Rennes: but usually the incentives were not strong enough to entice firms far from Paris to where they were most needed. Then in the 1960s de Gaulle's Government set a lead with its own major ventures, including space centres in Brittany, tourist and irrigation schemes in Languedoc.

In 1963 a major new government agency was set up, the Délégation à l'Aménagement du Territoire et à l'Action Régionale (DATAR), and for the next twenty years this exerted a crucial influence. With its compact team of young technocrats, always dedicated, sometimes fanatical, it acted as a ginger group, stirring ministries and other bodies into action: its dual role was to stimulate new investment where it was most needed, and to lay the ground for it by pressing for new infrastructures. It evolved a doctrine of making the best use of national space by siting new activities where they best fitted human needs and natural resources. It wielded a weaponry of incentives, with sizeable grants for areas such as Brittany, the Massif Central, Languedoc, the Pyrenees and Corsica. Its record has been variable, but it did do much to counterbalance the eastward drift of industry: in the period 1968–75 the growth of the west in terms of new jobs was four times the French average.

Since the 1980s the role of DATAR has declined. Much of the major work is now completed; money is tighter; and some of the initiative has passed to the new regional bodies, and to the EU. Yet there remains a lingering enthusiasm for *l'aménagement du territoire*. In the post-war decades it was elevated into a science and a philosophy, the subject of endless speeches, books and congresses. France seemed to present her planners with some of the exciting challenge of a virgin land. It was one of the few parts of western Europe where there was still the space, and the resources, for ambitious ventures. Steadily the state planners' enthusiasm percolated to more local bodies, chambers of commerce or town councils, whose parochial concerns widened into a sense of sharing in the exciting new schemes. In the boom years, this was the heady age of local debate about new airports, motorways and industrial parks. Today the concern with *l'aménagement* continues, but it is less eagerly expansionist, more concerned with preserving jobs and protecting the environment.

Regional planning has of course suffered from the usual French chasm between theory and achievement. Splendid blueprints may fall foul of ministerial rivalries, bureaucratic inertia or sheer lack of funds. Ask any Frenchman what he has done, and excitedly he will tell you what he is about to do – and yet, if only one of his projects sees the light, it is better than having no ideas or eagerness at all. Many local executives and *notables* seem mesmerized by geographical obsessions that sound weird to English ears. Towns are pieces on some huge chessboard, and the mere drawing of lines across a map yields some strange reality of its own. Translated into English terms, a local dignitary might talk like this: '*Swindon, bien que dans l'orbite londonienne, peut profiter d'une certaine vocation bristolienne, et tout en s'inspirant du rayonnement intellectuel oxfordien, elle se situe bien pour remplir un grand destin au carrefour des grands axes de demain – de l'agglomération birminghamoise jusqu'à Southampton aux portes de l'Amérique, et de l'hinterland* [in franglais] *galloise jusqu'à Harwich, plaque tournante de l'avenir scandinavienne.*' Does the mayor of Swindon talk like that?

Parallel to its industrial policies, the Government since the war has sought to stimulate the cultural and intellectual life of provincial cities, so as to counter the appeal of Paris. In the 1960s big new arts centres (*maisons de la culture*) were devised in some towns, not always with the happiest results (see pp. 433–7). Universities were encouraged to grow faster than those in Paris. And a number of Grandes Écoles and national research bodies were transferred from Paris. With many ups and downs, these policies have brought results.

DATAR's great period was in the 1960s and '70s. It may not have 'changed the economic map of France' quite as much as its directors claimed. But, thanks to its policies, much industry was shifted from Paris, and the provinces gained their full share of France's swift expansion in the boom years. The statistics are revealing. Whereas in 1954–62 the growth in industrial jobs was still as fast in the Paris region as elsewhere, in 1962–73 that region had a net loss of 77,000 jobs (about 5 per cent), while the rest of France gained 670,000, a rise of 15 per cent. This was quite a victory for the persistent efforts of DATAR, with new restrictions on the extension of plant in greater Paris. Big firms such as Renault thus devoted all their expansion to the provinces, and in some cases (notably Citroën) they transferred factories to the west. As Gravier had argued, it was a better use of national resources to put new investment in the regions, where costs were much lower than in Paris. And it was crucial to find new jobs locally for the hordes leaving the farms, who otherwise would again descend *en masse* on greater Paris.

The geographical pattern of post-war development in the 1960s–'80s was complex but clear. The towns fairly near Paris but outside its region – Caen, Rouen, Reims, Orléans and others – all did well in attracting new industry, and so did much of the south-east. But these were never DATAR priority zones. The already highly industrial regions of Lorraine and the Nord were well placed near the heart of Europe, but they faced the challenge of reconverting their older industries, coal, steel and textiles. In the under-industrialized west, the campaign to attract new investment did well in some big towns near the coast such as Bordeaux and Nantes, and in a few others inland such as Toulouse and Rennes. But in many of the less populated regions of the centre and south-west, far too few new jobs were created to cater for the steady rural exodus.

In fact, recent census figures show that the old notion of a France split down the middle – rich industrial east, poor rural west – has been giving place to a more complex pattern. The broad demographic outline is that population and activity have been tending to shift to the coasts: the principal zone of ageing and falling population, and of economic depression, is no longer the west as such, but a broad swathe of territory cutting across France from north-east to south-west: it starts in the Ardennes and Lorraine, takes in the upper Marne area, narrows to skirt northern Burgundy, then broadens to include most of the sprawling Massif Central and ends in the Pyrenees. Twenty-four *départements* today have more deaths than births, and most of them lie in this zone. This decline has roused recent Governments to take some action. Since the mid-1970s there has been a special programme for the Massif Central (see p. 416). And in 1995 DATAR was put in charge of a new project for aiding rural '*pays*' (see below).

When it comes to enticing new industry to the provinces, DATAR has always found that some firms hesitate for fear of not being able to persuade their senior staff to come, too. *Cadres* may today be readier to move from Paris, but are choosy about where they go. They may be enticed by the sunny south, but will think twice about settling, say, in gloomy St-Étienne or the grey-skied Ardennes. Often it is the wives who are most cautious about moving to a new town without friends, or without well-known seats of education for the children (it is major university centres such as Montpellier that have expanded fastest). Or a firm itself may be reluctant to move to a rural area where it fears not being able to find the right kind of skilled local workforce.

In order to combat such problems, DATAR has wielded a complex arsenal of incentives. Subsidies for new installations have been zero in a wide orbit around Paris and much of the south-east, but have ranged up to 25 per cent for many other areas, and have covered up to 60 per cent of costs for tranfers of plant *from* Paris. There have also been tax exemptions and other forms of aid. But seldom have these incentives proved decisive in choosing a location. Firms have found them a useful bonus: but other factors have usually weighed more heavily in the final resort, such as transport costs and labour. Generally DATAR has been left to apply the carrot as best it can, but sometimes the Government has stepped in at a higher level to use the stick, with threats or other pressures. This used to be relatively easy, in a land where the State controlled so much of the economy – witness the bullying of car firms to go to Lorraine (see pp. 111–12). And in order to induce one big electronics company to move to Brittany, the Government reportedly threatened to suspend its state contracts. But in today's more liberal era, this kind of pressure has become rarer, and less feasible.

DATAR had considerable success during its heyday of the later 1960s and '70s, when almost half the new industrial jobs in France were created in its 'priority zones'. But then economic crises obliged the Government to switch its top priorities from industrializing the west to the more urgent tasks of trying to rescue some older industrial areas. In 1978 DATAR launched a 3-billion-franc 'reconversion fund' for creating new jobs in the hard-hit steel and textile districts of Lorraine and the Nord, and in the shipyard zones around Marseille and St-Nazaire. These measures met with only modest success. But there is little alternative to this kind of policy. In America, when a big factory closes or an industry declines, the workers move off elsewhere. But in France this mobility, though traditional among peasants and now growing commoner among *cadres*, has spread little to industrial workers. Rightly or wrongly, they expect that the new jobs must come to them. At Decazeville in the Aveyron, when the coal mines had to be run down and the miners were offered jobs in state mines elsewhere, they refused. In protest, 800 miners even stayed at the bottom of a pit for several weeks over Christmas.

Having halted the industrial growth of Paris, the Government in the 1970s turned its attention to 'tertiary decentralization' – the transfer to the provinces of the central offices of some state bodies and private firms. Paris, with 20 per cent of the population, still had 40 per cent of all office jobs. So DATAR began wooing firms to make a move. The State set a modest lead with its own services: thus the Quai d'Orsay transplanted one minor department to Nantes, while some state banks moved services to the west. But only a few ministries or state agencies have managed to take this kind of step, generally because of opposition from their own staff: thus it took over fifteen years for the state meteorological office to complete its move to Toulouse. In 1992 the École Nationale d'Administr-ation was partially transferred to Strasbourg (see p. 93), but this expensive folly gave bad publicity to the entire policy.

Private firms have likewise proved reluctant to shift their head offices. One main reason is their wish to stay near the key ministries and sources of finance, which in turn will not budge – a vicious circle. The Ministry of Finance still shows little desire to grant more powers of decision to its own regional offices. However, the Government has had a little more success in its efforts to promote Lyon, Nice and Strasbourg as centres for headquarters of private firms, international as well as national. Near Nice, a big 'park' for scientific research and advanced service industries, Sophia-Antipolis, has been set up on an open 2,400-hectare site. Here Air France has transferred its global reservations service, and the CNRS has set up a big centre. After a slow start, the park has proved popular with foreign investors, too, today including Wellcome, Dow Chemical and Toyota.

Nowadays the golden age of *l'aménagement du territoire* is over, and DATAR has come to play a lesser role since about the mid-1980s. One reason is that the State has transferred part of its powers to the regional bodies, which have some scope for their own investment policies. Another is that France has opened its frontiers to a wider world where the EU itself takes regional initiatives; and many larger French firms now plan on a European or even global scale. Also, the slowdown in growth and the shortage of funds make it now less feasible for DATAR to carry out its grand schemes. Indeed, it has now fulfilled many of its planned objectives, so it is less needed. Its overall budget has been reduced more than that of any other state agency, and though its investment grants remain, they are fewer. In today's more liberal age, even under a Socialist Government, state *dirigisme* for major economic projects is no longer in vogue. So DATAR today has a humbler role, as partner and adviser in smaller-scale local schemes, often related to rural development or urban renewal.

Charles Pasqua, as Interior Minister with responsibility for DATAR in 1993–5, tried to give the agency some new tasks and a new lease of life. He sponsored a law that set guidelines for helping 'fragile zones' in the troubled *banlieues* and in some rural areas. This hard-line Jacobin was suspected by some critics of ulterior motives, that is, of wanting to create a framework that could enable his ministry to intervene in cities in time of trouble. But in itself the economic help that he planned was a useful step. His law allotted funds for creating jobs and new infrastructures in poorer suburbs, also in deprived rural areas where the population was falling. One of his aims was to provide more support for public utilities in those areas (he was a strong opponent of EU liberalism and of the plans to deregulate France Télécom and the EDF). Some aspects of his law were gradually put into force under Juppé.

Above all, the Pasqua law instituted a new rural concept, the *pays*. In a number of pilot schemes, groups of communes, maybe twenty to fifty in each case, have been invited to club together for new local ventures, economic, cultural or social, backed by special grants. The aims are practical, to enable villages to pool their efforts for development and to break through some of the usual administrative barriers between state services. The *pays* chosen are not random groupings, but real entities, for example the Redon district in Brittany, or the high Cévennes around Le Vigan. The project made a slow start, but many local *notables* have now shown some enthusiasm for it, and some 250 *pays* have been formed. Funding is allocated jointly by DATAR, the region, and the EU's 'Leader' programme.

In fact, one of DATAR's roles today is to administer the money that France receives from the EU's huge Structural Funds, mainly the Social and Regional Funds (the Common Agricultural Policy is different). 'This task has transformed our mission,' said one official. As in all member countries, the Government decides in detail how and where the money should be used in France, but within EU guidelines, and this involves endless negotiation with Brussels, largely done by DATAR. France may be one of the richer EU countries, but it has wide far-from-wealthy rural areas which qualify for aid under the EU's '5B' funds for rural development. Some older industrial areas, too, notably in Lorraine and the Nord, have been given special EU support.

Another new role of DATAR is to liaise with the regional councils. These have the power to devote part of their budget to their own development schemes, which can include transport and industrial invest-ment. And here a council can spend what it likes, within EU parameters, so long as it is prepared to raise the necessary local taxes. The effort is still modest, compared with that of the German *Länder*. But many regions are now taking their own initiatives, in areas such as hi-tech research and job creation. And some regional bodies are going abroad to canvass investment – a novelty for centralized France where previously all such work was done by DATAR's foreign bureaux. Thus Alsace now has a bureau in Tokyo which secured a lucrative investment by Sony. Some of the larger regions are forming links across EU frontiers: notably, Rhône-Alpes (capital, Lyon) has an active association with Baden-Württemberg, Lombardy and Catalonia, and has its own offices in Stuttgart, Milan and Barcelona. This powerful quartet has been lobbying in Brussels and Paris for some joint transport projects, such as a plan for a tunnel under the Alps for a new TGV line. Nord-Pas-de-Calais, likewise, is actively linked with Kent, beyond the Tunnel.

In sum, the regional reform has unleashed new local energies: the regions now compete against each other more strenuously, and some larger ones do their own direct lobbying in Brussels. In Germany, this kind of competition has long been a strength of the federal system. But DATAR, unused to it, is wary of what it sees as a possible duplication of effort, a trend that could increase the disparity between the rich dynamic regions and the poorer ones. So one of its ongoing roles today is to help the weaker regions, mostly with new infrastructure schemes. After years of patient effort, the west and south-west have been built up and some of the old imbalance has been reduced, just as Gravier hoped. But France's main focus still remains to the east, along the so-called 'blue banana' of big urban centres that runs from London via Paris, Brussels and Frankfurt to Milan. And now, with the opening up of Eastern Europe and the move of Germany's capital to Berlin, the EU's centre of gravity is again tilting east. In order to counter this, Europe's western regions have been planning to build up an 'Atlantic arc', running from Scotland and Ireland via Brittany and Aquitaine into north-west Spain and Portugal. This produces endless discussion, but practical progress is not so easy.

L'aménagement du territoire today still has a role to play, but a changing one, as some decision-making shifts to Brussels, or to the regions which have been gaining in autonomy – in Spain more than in France, and now in Scotland, too. We shall examine the real impact of France's regional reforms of the 1980s. But first, a look at environmental policies, which have also become a key aspect of DATAR's work. In fact, DATAR today comes directly under the Ministère pour l'Aménagement du Territoire et pour l'Environnement, with its influential Green minister, Dominique Voynet.

ENVIRONMENTAL CRUSADES:
BETTER LATE THAN NEVER

For the environment to be a key ministry, headed by France's leading Green, would have been far less likely even twenty years ago. The French were much slower than the Germans, or indeed the British, in waking up to environmental issues, and for many years the small ecology groups had only a limited impact. After all, France had so much space in which to build and expand, compared with overpopulated Germany or Britain; and for most people, economic modernization was the exciting priority. There seemed to be a contrast between the ever-anxious Germans, with their romantic vision of nature, and a maybe less prudent Latin nation for whom the countryside was more practical – a place for earning your living and getting the produce for lovely meals.

All this has been changing. The first major concern, in the 1970s, was over the spoliation of the coastline, of beauty spots and historic town centres, with ugly new buildings. But today the worries are less over aesthetics than over threats to human health and safety, covering pollution in all its forms, and to some extent nuclear fall-out. Pollution, from car exhaust, factories or unclean water, has become a big issue; and it seems to relate to the wider French worry about health, in an insecure and anxious age. Previously, the agitation over ecology came mainly from a few pressure groups who had to fight public indifference or even official opposition as they battled to protect some site or prevent some local hazard; and they were often regarded as cranks or political extremists. But today many of their ideas are the official policies of Governments or local authorities. All talk now of defending *le patrimoine* (the heritage of landscape and architecture), or of how best to site a new motorway or check traffic in towns. Some cities run by centre-Left councils – Nantes, Strasbourg, Grenoble and La Rochelle – have led the way in trying to curb the car and develop other forms of transport.

Politically, the Green movement in France has never done very well at elections, and has split into three. The main party, Les Verts, scored only 3.6 per cent in 1997. But as it allied itself with the Socialists, it was able to win eight seats and was rewarded with a plum job: its leader, Dominique Voynet, a doctor, lively and outspoken, became Ministre de l'Aménagement du Territoire et de l'Environnement. She promptly announced her intention of halting so many projects that she became known as *Madame j'arrête tout* (Madame I-Stop-All). She persuaded the Government to cancel the Rhône–Rhine canal scheme (see p. 138) and some nuclear schemes. She also promoted some useful plans for trying to limit car pollution in Paris. But she failed to induce Jospin and her Communist colleague, the Minister of Transport Jean-Claude Gayssot, to give up the scheme to extend Roissy airport. This is set to provide many extra jobs – the one priority higher today than environment. All over France, local 'green' militants have been finding that although their causes now generally find a more sympathetic official ear, this is not the case if a contested new project is to provide extra employment. There are other pressures, too, not only from economic interests, that can still work against environmental protection. Measures to check industrial pollution have sometimes been thwarted because they might harm productivity. And in 1996 the EU's new Habitat directive, on the protection of endangered natural sites, provoked such opposition from hunters, foresters and landowners that the Juppé Government shrank from applying it in France. Similarly, in 1998, under pressure from the large hunting lobby, Parliament voted not to accept new European restrictions on the right to hunt migrating birds. And in the 1999 European elections, a new political movement, Chasse, Pêche, Nature et Traditions, scored a high 6.7 per cent – almost as much as the PCF. With its charming name but reactionary ideas, it drew many former Front National voters.

In the post-war decades, the French were probably right to set their first priority on industrialization. But they have now grown more aware of its side-effects. Pundits are preaching what in a sense is the opposite of Gravier's warnings: that the *désert français*, having been made to bloom, might return to a desert, this time not through neglect but overexploitation. Back in 1970, one campaign dissuaded the Government from letting a promoter build a ski resort in the Vanoise National Park, in the Alps; then another foiled the siting of an oil refinery in the Beaujolais wine country. As one indication of how local opinion has shifted, a teacher in a village in the Midi told me recently, 'Ten years ago the mayor wanted to turn this place into a commuter suburb full of chic villas. I stood against him, but was defeated. Now he has come to accept the very ideas I defended. He has even discovered the charm of old houses he had planned to knock down.' Expansionists have steadily become ecologists.

★

Back in de Gaulle's time, the Government showed little concern for such matters: its creed was expansion. But even under Pompidou change began. In 1971 he created a Ministry of the Environment – the term was just coming into fashion – which spent its tiny budget on anti-pollution devices, etc. It was a start, even if it only nibbled at a huge problem. Giscard then came to power on a wave of environmentalist feeling. He was both a modernist and a nostalgist, and when in 1975 he produced his famous slogan, 'a more human kind of growth', he found a genuine public response. What today is normal policy in Europe was in those days quite a novelty for France. Among his various actions, Giscard notably set about trying to save France's beautiful coastline, threatened by overbuilding: an official report had warned that the Côte d'Azur was 'being obstructed by a wall of concrete'. Here, north of Antibes, a curving wall of ziggurat holiday flats, twenty-two storeys high and 800 metres long, the Marina Baie des Anges, had arisen by the beach, desecrating the view. It was too late to pull it down: but Giscard did veto some other mammoth projects. On the Vendée and Normandy coasts, he put a brake on the work of the notorious Guy Merlin, who had become France's foremost property developer by building ugly six-storey strips of holiday flats by the sea: they found ready buyers, but he was accused of 'Sarcelliz-ing' the coast and was forced to stop. And on the Aquitaine coast nine new tourist centres were built in gentler low-rise style, set just inland amid lakes and woods. So strict were the conditions that private investment was for a while frightened off.

Giscard in 1975 created the Conservatoire du Littoral, charged with buying up and then protecting some emptier stretches of attractive coast. This has had considerable success. It is somewhat like the National Trust in Britain, save that, this being France, it is state-run, not private. Backed by a 1986 law that can prohibit building schemes, the Conservatoire has been able to acquire land along some 500 kilometres of coast, much of it by the Mediterranean, plus 100 kilometres more inland, beside lakes. But in some places it has had trouble. At Cavalaire, on the beautiful Var coast near St-Tropez, a conflict broke out in 1995 between the UDF mayor, who planned to build a large new tourist complex, and environ-mentalist groups. They appealed, under the 1986 law, and a tribunal sus-pended the project. But the mayor hit back, and by 1998 the issue was still unresolved. As the project was expected to bring 200 new jobs, plus plenty of added revenue, many local people backed the mayor. It was typical of so many environment-versus-economy dilemmas in France.

Beach pollution has also been an issue. In the 1970s the new industrial complex at Fos, near Marseille, was pouring tons of sulphur dioxide daily over the area with its 2.5 million people. Yet the Government faced a dilemma: if it imposed stricter rules against pollution, would it not frighten away the new industries it was so eager to entice? A tax on pollution existed, but many firms found it cheaper to pay it than to install costly purifying devices, so they had a virtual licence to pollute. The whole Mediterranean was clogging up with filth from industry, sewage and tankers, the Italians being the worst offenders. An international campaign led finally to the Athens and Barcelona agreements of 1980, whereupon the French Government promised to spend 1.5 billion francs over ten years on cleaning up its south coast – much needed, for the Côte d'Azur playground had become a slimy mess. Strict pollution controls were introduced, which steadily bore fruit, and today the problem is almost solved. By 1997, some 93.5 per cent of French beaches were up to the norms of cleanliness laid down by the European Commission; and 108 communes, including seventeen on the Côte, could fly on their beaches the EC's blue flag of clean health. The remaining pollution comes less from industry than from pleasure-boats, used by many families as a summer home – '*Et ils font leur caca dans la mer,*' I was told by a po-faced official at the ministry.

Brittany is today one key environmental battleground. Along the coast, with its many holiday beaches, all has gone rather well. Ugly high-rise building has been averted; and although there are plenty of modern villas, mostly these are built in pleasant local style, with little of the 'bungalow blight' that has spoilt similar landscapes in Ireland. The Conservatoire has acquired ninety-five sites and has turned a few into wildlife sanctuaries. At the Pointe du Raz, Brittany's most dramatic headland, a horrific 'tourist village' had been built, with some fifty souvenir shops: but in 1993–4 it was pulled down by the local authorities, and the area was restored to nature. Inland, however, the picture is different, for Breton farmers are today among the least ecology-minded in France. Not only have large-scale pig-breeders polluted the water supplies with their excess manure (see pp. 342 and 398), but pesticides from the farms have caused the seaweed to stink along some beaches. And the removal of stone fences to enlarge the fields has caused soil erosion and flooding – the negative side of the official policy of urging farms to modernize. 'All this is the price we now pay for agricultural progress,' said one Breton.

However, away from the farms, many old Breton towns and villages have been tastefully restored, in their sober style of grey granite.

In the cities, concern for the quality of life has risen enormously throughout France. Much of this today relates to traffic pollution – the old vexed issue of public transport versus the private car. But effort has gone also into the restoration of historic town centres, and campaigns to avert new eyesores. One pioneer was the radical-Left mayor of La Rochelle, Michel Crépeau, a voluble idealist, first elected in 1971. His superb old Huguenot seaport with its Renaissance buildings has something of the quality of Bruges, or of Dubrovnik before the Serb shelling, and to my mind is the loveliest coastal town in France: but it was in danger of becoming a congested mess. Crépeau's first act was to shoot down a project for a monstrous eleven-storey block of luxury flats on the harbour front. Then he turned his sights on a projected giant suburb for 40,000 people. 'Work had started,' he told me, 'but I battled with the prefect and got the scheme reduced to 10,000 people. In place of one group of tower blocks I put a thirty-hectare lake. At the time I was looked on as a dangerous Malthusian, trying to limit growth: but I was simply the trendsetter of what is now official state policy.' Any visitor is sure to be impressed by what Crépeau has done for the city's historic heart, with its narrow arcaded streets and medieval harbour fortresses. Some dozen streets have been banned to traffic and attractively paved, while the stunning Renaissance town hall and other buildings have been handsomely restored. 'Pedestrian zones are now *à la mode* in France, but *I* did it first,' said Crépeau. 'Giving back the street to the walker is a return to an older style. All progress is a renewal of tradition.'

Some other cities have since followed suit, including Montpellier under Georges Frêche, Strasbourg under Catherine Trautmann, and Besançon. Lyon offers another striking case (see p. 352). Its beautiful medieval and Renaissance quarter was crumbling, and threatened by an urban motorway scheme. This was averted in the 1970s and *le vieux Lyon* was then finely restored, thanks to a campaign led by a local intellectual, Régis Neyret, who told me, echoing Crépeau, 'We were thought crazy at first. For most Lyonnais, *le patrimoine* meant just folk dancing. Today they are grateful.' Many smaller and more ordinary towns, too, such as industrial Poissy, west of Paris, have neatly renovated their little central streets, with smart paving, bollards and arty lamp-posts – maybe a little too contrived, in some cases.

Traffic in cities has proved a tougher problem, notably in Paris. Pompidou used to speak of 'adapting the city to the motor car', but that idea is now out of fashion. Instead, most people agree at least in theory that the car must be curbed, for reasons of pollution more than of traffic jams: and yet, in practice, many egoistic Frenchmen still prefer to drive in town if they possibly can. Public transport's share of journeys within towns has even been falling: by 1995 it accounted for only 15 per cent of all individual urban journeys, compared with over 50 per cent taken by car, 30 per cent on foot, 3 per cent by bicycle. Urged on by the State, towns are therefore constantly making efforts to improve their public transport: but how today can they best afford it? In the boom years, Lyon and Marseille built Métros; Lille followed suit with a fully automated all-electric light underground system, the VAL, then unique in the world, and very successful. Toulouse has now also built a Métro line. But since the mid-1980s, several other towns have preferred to return to the tramway, with new special rails: it may congest the surface more than a Métro, but is much cheaper, and simpler. These are not the old clanging trams that chimed with Judy Garland's heartstrings in St-Louis, but smart modern vehicles, swift, smooth and quiet. Nantes was the first pioneer, in 1983, followed by Grenoble, then Strasbourg (yes, these three pioneer towns again), and all have made the tram a popular success. In Nantes, which now has three lines, 95 per cent of inhabitants claim to be pleased with it. Orléans, Rouen and St-Étienne also have new tramways; Bordeaux is following suit.

Alternative individual means of transport are being promoted, too – the small non-polluting electric car, and of course the bicycle. So back to Michel Crépeau. 'The yellow bicycles of La Rochelle' may sound like the title of a Jacques Demy movie, with Gene Kelly and Catherine Deneuve pedalling tunefully in the rain, but in fact the phrase in the 1970s became a symbol of the new ecology. Crépeau looked at Amsterdam with its free bicycles, and at Orly airport he saw how easily a visitor picks up a luggage trolley, then leaves it where he likes. So he bought 250 bicycles and had them painted bright yellow. Today the scheme still operates, modestly: the municipal bicycles, kept in special parks, are lent free for the first two hours. Sometimes they get stolen – one was found by the Lake of Geneva – but mostly abuses are few. The bicycles are used more by tourists than by locals, and as a practical means of reducing car traffic, they may have been little more than a publicity trick. No other town has taken up free bicycles. But Crépeau's enterprise, in this and his other actions, was rewarded nationally in 1981 when Mitterrand appointed him Minister of the Environment.

The intrepid Crépeau, ahead of other French mayors, has more recently been pioneering the electric car. In 1995 I found a fleet of fifty tiny Peugeots gliding silently around town, hired out cheaply to selected citizens. 'They don't pollute,' he said, 'they take up little road space, they don't require much upkeep, they are comfy, and they are silent – so quiet indeed that they have to be fitted with some artificial noise, or people might get run over.' What more can you want? – save that the batteries need recharging every 1,000 kilometres, which can make running the car expensive. Renault's Clio, Peugeot's Tulip and Citroën's Saxo are all being built with some electric models, to rival the output of Fiat, Audi, etc. Grenoble and Tours are now following La Rochelle's lead; and in October 1997 St-Quentin-en-Yvelines, a new town near Paris, started a system of hiring out electric cars cheaply by the hour, rather like the yellow bicycles. The Government has been offering incentives, too. But, despite its advantages, the petrol-free mini-wonder is catching on only slowly with the French public. By 1997 only sixteen had yet been sold to private individuals, although big firms and public bodies had acquired some 3,000.

A wider effort, after a late start, is now going into encouraging people to use their own bicycles in town. The 1995 transport strikes in Paris had some effect, when many employees found they had little other option; and today some town councils are using the slogan, 'Travel more slowly to save time'. But still only some 3 per cent of urban journeys in France are by bicycle, compared with 30 per cent or more in Amsterdam, and in Basle, so close to France. Perhaps the main reason is that French towns have been extremely slow to build cycle lanes down main streets. Grenoble began in the 1960s, but its venture at first had little sequel. Today, however, it is Nantes and Strasbourg – where else? – that vie for the *maillot jaune* of Cycle City (yellow being evidently the colour both for racing cyclists and for bicycles). During the 1990s Nantes has built 180 kilometres of lanes, and Strasbourg had completed 90 kilometres by 1995 in this industrial city on a plain where air pollution can be bad. Strasbourg claims that 15 per cent of its urban travel is now by bicycle. Even Paris, under Jean Tiberi, has now made its own modest start. And in 1989 a Club des Villes Cyclables was founded by towns pledged to helping the cyclist: its membership had reached over 200 by 1997. So finally the bicycle is making progress in this normally car-mad country.

Later than in many big European cities, air pollution caused by car exhausts has finally come to be seen as a serious problem in Paris and some other French towns. Until about the mid-1990s, most Parisians had turned a blind eye (or blocked nostril), believing theirs to be a 'clean' city; periodic smog or fumes were blamed on the climatic oddities of Paris in its basin, where breezy winds alternate with phases of static air. Then citizens came to accept that Paris had problems as bad as Rome or London, when a series of reports and warnings, from the police, medical authorities and civic leaders, shook them out of their lethargy. The first moves were made by the Right, before Voynet came to office. Jean Tiberi, on becoming mayor, warned that use of cars in Paris might have to be restricted when pollution levels rose high: he was greeted with angry alarm by many tradesmen. Then in March 1997 one of the last acts of the Juppé Government was to push through a 'clean air' law: this laid down, *inter alia*, that if the dioxide rose to 'level 3', then half of all Paris motor traffic would be banned, on an alternation basis, odd-numbered licence plates one day, even the next. It was a system already in force in Athens and some other cities.

After some bad smog during the summer, the fatal 'level 3' was reached in October and the new law was applied for the first time. The odd-numbered cars were forbidden to drive in Paris and some adjacent communes, and public transport was free. Some 10 per cent of drivers disobeyed: but the police were ordered to be lenient in imposing the authorized 900-franc fines. Next day, the pollution eased, so the ban was ended. Nearly all Parisians judged it a success: they breathed more easily, traffic was lighter, buses and Métro were not too overcrowded.

Meanwhile, Madame I-Stop-All was preparing longer-term changes: 'We must end thirty years of the rule of the car, all mentalities must change,' she said. Of her two main proposed measures, one was to raise the surprisingly low tax on diesel. This until now has been little more than half the tax on petrol, leaded or unleaded, so that a litre of diesel costs, net, only 4.40 francs, against 6.50 for super leaded, a far wider margin than in most countries. It is one main reason why up to 50 per cent of French vehicles run on diesel, which is dirtier, so drivers have simply had a tax incentive to pollute – absurd. The minister's second and more important measure, which came into force in August 1998, is to introduce the so-called *pastille verte*, a certificate awarded only to non-polluting vehicles running on lead-free petrol with a catalytic converter. These, about one-third of the total, will be able to run at any time. The others will still be subject to the alternating ban whenever pollution reaches 'level 3'. The haulage industry has protested, likewise car makers, notably Peugeot, the world's leading producer of diesel vehicles. But Voynet's significant measure could make quite a difference, and the public does not appear too hostile. An opinion survey by Sofres has shown two-thirds of the sample ready to make more use of public transport and accept limits on the use of cars. But, when it comes to the cherished *bagnole*, belief and practice are not always the same.

Ecology pressure groups did not emerge in France until the late 1960s. Some were born of May '68, others were influenced by the United States or Germany; nearly all were linked to the growing disillusion with politics and the older parties. Today they are grouped in three political movements, of which 'Les Verts' is the largest. There are various splinter factions, and as they are often quarrelling, this weakens their political impact. But the main groups have won many seats on local councils, where they generally ally with the Left. Sometimes their proposals are extreme and unrealistic, like wanting to close airports: but often their actions have been helpful, if costly. Thus the new A86 ring motorway outside Paris was held up for years on its western side by a campaign to preserve the forest of St-Germain: finally, it was agreed to build a tunnel under the forest, at great extra expense. Generally, actions against planned new motorways have been less militant than in Britain. But some groups have fought against nuclear power stations, chemical pollution, unsightly building schemes, or the spread of new electric pylons caused by the growth of mobile telephone networks. Ecologists have tried to preserve wildlife from French huntsmen; and they urge town councils to recycle their refuse, a sector where France is still backward.

   Until the 1980s, one trouble with many of the local field crusades was that they soon got confused with other issues, such as the long-running feud between the public and a technocratic State. A common scenario was this. The State in its high-handed way would announce some project without proper consultation. The local inhabitants would object and *les écolos* would leap to their aid; the State then dug in its heels, and there ensued a battle of wills; in the process, the real ecological issues were not debated on their merits, but became submerged beneath the weight of fury at the technocrats' arrogant tactics. By law a public inquiry had to be held locally: but this was only consultative and often just a formality. If the inquiry revealed great local opposition to the project, the State was much less likely than in Britain to take account and back down. However, the Socialist reforms, by transferring many decisions to local authorities, then broke this pattern to an extent. And today Governments both of Right and Left have become more responsive to public opinion on these matters, and more environmentally conscious themselves. The issues are now more often thrashed out at a council meeting, rather than in militant physical confrontation. So there has been improvement. Even so, it is worth recalling some of the famous conflicts of the Giscard era.

In 1979 at Castries, a small town near Montpellier, the state-owned Gaz de France company carried out some secret seismic tests, then announced it was planning to use natural underground cavities as storage for 400 million cubic metres of gas. The population, aware of geological faults in the area, formed a committee to fight the project, and sent a petition with 4,000 signatures. But Gaz de France's technocrats at first refused even to discuss the matter: '*We* know what we're doing, *you* don't: just trust us,' they said, in effect. Then the company did hold a public inquiry, as by law it had to. 'We knew it would be a farce, so we boycotted it, and so did the local mayors,' one committee leader told me. 'But after weeks of suspense we learned that Gaz de France had dropped their project. They claimed that their seismic surveys had revealed faults. But these had been done months ago: so we felt sure that the real reason was our protest, and they didn't want to lose face by admitting they had backed down under pressure. But we scored a victory over their arrogance, by proving that popular action of this kind *can* bring results. Usually, in such conflicts, the State wins. But the danger is to believe that the citizen can never win, for people then lose the nerve to fight.' That was typical of the mood in those days. When I met my friend again in 1997, he said, 'The State and its technocrats do nowadays consult far more readily. And yet, in today's climate, if job creation is involved, it can be even harder to win a case of this kind. Recently a big stone quarry was to be opened near here, likely to produce dust and noise. We made a fuss, but we lost – for those reasons.' Jobs *versus* ecology – the usual dilemma.

A better-known *cause célèbre* of the 1970s was the Larzac affair. In 1971 the army announced its plan to extend from 2,800 to 17,000 hectares its tank firing range on the Larzac plateau, near Millau in the southern Aveyron. The 103 sheep farmers involved were due to be compensated: but they did not want to be driven off their ancestral lands, so they protested. And their cause was quickly taken up by a score of ecology and anti-militarist groups all over France, as well as by the Occitan regionalists: their slogan, '*Gardarem lo Larzac*' (save Larzac) was daubed across the Midi. Ecologists, by way of peaceful protest, would lie down in the path of the tanks. In face of this unexpected barrage, and of legal obstacles, the army prevaricated, and the dispute dragged on for years. Larzac became a national crusade, a pilgrimage centre drawing thousands each summer to take part in the protest and listen to lectures by Greens.

The evolution of the affair is significant. It began as a local movement of self-interest led by farmers. It was then taken up as an anti-Paris regional issue, and as a test case for ecology: the Greens who jumped on the bandwagon became more militant about Larzac than the farmers. And the Ministry of Defence made all the usual blunders of failing to consult, failing to state its case clearly or indicate the compensation terms. 'We are not against French national defence,' said one farmer; 'what angers us is the way the plan was imposed on us.' But as in similar cases, the Government was caught in a dilemma. If it bulldozed the scheme through, as it could, it would risk even greater unpopularity; if it backed down, it would appear weak and so encourage other protests elsewhere. But Mitterrand was not bound by this. Like any incoming ruler, he was able to change his predecessor's policy without loss of face. So one of his first acts in May 1981 was to cancel the army's scheme totally.

Some of the Larzac militants stayed on and settled in the area (see p. 425). And by chance they have recently found another big cause locally: to oppose the building of the tallest viaduct in the world. Designed by Sir Norman Foster, with seven giant 270-metre pillars, this will carry the new A75 *autoroute* over the lovely river Tarn at Millau, close to Larzac. In this tourist bottleneck, the old main road through Millau gets blocked with vast traffic jams in summer, and local *notables* have been battling for the *autoroute*. But some others, local worthies as well as ecologists, have argued that the viaduct would be too expensive, not entirely safe, and damaging to the spectacular scenery near the Tarn Gorges. The conflict has been intense: in the old glove-making town of Millau, the gloves were off! In 1997 I met Alain Desjardins, a Picardy-born Larzac veteran and self-styled *insurgé permanent*, now a local farmer, *aubergiste* and Green activist: 'This planned eyesore has become a hated symbol for us, as the Larzac camp was. Experts say that in high winds it could be dangerous, and the cost could go up to 7 billion. Most local people think it could help the area, but we *néo-ruraux* are all hostile.' This lobby put forward a counter-plan for a smaller viaduct in a gentler part of the valley, to the west. But the Government said it was too late to change the path of the A75, the final link in a great Paris–Barcelona motorway. And the new Communist Minister of Transport, as ever more concerned with jobs than ecology, gave the green light for a project now slowly going ahead. So this time *les écolos* lost. But how strong was their case? The project cannot be charged with Pompidolian gigantism, for its height was dictated by the depth of the valley at this point. The real issue is an old one: does a huge modern structure – in this case, elegantly designed by Sir Norman – enhance or harm a lovely landscape?

In the Giscard era, nuclear power became one of the main targets of the ecological protesters. When the Superphénix fast-breeder reactor was being built near Lyon in 1977 (see p. 116), some 30,000 demonstrators from many countries clashed with riot police: over 100 people were injured, and one died. The authorities claimed that the 'trouble-makers' were led by a commando of German extremists. And work on the reactor went ahead. The next battlefield was in sensitive Brittany, where the Government was keen to build a power station in a region that produced only 6 per cent of its own energy needs. A site for a huge 5,200-megawatt station was chosen on the rugged Cap Sizun peninsular. The regional council and the Finistère *conseil général*, both with pro-government majorities, voted in favour of the project, if only for the new jobs and investment it could bring to this poor corner of Brittany. But the adjacent village of Plogoff thought otherwise. The mayor claimed that the first he heard of the plan was by reading the newspapers. As at Larzac, the ecologists and the regionalists took up the cause, and the stage was set for another showdown with the State. Électricité de France, in charge of the project, produced soothing hand-outs to explain that there was no danger to the village. But the locals were not satisfied. In 1979, as the EDF's field studies went ahead, so did the protest rallies. I attended one, a good-humoured, relaxed affair with a holiday spirit and *les flics* discreetly out of sight. Young ecologists had come in thousands, many from Paris. There were Breton nationalist flags, and banners with slogans such as '*Oui aux moutons, non aux neutrons*'.

By the time the ritual public inquiry was due to begin, the villagers were seriously worried. They knew that in other such nuclear inquiries, local rejection had counted for nothing: at Nogent, near Paris, 45,000 voted against, 1500 for, yet the power station went ahead. So the local mayors staged a boycott, closing their *mairies* to the inquiry. But the

State, with nuclear power at stake, staged the inquiry itself, in mobile booths. Then the villagers' wrath exploded, in true Celtic fashion. Some 600 armed gendarmes, backed by riot police and paratroopers, were sent to protect the booths, and for six weeks Bretons and ecologists fought a pitched battle with them, hurling rocks and explosives. But the Government stuck to its guns. When the 'inquiry' had ended, its officials noted that no votes had been cast against, so the project could go ahead. The villagers maybe had a case, but the case against them was summed up to me by one pro-Giscard Breton leader: 'Of course no commune will ever vote for a nuclear station on its soil, that's normal self-interest. So decisions have to be taken on a wider level – and note that the Breton elected leaders *have* voted for the project. Even towns thirty kilometres from Plogoff are in favour. So what right have local villagers to dictate to all Brittany? And where else is our energy to come from? These anti-nuclear kids drive in their little cars to the demos: they'd be the first to moan if France had no fuel left. There's a lot of hypocrisy in ecology.' This frantic dialogue of the deaf was then ended by Mitterrand in 1981, who put a stop to the Plogoff project and to four others where work was about to start.

Ever since then, although work on other nuclear stations has gone ahead, there have been few mass rallies and sit-ins of the kind seen at Plogoff. The reasons are complex. It could be argued that the Plogoff and Larzac campaigns were essentially regional and political, more than ecological. And some local mayors and their voters, unlike at Plogoff, have welcomed nuclear plant for the jobs and money it can bring: just six weeks after Chernobyl, the mayor of a village close to Superphénix said, 'Yes, there's a risk, but it's worth taking. We have done well from the extra work and tax revenue.' Another factor is that the old official taboo about nuclear policy has been lifted and the whole debate has become more open in the media and in politics. Many ecologists thus feel less need to trudge the fields with their banners to make their voice heard. Today, under Jospin, nuclear policy is still in state hands: but the Green-led Environment Ministry now has just as large a voice as the EDF. And the devolutionary reforms of the 1980s, too, have made it easier for these issues to be debated democratically at local level.

DEVOLUTION AT LAST — A MIXED BLESSING

France has a new, less centralized structure of local and regional government. But has this really brought the improvements intended? Opinions today vary — just as they always varied on the outgoing system, complex and devious, which persisted with few alterations from Napoleon's day until the reforms of the 1980s. And it is not easy to make a fair evaluation. On the one hand, many leaders in other countries always admired France's prefectoral structure and envied the power it gave the State to initiate projects in the regions, as well as the stability it provided in times of unrest and the safeguards it offered against local corruption. These were clear assets. On the other hand, many French people came to ask whether the Paris-appointed prefect, political servant of the Ministry of the Interior, was really the ideal figure to be in charge of local affairs in a modern democracy. Nor was the prefect fully master in his own domain: both he and the locally elected mayors of towns were often victims of the same heavy state machine whereby rival ministries spread their tentacles through the provinces, jealously guarding their separate local fiefdoms, causing delays and muddles. The prefect had only partial control over this bureaucracy, which could sap the spirit of civic initiative.

During the 1960s and '70s the economic and cultural revival of the regions, plus other modern developments, led to growing pressures for a formal reduction of state control, both at the local level of towns and villages, and at a wider regional level. Pompidou responded with a few modest changes. But most Gaullist barons, Jacobin-minded, did not hide their fears that true devolution would 'cause the State to fly apart'. Yet many others, both of Right and Left, were by now of the view that France could not become a modern open society without some real reform of this kind: it could not stand aside from a trend towards regionalization that had been gaining ground in Italy, in post-Franco Spain, and elsewhere. The Socialists then came to power with an elaborate blueprint, which they saw as the most important of their reforms for reshaping French society. Pierre Mauroy called it '*la grande affaire*' of Mitterrand's first mandate. And today it seems clear that, whatever its inadequacies, it will go into history as a major achievement of their years in power.

It came into effect in stages in 1982–6. The prefect was stripped of some of his executive power, and a number of his responsibilities for local affairs were transferred to elected bodies in the regions, *départements* and communes. But the State retained strong reserve powers, and the devolution did stop short of creating a federal system on the German or American pattern. In fact, the feeling today is that the new regional assemblies, first elected in 1986, have not been granted sufficient power for there to be much danger of the State 'flying apart'. Many people would say that in this respect the reform has been too timid: it has not given the regions adequate scope for competing properly with their major counterparts in the EU, say with Bavaria, Lombardy or Catalonia, let alone Scotland, where devolution is now going further than in France. The regional trend in Europe is in part a bid to strengthen democracy at the lower levels, so as to balance the growing central power of the EU bodies. This is accepted by the Jacobin elements still so strong in France: but they would rather give more power to the lower tiers, the communes and *départements*, than to the regions which could prove greater rivals to the State. Hence the reform has strengthened the *département* as much as the region, resulting in what many anti-Jacobins see as a cumbersome compromise.

The reform has been criticized also for creating too complex, expensive and top-heavy a structure, with overlapping functions; for failing to merge the many small village communes into larger units; and for facilitating local political feuding, even corruption, now that the prefect has less power to intervene. But imperfect though the reform may be, opinion surveys suggest that it seems to be roughly in line with what most people want. The time is ripe for devolution to have its chance, whatever the risks among a people as contentious as the French. State centralism, for all its assets, was too powerful for too long, and the spirit of the times demands more scope for local initiative. So let us first look closer at the outgoing system, its weaknesses and strengths.

Local government has not lost its basic three-tier structure. At the bottom level, the country is divided into 36,763 communes, most of them villages, some of them big towns like Lyon. Unlike the *départements* created artificially in 1790, the communes are deep-rooted historical entities, often with a strong local pride. Each has its mayor and council, elected every six years. Mayors play a far greater role than in Britain, and many of them retain office for decades, becoming local father figures. Yet the mayor is also, in some ways, the servant of the State in the commune. The middle tier is that of the ninety-six *départements*, each with its elected council (*conseil général*). Above are the twenty-two regions, created in 1964, each grouping a handful of *départements*. Each *département* has its prefect, and each region its super-prefect, who is also prefect of the *département* where the region's capital is located. The Socialists' reforms retained these same three tiers, while granting to each more autonomy.

The regional prefect's main role has been to help coordinate economic planning. But under the old system the departmental prefect was more a political governor. As conceived by Napoleon, his first task was to maintain law and order: he controlled most of the police and was expected to keep the Government informed on local opinion and political developments. He would even act as a kind of electoral agent for pro-government candidates. But in post-war years this aspect of his work declined, as increasingly he became caught up in economic duties. Besides coordinating the ever more complex activities of the many ministerial services within his borders, he had to supervise the *conseil général* and the communes. His working relations even with anti-government mayors were generally quite sound: but each possessed a tacit veto on the other's projects and often would use it.

At first sight the system might seem to have been heavily weighted against the commune's freedom of action. The prefect had the right to suspend a mayor or councillor from office (and occasionally would do so). The revenue that a town could raise from local taxes was so limited, by law, that even in matters where it had some autonomy – roads, culture, sport, etc. – in practice it had to rely on financial partnership with the State, which through loans or subsidies provided some 70 per cent of the finance for local projects. And to obtain one franc the commune had first to secure state approval of the project as a whole. It could in some cases go ahead on its own: but seldom would it feel it had the money to forgo state aid. So it was at the mercy of ministerial delays, or arbitrary last-minute cuts by the Ministry of Finance. Or its projects could be vetoed. This might sometimes be sheer vindictiveness, if its electors had *mal voté*: but more often the factors were bureaucratic caution or parsimony, or sheer muddle and inertia. Urban-renewal schemes could wait many years for the go-ahead: Rouen once had to wait thirteen to rebuild a main square.

Until 1971 a commune had to present its annual budget in full detail to the prefect for his prior approval. This was then modified: accounts were now scrutinized in advance only where state money was involved or some irregularity was suspected. Yet in other respects the State's formal powers of control remained enormous. If a mayor wanted to erect a public monument, or even change a street name, or alter the pay rates of his staff, the relevant ministry could intervene. Many communes ended up resentful, and might in turn block state projects for their area. The State might have the legal power to override this, but in practice it tended to be cautious for political reasons and preferred the carrot to the stick. In fact, one of the roles of the prefect was to mediate between mayors and ministerial bureaucrats. For the prefect, after all, was a kind of diplomat, moved from post to post every few years, partly for promotion, but also to prevent him becoming too involved with the natives. Today he may have lost some of his formal powers: but he still has a lavish flat in his stately *préfecture*, where he entertains in style, and he presides in gold-and-blue uniform at major ceremonies. Prefects, nearly all of them *énarques*, may often share the limitations of the technocrat: but the better ones are men of culture, commonsense and personal presence, skilled at persuasion in a local world of wheeling-and-dealing. This may help to explain why, under the old system, there was often so much complicity and interdependence between mayor and prefect in daily practice. Despite the strong powers of the State, some mayors and other *notables* were in turn able to exert quite an influence on Paris in diverse ways. Mayors and prefects, though rivals, needed each other, and they generally knew how to reach a *modus vivendi*. A good prefect and a go-ahead mayor often shared common aims, whether of economic expansion or 'quality of life'; they also had a joint interest in preserving peace and avoiding disruptions that could discredit them both.

Above all, the tradition in France – unlike that in Britain – has long been for an ambitious politician to try to build a strong local power base, often by seeking election as mayor of a big town; or, put the other way, it can be the mayors of big towns who have found it easiest to climb high in national politics. For whatever the limits in the old days on a town's autonomy, within it the mayor has always been a big boss, *un patron*. Jacques Chaban-Delmas in Bordeaux, Gaston Deferre in Marseille, Pierre Mauroy in Lille, not to mention Jacques Chirac in Paris, are among the many recent examples of big-town mayors with a national role. And, unlike a prefect and his senior staff, a successful mayor usually stays in office for many years, often decades, thus becoming a focus of local loyalty. What's more, the French have hitherto followed the tradition of the *cumul des mandats*, whereby the more offices you held simultaneously, the more power you might be able to wield: thus a prominent mayor might not only be a deputy or senator too, but also maybe president of the *conseil général*, or an MEP in Strasbourg. These leaders have generally carried terrific clout in Paris. And so a prefect or other official would be careful how he handled a strong local *notable*, who could go above his head to a minister or even to the Élysée, or who one day might become his own master in Paris. This *cumul des mandats* was open to abuses, and has now been restricted under the post-1981 reforms (see below).

A clever *notable* was often able to play off one government service against another. For the State, that centralizing monster, was also a hydra whose diverse heads were frequently in conflict or at cross purposes; at national and local level alike, there were (and still are) long-standing rivalries between certain ministries and agencies. Officials would often prefer to deal with a *notable* than with each other, and this increased the latter's power. So it was small wonder that the freemasonry of local *élus*, loud though they might complain against state tutelage, would in practice oppose any reform that threatened their vested interests. This convoluted system was workable and had its strengths. But as the sociologist Michel Crozier, a strong critic of the State, pointed out in his book *On ne change pas la société par décret* (1979), 'This honeycomb network of power and decision-making confines *notables* and civil servants within an enclosed circuit; it prevents the citizen from intruding into public affairs, it creates and perpetuates the game of favours and privileges . . .' Crozier's view and that of other critics – myself included – was that the system was lacking both in democracy and efficiency. The *cumul des mandats* concentrated too much power in too few hands and gave the busy potentate too little time to concentrate properly on any one of his duties. Also, as Crozier suggested, the system even incited a mayor to be an autocrat in his town:

An astute mayor knows it is not a wise policy to invite the citizens to participate. The mayor owes his power to the fact that he alone has the ear of the state administration. In order to keep his power, he must remain as the indispensable intermediary, and this requires aloofness, secrecy and citizen non-participation. Universal suffrage designates a small number of *notables*, who then organize among themselves a relatively hermetic style of decision-making. (pp. 132–3)

Maybe Crozier put it too strongly: but rare in those days were the liberal mayors who attempted a different style.

Some other structures of local government had also become archaic. The departmental *conseil général* had been devised for the old rural France and never properly updated for modern needs. This enfeebled version of an English county council was directly elected and had its own modest budget for some services, such as secondary roads. But it met only twice a year, its budget and agenda were prepared by the prefect, and it usually did his bidding. It might have had more influence, were it not elected on a 'rotten borough' basis, weighted in favour of rural areas: for example, in the Haute-Garonne, Toulouse with two-thirds of the population elected only four of the thirty-nine councillors. A *conseil général*, its members mostly elderly, remained a bit of a joke – until the Socialists' shake-up.

A more serious weakness, and one that the Socialist reforms failed to tackle, is that most village communes are far too small for modern purposes of local government. This flaw cannot be blamed on the State: it is largely the communes' own doing, for they have refused total mergers, and many are even reluctant to regroup rationally. There are two types of problem: (a) the spread of conurbations has engulfed small surrounding communes which cling defiantly to their independence, sometimes obstructing the growth of an urban area's joint services; (b) many rural communes, now depopulated, no longer make sense as administrative entities. The map of France's communes has barely altered since the last century. There are still 36,763 of them, more units of local government that in the rest of the EU together. Some 22,700 have fewer than 500 inhabitants; one has only three, and most of its statutory council of nine live elsewhere! The smaller communes generally lack the finances and know-how needed for today's tasks: yet to persuade them to merge has not proved easy. Not only do mayors and councillors want to avoid losing office, but the citizen, too, is emotionally attached to his commune. The village *mairie*, the mayor with his sash conducting a wedding or opening a fête, this is something very real, especially in a time of rediscovery of rural traditions.

So, for electoral reasons, Governments have rarely tried to enforce mergers. Exhortation has been attempted: a law in 1971 allowed sizeable loans and tax benefits to communes agreeing to merge, but the response was feeble, and fewer than 1,000 communes have since disappeared. Small ones fear that to be swallowed up by a bigger one would mean the loss of 'human scale'. When one village was invited by the prefect to integrate with either Lille or Roubaix, the mayor retorted, 'We are like Poland in 1939, trapped between Germany and Russia!' – and all over France, you could almost hear the bells of the little Clochemerles tolling their sympathy for this *esprit de clocher*.

Communes, however, have reacted more readily to the policy, begun in the 1960s, of grouping together in associations for joint planning, services, etc. This has been especially necessary in the big conurbations, where de Gaulle's Government in 1967 did impose a new structure, the *communauté urbaine*, on Bordeaux, Lille, Lyon and Strasbourg: here the central and suburban communes each keep their own identity and mayor, with many responsibilities, but they also unite to form a joint council with its own budget, in charge of town-planning and many services. The system has worked fairly well, and has since been copied voluntarily in some other places. Generally, the central commune provides the main impetus, and its mayor is president of the *communauté*'s council. Some other conurbations, including Nantes and Montpellier, have preferred a looser formula, the 'district', which provides less scope for joint town-planning. Owing to rivalries between communes, and not only between Right and Left, some urban areas failed for many years to create even a 'district', despite the inconveniences. In Toulouse the arrogant Louis Bazergue (see p. 358) was on such bad terms with the suburban mayors, even his fellow Socialists, that he refused all cooperation on such matters as water supplies, and would not even extend the city's bus routes outside its borders. Then he took fright that Paris might impose on him a *communauté urbaine*, so he reluctantly changed his policy. Amazingly, it was the first time that he and the other local mayors had sat round a table together. After his fall from power, the conurbation evolved into a 'district', and it was no longer necessary to change buses at the city boundaries as if one were crossing a national frontier!

In smaller urban areas and rural zones, some 9,000 communes have formed groupings. Of the several possible legal formulae, some impose few obligations while others are tighter and oblige more sharing of finances and tax-raising. These are the ones officially encouraged, and they enable a group of smallish communes to do much that they could not afford individually: in rural Burgundy, in 1996, the president of one such association showed me proudly the new *salle des fêtes* and civic advice centre that they had been able to build jointly. However, many mayors and councillors remain afraid even of this degree of shared responsibilities, which they fear would weaken their freedom and identity. Yet the communes' increased duties under the regional reform, and the

pressure of today's economic problems, make it ever more important for
them to cooperate closely. Many senior politicians, of both Right and
Left, are today urging just this. 'By all means let the commune keep its
identity, for such matters as fêtes, marriages and war memorial ceremonies,' said one Breton *centriste* leader, Pierre Méhaignerie, 'but for
economic matters we need to move towards the German system of the
Kreise, or the British rural or urban district. It's increasingly absurd to
have so many autonomous communes' – a widely held view.

Another issue, more directly political, is regionalism. Here various
piecemeal reforms of local government were made under de Gaulle,
Pompidou and Giscard. The most important, in 1964, gave birth to the
'region', in a limited form: it had become clear that the little *départements*
were no longer suitable units for modern economic planning, so they
were grouped into regions, solely for that purpose. France's *départements*
are all much the same size (except around Paris), though their population
varies from 2.5 million to under 75,000. Their scale was conceived in
Napoleon's day so that an official in the main town could travel by
stagecoach to any part of his domain and back between sunrise and
sundown: but later the train and car killed all that. It was also evident by
the 1960s that big projects such as the Languedoc canal, extending
across the old borders, required a wider framework of coordination and
decision-taking than the *département*. So regional *préfectures* were created.
In each region a body of local worthies was set up, to 'advise' the prefect,
but these proved to be cyphers.

By the late 1960s the feeling was growing that France needed a
democratic regional structure: this was even one of the motifs of May
1968. De Gaulle, who understood these aspirations, put forward a project
of this kind in 1969: but it was defeated, largely for other reasons, and
he resigned. Pompidou then revived the idea in 1972, in a different form.
By now regionalism was gaining ground in Europe, and the Gaullists
conceded that they must do something. So a new assembly was set up
in each region, comprised of the local deputies and senators plus a few
other *notables*. It had a small budget of its own, derived from local taxes,
which it could use for funding some projects on its own initiative. So
the reform did mark a small step forward: the region was finally legalized
as a political institution. But in practice the new bodies had little scope:
it was still the prefect who had the money and power for the real projects,
and he tended to present them as *faits accomplis*. A few Socialist-led
assemblies, notably that in Provence chaired by Defferre, did manage to

stand up to the prefect: but it was rare. An assembly had no real popular mandate, being indirectly elected.

Giscard, at his election, indicated a readiness to move on to the next crucial phase: direct regional elections. But then came separate flare-ups in Brittany, Languedoc, Alsace and Corsica: Giscard rapidly backtracked, apparently under Gaullist pressure, and swung against regionalism. When I visited him at the Élysée in 1979, he told me, 'The French are so contentious that regional devolution would create local fiefdoms opposed to the State. France is like that. So we cannot yet take the risk. As for the aspirations of the Bretons and others, they can be satisfied by economic and cultural measures.'

The Socialists then inaugurated a new era. Once in power, they gave priority to a long-prepared masterplan, which they saw as central to their declared philosophy of creating a more participatory society and – as Mauroy put it in June 1981 – of 'giving the State back to its citizens'. They also saw devolution as a reform that could win the broad consensus of the nation; unlike many of their economic measures, it was not based on any left-wing dogma. The man charged with carrying it through was the veteran Gaston Defferre, who was given the title of Minister of the Interior and of Decentralization (in a French traditional context, something of a contradiction in terms?). He had long been mayor of Marseille, as Mauroy was of Lille: so they had seen state tutelage at first hand. Both were keen regionalists; and Mitterrand, though much less of one, backed them. He said, 'France, to come into being, needed a strong central power. Now it needs strong local powers to avoid falling apart.'

The reform was presented to Parliament in June 1981; then it gradually came into application, culminating in the first direct regional elections of March 1986. And it is still in force today, largely unchanged. It formally abolished the *tutelle* of the prefect, who can no longer tell a council what to do but can only interfere *post hoc* by appealing to a tribunal, if he suspects irregularity. He keeps the title of prefect and can still wear his uniform at ceremonies: but his role is now mainly confined to coordinating state services in his *département* and to helping the village communes with their affairs. The State has transferred certain of its duties to the three tiers of local government, and of these it is the *conseil général* of the *département* that is the main beneficiary. This previously feeble body now has a hugely increased budget, and its elected chairman has taken over the prefect's executive powers and budgetary control. He has thus emerged as a major figure on the French scene, equal to the mayor of a large city. 'The reforms have brought a big change to our daily relations with the *préfecture*,' a councillor told me in Amiens; 'local state officials used to be arrogant and secretive. Now they are more respectful and consult us more.'

To the region the State has handed over responsibiity for adult education, professional training and the building of *lycées*, as well as for some aspects of culture, tourism, road-building and aid for industrial development. An average-sized region might have an operational budget of about 2 billion francs per year, of which roughly half will come from its own fiscal resources and half from the State in a lump sum. Though it must fulfil all its basic duties, it does also enjoy a certain flexibility in how it spends its money: thus some regions will do more for culture than others, or for industry or helping smaller communes. The *département* has now been given the huge task of running the public welfare and social services, with big budgets involved; it is also in charge of some infrastructure and of *collège* buildings. And the communes have gained responsibility at last for their own town-planning schemes and the granting of building permits. Environmental concerns are shared between *département* and commune. All local bodies now have more power to raise extra finances, from loans or higher taxes. And another big change is that the State's subsidy for investment projects is no longer allotted per item but comes in an annual lump sum for the council to spend as it pleases. 'This gives us far more freedom,' one mayor told me; 'if we want a new swimming pool, we can now choose the kind we like, and build it in our own time.'

Yet it would be wrong to think that these reforms have recklessly disbanded the State. The prefects' political role, as watchdogs of the Ministry of the Interior, has ended; but they are still in charge of law and order, and of the national police (there are some municipal police, too); and they retain some reserve powers in case of trouble. Moreover, the State has kept control of certain key matters that in Britain or Germany are largely or partly in local hands – most notably education (as opposed to school buildings), health (as opposed to welfare and hospital buildings), and the supervision of justice.

The Socialists' reforms have not marked any revolution: but they have hugely modified the nature of French local government. They have been much criticized: but today most politicians and *notables*, of all political colours, do see them as at least a step in the right direction. Most citizens, too, seem to feel that administration has been brought closer to them and made more open and human. A survey published in *Le Monde* in February 1997 showed that over two-thirds of the large sample judged the reforms to have been positive and to have improved the quality of local affairs. Yet there are some major question marks. The reforms are thought to have produced a structure that is too complex and ill-defined. They have not always been well applied, and have produced some negative side-effects.

Notably, devolution may in some cases have facilitated the recent spread of civic corruption. For example, in the granting of building permits or public contracts, the prefect hitherto had the last word – and prefects in France, and their senior staff, have nearly always been above corruption. Now the mayor takes the decisions; and a weak mayor can yield to pressures of bribery, while an unscrupulous one can exploit his new freedom. Could Alain Carignon in Grenoble (see p. 347) ever have got so far in his machinations, under the old system? A prefect can bring a matter *post hoc* to a tribunal, if he suspects illegality, and some have done so: but this takes time, and by then the corruption has already spread its poison. On a wider level, too, devolution may have tended to increase clientelism and wheeler-dealing. A village mayor in Burgundy told me, 'We are under lots of new pressures, and it's harder for us to resist than it was for the prefect, who could be more impartial. To refuse an elector a building permit can be highly invidious.' In Germany a town mayor is a full-time professional; in France he gets a small salary, and expenses, but usually he has another job too, maybe in business. This can make him more vulnerable.

These and other problems have led recent Governments to reimpose the *tutelle* just a little, at least by instructing prefects to make fuller use of their residual powers and to give more practical help to smaller communes that may need it. Often this has been welcomed. In the 1980s many villages soon realized that that they lacked the expertise to make proper use of their added powers: so in 1985, under pressure from the mayors themselves, the Socialist Government felt obliged – in the case of those with fewer than 2,000 people – to modify the new law and go back to the previous system, whereby the State's annual top-up budget is not given in a lump sum but is worked out with the prefect item by item. The prefects thus recovered some of their lost power: nanny was found to be still necessary, after all. 'We accept that we need our prefect,' said one village mayor, 'as a provider of technical services, and a protector.

We just don't have the know-how ourselves.' Similar help is now given to the groupings of smaller communes.

The Defferre reforms have sometimes been criticized for bolstering local autocracy by giving too much power to mayors. This may be true in a few cases. Yet, in other ways, the reforms have clearly strengthened local democracy. First, town councils have returned to proportional representation. The Gaullists in the early 1960s had invented a single-list system for all towns of over 30,000 people, whereby any party or coalition won all the seats, or none. The Gaullists did this cynically, in the days when they were strong, knowing that it would help them and their allies to control most cities. Later it rebounded against them when the Left swept the board in 1977. But whoever won, there was never any true opposition on a council – in Bordeaux not a single left-wing councillor to gainsay Chaban-Delmas, and so on. It was a mockery of democracy. It also meant that, after a change of power, the new team would arrive at the *mairie* without experience of the council's affairs, and could make mistakes through ignorance. The system was modified in 1977 for larger cities. But it was left to the Socialists in 1982 to reintroduce PR to all local elections. So the mayor is now kept in check, not so much by the prefect as in the old days, as by an elected opposition. A victory for democracy.

Secondly, the Socialists in the 1980s began to restrict the notorious *cumul des mandats*. Their reform prevented a politician from holding more than two elective posts: so a mayor who is a deputy cannot now also be head of the *conseil général* or regional assembly. Jospin in 1998 set about tightening this rule, so as to make it illegal to be mayor *and* deputy or minister. The Socialists were already applying this voluntarily in their own ranks: thus in 1997 Catherine Trautmann ceased to be mayor of Strasbourg when she became Minister of Culture. It was quite a break with tradition. The purpose of the reforms is to put a check on empire-building, and to oblige mayors and other leaders to concentrate on one job at a time, rather than disperse their energies. But when Jospin's new bill came before Parliament, it faced strong opposition from politicians alike of Right and Left, who did not want to see their influence cut back. In late 1998 he was still trying to negotiate a compromise.

The earlier reform may already have helped to improve the quality of local affairs. But it may not have checked the tendency of French mayors to be little autocrats within their own fief. The Defferre reforms may have brought decision-making nearer home: but some mayors and *notables* have been hugging the new powers to themselves, rather than share them with the people. Citizens have the ability to prevent this, if they choose to participate more assertively: but they tend in France to leave the daily running of affairs to those they have elected. And mayors expect this: '*You* chose us, so stop interfering and let us get on with it', is their attitude. Defferre had a plan for setting up local ward councils that would oblige a mayor to consult more closely: but it was strongly opposed, then dropped. It has since been adopted voluntarily by some town councils, mostly those that are Socialist-led.

A related problem is that the granting of more power to local bodies may have increased the frictions between them: has local life become too politicized? In some *départements* feuds have developed between the larger towns, often in left-wing hands, and the local *conseil général*, more usually on the Right because of its rural electoral bias. And at this level the prefect cannot so easily arbitrate as he can between smaller communes. Since part of a town's budget consists of subsidies from the *département*, the result can be endless infighting. A Socialist councillor in Amiens complained, 'The right-wing *conseil* is victimizing us by holding back the money due for a road scheme.' And in the Vienne (capital, Poitiers) a battle royal broke out between the imperious chairman of the *conseil général*, René Monory, a Giscardian ex-minister, and the petulant Édith Cresson, Socialist mayor of Châtellerault. 'That boorish garage owner!' she told me. 'He cares only for exploiting the Vienne as his fief and scoring points off me. He's cut back on my town-planning subsidy.' But such vendettas are frequently more a matter of flamboyant rival personalities than of serious policy issues. Maybe they add a Latin spice to local life without doing as much real damage as the previous more insidious tussles between Paris technocrats and the provinces. And after the difficult first few years, matters today seem to be settling down. The pattern varies greatly: while near-war may still rage in Languedoc between the regional council and the mayor of Montpellier (see p. 381), in Alsace and Brittany, regions with a calmer, more northerly style, cooperation today is smooth, even cordial, between the centre-Right presidents and the Socialist mayors of the big towns.

The Defferre reforms also threw up the risk that enlightened state planning might now lose ground to petty self-interest and the *esprit de clocher* in some areas. This was one argument of the Jacobins against devolution: after all, much post-war progress in the provinces did come from the derided state technocrats. A local politico, under electoral pressures, may fail to take the longer-term view. Nor did the councils of the regions and *départements* find it easy at first to recruit the qualified staff needed for their complex new tasks. But gradually these problems have been sorting themselves out. Many councils have hired ex-prefects, or *polytechniciens* from the Grands Corps, to help them run their affairs. And regions and *départements* have mostly made sensible use of their new powers. This has been true even in the cultural field, where the ministry has now handed over some responsibility to the regions. It was apparent back in the days of André Malraux as Minister of Culture (see p. 434) that a local authority might not have the same broad vision of cultural needs as the ministry in Paris, and Jack Lang later echoed this fear to me: 'I had to fight to dissuade Defferre from transferring too much to the new regional bodies, which might prefer to spend the money, say, on new roads, not on the arts. I'm in favour of devolution, but it does carry drawbacks. In Germany, the *Länder* and cities shower money on culture, but they have a long tradition. In France, the patronage has till now come from the State, and it may take the regions some time to learn.' In practice, fifteen years later, it seems that the regions have been playing their part quite well, in giving subsidies to theatre, opera, and so on (see p. 437). The town councils play a larger role: some of them spend huge sums on culture, even in a time of tightening of budgetary belts.

In fact, another hazard of the Defferre reforms is that the overall financing has become a serious problem and many towns have run heavily into debt. They complain that Paris has been keeping them short of the extra money they need for their new tasks, and in a sense this is true. Basically, the Government is committed to ensuring that councils receive the same level of funding, through state subsidies and their own local taxes, as it previously spent itself. And this it has not quite done. The reform may have largely fulfilled its objective that local authorities' direct share of overall fiscal revenue, formerly a mere 17 per cent, should rise to some 33 per cent (in Britain it is 50 per cent, in Germany 80 per cent). But as the State's global budget for 'rates topping' is indexed to its income from VAT, and this has been falling, so there has been a shortfall. 'Juppé is cheating us: he expects us to pay for more, yet he gives us less,' said one big-city RPR mayor in 1996.

But the budget crisis has often been the mayors' own fault, for in the boom years of the early 1990s many of them went on a spree of overspending on prestige projects. They built new industrial parks, and golf courses to entice the *cadres* of the new industry: in 1992 some 400 new '*golfs*' were being created! They built leisure complexes and lavish *salles polyvalentes* (multi-purpose centres). These projects were often useful, but it meant that mayors had to take out big loans – and the prefect could no longer say 'no'. Mayors today have free access to financial markets: but the loans can put them heavily in the red, and many have felt obliged to put up local taxes faster than inflation. The real solution awaits a long-promised overhaul of the whole system of local taxation.

Above all, a reproach made widely of the Defferre package is that its three-tier structure is proving cumbersome and archi-complex, with responsibilities that too often overlap and are not clearly defined. Many operations are jointly financed by the three levels, and it is unclear who should pay for what. Or different new bodies deal with the same matter, and the law has left vague their precise duties. Top-heavy and expensive, the structure requires phalanxes of extra bureaucrats. 'Here in Lyon,' one councillor told me, 'we have the local ward councils, the city council, the *communauté urbaine*, the *conseil général*, the regional council, then Paris, and for many matters the EU in Brussels. Seven tiers! Crazy!' And a teacher added, 'It's absurd that responsibility for school buildings and equipment should be shared out between three levels.' Governments have repeatedly been urged to clarify and simplify the whole system: but in face of so many local interests, they find it difficult to do so.

The crucial factor here is that the reformers failed to make a choice between region and *département*, but instead promoted both equally. This, in the eyes of many critics, is the biggest weakness of the entire devolution package. Defferre, a convinced regionalist, had initially wanted to down-grade the *département* and endow the region with really strong powers. But his plan was actively resisted by the prefectoral corps and his own Ministry of the Interior, charged with preparing his reform: they took the Jacobin view that this would build up dangerous centres of opposition to the State. And Mitterrand, decisively, took their side. So the final text was a deliberate compromise: it assuaged the fears of the Jacobins, who judged that the State could now play off one tier against the other – *divide et impera!*

Regionalists, however, have long argued that the *département* is too small and artificial a unit to provide the framework for effective devolution, especially in the new Europe of large, strong and very real regions, from Bavaria to Scotland and Catalonia. The *département*, after all, is no more than the result of arbitrary strokes on the map by the Revolution's technocrats in 1790, while the regions – or most of them – have deep roots in the ancient soil of France. When a man from Avignon says, '*Je suis du Vaucluse*,' he is stating a legal fact, but when he says '*Je suis provençal*,' he is making an emotive and cultural statement; ditto a Norman speaking of the Eure, or an Alsatian of the Bas-Rhin. True, a few *départements* do inspire local patriotism, such as the Lozère (see p. 418); and conversely some regions such as Midi-Pyrénées or the poetically named Centre are hybrids with boundaries crudely drawn in 1964: but most others, from Burgundy to Brittany, from Picardy to Aquitaine, do roughly correspond to the old provinces and have a historical reality. 'The new structure is top-heavy,' one leading regionalist told me; 'not only does the *département* obstruct the region in practical matters, and vice versa, but the citizen is left with no clear focus of loyalty.' Under the Defferre reform, a *département* generally has about three times the budget of a region per capita; and its *conseil général* is likely to have the more imposing offices. So inevitably the citizen tends to see his *département* as the greater political unit, even if he identifies more with his region. It is a paradox that varies considerably from one region to another.

Nor have the regions thrown up their own political parties. In the votes for the regional assemblies in 1986, 1992 and 1998, virtually all the elected councillors have come from the main national parties, while locally based movements have done badly. In Brittany, for instance, the autonomist Union Démocratique Bretonne was eclipsed, though previously it had won some seats on town councils. These results, all over France, have brought some relief to those who had feared that the reforms might encourage separatism. Michel Debré, Jacobin-in-chief, Prime Minister under de Gaulle, once warned, 'There are several ways to kill a nation, and regionalization is one of them' – but how real is this danger today? One Jacobin argument has always been, 'Give separatists an inch and they'll take a mile': but even in Corsica this has not happened.*

---

* Corsica's troubles are still unsolved. In 1982 Paris rapidly granted that unruly island a slightly greater degree of autonomy than it later allowed to the mainland regions. So Corsicans elected their own assembly, with some resulting confusion but not any advance for the separatist cause. The terrorist Corsican National Liberation Front was outlawed in 1983 and has since split into three rival factions. Today these still conduct sporadic bomb attacks and murders: but very few islanders, perhaps 2 per cent, support their ideals of total independence. Many Corsicans, however, do call themselves 'nationalist' and want greater autonomy within France. The main moderate nationalist movement has been pressing for more legislative powers, the teaching of the Corsican language in schools, and for Paris formally to

Nor has the reform produced any serious test of conflict between the regions and the central Government. After 1986 most of the regions elected centre-Right councils, and in 1992–8 the Socialists controlled only two, Nord-Pas-de-Calais and Limousin. Then in 1998 they won several large ones, including Ile-de-France and Provence. But these various changes have had little impact on the alternations of power in Paris; and the kind of trial of strength between State and regions that the Jacobins feared has just not happened.

Instead, a different and very serious problem has arisen, which was not foreseen at the time of devolution when the Front National was still weak. After the elections of March 1998, four centre-Right regional presidents formed virtual coalitions with the Front in order to be able to stay in power (see p. 39). And this has led to some severe tensions, notably in the Rhône-Alpes region (capital, Lyon): here the president, Charles Millon, placed Front members on the council's committees, and they managed to block many decisions, for example on grants for students. Many committees preferred not to meet, and the council's work was seriously disrupted. A feud also broke out between Millon and his former political ally, the redoubtable Raymond Barre, mayor of Lyon, who publicly 'deplored' his policy. Finally, in January 1999, Millon was pressured into resigning, much against his will, and a staunchly pro-Barre

---

recognize the 'Corsican people' as a 'national minority'. Paris has refused this. But in a bid to assuage local feelings it does give special economic aid to this rather poor island. And it has stepped up police action against terrorism.

In February 1998 the regional prefect, Claude Érignac, was shot dead in Ajaccio by gunmen thought to belong to an extreme splinter group, maybe with Mafia connections. It was Corsica's worst political murder for many years, and it drew huge rallies of shocked islanders, calling for an end to violence. Most Corsicans are law-abiding, but a handful live by gangsterism; and as in Ulster during the Troubles, political terrorism and Mafia-type crime are closely bound up, each fuelling the other. Bomb attacks and shootings rarely kill indiscriminately: they are targeted against individuals, or else against vacant buildings. The extremists hate 'colonization' by French or other commercial interests, and they even dislike French visitors. Hence hotels or other tourist projects have sometimes been attacked (a Club Med village was once destroyed). Many Corsicans feel a sneaking sympathy for this campaign, as they do not want their paradise to be spoilt by the kind of mass development that has ruined many parts of the Mediterranean. Even so, as this lovely island with few other resources depends so much on tourism, officially the attacks are deplored as sheer perversity. It is Corsica's long tradition of violence, some of it based on ancestral family feuds, that makes it so hard to reach solutions.

councillor, Anne-Marie Comparini, was elected president in his place – with the help of left-wing and centrist votes on the council, but against those of the Front *and* the RPR! So moderate democracy triumphed, even if Comparini then found it hard to patch together a viable coalition. Similar if lesser tensions have arisen in other regions where the Front is able to hold the balance and thus disrupt – and all local political life is poisoned. If this kind of problem is not solved, maybe through a better system of alliances, or a change in the electoral law, then the entire experiment in regional devolution could be jeopardized.

Until this crisis, the reforms were working fairly well, and had managed to dampen the old fires of anti-Paris resentment in those mainland regions with a strong sense of identity – led by Alsace, Brittany and Languedoc. Local self-confidence has increased; separatism is no longer much of an issue. In this respect, they have been a success. But the debate on region versus *département* remains alive. The regionalist lobby still presses for some downgrading of the *département*: but this is opposed, not only by Jacobins in Paris but by a majority of conservative *notables* in the provinces. The RPR-led Juppé Government favoured the status quo. The Socialists, more regional-minded, now talk of taking the Defferre reforms a stage further. But they, too, are divided. No major change seems likely before monetary union is in place.

Many advocates of devolution have long argued that twenty-two regions are too many. They should be regrouped, and reduced to about eight or ten: this would give them far more strength and authenticity. I would agree. It seems absurd that Normandy, for instance, should be two separate regions. Some others, such as Limousin or Champagne-Ardennes, are too small and weak to fulfil their role properly, or to make good sense in the new contest of a Europe that has been regionalizing. As some power moves up from the nation State to the EU, so other powers should move downwards to the region, in the interests of promoting a human scale and local decision-taking. This is the argument of 'Europeans', who see the regions as an essential element in a United Europe.

Federal Germany has powerful historic *Länder*; Italy has been regionalizing, also Spain, where Catalonia, Andalucia and other provinces are now semi-autonomous. Even Britain, after lagging, has now taken a big step for Scotland and Wales. So France too, if it is to share in the new framework, needs sizeable regions with proper powers: if not, it could lose out, both in terms of economy and democracy. Or so it is widely argued. In Lyon, one centre-Right city worthy suggested to me,

'It is in the logic of Europe for the region steadily to grow in power, at the expense of the *département*.' Most Socialists, and the Greens, also argue for fewer and stronger regions. And in 1998 their coalition was starting to work out a new reform that might give added powers to the regions. But other potent forces, even within Socialist ranks, are fighting to keep the status quo: the *notables* of the ninety-six *conseils généraux* want to protect their influence and vested interests. So the old debate, region versus *département*, is still very much alive. This will be an issue in the years ahead, in a regional reform that was always meant as a long-term evolutive process, not a once-for-all measure. It may be far from perfect, but on balance it is popular. And already it has done much to pull France from the old strait-jacket of centralism.

So now we shall look first at Paris and its multiple problems today; then at a few of the more interesting French regions and larger towns, in the light of economic progress, local initiative and political reform.

PARIS, ADORED MONSTER:
MITTERRAND'S MIGHTY MONUMENTS — BUT WHAT
ABOUT URBAN SPRAWL?

Paris, as everyone knows, lives at a much faster tempo than London. People drive more assertively, they often seem in a hurry or are snappy down the telephone; and if they are brusque to visitors, this may not be xenophobia, as many foreigners suppose, for they can be just as bad with each other. They generally lack a community spirit of mutual self-help. All this is a matter of temperament, of course, but also of conditioning, for under some special circumstances they can be quite different. During the strikes of December 1995, Paris was deprived of public transport for a month; and in order to get to work, people had to improvise in various ways. It brought out an unaccustomed solidarity, trustfulness, even gaiety. Colleagues in the same office, who were not friends, would lend each other bicycles or a bed for the night; neighbours offered free baby-sitting; social barriers fell as directors gave lifts to their workers; everyone stopped for hitch-hikers or shared cars (the term *le co-voiturage* was coined). This all might seem normal in London, with its tribal memories of the Blitz, but was amazing for Paris. And, despite the horrendous traffic jams, many people even enjoyed the break from routine, and the chance to be more convivial with strangers. '*Tu sais*, les autres, *ils sont vachement sympas*,' said one typist, as if she had encountered some new human species. And when the strike ended? – it all went back as before, but not quite. Some lesson had been learned.

The zestful nervous vitality of Paris can be hugely stimulating. But it can also lead to daily tensions, in a city where high population density unites with the restless, self-willed temperament of its people. Many Francophiles like myself therefore find it a fascinating city to visit for a month or two, but not to live in for years, as many expatriates chose to do before the war. However, it has greatly improved in many ways in the past four decades. When I first lived there in the later 1950s, the mood was much more strained than today. Parisians, still scarred by the trauma of Occupation, had to face a fearful housing shortage, archaic public transport and gloomy blackened façades along main streets. But then steadily came greater prosperity. And from the early 1960s, after a grave neglect of town-planning for nearly a century, the Gaullists began to renovate and modernize on a grand scale. This applied to the rapidly growing suburbs, also to the city proper 'within the gates', the Ville de Paris with its twenty *arrondissements* (districts). So today Paris in most ways is impressively modern (at the cost of some of its old charm, *soit*). The public transport system, hugely improved, is judged to be the best of any major world city (but the car-traffic problem is less well solved). Recent Presidents have endowed Paris with a dozen or so super-ambitious modern cultural buildings, some less beautiful than others, from Pompidou's 'Beaubourg' to Mitterrand's Louvre pyramids, La Villette museum and the much-denigrated national library. Chirac, as mayor in 1977–85, was also criticized (and his scandal-prone successor, Jean Tiberi, even more so): but he did improve the 'quality of life' in various ways. Paris has become a beautifully clean city – save when a terrorist attack prompts the police to take the security measure of sealing up all pavement refuse bins, causing much scattering of litter.

For many years now, growing affluence and commercial activity have made the city glossier, livelier, but even more hectic. Old buildings have been beautifully restored, but quiet *vieux Paris* is less in evidence; and some inhabitants have preferred to move off to a calmer life in the provinces. Parisians' feelings remain deeply ambivalent towards a city that has always inspired deep loyalties and still casts a personal spell: 'Paris, what a monster,' they say, almost lovingly. They have seen it change so much, and it is still changing.

★

Some districts have been radically altering their character, under the impact of fashion or of commercial pressures. Most striking, and most regretted by many, has been the 'Champs-Élyséefication' of St-Germain-des-Prés, the old intellectual quarter. First in 1965 a glossy multi-storey 'drugstore', with slick boutiques, implanted itself right opposite the cafés once haunted by Sartre, the Flore and Deux Magots. Later it became accepted as part of the landscape. But now it has been supplanted in its turn by Giorgio Armani, who in 1998 opened an *emporio* on the site, largest of his trendy fashion shops around the world. Across the square, the highbrow bookshop Le Divan has closed, yielding place to Christian Dior; Vuitton and Sonia Rykiel have arrived, too, and the famous La Hune bookstore is menaced. The splendid Buci street market survives, as does the Brasserie Lipp, beloved of politicians, and the Flore and other cafés: but their clientele has changed. The old intellectual intensity has gone from the area. But then, in Paris, not much is static: St-Germain itself, an old aristocratic quarter, did not become a haunt of writers and artists until the 1930s, when the Flore was still a rendez-vous of the fascist Action Française!

'The streets of Paris are becoming uniform and commonplace,' wrote Emmanuel de Roux in *Le Monde* (23 November 1996) – 'the same clothes shops, the same restaurant chains, the same décors, are almost everywhere.' From a lover of *vieux Paris* this was an understandable reaction, but maybe too harsh, for many quarters do keep an individuality. So where today is intellectual Bohemia found? Answer, it has become more dispersed, less visible – at a time when Paris intellectual life as a whole is not what it was (see p. 427). The *cinquième* district, around and behind the Sorbonne and the Panthéon, is still a genuine *quartier latin*, where students swarm and off-beat cafés, cabarets and art-house cinemas stand below the walls of ancient academic institutes. Modern restoration has added to the area's vitality, without spoiling it. Some other Bohemian and youth-culture life, if not always so 'intellectual', has moved across to the Right Bank's eastern sector, spurred by the creation there of the Pompidou Centre (see below) and the Opéra de la Bastille. Here in the networks of tiny streets, far from the brasher Champs-Élysées to the west, are lots of vaguely trendy new art galleries, late-night cafés, foreign restaurants: the *onzième*, east of the Bastille, where Cédric Klapisch set his charming film *Chacun cherche son chat*, once the quiet abode of artisans and tradesmen, is now called *le quartier le plus branché* (switched on). But the serious philosophers ready to remake the world? They are too scattered to have any obvious citadel.

St-Germain is the latest but not the only victim of change. Montmartre, with its steep steps and quaint alleys, still keeps its visual charm: but few artists live there now, and a *lapin* needs to be amazingly *agile* to hop away from the milling tourists. The great cafés of Montparnasse, the Dôme and others, still have their *literati* devotees: but Paris's tallest skyscraper, and multi-screen cinemas, now overshadow the scene. As for the Champs-Élysées, it is now the stronghold of the advertising, public-relations and fashion-model worlds, the movie business and the travel agencies. The avenue's stately façades are lined with giant car showrooms, airline offices, fast-food eateries and multi-screen cinemas, while the Edwardian elegance of Fouquet's survives in their midst, still a showbiz haunt. On the other hand, various previously dull residential quarters have become more lively and diverse: in unlikely corners of sedate Passy or workaday Alésia, you might find ambitious restaurants or nightspots; and out in the humdrum suburbs some avant-garde theatres are among the best in France. The central entertainment areas – from the Étoile to the Boul' Mich', from Montparnasse to Bastille and Pigalle – are still full of nightly animation, on a grander scale than the equivalent zones of London or New York. Living late, full of street glitter, the city remains a powerful magnet for pleasure-seeking tourists or suburbanites.

Living in the city centre has always been chic, and costly restoration of areas such as the Marais or the Ile St-Louis has endorsed this vogue. Dukes and film stars vie with each other to buy, at huge prices, the smart apartments in and around the Place des Vosges. Elsewhere, the *haute bourgeoisie* retains its fiefs in the eighteenth-century *septième*, the nine-teenth-century *seizième* and modern Neuilly. However, many districts have long tended to be more socially mixed than in London, partly because of the way the Haussmann-era blocks were built, with flats of varying sizes and quality under the same roof. Then, in the days of acute housing shortage, many middle-class people took flats where they could find them, and if the controlled rent was low, they felt disinclined to move. So even today you may find a 'good' family living at a 'poor' address, say behind the Gare de l'Est, and it compounds their reluctance to entertain at home. But rebuilding has brought changes. Many previously humble areas, for example in the *quatorzième* or *quinzième*, have been growing more middle class, like Fulham or Lambeth. This is due less to the conversion of old homes than to the new privately built blocks: here professional couples with good incomes will often live in quite small modern flats, and maybe pay a high rent, too. The lure of living centrally remains strong for Parisians. Later, when they have children, they may choose to move out to somewhere roomier in the suburbs. Commuting has finally become a norm.

In administrative and in physical terms the Paris conurbation is in two separate parts, divided by the ring motorway of the Boulevard Périphérique. On its outer side are the tentacular suburbs, with a population today of about 7 million; inside is the commune of the Ville de Paris. With urban renewal, its population has been falling steadily, from 2.9 million in 1911 to 2.1 million today. It has since levelled off, but is still very dense: 20,400 people per square kilometre, against some 8,000 in the equivalent area of London. Green parks are few and small, except on the edges, at Boulogne and Vincennes. And the city has had to struggle to overcome the legacy of very poor planning and local government in the period 1870–1960.

Baron Haussmann, prefect of the Seine in 1853–70, modernized Paris radically, driving his boulevards through the teeming bowels of the old city. To some he was a vandal: but the commoner verdict is that he turned Paris into the best-planned capital in Europe. Yet from his day until de Gaulle's, little more was done for modern planning, save to build a Métro; and one reason was the feeble state of local government. From 1871 the municipal council had even less autonomy than a small village commune; it was allowed no mayor, and was ruled directly by the prefect of the Seine *département*, for Governments were haunted by memories of 1789, 1848 and 1871, and were keen to grant as little power as possible to the 'dangerous' Paris populace. With no mayor to lead them, the mostly conservative councillors left the Government to take the main planning initiatives. But, aggrieved at their dependence, they made free use of their powers of veto; and it was the consequent stalemate between council and State, persisting through the Third and Fourth Republics, that led to the virtual absence of effective new planning. Thus an essential measure to decongest the centre by removing the huge food markets, Les Halles, first mooted in the 1920s, was repeatedly blocked by the council right up until the 1960s. Yet traffic and business activity in Paris had by then been growing fast; and the failure to deal with the ensuing problems was one factor that led the EEC to choose the more manageable city of Brussels. Paris quite simply muffed its chance to become Europe's capital.

De Gaulle's return at last brought a more forceful approach. And the council, Gaullist-led, this time acquiesced in the new plans – de Gaulle stood no nonsense! So the 1960s saw serious efforts to bring Paris in line with modern needs, without spoiling its beauty. Les Halles *were* removed, to the suburbs. Blackened buildings were scoured clean, and a start was made on restoring run-down historic areas, such as the Marais. At the same time, much-needed new expressways and office complexes were built or projected. Today's needs may be very different: but in those days, these changes were seen as essential, if Paris was to prosper as a modern city. So the aim was to keep a sane balance between practical and aesthetic priorities, in a city with so much worth preserving; and in the 1960s this policy seemed to be working well. Under de Gaulle there was less ugly piecemeal rebuilding of central office areas than in London: one of the few new monstrosities was the 209-metre skyscraper that surged up from the heart of Montparnasse in 1969, dwarfing nearby monuments such as the Invalides. 'The charm of the view from my office,' joked one executive on its forty-eighth floor,' is that this is the one place in Paris from which you can't see it.'

André Malraux himself, as de Gaulle's Minister of Culture, is said to have approved of the tower – an odd lapse of taste. But apart from this, he did much good work for Paris, notably by leading a campaign to bring back more spruceness and light to the so-called *ville lumière*. In the 1950s this supposed European capital of gaiety and chic was suffering badly from dirty façades and lack of paint. Parts were picturesque, as in the Latin Quarter, but much was simply depressing. Then, with rising prosperity, a number of shops and cafés began of their own accord to brighten their fronts with fresh paint, or less elegantly with chromium. But above them, the façades of upper floors were still black and peeling. So in 1958 de Gaulle's new Government issued a warning: not only was the decay unaesthetic, it was also eating at the fabric. But it was hard to act, for ground rents of most older buildings were still pegged so low that landlords had a valid excuse for doing little (see p. 200). So a law was passed allowing phased rent increases so long as part of the money was spent on cleaning housefronts and courtyards; and a forgotten law of 1852 was cunningly revived, which made the cleaning of façades compulsory every ten years. This was effective: within a few years, the façades in most central areas were scoured pale – a policy still in force today. Malraux's ministry also set about cleaning public buildings and monuments: the Louvre, the Opéra, even Notre-Dame, were restored to their original sandstone hues without damage to their fabric. This brightening up of Paris (with similar work in many other cities) was outwardly one of the most striking changes in de Gaulle's France. It made Parisians feel more cheerful, and it did something to revive the tarnished image of 'Gay Paree'.

Malraux notably restored the lovely but neglected Marais. This district in the seventeenth century was highly fashionable, but by the 1960s much of it was a slum; many of its elegant buildings had been carved up into tenements or workshops. Malraux enforced a law obliging landlords to share in the work and cost of renewal; helped by the city council and some rich private owners, he was able to restore some handsome buildings to prime condition, and today the Marais is again a chic address. The fashion-conscious Jack Lang has an apartment there.

Pompidou's regime then showed itself less aesthetically conscious than de Gaulle's, and more lenient towards high-rise developers, in the interests of boosting Paris as a business metropolis. The new economic boom led to a shortage of modern office and commercial space, and developers complained that rising land prices and other costs were such that they needed to build high. And so, as Parisians voiced alarm at the prospect of 'Manhattan-sur-Seine', a debate grew as to whether tall modern buildings would always be out of place in a city of such classic harmony, or whether, if well designed, they could enhance its beauty. After all, the Eiffel Tower caused fury in its time, but today few lovers of *vieux Paris* would want it pulled down. In central Paris until the late 1960s, the few notable new post-war buildings tended to be rather elegant, not too tall, and in tune with their setting: for example, the Y-shaped UNESCO headquarters near the École Militaire. But then all began to change.

Under Pompidou work began on a whole cluster of 80-metre towers near the Porte d'Italie. At least this was well away from the city's beautiful centre. But another project, for a row of 85-metre blocks, was right by the river near the Eiffel Tower, on the Quai de Javel. At least these are well spaced, set on multiple levels amid small gardens, and grouped in some harmony: in terms of urban renewal they have much improved this former slummy area. But they and other new schemes were much criticized in the 1970s for turning Paris into one more high-rise city. Necessary and overdue urban renewal suddenly became high-rise smallpox, as over sixty new buildings qualified as skyscrapers and the familiar Paris skyline changed fast.

Giscard then came to power, with views that happened to coincide with an ecological shift in public feeling. Clamping down on the *laissez-faire* policy of 'gigantism', he called a halt to the half-completed Italie venture and vetoed other skyscraping projects too. Ever since his day the building of high-rise blocks within the Ville de Paris has been checked, and formal rules on the height of new projects have been mostly respected. The exceptions are one or two of Mitterrand's cultural *grands projets*, such as the new national library (see below). So if you survey the city today from any high central point, you will see, apart from the Montparnasse tower, little in central Paris that recalls Chicago or even Frankfurt. The new office blocks at Bercy, near the Gare de Lyon, are large but not very tall. And the few high-rise clusters are on the periphery – most notably at La Défense, five kilometres west of the Arc de Triomphe.

This spectacular grouping of thirty skyscrapers, all different, is in the suburbs but integrally a part of Paris in commercial terms. It combines modern offices with big shops and blocks of flats. It is grandiose, yes, but harmonious, centred around its giant new cube-like 'Arche'; and though still much criticized, La Défense is undeniably one of the most ambitious and exciting urban ventures in post-war Europe. Surprisingly, it was conceived under the Fourth Republic, to be an office overspill for the Champs-Élysées area and a new focus for the city's business life – thus continuing the historic tendency of Paris at that time, as of London, to shift its centre of gravity westward. A 690-hectare site was chosen astride the tip of the famous axis that runs from the Louvre up the Champs-Élysées to Neuilly. Here, beyond Neuilly, the three communes concerned were persuaded to collaborate with a state development body. First the existing mess of shacks and tenements was cleared, then the high-rise towers were built in stages over thirty years. In all shapes and sizes, some more than forty storeys high, they stand today around a wide traffic-free piazza: here many leading firms have offices, some 120,000 people work by day, and 38,000 live in high blocks, mostly around the edge. A mammoth shopping centre of 105,000 square metres, claimed to be Europe's largest, includes Marks and Spencer and a hypermarket. Below ground are acres of car parks and a grandiose Métro and RER station. No cars enter La Défense at ground level: there are ring roads and a new motorway tunnelled through the bowels.

Marvel of intelligent modern planning, or soulless folly? Verdicts still vary. Many of the towers are dull and squat, but some of the taller ones are strikingly original, their façades made of opaque reflecting glass, steely blue or golden brown, gleaming in the sunset. They prove again that French architects are generally more successful in a modern glass-and-steel idiom than when following more classic styles. Had this ensemble been set in central Paris, it would of course have ruined the townscape: but as an entity on its own, it has many merits. And the planners have made efforts to enliven the wide central piazza with colour and movement. It is a veritable outdoor modern art gallery: a huge scarlet stabile by Calder, a fresco by Atila, gaudy grotesques by Miró like figures from a carnival float, and a polychrome ornamental pool by Agam where musical fountains rise and fall. Attempts to include a souk and flea market were not successful: but there are outdoor cafés, concerts in summer, a museum, a giant-screen cinema. It may be all a little contrived, but is not dull. Some blocks of flats are in ziggurat form, with bold stripes of red, blue, green and orange; others, by the idiosyncratic Émile Aillaud, are a series of round or petal-shaped flowers with random circular windows, their walls 'camouflaged' with stylized cloud patterns in white, sky-blue and violet.

It was always agreed that La Défense should be crowned by some special building, a backdrop to the central vista. And after long debate work finally began on a striking project, designed by the Danish architect Otto von Spreckelsen. Inaugurated in 1989, for the Bicentenary, this Grande Arche de la Défense is a cube 105 metres high, with thirty-five storeys holding offices. Coated in white Carrara marble, it lies as it were on its side, with a big hole in the middle, so that from central Paris you can see through it to the sky beyond. The hole is criss-crossed by wires, to deter aviators from flying through as a stunt or suicide bid (two did, and died). Though it has been likened to 'some gigantic television set', the Grande Arche is certainly impressive, a fitting centrepiece to the grandeur of La Défense. It has its place among Mitterrand's *grands projets*.

But is La Défense also a commercial success? Initially, several big firms leapt at the chance to move out from congested central Paris, and the first towers were rapidly rented. But waves of economic crisis, notably in the mid-1970s and early 1990s, put brakes on the Paris office boom, and there were times when some completed towers were half empty. The Government even found it hard to persuade its own ministries to make the move, as planned: Education and Finance refused to transfer to La Défense, as their staff felt it was too far away. Finally the Ministry of Equipment and Housing (appropriately) agreed to move from the *seizième*, and is now in the Grande Arche, with 2,500 staff. As for big firms, of those that moved initially, some later found the rents too high, so they built or hired premises in cheaper suburbs such as St-Cloud. But others have taken their place. Recently, Fiat, Esso and Thomson Multi-Media have gone: but Total, Elf-Aquitaine, Mobil Oil, Framatome, IBM, Société Générale, First National City Bank and others have all remained or arrived. Today there are still some new towers standing half empty: but the proportion of vacant office space is claimed to be lower than in the Paris region as a whole, where it is 15 per cent. In sum, La Défense has broadly succeeded in becoming, as planned, the second business pole of greater Paris. It remains a notable example of the French flair for imaginative planning on a bold scale. And although such grandiosity is now out of fashion, it has enabled Paris to expand as an economic metropolis without high-rise development of the older office areas near the centre.

In central Paris the two major renovation schemes in the 1960s and '70s – Les Halles and Beaubourg – both caused a welter of controversy. For years a prime cause of the city's congestion had been the absurd concentration, in its very heart, of the nation's central food and wine markets. Fourth Republic Governments had repeatedly failed in their efforts to winkle the wine-traders out of their old stronghold near the Jardin des Plantes: then de Gaulle banished them by decree to a site in the suburbs, and in their place he put a much-needed but ugly new university block. The central food market, Les Halles, in an ancient and teeming district near the Louvre, took longer to shift. Zola had called it 'the belly of Paris', and every morning it blocked whole square kilometres with its lorries. Whereas London's little Covent Garden was simply a market for samples, Les Halles physically handled one-fifth of France's fruit, vegetables and meat. But the middlemen resisted change: they made fat profits out of the organized chaos and they had a powerful lobby. Finally, after years of pressure, a transfer was agreed, and in 1969 the fruit and vegetable market was moved out to a spacious modern *marché-gare* near Orly, and the meat market to La Villette. Today tourists who come to drink onion soup late at the Pied de Cochon, after a show, can no longer jostle with *les forts des Halles* in their blood-stained aprons. Picturesqueness has taken another knock: but central Paris breathes more easily.

The future of the prime 35-hectare site thus vacated was then the subject of a scarcely credible eleven-year wrangle, due to the widely varying interests of the general public, big business and state prestige. Hundreds of architects were consulted, scores of plans were eagerly adopted then bitterly discarded. A commercial lobby first demanded a big world trade centre, and Pompidou agreed. Defenders of *vieux Paris* were shocked when they realized that demolition of Les Halles would involve the tearing down of Victor Baltard's famous wrought-iron pavilions, but Pompidou rejected a proposal for some of these graceful structures to be incorporated into the new project. Once again, public opinion proved its weakness in France. Work began on a big station for the new RER express Métro, and for this a giant hole was dug and left gaping open: it became a stock Paris joke, this Halles hell-hole. Finally Giscard came to power, with a different vision from Pompidou's: he listened to local action groups, and cancelled the trade-centre plan, which he agreed was inhuman and out of scale with the area. At last it seemed that ecology-minded Parisians were influencing the planners – still rare in those days. It was impossible to save the Baltard halls: but Giscard did approve a plan for a classic garden, much needed in this dense area, plus a big underground shopping centre. Today this unusually designed mall, Le Forum, does a brisk trade, with its 200 boutiques and huge FNAC bookshop (see p. 638). Next door is the small formal garden, plus a museum, library and sports centre. The garden should have been larger: but the overall scheme does bring new amenities and a bit more sense of space and style to this cramped quarter of central Paris.

Four blocks to the east stands one of the most famous modern buildings in Europe, the Georges Pompidou cultural centre, a giant block of glass, steel and coloured pipes, often known by its nickname of 'Beaubourg'. Pompidou, apostle of high finance, was also a lover of contemporary art, and in 1969 he proclaimed his desire to endow France with a modern multi-purpose cultural complex of the first rank. The site chosen was the Plateau Beaubourg, in a seedy area; and out of 681 entries the winning design was by the Anglo-Italian team of Richard Rogers and Renzo Piano. Their bold modernism horrified many city councillors and high officials, who even tried to block building permits: but Pompidou pushed the project through, and the centre opened in 1977. Its critics have called it 'an arty oil-refinery': swathed in scaffolding and piping, it deliberately wears an unfinished look. Its architects call it 'an inside turned outside': i.e. all the service apparatus which is normally hidden in a building is here displayed outside, in bright colours. The water mains are green, the electricity cables yellow, the air-conditioning ducts blue – just as on architects' charts. The main escalator, too, is on the outside, set in a glass tube that rises diagonally up the six-storey façade, providing views over Paris and over the interior of the building, whose walls are also of clear glass. Inside is France's largest modern art museum, a 400,000-volume library, and vast spaces for special exhibitions, next to Pierre Boulez's music research centre (see p. 448).

Like the Eiffel Tower, another skeletal structure just as modernistic in its day, Beaubourg at first caused a furore but has now come to be accepted. Its success with visitors has been twice greater than expected: an average 23,000 it enter each day, more than the Louvre and Eiffel Tower combined. Most come to use the library, others to see the museum and special exhibitions (Matisse in 1993 drew 735,000); some are drawn by mere curiosity. Many young people are fascinated by Beaubourg's see-through, let-it-all-hang-out quality, and by the snook it cocks at normal palace-like museums. Its influence on recent museum-building around the world has been huge. In fact, the main objections in Paris today are less to the edifice itself than to its siting: 'It is not very tall, but it clashes grotesquely with the older buildings nearby, especially in the elegant Marais,' said one critic. Others find this contrast exciting. However, the exposed nature of the structure, plus its massive use by the public, have led it to weather badly; and in 1997, just twenty years old, it was virtually closed for the next two years, for a 440-million franc renovation. Its detractors cried, 'We told you so! – of course it was wrongly designed for its purpose.' And Lord Rogers – today one of Britain's most revered living architects, thanks in part to Beaubourg, which made his reputation – replied, 'The renovation is normal. The centre's interior has been worn out because of its very success.' This huge building is in fact too small for its multiple activities. It is now being redesigned to allow almost twice as much space for the museum.

Like Mitterrand's projects which followed, Beaubourg has been a token of the French readiness to innovate imaginatively on a grand scale. Equally remarkable, the often chauvinistic French resisted the temptation to make it simply a showcase of national talents. Not only were the architects foreign, but the steelworks and engineering contracts went to British and German firms, a Swede was the first museum director, and many of the new art works bought for it were American. Pompidou said he wanted an international flavour, and he got it. What's more, Beaubourg has also become, as intended, a focus of local animation. It has revitalized a moribund district and encouraged vital activity all around. Until its 1997 closure, the broad paved piazza in front of it would fill up on fine days with musicians, conjurors, clowns, even orators, all attracting visitors with their sideshows. It has marked a renewal of the Paris street tradition of *Les Enfants du paradis*. And the little traffic-free streets between Beaubourg and Les Halles have blossomed with antique shops, art galleries, modish bars and restaurants. The area has become a *de facto* overspill for St-Germain-des-Prés.

Since 1977 Paris has at last had its own mayor. So what difference has this made to the city and its problems? When Giscard came to power, he announced that it was time to end the absurd historic anomaly of this big city having no elected mayor of its own. He planned for a friend to fill the post: but Parisians instead voted for his arch-rival, Jacques Chirac. Then the Left's regional reforms gave the city council the same added powers as in other French towns. This was to lead to repeated friction. On some matters the Socialist Government was able to put its foot down: but generally Chirac proved himself the strong and undisputed boss of his own realm during his eighteen years as mayor. That is why he chose the job – as a power base for his ambitions to become President. He had many enemies locally, but he was mostly popular with Parisians, who re-elected him twice, in 1983 and 1989.

Chirac treated being mayor as anything but an honorific role. Except when also Prime Minister in 1986–8, he devoted a large slice of his famous energy and dynamism to its practical daily tasks, working long hours late at night in his sumptuous office in the huge Hôtel de Ville. If he met a baby, he smothered it with kisses; if there was an old folks' home to be opened, or a charity concert to be held, or a foreign ruler to be fêted, Chirac was toweringly there, with his generous handshake and his thrusting rhetorical optimism – *le Maire-Soleil*, he was called. He was a demagogue, anxious to be liked: but as mayor his concern for the less privileged and for quality of life was probably also genuine. 'Certainly he did do a great deal for old people, and for the poor,' one bitter critic, a left-wing councillor, admitted to me. He arranged free outings and holidays for the aged, gave them free telephones, and used the city budget to top up their state pensions; he even gave the poorer ones a box of luxury chocolates each New Year. He also granted *RMIstes* a special credit card for free medical aid. He saw to it that the public flower-beds were more colourful, and the pavements swept cleaner, than ever before. He even struck a blow for modern hygiene, and against picturesque squalor, by getting rid of the notorious old iron male urinals, the 300 *vespasiennes*, and replacing them with sleek unisex *sanisettes*, perfumed and heated. Decreeing that 'Paris must be *en fête* every day of the year', and that 'poetry must reanimate its streets', the sun-mayor also revived several traditional festivals long lapsed, such as the fair on the Pont Neuf in June with its folk-dancing and crafts. He built a new sports complex with a 17,000-seat stadium at the Quai de Bercy, in eastern Paris, part of a general policy of trying to aid the poorer eastern areas of the city and to shift its balance back from the west. And he completed some 60 hectares of small new parks, in a city centre that has much less greenery than central London or even Manhattan.

This record looks impressive. But when it came to housing and office-building policy, his touch was less sure. He did, it is true, go ahead with slum clearance. This had begun in the 1950s (see p. 200), but only about 25 per cent of the real slums had been cleared by the mid-1960s: then you could still find plenty of stinking alleys with crumbling façades and dank courts, where large families lived in Zolaesque squalor without running water. Just as wartime destruction had helped France's railways to become more modern than British ones, so Paris planners sometimes envied London's East End for the Blitz! But steadily the slums were pulled down. Between the 1968 and 1990 censuses, the percentage of homes without indoor flushing lavatories fell from 45 to 17 per cent – still shockingly high, you could say. Chirac did build about 2,500 new flats a year at the cheaper end of the subsidized 'social' sector. But, as his critics pointed out, this was not nearly enough to meet needs, and it scarcely increased the total, for many older dwellings were demolished. Moreover, Chirac's 'liberal' economic policy for the city encouraged the building of expensive private flats. So, as rents and land prices rose, the historic tendency increased for poorer people to leave for new homes in the suburbs – and Chirac, like others before him, was accused of trying to develop Paris as a bourgeois fief for electoral reasons. Many younger middle-class people left, too, finding central Paris prices too high.

Chirac was notably criticized for razing to the ground some poorer districts and replacing them with offices or better-class flats, rather than rehabilitating the old housing. This is a familiar issue in many western cities today. It concerned notably the Belleville quarter of eastern Paris, which was partially demolished in 1991, amid outcry. Chirac was keen on office-building, not only to spur economic growth, but because his council's revenue came largely from the *taxe professionnelle* on businesses. So, in the boom years, the formal restrictions on new offices in central Paris were often flouted, as modern blocks mushroomed or Haussmann-era mansions were converted from flats into brash open-plan business premises behind their stately façades. The council grew richer in the process, and so could keep housing rates much lower than in most French cities. 'Don't we have a clever mayor?' said the contented bourgeoisie. But then the recession of the early 1990s sent the property market into slump: so the city's finances tumbled, too, and when Chirac left in 1995, the Council was in debt. By then he was also being assailed by rumours of his connivance at sleaze in the city's housing policies.

Chirac's majority on the council was able to brush the left-wing opposition aside, thus helping him to rule autocratically. The Socialist Government was itself partly responsible for this: in 1982, as part of its devolution package, it set up a ward system in Paris, Lyon and Marseille, under the so-called 'PLM law', whereby each *arrondissement* would also have its own local mayor. But this honest bid to decentralize backfired against its authors: in 1983 Paris voted more massively than ever for Chirac and his supporters, enabling them to assume control of *all twenty* of the new local *mairies*, including those in working-class areas. It was a striking vindication of his popularity. The city council, with 141 seats for the centre-Right against 28 for the Left, became more of a rubber-stamp body than ever. And the *Maire-Soleil* – to mix historical metaphors – became 'greater than Napoleon, at least in physical stature', in the words of one Socialist. In sum, Chirac was in many ways an excellent mayor, in practical terms, with an unsurprising popularity in this mainly middle-class city. And it was high time indeed that Paris did have its own mayor. But maybe the French system allows such a figure too much personal power for the good of democracy – and Chirac in the nation's capital, natural autocrat as well as charmer, was bound to exploit this for all it was worth.

Before he became President, the successor he 'chose' was Jean Tiberi, a Paris-born Corsican, tough and somewhat taciturn, who had been his *adjoint* in charge of housing. In the 1995 municipal elections, Tiberi's centre-Right coalition found its majority much reduced, winning 98 seats against 58 for the Left. And six of the twenty *arrondissements* now elected Socialist mayors. But these were soon complaining that the council was failing to apply properly the 'PLM law' by withholding part of the funds due to them for running some local amenities in their areas. This grew into a major row. However, the local mayors did have great moral influence within the council, where debates were now livelier. So true democracy penetrated at last into the Hôtel de Ville, after the rubber-stamp years.

The Left inveighed against Tiberi over his budget and town-planning, and over some amazing scandals that emerged. One was the affair of the so-called '*domaine privé*' – a collection of about 1,400 flats which the council owned, some of them formerly confiscated from Jewish owners under Vichy. It was alleged that some had been let out at rather low rents to members of Chirac's political élite and their friends, including the families of both Juppé and Tiberi. The mayor then promised that the *domaine*'s flats would be sold on the market. Other more serious scandals concerned the alleged fraudulent funding of the RPR and the alleged improper payments to Madame Tiberi. Today judicial inquiries are still continuing. The mood is sour, and it is hard to avoid the impression that Tiberi, Juppé and even Chirac may all have connived in affairs stretching back over several years. For the municipal elections of 2001, the Right's candidate for mayor is not yet chosen, but on the Left one contender seems likely to be Danny Cohn-Bendit, the German Green, who is applying for French citizenship (he was born in France).

Whatever his faults, Tiberi after 1995 in some ways began to prove quite a good mayor. He had new policies on curbing car traffic (see below) and on urban renewal. And he had the courage to give a needed hike to rates and other taxes, by about 10 per cent a year, so as to pay for his schemes. But the Socialists were sceptical. Georges Sarre, a prominent left-wing councillor, told me in 1997, 'Chirac managed the city's finances tightly, as a good *père de famille*, like Balzac's Grandet. But when the economic situation changed, he was caught in his own trap. Tiberi has now changed that policy, but he had no choice. He simply lacks the money for his programme.' The new mayor promised to end the policy of demolishing flats in poorer quarters, and instead to modernize existing dwellings: this costs more, but is more in line with what people now want. At Belleville, where Chirac had put up six-storey blocks, Tiberi went to talk with the locals and ecologist groups, and accepted many of their arguments: 'The trowel will now replace the bulldozer,' said someone.

A fiercer debate arose in 1996–7 over the future of the so-called

'*ZAC du treizième*', a big urban renewal project (*zone d'aménagement concerté*) for a mainly empty 140-hectare wasteland by the river in the thirteenth *arrondissement*, on the Left Bank opposite Bercy. It had been conceived by Chirac as part of his overall plan to upgrade the city's poorer eastern districts; and it was to include big office blocks, as well as flats and much else. Then the slump in the property market forced Tiberi to freeze or reduce large parts of the project: many of the planned new offices were not finding developers. The Left argued that the ZAC was entirely misconceived. The city planners replied that there was still a big demand for new high-quality offices, even if many older ones in central Paris were lying empty. Indeed, the market has now revived since 1997, and the total of unused office space in Paris, though still large, has begun to fall. So today the plan remains to build, eventually, some 900,000 square metres of new offices in the ZAC, plus housing for some 25,000 people. But it will all take far longer than first planned, and the Left is still warning of financial disaster. The ZAC is due also to contain cultural centres and university buildings. Already, in the heart of its wasteland, there towers up the largest of all recent Paris creations – the new national library, a memorial not to Chirac's reign, but to Mitterrand's.

More than other recent French Presidents, Mitterrand revived a tradition dating back to Napoleon and the monarchy: that of endowing the capital with major new architectural works. De Gaulle had done surprisingly little, but Pompidou then took up the trend with Beaubourg. As a project may take up to ten years between inception and completion, one President's idea may have to be finished by the next, and both will try to claim the credit. Giscard may have completed Beaubourg with reluctance: but Mitterrand then eagerly took over and extended two of Giscard's ventures – La Villette, and the transformation of the derelict old Gare d'Orsay, on the Left Bank, into a superb museum of nineteenth-century art.

Mitterrand during his two mandates carried through a super-ambitious strategy, with eight or nine *grands projets* at a total cost of some 30 billion francs. Some are beautiful and successful, some much less so. Almost all are cultural buildings. He saw them as central to his plan for promoting a French cultural renaissance based on Paris (see p. 457): 'We are laying the basis for a new urban civilization,' he claimed; 'for me, architecture is the premier art.' He would closely scrutinize the draft designs, sometimes imposing his own tastes on the architects, many of them foreign. As for his critics, Chirac confessed himself 'appalled' at the level of public spending, while Barre spoke of his 'Louis XIV complex', and Giscard sneered, 'He is trying to leave monumental traces of himself so that his other deeds can be forgotten.' These *grands projets*, if they physically survive, may indeed be what Mitterrand is best remembered for – and he cared so much for his future place in history. In the process he has endowed Paris with a variety of monuments, museums and art works of glittering sophistication in the post-modernist mode. No other European city comes anywhere near to rivalling it.

One of the first and most exciting of these ventures is out on the drab north-eastern edge of Paris, at La Villette. Here a big new abattoir had been built in the 1960s, next to the main Paris meat market: but by some crazy miscalculation it became obsolete. So in 1980 Giscard decided to turn the forlorn 50-hectare site into a science museum, designed by a French architect, Adrien Fainsilber. Mitterrand then extended the project into a huge science-arts-and-leisure complex, which opened in stages after 1986. Now complete, it is a delight of variety, ingenuity and fairground fantasy. The science museum, claimed to be the world's largest, fills the abattoir's main hall and is *three times* the size of Beaubourg: Fainsilber's conversion of the building shows clearly the influence of the Rogers/Piano concept, for here, too, are painted pipes and girders, plus brilliant use of glass walls and mirrors to give an effect of shining light and soaring cathedral-like spaciousness. The museum itself is equally original, in contents and presentation, with plenty of knobs to press and computers to operate – a thrill for any schoolchild. My only grouse: the stress on recent French hi-tech achievements does seem a little chauvinistic.

Outside is the Géode, a giant sphere of reflecting steel that houses a panoramic cinema using the Omnimax system, as at the Futuroscope (see p. 627). The large amusement park next door is strewn with bizarre-shaped bright-red follies. Close by, the huge former hall for cattle is now used for exhibitions and cultural events, while the Zénith is a major new venue for pop concerts. Across a broad piazza is the elegant new Cité de la Musique (see p. 445) and the new home of the Conservatoire de Paris. And so, to adapt the slogan of one big Paris store, *vraiment, on trouve tout à La Villette!* It is large-scale, yes, but not unpleasantly grandiose, and has been a massive success: 3.5 million visitors came to the science museum alone in 1995.

Far more controversial has been Mitterrand's glass pyramid for the

Louvre. Clearly some urgent renovation was needed for Europe's largest art museum, which had become inadequate for dealing with its growing millions of visitors and for properly displaying its treasures. So the President decreed that the Ministry of Finance should quit its historic headquarters in the north wing: its officials at first dug their heels in, typically, but were finally induced to move out to their glossy new premises near the Gare de Lyon. Their part of the Louvre has now been turned into galleries, and the museum's pictures have been rearranged, with much more space. There is more daylight, too, in parts: Mitterrand's major coup was to invite the famous Chinese-American architect Ioh Ming Pei to come up with something special for the main entrance, and special indeed was the result – a five-storey glass pyramid which has not ceased to startle the world. When it was opened in 1989, Pei cheekily told the *Daily Telegraph*, 'The Louvre is a mess, it doesn't work . . . Across 800 years it has been rebuilt constantly. This gave me the feeling that it could change again, and this was maybe the moment.' His see-through pyramid brings daylight cascading into the loftily spacious new marble-clad entrance hall below, and for this it is widely admired. Parisians of course remain divided about its exterior location, where it contrasts dramatically with the classic Louis XIII/XIV façades of the central courtyard. But as with the Eiffel Tower or Beaubourg in their day, it is slowly becoming accepted as part of the landscape.

Argument has also shrouded a *projet* rather more *petit* – the decoration of the graceful seventeenth-century courtyard of the Palais Royal. Jack Lang, as Minister of Culture, was keen to promote the work of modern French artists: so, with Mitterrand's backing, he accepted a design by the young avant-garde sculptor Daniel Buren, for 260 black-and-white striped pillars of varying lengths – 'the sawn-off stumps of what appears to have been a peppermint or liquorice forest', wrote one critic less than amicably. Again, many Parisians were horrified. The Académie des Beaux-Arts and other bodies all protested to Mitterrand – but in vain. Today tourists come to gawp at these pillars, and children play hopscotch on the shorter ones. Some of them, in a basin of running water, are lit up at night in luminous blue. Richelieu might be startled: but in their way they *are* rather lovely.

Other *grands projets* have included the Grande Arche; the much-criticized Opéra de la Bastille (see p. 446); and the elegant Institut du Monde Arabe, on the Left Bank, a cultural centre superbly designed by Jean Nouvel. This trendy showman is one of the few modern French architects today with a world reputation. There are not many others: recognizing this, Pompidou and Mitterrand, to their credit, rejected a narrow chauvinism and chose foreigners to design several of the new projects intended for the greater glory of Paris. It has been a prime example of the admirable open internationalism of this city today (see p. 457). Some of the new buildings may seem pompous: but they have added much to Paris, and they represent a brief architectural golden age which may now be ended (Chirac has no such plans, save a fairly modest one for a museum of African art). And the public? Despite initial scepticism, for example over that pyramid, it has warmed overall to Mitterrand's grand design.

But was there not one final mighty blunder? There it stands today, upstream by the Seine, a colossus of four glass high-rise towers, designed to look like open books – the most recent, the largest, most ambitious, and possibly the least well conceived of Mitterrand's grand pharaonic gestures. The final dream of a literary man. The venerable old Bibliothèque Nationale, in the heart of Paris, had grown inadequate: it was cramped and badly catalogued, and academics often had to queue for hours to get a seat. A new national library was clearly needed. So a young French architect was hired, Dominique Perrault, and a spacious site was chosen – a derelict railway yard at Tolbiac, by the Left Bank near the Gare d'Austerlitz, within the *ZAC du treizième*. The unfinished building was inaugurated by Mitterrand in March 1995, just before he retired, and was then partially opened for use in December 1996. Costing 7.5 billion francs, it had suffered some of the same problems as the new British Library, but less serious, for the governmental backing to get it built was far greater. So the delays were not too bad. It has been criticized more for its design, for its expense (its running costs will eat up a tenth of the annual French culture budget), and for being poorly adapted to its use by researchers and the serious public.

The four 80-metre towers have been built to house the 10 million books from the old library, but their readers sit in caverns below ground – not ideal, you might think. What's more, the luminous glass façades were intended to reflect the light, shining in upon the books: Mitterrand thought this would look just lovely, viewed from across the river. Then it was realized that sunlight could damage the rare works, so wooden shutters were installed inside the glass walls, thus destroying the effect planned. It was a crazy imprudence. The library stands around a beautiful sunken garden, with graceful trees: but its interior as a whole is heavy and uninviting, with vast staircases, and a reader may have to walk some way to reach the part he wants. It is the world's second largest library, with fewer books (10 million) than that of Congress in Washington (25 million), but with more seating space (4,500 places), and a staff of 2,400. The old Bibliothèque Nationale will retain special collections of maps, prints, etc.: but its main store of books was in 1998 moved to Tolbiac, which acquired some 400,000 new ones too.

In fact, whereas the old library was solely for research, the new one also has a large section for the general public and students. Books cannot be borrowed: but there is shelf access, plus a modern computer system whereby books can be ordered in advance from home. Cataloguing, with the Dewey system at last installed, is far better than in the old library. In short, the new one has various facilities that its encrusted old predecessor did not. But it has had teething troubles and is not yet very user-friendly. In late 1998 its staff, haughty and dissatisfied, went on a lengthy strike against their working conditions and especially the awkward computer system. And even some scholars talk of an 'inhuman' building, a 'folly' unrelated to real needs, with awesome interiors. Yet this Bibliothèque François-Mitterrand (now its official name) may one day prove its real worth. Access to it finally improved late in 1998, with the opening of a new Métro line from central Paris.

This brings us to the crucial issue of transport in Paris and its region. As with the *grands projets*, matters here are more in the hands of the State than the city council. The latter deals with the building and upkeep of roads: but the police are in charge of traffic and parking, while public transport is run by a body responsible mainly to the Government.

Today the steady growth of car traffic in Paris, long tolerated, has finally come to be regarded as an urgent problem – more because of pollution than time-wasting congestion, though both are serious. Fewer people may live inside the Ville de Paris than in the old days, but more of them own cars; and though only 13 per cent use these to go to work, many others drive in daily from the suburbs. The Frenchman still tends to regard regular use of his car as a basic human right: he may drive it to town in the imprudent hope that that he, unlike the next man, will somehow beat the jams and find a parking space. So the authorities have faced a familiar modern dilemma: is the answer to pander to the motorist by building yet more freeways, tunnels and car parks? – or is it to restrict the car and provide alternatives? For long the policy in Paris was the former. But for thirty years now, serious efforts have been made to entice the citizen away from his beloved *bagnole* with better public transport. This has improved marvellously, but has still not solved the problem.

Various measures in the 1950s and '60s made it possible to keep abreast, just about, of an annual 10 per cent increase in the volume of traffic. Some streets were widened, and the one-way system was made Europe's most extensive: even major avenues like the Boulevards St-Germain and Sébastopol are now *à sens unique*. An urban ring motorway, the Boulevard Périphérique, was completed in 1970, around the edge of the Ville de Paris. Linking with this, exitways from the city were improved. An expressway was built, west to east, along much of the Right Bank. Plans for a similar route along the Left Bank, east to west, caused an outcry at the threat this posed to the Notre-Dame area with its lovely *quais*: Giscard on coming to power banned the project. But in general, the main roads along the river on both sides have been much improved, with underpass tunnels, and quayside roads away from the beauty spots. There will still be traffic jams at peak hours: but mostly it is easier than in London to cross the city centre beside the river, quite fast if you wish. MAYBE TOO FAST! – was not the Tunnel de l'Alma, by the Right Bank, the scene in August 1997 of the most notorious fatal car accident in world history?

The rate of traffic in Paris is highly uneven. You can sweep majestically along some boulevard, then get stuck in the honeycomb of little streets towards Les Halles or the Gare de l'Est, caught in a cortège of horn-blowing Gallic frustration. This is one legacy of Haussmann: a few broad roads that mask a maze of narrow ones, often obstructed by cars parked illegally. Parking, in fact, is a worse problem in Paris than traffic. Some 100 underground car parks have been built since 1970, and they can accommodate 64,000 cars: but this has only partially eased the evening agony of trying to park in many entertainment or residential districts, where the narrow streets between high blocks were not built for the motor age, in a city that still has twice the population density of London. However, daytime parking in business areas has been eased by the introduction of pay-machines. Four times in the 1960s the city fathers had rejected police proposals for parking meters: they judged them too ugly for graceful Paris, and they thought Parisians would never tolerate such an assault on their 'right' to free parking. By 1970 Paris was the only world city without pay-parking: but finally the police got their way. The first meters were met with a wave of sabotage: paper-clips or chewing-gum were shoved into them, some were sawn off in the night by angry motorists. So they were gradually replaced by pavement machines selling timed parking vouchers – less ugly, and harder to vandalize. These are monitored by smart women dishing out fines of 75 francs for overstaying, 250 francs or more for 'obstructive' parking. There is no clamping, but serious obstructors may find their car towed off to a pound, where the fine is higher. It is reckoned that some 75 per cent of Parisians do buy their vouchers or pay their fines: but of those coming from outside the city, 55 per cent do not. And the wardens and police are regarded as lax in writing out fines or chasing up the unpaid ones.

Fewer people might use their cars, if taxis were more numerous. The total was pegged at 13,000 in 1937, and since then it has risen only to 14,800. The powerful taxi-driver lobby has always operated a closed shop, and if the authorities propose a major new issue of licences, this is met with strikes or a threat of strikes. Moreover, the drivers, like other French, prefer to stick to their classic meal-times, so taxis tend to become hard to find just when they are most needed. The drivers claim that to raise taxi numbers would put many of them out of business: they seldom accept the argument that it could reduce the use of private cars, and so increase their own trade. The city council claims that the answer is to curb the car, enabling taxis to move faster and thus do more business.

Meanwhile a visitor to Paris might be advised to take a bus or the Métro, rather than wait around for a taxi. Thirty years ago, London's public transport was better than Paris's: but now the reverse is true, as London's buses and tube trains have grown dirtier, slower, more infrequent. Is this a symptom of the two nations' attitudes to public services? London Transport has been investing only about one-third as much as its Paris equivalent, the Régie Autonome des Transports Parisiens (RATP), which has a more dynamic long-term development policy and gets a big subsidy. Its bus service, once ramshackle, is now a joy: new and more comfortable vehicles have been introduced and their frequency increased. Down many boulevards there are now bus corridors, enabling the green single-deckers to move at a spanking pace along much of their route. At bus stops, the numbered queue-slips have long departed: you now queue in an orderly Anglo-Saxon fashion. There are no more conductors, for all buses have automatic punchers; and the *carnets* of tickets or zoned season tickets are usable alike on bus or Métro. Thanks in part to these and other improvements, the total of passengers on Paris buses, which had been falling heavily, has more than doubled since 1974. One recent innovation, taken from America, is a phasing system that enables buses along the same route to be spaced out more evenly, thus avoiding the crazy London situation where two Number 9s can arrive together and the next one half an hour later!

Buses have long been acceptable to the bourgeoisie. But the Métro in the old days, with its garlicky stench, prison-like automatic barriers, and sad ticket-punchers like *tricoteuses* at the guillotine, was defiantly a working-class institution. 'Sorry I'm late,' said Marie-Chantal, archetypal Parisian deb, in a joke of the 1950s, 'but my brother Claude had taken the Jag, Pierre had taken the Mercedes, so I took the Métro – *tu le connais?*' London's debs have been cheerfully boarding trains at Sloane Square since W. S. Gilbert's day: but London tube trains with their plushy seating were a cut above the Métro. So what would Marie-Chantal make of it today? She would find sleek new trains, rather less spartan, and many stations given a facelift with arty décor that mirrors their *quartier* (e.g. classical art along the Louvre platforms). Gone are the barriers, the ticket-punchers, the stench; trains go fast, and with superb frequency, except in the late evening. The chief snag, due to the way the Métro was built in the 1900s, is the long walk needed to change platforms at some larger stations, with their gloomy corridors. Some passengers are irritated by the RATP's leniency towards the long-term unemployed, who come regularly into carriages to beg and to harangue you on their fate: but perhaps this is salutary. On the plus side, one asset of the Métro is its cheapness, compared to London: bought on a *carnet*, a flat-rate ticket for any journey cost, in 1998, just 4.6 francs. But the passenger is paying only 35 per cent of the real cost: the rest is met by the RATP's big subsidy from the State and local bodies, i.e. from the taxpayer. Tourists thus get this bonus for free, which some Parisians think unfair: but the city benefits indirectly from the trade they bring. And the subsidy helps towards a better Métro service: it carries 4.5 million people a day, against London's 2.5 million.

Above all, the rail network has been hugely extended since the 1970s, with new express trains going far into the suburbs. Previously, the Métro itself barely penetrated outside the Ville de Paris. It had been built in 1900 on a different gauge from the SNCF (state railways), which was bitterly jealous of its new rival and managed to place limits on its expansion and to retain a monopoly of suburban traffic. But the SNCF's local services were slow and clumsy, and with the post-war growth of the suburbs, something new was needed. So the State allowed the RATP to develop the Réseau Express Régional (RER), which began in 1977 and today has four main lines, traversing Paris and extending to such crucial destinations as Versailles, Charles-de-Gaulle Airport and Disneyland. Trains are large, and fast: the 25-kilometre journey from St-Germain-en-Laye to the Opéra, with several stops, takes twenty minutes. The RER links up at some points with the Métro, and their main junction stations, such as Châtelet, Étoile or Grande Arche, are of a size and brash metropolitanism that make Baker Street or Embankment look quaintly provincial. Châtelet-Les Halles, a 3-hectare cave-palace of space-age design, is claimed to be the largest and busiest underground station in the world. What's more, the RER has the same gauge as the SNCF: the old SNCF/RATP feud has ended, and the RER lines are run jointly, on an integrated basis. So the old main-line SNCF termini are no longer culs-de-sac but part of a trans-Paris system, as the RER from Roissy airport stops at the Gares du Nord and de Lyon on its way to Melun. London, too, is now beginning to limp in this direction, as best it can. The SNCF has now linked the Gares de l'Est and St-Lazare into this system with a new short stretch, called Éol. And the RATP in 1998 opened a fast, fully automated new line, called Météor (MéTro Est-Ouest Rapide), from St-Lazare to the national library at Tolbiac. This is all very expensive, and some critics argue that priorities should be elsewhere. But many transport experts believe that Paris has developed the world's best subway and suburban system.

Yet the problem remains: what to do about the motor car? Chirac as mayor was lenient, knowing that his bourgeois voters and his business allies wanted to keep their freedom to drive: so he encouraged road improvements and new parks for cars, but did little to deter their use. Yet traffic within Paris has gone on slowly rising, due largely to the daily influx from the suburbs; and the public has become more pollution-conscious. Tiberi seems more sensitive to this than Chirac; and whatever his other faults, he has embarked with apparent sincerity on a policy of at last trying to dissuade motorists. But it is not easy. In 1996 he opened the first bicycle corridors in Paris, with promise of more to come: but it was on a modest scale compared with what German and other cities do. He also began to develop a few *zones tranquilles* in local residential areas, where cars are now limited formally to 30 km.p.h. and are slowed down by 'sleeping policemen' – as in some parts of London. Above all, he planned a new scheme to deter cars from entering Paris from the suburbs, not by tolls or other controls (nor by park-and-ride incentives, which had been tried but never caught on), but by filters on access roads. This idea led him into conflict with the mayors of adjacent communes, who complained that he was trying to offload his traffic jams on to them; and discussions faltered. Tiberi thus faces various kinds of opposition, not least from the car-loving electorate he has inherited from Chirac. And many of his schemes are expensive. However, growing public concern about exhaust fumes did lead the Juppé Government in 1997 to decree a partial ban on cars whenever air pollution rose above a certain level. Then, after the elections, it was the new Environment Minister, Dominique Voynet, herself a Green, who eagerly and successfully applied this ban for the first time (see p. 276).

Transport in the wider Paris conurbation, with its huge post-war growth, has posed different problems. Eight motorways today radiate from Paris towards other cities, all linked to the Boulevard Périphérique. This is often saturated at peak hours, and since 1986 a second ring motorway, the A86, has been slowly constructed, about 6 kilometres out: it has met with every kind of obstacle, budgetary, legal and environmental, and is still far from completed on its western side. A third radial *autoroute*, the '*Francilienne*', some 10 kilometres further out, has now been finished on its eastern side. This whole spider's web is open to criticism, but has done much to ease commuter traffic in a region where public rail transport is still much too centripetal. The RER lines may go far out, but none is radial; and only since 1992 have two strips of fast tramway been built, linking a few suburbs. There are plenty of transversal bus lines, but they are not fast. Yet many people today live in one suburb but work in another, and thus feel obliged to use their cars, either for this or to go to work in central Paris, if they are not near an RER station. The figures are remarkable. Car traffic in the region has doubled since 1970, and has been rising *six* times faster than use of public transport: this latter accounts for 62 per cent of all journeys within Paris, but less than 20 per cent of inter-suburban ones. So the authorities have come under criticism for not doing more, and sooner, to fight this trend. One complaint: 'Why spend so much on new underground parking, drawing yet more cars into Paris, rather than on more suburban railway lines?' Others point out that the two new tube lines in the heart of Paris have since 1994 eaten half of the budget for developing public transport in the Ile-de-France. Today region and State have finally promised to make more effort towards improving suburban links, and the new Minister of

Transport has made this a priority. But it will take time, and much money, to make a real change.

Outside the Ville de Paris are the suburbs, which have been growing fast since the war while Paris's own population declines. Today the whole conurbation of about 9.5 million lies within the new Ile-de-France region: they are known by the expressive nickname of '*franciliens*'. The region, with 12,000 square kilometres, is partly rural. It comprises 1,278 communes and eight *départements*: Paris, both a commune and a *département*, has a prefect as well as mayor.

Baron Haussmann's rational replanning of central Paris was never extended to the new industrial suburbs, which after 1870 grew up higgledy-piggledy outside the gates. Aubervilliers, Les Lilas, lovely names for ghastly places: these and scores of other townlets arose while Paris was sucking the blood from the rest of France. They 'presented almost the limit of urban degeneration', as one critic put it. After 1918 this growth slowed: but, with land prices low, another kind of excrescence now appeared in the suburbs, the individual *pavillon*. The *petit bourgeois* found that he could afford to realize a dream that he secretly shares with the Englishman: a suburban cottage with a garden. But instead of the English ribbon-development of that period, there was anarchy. Some 80,000 little red-roofed *pavillons* spread their rash of assorted shapes across the outer suburbs. Then after 1945 the population again rose rapidly, so hundreds of new blocks of flats were flung up piecemeal. But until the 1960s not much was done to plan these new suburbs coherently. At first, stray blocks were planted anywhere; nor was much effort made to provide these sad new dormitories with proper equipment such as hospitals and playing fields. Suburban public transport was appalling, too. Yet in a time when housing was still scarce, many people had to live far from their jobs. So a worker might have to rise at 5 a.m. to make a two-hour train journey via central Paris to his factory on the far side of town, arriving back home at 8 p.m.

It was de Gaulle's Government, typically, that finally took action, after the Fourth Republic's *laissez-faire*. The Paris region's population was then growing by over 130,000 a year. So a new planning office was set up, under Paul Delouvrier, a leading technocrat; and he prepared a grandiose master plan, the Schéma Directeur, which remained the basis of action for many years. The essence of its thinking was that Paris would be asphyxiated unless it were made polycentric. The British post-war solution of 'new towns', previously rejected as not being in the French tradition, was now espoused on a giant scale, and the Schéma decreed five new cities: St-Quentin-en-Yvelines to the southwest, Cergy-Pontoise to the north-west, Marne-la-Vallée to the east, Melun-Sénart and Évry to the south-east. These towns, essentially part of the conurbation, are only twenty-five to forty kilometres from the city centre, nearer than, say, Crawley is to London. Building began in the early 1970s, and today the towns are nearly completed and quite a success (see pp. 208–9). Each has a population of some 80,000 to 200,000, and is well endowed with amenities and local employment.

The Schéma also decreed new transport networks, the transfer of some activities from the city centre, and measures to absorb and renovate gradually the existing ugly suburban mess. France's economic boom of the 1960s made funds available: so outer Paris was at last able to receive the community services it badly needed. For example, whereas no new hospitals at all were built in greater Paris in 1934–60, ten were completed in the 1960s. New theatres, colleges, swimming pools and libraries at last began to enliven *la triste banlieue*, which had lacked such luxuries, save in a few richer reserves such as Versailles. Some leading Grandes Écoles, including Polytechnique and HEC, were moved from their cramped downtown quarters to spacious new premises outside the city. Today, while the Paris suburbs still have their social problems, and some serious pockets of poverty and poor housing, they do not lack modern public amenities and equipment.

In 1964 Delouvrier became super-prefect of the newly formed Ile-de-France 'region'. He and his officials imposed their Schéma rather high-handedly, in the manner of those days; and of course they ran into opposition from local communes, many with left-wing mayors who complained with reason that they had not been properly consulted. 'But how on earth,' said one lofty technocrat, 'can you expect the mayor of some piffling suburb to grasp *our* real problems? His arguments would simply have held things up.' Today this pattern has changed, under devolution, and there is far more consultation (see below). But the first Schéma, though hardly democratic, did bring results and was on the whole successfully applied. And so, by the 1980s, the race against time to save greater Paris from asphyxia seemed to have been won. Today the sprawling Paris suburbs present a bewildering variety of urban styles. Old villages have been engulfed by high-rise estates, yet keep something of their village character. The California-style garden cities around

Versailles, with their *piscines* and sun terraces, contrast with the dour 1950s HLM blocks of the 'Red' eastern suburbs. New flyovers swoop over the surviving jumble of pre-war *pavillons*; glossy modern factories stand beside crumbling old workshops. Some at least of the old vacant lots and seedy shacks have been steadily replaced by ritzy hypermarkets, civic sports centres, theatres, clinics, or imposing new *mairies* and *préfectures* of glass and steel. And some town centres have been smartly renovated with cobbled pavings and arty lamp-posts – rather too artificial for some tastes.

A few huge-scale new projects, for commerce or for mass entertainment, have marked the region in recent years. While La Défense had continued the old trend of Paris to develop westward, the authorities have now felt it important to move the balance towards the east. Within the city, Bercy and the *ZAC du treizième* have formed part of this policy; further out, the new Disneyland (see p. 628) was assigned to the edge of the new town of Marne-la-Vallée. To the north-east, the modern Paris airport of Charles-de-Gaulle was opened in 1974 at Roissy, to share traffic with the older airport of Orly, to the south. With its two big circular termini, Roissy today handles 24 million passengers a year, and Orly 22 million: together they form Europe's second largest airport, behind London's (71 million in 1993) but ahead of Frankfurt (32 million). Roissy is now nearing saturation, and in 1997 it was Jean-Claude Gayssot, the new Communist Transport Minister, who gave the go-ahead for building two more runways, despite fierce opposition not only from environmental groups (led by his own colleague, Dominique Voynet) but from local politicians of all colours, representing their noise-scared constituents. Measures are now promised against night flights, which till now have been allowed at Roissy, though not at Orly, nearer to built-up areas. Jospin overrode the ecologist and local lobbies because of the need for more jobs and trade in the area, as a clever cartoon by Pessin in *Le Monde* pointed out (25 September 1997): 'Aircraft taking off, 90 decibels; unemployed couple, 180 decibels' (they are shown screaming loudly).

On the same side of Paris, at St-Denis, is the Stade de France, today familiar to over a billion football fans via television. Seating 80,000, this graceful oval-shaped stadium, super-modern, with its shimmering white roof, was designed by French architect Michel Macary and three colleagues; it was then built by a French consortium (led by the huge Bouygues group), at a cost of 2.7 billion francs. And the story behind it is curious. When France in 1991 was allotted the 1998 World Cup, it was clear that the existing Parc des Princes near the Bois de Boulogne would be inadequate for the Paris matches, so a new and more prestigious stadium was needed. The Government wanted St-Denis, so close to Paris: but its Communist-led council at first said no, and another site out at Melun was prospected. Then St-Denis woke up to its folly just in time, and agreed – so long as the stadium was to be part of a wider renovation scheme. On this basis, work went ahead. St-Denis itself, the foremost town close to Paris after Versailles, may be a historic city with a famous basilica: but it has long been the centre of a poor working-class area, where eight of the nine local communes are Communist. The Stade is in a grim area, La Plaine-St-Denis, between the gates of Paris and St-Denis centre. Before 1939 it had been a thriving zone of small industries, but gradually it became woefully run-down and desolate, and many factories were empty. In its prime position, it was ideal for redevelopment. St-Denis council had insisted contractually that 25 per cent of the work on the Stade would go to local building firms, and though this quota was never met, the town has certainly benefited hugely. The A1 *autoroute* to Lille, dividing La Plaine in two, has now been put underground; new blocks of flats and offices, new small industries, have begun to enliven this former wasteland, bringing in new jobs. The St-Denis council, which for years had been virtually at war with the State, started to cooperate even under Juppé, and is now doing so actively.

Two wider factors have recently changed the picture in the Ile-de-France. First, like other French regions, it now has its own directly elected council, with some autonomy. So the revised Schéma Directeur, adopted in 1994, was not imposed by the State but was drawn up jointly with the council. And instead of promoting growth at all costs, as Delouvrier's document had done, it puts a stronger emphasis on the environment and quality of life, in line with the new mood among *franciliens*. Until 1998 the council had a centre-Right majority, with an RPR chairman, Michel Giraud. But many larger communes such as St-Denis have always been left-wing, and both electorates have needed to be catered for. So the new Schéma puts an accent not only on social housing and jobs, but on the preservation of peripheral forests and farm land, which concerns many middle-class voters. A proper green-belt policy is at last being developed. In the March 1998 elections, the regional council fell into Socialist hands, under Jean-Pierre Huchon, former *directeur de cabinet* of Rocard at Matignon.

The second factor has been changes in the population growth. Since about 1960 this had been slowing right down, from 130,000 a year to some 24,000, below the French average. This was due to the impact of DATAR's policies, plus the new trend of some Parisians seeking a life in the provinces. But in 1982–90 the growth rate of the Ile-de-France rose again by 580,000 – faster than the national average. A setback for DATAR? May be: but the new 1998–9 census has shown that growth has slowed again to 325,000 over eight years, just below the French average. Today the number of *franciliens* is nudging 11 million, of whom some 9.5 million are within the Paris conurbation. If numbers are still rising, this is not due to new net immigration, but rather to a high birth rate in the region, with its youthful population and many ethnic immigrants. Even so, it is a blow to DATAR policies. And although 1994 Schéma pledged itself to 'controlling growth', how this can be done without the anathema of trying to limit job creation is not entirely clear.

In 1998 an official report by INSEE showed that the Paris region still has much the greatest concentration of economic power in the EU, ahead of Lombardy, Greater London and the Ruhr/Düsseldorf areas, which come next in that order. It is not that Parisians are personally the richest, but the economic might is centred on the capital, more than in other countries – which shows that decentralization in France still has its limits. And so today the old debate continues as to whether or not to try to check the growth of the Ile-de-France, where three-quarters of jobs are in the tertiary sector. Jean Voisard, a leading DATAR figure, told me in 1997, 'The Government could do more to prevent Paris from growing. But its own ruling élites are here, 40 per cent of all senior French *cadres* are here, and the State puts so much money into Paris that taxes here are lower and living is cheaper, at least in the suburbs: so of course people are drawn here.' Not all would agree, but many *élus* want to have it both ways. They speak out against the tentacular growth of Europe's second largest conurbation: yet understandably they want nothing done to limit job creation. In other cities and regions, life may be gentler.

BRITTANY RESURGENT:
A NATION ONCE AGAIN?

Brittany has changed more strikingly since the 1960s than any other region of France. Its proud Celtic people see themselves as a nation, like the Scots, so they harboured the sharpest sense of grievance at the old French centralism – at a colonizing Paris which refused them any autonomy, tried to suppress their language, and left their land to be the eternal economic victim, out on its lonely peninsula. But today all is different. This formerly poor and backward province is now one of France's most modern and successful. It may have its problems, but it breathes an aura of prosperity, evident in the neat villages of the coastal plains, the fine new roads and factories. It has below-average unemployment and is France's top region for agricultural output and for telecommunications. The progress has been helped by special government aid, but is due also to the Bretons' own hard-working efforts – a people almost as dreamy and passionate as the Irish, yet as tough and industrious as the Scots.

Just as the previous lack of autonomy was resented most keenly in Brittany, so the Defferre reforms of the 1980s have worked better here than in most regions: by at last giving Bretons more control over their affairs, they have assuaged the old 'colonial' complex. Bretons are now free to express their Breton culture as they wish – and the Government even helps! Few of them are separatist: but many at heart feel Breton first, French second. The Breton persona is vibrantly *à la mode*.

With my Irish roots, I feel more at home here than in other French regions. This is France's Celtic fringe, a wild mysterious poetic land where the desolate central moorlands slope down to fertile plains, and Atlantic rollers break on rocky headlands. In many villages, the curious stone calvaries and ossuaries, with ornate carvings, bear witness to a special religious past, linked to the terrors of death at sea. Brittany was not annexed to France until 1532, later than most provinces. Its people retain more sense of a separate identity than others in mainland France, while the visitor may find this region more 'un-French' in character than any other save perhaps Alsace.

When Bretons put on their costumes for summer festivals, it may be with an eye for the tourist trade. Yet their concern for their traditions is powerfully real, and has been reviving ever since the 1960s, especially among the young. Some young poets, writing in Breton, relate modern political themes to the ancient legends of Merlin or Tristan and Isolde. And when teenagers hold a 'hop' in a village hall, they use the stately slow-swaying Breton dance forms, plus traditional music which somehow gets transmuted into Breton pop. Bretons have become assertively self-confident about their culture, while a few older ones still brood on past injustices. 'In the 1940s I was punished if I spoke Breton at school,' said one professor. 'The French tried to destroy us. They gave us an inferiority complex. For me, France is a foreign country.'

In the 1960s a hard-core of nationalists took to violence, like the IRA or the Basque ETA but on a smaller scale. This Front de Libération de la Bretagne carried out sporadic bomb attacks on public buildings, even on the palace of Versailles; scores of activists, including priests, were arrested and some were given prison sentences. But while many Bretons felt a sneaking sympathy for the FLB, its violence was deplored and its separatist aims were not widely shared. Today it has virtually disappeared. Most Bretons have always accepted that outright independence for Brittany would not make economic sense. They have been ready to remain French, so long as Brittany gets a better deal – as it was given economically from about the mid-1960s, and then at last politically under the regional reform, which has led to a right-of-centre majority in the new assembly in Rennes since 1986.

This reform, though less radical than some would have liked, has satisfied the major part of Breton opinion, and has defused any lingering separatism. 'It is not perfect, but it's a big step forward, and has changed the nature of our links with Paris,' I was told by Claude Champaud, an RPR leader; 'we still depend on Paris in many ways, but we're far less subservient.' In every Breton regional election since 1986, the elected candidates have all been from the main French national parties, whether of Right or Left: the local 'regional' lists, representing purely Breton interests and demanding a more radical devolution, have done badly and won no seats. This might seem strange, for there is nothing to prevent a region from developing its own political parties, so long as these do not advocate secession, which is illegal. But most Bretons have now ceased pressing for greater autonomy: their main local anxieties today are economic, not political. And Le Pen's party fares poorly in his own homeland, where immigration is low and people are generally tolerant. The regional council is more effective than most in France, perhaps because Brittany is a *real* region, unlike others. This right-of-centre council has collaborated quite easily with the main town councils, which are Socialist-led. Bretons are less given to political feuding than many French. And when it comes to confronting Paris on some issue, rival politicians tend to unite in solidarity, putting Brittany first.

The cultural renewal has had counterparts in some other regions, and abroad in Ireland and elsewhere. In the 1970s many Breton leaders and intellectuals, frustrated at the lack of progress towards political reform, felt that they must first channel their campaign into economic or cultural action – as the nationalist poet Xavier Grall told me: 'Our best course is to build up our culture as the spiritual basis for a political thrust when the time is ripe. Many nations have done this under oppression – the Irish under Britain, the Slovenes under Austria.' The self-expressionist ideals of May '68 also helped to foster the renewal, which has since taken diverse forms. Groups of intellectuals have been seeking through arts and literature to counter the inevitable decline in day-to-day rural folk culture as the peasantry disappears: while the *coiffes* die out in the villages, the poetry clubs grow in the towns. Today three or four new novels in Breton are published each year, and their sales have been rising, maybe up to 4,000 copies; literary reviews have been started; a few theatre groups act in Breton. But this modest movement is riven by rivalries. For example, the true Breton speakers tend to look down on the rest: Grall, most ardent of Bretons, felt a sense of shame that he was brought up in a French culture and could not write his poems in Breton. But Brittany's best-known modern writer, Pierre-Jakez Hélias, who died in 1995, wrote in both languages: in his wonderful saga of his own peasant family, *Le Cheval d'orgueil* (1975), which sold 1.2 million copies in France, he told how he felt uprooted when sent to school and forced to learn French: 'We are immigrants despite ourselves in a civilization that is not our own.' And there was the poet-singer Glenmor, who died in 1996, a charismatic figure, burly and bearded, who could magnetize an audience with his growling voice and the stern rhythms of his own Breton songs . . . '*Deiz ha deiz, hir ha berr, o youc'hal* . . .' It was enough to set any Celt's pulse racing, from Quimper to Connemara, from Lorient to Llangollen.

The past thirty years have also seen a craze for popular Breton music among young people. Nearly every village has its *fest-noz*, a fête where groups play Breton instruments such as the *bombarde* (a kind of oboe) or bagpipes, and the dancers sway in slow rhythm. The trend began spontaneously, then grew commercialized as Breton folk-song merged into a more hybrid Breton pop and rock. *Le bretonnisme* became fashionable and even created an export industry, a mini-Nashville: Alain Stivell, a folk-singer in a lighter vein than Glenmor, became a cult hero, selling millions of records not only in Brittany. Today the guitarist Dan ar Braz, who worked with Stivell, is also popular: influenced by Irish groups such as U2, he has developed new rock styles based on old Breton themes.

In 1996 he assembled a large group of Celtic singers and players, including Irish and Scots, to represent France with a song in Breton for the Eurovision contest – to the indignation of some Gaullists in Paris. Traditional Breton music and its new rock versions today coexist. Some older people of course dislike the rock, while the modernists consider the traditional approach too formal, slow and heavy. They believe that lighter, faster rhythms can also be genuinely Breton.

A smaller minority of young people are involved in the language revival – a complex issue. Breton used to be Brittany's main language, but then in the late nineteenth century Paris began an assimilation policy: it won over the bourgeoisie to French, then tried to stamp out Breton among the peasantry. State teachers would punish pupils who spoke Breton in school. This terrorized many Bretons, who looked on their teacher as 'superior', and it produced a sense of inferiority: young men joining army units on military service found themselves mocked if they spoke Breton or could not manage proper French. And so, until recently, humbler parents who spoke Breton among themselves would try to prevent their own children from learning it, wanting to protect them from this 'handicap'. I met one man whose Breton-speaking parents had taught him only French. When as a teenager he began going to *fest-noz*, he wept with joy to discover his heritage, then went to college and learned Breton on his own. His father was furious: '*Fiston*, after all we've done for you, why shame us like this?'

These attitudes have now changed, and Paris has ended its campaign. But the legacy of its war of attrition is that Breton has been steadily dying out as a daily language; and the rural exodus has hastened the process. Today Breton is spoken just between close friends and relatives, mostly older people, and is no longer a *lingua franca*. In 1930 about 1.2 million people (half the population) still spoke it fluently: today the figure is under 600,000, mostly in the western areas (*la Bretagne bretonnante*). And the figure is still falling, as the older peasants die. However, a modest revival has now come from a very different quarter: Breton intellectuals, and the young.

The Government, too, has softened its policy. In the 1960s it began to tolerate Breton and other French regional languages; Giscard, as President, formalized this in 1977 in his 'cultural charter for Brittany'. Ever since, the Ministry of Education has even been helping Breton a little, rather than trying to wipe it out. A state university in Rennes offers a higher diploma in Breton, which can also now be studied in state *lycées* and is an option in the *baccalauréat*. Since 1977 the pioneers of the campaign for Breton have opened a chain of private junior schools, the Diwan, state-recognized, where the teaching is mostly in Breton. There are also bilingual classes in some state schools. The numbers who follow these streams have been increasing steadily, but are still less than 2 per cent of all pupils. Some parents complain of the shortage of suitable teachers in the state schools. One Breton activist told me, 'Paris no longer sees our language as a threat to French unity, but expects that as a daily vehicle it will die out of its own accord, or be limited to a harmless minority of intellectuals and students. So it's prepared to help us a little, but grudgingly.' France remains one of the few countries not to have signed the Council of Europe's charter on protecting minority languages. Chirac promised to do it on a visit to Brittany in 1996, but did little. Finally Jospin in 1998 planned to have the charter ratified quite rapidly. But in June 1999 the Constitutional Council declared that it was not conform with the Constitution (which says that French is the only language of the Republic). And Chirac himself, backed by diverse 'nationalists' of Right and Left, opposed any revision. So the Socialists in the Assembly decided to put forward their own amendment. In practice, the new charter will change little that is not already in force: so the conflict is somewhat absurd. But it shows how anxious some French have become about national identity in face of the new global threats.

Much of the pressure for more teaching of Breton comes from parents. I know one couple (the wife is half English, half Russian Jewish, but devotedly *bretonne*) who have put their three daughters into an *école bilingue*. They also go round the villages, tape-recording old folk's stories and folk-songs of the older generation, before they disappear. Many other parents still think that learning Breton is a waste of time. Often the initiative comes from the teenagers themselves, once they have grown aware of their heritage. But are they numerous enough to balance the decline among the old? 'The Breton language which I love,' Hélias told me, 'is bound to go on dying out from daily use, despite the efforts of a few intellectuals to revive it.' Many others are equally pessimistic, knowing the problems of keeping a regional tongue alive in an age when there are pressures to learn 'useful' major languages, such as English. But does a nation, or an autonomous people, really need its own language? After all, nationalism is more active in Scotland, where hardly anyone speaks Gaelic, than in Wales with its hordes of Welsh speakers; and today Irish has much the same problems as Breton. 'But the Irish case just proves my point,' said one nationalist professor I met, Per Denez. 'Once a people is free, it can go its own way. But a people struggling for survival needs a language as a weapon and focus of identity.'

Bretons' links with their Celtic neighbours, in trade and tourism as well as in culture, have much increased recently. They are rediscovering an ancient tradition, which had lapsed in the centuries following France's annexation. Each August, the huge pan-Celtic folk festival at Lorient draws exuberant crowds of up to 350,000. Breton groups today tour other Celtic lands more often, while the new Breton music is sometimes influenced by Irish. Paddy Moloney, leader of The Chieftains, spends his summers in a cottage near Lorient: 'I feel closer to the Bretons than to the Welsh or Scots,' he told me. Various Breton links with Ireland are today especially warm (the two Celtic peoples have in common the memory of long and harsh 'occupation' by a larger neighbour). The number of Breton/Irish town-twinnings (they include Rennes/Cork, Lorient/Galway, Quimper/Limerick) has grown since 1980 from ten to 102: Ireland has more with Brittany than with the rest of the world together! And some Breton firms are beginning to set up factories in Ireland.

On the economic front, local leaders have been trying since the 1960s to develop new trade links with the world, and thus 'liberate' Brittany from overdependence on Paris. The province lies at the western extreme of a France whose focus has been shifting eastwards, under the EU: so Bretons are bound to feel disadvantaged, if their main economic links remain via Paris. Their leaders stress the importance of turning the focus seawards again, to Britain and Ireland, to Spain and across the Atlantic: that is, to resume the old maritime trading role that Brittany held before the bear hug of Napoleonic centralism. Claude Champaud, president of the region's economic and social council, told me, 'Brittany knew three golden ages: in Druidic times and under the Roman conquest, and in the post-Renaissance era. In these periods it was a great trading centre, our textiles and tin mines flourished. These were times when Britain and Spain were flourishing, too: we *need* these lands. We are weak when France forgets the sea and pursues a "Lotharingian" policy. Today, with or without Paris, we must return to the old ways.'

Some dynamic Bretons have been putting this into practice. One key local figure is the amazing Alexis Gourvennec, a man who in his time has been peasant, shipping magnate, pig-breeding tycoon, ruthless riot leader and pan-Celtic visionary, and has done more than anyone to rescue Brittany from poverty and forge new economic links. He grew up on a small farm near Morlaix, in north Finistère. In 1961, aged twenty-four, he won national fame when he led his fellow peasants in riots against the middlemen, then pressured Paris into reshaping its farm policies, and went on to build up a huge cooperative of vegetable growers (see pp. 387 and 397). His toughness is typically Breton; his economic foresight is more unusual. Realizing that farm progress alone could not solve local problems, he set up a local body that lobbied intensively in Paris, and in 1968 was instrumental in persuading the Government to allocate massive new funds for Brittany, including money for building a deep-water port at Roscoff.

Gourvennec was gambling on Britain's entry into the EEC and the new trade that would follow. But the cross-Channel links in the west hardly existed. A direct ferry from Roscoff to Plymouth seemed the answer – but who was to run it? Gourvennec approached shipping firms which all turned the project down. So the farmers' cooperative decided to launch their own company (today called Brittany Ferries), to the scorn of other lines such as Townsend Thoresen which expected them to flop – '*Vous n'êtes pas des armateurs, mais des amateurs.*' But by hiring the right technical skills the farmers succeeded. In 1973, when the new deep-water port was ready, they opened the daily ferry service to Plymouth which has done so much to develop trade and tourism between '*la petite et la Grande Bretagne*'. BF has since started other successful routes: Portsmouth–St-Malo, Portsmouth–Caen, Roscoff–Cork and Plymouth–Santander. The boats and their food and service are excellent, the crew are mostly Breton, and charming. So, as I have found on the 26-hour trip to Santander, the first day of your holiday in Spain is *de facto* a holiday in Brittany, very delightful. Today Gourvennec's farmers still own some 64 per cent of BF's shares, while the regional council and other local interests own the rest. It is believed to be the only example in Europe of farmers starting their own shipping line, and taking the lead in regional local expansion.

Of BF's 2.7 million annual passengers, 75 per cent are British. There is also a big two-way traffic in meat, eggs and heavy freight, while the farmers' cooperative uses the ferries to export to Britain each year some 50,000 tons of its potatoes and 20,000 tons of cauliflowers. A success story, yes: but today's tougher times have brought problems, inevitably. The opening of the Tunnel, to the east, has increased cross-Channel competition (see p. 146), affecting BF's services from Caen and St-Malo.

And BF's leaders are indignant at the British ferry lines' much lower labour costs, which permit lower charges: 'It's unfair competition,' I was told. In 1996 BF's traffic fell badly: but the Government, ever anxious to keep Brittany sweet, stepped in with a large special subsidy, approved by Brussels.

Gourvennec did not use violent tactics to get his way: but he had often done so in the past. In 1975, when the TT line of Hamburg had the impudence to start a rival St-Malo–Southampton ferry, he sent in his own commando force to prevent the boat from landing: he claimed it was a flag-of-convenience vessel with an underpaid Filipino crew, and he had the right to act. Bonn lodged protests, but Paris took no action: Giscard preferred to keep powerful Gourvennec as a friend. Though proudly Breton, he is no separatist but has purely economic aims, so Paris has always found him useful. Today, ever controversial, he has plenty of local critics who will brand him as 'arch-capitalist' or even 'fascist', and claim that he has become less the idealist, more the ruthless tycoon. But in 1996 I found him still full of plans for Brittany's geo-economic future: 'The new Europe is developing too much to the east, especially since the fall of Communism. To counter this, we must build up *le Grand Ouest*, a great axis from Scotland to Portugal – and our ferries will play their part, linking the Glasgow–Plymouth motorway with another from Brittany down into Iberia.' Other leaders, too, along Europe's western fringe, have begun to promote this idea of a so-called 'Atlantic arc' and are lobbying for it in Brussels. As one practical step, a modern expressway has finally been completed from St-Malo down through Rennes towards Bordeaux. Some Breton leaders are urging that Nantes be detached from the hybrid Pays de la Loire region and brought back into Brittany, its true historic home. But for political reasons this is unlikely to happen.

Assertive, tenacious, but not always realistic, Bretons for years had blamed their economic woes on Paris's neglect. But from the 1960s the charge ceased to be so justified. De Gaulle loved the Bretons, who had sent him so many of the Free French; and after his return to power in 1958, the Government proclaimed for Brittany an 'electronics and nuclear vocation'. It built a major space-communications centre at Lannion, by the north coast; it persuaded electronics firms to set up plant in Brest, Rennes and other towns; and it created a nuclear power station in Finistère, one of France's first. This was all a new departure, for a region with little industrial tradition. But the Bretons were still not satisfied.

In response to serious agitation and violence in 1968–9, a worried Government then launched a more extensive programme, and during the 1970s it poured more money into Brittany than any other region. The telephone system was fully automated; new research centres were set up and Grandes Écoles transferred from Paris; a giant new dry dock was built at Brest, able to repair 500,000-ton tankers; and work was begun on a network of new toll-free expressways, today completed. DATAR offered handsome grants to woo investors, notably to the west, and some firms responded. In the booming 1970s industry was creating some 5,000 extra jobs a year in Brittany. Whatever the motives, Paris had certainly repaired its long neglect.

In today's harder times the efforts have continued, but with ups and downs. Half of all French research in telecommunications is done in Brittany, much of it by the Centre Commun d'Études de Télécommunications et de Télédiffusion (CCETT) in Rennes, an imposing ultra-modern state-owned operation: this has had a 'locomotive' effect, drawing similar new investment from Paris, Germany and Japan. Also at Rennes, Citroën was persuaded back in the 1950s to install a large new provincial factory; and this still flourishes, despite the more recent troubles in the French car industry. Whereas Citroën elsewhere has been laying off some workers, in Rennes it has built up its plant, today with a staff of 12,000. And its success has encouraged spin-off investment, some of it by foreign firms, Belgian, American and Japanese (Canon, Mitsubishi). They report that Breton ex-peasants, hard-working and disciplined, have adapted well to their new role as industrial workers. So Brittany has come a long way in the past decades, and is full of spruce new buildings. Except in parts of the wild interior, it does not *look* a depressed area. Yet there are some real problems, notably in the naval dockyards of Brest and Lorient, in the fishing industry, and in the spread of pollution. And of course the new prosperity is unevenly spread. It is most evident in the richer farming areas, in tourist spots, and in the eastern part of the province nearest Paris.

Here Rennes, the capital, provides a good case study in how provincial cities have changed since the war. From 1953 to 1977 it was lucky to have one of the most enlightened and active of French mayors, Henri Fréville, a local history professor and a *centriste*; and his Socialist successor, Edmond Hervé, has since continued many of his social policies. When Fréville took office, this dignified town of old grey granite buildings was sleepy and rather poor. It had long been a centre of army, law and learning, but had no industry to provide jobs for the emigrants pouring in from the overpopulated farmlands. It was then Fréville who enticed Citroën to Rennes; other industries followed, the university and scientific milieux expanded, and the city won new confidence. Its population has grown since the war from 95,000 to 245,000 (with suburbs). Fréville built housing estates of above-average quality, and made efforts to endow them with better social and leisure amenities than were usual in the new French suburbs of that time. Thanks to this and to other more spontaneous factors, Rennes grew more lively. 'It used to be dead after seven, but now some cafés are full after midnight,' said one Rennais. 'In the '50s the shops were seedy, their window-dressing unchanged since 1910; now there are plenty of slick boutiques. And the Breton *coiffes* are gone from the streets – sad in a way.' Fréville took the initiative for building a big *maison de la culture*, now the Théâtre National de la Bretagne. And in this city of 60,000 students, cultural life is vibrant, with avant-garde plays, an opera company and Breton folk clubs.

Edmond Hervé, mayor since 1977, is as much a devoted Catholic humanist as Fréville was. The degree of continuity in policy, despite the swing to the Left, has been unusual for France, but not so untypical of Brittany, with its sense of patriotic solidarity. Hervé told me in 1996, 'Fréville was a good man, and I have been happy to follow many of his policies, for example by improving and renovating the poorer housing estates. In Rennes we have few of the social problems of *la banlieue*, found in other cities. Most of our immigrants are not foreign but Bretons from our own rural hinterland.'

While Rennes remains a boom town, the west of Brittany today fares less well; and the growing imbalance is causing worry. It is partly a matter of geography. The TGV from Paris goes by swift express line as far as Le Mans, then glides on more slowly to Rennes and Brest: this puts Rennes a bare two hours from Paris by TGV, while to go from Brest to Paris takes over four hours. Inevitably, investment is attracted mainly to the Rennes area. In fact, Ile-et-Vilaine, of which Rennes is capital, is one of the few French *départements* to have registered a net gain in industrial jobs in the 1990s. An executive in Brest told me, 'We feel our remoteness keenly. One used to speak of Brittany's isolation, but now it's just Finistère's. We have good roads but bad air links – and if the plan succeeds to extend the fast TGV line as far as Rennes, Brittany's capital will be just seventy-five minutes from Paris, and Brest will seem in another country.' During the 1990s recession, several factories in the west closed or made lay-offs. Notably, but not for reasons of geography, the big naval dockyards and arsenals of Brest and Lorient have been affected by the restructuring of France's defence industries with some 1,800 jobs due to be lost out of 6,000. It is a reminder of how much Brittany remains dependent on state economic support.

Lorient has been hit also by the sporadic crises in Europe's fishing industry – another complex issue. Nearly 30 per cent of France's fishing is done from south Brittany, mainly from the three big ports of Lorient, Concarneau and Guilvinec; and much of it is expensive high-quality fish – bass, John Dory, monkfish, red mullet. Fishermen there, as elsewhere, have suffered from growing foreign competition, shortages due to overfishing, and periodic price collapses caused by cheap foreign imports, often Russian. The EU's fishing policy does little to protect prices, but it imposes zonal quotas; and Brussels has been trying to oblige member states to reduce their numbers of fishermen and vessels, for some stocks are in danger. The French, among others, have grown angry with Spain's huge fleet for allegedly poaching and not respecting the quotas or rules on fishing-net mesh: but in fact other countries cheat, too. French fishermen have also been disturbed at Atlantic overfishing by Russian and Polish crews, who dump cheap white fish on European markets.

Matters came to a head in 1993–4 when fishermen took a cue from the farmers and began to riot. At one demonstration in Rennes, the historic Breton parliament building was burned down, seemingly by accident. The Balladur Government appeased the fishermen with substantial concessions, including special aid to Lorient for modernizing its decrepit fleet: the port was thus saved from possible closure. Since then, all has been calm, but fishermen remain anxious. Their numbers in France have fallen from 40,000 to 15,000 in ten years, and this may continue. At Guilvinec, a port that does better than Lorient, as I watched the picturesque sight of the langoustine and lobster boats returning at sunset, one sailor told me, 'This is a tough profession. We have to work ever harder to compete and earn a living, and I'm not optimistic. For centuries, we Bretons have lived from the sea. But today we urge our sons to go off and do something else.'

Agriculture fares better. Pierre-Jakez Hélias has movingly described the pre-war poverty of the peasants of his corner of the Bigouden country, near Guilvinec, when subsistence farming covered most of Brittany. Today the region has thousands of large modern farms: it is France's foremost agricultural producer, a big exporter too, and has also moved ahead in food-processing. But there has been a price to pay, ecologically. Breton farmers have today come under widespread criticism for their environmental thoughtlessness, even greed. The removal of stone fences to enlarge the fields is causing soil erosion. Worse, the intensive development of piggeries and of battery poultry breeding, together with the excessive use of pesticides, have contaminated the water supplies (see p. 398). From poverty to pollution – that is the story of Breton farming since the war. The pesticides have infected the seaweed, causing a foul smell along a few beaches, and there are fears that this could harm tourism, also crucial to Brittany. Along its coasts, neat new hotels and holiday villas dot the meadows and woodlands beside rocky coves and sandy beaches.

Like Ireland, Brittany with its poverty and big Catholic families has had a long tradition of emigration – to Paris and elsewhere. With prosperity this changed, and the census figures of 1976 and 1982 showed that for the first time fewer Bretons were leaving than returning – to take jobs in their homeland, or to retire. But today the net exodus has resumed. Although unemployment is slightly below the national average, many of the brightest young job seekers are emigrating. 'We used to export sailors, farm hands and servant girls,' said one economist, 'but today it's a brain drain. Our young are highly educated, we are first in France for the numbers passing the *bac*: but there aren't enough top-level jobs for them here.'

The region may have suffered less from economic cutbacks than some parts of France, but there are worrying signs. In 1996 the telecommunications centre at Lannion, pride of the new Brittany, took a blow when Alcatel announced it would cut its staff from 2,300 to 1,700. Brittany today has several dynamic firms of its own, such as the ferry company, or a locally owned factory in Quimper, making sailor-style shirts and jerseys, which has increased its turnover by 50 per cent in ten years, in the cut-throat world of textiles. But – a familiar problem in many countries – too many other firms are dependent on decisions taken in head offices far away, by Alcatel, Citroën, Mitsubishi . . .

In culture, in local affairs, in many economic sectors, Bretons have won a new emancipation from Paris, and have gloriously reasserted their identity and their values. Now this seafaring people, used to travelling the globe, faces in its homeland the challenge of globalization.

GRENOBLE:
THE FANTASTIC 'LEGEND' LICKS ITS WOUNDS

The post-war growth of the larger French towns has altered their character. It has brought a new vitality, but also serious problems of planning, housing, transport and social cohesion. Towns have been coping in different ways. Some of the most successful have had Socialist mayors, such as Hubert Dubedout in Grenoble in 1965–83, or more recently Catherine Trautmann in Strasbourg, Jean-Marc Ayrault in Nantes. Today the growth of towns has slowed right down, and only the ebullient Socialist mayor of Montpellier, Georges Frêche, is still pursuing grandiose dreams of development. But in the boom years, towns were changing fast under the impact of new industry, new ideas. Some of the impulse came from state-directed schemes, as in Toulouse; in other cases, the growth was more spontaneous – as at Grenoble.

Grenoble for many years was somewhere very special, ahead of other French towns. In the 1960s this 'little Los Angeles in the Alps' became a legend, first for industrial and scientific boom, then for a new kind of municipal enterprise. 'What Grenoble does today, France does tomorrow', went the saying. It was helped by its splendid setting, in a valley below the ski slopes of the high Alps and the jagged Vercors massif. This, and the growth of big new hi-tech factories and research centres, drew thousands of young newcomers. Some were attracted also by what seemed to be a more modern and open style of provincial life. The population, 80,000 in 1945, reached 400,000 (with suburbs) by 1975.

Later, the euphoria waned. The pioneering mayor, Hubert Dubedout, began to prove a disappointment: *Grenoble, le mythe blessé* was the title of a book published in 1979. Some other towns were starting to copy Grenoble, or to catch it up, making it seem less special. Then, far worse, the new Gaullist mayor, Alain Carignon, elected in 1983, provoked one of the most serious French corruption scandals of the 1990s, and was convicted and sent to prison. Today the legend is still licking its wounds. Yet Grenoble remains a stimulating and unusual city. Eight people in ten are immigrants to a city that is highly cosmopolitan, with a huge student population in its renowned universities. The exceptional degree of mobility gives local life a slightly Californian style, in some ways rootless, but informal.

Long before the war Grenoble had already been a pace-setter, in some cases by accident. It created the first funicular in France, the first scheme of family allowances, the first hydro-electricity, even the first stirrings of the French Revolution. And in 1960 the first French family-planning clinic opened there, semi-illegally. Then in 1965 it was the first big French town to stage a municipal 'revolution', by electing a young mayor from among the new immigrant technocrats, rather than from the local bourgeois *notables*, as had been the French tradition. This bourgeoisie had earlier been given a bad name by the town's most famous son, Henri Beyle, better known as Stendhal, who was born there in 1783, the son of a barrister. In his autobiographical *La Vie de Henri Brûlard*, he wrote, 'Everything that is mean and vulgar in the bourgeois way reminds me of Grenoble, everything that reminds me of Grenoble fills me with horror.'

So what has later made Grenoble so special and attractive? One answer lies in its mountains. The town's industrial strength originates from the nearby invention of hydro-electricity in the 1860s, and nowadays it is the skiing and scenery, above all, that attract the new élites: no other French town is so near the mountains. The rest has been a snowball effect. This was no more than a quiet burg noted for its glove-making when some engineers experimented with new ideas of drawing electricity from the waterfalls of the Chartreuse massif. Factories then settled near this new source of power: some were little paper mills, still visible in the steep clefts of the massif. Grenoble's population then doubled from 1872 to 1926, at a time when most of France was static. By the 1950s the largest firms were Merlin-Gerin (electro-metallurgy) and Neyrpic (turbines and hydraulics), both leaders in their fields. The university was also expanding fast, notably in science, and this prompted the Government in 1956 to choose Grenoble as the site for France's principal research laboratories. Then in the 1960s industry took a new direction. Some of the older mechanical firms, based on hydro-electricity, were past their prime. But more advanced industries arrived to work with Grenoble's pool of research scientists. Péchiney opened an electro-chemical research centre; American investors included Caterpillar and Hewlett-Packard. Grenoble at that time proved the best example in France of the 'multiplier effect'.

It also took the lead in promoting cooperation between universities and local industry. In the US or Britain this had long been common, but French professors with their ivory-tower attitudes had tended to scorn practical work, hence the lag in applied research. In Grenoble, since the war, firms have commissioned local institutes and science faculties for special research work, while academics have made use of companies' laboratories and know-how. This liaison encouraged new investment: thus the invention of a new power magnet by one famous local physician, the late Louis Néel, led to the creation of two factories. Eventually, the economic 'revolution' made its impact on civic life. The new high-powered immigrants became steadily more numerous and assertive than the native nucleus of lawyers, doctors and others who would normally rule the roost in a French town of this kind. And this led to Grenoble's second 'revolution', the municipal one. Initially, through the boom years of 1950–65, the *mairie* had remained in the hands of the old guard of Grenoble-born *notables*, in turn Socialist or Gaullist but all conservative. Little was done for town-planning. The city spread its tentacles along the valleys, and rents and land prices shot up unchecked. I saw a new ring of skyscrapers on the outskirts in 1959, and came back six years later to find that other rings had grown beyond them, as in a tree. It reminded me of posters in Texas: 'Don't park your car in this lot: there'll be a new building in an hour.' All exciting, but inconvenient for people living in a city that had vastly outstripped its public services.

Then in 1964 a certain Hubert Dubedout of the nuclear centre found that his water supply kept failing in his fourth-floor flat. Thousands were in similar plight, for the mother city of hydro-electricity was served by a water system unchanged since 1883. Dubedout launched a campaign to get the mayor to act, and succeeded. He and friends from the scientific élite then formed a non-party group to contest the 1965 local elections. Allying with the Socialists, they succeeded against the odds in defeating the Gaullist-led ruling coalition. The egg-head blow-ins had found their force at last: nearly all voted for Dubedout. His team then worked to get Grenoble ready for the 1968 Winter Olympics: this involved a huge new ice rink, a new airport and railway station, and an Olympic village to house 4,000. Much of the 1,000 million francs cost was borne by the State: the town had to find most of the rest, and some of the burden fell on rate-payers. But Grenoble acquired in two years a modern infrastructure that otherwise would have been spread over twenty.

Dubedout, who stayed in office until 1983, was one of the most remarkable mayors in post-war France. An ex-naval officer and engineer from Pau, urbane and disdainful in manner, he was a world apart from the traditional French big-town mayor. When I first met him, at a formal lunch in the *préfecture* for elderly *notables* from nearby villages, he winked at me in front of the prefect as if to say, 'I feel as much an outsider here as you.' His 1965 victory was greeted by some observers in Paris as a national portent, a breakthrough into local politics by the kind of non-party pragmatist who normally steers well clear of the world of municipal intrigue. Some lesser towns did then throw up their own Dubedouts, if not of the same calibre. But Dubedout himself was soon forced to become more of a party political animal than he had intended. He found it impossible to retain a non-party stance in this highly politicized town. His sympathies were radical-progressive, so he joined the Socialist Party. In face of the Right, he was obliged to rely on Communist electoral support, grudgingly given: so after 1977 he ruled in uneasy coalition with the PCF, while also being harassed by campus *gauchistes* and the bourgeois Right, each accusing him of being the creature of the other. His path was never smooth.

None the less, helped by a dedicated team of Socialist councillors, mostly non-Grenoblois like himself, he went ahead with a series of civic innovations that in their French context of the time were remarkable. His smart new *mairie*, all fountains, modern art, glass and marble, was no mere showpiece but the headquarters of a campaign to create a new style of local administration. It met with variable success (see below). He tried to break down some of the usual French barriers, and to associate citizens more actively with daily government, rather than merely 'administer' them in the French manner. He encouraged neighbourhood associations to play a more positive role. He was the first French mayor to persuade suburban communes to group with the big city for some joint planning and services, a scheme then widely copied. He began to restore the old town, and poured money into varied cultural activities, crowned by a large *maison de la culture*. Above all, he built his utopian new town of L'Arlequin (see p. 217), with the aim of forging a new kind of social integration. All this was revealing of Dubedout's own spiritual odyssey at that time. A friend of his said to me, 'He came to power as a cool believer in efficiency. But gradually he has moved towards a real concern for human suffering and underprivilege. Beneath that disdainful mask, he's a humanist.'

Dubedout's very qualities and idealism added to his problems, in this town of factions. He tried to achieve a broad consensus for his policies, but this ran into trouble – one aspect of *le mythe blessé*. Soon he was under pressure, alike from his Communist 'allies', who hated him, and from the Government. De Gaulle in the late '60s had backed Dubedout and his reformism: but then, under Giscard, Paris took a harder line with left-wing towns, and the prefect became less cooperative. Under the Socialists, Dubedout's path at first grew easier. But in the 1983 local elections Grenoble swung to the Right and he was defeated. Many of his former supporters had turned against him – first, a number of yuppie *cadres* who disliked his move to the Left in alliance with the P C F (what irony); also working-class voters who resented his help for immigrants, so they switched to the Front National. 'I was hit by a racist backlash and caught in a trap between Left and Right,' Dubedout told me bitterly. Perhaps he was too sincere for the brutal world of politics. He died in a climbing accident in 1986, a partly disappointed man.

Then came the fearful saga of his successor, the young Alain Carignon. He, a local man from a modest background, was a protégé of Chirac's and a disciple of the Thatcherite ideas then gaining ground in France. So he set about privatizing some services; and his public spending axe fell heavily on Dubedout's network of social and cultural schemes. But he kept some of the modern town-planning projects and applied Dubedout's idea for a modern urban tramway. He was even made Minister of the Environment by Chirac in 1986–8. For some years, he seemed to be doing well, in his own style, and was quite popular in Grenoble, especially with those *cadres* and tradesmen who had never liked Dubedout the technocrat. But others disliked Carignon's prestige-hunting and wheeler-dealing.

At one point, a mysterious series of 'false' invoices were discovered in the *mairie*'s files. The local judiciary were slow to act: apparently they were under pressure from Carignon, then Balladur's Minister of Communication. But finally in 1994 the mayor was arrested on a corruption charge: eager to privatize the city's water supply, he allegedly had solicited and obtained lavish gifts from the big Lyonnaise des Eaux company in return for giving them the contract. It was the first time in France since 1898 that a serving mayor and deputy was sent to trial for corruption (another 'first' for Grenoble? – and again, the crisis was over the water supply!). Carignon, protesting his innocence, remained mayor until the municipal elections of June 1995, but finally agreed not to stand again, and the Socialists won back the *mairie*. In November 1995 he was found guilty and sentenced to four years in prison. He then appealed.

It was a tale of the lure of power and money. Carignon came up the hard way, and did not even have the *bac*: but he was very bright, charming, plausible, and often went out of his way to praise Dubedout in public. However, power went to his young head, especially after he became minister as well as mayor. With the money from the bribes, he took a smart flat in Paris, where he cut a trendy figure. Though married he was also gay, known in Paris as '*une folle*': but he managed to keep this side of his life hidden in Grenoble. In court some agents of the Lyonnaise des Eaux were sentenced, too: but the judges suggested Carignon was the more guilty for seeking out the bribes, which included air travel in private planes. He wanted the gifts for his own lifestyle, but also to offer to his pals, in return for their loyalty. He was the arch-clientelist, with a tight network of cronies. Yet his image and influence in Grenoble were such that, up to the last moment, few people could believe that he was guilty. Not only the local right-wing daily, *Le Dauphiné libéré*, but even *Le Monde*'s correspondent, were discreetly non-committal until the trial. The affair also showed up one possible negative aspect of regional reform: under the old system, when the prefect's *tutelle* over local finances was stronger, corruption of this kind was rarer.

Most amazingly, Carignon even in prison was able to remain president of the *conseil général* of the local Isère *département*, a post he had held since 1985. In this right-wing council a majority of its members continued to support him, either out of genuine loyalty, or in some cases, maybe, because they knew that he could ditch the dirt on them (the Lyonnaise's intrigues were not confined to Grenoble). And the public could not understand how this condemned criminal was able to remain in his lofty post, masterminding the council from jail. It was due to an anomaly in French law: the regional reform had not foreseen a case such as this, so there was no legal means of forcing him to resign until the legal process ended. But then in October 1997 he lost his appeal, so at last he had to stand down. Even so, the council remained on his side. And today, from its offices opposite the Socialists' *mairie*, it still conducts a kind of vendetta: on matters where the city or region requires its cooperation, it sits on dossiers and takes no decisions. Thus it has blocked a useful project for transferring parts of the university from its ghetto-like campus into new premises in adjacent communes. As one town councillor put it, 'Carignon carries out a scorched-earth policy against us, partly out of sheer spite.'

The new mayor, Michel Destot, is a former engineer. He lacks charisma or bold ideas, but is solid and sensible, and is quietly trying to repair the damage of the Carignon era. He sees his role as, first, restoring Grenoble's battered image in the world. Secondly, as he told me, 'Carignon badly neglected the city's public equipment, so we have to put money into building more social housing, primary schools, and so on.' Thirdly, Carignon the Thatcherite somehow overspent, leaving the city's budget with a debt of 1.7 billion francs. He liked big financial projects, and built a huge glossy commercial centre, Europôle, which loses money. Amid these and other problems, Destot has no special plans to pursue the civic and cultural innovations of Dubedout. He has other more urgent priorities, at a time when high unemployment makes ventures in local democracy seem less relevant. Destot's welfare services work hard to help the jobless or homeless, but there is no longer a large well-paid team of *animateurs* spreading culture in suburban streets. That was possible in the 1960s, not today. And though Dubedout's neighbourhood councils still exist, they have suffered from the heavy politicization of recent years. But the conurbation's *communauté urbaine*, which Dubedout initiated, is working well. So what will survive in Grenoble of his legacy? Of his social schemes, probably not much; of his ideas for town-planning and open government, rather more. Above all, his pioneering style of mayorship has had a big influence on many other French towns, such as Lille and Nantes. They have now moved ahead of Grenoble in their sense of civic enterprise.

Is this city amid the Alps still a special place? Municipally, no: but in its sharp tempo, hi-tech prowess and cosmopolitan spirit, probably yes. Industrial expansion has now slowed, as elsewhere: but high-level research still flourishes, and here Grenoble is ahead of any other French town outside Paris, except Toulouse. It has thousands of foreign students, and over 6,000 researchers and scientists, many from abroad: this milieu still lends the city its aura of an open, mobile, and youthful society. It is now a major European centre for new information technology, as well as for computers, electronics and nuclear research. The Institut National pour la Recherche de l'Informatique et l'Automatique, recently opened in a splendid white ziggurat structure below the mountains, claims to be a world pioneer of Internet and the information highways. Much of the new private industry is foreign-owned, including Rank Xerox, and Hewlett Packard (with a staff of 2,100), and links between firms and university are still close. In one or two cases, the Carignon affair has deterred new outside private investment. But mostly the milieu of industry and science is too cosmopolitan to be bothered with what it might see as local scandals.

The city's urban growth has come close to a standstill, after nearing saturation on its confined mountain-girt plain where three valleys meet. Traffic can be very bad in places, and much of the high-rise building of the boom years now looks tatty. In fact, apart from its setting, this is not a beautiful city. But it has been improved by certain recent ventures, some of them Carignon's. He has carried through an idea of Dubedout's for a new museum of art – and splendid it is, one of the best in the provinces, housing the city's large historic collection. But Carignon spurned other more 'dangerous' forms of culture, notably the *maison de la culture*, renamed Le Cargo, which Destot is now expensively renovating. As for the smart new tramway, in France it was Grenoble that pioneered this modern version of an old means of urban transport, now fashionable: this, too, was Dubedout's project, which Carignon then built. It has eased some traffic, and it provides a new fast link with the big university campus in the suburbs (see p. 565). The building of the campus in the late 1960s, though badly needed, deprived the old city centre of much of its evening animation. But now more students are again living there, or they throng the bars and *bistrots* of the charming historic area by the river Isère. So Grenoble has got back its *quartier latin*. Its tiny squares are lively with open-air cafés, and on a warm night the Place St-André is magical.

Since the Dubedout era, Grenoble has lost the sense of being in the vanguard of a new kind of French society. Some other towns have caught up, in various ways: the social informality, in the 1960s so novel for France, has become more general. Yet there remains a certain intensity, in daily and working life, perhaps enhanced by the heady Alpine setting. 'Human contacts are easier here,' one scientist told me, 'and I'm sure that the skiing helps. It's easier to iron out your problems with some tycoon or civil servant when you're up in a funicular with him.' Or you can wear ski-clothes in a smart restaurant, and no one will mind or notice, as they might in Lyon. It is a town with an unusually active *vie associative* of private clubs for sport, culture, leisure, maybe because so many people do not have family roots here. And it is cosmopolitan at all levels. The Italians have long been numerous, and even have their own mafia, with occasional violence. There are plenty of Americans, Europeans, Africans, Asians. Destot is even creating an international *lycée*, one of the few outside the Paris region. Grenoble still feels that its future lies with Europe – like its larger neighbour and longtime rival, Lyon.

LYON:
TRADE FOLLOWS THE NEW FLAG OF EUROPE

France's second city* has long suffered as much as almost any from overdependence on Paris, and its pride has been hurt. Even today, so its leaders feel, regional reform has not brought as much change as was hoped. Take an early morning TGV to Paris, and you may well travel with several hundred identikit executives, all in the same neat suits. And on the evening trains they all return, their briefcases hopefully full of those vital dossiers secured in government offices. Once I called on a Lyon city councillor. 'Don't put through any more calls,' he told his secretary – 'unless of course it's the Ministry of Finance in Paris.' I smiled. He smiled, too: 'Sorry, that's France for you.'

Today Lyon has an exceptional mayor, Raymond Barre, former Prime Minister. An eager 'European', he is striving to forge new international links, economic, even political, as the best way, he believes, of weakening the hold of Paris centralism. Thus Lyon could come again to play a proper world role equal to that of its peers, say, Turin or Stuttgart. But it is not easy. It is not so much the legal framework that needs further change as a whole network of entrenched attitudes and practices.

This dignified old mercantile city, where the Rhône and Saône meet, has a keen sense of its own mighty past. Lying on western Europe's best north–south trade route, it was for centuries a leading European centre of banking and commerce, and its silk industries were famous. Its Bourse dates from the fifteenth century, before that of Paris. Then, with the first industrial revolution, many of France's leading engineering and chemical firms were born here, such as Rhône-Poulenc and Péchiney. But the later nineteenth century was also the period of concentration of decision-making in Paris: most larger firms felt obliged to move their head offices there, including the great bank that bears the city's name, Crédit Lyonnais. Lyon's banking prowess waned, and the city lapsed into a strait-jacketed provincialism. 'Paris has always hated us and tried to cut us down,' said

---

* The population of the commune is only 415,000, but that of the conurbation is 1,262,000. Marseille is a larger commune (800,000) but a smaller conurbation (1,231,000) and a town less wealthy than Lyon, less important economically or culturally.

one local historian, 'especially after 1789, when we fought against the Revolution.'

In the 1960s Lyon finally began to reassert itself. It could not cure its administrative dependence on Paris: but this hitherto rather stuffy town did become again more outward-looking, and gave itself a modern facelift. Much was due to Louis Pradel, the *centriste* mayor in 1958–76, one of the most enterprising in post-war France. He was not a social idealist like Dubedout, but a builder and modernist, who believed that Lyon must first obtain the right infrastructure before bidding for a wider role. Ring motorways were built, and a big new international airport; the comfortable Métro, opened in 1978, gave the Lyonnais some hint of living in a modern metropolis. Above all, Pradel built an enormous office complex, La Part Dieu, with a 170-metre pepperpot skyscraper and other high-rise blocks of glass and steel, holding a big public library, a 2,000-seat concert hall and a vast shopping centre – the kind of gigantic expansionism then in vogue in France. Today it still does well, despite the decline in the market for office space that has hit Lyon as well as Paris.

Pradel was less interested in old buildings and the environment. It is true that in his day some of the Renaissance façades along the quays of the two rivers were repainted in their original pastel shades, pink and yellow, making Lyon look less grey. But other Renaissance houses by the Rhône were pulled down, and Pradel even planned to push a motorway through the heart of the historic *vieux Lyon* quarter, by the Saône. He was thwarted by a local campaign. More recently, *vieux Lyon* has been sensitively restored and it is now a tourist venue: its handsome old palaces, with their courtyard galleries and balconies, once the homes of silk merchants, are now in some cases luxury hotels. Michel Noir, mayor in 1989–95 (see below), did much to beautify the town with illuminated fountains: one of his new underground car parks won a first prize as Europe's loveliest and best designed!

Noir also hired the fashionable Paris architect Jean Nouvel to redesign Lyon's distinguished Opera House (see p. 450). It was given a curious new curved metal roof which makes it look like an aircraft hangar, and many Lyonnais hate it: but the acoustics are marvellous. It is the main focus of a cultural scene that has become extremely lively, even upstaging Paris in some respects. France's leading theatre manager Roger Planchon (see p. 433) has his base in the town, which houses some fifty theatre groups. The art of gastronomy remains one key local speciality, while modern dance has now become another, led by Guy Darmet. His biennial festival had a Brazilian theme in 1996, when he got 200,000 Lyonnais out on to the streets dancing sambas – not the world's usual image of this supposedly staid city.

Lyon has been changing, socially. In the old days, the silk traders were voyagers with an open outlook. But later the city's bourgeois society came to be regarded as the most enclosed, stuffy and formal in France: even married couples would call each other '*vous*'. The élite of bankers and industrialists were known for their conformism, secretiveness and outward puritanism (save in their famous love of cuisine); they never showed much interest in the outside world, nor made outsiders feel welcome. But more recently so many newcomers have settled, from Paris and elsewhere, that a more mixed and open society has developed: the proportion of inhabitants born in the city has dropped since 1950 from two-thirds to one-third. On a warm night, the piazzas and little streets of *vieux Lyon*, with their masses of outdoor cafés and *bouchons* (*bistrots*), are a kind of St-Germain-des-Prés, crowded with the sophisticated local *jeunesse dorée*.

Commercial growth and improved transport links have also served to make Lyon more cosmopolitan. Satolas Airport, now an Air France 'hub', has direct flights to seventy towns around the world. Some big foreign firms have arrived, and Lyon has become the central headquarters of two world bodies. The International Cancer Research Agency moved here under Pradel. Then Interpol, the police agency, chose Lyon rather than Nice or Geneva when it moved from Paris. This had no connection, I was assured, with Lyon having by now distinguished itself as a notorious centre of organized crime and prostitution – a sure sign that it had entered the big-city league at last.

Yet such 'progress' is not the same as liberating Lyon from the hold of Paris, in being able to run its own affairs. For decades, Lyonnais had groused but done little. Then in the 1970s a few senior businessmen put pressure on the Government to help them reactivate the city's historic role as a centre of banking. DATAR did show some response, proclaiming a desire to build up Lyon as 'an international service centre', and a few modest results emerged. Some big state banks either increased their ceilings on transactions that could be decided locally, or they physically transferred departments, so that decisions affecting the region could at last be taken locally, not in Paris. The Banque de France set up a special office in Lyon, and in 1978 a new autonomous body, Siparex, was created to raise local finance for local medium-sized firms. Some thirty companies were introduced on to the 'second market' of the Lyon Bourse.

However, in the 1990s these brave moves have tended to slow down or even go into reverse, for various reasons. In the case of Crédit Lyonnais, its débâcle has made its worried directors feel the need to reinforce central control. Next, as elsewhere in Europe, electronic progress in banking has made it more sensible for the work to be done centrally, so physical decentralization has lost much of its meaning. Some seventy-five banks are represented in Lyon, where the banking scene remains livelier than thirty years ago, and Siparex still does quite well: but the bid to develop a 'second market' has not had much success, for most local firms prefer to deal on the Paris Bourse.

Efforts by DATAR to persuade industrial firms to put some or all of their head-office activities in Lyon, rather than Paris, have met with similar problems. At first, the policy made some progress, and in 1977 DATAR was thrilled when the giant Rhône-Poulenc, Lyonnais by origin, transferred the head office of its fertilizer division to Lyon, where it still is today. A few other big firms, notably Framatome and Péchiney, made similar moves. But powerful economic pressures have been pushing in the opposite direction. Berliet, the Lyon lorry-maker, always prided itself on being one of the few big French firms to keep its head office at its provincial plant: but then Renault took it over and in 1978 moved this office to its own HQ in Paris. It was a blow to Lyon's pride, and to its coffers: Berliet provided 12 per cent of local banks' turnover. Today a few foreign firms have their European HQ in Lyon: but larger French ones still prefer to keep their head office near the vital ministries and financial centres in Paris. So long as the State fails to decentralize its own civil service, notably the Finance Ministry, this is unlikely to change. Some leading Lyonnais even detect signs of some recentralization in the past few years, in various spheres, due to economic cutbacks and other factors. 'Firms and state bodies in Paris are tending to claw back decision-making,' one executive told me. 'Not on any legal basis, but because they find it's easier and quicker to take decisions centrally. Local people could fight this, but usually they can't be bothered. There seems to be no longer the time or money for all those sympathetic little decentralizing experiments of a few years back.' One small example: both *Le Monde* and *Libération* recently launched regional editions, but these were soon abandoned.

Most senior businessmen and officials must still go to Paris once or twice a week. In 1981 the two towns became linked by the new TGV express, which cut the former four-hour journey to two hours and has made it quicker to go by rail than air between city centres (90 per cent of passenger traffic is now by TGV). This was officially trumpeted as another step in Lyon's modern progress: but although the TGV is certainly useful, some Lyonnais today feel that in terms of centralization it has proved somewhat counterproductive, bringing the city even closer to the orbit of Paris. As for the 1980s regional reform, many local leaders today claim that, in terms of relations with Paris, it has done much less for a big city like Lyon than for the regions, *départements* or smaller towns.

So does this mean that even a strong mayor has only limited scope to improve the power balance? Michel Noir was an excellent mayor in many ways, charismatic, popular and stunningly handsome. He did a lot for Lyon, and was being tipped as a possible future Prime Minister. But he fell out with his party, the RPR, and became stupidly involved in one of the many sleaze affairs of the time, so he ended in disgrace. Raymond Barre, already seventy-one when he took on the job in 1995, was at first hesitant: but he seems to have come to enjoy it. A true statesman, and a moderate, he has achieved good working relations with the local Socialists, and he is fairly popular – save that many on the Left call him a philistine, claiming that his budget cutbacks are harming Lyon's rich cultural life.

Barre's principal strategy is to build up Lyon's external relations, not so much with Paris as with other places. 'Stop whingeing,' he tells Lyonnais. 'Go out and make new friends, as you did in your silk-trading heyday.' Notably, he has ended the long feud with Grenoble, second city of Rhône-Alpes and only 100 kilometres away (for thirty years, no Lyon mayor even paid a visit). Barre gets on well with Destot the Socialist, and lent him support after the Carignon *débâcle*. Today the two mayors are forging a new 'network' of the main towns of the region for economic and cultural development. Barre is also working with Jean-Claude Gaudin, the powerful RPR mayor of Marseille, to develop what they call '*le Grand Sud-Est*'. '*C'est un grand axe de demain!*' I was told euphorically by one of Barre's *adjoints*. 'It will link Lyon and Marseille with Barcelona, also Genoa! *L'arc méditerranéen!*' (My 'Swindon syndrome' again?)

The Rhône-Alpes region, France's largest and richest after the Ile-de-France, has for some years been working with three other big and wealthy ones – Baden-Württemberg, Catalonia and Lombardy – to build up a major association. This has been slow to achieve much, in practical terms

– and in 1998 the region's deal with the Front National caused some setbacks. But in Europe as a whole, the new idea of cross-frontier groupings is not likely to go away. And Barre holds the view that Lyon's dependence on Paris will not change from inside France, but only under outside pressure, as new European realities weaken the old national structures. Many of Lyon's leaders today believe this, too, or hope for it. Maître André Soulier, a senior *adjoint* of Barre, suggested to me, 'I know well, as a lawyer, that if you build up a new *de facto* situation, then finally the law will yield to it and change accordingly. Even after regional reform, the Quai d'Orsay was still trying to prevent Rhône-Alpes from forging its own new foreign links, claiming that this poached on its own preserve. But finally it has given way.

'Europe today,' he went on, 'is Lyon's historic chance. Fernand Braudel wrote that the city always does best when it looks abroad, as in the silk-trade days. Inevitably, as Europe develops, even France will have to move towards the decentralized German model. The Defferre reforms are not perfect, but they mark a step forward and are irreversible. Our regions still have only limited powers, but the logic of history is on our side.' This talk of a *Europe des régions* is not new: but now it has begun to seem less fanciful. Lyon has a chance of moving into a higher European league as a major economic capital. Already, when the phone rings from the ministry, Soulier no longer trembles so much.

TOULOUSE:
MEDIEVAL PRIDE VERSUS SPACE–AGE AERONAUTICS

'The name "Toulouse" used to evoke cassoulet, rugby, siesta and bel canto. Today it's Airbus and Ariane space rockets,' said one inhabitant. This city vies with Grenoble as the leading French provincial centre for high-technology research and modern industry; it has some 10,000 researchers, many of them in the National Centre for Space Studies, and it likes to think of itself as Europe's capital for space industry and aeronautics. Yet fifty years ago it was still a sleepy market town, and its pride was focused mainly on its medieval glories.

Toulouse and Grenoble are the two French cities to have grown and changed most radically since the war – but in different ways. While Grenoble's boom was largely spontaneous, Toulouse was pushed into it by a concerted state policy, helped by the local exodus from the land. In

Grenoble, the municipal dynamism came from the new élites, led by Dubedout. Toulouse, too, has its newcomer élites: but the *mairie* has remained in the hands of the 'native' Toulousains, and for years its style of government was unequal to tackling the problems of rapid urban growth.

In their ancient and lovely city of mellow rose-pink brick, Toulousains have an exceptional local patriotism, and a long history of hostility to Paris. They were also long suspicious of modern industry and commercial profit, and lacking in a sense of enterprise. Yet the Government from the 1950s used Toulouse as the foremost pilot zone of its campaign to promote new industry in the less developed provinces. The result was a fascinating example of the paradoxes inherent in the conflict between state regional policies and local aspirations. Was this government dynamism versus local inertia? – or local tradition fighting cruel Parisian centralism? Or both at once?

Toulouse's population, 180,000 in 1939, had risen to 450,000 by the 1970s and is 650,000 today, suburbs included. Not only did the city draw many thousands from the farms of its backward hinterland, but in the 1960s it took 30,000 *pieds-noirs*, to add to the 25,000 Spanish refugees from the Civil War. Executives, scientists and others came from Paris and elsewhere, lacing the city's parochialism with a new cosmopolitan air. Around the 1970s Toulouse seemed to cross that mysterious threshold where a medium-sized town takes on the ambience and lifestyle of a metropolis, as the suburbs grow larger than the main part of the city, and townsfolk become commuters.

The post-war state planners found that economic development was hampered not only by the local lack of enterprise but by sheer geography. Toulouse is not on the sea like Bordeaux, nor on a major river route (the Garonne here is barely navigable), but lies in a cul-de-sac: Spain is quite near, but across the high Pyrenees, and until Franco's death in 1975 it seemed an alien, far-away place. So why should new industry want to come to the city? To counter this problem, the planners in the 1950s began special efforts, using as their base the armament and aircraft factories that had been set up here around the time of the First World War, so as to be as far from the Germans as possible. In the 1920s the city's aerial vocation had taken another stride when Mermoz and Saint-Exupéry pioneered flights to Africa. Then after 1945 the Government developed it as the capital of the French aircraft industry, first with the Caravelle, then the ill-starred Concorde, now the successful Airbus.

The Government in the 1960s also made Toulouse the focus of its drive to expand the electronics industry, and it enticed several big firms including Motorola. Parallel to this, the city was made France's leading provincial centre for hi-tech R&D. The three aeronautical Grandes Écoles were moved from Paris, also the National Centre for Space Studies; scores of other scientific institutes were set up, and the science faculties were greatly expanded (the overall student population, 110,000, is the highest outside Paris). The aim was to sidestep geographic isolation by making this '*la capitale de la matière grise*', where advanced industries and research centres could help each other. And still today the grey matter migrates here quite willingly. Modern élites have come massively from other parts of France and Europe. Yet this new wave has not pushed the old Toulouse society on to the sidelines and taken charge of the city, as in Grenoble. The 'real' Toulousains, born and bred here, at first looked with suspicion at the state-directed modernization of their city. Today they are more proud of it, and old and new Toulousains coexist quite easily. But they remain separate in many ways.

You can notice this contrast visually. Fly over the city as it sprawls beside the Garonne on its wide plain, and it looks like some giant vanilla-and-strawberry ice-cream: the old city of pink brick is ringed by a white circle of more recent flats, colleges, factories and laboratories, a gleaming superstructure grafted on to the old core. Here the two rival élites confront each other: on the one side, the energetic scientists, pilots, professors and managers, together with the resourceful *pieds-noirs* and other immigrant entrepreneurs; on the other, the 'real' Toulouse as it sees itself, a bourgeoisie of doctors, lawyers and landowners. They live within their graceful pink palaces in the heart of the city, patriotically involved in the living past of a city that once ruled all Languedoc, in opposition to Paris.

During the 1950s and '60s, the resulting coolness between mayor and prefect was a hindrance to local affairs. '*La ville rose*' had been a Socialist/ Radical fief since 1904, and until 1971 the *mairie* was in the hands of a left-of-centre coalition, fiercely anti-Gaullist. The mayor, Louis Bazergue, became a byword in France for a certain kind of old-style Socialist potentate of the Midi. He applied his Leftist principles by amassing a private fortune through property deals. Bazergue made urban improvements on lesser matters such as street lighting, where he was his own master: but for larger-scale projects requiring state/city cooperation, mayor and prefect tended to obstruct each other's schemes, and public services lagged far behind the city's rapid growth. When the prefect set up a town-planning unit for the area, Bazergue refused to cooperate. Yet his own planning relied too much on ill-prepared prestige projects. The largest was for a new super-suburb to house 100,000 people, the notorious Mirail. When Paris reduced its share of funding, the project fell far behind schedule, under the crossfire of ministerial vetoes and local bungling. 'The Gaullists victimize me,' Bazergue complained to me. 'Bordeaux under Chaban gets far more budgetary aid than we do.'

In the 1971 elections, Toulouse finally fell to the Right, and under its next mayor, Pierre Baudis, a gentle, courteous Giscardian, relations with Paris improved. Some projects were unblocked and carried through. Baudis was then succeeded in 1983 by his son Dominique, also a prudent *centriste*, who has since had correct relations with Paris, under all governments. So the old political in-fighting has much declined, despite some sharp electoral swings. Baudis, a former TV journalist, is an astute politician but also a genuinely pleasant, open-minded man. He is liked locally and takes the trouble to consult: he even held a referendum on the colour of stone to be used for repaving the city's celebrated main square, the Place du Capitole. He is a careful administrator, but he lacks any clear vision and seems mainly concerned with keeping the voters happy in this heterogeneous town full of problems. When in 1997 I asked what he saw as his three main achievements since 1983, he said, 'Balancing the budget, building a Métro and embellishing the city.' Thus he has given a much-needed facelift to his fine eighteenth-century *mairie*, the Capitole: its inner court, hitherto a messy parking lot, now has lively modern sculptures. He has also beautified the messy banks of the wide Garonne, in a city which had long turned its back on its river, unlike Bordeaux. And he has belatedly embarked on an ambitious programme of new cultural buildings – a sector where the town was seriously behind the times, despite its stately classic opera house (see p. 450). A big modern art museum, a new *cinémathèque*, a civic theatre, a huge hall for pop concerts and an aerospace museum are all now being completed, with funding from State and region as well as town. 'We must be visibly excellent if we are to be a true European city,' said Baudis. One museum curator was sceptical: 'We have had to fight for twenty years to get these projects, and we've now got them mainly because of their prestige value. Baudis at heart cares little for culture.'

He has been trying also to deal with the more mundane matter of road traffic, in this medieval city of central congestion plus far-flung new suburbs. He has built one long Métro line, which has reduced surface traffic a little; a second is being prepared. As for cars, most of the well-do-to 'old Toulouse' families – Baudis supporters – live right in the centre where streets are narrow. Yet the Toulousain feels that he has a sacred right to use his car, and in meridional style he has a fondness for 'wild' parking, often on pavements. Baudis has refused to annoy his own voters by banning cars, so the central area still has fewer pedestrian streets than most French towns. His clever compromise solution has been to put elegant black bollards along some pavements: this stops the 'wild' parking, while still enabling cars to move down the middle. Baudis told me, 'I want to leave my citizens a real choice between public transport, the car, the bicycle and walking. If I banned cars from the centre, it would die, and scores of restaurants and bars would close.' It is a choice contested by environmentalists. Nor has it cured the congestion, as motorists relentlessly make their way towards the many new downtown underground car parks that their thoughtful mayor has built for them.

Today the city's conurbation is a dusty, noisy, lorry-filled place. Driving through its suburbs, you pass kilometres of warehouses, hypermarkets, discount emporia selling utility furniture, and high-rise blocks of equally utility flats. Then in the medieval centre the ambience changes. Even in February the café terraces can be full of sunbathers at lunchtime, while after dark the rose-pink façades of the ancient churches and palaces glow under discreet floodlighting; and well past midnight some brasseries are still full and some boutiques still open. For many visitors, this southern scene is magical. Yet I do find the tall close-packed red-brick architecture a bit claustrophobic, as compared, say, with the cool pale stone of Montpellier. And in modernizing, central Toulouse has lost some of its true character: there are more shiny snack bars, fewer games of boules in little squares. But at least, in the Place du Capitole, the façade of McDonald's has been transmuted from its usual brash red and yellow to a sober pink – so as to blend with the setting!

The populations of 'old' and 'new' Toulousains are today moving closer, and antagonism has waned. Many 'new' residents, here for thirty years, are now well integrated. In 1995 Baudis even brought a few on to his municipal council, which is still mainly a fief of the older local bourgeoisie. Some other newcomers have even become pillars of local society. Serge Peignon, owner of one building firm, told me, 'I arrived from Savoie twelve years ago. Now I've been elected president of the local Patronat, and I don't feel treated as an outsider.' Among the young, this studenty town is a lively polyglot melting pot: but many of the older bourgeoisie remain more reserved and separate.

Industrially, most of the local impetus still comes from big firms implanted from outside. A much-quoted exception is Pierre Fabre, former owner of a modest chemist's shop at Castres, who patented a drug, then built up a pharmaceuticals firm that today is one of France's largest, still family-owned. A handful of other entrepreneurs have followed suit. But hundreds of other little local firms have closed in recent years, or have been swallowed up by outside groups. The major companies however still do fairly well, overall; and Toulouse at this upper level remains fiercely impressive, as its vast network of interrelated activity rings the outer city, in industry, research and high technology. Aerospatiale is again thriving, thanks to the success of Airbus Industrie where hundreds of British, German and other engineers work with their French colleagues at the head office near the airport. Motorola is still in Toulouse, with a staff of 3,200; Péchiney has pulled out but Siemens has arrived, while Alcatel is making space satellites. But there is some anxiety that the city is too dependent on its aerospace sector, employing scores of local firms. 'Will the last man leaving Airbus please turn out the lights of Toulouse,' runs a local joke.

Much of this new activity is European in scale. In this context, the entry of Spain into the EU since 1986 has helped to make Toulouse less peripheral: trade with Spain has much increased, and Baudis has been developing links with Barcelona. The blue-and-gold Euro flag flies over his *mairie*, where he claims, 'In embracing Europe, Toulouse is in the vanguard.' So the old *ville rose*, long enclosed and inward-looking, has now been pushed into a wider role. But the French city that has done most to embrace Europe, and is also today a model of civic enterprise, lies far off beside the German border.

ALSACE AND STRASBOURG: FRANCO-GERMAN HOPES AND DILEMMAS

In the prosperous wine villages near Strasbourg, people hang flags from their flowery balconies – and the *tricolore* is well outnumbered by the blue-with-gold-stars flag of the EU. It is good for tourism, also an expression of the Alsatians' real European feeling. For some of them at least, a United Europe appears an answer to their old dilemma of identity.

More than any other mainland region, except maybe Brittany, Alsace looks and feels different from the rest of France. Its Allemanic people, beside the German border, have a culture that is highly Germanic: yet they hated being twice annexed by Germany. They feel deeply attached to France, yet separate. So where do they belong?

The capital, Strasbourg, is today also a capital of Europe, seat of the Council of Europe and very symbol of Franco-German reconciliation; and in the 1992 referendum on the Maastricht treaty, Alsatians gave a stronger pro-Europe vote than any other region. In many ways the province seems un-French. The cosy, tidy prettiness recalls south-west Germany – as do the old half-timbered houses, the baroque wood carvings, the Germanic names and dialect, the wooded hills, even the style of the wines, white and dry yet fruity. Alsatians are Allemanic cousins to Badeners and Swiss-Germans, across the border. Many have hybrid names, e.g. Jean-Pierre Froelicher; or they use a mix of their own dialect and French (*'Voilà, ein Winstub'*). I have always found it easy to be seduced by a gentle and prosperous region that seems to unite the positive qualities of two contrasting races – Teutonic spruceness and efficiency with an overlay of Gallic stylishness and eagerness. Plus the gregarious hedonistic joviality often found in wine-producing areas.

The Alsatian dilemma of identity was not always within so peaceful a context as today. This disputed frontier region suffered heavily from the long Franco-German enmity. It was a Hapsburg realm, then was annexed by France under treaty in the seventeenth century. After the Franco-Prussian War, the new Germany took it back, together with part of Lorraine. Alsatians by now felt basically loyal to France: so they resented the Kaiser's 'occupation', and the women's black bat-shaped bonnets became a sign of mourning. The region was then restored to France in 1918. But in 1940–44 it was annexed again, and much more brutally, by the Nazis. They tried to Germanize it thoroughly: even children faced prison for speaking French. So Alsatians later acquiesced in France's post-1945 policy of Frenchification, under the slogan *'c'est chic de parler français'* and the dialect began to die out. Some Alsatians had been pro-German in the war, even actively Nazi, and a few had joined the SS of their own free will: this left a sour note, and troubled the Alsatian conscience.

These varied events since 1870 were traumatizing for many Alsatians. Those born in the 1860s and still alive in 1945 could remember having altered nationality four times. 'My great-uncle,' said one politician I met, 'was a deputy in the Reichstag before 1912, then my father was a senator in Paris after 1948.' And the great Albert Schweitzer, born in Alsace in 1875, was in 1940 interned by the French as an enemy alien at his leper colony in Gabon. Today, at the excellent museum of rural life near Mulhouse, a model classroom has been built where actors vividly play out scenes of how Alsatian children were taught at different periods: as *la patrie* and *Das Vaterland* play Box-and-Cox, the flags, anthems and doctrines keep changing. But the children remain, innocently bewildered. In Alsace now there still remains some residual resentment of Germans: but mostly a new generation has come to terms remarkably well with its troubled past – 'Our bilingual biculturalism used to be a handicap,' said one mayor, 'for the French looked down on us as not properly French. But in today's Europe, it may be an asset.'

As in Brittany, people enjoy expressing the region's personality through its traditions and folklore – the choucroute and wine festivals, the cult of the luck-bringing stork, the folk-dancing in flowery costumes, and the fêtes of '*le mariage de l'ami Fritz*' based on Erckmann–Chatrian's cosy 1864 novel about a local folk-hero. Strasbourg even has a thriving satiric theatre in local dialect, La Choucrouterie. This innocent folklore, quaint and self-admiring, appeals mainly to older people. But recently an intellectual debate has arisen as to whether it is healthy for modern Alsace. One group, Identité et Liberté, seeks to stress Alsace's separate ethnic identity, in terms of its culture and traditions. Another, Saisons d'Alsace, prefers to affirm Alsace's modern role as an integral part of France, a region like any other, and denounces its rivals as backward-looking. But this is something of a false debate, very abstract. There is virtually no political separatist feeling in Alsace, and it would make little sense in a small area of 1.6 million people. Most Alsatians want to be part of France, within Europe, and to have good relations with Germany without getting too involved. Some feel Alsatian first, secondly French; or else vice versa; or both equally. Many feel Germanic in their culture, but not German.

German tourists come in hordes to a region steeped in this culture. Its greatest artwork, the Issenheim Altar in Colmar (*c.* 1510), is by the German artist Mathias Grünewald. Gutenberg from Mainz devised his printing press in Strasbourg, where later the young Goethe came from Frankfurt as a student and loved a local village girl, whom he later deserted. One of his best-known poems talks of her *Schmerz*. Today, despite the *Schmerz* caused by later 'visitors', Germans in Alsace are on the whole well accepted – so long as they behave. In some areas, groups of them have bought weekend or commuter homes, where they form ghettos, make little effort to mingle, and often prefer to do their weekly shopping back in Germany. This can be resented in places where they are numerous. Or the trippers come over *en masse* to the towns and beauty spots, where they talk German loudly. Restaurants and shops are glad of their trade, but ordinary citizens are less pleased – it is the problem with brash trippers anywhere, witness British lager louts in Calais. Real historic anti-German feeling is today less than might be expected, except among some elderly people with wartime memories. And the authorities make efforts to develop links, with some success: the town-twinnings, led by Strasbourg/Stuttgart, work quite warmly. It is even French state policy in schools to build up modern German (not the local dialect) as an official second language of Alsace. But this makes slow progress, for most young Alsatians would rather learn English. And the dialect, quite similar to Swiss-German, though still widely spoken in rural areas, has been declining in the towns and among younger people. It is more of a spoken dialect than a written language; and the pressure from intellectuals to keep it alive is less strong than in the case of Breton.

Rather like Bretons, Alsatians used to being treated like poor relations within France. But they have now won more self-confidence, thanks to their economic success, and to Europe. This is one of France's richer regions and has the lowest unemployment rate of any, just 7.5 per cent in 1997: one reason is that some 60,000 Alsatians commute daily to well-paid jobs across the frontiers, in German industrial towns such as Karlsruhe, and in Switzerland around Basle. Commuters in the opposite direction are few. Alsace does have some problems with declining industries (textiles, potassium mines): but it has great economic assets, such as the quality of its white wines, produced in a string of lovely villages along the foothills of the Vosges. Above all, after Nord-Pas-de-Calais this has become the foremost region in France for attracting foreign industrial investment – thanks to its central position in the EU and the reputation of its labour force. In first place the Germans (Siemens, Bayer, etc.), secondly the Swiss (Roche, etc.), thirdly the US (General Motors, etc.), all have plant in Alsace, some of it new. In fact, foreign-owned firms account for some 40 per cent of industrial jobs there – too many, in the eyes of some critics. 'The authorities should do more to build up local firms, not just encourage outsiders,' one manager told me bitterly. 'Alsace has become an economic colony of foreign firms, and that's unhealthy.' Yet most local leaders stress the advantages for Alsace of its new international role. In 1997 the Socialist mayor of Strasbourg, Catherine Trautmann, told me, 'Europe enables us to link our old Germanic history with our French history – to reconcile the two and end the old dilemma.' The discourse of the Left and the moderate Right is pro-Europe. But among ordinary Alsatians, some doubts have been growing, as elsewhere. Some fear that France is not well placed to compete with the organized strength of Germany, so close across the border. Alsace still flies its blue-and-gold flags for Europe, but no longer quite so buoyantly.

So what of the Front National's advance? Although Alsace's pro-Europe vote in the 1992 referendum was the highest in France (68 per cent), in the presidential elections three years later its vote for the chauvinistic FN was also, amazingly, the highest of any French region: 25 per cent. In the 1997 elections this fell to 21 per cent (overtaken by Provence), but it was still well above the French average. Experts have endlessly analysed this phenomenon: why should this successful, disciplined region, relatively pro-European, vote so heavily for an extremist party? It is a complex issue. It seems that the vote was not essentially anti-European, nor anti-German except in a few areas where the Germans are numerous. Nor was it primarily a vote against local ethnic minorities: in fact, the FN tended to score higher in villages where there were hardly any immigrants than in some of the mixed poorer quarters of Strasbourg. The vote seems to have been fuelled by a fear of the unknown; also by fears of disorder and of France's weakness.

The head of the Front in Alsace, Yvan Blot, a sharp *énarque*, gave me a possibly accurate analysis: 'These Alsatians, many with a Protestant tradition, have a Germanic Swiss-like temperament that abhors disorder. Villagers had grow alarmed by the stories of car-burning and other violence in the Strasbourg suburbs – and by the political corruption that has spread to Alsace.' Adrien Zeller, the *centriste* president of the regional council, added other explanations: 'It was not an Alsatian separatist vote, but a patriotic French vote of frustration against the incapacity of Paris politicians to run the country properly. Without being anti-German, it was a vote of fear that France cannot get its act together in face of Germany. When doubts about Europe grow, Alsatians feel vulnerable.' And the Front, though nationalist, will cleverly play on regional fears and aspirations. Among older people, its support may even include a hankering for Nazi values, in a region that once had many Nazi sympathizers.

The FN's strength in Alsace prompted it to choose Strasbourg for its annual national congress in March 1997. Citizens were furious at this provocation in the home town of the Court of Human Rights. But mayor Trautmann had no legal means of stopping the party from going ahead, nor from hiring the main suitable venue, the big civically owned Palais des Congrès. Her answer was to hit back with a counter-manifestation. Anti-fascist groups, and a motley of democratic or Leftist groups, converged on the city from all over Europe for a huge rally on the same weekend, masterminded by the *mairie*, with the city dramatically draped in black. And the rally attracted so much publicity across Europe that the Front's own congress was almost overlooked. So for Trautmann it was a notable political victory (as even Yvon Blot admitted to me). It marked the climax of her eight years as mayor, which ended in June 1997 when Jospin appointed her Minister of Culture.

Strasbourg is a superbly handsome and historic city, crammed with culture, one of the most delightful in France. Like Alsace as a whole, it seems to combine the best of French and German traditions, with its ancient gabled wooden houses by the quiet river Ill, its soaring cathedral, its baroque buildings from the Louis XIV period, and the imperial art nouveau palaces put up under the Kaiser. Since 1989 it has been so well run that its qualities shine even brighter.

Trautmann took up some of Dubedout's ideas, and has been the most admired French mayor of the past ten years, as well as the only woman mayor of a large French town. 'La Reine Catherine' (one nickname) is from the Lyon bourgeoisie by birth, Alsatian by marriage, and a Protestant theologian by training. Socialist from her teens, she was briefly in Rocard's Government in 1988, then aged only thirty-eight she won the *mairie* of Strasbourg – quite a feat in a city that had long been seen as heavily conservative (Pierre Pflimlin, the *centriste* former Prime Minister, was mayor from 1959 to 1989). Trautmann is a good-looking, capable and energetic woman who speaks her mind bluntly and clearly; she generally gets her way, and she radiates practical social concern. She reminds me a little of Ireland's Mary Robinson, but has more flair for politics. She has got on easily with the Alsatian centre-Right establishment, and has had a varied following in Strasbourg where in 1995 some 25 per cent of Le Pen supporters switched their vote to her for the city elections.

Her record in 1989–97 was not spectacular, but effective. She helped to rejuvenate a city that had grown somewhat tired and gerontocratic. She did a lot for youth, culture, the poorer suburbs and quality of life.

In the wake of Grenoble, she pushed through a project for a modern tramway, with the aim of improving not only traffic but 'social cohesion', as she put it. These sleek green trams, together with a major programme of new cycle paths and pedestrian zones, have helped to remove many of the traffic jams that can so often clutter big French towns: as compared with Grenoble or Toulouse, the city is a delight in this respect. 'The tramway,' Trautmann told me, 'is a metaphor for closer human contact. It is part of a policy of curing isolation, bringing the suburbs in closer touch with each other and with the centre, thus restoring to this sprawling city a greater social cohesion.' This is certainly needed, for Strasbourg's suburbs have not been spared the youth malaise of recent years. There were some serious outbreaks of violence in 1995, when one of the trams was fire-bombed, and again in December 1997 (see p. 186).

Trautmann sought to decentralize some cultural activity, endowing the poorer suburbs with better social and cultural services (see p. 438). She made a bid to limit class or immigrant ghettos by putting mixed housing in some residential areas; she also helped immigrants' associations to have more influence (see p. 229), and she backed plans for building a mosque. As far as was possible, she tried to help the unemployed by insisting that firms under municipal contract should give some priority to hiring those without jobs. And she allocated a remarkable 22 per cent of the city's budget to culture, without it making her unpopular: even non-culture-consuming citizens tend to be proud that Strasbourg has the most developed cultural life in the provinces, along with Lyon. These varied policies the mayor managed to pursue without bringing the city too heavily into debt or raising taxes unduly. In her cheerful modern civic offices, she was helped by a local tradition of sound administration, Germanic in style, so different from the wheeler-dealing of the Midi.

One of her major battles has been to prevent the departure of the European Parliament. Strasbourg is proud of its European role. The Council of Europe has been here since its creation in 1949, with a fine modern palace on the edge of town; here the Parliament, too, holds most of its sessions, while the Court of Human Rights is in a building nearby. These institutions, though separate from the life of the town, are a good source of jobs and revenue (many hotels depend on them); and with their high-profile diplomatic activity they are good for the city's prestige. However, many members of the Parliament find it inconvenient to travel to Strasbourg, and would prefer it to be in Brussels, easier of access from London and most other capitals. Backed by the

Belgian government, they lobbied for a transfer, and made progress: some sessions are now held in Brussels, and most of the executive and committee work is done there. Trautmann fought back, with the support first of Mitterrand, then of Chirac, both keen for the Parliament to stay on French soil. Hitherto it had no building of its own, and had to borrow the Council of Europe's premises. But then France took the gamble of building a lavish new home for it, a grandiose golden palace of glass and steel, with a waterside setting opposite the Council. It was paid for by city, State and the Parliament itself, and was completed in 1998. Soon afterwards, the EU Governments formally confirmed that this, not Brussels, will definitely be the main seat of Europe's major democratic assembly. A victory for Strasbourg.

Queen Catherine told me, 'It would have been crazy to let bureaucratic Brussels swallow up all the EU institutions. Is not our great city the very incarnation of Franco-German reconciliation, still the cornerstone of our Euro-faith? Was it not here in 1947 that young French and Germans first danced together on the Rhine bridge at the frontier, throwing their passports into the river?'

France's four other main cities, also regional capitals, are Marseille, Bordeaux, Nantes and Lille. Gaston Defferre, suave bourgeois Socialist of the old school, was mayor of Marseille for thirty-three years until his death in 1986, and he ran the city as if it were his private property (he owned two of its main newspapers). Despite constant battles with the state bureaucracy, he did quite a lot for town-planning: a new Métro, a tunnel under the *Vieux Port* to help cure the fearful traffic-jams. But he also made many mistakes and he ran the city heavily into debt. He was followed by Robert Vigouroux, a somewhat colourless figure on the centre-Left. Then in 1995 the *mairie* fell to the Right, and the mayor is now Jean-Claude Gaudin, a likeable and dynamic *centriste* and ex-minister, who is applying budgetary rigour but also trying to renovate parts of the city centre, horribly run-down. Its main boulevard, La Canebière, once one of Europe's grandest streets, is today a tatty mess: here Gaudin in 1996 launched a massive renewal operation. This brash, torrid city of a million people is strongly proletarian, strongly Levantine, famous alike for its *bouillabaisse* and its mafia-style crime. Today the gangsterism and the drug-trafficking have both declined: but racism has increased, with a high Front National vote and a large Maghrebi population. Marseille is still the first seaport of the Mediterranean, if its big modern extension at Fos, to the west, is included. But like so many big ports its golden days are over; and it has not attracted enough new industry to make up for the fall in its ship-repairing role. Gaudin is fighting hard to improve his city's tarnished image.

Bordeaux is a lesser port with an equally celebrated former mayor, Jacques Chaban-Delmas, leading Gaullist, who ruled for forty-eight years until 1995, even longer than Defferre. Until about 1958 this had the reputation of being the least active of France's largest towns. Its narrow-spirited mercantile ruling class, straight out of the pages of François Mauriac, clung to the illusion of Bordeaux as a great seaport. But half its cranes were idle: it suffered from the loss of France's colonies and the decline of the timber trade, and the area had little industry save its wines. Then, after de Gaulle's return to power, Chaban's hour came. As president of the National Assembly, and later Prime Minister, he used his mighty influence to secure the right funds and decisions from ministries: in fact, no other big French town has ever benefited so blatantly from such favouritism. Firms dependent on state contracts were pressured to set up new factories, including Dassault and Thomson-CSF; in 1971 Ford Motors located here its first plant in France. Chaban persuaded the cautious burghers to accept this change of course towards modern industry; he also took the initiative for a big new deep-water port for tankers and containers at the mouth of the Gironde; and he revived Bordeaux's cultural life, with a prestigious annual arts festival.

Chaban retired in 1995, aged eighty, to be succeeded by another leading Gaullist, Alain Juppé, who had just become Prime Minister and wanted to build a strong local power base, in the French tradition. But within two years he was in political disgrace in Paris; and in Bordeaux he has not yet proved that he has the qualities to make a distinguished mayor. The city still has some successful industries: in fact, far more people work here in aeronautics (27,000), mostly military aircraft, than in Toulouse (16,000). But Bordeaux suffers from its peripheral position in the EU; and its prestigious wine trade has been harmed by fraud scandals. The city has not returned to its old stuffiness, but is no longer in a golden age.

Nantes, to the north, is another graceful city and big Atlantic port – and yet another example of how much a major French town depends on having a really dynamic mayor. Jean-Marc Ayrault, a Socialist and local teacher, has since 1989 been carrying out much the same kind of social and cultural policies as Trautmann in Strasbourg, and with a similar success. The big popular outdoor arts festivals are remarkable. Yet Nantes, like Bordeaux, is a town with a conservative tradition. In the post-war decades it expanded rapidly, gaining a new vitality. But then its shipyards closed, and today those at nearby St-Nazaire are also in trouble. Yet despite a decline in industry, Nantes has become the major services centre for north-west France, ahead of Rennes, its rival. Rennes is jealous: but Nantes in turn resents the fact that Rennes is the capital of a real and glorious region, while Nantes must content itself with the hybrid Pays de la Loire.

Over to the east is Lille. This fine old Flemish town by the Belgian border had long seemed peripheral in a purely French context: now it has been pitchforked into a central role in the new Europe, thanks to its strategic location. It was the capital of an area of classic heavy industry: but today the coal mines have closed, the steelworks have contracted, the big textile firms, though now modernized, have been forced to make cutbacks, and unemployment in the Nord-Pas-de-Calais region is above the French average. However, with the opening of the Channel Tunnel, 110 kilometres away, Lille has now become the hub of a new TGV network, linking Paris and London with Brussels and on to Germany. It is at the heart of the so-called 'Golden Triangle' (London/Paris/Ruhr), Europe's wealthiest urban mega-region. 'Soon these cities will be little more than *our* suburbs!' smiled one official at the *mairie* of Lille.

The Socialist mayor since 1973, Pierre Mauroy, supreme power figure of the region and an ex-Prime Minister, has long been ardently pro-European and has responded with energy to the new challenge. Next to the new Lille-Europe TGV junction in the heart of town, he has built Eurolille, a major new business centre, which is doing well. Now only two hours by train from London, Lille is the nearest to Britain of large continental cities; and plenty of new British investment has been coming in. The city's economic problems are still far from solved, but it has acquired a new lease of life. And beneath its workaday exterior, this birthplace of de Gaulle is a lively, go-ahead town, full of culture and Flemish festivals. Mauroy's number two locally, due to take over from him in 2001, is Martine Aubry, now deputy Prime Minister. She is the daughter of Jacques Delors – a further token of Lille's good Euro-credentials. So now down to the other end of France, to Montpellier, another city assertively ruled by a high-profile Socialist mayor.

MONTPELLIER AND LANGUEDOC:
THE NEO-CATHARS FIND A NEW DESTINY

Montpellier today is the town that has been trying hardest to take over the 'legendary' mantle of Grenoble. It is an amazing place, sophisticated, ebullient and exhilarating: yet the coastal region of which it is the capital, Languedoc-Roussillon, was till recently one of the most sluggish and backward in France, known for its vast output of cheap low-quality wine. In the 1960s Montpellier was still a charming but sleepy old city of 90,000 people: today, with suburbs, it has nearly 300,000, and is the fastest-growing of French towns. It has not much industry, but an array of new research and hi-tech service activities, centering round one of Europe's oldest and most renowned universities.

The boom has been due in part to spontaneous factors, such as the appeal of the sunny south to enterprising blow-ins from the north. It is due also to the remarkable Georges Frêche, Socialist mayor since 1977. He has created some grandiose new buildings, perhaps *too* grandiose, and has sponsored a mass of cultural and economic activity; and he has managed to imbue many of his team with his own manic enthusiasm. The town's new suburbs sprawl awkwardly across the plain and are not too well planned: but the city centre is enchanting, a blend of old and new. Here the narrow streets of the medieval kernel have been gracefully restored and freed of traffic; and students laze and chatter in the outdoor cafés of the lovely broad main square, nicely paved, known as 'Place de l'Oeuf' for its shape (pity about the red-and-yellow McEyesore). Even in winter the sun will shine warmly, and the easy spirit of the Midi seems to infect the crowds of young people. Unemployment is high, and of course there are anxieties beneath the surface: but, after so much Parisian *morosité*, I found it a tonic to visit a town with such an engaging youthful ambience, and such civic panache.

Frêche is a Socialist in a different style from Dubedout or Trautmann. A professor of history from Toulouse, he is famous for his braggart manner and love of rhetoric. 'Montpellier,' he told me in 1997, 'is the Rome of today!' – and he tends to speak of 'my economy' in 'my city', or the recent doubling in size of 'my airport'. Some Parisians dismiss him as a crazed megalomaniac: but in fact he is full of jokes, wit and warmth, and is quite unpompous. What's more, he has actually achieved a lot of what he promised: his claims are more than just rhetoric. And although sceptics wonder how he can have managed such ambitious projects in today's economic climate, he has not brought the city into great debt, nor has there been any sign of sleaze. Frêche is popular locally, and more astute politically than Dubedout was: since 1977 he has been thrice re-elected, each time with an increase in votes, in a town formerly held by the Right.

He has drawn round him a team of similarly excitable and eager people, councillors and officials: this can make a round of interviews at the *mairie* quite exhausting. Most of the leading ones are, like him, not local: they come from maybe Paris, Alsace, Flanders, even Germany, or are *pieds-noirs*. Some had worked with Dubedout in Grenoble and moved here after his fall. Frêche has not been as innovative in local democracy as Dubedout: but he and his team have a good record of helping the poorer suburbs, especially the immigrants, and of improving the quality of social housing. A massive sports and leisure programme for the young is aimed at the 'prevention' of delinquency.

Among the new buildings, the most eye-catching and highly publicized is Antigone, an enormous housing complex of unusual design by the trendy neo-classical architect Ricardo Bofill, from Barcelona. He has done other work of this kind in France, notably his 'Versailles for the people' at Marne-la-Vallée, near Paris – a nineteen-storey 'palace' and triumphal arch, with tall classical columns and 'Roman amphitheatre' – all built, believe it or not, as a municipal housing estate. Antigone, somewhat similar but even bigger, is a curvaceous complex of high creamy-white colonnades and piazzas, with gardens sloping down to a river; one square is based on Rome's Piazza Navona. Across the river is the palatial new home of the regional council, a lofty hulk whose mirrored glass reflects Antigone. Bofill's style may be too monumentalist for some tastes, including mine: but his 'Rome of today', now housing some 10,000 people, is certainly impressive. It is not out in some suburb, but was built on a stretch of wasteland close to the city centre. This makes it all the more remarkable that some 40 per cent of flats are social housing (others are more costly): 'My aim is to mix the social classes,' says Frêche. But Antigone has some drawbacks. Though central, it is clumsily linked to the main downtown Place de l'Oeuf area. And its shops and cafés, facing away from the main roads, mostly do poor business and some are closed: Antigone in the evening seems a dull dormitory with little animation. But a large Olympic-size swimming pool has now opened, and a big public library is to follow.

In the medieval town centre, Frêche has much extended the zone of pedestrian streets. Shop-keepers at first protested, thinking the ban on cars would harm their trade: but then they found that a small street with no cars actually attracts more shoppers. Frêche is also building a tramway, on the Grenoble model, while new ringways have improved road traffic. But he has not been able to control the chaotic growth of new suburbs, which started in the 1960s. Many of these are outside the city's own borders, but the conurbation's administrative 'district' has no effective joint planning policy, under the French system. 'I have to get the unanimity of all my local mayors,' says Frêche, 'and there's one little Astérix who always blocks everything.' He has also put money into cultural expansion: there are various summer festivals, including one for books and one for modern dance, internationally famous. For the resident opera company, Frêche has built his second most ambitious project: the Corum, a massive new centre with a 4,000-seat theatre and other facilities, used also for business congresses.

His critics ask how a city like this can today afford such schemes. He argues, plausibly, that its rapid growth breeds new wealth, through fiscal revenue. And the town does get some special aid from the State and the EU, like the rest of the region. Even so, the boom can seem precarious in today's uncertain times. Take the case of IBM. This giant in 1965 opened a factory at Montpellier, which grew to be its biggest industrial base in France, with a staff of 3,500. This was hailed as a dramatic breakthrough towards the overdue industrialization of Languedoc. But then in the 1990s IBM fell into trouble worldwide, and was forced to cut back radically on its output of large computers; its staff at Montpellier was reduced to about 1,000. Since then, some other industrial firms have moved in, including GEC/Alsthom: but to attract them is nowadays not so easy.

So Frêche and his colleagues have switched their main efforts to encouraging tertiary activities, mainly research, and with some success. With a great beating of drums, a fashionable new 'Technopole' has been created, focused on computer sciences, telecommunications, food-processing and pharmaceuticals; its innovation centre, Cap Alpha, helps small new firms to get going, and claims to have created 3,000 jobs locally in ten years. One large-scale and unusual venture, Agropolis, has 4,000 people working on Mediterranean food research, notably in bananas – 'It's a bid to fight famine in Africa – we are the world capital of the banana!' I was told. Another research centre deals in pharmaceuticals with a staff of 2,500, and it works closely with the university, whose specialization in pharmacy and medicine dates from the Middle Ages. This tradition has helped the modern growth of a town that today has four times fewer jobs in industry than in areas such as research.

Frêche talks eagerly about his city's rise in population as if it were a virtue *per se*. 'Most other big towns have stopped growing, but our conurbation goes up 1.5 per cent a year. Recently, our commune has risen from twenty-first to eighth place in the French league table of cities, and we are set to overtake mighty Bordeaux in the 1998 census results! Growth is due less to the high birth rate than to the influx of newcomers, most of them young. We are so attractive!' Only 20 per cent of the population were born in Montpellier, while 40 per cent have come from other parts of the region, and another 40 per cent from elsewhere; of today's new arrivals, two-thirds are from northern France.

But what is the intrinsic virtue of such growth, which of course causes problems? Unemployment, at 15 per cent, is well above the French average: although Montpellier has been creating new private-sector jobs faster than any other French town, there are not nearly enough of them to cater for the influx – and young people flood in simply because they have heard that this is a boom town offering jobs in a sunny spot near the sea. 'It's Frêche's fault for praising this place too loudly in public,' said one of his colleagues, while Frêche admitted, 'Yes, we are victims of our own image.' His leading alderman and guru, Professor Raymond Dugrand, always as euphoric as his *chef*, said when I asked him if he was worried about the unemployment, '*Mais, c'est un chômage de croissance, mon vieux!* We can't prevent people coming here, it's a Californian phenomenon. And is it so bad to be unemployed, here in the sun?' Of those registered for the dole or RMI benefit, some 95 per cent have come from outside, especially in summer. Many do odd jobs, or they go to the beach and do not look for serious work. Some turn to petty crime, which has blotted the image of Frêche's paradise. 'I used to adore this place, but I wouldn't leave a car on the street today in summer,' said one resident. But I have a happier tale to tell. When I left my wallet, full of money, in a downtown outdoor telephone booth, the next user, a young man, rushed up and gave it to me.

This city today, with its 55,000 students, is a breezy, open and cosmopolitan place, with some of the sophistication associated with Paris or the Côte d'Azur. In hotels and offices people burst into English at you if they hear your accent. The town's glossy publicity brochures speak of

'Montpellier, Euro-City', which is not just eyewash: its foreign residents include some 2,000 Germans, and it has active twinnings with Heidelberg, Barcelona, Louisville, and cities in China and Israel. Not surprisingly, the rest of Languedoc-Roussillon is today highly jealous of Montpellier, which has come in some ways to equal Paris as a focus of local resentment.

Languedoc is the one mainland province where anti-Paris feelings have long been even stronger than in Brittany. Like Brittany, it has a keen sense of its separate historical identity and has been in the throes of a cultural revival, while some people are trying to keep alive its ancient language. But this is not the misty north: it is the Midi, a land of cypress and cicada where old men play boules in dusty village squares and under the dazzling sun the pace of life has been easy. While Bretons are alert for progress, Languedociens have tended to be slow, lethargic and recalcitrant. So in the 1950s and '60s the state decided to take the lead in imposing its own big development schemes – with controversial results.

The term 'Languedoc' is ambiguous. Until Napoleon's day, the noble province of the 'tongue of *oc*'* stretched far to the west beyond Toulouse, its historic capital. But today's modern region of Languedoc-Roussillon is a hotchpotch: shorn of the Toulouse area, it consists of eastern or 'lower' Languedoc along the coast, plus Roussillon (French Catalonia) to the south, and bits of old Provence and the Massif Central to the north. It is a good example of how the 1964 regional carve-up ignored many of the old provincial boundaries. In the twelfth and thirteenth centuries, Bas Languedoc was the heartland of the Cathar heretics; and though the religious element has long disappeared, the dissident Cathar spirit has persisted till modern times, notably among the winegrowers of the coastal plain, who produce most of France's cheaper table wine (see p. 401). The vine used to be called 'Bas Languedoc's sole wealth, and its tragedy'. In the mid-nineteenth century factories thrived on this coast. But the vine killed this brief age of industry. When French wine consumption rose rapidly, Languedociens found they could produce plenty cheaply on their sunny slopes, and it was much less trouble than building factories. Vines and climate united to produce a sluggish temperament, excitable only when local interests seemed menaced – that is, when the wine

---

* So named historically because 'yes' in the Occitan language is *oc*, not *oui* as in standard northern French.

market was threatened or when Paris tried to introduce economic change. This fertile and thickly populated plain, lying on the main route into Spain, seemed to Paris ideal for development: so it chose Languedoc for two of its major post-war schemes: a canal that was the biggest irrigation network in Europe, and one of the largest state-sponsored tourist projects in history. It was a technocrat's dream, *carte blanche* to make bold new strokes across the map. But to involve the local population proved not so easy.

The monoculture of cheap wine was economically harmful: but without water, it could not be diversified for other crops. So in the 1950s the State set up a company that dug a wide master canal from the Rhône to Montpellier, and built dams in the hills to the west. A network of little canals began to transect some winegrowing areas. The company then persuaded a few pioneers to uproot their vines and show that the same acreage of apple or pear could earn six times as much, if irrigated. Other growers were invited to follow. And how did they react? They rioted in the streets, they formed 'committees of defence against the canal', they behaved in short like Victorian farmers who feared those new-fangled trains would run over their cows. Very few vines were uprooted. The canal ran into debt for lack of clients, and the company for a while had to sanction what it had regarded as anathema: use of the canal to irrigate vines. Many growers were later deterred from planting orchards by the seasonal fruit surpluses. But today the problems of excess cheap wine have been solved (see p. 404), and the canal has been finding its proper vocation.

The Government's major post-war effort for Languedoc was the tourist project, started in 1963. From the Rhône delta to the Pyrenees lay 200 kilometres of open sandy beaches, backed by stagnant lagoons. This coast had never been exploited, for the mosquito reigned supreme, and bathers were few. Yet the Riviera and Costa Blanca were nearing saturation, as the tourist hordes grew each year. So the Government decided to build a chain of eight big modern resorts, with a double objective: to give a needed boost to the region's economy; and to help France's tourist balance by providing an overspill for the Riviera and maybe deflecting some tourists from moving on to Spain. First, a chemical blitzkrieg destroyed the mosquitoes, the lagoons were drenched and purified, 3 million cypresses were planted to act as windbreaks; the whole coast was zoned in a massive blueprint, and land prices were pegged to avoid a gold-rush speculation. Georges Candilis, a disciple of Le Corbusier, was hired to draw up a masterplan, while local Sociétés d'Économie Mixte, associating chambers of commerce and other bodies, were charged with providing the infrastructure for each resort. Private developers then built the hotels, holiday flats, marinas and so on, to run them on a profit-making basis.

'Our aim,' said a planner, 'has been to avoid the anarchic development that has spoiled the Costa del Sol and parts of the Côte d'Azur.' And this has more or less succeeded, even if the bold visual style of the resorts may not suit all tastes. The project, now completed, has provided some 280,000 extra tourist beds, half as many as on the whole Côte d'Azur. All the resorts are busy in summer: the number of visitors to this coast rose from 500,000 in 1965 to some 4 million by 1998. But the project has provided less lower-cost 'popular' accommodation than was promised. Under pressure from the banks to amortize costs, the developers found it more profitable to sell holiday flats and villas by the beach to well-heeled Parisians, Germans and others, while cheaper flats and functional holiday camps were pushed inland. 'For Paris, this is a commercial victory, but a moral defeat,' said one left-wing sceptic. 'It shows how the social ideals of French planners so often get thwarted by the capitalist system.' So the resorts have more in common than was intended with the rich new developments round Cannes, even if most of them look very different from a traditional seaside town.

Deliberately, the resorts vary in style. Perhaps the most attractive is Port Camargue, to the east, where a vast harbour has been created out of marshland, so that the town seems built on water, like Venice: on the maze of little peninsulas dotted with villas, an owner can moor his boat by his front door. Cap d'Agde, near Béziers, is a pastiche Mediterranean fishing port, like an operetta stage set, with pretty buildings in pastel shades: artificial, but pleasing. Here a nudist holiday town, Europe's largest, has casinos, supermarkets, nightclubs, and housing for 20,000 bodies which more often resemble an ageing Hamburg *hausfrau* than the young Bardot. La Grande Motte, near Montpellier, is the best known and most sophisticated of the resorts – a space-age vision with motor yachts and beach parasols added. Coloured sun-blinds cover the honey-comb façades of the famous ten-storey ziggurat pyramids of holiday flats, row upon row. Some are in weird shapes and colours: one resembles a giant fairground wheel, painted purple. Not everyone might choose to spend a holiday in this surreal pop-art setting, however lavish the amen-ities. Yet La Grande Motte is now full in high summer: it can take 40,000 tourists, and its marina for 1,800 yachts is as busy as almost any on the Riviera. Folly or masterpiece, the resort will anyway survive as a monument to the heady modernism of the de Gaulle and Pompidou eras. Today its gigantism is out of favour (save maybe at Antigone?), and newer tourist projects, such as those on the Aquitaine coast, are more discreet.

The tourist project created some 25,000 new full-time jobs and many seasonal ones. In the 1960s Languedoc's economy was also much stimulated by the arrival of over 100,000 repatriates from Algeria – the *pieds-noirs*. They proved an enterprising breed, more so than most of the locals, and they took over many dying farms and businesses and made them buzz. Not surprisingly, they were resented at first: but finally they assimilated well. The absorption by France of over 800,000 *pieds-noirs*, mostly in the Midi, was one of the great French successes of the time: it was possible in that age of fast economic growth, but could never have happened today.

Languedociens are a strange people. Their complex of being 'colonized' by Paris may finally be waning today. Yet its historic basis survives, and ancestral hostility to Paris still runs quite high among older people. Tribal memories go so deep that Paris's brutal suppression here of the Cathar (Albigensian) heresy in the thirteenth century is still a live issue. The Cathars' specific doctrines of pious asceticism may today find little echo in the Midi: yet politically and psychologically their spirit of revolt lingers. The past years have seen a revival of interest in the Cathar period, as new books on the subject are bestsellers (starting with Le Roy Ladurie's *Montaillou* in 1978) and summer and university seminars are frequent. To this day people have not forgiven Simon de Montfort and Louis XIII for the massacres at Béziers and Montségur, the wiping out of the troubadour civilization, the annexation to the Crown by fire and sword. And by a strange telescoping of history all this became mixed up in local minds with modern discontents, notably those of the winegrowers, so that de Gaulle, Giscard and de Montfort were lumped together as responsible for what the growers' vitriolic ringleader, Emmanuel Maffre-Baugé, described to me as 'Paris's eight centuries of heartless colonization of our Occitan nation'. To the east, in the Protestant area from Nîmes to the Cévennes, resentment of Paris's crushing of the eighteenth-century Camisard revolt is also alive. All in all, it has made for a region that is not only anti-Paris but has often been cussedly eager to march out of step. Witness '*les Cathares du rugby*': because the game is normally fifteen-a-side, a number of thirteen-a-side rugby teams have emerged in the Carcassonne area.

The complex of being 'colonized' has some modern basis, too, for in Gaullist or Giscardian days the State was often tactless. Technocrats from Paris would impose their schemes without proper consultation (see p. 719), or would try to claim the credit without letting local people feel that they, too, had played a part. All this would raise the hackles of even the more reasonable local leaders. Raymond Dugrand told me in 1980, 'The State has done a lot for this region, but in the wrong way. It treats us as it once treated Algeria. Yes, we *are* an underdeveloped land, like southern Italy, we have no native industrial class, we lack the experience to solve our own problems. This creates an inferiority complex which paralyses our power of action – a familiar vicious circle. Here at least the Marxist analysis is perfectly valid.' The vicious circle could be summed up as follows. A state official, exasperated, said to me, 'The only way to get anything done here is for us to take the initiative and present the local *notables* with a *fait accompli*. If we leave it to them, all they do is quarrel and prevaricate. They're a hopeless lot.' And a *notable*, equally exasperated, said, 'We know that Paris despises us, but that doesn't help. They should try to encourage *our* ideas, not just criticize and treat us like kids. The economy may have improved since 1960, but the power balance remains unchanged.'

The winegrowers were the most conservative. Some were middle-class townees living in their decaying mansions – 'They are waiting for some golden age to return,' said one critic; 'the vine round here is considered *un métier noble*, not mucky like pig breeding.' In the 1970s the growers would rally round their flag-bearer, the flamboyant Emmanuel Maffre-Baugé, who epitomized the spirit of these '*Cathares de la vigne*'. This burly, jovial gentleman-farmer used to be a rightist Catholic: but fury at government wine policies drove him in 1979 to stand on the Communist list in the European elections, to the amazement of his friends. His reason: 'Only the PCF is protecting the growers by opposing Spain's EEC entry.' He was elected, and came to cut an incongruous figure as 'the Red Cathar of Strasbourg'. When I visited him, he poured me glass after glass of his very drinkable *vin de pays*: 'I'm disgusted at our victimization by Paris finance groups. We're ignored culturally, too – who in Paris knows of the wonderful Occitan poets? I feel deeply Occitan, my blood is the juice of these grapes, but I'm French, too, no separatist. For my beloved homeland, I want a French federal solution. If I want my cat to pee in this corner or that, I have to ask bloody Paris first. We waste half our time on endless journeys there, yet if we didn't go, our voice would never be heard.'

The regionalist trend that emerged strongly in the 1960s was charged with emotionalism. One small band of romantics began plotting a new Occitan 'nation'. Their leaders even nominated a provisional 'government', and produced historical maps to assert the reality of 'Occitania': but Occitania was never a nation, simply the medieval name for all the lands speaking the *oc* tongue, covering a vast area up to Lyon and Bordeaux and into Spain and Italy. Two more serious movements, if still limited, have been Lutte Occitane and Volem Viure Al Pais ('we want to live in this land'). The former still has some support among leftist intellectuals, while VVAP appeals to young ecologists. Neither has ever let off bombs, or today does anything more violent than daub walls with the 'OC' slogan. The movements never had a real political influence, and since the mid-1980s the regional reforms have cut the ground from beneath their feet. All the true local political leaders, of both Right and Left, are more concerned with making the most of the new self-governing powers.

Culturally, matters are different, and here the Occitan revival remains very lively today. In Toulouse and Montpellier, university centres of Occitan studies are working hard to rediscover the region's colourful cultural heritage, with its troubadour links. Occitan, cousin to Provençal, is still spoken in some rural areas, and the vogue for learning among urban teenagers is stronger than in the case of Breton: several thousand a year take it as an option in the *bac*. A few poets and novelists write in Occitan, while pop singers such as Marty have drawn eager audiences. Occitan theatre and folklore groups of some quality are also active, while the Occitan summer university at Nîmes draws the faithful by thousands from all over southern France to dance the *crozada*, to hear lectures on the Camisards, or to explore the troubadours' ballads. Even some of the new arrivals in Montpellier, *cadres* and scientists, have been showing a keen interest in Cathar culture and history. And some town councils have made their street signs bilingual. Or they now fly the red-and-gold flag of Languedoc over their *mairies* – the gesture is cultural, not political.

Party politics in Languedoc have long been contrary and paradoxical. For many years before 1981 this conservative people voted firmly for the Left, less from left-wing conviction than because the Government in Paris was centre-Right: in 1978–81, of the twelve deputies of the Aude, Gard and Hérault *départements*, six were Communist and five

Socialist. Later the pendulum swung to the right. But in the 1997 elections the Left swept the board more than elsewhere in France, and today the centre-Right has only one deputy. He is the formidable Jacques Blanc, a UDF leader from rural Lozère, and since 1986 he has also been president of the new regional council, which has stayed on the Right. In 1998 he was one of those who dared to use Front National support to gain re-election (see pp. 39–40 and 298) – and this aroused a storm of protest within his own ranks, as well as on the Left.

Today it is patently clear that the sharpest political conflicts are no longer between Languedoc and Paris but within the region – and notably between Blanc and Frêche. Montpellier's success is resented by some other local towns, and Blanc has been seeking to capitalize on this. Wanting to cut his Socialist enemy down to size, he has been trying to reduce regional funds for some of Frêche's projects. The ever-combative Frêche has been feuding also with a fellow Socialist leader, Gérard Saumade; and with Montpellier's smaller rival, Nîmes, where the dynamic right-wing mayor Jean Bousquet was condemned to a prison sentence for misuse of public funds and in 1995 the Communists regained the *mairie*. So intense are rivalries in Languedoc that the regional reform has been working less smoothly than in many parts of France, and poor cooperation has led to wastage of resources. And yet, oddly enough, though insults are hurled flamboyantly, there is also a certain conspiratorial mateyness between fellow Languedociens of all colours. As was often suggested to me, the world of local politics has a southern Italian flavour: it is a *commedia dell'arte* of role-playing and wheeler-dealing, where ideology counts for less than personality. After all, this is the Midi. But as Jacques Blanc may find as he takes up his long spoon, it can be a dangerous game.

Despite these political charades, a new and more positive mood has finally been emerging among the people of Languedoc over the past ten or fifteen years. They have become more self-reliant and self-confident, less resentful of Paris. The old Cathar spirit is waning at last. One factor is the change of generation, as new local leaders arise who are more realistic and modern-minded, and new entrepreneurs arrive from outside and begin to integrate, as in Montpellier. Secondly, now that DATAR keeps a lower profile and big state-imposed projects are fewer, Languedoc has less cause to feel dominated by Paris and accepts that it must do more to help itself. Industry is no longer scorned, but eagerly sought. Thirdly, the regional reform, by giving new powers of decision to local bodies, has altered attitudes to Paris. It may not have met all the aspirations of the keener autonomists: but it is seen as something to build on, and it has defused the separatist movement, as in Brittany. 'We have lost much of our old inferiority complex; we are more confidently in charge of our destiny,' says Raymond Dugrand. 'Yes, we remain colonized in a way, for most of the finance for development still comes from outside. But at last there's a real political will here to take our own future in hand.'

Fourthly, the stubborn world of the vineyards has finally come to accept today's realities (see p. 401). The growers have at last massively uprooted their poorer vines and switched to better produce; old-style demagogues like Maffre-Baugé have given way to younger, more open-minded leaders; wine, which used to dominate Languedoc's ill-balanced economy, today brings in less revenue than tourism or other new service industries. This is the latest element in a saga of modern change that had begun much earlier in other branches of French agriculture – to be explored in the next chapter.

5

A BOOMING MODERN AGRICULTURE – BUT CAN THE SMALL FARMER SURVIVE?

France today earns more from exporting cereals than automobiles. Agriculture has been called her *pétrole vert* (green oil), the supreme resource of a country with much the biggest output of any EU member. But despite its spectacular post-war progress, farming today still faces dilemmas. The big farmers mostly do very well, and they are the main exporters. The smaller ones, many of them, have also modernized and grown more prosperous: but they are anxious for the future, not without reason. They face new threats from world markets, as barriers fall. And in strictly economic terms, does France still need her army of smaller farmers? Would not the job be better done by a few thousand huge industrial farms across France? But in that case, what would happen to France's beloved rural traditions, and to the upkeep of the countryside? And where would the farmers go, in a time of high urban unemployment? This is the great debate today, between 'productivists' and 'ruralists'.

The sheer diversity of farming makes it hard to generalize. A vegetable grower of the fertile north Brittany plain faces very different problems from a struggling sheep breeder of the central highlands, while the well-to-do cereals and sugar-beet barons of Picardy are a world away from the producers of cheap Languedoc wine, or the cattle farmers of Normandy, disturbed by the impact of 'mad cow disease' on their markets. Until about fifty years ago, France still had 'two agricultures', quite distinct. The bigger farms of the north and north-east were already as rich and up to date as almost any in Europe: but across the rest of the country, smallholders survived on subsistence farming or upland peasants lived in stark poverty.

In the decades after the war, the major part of this poorer sector went through a revolution, technical, economic and social. In no other part of French life was change so dramatic, or the conflict between old and new so sharp. Farm mechanization soon began to make economic nonsense of France's vast peasant community, and the great exodus began to new jobs in the towns. Over 7 million people have now moved off the land; farming's share of France's active population fell from 35 per cent in 1939 to 8 per cent by 1987 and some 4.8 per cent today. The exodus has now slowed, but it continues. When farmers leave, they often sell their land to others, so the average size of a farm has trebled since the mid-1950s. But the difference between rich and poor farms, in size and in wealth, remains huge.

Even more important has been the change in attitudes. Most farmers used to be a social class apart, afraid of progress. But after the war a new generation of modern-minded younger ones, with a very different outlook from their parents, began to arise not from the rich estates of the northern plains but from the smallholdings of the south, west and centre. They promoted a new creed, entirely novel in this individualistic milieu, of technical advance, producer groups and marketing cooperatives. And it was largely thanks to their own efforts, more than to state technocrats, that productivity had grown sixfold by 1980. Today the old-style poor peasant, sozzled, semi-illiterate, does still exist in a few places: but he is a dying breed. Traditional peasant society, once so strong and picturesque a feature of France, has been passing away, and the new-style farmer is more like a small businessman. Maybe he has a handsome car and modernized home, and his children are scarcely different from town children. Thus the old class of *les paysans*★ has become largely integrated into society.

The EU's Common Agricultural Policy (CAP), introduced in the 1960s, greatly helped French farming as a whole, bringing new markets and big subsidies: but its support system has unfairly benefited the larger farms most. More important, the technical progress of the post-war decades, and the ensuing huge rises in productivity, while enabling most farmers to achieve decent living standards, led also to vast surpluses in dairy products, beef, wine and some other sectors – throughout the EEC – and these the taxpayer had to subsidize. So the farmers, after being encouraged for decades by Governments to produce more and to invest heavily in new equipment, were in the 1980s asked to cut back. It left

★ The word '*paysan*' denotes the whole social class of people who earn their living from the land, as farmers or labourers. It is a less archaic and pejorative term than 'peasant'. 'Countryman' might be a fairer description.

them bewildered and angry; technical progress, long seen as the panacea for farming, had taken a nasty revenge. Milk quotas were introduced, while other new CAP reforms have since managed to reduce the surpluses without hitting farmers' incomes. But today the CAP still benefits the rich most, and it is expensive: many farmers derive over half their income from the CAP grants, and some resent this system of 'charity hand-outs'.

The steady growth of modern large-scale farming is excellent for exports, but it threatens the smaller farmer. His children are wary of entering a hard profession with an uncertain future. So what will happen to French rural life? Some hope comes from a change since the 1970s in urban attitudes to the countryside, now *à la mode*. After their rapid post-war urbanization, the French are looking again to their rural roots: new jobs in the cities have grown fewer, and some young people prefer the idea of a simple country life. So the pendulum has been swinging back, and the whole question is now posed of how to make the best use of France's vast rural heritage. Many farm leaders insist on retaining the smallish family farm as the basic unit. They argue that the danger otherwise is of part of the landscape becoming a desert, while the rest is a series of vast, silent wheat fields and prairies operated by absentee capitalists, as in America. But farmers also accept that, under high productivity, less land is now needed for cultivation, and some must be turned over to other purposes. They are ready to join in helping to revive countryside and villages with new activities, based on tourism, leisure, crafts, forestry, modern-style cottage industries. And so, as France moves into the so-called post-industrial era, town and country will move closer together.

THE FARMING REVOLUTION: FAREWELL TO THE OLD PEASANTRY

Briefly, this is the story of farming's post-war 'revolution'. Before the war, while a few estates in the north were large and up to date, the rest of the country was a mass of archaic smallholdings, sunk in lethargy and a kind of fatalism. *Paysantisme* was a way of life, a doctrine that nothing could or should disturb 'the eternal order of the fields'. The laws of equal inheritance, dating from Napoleon and earlier, were a major cause of the absurdly small size of farms. And farmers were protected by high tariff barriers, adding to the stagnation.

In 1946 the first Plan set about trying to coax the small farms out of their archaism. It made farm machinery its top priority outside industry, with striking results: the number of tractors rose from 35,000 to 230,000 by 1954, and productivity soared, too. The much-needed rural exodus was also gathering pace. But in the 1950s inflation hit the farmer badly, provoking endless rural protests, led by right-wing demagogues of the old school. The weak Fourth Republic Governments gave special aid, but it was not enough. Discontent was marked by the burning of crops, tractors barring the main roads: it all gave townsfolk and foreigners a picture of the French farmer as a comic and ignorant anarchist, always complaining, his head firmly in the sand. Yet his plight was genuine, if partly his own fault. It was time for a new outlook, and new leadership.

And it came, in the late 1950s, from an unexpected source. Like so many of the progressive influences in early post-war France, it was rooted in militant leftish Catholicism: nearly all the new young radical leaders came from the Jeunesse Agricole Chrétienne (JAC), a youth movement which was founded by the priesthood to combat rural atheism, but then during the war took on a more secular tone. Among the very young sons of small farmers, there occurred one of those strange psychological changes that seemed to have marked the destiny of France at that time. The danger and responsibility of their wartime activities, often in the Resistance, gave them an early maturity and seriousness. Many began to ponder on how they could avoid a life of certain hardship and poverty, short of leaving the soil which was their home. Some, deported to Germany, saw there how small farms could be run on modern lines. But how to do it in France?

By 1945 the initiative in the JAC was out of the hands of the priests and the accent was on learning economics, self-help and sharing of labour – new and amazing in the peasant world. Local groups set about studying accountancy and new farming techniques. But the JACists soon found that to apply their ideas in practice was not easy: in this patriarchal society, on most farms the way was blocked by fathers who would have nothing of the new methods. So, rather than wait for fathers to retire, the JACists decided to carry their campaign into national farming politics. Under their forceful and visionary young leader, Michel Debatisse, son of a small Auvergnat hill-farmer, they began their assault. The main union, the Fédération Nationale des Syndicats des Exploitants Agricoles (FNSEA), was in the hands of the older rich farmers of the north: but in 1957 the Debatisse faction managed to take over the key posts of its moribund junior section, the Centre National des Jeunes Agriculteurs (CNJA) and began to use it as a militant pressure group. As a step towards breaking down the peasants' isolation, joint meetings were held with factory workers' unions – most unusual in France. The CNJA also formed links with the young technocrats who came to power with de Gaulle in 1958. They found a similarity of language and interest, and Debatisse was elected the youngest-ever member of the Economic and Social Council. The breakthrough was beginning. The CNJA proposed a new policy of investment and structural reform, with drastic measures to persuade older farmers to retire. The Government responded, and in 1960 a new law was passed. But its application then proved very slow.

In the very special region of western Brittany, the young farmers' rising irritation reached flashpoint in May 1961, when a seasonal glut knocked the bottom out of the potato and vegetable markets. At Pont-l'Abbé, farmers set fire to ballot boxes in local elections and filled the streets with tons of potatoes sprayed with petrol. Then, at Morlaix, 4,000 young farmers invaded the streets with tractors and seized the sub-prefecture. Many of them were prosperous vegetable growers on the rich coastal plain. When their leader, Alexis Gourvennec, was arrested by the police, sympathy riots spread throughout the west. It was the largest and most effective farmers' demonstration in post-war France, and it marked a decisive turning point.

For the first time farmers were protesting *for* progress, not against it. For the first time the riots were led by the new leaders, not the old demagogues. *L'agriculture de papa est morte*, read the triumphant banners. Gourvennec and his friends (see p. 337) were furious at the Government's failure to reform the archaic marketing system, notably in artichokes, causing price collapses in a good season. His area's problems were very different from those of a poorer upland region like Debatisse's. But both young leaders passionately wanted change. De Gaulle then responded quickly. As Minister of Agriculture he appointed Edgard Pisani, an ex-prefect, who in the next years proved the most forceful and far-sighted figure to have filled that normally unwanted post in this century. He created a new pension fund to encourage older farmers to retire; an agency for buying and redistributing land; and a system to help farmers to form groups both for marketing and shared production. His laws became the basis of all later government policy for modernizing agriculture. The young farmers then infiltrated the FNSEA itself, of which Debatisse was president in 1971–9. Their revolution helped to bring the smaller French farm into the modern age, where it could face the new problems of European and world competition.

The 1960s and '70s saw great modernization and structural change, some of it spontaneous: the steady exodus to the towns enabled those who remained to buy up or rent the land vacated, so that since 1955 the average size of farms has risen from 14 to 40 hectares. This and other factors – the CAP subsidies, improved production and marketing techniques, the domestic consumer boom – have all helped a majority of farmers to increase their standard of living greatly, with some ups and downs. Today there are still many unsolved problems, and great disparities between farms, but new attitudes have emerged. Whereas Debatisse left school at thirteen, farmers' children today stay on to take technical diplomas, or they get a degree in agronomy at one of the hundreds of new agricultural colleges. I met one small farmer whose son was a *polytechnicien*. At the same time, farm labourers have become far fewer, and those that remain now earn a decent wage. Many have had technical training.

Home comforts have steadily improved, and for good or ill the peasant's life has become 'urbanized', as in Britain, only later. On the north Brittany plain in 1979 I visited Jean-Pierre Le Verge, a local CNJA leader, in his comfortable modern farmhouse. 'We grew up in utter poverty,' he said, pouring me *un scotch*. 'My father had only 11 hectares, eleven cows – and six children. As a teenager I could not afford a five-franc ticket for the local fête. In 1960 we still had no running water, no heating save a wood stove, no TV or even radio, no car, just an old horse-cart. I left school at fourteen. But then my brothers and I persuaded my father to retire and let us modernize the farm. Now we have a big modern piggery with 300 sows for breeding, and we've enlarged the farm to 24 hectares. My income has soared: but there's a large loan to pay back on our investments. We have a new Peugeot 505, a colour TV, hi-fi, more gadgets than we need. The first holiday of my life was in 1975, but now we go to the Côte d'Azur. Yes, we see ourselves as having fully integrated into society, we live like townspeople – but we work longer hours, maybe sixty-five a week.'

In Auvergne I revisited a maize farmer who had built himself a neat new house on the site of an old barn. 'When I was a boy,' he said, 'our social life was with the other local peasants. But the village is now half derelict, and my own children make their friends in the nearby towns. Our horizons have become far wider, but some of the old warmth is lost.' At the height of the rural exodus, it was usually the girls who left the farms first for the towns. They hated the isolation, drudgery and sense of inferiority, and they rarely wanted to marry a farmer. A town girl would never think of doing so. But today over a third of young farmers marry the daughters of non-farmers! 'We have left our ghetto,' said Debatisse.

Whereas urban class divisions remain fairly rigid in France, in the villages and rural areas the structures have altered far more. In the very old days, the village was ruled by an élite of local *notables* – the *curé*, the teacher, the lawyer – who acted as intermediaries between the peasants and the rest of society. But these leaders have been drifting away or losing influence: *châtelains* today often have jobs in Paris, while the role of the *curé* has declined, and the calibre of local teachers, too. And the farmers, fewer but more forceful and educated than before, have taken affairs into their own hands. Many are now mayors or *conseillers généraux*. In an area near Nantes with a feudal tradition, a small farmer with strong left-wing views, Bernard Lambert, spoke to me bitterly of the 1930s when his father was a sharecropper (a system now abolished). 'He would lift his cap to the *châtelain* and call him "*Monsieur notre maître*". But our relations with the gentry have changed a lot. Some are quite human nowadays – you should meet my neighbour, the Comte de Cossé-Brissac!' So this Marxist lifted the phone: '*Écoute, mon vieux, je t'envoie un journaliste anglais – d'accord?*' Amazed by the *tutoiement*, I took leave of the Lamberts in their cottage and drove through the social barricades to the baronial hall where the young gentleman-farmer count sat me on a Louis XV sofa: '*Oui, c'est un brave type, Bernard – un peu excité, un peu farfelu, mais il est bien.*' This may be an extreme example: in some areas there is still suspicion between rich and poor farmers. But the barriers have been falling, both within the rural classes and between *paysan* and *citadin*. As the farmers become urbanized, so also the townsfolk penetrate into the country, buying up old houses as holiday homes (see pp. 626–7).

Modernization of farming would have been harder had not the Debatisse generation succeeded in making some inroads into the French peasant's deep-rooted individualism. Farmers have been learning to group together, for joint marketing or production. In Normandy a CNJA leader with a huge cattle and wheat farm told me, 'We formed a group of twenty-two farmers, and bought a silage machine, harvesting equipment and several tractors in common. We share all costs.' This kind of venture, new since the war, cuts across the peasant's traditional suspicion of his neighbour. The Pisani laws granted financial aid and a legal structure to groups sharing equipment, and there are now more than 6,000 of these. Besides helping to pay for modern equipment, the system brings other advantages. Now that salaried workers are scarce, it can provide a pooling of labour for many jobs, and the chance of rotas for milking or minding livestock that enable the farmer to take a weekend off, even a holiday. But the groups have not always worked smoothly. Some have failed and split up, either because the older members would not cooperate, or because the women could not get used to joint accounting. A different kind of state-backed group, the Groupement Agricole d'Exploitation en Commun (GAEC), facilitates the enlargement of farms by enabling the land itself to be jointly owned. There are some 47,000 GAECs, and generally they succeed when the owners belong to the same family. But GAECs between neighbours are much rarer; and often they collapse because the members do not trust one another.

Peasant conservatism has also hindered a solution of the problem of soil parcellization. Seen from the air, many parts of France used to seem like a crazy quilt of thin strips: even a modest farmer might have twenty or thirty tiny fields, not next to each other but scattered. This was partly the result of the equal inheritance laws, as farms were split up between sons and then the parcels changed hands. And it hardly helped the operation, say, of a combine harvester. The official remedy has been the controversial policy of *remembrement* (regrouping): by subsidizing up to 80 per cent of the legal and field costs, Governments have sought to encourage farmers to make rational swaps, and some 14 million hectares have been *remembrés* since the war. The results have been variable, far better in the go-ahead north than the sluggish south. In many small-farm areas older peasants resisted the scheme, often through emotional attachment to their own bits of soil: a farmer might accept the idea in theory, but then refuse to give up the field where his father taught him to plough or the apple-tree his grandmother planted. In the Aveyron, in 1963, the commune of Privezac had voted 90 per cent for *remembrement*, so surveyors arrived and drew up a plan. Then the village split into two camps, but across the traditional rural lines of Reds against Whites, teachers against priests. In the pro-*remembrement* camp, the young Catholic JACists were led by the Socialist mayor, an ex-teacher; against them were the older farmers, led by the deputy mayor, a Catholic ex-officer. When bulldozers arrived to tear down the hedges, the old guard charged them on tractors. The police made some arrests, and finally the work did go ahead.

Regrouping is not imposed on a commune unless over half the farmers are in favour. But in the Massif Central today only a minority of communes have yet been touched: I met one goat breeder with 34 hectares split into fifty far-flung parcels. But *remembrement* is less useful in these hilly livestock-breeding areas than on the crop-growing plains further north where much more has been done, making it much easier to work with machinery. Many farmers say that without the reform they could never have achieved a decent living.

Farmers have also been forming new groups to market their produce. In order to compete in the new Europe, France has been obliged to modernize its internal marketing system – a major change. The former chaos was legendary: produce might change hands several times on its way from farmer to housewife, or travel hundreds of kilometres from its country farm to the Paris markets, only to be sent back for sale near its point of origin. The isolated peasant was powerless in the hands of ruthless profiteering middlemen. Since the 1960s, however, the Government has sponsored the building of modern marketing centres, which have reduced the abuses. And the farmer himself has become more businesslike: by forming sales groups, he is now better able to combat the middlemen. Hundreds of these Sociétés d'Intérêt Collectif Agricole (SICA), state-assisted, have had good results in preventing prices from tumbling in a crisis. One Aveyron farmer told me, 'Our meat SICA saves us time and trouble. We don't have to go to the market individually: a SICA lorry collects our livestock and sells it for us, maybe abroad. And the dealers now cheat us less, for the SICA knows the markets as well as they do.' SICAs have been especially effective in fruit and vegetable sectors. But although the middlemen now have less power, the big hypermarket chains, by dictating their prices, are now seeking to exploit the producers in just the same way.

In the old days an absurdly high share of national produce transited via Paris – an aspect of France's centripetal legacy. So the Government in the 1960s built a dozen or so provincial *marchés-gares*, big modern markets by railways on the edge of cities. Linked by telex, they were able to direct produce where it was needed, and they certainly speeded up transactions and reduced dependence on Paris. In 1969 the Paris central market of Les Halles was transferred to a big new *marché-gare* in the suburbs, near Orly airport (see p. 309). Since Zola's day, this colourful market had been a huge spider's web of middlemen where vested privilege and muddle went hand in hand. But in their sleek new premises the middlemen could not so easily reconstruct their mafia. However, the vast improvement in French marketing since the 1960s has been due less to the *marchés-gares* than to growth of farmers' cooperatives, today doing their deals directly by fax or e-mail.

In marketing and techniques, in organization and in lifestyles, the post-war progress in farming was huge. And another major change was the impact of Europe's Common Agricultural Policy, from the end of the 1960s. But ironically the improved productivity led simply to surpluses – one of the main problems that the CAP has had to tackle since the 1980s.

BRUSSELS'S REFORMS, FOOD SURPLUSES AND MAD COWS

The EU's controversial Common Agricultural Policy has altered the entire focus of French farming since its introduction in the 1960s – 'If we have a grievance now, we go lobbying in Brussels more than in Paris,' say farmers. At the start, they set high hopes on the CAP: they saw that France was starting with the lowest wholesale prices of the Community and the largest production, so it seemed inevitable that the alignment of prices and dropping of internal trade barriers would benefit them more than others. Had not France agreed to the EEC partly because it felt that its gains in agriculture would compensate for Germany's likely gains in industry?

On balance the results have been positive for French farmers and remain so today. They benefit from a largely protected market of 370 million consumers, where prices are well above world levels. However, they have become much less starry-eyed about the CAP. One early disappointment was that France's partners much increased their own production, so the new market for their own vast output was smaller than expected – even if today 73 per cent of French agricultural exports go to other EU countries. Also some smaller French farmers have not found it easy to keep up with their more efficient competitors in Holland and Denmark, notably in the pig and dairy sectors.

During the 1990s farmers have been digesting the effects of the 1992 CAP reform, which aimed to reduce the cost of its absurd and much-criticized system of subsidies. This archi-complex system comprised a CAP levy on agricultural imports from outside the EU, redistributed to farmers in the form of export subsidies and price supports (covering essentially sugar beet, dairy products, most cereals, some fruit and vegetables). This protectionist system aimed to encourage EU self-sufficiency and to ensure a decent living standard for farmers regardless of market prices, and it helped mostly countries such as France that were net exporters. But it proved expensive for national budgets since the price supports and other subsidies were allowed to exceed by far the size of the levy, thus creating heavy annual deficits. This was because the EU, yielding to pressure from farmers' lobbies, fixed the prices for many products around the level of the highest then obtaining, not the average. Thus if wheat was cheapest in France and dearest in Germany, the German rather than the French price was chosen for the CAP. This encouraged farmers to overproduce in many sectors, knowing that their surpluses would be bought up anyway, then either dumped on world markets or expensively stockpiled. The notorious 'butter mountain' caused a scandal in the 1970s, resulting in the cheap sale of butter to Russia; and by 1986 the CAP's stocks had reached 15 million tons of grain, 750,000 tons of beef and 1.4 million of butter.

As the subsidies were paid on quantity of produce, inevitably the system benefited most the big rich farmers who needed it least. France's large northern farms, with their high productivity, did handsomely, while less efficient smallholders gained far less: some 80 per cent of all aid was going to just 20 per cent of farmers. It was the same in other countries, and clearly the CAP's unified price system was unfairly suited to a Europe with such diversified agriculture. Moreover, the cost of the supports fell heavily on the EU taxpayer, and the British in particular were aggrieved, understandably.

But British opinion has been wrong to suppose that 'it's all the fault of the French', or that the CAP is a conspiracy to bolster inefficient French farmers. The truth is more complex. Poor peasants benefit less than rich farmers – *including* British ones! And German farm lobbies have been more to blame than the French for the insistence on high prices, for Germany's farming today is on average more backward and small-scale than France's (see my book, *Germany and the Germans*, 1991, pp. 154–71). In fact, the majority of French farmers have not been blind to the injustices of the CAP and the need for change: but, like their Governments, they remain strongly attached to the basic CAP concept of a free, unified and protected market. They oppose the kind of moves to dismantle it that are favoured in Britain.

In 1983–4 the EEC finally began to take some concerted measures to oblige farmers to limit production, starting with milk quotas. French farmers' reactions were typically emotional and confused. Most accepted that cuts were necessary and that this would involve sacrifices: at the same time, they felt they had been badly misled across the years. 'Until recently,' one Norman dairy farmer told me, 'the Government was still urging me to increase my productivity. So I invested expensively in new equipment and ran up heavy debts. Now I'm told to cut back. We've been tricked, and I'm furious.' It was this sullen mood that led to sporadic violence in 1984, as farmers joined forces to protest against the milk quotas, plus British lamb imports, a drop in pork prices, threats of Spanish competition over wine and fruit, and so on. Farmers threw bombs at town halls, tore up railway lines, attacked British and Spanish lorries and spread dung in the forecourts of Paris ministries. The venerable tradition of French peasant protest, quiescent for twenty years, was alive and well. But the milk quotas went ahead: they worked quite smoothly, and gradually came to be accepted (see below).

By the late 1980s all EEC Governments recognized that quotas were not enough: more radical means must be found of revising the costly system of supports and buying of surpluses, without damaging the small farmer too much. Mounting American pressure in the GATT talks was adding to the urgency. So the Commissioner for Agriculture, Ray McSharry, from a small-farm Sligo background, drew up a bold scheme that would put a ceiling on aids for large farmers, thus narrowing the gap with small ones; and he was warmly backed in Brussels by the 'social-minded' Jacques Delors, who also had small-farm roots. But some key member Governments, notably Britain's, argued that any such cut in price supports for the big cereal exporters would limit their competitiveness and thus harm trade. So the scheme was rejected.

Instead, another solution was worked out, less socially generous, but innovative in its way. This important reform, adopted in 1992, switched many supports from the produce itself to the producer: in other words, notably in cereals, the CAP would now do less topping up of prices, and instead would give direct 'compensation' grants to farmers. As these were related to the size of their farms, not of their output, they might reduce their incentive to overproduce. The reform also introduced a system of 'set-asides', novel for the CAP, whereby farmers would receive subsidies for letting part of their land lie fallow each year. Thirdly, in the livestock sectors, the reform did retain one element of the earlier McSharry proposals: it set upper limits on the number of 'headage payments' (i.e. subsidies per animal) that any individual farmer could receive.

The reform managed to impress the Americans – often so hostile to the CAP – that Europe was at last prepared to reduce its protectionism. This made it easier to reach an agreement in the GATT's Uruguay-round talks, where the French had argued that the US was driving too hard a bargain: 'They'll screw us for every franc, they want to wipe us out,' said one farmer. The GATT crisis of 1993 drew out all the latent anti-Americanism of the French, among farmers, public and politicians alike. But Prime Minister Balladur finally achieved a compromise with Washington which he skilfully managed to sell to his own public as a French victory, while partly pacifying his farmers with special hand-outs. In the event, the GATT deal affected French farmers much less severely than they had feared.

The 1992 CAP reform has been judged a modest success by many French officials and farm leaders, but not all. Certainly, it has reduced the surpluses, notably in cereals. And it has made it possible to limit the wasteful system of 'intervention' buying, whereby the CAP would guarantee to buy up a farmer's excess produce and destroy it or sell it off cheaply abroad. The CAP's burden on the EU budget has been eased a little. And the cuts in export subsidies have induced farmers to sell more wheat for animal feed on the home market, thus reducing the EU's costly feed import bills – one main purpose of the reform.

Farmers were at first wary, suspicious of any system that smacked of 'deficiency payments', so alien to their tradition. But gradually they have learned to live with the reform: 'It's not been the end of the world, just the end of a world,' a CNJA leader told me. The big wheat barons, who stood to lose most, found that by happy chance the reform was followed by large rises in world wheat prices: so they have not suffered so much. One common objection to the reform is that, too bureaucratic, it demands too much form-filling. Another, more serious, is that the compensation payments are too much like charity, and this offends a farmer's pride. 'When the subsidy was disguised within the price paid, I didn't notice it so much,' a Normandy maize grower told me, 'but now it comes as a hand-out, about 2,000 francs per hectare, and I no longer feel that I've really earned it. We don't want to feel like *assistés*.' This is a common view. Many farmers derive over half their income from the CAP direct grants.

The set-aside scheme was also at first disliked, since taking good land out of production is instinctive anathema to a French farmer – 'It's like obliging a painter to destroy his canvas,' said one. But most of them now accept that the scheme does them little harm. Smaller farmers are exempt; even for the others it is not compulsory, though if you fail to set land aside you cannot claim the grants for it (maybe 2,500 francs a year per hectare). At first, 15 per cent of a farmer's land was to be set aside. Today, with improved world-market conditions, this has been reduced to some 5 per cent: so the problem is marginal. 'But in a starving world we remain hostile to set-asides on philosophic principle,' said an FNSEA official.

In 1998 the European Commission proposed yet another reform of the CAP, known as 'Agenda 2000'. This would end the set-aside system and further reduce guaranteed prices in beef, milk, cereals and other sectors. Farmers, except the largest ones, would be compensated by increased direct grants. The proposals marked a further attempt to bring prices closer to market realities, and to see that small farmers, not large ones, benefited most from the supports. Even so, France joined Germany in opposing the scheme, and so a strenuous debate began.

The earlier 1992 reform has not halted the trend towards larger and fewer farms. In fact, the compensation grants and the milk quotas allotted by hectare both increase the farmer's urge to buy up more land. Nor has the reform done much to reduce the gulf between rich and poor. But the huge variations by sector and by region make it hard to generalize about a complex farming world often shaken by specific crises – for example, 'mad cow disease', pollution by pig effluent, or distortions of the vegetable market. We should look at the main areas of production – cereals, fruit and vegetables, pigs, sheep, beef and milk.

France is the EU's largest producer of cereals, by far, with 30 per cent of the total: soft wheat is the biggest crop, followed by maize. Cereal exports are a major earner, much encouraged by the Government, so the subject is politically sensitive: hence the tough GATT negotiations. Most cereals are grown by large, efficient farmers on the plains of the north-east and the Paris basin; and though their incomes fluctuate, they are generally very well off. They farm on an industrial scale, a world away from the small hill-farmers of the Massif Central.

The fruit and vegetable sector is much less CAP-regulated than cereals:

so it is highly vulnerable to market fluctuations, and this can lead to drama. France's output has greatly increased in recent years, alike in the orchards of the south and on the big vegetable farms of the north-west, and elsewhere: but it remains far behind that of Spain or Italy. Since Gourvennec's victories in 1961, the growers have largely won their fight against France's own middlemen: but now they face severe foreign competition. When Spain joined the EEC in 1986, the fruit and early-vegetable growers of the Midi found their markets threatened by Spanish farmers with an even warmer and earlier spring, and lower labour costs. They managed to survive, but the problem remains far from solved.

Even in Gourvennec's prosperous west Brittany, there can still be serious trouble. After the 'artichoke wars', he and his friends created a SICA that is today the most powerful in France. With 2,500 members, it has a near monopoly in an area producing 70 per cent of French artichokes and cauliflowers, also tomatoes, leeks, endives, broccoli, etc.; much is exported to Britain and Germany. In their modern auction centre south of Roscoff, linked by fax and e-mail to the rest of Europe, the farmers can regulate their prices, using a stop-the-clock Dutch auction system; in periods of glut they sometimes withhold produce. But their tactics can be useless. In June 1996 I found hundreds of protesting farmers blocking the main road near Morlaix, causing me to be late for a friend's funeral; at Quimper they tipped tons of artichokes into the streets, and jovially thrust some through my car window. They were lovely for dinner.

The problem? A late spring, then a hot May, had caused a glut; and the farmers were again being undercut by producers from Italy and Spain where labour costs are far lower and the lira and peseta had recently devalued. Gourvennec, still the SICA's president, said to me, 'There's barely the glimmer of *une Europe sociale*, so a country like Spain, or Britain too, with lower social charges and wages, can produce more, much more cheaply. And in vegetables, labour is 50 per cent of the cost price. I'm furious with Brussels for not sorting this out. So roll on the single currency! Either we need a stronger Europe with tighter rules, or none at all.' But a Europe of unified social costs seems light years away.

In the livestock sector, pig breeding is an area without any CAP price control, and its problems today are less those of sales and markets than ecology. Until the 1980s France was outclassed by the big modern piggeries of the Danes, Dutch and Germans: but the larger French producers have now improved their techniques and increased their output, and France is no longer a net importer. Over half of French pigs are bred in Brittany, where Gourvennec has France's largest pig farm, producing 90,000 a year. He and some others are rich: but they now face a problem more daunting than artichoke glut: water pollution. Nitrates from the liquid manure have been seeping through the Breton granite into the underground streams and the water supply, causing a nasty smell along parts of the coast. The pollution occurs also in some other parts of France, but is worst in Brittany where breeding is most intensive: here the problem has existed for years, but only recently has it aroused such public concern. Many Bretons will not drink tap water, or they boil all water for cooking. Medical experts are unsure how far the nitrates are a threat to health. But the EU Commission has chosen the figure of 50 milligrams of nitrate per litre as the danger threshold, and has forbidden farmers going above this level to expand their production unless they can deal better with their manure. The French Government backs this policy, and in 1997 one Breton breeder was sentenced to a year in prison for breaking the rules.

Some older farmers think the issue much exaggerated: but most are now taking it seriously, and are helped by expensive government aid. Scientific research has been exploring the denitrifying, dehydrating or burning of the manure: but results in Holland have not been fruitful, and technology may need longer to produce a viable solution. Meantime, farmers are now spreading their manure over much wider areas, often using the arable land of neighbours. They stock and dry it first, which dilutes the nitrate level. But it all takes time and effort, often money, too. When in 1996 I revisited Jean-Pierre Le Verge, I found him a changed man. 'I now have a thousand sows and I'm rich, but I'm utterly fed up. If it weren't for my kids, I'd sell out, as many are doing. Of course there *is* pollution, and we're dealing with it. But it was worse twenty years ago, when no one cared: it is just that society and values have changed. All this ecological concern, it comes from Germany, it's too much and we just can't cope. And the new CAP rules, which prevent me from expanding, are hypocritical: wheat growers also pollute, but they aren't touched. I escaped the medieval poverty of my parents; I built up a big prosperous farm – but where am I now? Farming is at a crucial turning point.'

Sheep breeders are found mainly in the hilly parts of central France. They do well from the CAP subsidies. But since the 1970s they have suffered from heavy competition by British lamb, produced and sold more cheaply. France imports over half of the lamb and mutton it consumes, and much of this comes from the UK. Farmers have sometimes reacted angrily by attacking lorries carrying lamb from the Channel ports.

This was nothing, however, compared with the more justified anti–British fury over '*la vache folle*' in 1996. The beef market has always been a contentious matter in a land that has long been Europe's top beef producer – and top consumer, too. But in the 1980s the EEC's 'intervention' buying system, plus the impact of cheap foreign imports, meant that Europe was producing more than it needed, and the 'beef mountain' grew. What's more, the French public's consumption of beef was slowly falling, by 1 or 2 per cent a year, as a younger generation turned to other habits, or found pork much cheaper and just as tasty. But the CAP reforms of 1992 helped to ease the surpluses, and farmers also reduced their cattle herds: so the problem was under control. Then came BSE.

In the early 1990s there had already been sporadic cases in France of bovine spongiform encephalopathy ('mad cow disease'). But these were always hushed up by the authorities for fear of alarming the public and upsetting the markets: the herds were quietly destroyed and the farmers compensated, and the cases were not recorded. Then in March 1996, when the British revealed the extent of their own BSE disaster, it was found that in 1993–6 some 154,000 tons of the infected British animal feed had been imported into France as diet for French cows. All hell broke loose. Not only did France promptly ban all British beef imports (as Germany had done earlier), but the public was soon eating about 30 per cent less beef; and foreign markets for France's important export trade also collapsed. Breeders and dealers were on the streets, claiming they would go bankrupt and demanding special aid. In FNSEA-led protests, John Major was burned in effigy at Strasbourg, and British tourists arriving by ferry in Normandy were once blocked for thirteen hours by farmers. '*Cette catastrophe, c'est la faute des Rosbifs,*' said one ('*rosbif*' i.e. roast beef, has long been a French nickname for the English).

Then in 1999 a new crisis broke: when the EU Commission, judging British beef to now be healthy, decided to lift the ban on its import, Paris – under pressure from consumer groups and farmers – refused to go along with this, to the fury of *les rosbifs*. France received some support from Germany, where the ban was also still in force: but British wrath fell mainly on Paris. By December the dispute was still unresolved and it showed once again that France was prepared to flout EU rules in the defence of its own interests.

After the 1996 crisis, the French authorities did provide farmers with massive compensation. And the issue of France's own BSE was now out in the open. By mid-1998 there had been only thirty-seven known cases, it was claimed, and each time the entire herd had been slaughtered. Cattle on French farms are always carefully controlled, and each animal has its own written record and identity card. On the other hand, the meat market can still be prone to corruption and muddle, despite CAP measures. The farmers' own SICAs have made progress, but their battle with the middlemen goes on. And during the BSE crisis farmers were angry that although their own producer prices had fallen, those in the shops remained much the same (unlike in Britain). 'The hypermarket chains and the wholesalers exploit us with their profiteering, and we have no means of hitting back,' said one farmer I met in the Charolais. I heard the same in many areas.

Beef consumption today is a mere 10 per cent below its previous level. But prices for the producer are still 20 per cent below, so the farmer is hit. Some would be happy to switch to dairy farming: but they cannot, because of the milk quotas – today another stormy issue. These have in themselves been quite a success, in France as elsewhere, helping to reduce surpluses. France in 1984 was given its own overall quota, and this was divided between farms, whereby each cut its output by some 3 per cent. EEC loans were given to induce some dairymen to move out of milk production altogether, and many responded. As a result, the total of French dairy producers fell from over 200,000 to some 92,000 by 1993, with many mergers and enlargements. This was seen as a useful trend in a France where dairy herds were still on average too small, compared with Britain or Denmark. The total of milk cows dropped by some 30 per cent, whereas milk output fell by 5.4 per cent: that is, the cows became more productive.

Farmers, at first wary of the quotas, soon came to accept them. 'I see them as a necessary evil,' said one I met in Burgundy in 1996. 'I have fifty dairy cows, and an annual quota of 370,000 litres, which I sell at 2 francs the litre. I can just about make a decent living.' Butter and cheese producers are especially glad, since the quotas have helped to keep the market stable. But some farmers argue that the reform should have been done differently. Each pasture carries its set quota, which cannot be bought or sold separately: but this can add to the rivalry between farmers over land, and it makes the big farmers eager to acquire ever more land, so as to gain more quotas. This can make it harder for younger, small farmers to make a start. But at least overproduction has now ended – as in another important sector: table wine.

MIDI WINEGROWERS ACCEPT REALITY:
AN END TO UNSALEABLE PLONK

No other sector of French agriculture has changed so much recently as that of cheap table wines – notably in Languedoc. It has been a success story. 'Midi winegrowers riot again' used to be a common headline: the vast tribe of producers, stubborn and unruly, led by demagogues like Maffre-Baugé, would take little account of markets and expect large subsidies for disposing of their unsaleable surpluses. But today, with a change of generation, no other farmers have done more to adapt to new conditions. Accepting that the consumer no longer wants their poor-quality plonk, they have uprooted many inferior vines, planted better ones, or switched to other produce. Languedoc now produces mainly good wine, and is fast increasing its exports.

France has long had two wine industries, rich and poor, with separate problems. One is the minority of more expensive wines, led by Burgundy, Bordeaux and Champagne. This élitist little world is highly efficient, and does not riot. Its sales both in France and abroad have been rising happily, and only seldom – for example, during the fraud scandals of 1974 and 1994 – does it cause the Government any headaches. The medium-priced *appellations*, such as Bourgueuil, Cahors and Côtes-du-Rhône, also find ready buyers.

The second group has been the producers of table wines, which used to account for two-thirds of France's average annual output of some 70 million hectolitres. They numbered hundreds of thousands, about half of them in Languedoc (see p. 375): most were smallholders who for centuries had gained a modest living from producing their plonk on a few ill-organized hectares. Repeatedly they panicked at the threat of falling prices in a bumper year, or of cheap Italian imports: their lobby was powerful, and Governments generally pandered to it.

After the war, Paris made varied attempts to solve, or at least mitigate, the chronic overproduction. It spent millions of francs on buying up and destroying surpluses. In 1953 it launched a more constructive policy of grants for uprooting poor vines, but this at first met with a weak response. Later it began to encourage the replacing of poor vines with 'noble' ones, more likely to find a market, and this became CAP policy. With the ending of tariff barriers in the 1960s, France discovered big new markets in countries such as Germany and Belgium, but mostly for its better wines. At the lower level, farmers soon found to their horror that their Italian rivals benefited most from the new open market. Italian wines, more cheaply produced, less carefully graded and often more robust than French ones, began to flood France's own market. Under EEC rules the Government could not stop these imports, nor prevent big firms such as Nicolas from fortifying French wines with the stronger south Italian ones.

In the summer of 1975 came the inevitable explosion, as the Languedoc wine lobby yet again used violence to obtain its ends. Growers disrupted tourism by blocking out signposts; they blockaded the port of Sète, entry point for much Italian wine. The Chirac Government, scared of social unrest in a time of economic crisis, yielded to their demands by flouting EEC rules: it put high import duties on Italian wines, to the fury of Rome and Brussels. But this did not reduce imports enough to satisfy the growers: 1976 saw more and worse riots throughout the Midi, with a farmer and a policeman killed near Narbonne, attacks on lorries and depots of importers of Italian wine. Finally, a scared Government made further concessions. Once again, the Midi found that violence can pay.

Soon, however, the EEC Commission managed to persuade the Paris and Rome Governments to seek joint solutions to overproduction by banning all planting of new vineyards and granting more subsidies for uprooting poor vines. This bore some results. And growers were pacified by a new CAP scheme that offered guaranteed payments for the distillation of surpluses. But the real problems had merely been expensively patched over, not solved. The French complained that the Italian authorities, unable to control the Mafia, were not applying the rules properly – a familiar story. And many small French producers found it easier to live off the distillation subsidies than plant better vines. This was because, under French rules still valid today, the lower classified *vin de pays* grades were limited to outputs of some 8 to 12 hectolitres a hectare, whereas for unclassified *ordinaires* there were no limits, and yields in some years could exceed 50 hectolitres: yet price differentials were rarely more than 25 per cent for the producer. So the distillation scheme gave him some incentive to go on producing unsaleable plonk.

A turning point came in 1983 at the EEC's Dublin 'summit', when the French and Italian Governments were persuaded to scale down the distillation subsidies. In the next three years these were reduced by half. This change of policy was a political risk. But it did coincide, remarkably, with a gradual change of attitude among winegrowers. The old reactionary demagogues were losing influence and a new generation was coming up, far more realistic, modern-minded and European in outlook. One of their leaders, Jean Clavel, director of the big Coteaux du Languedoc association near Montpellier, spoke to me in a language inconceivable in that area ten years previously: 'The EEC has wasted money scandalously on subsidizing bad wine. What's more, the special aid from Paris and Brussels has hindered this region's evolution, as the lazy growers saw it as their due. But now they have seen the mines and shipyards closing, and finally they realize that their own industry cannot go on being treated as a special case. They have to adapt. More are now moving to a strategy of small-scale higher-quality production.'

Many producers have now pulled up their vines and changed to other crops, with the help of grants. In Languedoc most hillside vines can produce tolerable wine: but on the plains are wide areas where the terrain does not permit improvement, and here some 20,000 hectares were uprooted after 1978. West of Nîmes, one wine cooperative has diversified into selling apricots and asparagus produced by its members. Other growers have kept their vineyards but replanted, so their wines can be upgraded. They have also improved their marketing and promotion, which used to be so archaic that the region's better wines were always underpriced. A Corbières selling in a shop for 15 francs is often just as good as a Beaujolais or Bordeaux at twice the price, but only now has Languedoc been pulling free of its old reputation as producer of the working man's *gros rouge* and little else.

Wines in France are carefully controlled and graded by the authorities, and for some years the policy has been to improve quality, and to upgrade where justified. The top classification, *appellation d'origine contrôlée* (AOC), today accounts for 45 per cent of all French wines, against only 16 per cent in 1966; some 25 per cent are in the middle category, *vins de pays*, very drinkable; only 15 per cent are unclassified *vins de table*, which used to be the majority. The rest of the output is for brandies such as cognac. Some wine experts argue that the authorities have been too generous in according new *appellations* and that the AOC label, so well-known abroad, is no longer so reliable a guarantee of quality. There may be some truth in this, for sometimes growers can be careless in the preparation of their wines, even in the Bordelais or Beaujolais. But at the lower level, in areas such as Languedoc, there is no doubt that average quality has greatly improved – and this reflects the big changes in French drinking habits. Today there are fewer manual workers expecting their daily litre or two of *gros rouge*, and in all classes people want to drink less but better wine. Wine consumption per head has fallen by exactly half since 1960 (see p. 160).

Production has fallen, too, from some 70 million hectolitres in the old days to about 55 million in an average year. This is less than the fall in drinking, but exports have gone up, filling the balance. Today there is not much overproduction, and little subsidized distillation except in a bumper year; and the policy of grants for uprooting, having achieved its aims, has ended, too. The total area of vineyards has been reduced by over 10 per cent since 1987, and in Languedoc the figure is higher: here the AOC percentage has gone up from 4 to 15 per cent. 'We have achieved our revolution, there's no more really bad wine here,' I was assured in 1997 by Jean-Philippe Granier of the Coteaux du Languedoc in his smart new office. 'Some of our growers are still lazy, but most see that they are better assured of a sale with a *vin de pays* than a poor *vin de table*. Today we operate by the law of the market, and that's healthy. And we export 30 per cent of our product, much of it to the United States, where our wines are appreciated – more so than in France, where they still carry the bad-plonk image of the past.'

The issue of Italian imports has been mainly solved. Nor have Spanish imports proved such a threat as was feared when Spain joined the EEC in 1986: French drinkers do not care much for Spanish wines. Growers still complain about Italian and Spanish illegal overproduction: but this relates mainly to other markets, not to imports into France. Meanwhile, French exports have doubled in volume since 1975, because secondary regions such as Languedoc have now joined the 'noble' wines in the growing battle for world markets. Amazingly, 10 per cent of all French exports consists of sales to British motorists at Calais and other ports, now that large quantities can be brought into Britain duty-free under single-market rules.

The Languedoc growers have come a long way in a short time. Within the EU, they are confident of holding their own against the Italians and others. But they know, as they told me, that the coming battle will be with the decent medium-priced wines of countries like Australia, South Africa, Bulgaria and Chile. Winegrowers are becoming caught up in globalization – like so much of the French farming world.

NEW ROLES FOR THE SMALLER FARMERS

After its huge transformation, most of French farming is today modern and efficient in its way, and most farmers earn a decent income, despite the price fluctuations. So in a France open to world markets and obsessed by exports, the main remaining unsolved problem is how to assure a *raison d'être* and a future for the smaller family farm. Some peasant farmers, it is true, remain in poverty: but their numbers have dwindled, they have become a social rather than an economic problem. And farming is no longer the central political issue that it used to be when it made and unmade Governments under the Third and Fourth Republics. As the farm lobby wanes in size and thus in influence, farming has slipped towards the sidelines of national life, overtaken by more urgent problems such as unemployment.

French farmers have become far more export-minded. Curiously, until about 1968 this mighty farming nation had a net trade deficit in food and drinks: by tradition, exports were limited mostly to quality wines and spirits, some cheeses, and suchlike. But the trade balance cannot live on Moët and Martell alone, nor on bicycling onion-sellers. The EEC and the productivity boom of the 1970s gave French agriculture new opportunities which it took: the overall trade surplus in food and drinks, a modest 8 per cent in 1970, had risen by 1985 to over 50 per cent, mostly accounted for by cereals. By 1995 the surplus in farm trade had reached 52 billion francs. Besides cereals, France is also a heavy net exporter of wines, sugar and live animals, but it has a deficit in fruit and vegetables. Most of the exporting is done by the large farmers, eagerly encouraged by the Government.

So this is the central dilemma of French agriculture today: should France become a land of large-scale industrial farming in the American manner, with relatively few but highly efficient farms? – or is there still an important role for the smaller family farm? It is the fundamental clash of philosophies between 'productivists' and 'ruralists'.

Today the trend is still for farms to grow ever fewer and larger. When a farmer retires, in many cases he has no successor, so his land is sold to another nearby. This tendency has till now been encouraged, for in many areas farms have been too small to allow their owners a decent living. But many people now argue that the process is in danger of going too far, for human and environmental reasons: if the small farm fades away, then a whole rural tradition is threatened, and the countryside becomes either a wilderness or the joyless instrument of absentee capitalists. This is the 'ruralist' position. The 'productivist' view, held by a minority, is that France's own food needs, and her export potential, are best satisfied by modern large-scale farming, and smaller non-viable units should not be kept alive artificially. Both priorities are valid: the issue is what balance to draw between them. This has been the main focus of recent discussion, within the farm unions and between them and Governments.

Some 60 per cent of French farmers belong to the main union, the FNSEA, where the balance of power tends to fluctuate between the richer ones of the north and the poorer ones of the south and centre. In the mid-1990s its president, Luc Guyau, a big cereals producer from the north-west, was in conflict with smaller farmers from the Massif Central, closer to Debatisse's ideas on the family farm. A second union, Coopération Paysanne, with left-wing views, has developed strongly among small farmers in some areas since the 1980s: it wants guaranteed minimum earnings, and limits on the income of rich farmers. A third group, Coordination Rurale, right-wing and rather Poujadist, is influential in parts of the west: it is anti-European, and many members vote for the Front National.

During the de Gaulle, Pompidou and Giscard years, the FNSEA leaders believed that a policy of wary cooperation with the Government was the best way to ensure that it came to their aid, and generally this tactic paid off. Then the picture changed under the Socialists, who were less dependent on the farmers' vote and tried at first to take a tougher line. Édith Cresson, the abrasive and outspoken Agriculture Minister, began to consult with small leftist groups such as Coopération Paysanne, and refused to treat the FNSEA as the ministry's sole privileged partner. She was soon in sharp public conflict with the FNSEA president, François Guillaume, a wealthy cattle breeder from Lorraine. Also abrasive, and a male chauvinist like many French farmers, he spoke derisively of 'this woman who knows nothing about farming'. Rallying his troops, he forced Cresson to back down on her radical plans for land distribution. She was replaced by Michel Rocard, and he by Henri Nallet, both pragmatic social-democrats. In line with the new CAP campaign against surpluses, they made efforts, as Nallet put it to me, 'to persuade farmers to think of themselves as ordinary economic agents like other business people, rather than as a special case endlessly needing public aid'. This brought some results: Rocard in 1984 was the EEC's chief architect of the milk-quota scheme.

When Chirac became Prime Minister, he provocatively chose Guillaume as his Minister of Agriculture. This pleased French farmers, but it caused dismay in Brussels, where Guillaume was known as a militant demagogue. On one famous occasion, when demanding higher milk prices, he and his friends had led a cow up to the EEC council chamber where, paralysed with fear, it expressed itself as only a cow knows how. Would he now, as minister, try to renege on the new policy of limiting output? – some EEC officials were also going weak in the bowels. But in fact once in office he took a fairly cautious line: Chirac, so it was felt in Paris, had been astute in buying the farmers' support by appointing him. Indeed Jacques Chirac, himself a popular former Agriculture Minister, with some roots in the rural Corrèze, has always been clever at parading as the farmers' champion while trying to stop them getting out of hand. In the 1990s, after Balladur had pacified the farmers with his GATT compromise, Chirac as President continued to win their qualified support. Within the bounds of the tight CAP rules, Governments recently have pursued the dual strategy of (a) promoting exports, and (b) helping the small farmer and checking excess drift from the land. The Socialists, with Louis Le Pensec from Brittany as minister, are today following this.

Rural emigration has had a varying effect. In some areas already thinly populated, it has now reached or even gone beyond its safe limits. But in others, for example Brittany and parts of Poitou-Charente, there are still too many people on the land in economic terms, and the exodus continues. Everywhere it has slowed down: young people are less anxious to leave the land than thirty years ago now that farmers' lifestyles have improved and jobs in the towns are harder to find. But many still shy away from inheriting the family farm. In Normandy, in 1997, I met two brothers with a large farm and a total of seven teenage sons, *none* of whom wanted to stay on the land. So the mergers continue. The total number of French farms, 1.6 million in 1970, was down to 730,000 by 1997. 'It seems inevitable that the process will continue,' I was told by Dominique Moreau-Ferellec, director of the CNJA. 'Our aim is for it to level off at about 550,000, with a total of 3 to 4 per cent of people employed in farming, against 4.8 per cent today. We don't want to go lower, and become like Britain with less than 2.5 per cent.'

So the issue is how to persuade more bright, educated young people to stay on the land. There has long been a fund to encourage older farmers to retire and make way for the young: this has borne some fruit, but even today 40 per cent of *chefs d'exploitation* are aged over fifty-five, and this is seen as far too many. Recent Governments, strongly backed by the CNJA, but less so by the barons of the FNSEA, have been promoting a policy of '*l'installation des jeunes*', a phrase heard on everyone's lips at farm congresses. Briefly, young farmers wanting to settle can receive special loans to help them with land or equipment. Less than 10 per cent of those using the scheme have come from outside agriculture or from abroad (a few are British or Dutch, see p. 700) even though the corporatist prejudice against newcomers in the profession has today waned. Nearly all applicants are the children of farmers wanting to take over: 'We used our loan for buying papa's farm from him and building a new dairy unit. It was essential to make the business viable,' said a young farmer in Burgundy. The scheme worked badly at first, for the fall in farm incomes in the 1980s, plus the uncertainties about CAP reform, were a deterrent. But today some 8,000 *jeunes* are being *installés* each year. This is seen by the CNJA as still far from enough, if the family farm is to be kept alive and healthy.

Some are deterred by the high level of technical skill and expertise needed for modern farming, even if so many of them now have had suitable training. And though much of the old physical drudgery has gone, it is still a profession requiring hard work and long hours, maybe alone. In the old days, a wife always worked alongside her husband on the farm: but since 1980 the number of wives with other jobs has risen from 5 to 50 per cent. Either they reject farm work or else, with rising expectations, the couple feel that they need the second income.

Then there is the fearful problem of the cost of buying or renting land – 'the bane of our *métier*', said one farmer. In most sectors, the minimum viable size of a farm has been rising for those who expect a good income: if 25 hectares were enough in the 1970s, today it might be 35. But how to acquire the land? Few young farmers have much capital, and mortgages are a burden, so most of them prefer to rent: some 55 per cent of farm land is today rented rather than owned by the farmer. Those who do prefer to buy can always turn to Crédit Agricole, the world's largest farm bank, which has done much to fund the modernization of French farming: but the loans that it offers, for buying land or modern equipment, have simply drawn many farmers into piling up large debts. They have the satisfaction of acquiring a permanent estate, as they do not with rented land: but the repayments are heavy – 'When I'm dead, I'll be rich,' some say. This was especially a problem in the 1970s, when land prices were rocketing. Since then prices have fallen by some 30 per cent in real terms: land now costs about 3,200–4,000 francs a hectare in average cultivable areas, less than in most wealthier EU countries. The level of indebtedness has fallen, too.

In pre-war days feudalism was still common, and some farmers were *métayers* (sharecroppers), paying their landlords a tithe – a system abolished in 1946. Other farmers owned their own ancestral land, and on their retirement, sons would each tamely receive his own portion under the equal inheritance laws: these still exist, but are obsolete in practice. Under the Pisani laws of 1961, regional agencies called SAFERs were set up (Sociétés d'Aménagement Foncier et d'Établissement Rural), with powers to buy up land as it came on the market, to make improvements and then resell to the most deserving, maybe a young farmer. The SAFERs are still active. They have some rights of pre-emption, at fixed prices, and so in some cases have been able to curb speculation, or to prevent land being sold to non-farmers for other purposes judged unsuitable. They were greeted at first as the heaviest blow ever struck in France at the sacred rights of property: but the scheme has worked patchily, impeded by the usual French legal delays. And younger farmers complain, once again, that even land handled by the SAFERs has in practice gone mainly on enlargements.

Farmers' incomes rose steadily until the later 1970s, then fluctuated during the 1980s, but have been rising again since the CAP reform. In 1995–7 they rose on average by 8 per cent a year, thanks to three good harvests which especially helped the growers of cereals and other crops. Most farmers today make a respectable living, though of course they grumble, as farmers do. The old-style poor peasant does still exist in some areas, but he is a dying breed. In parts of the Massif Central, you can still find grim hamlets where the soil is stony and the younger people have left. Those who stay eke out a living from useless polyculture, that curse of so much poor-soil farming: a patch of vines for their own vinegary wine, a cow or two and some mangy chickens, cabbages struggling to grow on a chalky hillside. This today is a social problem of *exclusion*, more than an economic one.

Most farmers are now integrated into society and have become businessmen. They still have their own lobby, like lawyers, or doctors, and their own specific problems: but they are less corporatist than they used to be. For example, they will now less often try to prevent dedicated outsiders from entering the profession. I know an educated young Toulousaine who wanted to go into farming, so her well-to-do father bought her a 50-hectare sheep farm in the Dordogne, which she now runs herself. 'The older farmers were amazed, and they still can't take me seriously – what? a *girl* from a *city*, breeding sheep? The younger ones, too, were suspicious at first. But they fully accept me now they see that I am trying to be a serious professional like them.' However, farmers are still strongly opposed to 'unserious' part-timers. One farm owner in five has another, full-time job: usually these are people living near towns, who work in an office or factory but use their old property for their family needs, with maybe some vines, a few cows and vegetables. As in Germany, where the practice is far commoner, the Government favours part-time farming, which it sees as a means of alleviating urban unemployment. But real farmers are indignant at these 'dog-in-the-manger amateurs'. Even more they dislike the firms or individuals in towns who acquire a farm, then install a manager to run it for them: these absentee landlords are so strongly opposed by the farm unions that they are still very few. But there are signs that the trend may grow.

Above all, smaller farmers are worried that the new global competition will inevitably favour large-scale industrial farming at their own expense. It is ironic that just when the family farm has largely completed its own revolution – social, economic and technical – it should now be threatened by these outside forces. The issue has set some small farmers against the big ones – a conflict at its sharpest in north Brittany. Here Alexis Gourvennec, former radical champion of the small grower, has evolved over the years into a prime advocate of big-scale capitalist farming, even if his giant pig farm is still a family business. He has clashed with the local firebrands of Coopération Paysanne, who raided and damaged his new piggeries and have even rallied enough support to win control of the Finistère branch of the FNSEA – this, in Gourvennec's own heartland! One of their leaders, with a smallish dairy farm, said to me in 1997, 'We want ceilings put on grants, to help limit the size of farms. The CAP reform did the opposite – a catastrophe.' But Gourvennec scoffed: 'These silly Leftists have their heads in the sand. Farming is now a business like any other, so it must follow economic rules and the law of the most efficient. A farmer has a right to expand, like any industrialist. If the car industry were made up of thousands of small producers, how could it survive? Finistère still has thousands of small farms that will have to die, and it's silly to go on urging the young to settle.'

The same dispute erupted in 1996 within the leadership of the FNSEA itself, where the 'productivist' ideas of the large farmers were openly contested by a 'ruralist' group. Michel Fau, a pig breeder in the Aveyron, summed up to me the 'ruralist' position: 'For these big barons, what matters for French farming is being competitive on world markets. But *we* believe that agriculture also has a human role; to provide jobs enabling lots of farmers to remain in the rural world and keep it alive. It would be terrible if the land became too depopulated. The CAP reform, and its low-price policy, may help exports but it harms the countryside, by increasing the gulf between large and small farmers. The excellent McSharry proposals were betrayed. This is true especially in cereals; and the milk quotas, too, encourage farmers to buy up more land, so as to get more quotas. In livestock, it's not so bad, because the headage subsidies are limited to 100 animals per farm.'

The argument against excessive depopulation is a strong one. But if small farmers are to be helped to stay on the land, how is it to be paid for? One answer could be for some of them to diversify, maybe into crafts or rural tourism. But even within agriculture, a small farmer can become so efficient a producer that he, too, is fully competitive. Many experts today believe this, and hold that part of the answer lies in greater specialization. That is, while bigger farms continue their capitalist expansion, smaller ones should concentrate on specific quality produce that can find niche markets, both at home and abroad. And this, it is argued, corresponds to changes in consumer habits. Shoppers are becoming more choosy, more concerned with quality, whether for reasons of health and hygiene or of physical taste: witness the trend to better-quality wines, or the belated move in France towards organic produce. In response, many hypermarkets have successfully opened specialized counters with higher prices alongside their routine cheaper offerings. And the FNSEA and Government alike are urging farmers to put more stress on the value-added, and on prestigious local *produits du terroir*. For domestic or export markets, these might include specialized poultry, or charcuterie, or even foie gras where amazingly France has a deficit and imports from Israel and Bulgaria. Or indeed some of France's 300-odd different cheeses, thirty-six of which have their own *appellation*, like wines. Witness, for example, the success of the new Laguiole cheese cooperative in the Massif Central, which has saved eighty local farms from ruin (see p. 413).

This trend towards specialized quality could save thousands of farms across France. But its impact is bound to be limited. It cannot possibly solve the whole problem of the more remote areas and the smaller farmers. Most of them today remain anxious. They have digested the CAP reform and the GATT accord. But they are wary of the next round of GATT talks, and of the opening up of the EU to eastern countries like Poland, with its huge low-cost farm sector. In fact, they are fearful of the whole trend towards the globalization of agriculture, and in 1999 they were again demonstrating violently against American commercial practices.

One of their spokesmen is Raymond Lacombe, an ally and contemporary of Debatisse. He is a stocky peasant with a smallish dairy farm in the Aveyron (and a *polytechnicien* son with a doctorate from Stanford); and like Michel Fau he represents a 'ruralist' view within the FNSEA, of which he was president in the late 1980s. I revisited him in 1997: 'Basically, we have saved the family farm, but I'm worried about its future. The new world trends have been creating a *sauve-qui-peut* outlook among farmers, which goes right against the spirit of cooperation we built up after the war. Farmers believe that productivism will triumph, so they keep trying to get bigger, and push the smaller ones aside. It could ruin this region' – and he took me on to his balcony, above a rolling landscape of little fields and farmsteads. 'To keep this lovely countryside from becoming a desert, we need plenty of small farmers to stay. I have founded a national movement to fight against rural depopulation and the growing urban concentration. We farmers are *de facto* the guardians of nature. Perhaps we should get paid for it.'

So today there are two related problems. First, if very large capital-intensive modern farms replace the small ones, this might add to efficiency, but would also damage the fabric of rural life. Secondly, in a new era of high productivity, a biggish country like France no longer needs so much land for agriculture. In the poorer upland areas at least, more of it should now be turned over to other uses, including industries, crafts, etc., in the villages and townlets. And should not farmers be encouraged to stay, diversify, and take part in this activity? The EU is now thinking along these lines. It is a debate that ties in with changing French attitudes to the countryside, as new urban generations vaguely dream of 'a return to nature'.

BACK TO NATURE:
THE CRUSADE TO SAVE THE RURAL 'DESERT'

The hilly Aveyron, in the south of the Massif Central, is typical of those *départements* of rural France that have been steadily losing population – from 415,000 in 1886 down to 270,000 at the 1990 census. So many young people have left that there are more deaths than births. However, the past twenty or so years have seen signs of a new spirit, and of change. The decline in population has now almost levelled off. Some Aveyronnais have even returned from Paris to start up new industries, in what is not a poor area. And a few dynamic farmers and business people have set about trying to revive their *pays*.

The star case is Laguiole (pronounced 'lai-yóll'), a townlet on the rolling Aubrac plateau, by the main road through the wilds from Toulouse to Clermont-Ferrand. Here farmers have created a big cooperative to make and market the local cheese, creamy and tangy, a bit like Cheddar. What's more, the local knife-making industry has been reborn, and gastronomy and tourism are booming, too. The driving force is André Valadier, a dairy farmer now in his sixties, a burly, handsome man of great energy and charm. 'When we started our cooperative,' he told me, 'people said we were crazy and the famous Aubrac cow was just folklore. But if you love your *pays*, you must work to improve the quality of its produce. The Aubrac strain was fading away, and Laguiole cheese, too. So we bred new Aubrac and bought new strains, and we put the cows on to grass where they can ruminate: it improves the quality of their milk. There's a local saying: "For the cheese to be good in its rind, the milk must be good in its pee. For the milk to be good in its pee, the cow must be *bien dans sa peau* [at ease]. For the cow to be at ease, she must also be happy in her *pays*." Here, I think she is.

'When the milk quotas came in, at first we didn't have nearly enough, so we urged our members to cheat and overproduce, and the cooperative paid their fines. Then, by gaining an *appellation* for our cheese, we got extra quotas. Now we have this big modern cheese factory: a hundred local farmers bring us their milk, we pay them well, our cheese sales have risen thirtyfold, to 750 tons a year – and these dying uplands are reborn. We have saved eighty farms. My own sons, and one has a posh degree, are keen to take over mine when I retire.' In the town square he showed me the bronze statue of an Aubrac bull, dating from 1947, the fallow period: 'We used to call it "*le monument aux morts*". Now it's the symbol of our renewal.'

Some of the cheese is sold to make *aligot*, a simple local speciality of cooked cheese and bread, a bit like fondue. Seven new restaurants in Laguiole now put it on their menus ('We *inflict* it on our tourists!'). Much the most renowned is that of Michel Bras, who taught himself to cook in his father's local café, then opened a restaurant. This now stands on a hill above town, very luxurious, with striking modern design, and is the most prestigious in the region (two Michelin rosettes). Bras is passionate about his creative use of every kind of local produce, and he draws a trendy clientele from Paris and further afield. Laguiole, fancifully called 'the St-Tropez of the Massif Central', now draws some 250,000 tourists annually. They come also to buy its famous knives. This elegant small farmer's knife, Spanish in origin, its handle made of bull's horn, was produced here from the 1820s, but recently the industry died away. In 1983 it was revived under local impulse – rather like the cheeses – and today a new factory employs 180 people and sells 250,000 knives a year. The trendy Parisian designer Philippe Starck is involved. And the knives are sold by twenty-five shops in Laguiole, where the population has risen and a new school has opened.

'The triumph of Laguiole shows *la force d'un site*, the power of genius loci,' says Valadier. 'Today, when other values prove illusions, urban society needs a rural *terroir* as a value to cling to – and that's what we offer. We have proved the worth of partnership between agriculture and other dynamic local forces: farmers were wrong to be corporatist for so long. Nor should we be defeatist about the handicaps of our mountain isolation. It is silly to expect everything to come from Paris and Brussels: they can provide oxygen, but the rest comes from our own energy.' Laguiole is exceptional: in few other places has local initiative borne such fruit. But it has set an example.

Another sign of local renewal is the trend for some Aveyron *émigrés* to return and work in their homeland, if they can: it is the rural exodus in reverse. Consider the remarkable case of Michel Poux. His parents were small farmers who found it hard to make a living in the uplands near Rodez, Aveyron's capital. When he was seven they moved to Paris, where he had a technical education and got a good factory job. 'But my *idée fixe*,' he told me, 'was always to return to live here, *dans mon pays*. I loathed Paris. I would come on holiday to my grandparents and only here amid these gentle hills did I feel alive.' But there was too little industry in Rodez to suit his skills; he tried in vain, repeatedly, to get a job. Finally, he took his courage in his hands, built a house near Rodez on a mortgage, and started a workshop on the ground floor, producing machinery parts. Against the odds, he succeeded. He gradually expanded, and in 1991 built an imposing new factory outside Rodez, with a staff of 120, making motor parts for Bosch, Ford, St-Gobain and other big firms. 'With our light precision products, we don't need much heavy freight, so we are little handicapped by our isolated location. And I still have this happy feeling of being all the time on holiday! Nor am I the only case. My brother and his wife had a prosperous small business in Paris, but they've moved back here at a lower income. They couldn't stand any more commuting – *métro, boulot, dodo*.'

For the Aveyron, after a century of emigration, this is a revolution. There are still more Aveyronnais in Paris than back home. It was normal for the bright ones to emigrate, men like Marcellin Cazes, who arrived penniless and illiterate in Paris in the 1920s and later became the famous owner of the brasserie Chez Lipp. But Aveyronnais also retain a loyalty to their *pays* that is exceptional even by French standards. One Paris industrialist, needing to relocate his factory, chose Rodez because that was where he came from. Traditionally, Aveyronnais went to Paris to work in cafés, or run cafés: but recently the Paris café trade has been in recession, so some *émigrés* have now returned.

Other parts of rural France can tell similar stories. The message is clear: the growth of cities has produced a reaction since the 1970s, as *déracinés* ex-peasants crave a return to their origins, generally not to the farms where scope is now limited, but maybe to smaller factories or offices near their beloved *terroir*. The numbers involved in this new urban exodus are only a few tens of thousands, but they mark a shift in French attitudes towards rural areas. And the rise of urban unemployment, plus the problems of *la banlieue*, have intensified the vogue. So there are two opposing currents of migration: some wilder areas are still depopulating, but in others new inhabitants are arriving, eager to create new kinds of activity, if they can. For example, one young engineer from Toulouse opened an electronics workshop with a staff of twelve in a village of the upper Lot valley.

Even within the Aveyron, the pattern varies greatly. It has impressive modern roads and big new shops; Rodez (pop. 45,000, with suburbs) is a prosperous city with some sizeable industries, notably Robert Bosch. Unemployment is well below the national average, and new small firms are still being created. But the lonelier plateaux to the south are full of dying hamlets. Here, as in many other parts of the Massif Central, of Savoy, the Jura and Pyrenees, the population has fallen below the minimum needed for keeping up services and a social life. If the farms become too depopulated, then the village schools and shops close, and churches and post offices, too. It is especially hard on poor elderly people without cars. The young no longer leave so gladly as in the 1960s, but often they have no option. The old remain, and they die off. Go into many areas untouched as yet by tourism or holiday homes, and you find these sad, derelict villages. In one, in Burgundy, a farmer complained to me: 'There are no more local fêtes, for the young are all gone. Some townsfolk bought up farmsteads as weekend or retirement homes: but they found the place so gloomy outside high season that they sold and left. For me, keeping a network of lively, friendly neighbours is more important than getting a larger, richer farm.'

The problem has caught the attention both of public opinion and of the State. In 1975 the Giscard/Chirac Government launched a long-term development programme for the Massif Central, where both those leaders had roots, it so happened. The Socialists then broadly continued the plan, which at first was managed by D A T A R . Since devolution, some aspects of it are now handled by the four regions that share the Massif. But its four main aims remain: (a) To promote small industries and traditional handicrafts, notably those using local materials. This has had some success. (b) To develop forestry and wood industries, in a *massif* whose huge resources are ill-organized. Progress here has been slow. (c) To build new motorways and main roads. Despite protests from ecological groups, this has gone ahead well: in these remote areas, communes usually vie with each for the advantage of a new trunk road. The new A75 *autoroute* cuts through the Massif from north to south, and a huge viaduct is being built over the Gorges du Tarn (see p. 279). (d) To promote tourism, especially the deceptively simple back-to-nature holidays now in vogue with French sophisticates.

Here the Club Méditerranée has set a lead with its upmarket holiday village devoted to horse riding at Pompadour (Corrèze). Elsewhere, old farmsteads are being fitted out as holiday homes; or you can hire a horse and carriage and jog for days down forest paths, like gypsies – very chic. Some farmers find that it adds usefully to their income to convert an old cottage or stable (with the help of state grants) as a *gîte rural* for tourists. City dwellers come eagerly to these country lodgings, and they sometimes form lasting friendships with the farmers; it is one more aspect of the narrowing of the old gulf between *paysan* and *citadin*. I found a farm where for a fee you can spend a week learning how to milk cows, clean their sheds, make hay and practise local recipes – ideal for the weary tycoon. And clever farmers who actually get paid for their extra summer labour!

The tourist season is short in these uplands, and in winter the farming families can face months of relative isolation. The French rural world is only now emerging from a difficult period of mutation between two cultures: the old folk culture now largely vanished, and a new modern one that cannot so easily penetrate to remote villages save through television. In the old days there was poverty, but also a warmth and tradition that helped make it bearable. In Breton moorland farmsteads young people drew round the fire on winter evenings to hear grannies reciting Celtic legends. In some other regions there were *veillées* in winter, where neighbours would gather in one farm to weave baskets or shred maize, and make it the excuse for a party. And at harvest-time there were huge parties for the labourers, whereas today the work is done by combine-harvesters. Folk festivals have been revived in many villages, but this can be self-conscious. Gillian Tindall, in her excellent book *Célestine* (1995), about social change in a village of the Berry, describes a modern festival full of medieval jugglers, bagpipes, locals in blue smocks and lace caps, as well as pony traps, early tractors and an old threshing machine persuaded to function again. The villagers, she writes, were puzzled but gratified 'to find themselves suddenly tourists in their own past'.

Much of the year-round social and other activity has been regrouped in the country towns or the bigger villages – like Laguiole – and a family within range of these has a leisure life now urban in style, as in Britain. One local leader told me, 'We are only five kilometres from Baraqueville, and it's become a lively place, with tennis, a dance club, a big disco and summer festivals. Our own village school is closing, and our younger boy gets picked up by school bus and taken to Baraqueville.' But this existence is relatively privileged. Many hill farms and hamlets are much further from the nearest lively *bourg*; and the local primary school, if it is still open, will have just one class spanning the whole age range. Remote farmers have little to do on winter evenings but watch TV.

In the really isolated spots, could the solution be an American one, where the families regroup in or near the small towns, and the farmer commutes by car to his fields? It is now happening in some places. To study the problem at its most dramatic, we should go to Aveyron's neighbour, the lonely and lovely Lozère, the most appealing, the most individual, of any French mainland *département* that I know.

Lozère, the size of Norfolk, has only two sets of traffic lights. Sheep are far commoner here than people. But the air is pure, the light is clear in this high rolling wonderland, which is luxuriantly green in summer and scenically not unlike the Scottish Highlands, with some of the same problems. Geologically, its northern half belongs to the granite plateaux of Auvergne, where stony pastures alternate with sweeping forests of pine and beech. South, across the upper Lot valley, the landscape is even more dramatic. Here the limestone plateaux of the *causses* are cut by the deep Tarn gorges, while eastward lie the forested heights and narrow fertile valleys of the Cévennes. Here the Cévenol peasants are still in majority Protestant, still aware of forming a kind of enclave, still bitter at the memory of the eighteenth-century wars against the *Camisards*. But today their relations with Catholics are perfectly friendly.

Partly as a result of its historic isolation before the days of train or car, Lozère retains a stronger sense of identity and local patriotism than almost any other French *département*. This is the kind of feeling normally reserved for a region, not an artificial *département* (see p. 297). But Lozériens have their own mountain realm – 'a kind of land-locked, non-violent Corsica', said one newcomer. It is today part of Languedoc-Roussillon: but Mont-pellier is a world away across the Cévennes, and Lozère in practice forms a kind of no-man's-land between Languedoc and Auvergne. Did I say *no*-man? Well, there are a few of the species left, and intriguing they are, too. The locals, of sturdy mountain stock, have been joined by a colourful assortment of newcomers – silk-screen printers, bee-keepers, militant Greens, religious prophets, *fils à papa* fleeing the shame of their wealth.

It is the least peopled of any *département*, with a density of 14 per square kilometre. The population, 140,000 in 1900, dropped to 72,800 by 1990. This drama, coupled with Lozère's unspoilt beauty and peasant character, has made it into something of a cult. Sociologists, reporters, state techno-crats, do-gooders of various kinds, have come to visit or stay. Lozère is a problem child, almost a lost tribe, scrutinized and subsidized as though it were somewhere up the Amazon. The State and the EU have poured in special funding, plus various kinds of priority treatment. Thanks to this, and to their own efforts, many Lozériens today feel that they may have finally turned a corner. The population has started to rise again, by a modest 300 since 1994. Some new small industries have arrived. Unemployment is only 5.5 per cent. And certainly the area does not look run-down. Mende, its tiny capital, is quite a sophisticated place, with smart shops. In summer the tourists arrive *en masse* and the moors and forests are specked with the blue-and-orange tents of *les campings*. But the season is only June to September. Through the harsh months out of season, Lozère can wear a different mask. The simple rural tourism cannot itself produce the extra resources needed to balance an economy still heavily dependent on outside aid.

For the economy, does the best answer lie with more specialized livestock farming? Or with trying to attract more light industry? Or with the development of forestry, which has a big untapped potential and could create jobs? Some 45 per cent of the Lozère is covered with forest, mostly pine, also oak, beech and chestnut. Some forest land belongs to the State, some to big private estates, but mostly it is parcelled out between small owners. Moreover, the land is hilly, not flat as in the Landes, and this does not make large-scale tree-felling easier. Yet there is much that could be done. The national forestry office has been trying to teach the small owners to tend their trees properly, and to persuade them to regroup rationally (as on the farms). But this arouses the usual resistance.

France, despite her big forests, is oddly enough a net importer of both wood and paper by about 30 per cent. The official aim is to increase output, and land under forest is growing by about 1 per cent a year. But in Lozère, most of the wood is of mediocre quality: it is good enough for fencing or timber, but not often for furniture; and today, at a time of world oversupply, it suffers growing competition from Eastern Europe. It should be possible to increase local processing: but in the whole of the forested Massif Central there is not a single wood-pulp factory or paper mill, and Lozère's own wood for pulping has to be sent to a factory in Provence that sets its prices. One plan for a wood-pulp plant was torpedoed by the local population, fearing pollution.

Such reactions can present a problem for those trying to attract new industry. Older Lozériens, maybe living in Paris, want to come home and retire peacefully: they are emotionally opposed to seeing their homeland change, and they find support from the Greens who have settled in the area. But others believe that forestry, farming and tourism will not be enough to 'save' Lozère and industry is essential, too. There are plenty of *cadres* and engineers in Paris who would love to come and work here. And some light industries could be enticed by the local raw materials and greenfield locations. Recently, there have been some successes. One little firm is using local herbs for perfumes; a Swedish company is making wood products from local timber. All such new investments secure generous aid from Brussels; and so do the farms and villages, through the EU's 'Leader' programme for rural development. This, for instance, will give grants to keep a village café or shop alive; and many farmers say that more than half of their gross income is from the EU, in one form or another. Lozère is one of the few French *départements* to be fully included in the EU's '5B' zoning for remote upland areas. And its recent progress is due quite largely to EU aid.

But for how long will Europe be prepared to go on shoring up such areas? In Lozère, only a few fertile valleys are really suited to modern farming. Where the land is poorer, on the wide plateaux, the family farm will always have to struggle. Many people believe that the uplands should be reforested, and tourist amenities and parks developed. But the farmers do not want to leave – and they have some powerful local support. For many years, the pillars of the Lozère rural world have been François and Jeannine Braget, a sympathetic, generous-hearted couple, both from local farming families. He, now president of the *conseil général*, said to me, 'Even if it is costly in terms of roads and so on, it is essential to preserve the human tissue of hamlets and farmsteads that has existed here since pre-Roman times. A solution of regrouping the families in the big villages might work in a wheat-growing area, but not in one of livestock, where the farmer must be near his pastures. Yes, the United States has miles of emptiness, but those are virgin lands of conquest, not of an ancient tradition of habitation. So the nation must help pay to keep the farms going. If the human tissue went, there'd be no more need for Mende, or the prefect, or the bishop.'

One solution preached by the Bragets is pluri-activity. That is why Jeannine set up her cooperative for reviving rural handicrafts, and has urged farming families to practise traditional home crafts in the winter, thus adding to their income. The crafts were dying out, but trained artisans were hired to help the farmers relearn them, using local materials. They make pottery, rugs, baskets, wooden lampshades, iron candlesticks, and so on – mostly in the austere but authentic local style. Members' work is sold in the cooperative's shops in Mende, Paris and Montpellier. The results are modest, but Jeannine Braget is sanguine. 'We want to help people stay in their *pays*, not on charity but through their own work of which they can be proud. It's a renewal of a medieval tradition. And country people are happier than factory workers, so long as they have the basic comforts.' Revisiting her in 1997, I found this sturdy Joan of Arc still in good spirit: 'Lozère today feels less remote and isolated, we have good new roads, and less sense of self-pity. I think we are winning our battle to save Lozère. We have the lowest crime rate in France: I leave my doors unlocked.'

In the 1970s Lozère and some other areas received a shot in the arm from an unexpected source. Thousands of middle-class students and young intellectuals, from Paris or elsewhere, made their bid for a new rural utopia: they gave up their studies, or their jobs maybe as teachers, to opt for a purer, simpler life, scratching a living from hill-farming on a few stony hectares, or from handicrafts, or both. It was a stirring saga, a bit like Arnold's scholar gypsy, and it was typically '1970s'. In the Cévennes alone there were some 2,000 of these '*installés*' (settlers), or '*marginaux*' (drop-outs). '*Les margi-bouseurs*' (*bouse* is cow dung) was the scornful term for them in Latin Quarter circles. But the scorn was often based on jealousy: for every pioneer who made the radical break, there were ten others who dreamed of doing so. Many of the settlers failed and went back home, but some stayed and adapted, and a few new ones have since arrived. The trend has done a little to help revive areas such as Lozère, even if it has led inevitably to culture clashes between *installés* and natives. And some, who came to invent a new autarkic way of life, found that the adventure led them down expected paths.

Witness the strange case of Ginette Lespine, hippy turned *notable*. In 1972 she and a few other Leftist students bought a derelict farmhouse and a patch of land on a steep slope of the Vallée Française, in the Cévennes. Here they set up a commune (in the Anglo-Saxon sense: the French word is *communauté*). The aim was to live in isolated self-sufficiency, rejecting all society. The dozen members shared everything, work, property and each other, while shocked rumours spread among the Protestant peasantry of the free-love lifestyle of these long-haired '*zipis*' (French for hippies). For a while, all went well. But then quarrels broke out within the group – over money, work, relationships – aggravated by their isolation. The rural idyll went sour as they found it impossible, knowing nothing about farming, to make even a subsistence living on this stony hillside. The group split up, most members drifted back to the cities. But four of them decided to stick it out: they divided the property, lived as two separate couples, and decided to try to adapt to local ways. They had goats, rabbits, beehives; they sold cheese and honey, and did weaving in winter. They remained poor, but survived. Ginette, who had come with a *licence* in psychology, obtained a diploma in farming, and won grants for improving the farm.

They came as rebels against society, hating the State and all its works. But then their idealism changed course: they grew sympathetically involved with the Cévenols, and dedicated to helping the area. Dynamic and resourceful, they took the lead in forming a young farmers' cooperative. Above all, Ginette was invited by the local mayor, a Socialist doctor, to join his list. She has become a pillar of local society, municipal councillor in charge of public relations, editing the village news bulletin. And the locals have fully accepted her.

To the Cévennes and elsewhere the settlers came with a variety of motives. The first main influx, in 1968–71, was made up largely of young people disillusioned by the failure of May '68 to change urban society. So they set out to build their own mini-utopias, or they went in hopeful quest of a traditional rural world untainted by the wicked city. And they sought out depopulating areas where land and dwellings were cheap. Some even found a spiritual affinity in the Cévennes, 'a land of historic resistance to Paris', said one. These pioneers were influenced by the counter-culture movements in America, but in France they faced a different situation. America still has vast virgin spaces, as well as a tradition of pioneer settler communities. In France, wherever they went the settlers came up against the ancient tissue of peasant society, as well as a pervasive public administration. They had less freedom of manoeuvre.

The style of group living in communes is not in the French temperament or tradition, and Gallic individualism baulked at the sharing out of property or chores, let alone shared intimacy. Of the commune members who stayed, most ended up living as couples. And today few communes survive, save those with a disciplined religious basis (see p. 586). The early arrivals soon found, too, that hill-farming was not the easy idyll they had imagined. They had no training, and little aptitude, for its daily drudgery. But then other waves of settlers arrived, less dilettante. In the mid-'70s came the ecologists and artisans, with thought-out ideas on how to make a living in the country. Of those who have stayed, most have tended to integrate into local society. In fact, the early utopian vision of a 'return to the desert' to create a counter-society, has steadily given ground to the different ideal of rediscovering an existing rural society and helping it to survive, or else to a simple personal desire to live and work in the country, with no special sense of mission.

Some *installés* have changed their trade completely, like the former TV producer who is now a cabinet-maker. Others brought their trade with them, like the state nurse from Paris who continued nursing, while her husband, an ex-teacher, minded the goats. In a hamlet on the *causses*, I met a couple of screen printers who had tired of working for design firms in Paris, so they came to Lozère, which they knew from their holidays – 'We've simply transferred our job to the countryside, and we're far happier now.' Another case is that of a young *polytechnicien* from the proud Ponts et Chaussées corps: bored with élitist careerism, he put all his money into starting a restaurant in the upper Lot valley, but he failed, so he worked as a labourer in a nearby quarry. As an 'X' engineer he was so much more talented at quarrying than anyone else around that with a loan he was able to buy up the quarry, and grew prosperous. But I also found some authentic bourgeois drop-outs, like the failed writer and his arty-crafty wife living in a derelict cottage and surviving on hand-outs from their shocked but indulgent parents. 'Our only motivation is sheer laziness,' they said cheerfully. I found them gentle, relaxed, amusing, seemingly happy. And when I asked the kindly Jeannine Braget about these 'parasites' in her Lozère, she said, 'I am fond of that couple. Laziness has its own moral value. And Lozère has room for all types.' In fact, almost all the many *installés* I met seemed to me remarkably amiable, tolerant and friendly, so different from what they might have been in Paris.

The reactions of the natives to the settler invasion have varied. At first it came as a cultural shock to these good peasants who had lived in isolation for so long. They were horrified at the idea of group sex and drug addicts defiling their virtuous valleys; a few mayors even held up the supply of water and electricity to the communes. Some of the early settlers also made clumsy attempts to 'civilize' the locals with avant-garde theatre shows ('we played Mayakovsky on the farms') or by trying to convert them to organic farming. But the conflicts subsided, and most settlers told me the same story: 'Like all mountain folk, the Cévenols may be suspicious of outsiders, but they also respect hard work. Once they see that we are here to *work*, they accept us.'

Some ambivalence persisted, however, for the Cévenols have seen the settlers both as a threat and an opportunity. 'They're so ready to help;

they've given this village a new lease of life: thanks to them the school won't be closed down', has been one reaction. But another might be: '*Our* kids have had to leave home to find work, and here are these newcomers taking over the land. With their degrees, they could have had good jobs in town – why come here begging for subsidies?' What has puzzled and often angered the Cévenols is that the settlers came rejecting those same urban values which they themselves had been taught to respect as their life's goal. To win a good diploma, to find a salaried job, to improve your social status, your speech, your dress, to acquire consumer gadgets, to become more like townsfolk – this had been the trend of the French peasantry since the war. And now, townees arrived turning all this on its head. While country people ape town values, people from the city ape what they suppose to be country ones – all very bewildering! The more sensitive *installés*, aware of the dilemma, tried to be tactful. 'When our neighbour said how thrilled she was that her son had just passed his *bac*,' one of them told me, 'we said yes, yes, how lovely, and kept back our views on the absurdity of the whole *bac* rat race that we've rejected.'

Several settlers are now mayors, or they run welfare centres or clubs for old people. But many prefer to stick within their own little colonies, especially the professional artisans. Some would-be farmers tried at first to live in autarky, rejecting all dependence on a market economy or even public utilities. But they soon found this did not work. So they had to take training courses, or seek help from the SAFERs, if they were to make a go of farming. François Braget, once director of the Lozère SAFER, told me, 'These newcomers can be a real asset. They can help to recultivate dying areas, they can give new heart to our own youngsters and encourage them to stay.' And Dr Monod, the mayor who brought Ginette Lespine on to his council, agreed: 'After our steady fall of population, new blood is essential. After their brave battles across the centuries, the Cévenols had been growing defeatist, they felt their home-land was doomed; some were giving up the struggle, selling off their land or houses cheaply. But now the mood has been changing, partly thanks to the *installés*. They have shown that success *is* possible here.'

Some settlers have been collaborating with the state-owned Parc National des Cévennes, whose officials have carried out intelligent policies of conservation and land restoration. Settlers often find much in common with these technocrats, many of them also radical idealists in their way. But the irony is not lost on the newcomers: they came to avoid the State and have ended up its accomplices – is this necessary pragmatism, or a betrayal of ideals? One said, 'We fled as far as possible into the heart of the forest, and what do we find here but the State.'

Today, in the late 1990s, the new *émigrés* from the towns are less numerous, and few are motivated by any special idealism. They come for more practical reasons, to escape from urban unemployment or the tensions of *la banlieue*, or simply because they fancy country life, with its lower living costs and gentler rhythms. Many are from working-class milieux. They manage to survive on the RMI, or by doing odd jobs.

Yet there are still a few new arrivals of the older kind, today known as '*les néo-ruraux*'. On a remote plateau of the Cévennes, in 1997 I visited Philippe Galzin, young graduate from Montpellier and son of a business executive: he and his wife Catherine took over a big ruined farmhouse, converted it, and now run it as a *ferme-auberge*. They produce poultry, lamb, honey, fruit and vegetables, and sell this to their guests. They have three adopted Tahitian daughters, all at local schools – 'And we're delighted to find that there's no racist feeling among these Cévenol peasants,' said Galzin. 'We do feel a sense of vocation to revive this area. We have persuaded some local farmers to start *auberges* or *gîtes*, and have encouraged some outsiders to settle here as we have done. So the population has at last been rising again.' And on the Larzac plateau, veterans of the 1970s campaign against the army (see p. 279), most of them Greens or other militants from the north, have bought up farms and established a kind of colony. Here some of them organize cultural events, social work, political debates, and they champion local environmental causes. 'I am peasant, hotelier and *animateur politique*,' said one, from Picardy.

So what is to be the future for rural Lozère, and other such remoter areas? In 1996 the EU Commission came up with proposals for the funding of non-farm activities in some of these places, and for paying farmers to stay and take part. It was just what some French leaders had been proposing. But Europe's richer farm lobbies opposed the scheme, fearing that it would mean a reduction in funds for their own direct grants.

Even so, it seems inevitable that the future will lead this way, with or without any special EU aid. In France, farmers in areas like Lozère accept that a rural economy must become less dependent on farming alone. They are suspicious of theme parks, vulgarizing the countryside: but they have grown readier to take part in other kinds of tourism and pluri-activity, as well as in specialized farming for niche markets. In today's age of fax and Internet, it should be possible for many a small modern business, not dependent on heavy transport, to succeed in the countryside or in villages – and some have done so. It enables refugees from urban stress to realize their dream of country living. Or farmers and their families can themselves take part in such activities. In any case, depopulation can only be halted by using the country for other purposes, as less land is today needed for cultivation, and as farms continue to grow fewer and larger. The ideal of a network of little farms is no longer realistic. But nor do the French want too much of their country to be given over to large-scale industrial farming, or to endless forests for wood pulp, or empty nature reserves. France is not destined to share the vast silences of Wyoming.

6

CULTURE AND INTELLECTUALS:
VIGOROUS PERFORMING ARTS –
BUT WHERE IS THE NEW CREATIVITY?

On the opening day of the World Cup, the French authorities held a stylishly exotic parade in central Paris, costing 50 million francs. There were dragons, ostriches, dancing orange fireballs, 20-metre plastic giants weighing 38 tons, 4,500 extras and much else – all to show that in France sport is not complete without culture too, of a sort. Just before the final match, 300 fashion models of Yves Saint-Laurent then paraded on the pitch. Previously, Mitterrand had endowed Paris with some lavish modern architectural works, as part of his plan for a French cultural renaissance. In short, the French can still dazzle with spectacular style, when they try. Yet where are the new creative novelists, playwrights and painters of real quality? Or the new philosophers?

In France, more than in most countries, this seems to be the age of the performing arts, rather than of profound individual creation. Or rather, as some might see it, much of the best creativity is now of a different kind. Instead of the solitary poet or painter producing great works in his study or studio, the accent today is on eager innovation by little groups of actors, dancers and musicians, or workshops of sculptors, weavers, decorators, video directors, all in close touch with their public. It is a culture that is less philosophical or spiritual, maybe more ephemeral, and certainly more social, than the classic one. And it is encouraged by the strong tradition of state patronage of the arts, which has spilled over into helping all kinds of local activities.

The revival of the performing arts, and of enthusiasm for them, dates from just after the war, when theatre in the provinces had a striking renaissance. Then came André Malraux's *maisons de la culture*, and then, in the 1960s, the new blossoming of musical activity, in a nation formerly not so concerned with music. Museums and art exhibitions, too, have been attracting wider attendances. And yet, I repeat, where are the major new playwrights, novelists, poets or artists? Even the cinema, though still Europe's most active, is no longer in the golden age of the *nouvelle vague*. And although television has been freed from state control, this has led it into a dull commercialism, rather than down fertile creative paths as in Britain.

Of course, this whole situation is not unique to France. In the 1995 edition of my book *Germany and the Germans*, the parallel chapter bears much the same title, 'lively activity, low creativity'. And maybe it is hard to judge one's own age: were not critics in the past complaining that Impressionism was killing art, or that cinema would kill theatre? But in France the cultural staleness today seems pervasive, and many French will admit to being worried about it. In philosophy and literature, as in the classical arts, France no longer appears as the champion of the West, the unrivalled powerhouse of new ideas, new expression. The leadership has passed on – maybe to New York, or even London. And French writing and thought have lost much of their old radiant universality, as the humanism of Camus or Gide yielded first to the arid algebra of structuralism, and today to a loquacious parenthesis on the Paris intellectual scene.

The reasons are not so clear. It may be that the arts and ideas, in any country, flourish best either in a time of serene prosperity, or under oppression or austerity, but not in a time of economic transition, social change and unease, as France is still experiencing. One left-wing writer suggested to me, 'Since the 1950s the ruling bourgeois élites have opted for the economy rather than culture. In former days many senior diplomats, for example, were also writers – Saint-John Perse, Claudel and others. But ENA has killed all that. It turns out automata who are not interested in culture save for the snob value of a visit to the opera.' That may be true of some. But today many more French people, mostly young, have been turning away from the old gods of technocracy and economy, towards quality of life, serious ideas, fulfilment through private enjoyments. They would be fertile soil for a true cultural revival. Various small-scale novels and films, sensitive, personal and humanist in the French manner, but not ambitious, are still appearing – I could cite Robert Guédiguian's tender uplifting movie *Marius et Jeannette*, or Marie Darrieussecq's provocative fantasy tale *Truismes*. Who knows where the trends might lead? 'The present negative phase may be valuable. I'm full of a *pessimisme joyeux*,' one intellectual, Yves Hersant, told me in 1997.

STATE PATRONAGE:
JACK LANG'S SHOWY FIREWORKS, A HARD ACT
TO FOLLOW

After Malraux's forceful reign in 1959–69, the State's effort for the arts declined, and under Giscard's presidency the Ministry of Culture's share of the national budget fell from 0.61 to 0.47 per cent. But Mitterrand, a deeply cultured man, arrived with the stated aim of promoting a renaissance: he planned to make full use of state patronage of the arts, a tradition in France since Colbert's day. He was pledged to doubling the culture budget, and gradually he did so: the figure went up to 0.76 per cent for 1982 and by 1986 it had reached 0.92 per cent, some 10 billion francs (for 1998 it has nudged up to 0.97). It was a remarkable policy in a time of recession when most European Governments were reducing their support for the arts. Mitterrand had national prestige in mind: note his architectural projects for Paris. But he and his amazing young Culture Minister, Jack Lang, were guided by other motives, too. Lang wanted to popularize the arts, to bring them closer to daily lives. He also hoped that a better cultural climate might stimulate new creative work and revive the flagging French genius. But that could be harder to ensure.

Mitterrand was a traditionalist and literary man. But Lang, then in his early forties, had modern tastes, exuberance and a sympathy for the desires of a younger generation. As a student he had founded the Nancy experimental drama festival. Later he ran the Théâtre de Chaillot in Paris and entered politics, becoming a personal friend of Mitterrand. He came to power brimming with ideas, some sane, some zany – what a contrast he made to the smoothies who had been ministers under Giscard! He was a bit of an erratic maverick, given to a hyperbole that could make his critics snigger, as when he joyously proclaimed to Parliament in June 1981, 'The French have crossed the frontier separating darkness from light!' But around him he did create an infectious mood of enthusiasm in the cultural world, among professionals and public alike. His role under Mitterrand was compared by some to that of Malraux under de Gaulle, for both of them believed in the mission of the State as guide and evangelist: but there were big differences of style between Malraux the lofty mandarin and whizz-kid Lang, who told me, 'The basis of our thinking is that *all* the arts matter, even minor ones, and culture must be truly popular.' So he extended state patronage to spheres it had previously ignored. He set up a school for circus performers, a costume museum in the Louvre, a school for photography at Arles, a gastronomic institute in Lyon; he helped the traditional porcelain and tapestry-weaving industries; he put money into jazz, rock, *chanson* and variety. He gave some help to individual creative artists, but he put a bigger stress on the performing arts, and on 'participation' of all kinds, including amateur activities. He made a special effort for museums and for public lending libraries, badly developed in France.

Lang was an unusual politician, loved by many, derided by some. With his shock of black hair, his film-star good looks and his love of fine clothes (pink shirts, Thierry Mugler suits), he cut something of a dandy figure; he still lives in a big lovely flat in the fashionable Place des Vosges, and as Minister of Culture he surrounded himself in public with a coterie of trendy actors, singers, writers and artists. It was radical chic, what the French call '*la gauche caviar*': but it was linked to hard work and real dedication. He could be too outspoken, even vulgarly show-off; and he and his assertive wife ('*la mauvaise Lang*' to her critics) were sometimes accused of manipulating cultural figures for political ends. But although by nature polemical, he was not over-sectarian in his choice of causes to support. And he became hugely admired abroad: before the 1986 elections, some hundred celebrities including Samuel Beckett, Ingmar Bergman, Graham Greene and Arthur Miller, signed a petition praising his policies for breathing new life into the arts and urging that they be continued. In France, opinion polls showed him to be the most popular of Mitterrand's ministers; and he in turn made the arts more popular, proving that they could win votes. But how far did he, or could he, stimulate a rebirth of true creativity? Certainly, there was a new groundswell of innovation and experiment, notably in performing arts such as modern dance, and in areas such as sculpture and tapestry. But, as Lang knew well, the rare jewel of genius cannot be produced by state decree, nor even by state funding. Of a revival in literature, play-writing, painting, even cinema, there was not much sign in his time.

His top priorities were elsewhere. 'What we have done,' he told me, 'is to give a mass of local people, in all the arts, the feeling that society appreciates them. This is as valuable as the money we grant.' He was more interested in this grassroots work than in helping the venerable institutions: he rather neglected the Comédie-Française. As his director of the visual arts, Claude Mollard, wittily suggested to me, 'The French love to create Orders, such as the Order of Architects, but these formal bodies tend to sterilize creativity, so that an avant-garde then rises up against them, as the Impressionists did in the nineteenth century. Our aim at the ministry has been to dis-order French culture – to promote what Lang calls "*un désordre créateur*"!' Indeed some disorder usually trailed in the wake of Lang, not the most methodical of organizers.

He was Culture Minister for the two full terms of the Socialists' ten years in office, 1981–6 and 1988–93. The first was his main period of innovation; in the second, he tended to repeat himself. 'With my huge budget, and my direct line to my friend in the President's chair, I had all that I'd ever dreamed of to fulfil my ideals,' he told me later. So what is his legacy today? Some 5,000 local associations of all kinds benefited from his largesse, as well as over 500 professional theatre groups. And some critics accused him of extreme *saupoudrage*, the wasteful scattering of resources – 'He subsidizes everything that moves,' wrote *Le Point* – while others felt that his ministry was too meddlesome. Today in some towns I have heard the view that by helping so many little troupes, so many projects, Lang served to create more activity than the public could sustain. 'Here in Grenoble,' said one official, 'we have far more theatre and music groups, more galleries and so on, than audiences can cope with. So many of them are doing badly. This has been partly Lang's fault.' But though he may have painted with too broad a brush, his overall legacy in the arts has undoubtedly been positive.

The centre-Right ministers after Lang put less stress on the kind of fringe or experimental ventures (e.g. graffiti art) that he had promoted. But in many other ways they continued his main policies. After all, they were ambitious men, and they felt that if Lang had won such popularity through helping the arts, then they could, too. Yet his was not an easy act to follow, and they lacked his charisma. François Léotard, in the *cohabitation* period of 1986–8, cut back slightly on the live arts: but he did put a new emphasis on *le patrimoine*, i.e. the restoration of old buildings and monuments, which Lang had somewhat neglected. Being a free-marketeer, Léotard also urged performing bodies to seek more help from '*le sponsoring*' by local firms – a system that is not in the French tradition and has still not caught on widely.

Jacques Toubon, under Balladur, was a good minister who kept Lang's major policies going. Then Philippe Douste-Blazy, under Juppé, was more controversial. This charming young doctor was full of generous promises which he seldom carried through: one reason was that all ministries were now under heavy pressure to make cuts, and this time culture was not spared. Its overall budget was not reduced greatly: but as the ministry's scope was extended to new services (architecture was transferred from the Ministry of Equipment), the butter had to be spread more thinly. The main cuts were in *le patrimoine*, while the performing arts suffered less: but many theatres and music groups had their grants frozen or reduced. Cultural leaders and artists growled and held protest rallies, but to no great avail. Notably, some 100,000 part-time performers and freelances, *les intermittents*, were menaced by a scheme to abolish their special dole/insurance system: without it, they felt that they could not survive in their precarious world. So they staged sit-ins in theatres and arts centres. They won a reprieve, but by mid-1998 the issue was still not finally solved. All in all, the cultural mood in the Douste-Blazy period was not bright. And Chirac himself has never been known as a major champion of culture – save for his love of poetry, military music and African art.

When Jospin came to power he chose Catherine Trautmann, who as mayor had done so much for culture in Strasbourg (see p. 438) and had a high reputation. But as minister she then disappointed even many of those who shared her Socialist views. She promoted a new law to protect the diversity of television, and she made administrative changes within the ministry. But she was given little money for major new schemes, and seemed to lack any clear vision or ability to inspire: so there was no return to the *élan* of the Lang era. Trautmann's main struggle was to sustain the great effort made by the State in the provinces.

IN THE PROVINCES: MALRAUX'S '*MAISONS*', AND TODAY'S HIGHBROW VERSUS LOWBROW BATTLES

Shakespeare in Breton villages, modern dance in Montpellier, avant-garde sculpture in the sombre steel towns of the Nord . . . the list is endless. The cultural scene in the provinces is today ten times livelier than in the old days, when the gulf between Paris and its 'desert' used to be nowhere so evident as in the arts and intellectual activity, and almost any ambitious creative artist or performer, in any field, would make for the limelight of the capital. But the tide has turned since the 1950s.

The growth of universities and industry in the regions has produced big new potential audiences, while the State has weighed in with sizeable subsidies, as one facet of its *aménagement du territoire*, and town councils have followed suit. Two ministers especially, in their different styles, first Malraux with his *maisons de la culture*, then Lang with his more eclectic approach, have left their mark as dispensers of state patronage. But a large part of the trend has been more spontaneous. Paris may still exert its lure: but much of the best theatre and music is now to be seen and heard in the provinces, where many talented artists and producers are readier to make a career. And much of the scene is outward-looking, international, not parochial: a Czech play on tour in rural Normandy, a street festival in Nantes on the theme of modern Argentina or Egypt, a major Spanish art exhibition in Grenoble . . . These are recent examples.

First, in the early post-war years, a few talented young actor-producers decided to forgo the Parisian rat race and set up 'reps' in other cities. It was one token of the rebirth of France in that period, following the inter-war period when provincial theatre was virtually dead, killed by local apathy as much as by the cinema. For these pioneers, the struggle at first was tough: but soon the State and some councils were providing regular grants. In Rennes the Comédie de l'Ouest patiently created an audience for serious drama in a region with little such tradition. It took Brecht, Strindberg and the equally unknown Shakespeare to the far corners of Brittany. Here in the 1960s *Look Back in Anger* and *Waiting for Godot* caused a furore, as Catholics distributed tracts against them: but times have changed, and Beckett is now on the *bac* syllabus. In the 1950s the young Roger Planchon founded his remarkable theatre in the working-class Lyon suburb of Villeurbanne: here he built up a popular audience, staging lunch-hour excerpts in factory canteens and bringing busloads of workers to his theatre amid the HLMs. The bourgeois theatre-goers of Lyon at first ignored this Bolshevik crank. When he became famous and began to do seasons in Paris, they would go to watch him there: but few would venture in their glad rags to sit among the workers on their back doorstep. Planchon was the greatest and most influential pioneer of the provincial revival; and he and his company, still at Villeurbanne today, were honoured by the Government in 1972 with the mantle and title of the Théâtre National Populaire.

Many of the early post-war reps had no adequate theatre, and in many major towns the live arts were very badly housed. This inspired André Malraux in the early 1960s to embark on his grandiose policy of building a network of big multi-purpose arts centres, the notorious *maisons de la culture*. This project was not a total success, and has since been suspended:

but its story is worth telling. The formula was that of state/municipal partnership, with each going fifty-fifty on costs and subsidies, and the *maison*'s artistic director responsible to both patrons. The enigmatic Malraux, successively man of the Left, man of action, visionary mandarin of art and prophet of Gaullism, was a fanatic with his own special ideals, and several of them were evident in his scheme for these arts centres, which, he declared, would enable France 'to become again the world's foremost cultural nation'. (Was he admitting that she had ceased to be so?) It was his lofty aim that the *maisons* should present only works of quality and spread Paris standards across France. His second purpose – and here spoke the man of the Left – was to destroy the notion of culture as a bourgeois preserve and draw a new social class into theatres and galleries. But Malraux, mandarin of art, went further: art was a means whereby the soul attains to God (see *Les Voix du silence*), and so with a Gaullist missionary zeal he sought to colonize the French desert with this divine truth. It was a matter of doctrine that the *maisons* should be highbrow and not offer a place, as some would have liked, for mere entertainment. They were to provide for 'interpenetration of the arts', he said, with many activities under one roof: thus a film lover, once drawn inside, might begin to take an interest in sculpture, or an opera fan in poetry. But this sensible idea did not solve one of the basic contradictions of the whole policy: the highbrow doctrine was hard to reconcile with that of bringing culture to the masses. It presupposed that workers must needs love the highest when they see it, and would flock in. Which of course they did not.

Malraux's doctrine also brought him into conflict with his partners, the town councils, who were well aware that their electors might not be too keen on the austere diet proposed to them. It was to his credit that, regardless of politics, he chose as artistic directors the best talent available, and many were anti-Gaullist men of the theatre. A serious conflict arose at Caen, where the lively director, Jo Tréhard, launched a programme of modern plays, concerts and debates, and picked up an eager student audience. But the older bourgeoisie were furious: their idea of theatre was operettas and boulevard comedies on tour, such as they had before the war. And the right-wing council supported them, with an eye on votes, and began to plot Tréhard's removal. He at first survived by making concessions ('I put on *The Merry Widow*, though I'm ashamed of it,' he told me). But in May '68 he sided with the rebels, and the council found this too much and had him sacked. The State replied by cutting its funds, so the splendid new *maison* became a routine municipal theatre. Jo Tréhard was left gamely trying to salvage his policy in a tawdry church hall in the suburbs. It seemed a local tragedy worthy of Brecht. Some other towns saw similar disputes, either over politics or 'brow', or both – in a land where the provincial public is often no more devoted to 'culture' than in Britain, even if it pays greater lip service to it. In the aftermath of May '68 the *maisons* fell easy prey to the French talent for polarization: the bourgeoisie would denounce them as hotbeds of Leftism, while the *gauchistes* boycotted them as too 'establishment'. The directors were caught in the crossfire.

The quarrels subsided; and after Malraux left, the State's role became less evangelical. But other problems arose. It soon became apparent that these 'cultural cathedrals' had been conceived on too grandiose a scale, and their overheads were too heavy. The biggest ones – at Grenoble, Rennes, Reims and Amiens – had three theatres, huge foyers and galleries, and they required a huge staff. Not only was this costly, but the oppressive scale of the buildings did not make for a warm, inviting atmosphere – one reason why so few workers were drawn to enter these *temples de la culture*. So Malraux's ideal of wooing this class was seldom fulfilled. In 1971 the ministry gave up the policy of building 'cathedrals' in favour of new centres of a more modest kind, and this was continued by Jack Lang in the 1980s. Only twelve *maisons* were ever completed. But Malraux's dream need not be written off as a failure: the surviving *maisons* today, though cumbersome, do present interesting creative work, and they draw good audiences. Most are now called '*scènes nationales*', with a new statute, and essentially they are big regional theatres. They concentrate on plays and dance, plus some concerts and films: but rarely do they offer art exhibitions, or debates or poetry readings, so the 'multi-arts' ideal of Malraux has not quite worked out.

In some towns, the sheer size of the buildings still works against them, especially in a time of budget restrictions. The *maison* at Grenoble, the largest, cost 30 million francs back in 1968 – an unlovely palace of glass and concrete, grander than London's Royal Festival Hall, with a revolving auditorium. The centre at Rennes also has three theatres, a cinema, art gallery, and much else. After a financial crisis, some activities have now been privatized and the staff has been cut from ninety to forty. Even so, as elsewhere, the overheads limit the amount of money available for programmes. At Grenoble, of an annual budget of 50 million francs, some 70 per cent comes from state and local subsidies and 30 per cent (quite a high figure) from the box office. But much of the total goes on staff wages and upkeep, leaving only 35 per cent for artistic creation. Yet such is the stern arithmetic of subsidized culture, as in most countries, that if seat prices are to be kept within reasonable levels, then any performance, however popular, will run at a deficit and need its share of the subsidy. This applies mainly to large-scale drama, orchestral concerts and opera. 'It's an absurd irony,' said one director, 'that we could play *Tosca* to full houses for four nights, but we can't afford it, so we keep the run to two nights – and many of our subscribers can't get seats.' I heard the same story everywhere. Many centres have thus been forced to limit their programming, and hence are used well below capacity – but not for want of audiences. There are many evenings when a centre is closed. At Grenoble I found doors being locked at 9 p.m. as the last customers left the big, uninviting cafeteria; and I compared this with the jolly club-like ambience of some more modest centres in other towns, more attractively designed, with lower costs, thus able to afford more activities. Had Malraux managed the clever feat of turning a cathedral into a white elephant?

So is the answer to raise seat prices drastically? Or to open the *maisons* out to wider uses, so as to share overheads? Under Lang, less of a highbrow than Malraux, the centres were encouraged to broaden their programmes. They can now invite cabaret artists and pop singers of the more respectable kind, as well as hold jazz concerts, or even hire out rooms to business conferences. But amateur dramatics and singing clubs are still taboo: the argument, very un-British, is that professional and amateur standards must be kept distinct. Touring commercial shows are also rarely allowed: 'This could damage our image and confuse our public,' I was told in Rennes; and at Amiens I found *The Merry Widow* on tour relegated to a local fleapit, while the *maison*'s larger theatre stood empty. Lang did encourage the raising of prices from a previous very low level: at Grenoble a seat now costs on average 70 francs. Ministers since Lang have continued this policy, urging the centres to become more profit-geared, while accepting that they have a public-service function and cannot charge full commercial prices.

Lang tried a strategy of building up the *maisons* and *scènes nationales* as foyers of artistic creation, mostly in theatre and music, and this has paid off. The centres do not have their own rep companies, but they mount their own productions, using outside talent, or they invite shows from elsewhere. It can be very stimulating. The Rennes centre, now called the Théâtre National de Bretagne (which nation? – a nice ambiguity), is run by François Le Pillouër, an eager, dynamic man, full of ideas. In 1996 his programme included *A Midsummer Night's Dream*, directed by the brilliant Stanislas Nordey; a Marivaux acted in Italian by the Piccolo Teatro di Milano (director, Giorgio Strehler); three new experimental French plays, one directed and partly written by Georges Lavaudant; dance companies from Vietnam and Japan; orchestras from Amsterdam and Armenia; films by Pasolini, Resnais, Kurosawa. 'We have invited directors such as Brook and Strehler to meet our public, to do open rehearsals and transmit their *savoir* – as in the Florentine Renaissance,' Le Pillouër told me excitedly. 'Deborah Warner will do *A Doll's House* with Huppert. We are nothing if not Europe-oriented! And our audience level averages 80 per cent in the three *salles*, totalling 1,600 seats.' In Grenoble the ex-*maison de la culture*, now curiously named Le Cargo, was recently run by a leading choreographer of modern dance, Jean-Claude Gallotta, and is being expensively renovated. Like many of the other centres, it has an international programme and draws large local audiences. Here, at least, Malraux would not be disappointed.

These Malrauxesque ventures are only a small part of the full cultural life of the provinces. Some towns, including Lyon, Strasbourg and Toulouse, have preferred to build their own smaller centres, or to renovate their existing theatres or opera houses. In fact, the balance of the partnership for arts patronage has been shifting in recent years, away from the State and towards local authorities. Under the Defferre reforms, the regional councils now have some responsibility for culture and its funding, while the *conseils généraux* put money in, too. But much larger sums come from the main cities, which since the 1970s have increasingly been taking charge of their own cultural policies, while the State provides support. Here France has been following the model of Germany, where the arts are seen as a focus of municipal prestige and of intense inter-city rivalry. And most leading town councils, especially those in Socialist hands, are far readier than their British equivalents to spend huge sums on culture to suit every 'brow'. In Strasbourg it is 22 per cent of the municipal budget, in Grenoble 18 per cent, in Bordeaux 15 per cent (these figures normally include museums and libraries). And of the total public spending on culture in 1996 (73 billion francs), some 41 per cent came from town councils, 9 per cent from the regions and *départements*, 50 per cent from the State. Of course the odd voice is heard protesting that the sums could be better devoted to schools or housing; or, as 'liberals' argue, that they should not come out of the public purse. But seldom is the spending of ratepayers' money on the arts the electoral suicide that it can be in Britain. Culture is in demand, and is a matter of local pride, a status symbol, like having a good football team. Even the dull industrial town of Maubeuge, by the Belgian border, has put itself on the map with a major annual international festival of music and drama, created in 1987 by a lively local theatre man, Didier Fusillier.

During the past forty years, the cultural map of France has been transformed by the building of new equipment – theatres, museums, concert halls, arts centres – or the renovation of older ones. Malraux gave the first impetus, then Lang followed, urging towns to invest. But some of the movement has been local and spontaneous. Grenoble refurbished its arts scene under Dubedout in the late 1960s. More recently, Lyon rebuilt its opera house and some museums, while go-ahead Montpellier has created a big modern opera house-cum-congress centre. At Toulouse, the conservative but prestige-conscious mayor, Dominique Baudis, has belatedly lavished money on some major new buildings and arts centres (see p. 359). His council also provides 80 per cent of the 120-million-franc subsidy for the classic opera house.

There can be a contrast between the cultural policy of a right-wing town like Toulouse and that of, say, Strasbourg or Nantes, in Socialist hands. Witness the case of Royal de Luxe, a street theatre group in Toulouse that staged provocative 'happenings'. One day in 1996 it took a derelict bus and set it ablaze: the local bourgeoisie were shocked, so Baudis expelled the group. It moved to Nantes where it was welcomed by the Socialists. This city's council has done much to promote popular culture in the poorer suburbs: 'The difference between left- and right-wing councils,' I was told by Yannick Guen, councillor in charge of culture, 'is that *we* try to help the live arts and creativity, while *they* put the stress on buildings and on posh institutions like opera.' Nantes's lively cultural scene today owes much to Jean Blaise, a dynamic *animateur* who runs a civic theatre in an ex-factory. He has also staged 'Les Allumées', a lavish annual outdoor festival of dance, music, song and drama, which each year has taken some far-off city as its theme and invited special troupes – from Buenos Aires, Cairo, St Petersburg, etc.

At Strasbourg, Catherine Trautmann as mayor put the accent alike on élitist institutions and on more populist local activity. She and her team managed to rejuvenate the opera house which had grown stagnant, with an ageing public. She launched a major new museum of modern art, and she helped the famous annual festival of contemporary music. 'As a European capital, the city needs prestigious institutions of high culture,' she told me, 'but we also want to make the arts more widely accessible.' So part of her effort went on creating new popular cultural centres in the workaday suburbs: a former municipal dairy was turned into a popular music venue, geared towards the young. At Lyon, the balance has been different. On the one hand, Guy Darmet's popular modern dance company, state-backed, has done much to help little local dance troupes in the city, and to bring dance to the people. But under Raymond Barre the city council's own emphasis has been more on the costly institutions – to the anger of some radical Lyonnais. 'It's a disgrace,' said one, 'that three-quarters of the city's huge culture budget goes on the opera, orchestra and big theatres, while the many smaller local troupes are struggling to survive.'

So this leads to the issue: what is culture, and whom it is for? Alongside the serious professional work of the main opera houses, theatres and other such centres, the past decades have seen – as in Britain – a flowering in France of all kinds of smaller-scale local activities, often spontaneous or ephemeral. Some are in the modes of pop or rock, rap or jazz. Some are folkloric, based on old regional cultures. And some, more than in Britain, are wordy, intellectual, or avant-garde. Much of this work has been helped and encouraged by town councils, and by the State, especially under Lang. Over 1,000 little troupes of young professional actors have emerged, generally struggling on a shoestring, often short-lived, seldom with a theatre of their own, and Lang gave aid to some 500 of them. In Brest, the Théâtre de l'Instant has for twenty years been operating from a poky little flat, whence the four actors sally forth on their 'civilizing mission', introducing Bretons to Handke, Horvath or Synge. Other groups, with a more populist approach, tour the HLM suburbs with their own home-grown playlets on local life: it is their bid to bridge the notorious cultural gulf that kept the workers away from the 'cathedrals'. At one *maison de quartier* in Rennes, the staff *animateur* created an amateur drama group which wrote and acted a play about housing, with the chorus, '*On a des HLM, Vive la Bretagne!*' These homespun attempts to relate culture to local life may seem old hat to British readers; but in a France long dominated by the reverential approach to '*la culture*' taught in schools, it has all been new and exciting.

In Grenoble's golden age under Dubedout, the councillor in charge of the arts, Bernard Gilman, was a self-educated ex-worker with ideas on how to open culture to the people. His policy, unusual in the 1960s, was to release it from its temple-like enclosures into street and suburb. He launched a summer festival in squares and piazzas, with plays, concerts and even debates on such subjects as abortion reform. He sent *animateurs* into the youth clubs and *maisons de quartier*, where they held street shows, or classes in weaving for Muslim women. And he encouraged mobile groups of professional actors to live for a while in some suburb, then devise plays on its own themes (as in Brittany), expressed in its own language, maybe about housing or delinquency. In a school hall at L'Arlequin, I sat with a working-class audience to see one of these plays, about abortion. It was not exactly of Comédie-Française standard, but it was original. Later, Carignon abolished the Gilman projects, which have not yet been revived. Grenoble's cultural leadership has now passed elsewhere. But Gilman's ventures had a pioneering influence at the time, on some other towns, and on the Ministry of Culture

This for some years now has been placing the emphasis on what is called '*le socio-culturel*'. Especially in the Lang era, its *animateurs* were everywhere, organizing a festival here, starting a pottery class there, granting funds to spontaneous projects. Budget cuts in the 1990s have now reduced this activity a little. But the *animateur* remains part of a key French profession that has no real equivalent in Britain: these are the people who stir up happy activity, strive to break down public apathy. In some places they have been filling the gap left by the declining roles of *curé* and *instituteur*. And rural *animation* takes many forms: in the Massif Central, for example, some *néo-ruraux* (see p. 423) have been given funds for going round youth clubs and social centres, reciting their own poetry or even urging the villagers to write poems, too. But today the main accent is on helping *la banlieue* and its young unemployed. Here Douste-Blazy as minister put 44 million francs into a fund for assisting thirty projects: in some, actors, artists or directors would go to a poor suburb for a period and work with young people, maybe making a film with them, or improvising a play. Comédie-Française actors did this near Paris, and the veteran left-wing director Armand Gatti did the same at Sarcelles. 'Our aim,' said the minister, 'is to open up the world of creativity to youngsters normally excluded from it' – generous words, sincerely spoken. But his critics thought his scheme poorly applied, and a mere drop in the ocean.

This trend to *animation* and popularizing of the arts raises disputes over doctrine. Many people see it as important social work in today's France. But others are more élitist, preferring to offer a more highbrow diet to a narrower audience. And this can lead to clashes when public funds are limited. At La Rochelle, the mayor Michel Crépeau launched an international annual festival of contemporary music, very serious, which won world renown. Then a Communist took over the *maison de la culture*, and claimed that few local workers had much interest in the festival's arty offerings. Crépeau, under pressure, backed down and widened the scope of the event, which today is a big festival of pop and rock. At Grenoble, similarly, the *maison de la culture* under Georges Lavaudant was denounced by the extreme Left as 'run by an élitist clique as a highbrow ghetto, out of touch with popular needs'. Lavaudant, too, was on the Left, but in a Parisian intellectual way – 'He's more concerned by what the Paris critics write about his shows than whether local people enjoy or understand them,' someone remarked. But this arrogant, gifted genius did stage some remarkable avant-garde creations, based on his own texts.

The avant-garde or consciously highbrow does have a larger following in the French provinces than in Britain. In Caen, twenty-five years after the downfall of Tréhard, I found a state-backed theatre doing well with a serious programme focused on the modern German authors much admired in France today. Its director, Michel Dubois, said, 'We've done Kleist, Kroetz and Fassbinder, also Bond and all sorts of neglected "difficult" plays. And we get good student audiences. We even toured fifty Normandy towns with a new Czech play. Tréhard is dead, and his old *maison* is the municipal theatre, showing mere "boulevard" plays on tour. But here we keep his flame burning. You see, there are two ways of doing theatre which just do not meet.' Like the Germans, the French tend to make a sharper distinction than the British between 'entertainment' and 'serious' culture. And in many towns there are sizeable audiences who are curious about what is new or 'difficult', French or foreign.

If one schism is between serious and lowbrow, another, very different, is between classical and modern concepts of culture. Grand opera survives in the French provinces, less than in Germany but far more than in Britain; and some towns relish the status symbol of having their own company or mounting operatic seasons. But this has led to conflicts with those preferring less expensive arts. At Nancy, the old operatic tradition of this historic city had been crumbling, whereas the town had begun to shine in other fields. In 1962 a certain Jack Lang, then a local student, founded an international festival of experimental drama, which became world famous and helped to launch him on his glittering career. Then in 1973 some other young local people started a biennial jazz festival which had almost equal success. Both events secured big civic subsidies. But in 1977 a new mayor took power, an elderly right-wing figure, Claude Coulais, who decided that a revival of opera and ballet would be better for the city's gracious image – and more popular with his own voters – than those messy long-haired types disturbing the place with their noisy music and subversive Leftist drama. Better Berlioz than the Bread and Puppet. So Coulais hired a prestigious new director for the civic opera house, Jean-Albert Cartier, who brought his well-known state-backed ballet company. He renovated the opera company and began to stage lavish productions in a bid to outdo the opera at Strasbourg, Nancy's grander rival. Coulais gave him a 30-million-franc annual subsidy, which meant severe cutbacks in civic support for the two festivals, and the jazz festival had to reduce its scope.

'That bourgeois swine, Coulais, is killing the cultural life of this town,' Lang told me in 1979. 'Ten days of jazz in the streets, giving pleasure to 100,000 people, cost the town no more than the décor for one Verdi production. It's a criminal switch of priorities.' So Nancy became the scene of the sharpest cultural policy conflict in France. Cartier's operas were good, yes, and were popular with a certain public. But the other festivals not only appealed more widely and cost much less: they were also original ventures, whereas Coulais was simply adding one more decent opera-house to the hundreds in Europe. What was the point of Nancy trying to rival nearby Strasbourg? So when Lang became Minister of Culture he was able to take a sweet revenge. He used state funds to rescue the jazz and drama festivals, and he put limits on ministry support for the opera. Today the quarrel has subsided. Under a new mayor and new director the opera survives, more modestly (see below), while the town has a splendid new civic theatre which has taken charge of the drama festival. In all France, jazz, opera and much else today form part of a lively musical renaissance.

MUSIC:
JOYFUL NEW ENTHUSIASMS

Not only does Paris have a grand new opera house and a lively and informal new Cité de la Musique: even a lesser town like Orléans today houses a modern dance troupe, while Montpellier's resident opera company performs everything from Monteverdi to Bartók. After many decades of stagnation, France today is again alive with the sound of music – a revival that has been the most cheering cultural development of the past thirty years. It has even surprised the French themselves, who had come to think that Malraux might have been right when he said, 'France is not a musical nation.' And it has impressed foreign critics: the judicious Peter Heyworth devoted eight columns in the *Observer* of 6 January 1980 to a glowing analysis of the 'remarkable surge of activity in France's musical life'. He commented, 'Music in the French provinces is on the march. *Die Meistersinger* in Toulouse! It's enough to put Bernard Levin off his cassoulet.'

The renaissance has been both at grassroots and élite level. Paris has again become a major city of serious music, thanks in part to Pierre Boulez's return in 1972. But equally striking, all over France, has been the new popular passion for music of all kinds. This was stimulated by massive new official funding, first in the 1970s, then under Lang in the 1980s, if rather less so today: but the popular vogue continues. Not only are the French *listening* to serious music much more than before; they have also shifted back to the tradition of amateur *playing*. Sales of pianos have risen more than sixfold since the 1960s, and provincial *conservatoires* are crowded with eager part-time pupils. So this is a revolution of those who want to be more than passive consumers. At a festival of modern dance in Lyon in 1996, on a Latin American theme, some 200,000 citizens were dancing sambas in the streets.

The musical explosion has been comparable to that in wartime Britain. Standards of performance both professional and amateur are still variable, often mediocre, for France still has leeway to make up after her long neglect. But the enthusiasm is there. New state support has helped: but above all the revival since the 1970s seems to be an expression of the new mood of the French, of that return to private pleasures and fulfilments that is a theme of this book. One musician suggested to me, 'In the post-war decades, until after 1968, the French were preoccupied with ideologies and political issues, and this climate favoured the art forms which best deal with these, such as literature and theatre. But today people shun political idealism: they'd rather seek an inner world. So they turn to an art form that appeals joyously to the heart and senses more than the intellect.'

Two centuries ago France was a leading musical nation. Chopin, arriving in Paris in 1831, said that he found there 'the best musicians in the world'. But the reformers of the 1870s period then starved music of official funds; they gave it only a marginal place in the new school curriculum, so that French schoolchildren were to grow up with virtually no musical education. After 1945 regional *conservatoires* still existed for devotees, but they were run on stuffy academic lines, shutting their doors to any spirit of free enjoyment. Concerts were few and ill-organized. André Malraux, as Minister of Culture, at first did nothing to improve matters. He was not a musical man, and he told Stravinsky that music was 'a secondary art'. His ministry, as all musicians complained, treated this as the poor relation of the arts. Yet it was absurd of Malraux to write off the French as 'not musical': in this *étatiste* land they had simply not been given the training or the means.

Finally, in 1966 Malraux grudgingly did something: he gave music its own department under Michel Landowski, a minor composer, who was to make a huge impact. He, more than anyone, prepared the groundwork for the musical revival. He drew up a masterplan to provide France with a much-needed infrastructure, and during his eight years in office he set about applying it. At first he lacked funds, but after Malraux's departure in 1969 the ministry vastly increased its budget for music: this soared from a mere 11.5 million francs in 1966 to nearly 400 million by 1979. Landowski created twelve new orchestras in France; he promoted a revival of the twelve provincial opera companies; he poured money into renovating and expanding the thirty *conservatoires* and helped to found scores of new ones. Classical in his own tastes, he was criticized by modernists such as Boulez for putting the accent more on quantity than quality, but he felt that he had no choice: French musical life was in so moribund a state that the first priority, he felt, was simply to provide massive new resources.

While Landowski was thus at work amid the grassroots, helping to initiate a local public in the standard classics, in Paris a different type of musical revolution – more avant-garde – was being prepared. In Malraux's day, so great was the official prejudice against modern music that France's major composer-conductor, the serialist Pierre Boulez, was for many years spurned in his own land. To study French serialism, you had to go abroad. And Boulez, furious with Malraux's policy, went to live in Germany, and to conduct leading orchestras in London and New York. But the Government later grew remorseful at having lost such a genius: in 1972 Pompidou personally persuaded Boulez to return and to run an ambitious new research centre for modern music as part of the new Beaubourg arts complex. This Institut de Recherche et de Co-ordination Acoustique/Musique (IRCAM) was opened in 1977. Boulez also set about playing a full part in Paris's musical life (he conducted Berg's *Lulu* at the Opéra); and with his usual dogmatic fervour he began to evangelize the city with his passionately held theories on modern music (see below).

Pompidou's second coup in 1972 was to persuade Rolf Liebermann, the great Swiss manager, to take over the Paris Opéra. Once so glorious, this had been in decline for many years, suffering from feeble management and inadequate funding. It had become a European laughing stock and even its own public was leaving: audiences were down to 69 per cent capacity. Oddly, de Gaulle (maybe under Malraux's influence) never seemed too worried about this blot on French national prestige. But Pompidou cared more for music; and a key element in his overall policy of trying to restore Paris's cultural pre-eminence was to pull the Opéra back to the front rank. The building itself, the sumptuous Palais Garnier, was expensively renovated. And Liebermann, formerly in charge of the Hamburg Opera, was enticed with a huge salary and subsidy to turn down similar offers from Berlin and the New York Met. During his years as artistic manager, 1973–80, Liebermann pursued a policy of hiring the world's leading singers, directors and conductors, at fees often extravagant even by opera standards – and he could do so, for he now had the largest budget of any opera house in Europe. Mostly the policy paid off. Even many foreign critics (but not all) were soon agreeing that the Opéra at its best was again the equal of La Scala, the Garden or the Met. Some productions were superb – for instance, Giorgio Strehler directing *Figaro* under Georg Solti's baton; or, in a rare excursion by the Opéra into the modern field, Patrice Chéreau and Boulez (as conductor) mounting the first-ever production of the full version of Berg's *Lulu*. Some other ventures were less successful. But at least the public returned, as box-office takings moved up to 98 per cent capacity. A night at the Opéra was again the height of Parisian chic.

After Liebermann left in 1980, there followed a succession of artistic managers of no great distinction, and quality became again more humdrum. Much of the best work was done by the resident ballet company, which Nureyev ran from 1983 to 1990. The Opéra itself remained a problem child: its unusually high costs stemmed in part from its notorious administrative and union problems, which managers were never given the brief to solve. It still lumbered under an archaic bureaucracy, whereby the spending of every franc had to be approved by the Ministry of Finance. And the left-wing staff unions insisted on work schedules that made flexibility of rehearsal very hard: for example, a musician had the right to appoint a substitute who had not even attended rehearsals. One day, this so infuriated the conductor, Roberto Benzi, that he threw his baton at the orchestra and walked out. The unions perpetuated an absurd level of overstaffing, and as their members had civil-service status, they could not be dismissed. In addition, the opera house built in the 1860s by the great Charles Garnier, though supremely elegant, had become unsuited to the kind of modern large-scale productions now in fashion. Its backstage facilities were appalling.

These and other factors prompted Mitterrand, with the eager support of Lang and Boulez, to dream up a scheme for an ambitious 'twenty-first century' opera house, that in the right hands could again bring Paris into the first operatic rank. A site was chosen at the Bastille, and an apt opening date was set: 14 July 1989. Designed by the Canadian architect Carlos Ott, this new 2-billion-franc palace would have a big auditorium with 2,500 seats, plus a smaller *salle modulable*. There would also be space for cinemas, exhibition and lecture halls, with the aim that the building should be rather like the Lincoln Center in New York. Work began. But when Chirac became Prime Minister under the *cohabitation* of 1986, he and Balladur wanted to cancel a project that ran counter to their policy of spending cuts. Chirac, too, is no lover of classical music; and though it seemed odd that as mayor of Paris he would want to miss a chance to enhance its prestige, he was also none too keen to abet Mitterrand's personal bid for glory. Other strong lobbies, too, were at work against the project – from older opera-goers who were sentimental about their beloved Garnier, and from the staff unions who realized that the transfer might lead to many dismissals and a weakening of their power.

Chirac was overruled by Mitterrand, who knew that to scrap the scheme would cause an international scandal. But Chirac secured a money-saving compromise: some of the building's planned features, including the *salle modulable*, were postponed *sine die*. The formal opening in 1989 was kept, but performances did not start till later. Today this massive white hulk looms out beside the Place de la Bastille. Inside it is no beauty, and it has not yet found a way into Parisian hearts: but the acoustics are fine, and the backstage is said to be the second largest in Europe, making it suitable for grand productions. These are generally a success. But the plan for a lively multi-purpose venue on Lincoln Center lines has not worked. As for Garnier, whereas the original plan was to use it just for ballet, instead it was lavishly renovated and is now used with success for some smaller opera productions that do not need the Bastille's scope. Parisians are happy with this, and the two houses are run as one company.

When the Opéra Bastille opened, the artistic quality did not immediately revive: the post-Liebermann phase of incoherent policy persisted, with four managers in eight years. But then in 1994–5 Hugues Gall took over. An able, outspoken man with a Bavarian father and Norman mother, he had been Liebermann's assistant, then ran the Geneva opera. At the Bastille, he established himself as a tough administrator, and was able to do something to improve the situation with the unions and his 1,400 staff. But he still had problems. 'We now do Sunday matinées for people from the provinces,' he told me in 1997, 'and I've just endured a four-month partial strike by the stage technicians, who wanted to be paid *ten* times extra for this Sunday overtime. So we had to do our *Lohengrin* with no sets. The staff always seem to think they can gain something by striking, and even many of my musicians seem to have no sense of pride in making this house work. Some singers and players I'd love to sack, they're old and tired: but they have civil service tenure.'

Gall has built up a full repertoire, which the Opéra had lacked for many years. 'My selection is classical, which reflects my own personal taste, but also that of most of my public,' he told me. Indeed, Verdi, Puccini, Mozart or Bizet achieves virtual full-capacity audiences, alike at the 2,700-seat Bastille or the 1,800-seat Garnier; but Britten's *Billy Budd*, less known in Paris, reached only 84 per cent. As yet, Gall has not often tried a modern or controversial work, though in 1998 he premièred *Salammbô*, based on Flaubert's novel, a new opera by the French composer Philippe Fénelon; and this will be followed later by Berg's *Lulu*. The directors that Gall has hired or inherited include Jorge Lavelli (*Faust, The Merry Widow*), Giorgio Strehler (*The Marriage of Figaro*), Robert Wilson (*Madame Butterfly*) and Jonathan Miller (*La Traviata*), and he has built up a fine orchestra. His somewhat conventional policy is certainly popular. Average capacity for the two houses runs at 91 per cent, and as much as 30 per cent of receipts comes from the box office: the subsidy (521 million francs for 1998) is entirely from the State. In short, Gall has revived and stabilized the Opéra, but few of its new productions are brilliant. He has not brought it up to the level it knew under Liebermann, nor to the highest world rank.

The Opéra's smaller rival, the Théâtre du Châtelet, has pursued a more creative and stimulating policy over the past ten years with great success under its dynamic manager Stéphane Lissner. He presented works such as Berg's *Wozzeck*, directed by Chéreau, and some modern operas. But in 1997 he fell foul of politics and was virtually pushed out (Châtelet's main patron is the Paris city council). In part he was victim of the curious feud that has marked French musical life since the early 1970s between the supporters of Landowski and those of Boulez. The former tend to be closer to the Gaullist RPR, and the latter (including Lissner) to the Socialists. And in the mid-1990s the Landowski clan were regaining ground lost to the *bouléziens* in the Lang era. But the feud also cuts across party lines and is more a matter of two approaches to music: paradoxically, Boulez, closer to Lang, appears the more élitist, and Landowski more populist. The quarrel is in some ways absurd, for both approaches are valid, and complementary: while Landowski did a huge amount to revive daily musical life, Boulez brought in new ideas, and opened French music to modern trends.

Even before his return, a small but devoted audience for modern music of various kinds had existed in France for some years: the late Olivier Messiaen lived in Paris, and Iannis Xenakis still does, and their concerts have drawn keen audiences of mainly younger people. Thanks to their groundwork, and more recently to Boulez, modern music has been slowly reaching a wider public. This is still small, but possibly larger than in London, and Boulez's chamber concerts have often drawn 1,000 people. One factor may be the habitual French fascination with the new and avant-garde. But it could also be that the poverty of classical musical education in France has meant that the French are less inhibited in their approach to new concepts of music.

Boulez's great influence has of course been controversial. He created a chamber orchestra for modern music, the Ensemble Intercontemporain, which has been very successful. He also built up his research centre, IRCAM, which includes an experimental studio with mobile acoustic panels: by altering their position, one can change the whole tone and texture of the music. At IRCAM, musicians and scientists have worked side by side in evolving new approaches to music. The centre, handsomely funded by the State, has been criticized as being too esoteric: but today it is widening its scope and becoming more accessible. Boulez himself, now in his seventies, also gets criticized – even by many who admire his work – for his dogmatic manner and his possibly inhibiting influence on some composers who do not share his approach. Yet in a wider sense he has made a huge positive impact by championing new institutions – not only the Opéra Bastille, but the excellent new Cité de la Musique.

This is a large, lively multi-purpose music centre, on the new La Villette cultural site in north-east Paris (see p. 317). Like the Opéra Bastille, it was a Mitterrand/Lang project which under Chirac was nearly cancelled, but Boulez and others managed to save it. Spacious and modern, it has a lovely setting by a broad piazza, and a delightful informal ambience; and it regularly draws large audiences to its varied programme of concerts and other performances. Some of these may be of modern music, but they range more widely, as its director, Brigitte Marger, told me: 'Our aim is to offer diversity and attract a very mixed audience. Some are the bourgeois concert-goers from the *beaux quartiers*, but many are young people who want something more radical and, I'm glad to say, many are poorer people from this working-class part of Paris.' In the fine big *salle modulable*, I attended a superb concert performance of Gluck's *Armide*, with an orchestra from Grenoble; in the same season there was plenty of Bach and baroque, also jazz, *chanson* and marionettes, a flamenco group from Andalusia, and a few Boulez concerts. Marger draws her performers from far and wide; she has no resident orchestra. There is also a splendid new museum, featuring many old instruments.

The Cité is perhaps the best place in town to observe the French musical revival in full swing. Elsewhere, Paris's weakest point is the average quality of the six full-time symphony orchestras. The Opéra's is probably the best, but the others do not reach a high international standard. They suffer from a lack of good modern concert halls, a poor policy of hiring conductors and lack of discipline during rehearsals. Apart from the Opéra, the most worthwhile musical venues are not those with their own orchestras, but the ones that hire performances, often from abroad – like the Cité de la Musique, or the excellent Théâtre des Champs-Élysées under Alain Durel.

*

In the provinces, as in Paris, state and civic money was poured into new musical activity during the 1970s and 1980s, under the impulse of Landowski, then of Lang. And the public responded eagerly, packing out the opera houses and concert halls. Today budgets are a little tighter, but the enthusiasm continues. Lyon and Strasbourg have been in the forefront of the resurgence; also Toulouse, which makes a remarkable case study.

This proud city has a fine musical tradition, notably for opera (*le bel canto*, it is called locally): but by the 1960s this was fustily decadent. The revival was then led by Michel Plasson, a gifted young conductor from Paris who took charge of the city's orchestra, then for a while of its opera company, too. When he arrived in 1968, the members of the orchestra had an average age of sixty-five, and its concerts had thirteen regular subscribers: today the age is thirty and the subscribers number 2,000. The opera plays to over 90 per cent capacity, and keeps up a decent standard; lavishly renovated in 1996, it receives a modest subsidy from the State and a giant 100-million-franc grant from the city council under Dominique Baudis, happy to promote Toulouse's cultural prestige. Plasson also converted a disused hexagonal cornmarket, seating 3,300, with excellent acoustics, and here his Orchestre National du Capitole holds seasons of classical music, with such visiting soloists as Igor Oistrakh. The success has been great: for Plasson's Beethoven cycle, the capacity audiences of mainly young people were larger than for the Rolling Stones. His own taste is conservative, like that of much of his local following: but he has also put an accent on reviving some French composers long neglected in their own country. His orchestra, with 104 members, is among the most highly regarded in Europe. He told me in 1997, 'Despite the current state parsimony, France's musical renaissance is still alive, thanks above all to the eagerness of our younger audiences.'

France's new vogue for opera continues, but amid financial troubles. With ten full-time companies, the provincial scene is livelier than in Britain, but can hardly compare with Germany and its ninety or so companies. Lyon has the best opera, which in 1995 was awarded the status of Opéra National, and its building has been expensively rebuilt in modern style. The Opéra du Rhin, at Strasbourg, also has a good reputation. But elsewhere standards are variable: some companies are frankly mediocre and some towns, as we have seen, have been trying too hard in the battle for prestige. The operas of Bordeaux and Marseille have been in crisis, while at Lille and Rouen the resident companies have just closed, both towns being too close to the orbit of Paris (Lille has the TGV). Nancy, after its furore, is now likely to share facilities with Metz. Down in the Midi, however, at Montpellier, mayor Georges Frêche is undeterred: he has brought in a manager of German origin, Henri Maier, who has adventurously staged some neglected classics, baroque operas and unusual modern ones. Wagner, too: 'A Midi public adores him,' Maier told me.

Summer festivals are also now playing a big role in French musical life, and scores have emerged in the past forty years. The annual classical festival at Aix-en-Provence, founded in 1948, claims to be in the same league as Salzburg, with Stéphane Lissner as its new director. Orange has an opera season, while Strasbourg's 'Musica' celebrates contemporary music. Many a little town has eagerly sought the kudos of mounting its own festival: but often they run heavily into debt, then vanish, for there just is not enough subsidy to go round.

The public taste in serious music is remarkably catholic. As the classics are so little taught in schools, many young French can turn to Beethoven, Brahms and others as exciting discoveries, and take them less for granted than in Britain. Indeed, one reason for the joyous new French approach to music could well be that it is *not* associated with dull classroom hours. French taste is not chauvinistic: but recently Berlioz, long ignored in his native land, has been rediscovered and Lyon (the great man was born nearby) has staged some major Berlioz festivals. The French have also been showing a new enthusiasm for baroque music, and for Renaissance and medieval music, and numerous groups have been formed. An American, William Christie, runs the influential baroque music centre at Versailles.

One heartening aspect of the music revival has been the boom in amateur activity – in choral singing, and especially in the learning and playing of instruments, previously much neglected. The key factor has been the expansion of the *conservatoires*. These are music schools, some state-run, some municipal, others independent, and they fulfil two main functions. A few major ones, such as the Conservatoire de Paris, train future professionals, full time; but the vast majority of the schools' overall clientele is made up of part-time pupils, some adults, mainly children, who come for the musical education they are denied in school. If you want to learn the violin, or singing, then when classwork is done you go to your local music school, and your parents must help pay for it, which means it is still something of a middle-class privilege. The music schools have trebled in number since 1960 – there are some 200 in the Paris region – and the number of their pupils has risen from 250,000 to over a million. In fact, the increase in their state or local subsidies has not kept pace with rocketing demands, and many applicants have to be turned away.

The piano is the most widely played instrument, with flute and clarinet not far behind. Choral singing is on the increase, but remains less common than in Britain or Germany, with their stronger tradition of amateur choirs. 'We French talk a lot, but we don't so often burst into song' is a common remark. But many people have now gone crazy for dance and ballet of every kind: some 2 million attend classes. In short, today's anxious France has perhaps been seeking in music some kind of *douceur de vivre*, and the echoes can be heard on every side: medieval ballads in the floodlit courtyards of old castles; sounds of a Debussy prelude floating through the walls of an HLM; balletomanes practising in village halls; and, in a few families, a revival of the charming Victorian habit of making music together after dinner. Music rivals cuisine as a new *mode*. Boulez and Béjart, as much as Bocuse, are the pied pipers.

Among the many contributory factors, four are worth stressing. One, the upsurge in official support. Two, the role of the previously abused state radio: two networks, France-Culture and France-Musique, better than the BBC's Radio 3, have for years provided a worthy output of serious music of all kinds, and this has done much to stimulate and educate public taste. Three, music is an aspect of the affluent society: the boom years brought new money for spending on opera-going, hi-fis, pianos, and so on, and as much as 17 per cent of records sold are of classical music. The fourth factor, perhaps the most important, is psychological. The music revival has clearly been linked to the rise of ecology and the revulsion against ideologies and politics. One critic, Pierre Billard, wrote in *Le Point*, 'In this age of uncertainty, technology-dominated, the return to music marks a withdrawal into intimate, individualist values, a recourse to comforting romanticism in face of the tough world outside.' Escapism or liberation? The vogue for music has been at once private and gregarious, and thus symptomatic of two recent French trends, the *repli sur soi*, and what the French see as the growth of *la vie associative*. They may at home be turning to music as a personal solace: but in coming together so eagerly in public, to hear it or to make it, may they not also be giving expression to their yearning for a new social warmth and community?

Yet if France is again a musical nation, the average quality of performance remains to be improved: here the French do not yet match the
deeply musical Germans, nor even the British, whose revolution occurred
earlier. The French have produced a few artists of world rank, such as
the cellist Paul Tortelier: but their long neglect of musical education has
been such that they cannot yet equal their neighbours' regular output of
first-rate singers and players. In the Franco-British musical exchanges
now so active, the French are often enviously aware of the British
superiority. So the authorities are making efforts to improve standards,
but it is a slow process, and there is still a serious shortage of good
teachers.

More than any other of the arts, music accorded with Lang's philosophy
of joyous popular participation, and it benefited especially from his
largesse. He trebled the Ministry of Culture's budget for it, leading his
less kind critics to claim that he was cashing in on the music boom for
political ends. All kinds of music were supported, even classical opera.
But his major effort went on encouraging youth activity (a National
Youth Orchestra was formed, on the British model) and on widening
state patronage to embrace less highbrow kinds of music, even rock and
pop. This was a break with Landowski's approach, and it revived the
debate as to which kinds of music are part of 'culture' and which are
not. Lang's excellent director of music, Maurice Fleuret, told me, 'The
ministry had always boycotted jazz, folk and *chanson*, and Landowski
cared just about classical music. But I said: why not the electric guitar,
or Indian music, or Breton bagpipes?' So the ministry created a major
jazz orchestra, it paid for new jazz classes in the *conservatoires*, it built a
giant stadium for jazz and rock at La Villette, and it opened a training
centre for variety performers. 'If France is to escape the Anglo-American
domination in modern popular music,' said Fleuret, 'then we must
seriously help our young talent, as they do.' But despite these brave
words, the domination today continues (see p. 706).

Above all, Lang gave support to the remarkable creative flowering of
modern dance in France. Fleuret said to me, 'This had long been frozen
in a neo-classicism represented by Lifar. Then the American influences
arrived, led by Merce Cunningham and others, and now a new French
generation of choreographers have responded, developing their own
styles and ideas. Nearly all are in the provinces. Even a town like Orléans
has come to us saying, "We want an avant-garde ballet."' Today the

ministry supports some forty dance companies: most were created since 1981 and are devoted to modern, not classical dance. One of the leading new choreographers, Dominique Bagouët, died of AIDS in 1992: but others are still active, led by Jean-Claude Gallotta at Grenoble, Guy Darmet at Lyon, Maguy Marin at Créteil near Paris, and Mathilde Monnier at Montpellier, which has a major annual dance festival. 'A century ago I might have been a painter, and fifty years ago a film-maker, but modern dance is the true art of today,' I was told by Gallotta, who has taken his company as far as China and Japan. This French creative movement is eagerly followed in France and has even won a high reputation abroad.

Lang and Fleuret also gave money and recognition to many of the 650 folklore troupes that try to keep alive the old music and dances of Alsace, Auvergne, Brittany and other regions. Grants were given to some of the sixty workshops that still make the *vielle à roue* (hurdy-gurdy). And encouragement was given to the amateur music-making (choirs, brass bands, chamber groups) that Landowski had largely ignored. Notably, Lang instituted an annual Fête de la Musique, which since 1982 is now held every 21 June. Amateurs and professionals take part together in this mammoth popular fête – some 10 million people, more than for the 14 July celebrations, it is claimed. There are concerts and singalongs of all sorts in streets and parks, in prisons and hospitals, in cathedrals and railway stations – a great mishmash of sonatas and sambas, Mozart and rap, requiems and rock. 'It's a political gimmick, *la journée la plus Lang* [the Langest day],' said the Right at first. And today some leading musicians still boycott the fun because they dislike the mixing of genres. But the public feel otherwise – and recent centre-Right Governments have wisely not tried to cancel the fête. In fact, in music policy as a whole, they broadly continued the line set by Lang, and they cut his subsidies for performance only slightly.

For some years now French pop music and rock have both been in a poor uncreative state (see p. 572). However, the 1990s have seen a remarkable flowering of rap and hip hop in France, where ethnic singers have adapted an American genre and made it their own. France is now the leading world market for this kind of music, after the United States, and some albums have sold up to 700,000 copies. The major star has been the Dakar-born poet M C Solaar, whose wistful, angry yet humorous songs display a striking talent and have made him hugely popular with the young.

The best-known rap group is IAM from Marseille (its initials stand for Imperial Asiatic Man, or Invasion Arrivant de Mars), whose multi-ethnic members are by origin Italian, Spanish, Algerian, Senegalese and *pied-noir*. Many of IAM's songs, like Solaar's, evoke the malaise of *la banlieue*, the problems of racism and youth today, but while Solaar can be gentle and ironic, IAM and some other groups are more provocative and verbally violent. Two of them, Nique Ta Mère (see p. 252) and Ministère Amer, have been prosecuted for inciting their audiences to attack the police. Rap groups have benefited from the new official quotas for home-grown popular music on radio (see p. 706), which have made them in greater demand with producers. Above all, somewhat like the ethnic players of the World Cup team, the popularity of some rap stars has helped a part of French youth to become more sympathetic to immigrants. But of course rap is fiercely denounced by Jean-Marie Le Pen and his friends.

One major issue facing all recent Culture Ministers has been how to improve the woeful level of music education in state schools. This, so it is widely felt, has held back the rise in standards of playing, despite the new public enthusiasm. Here the villain of the piece has long been the Education Ministry, which has hesitated to liaise with its rival or allow music a place in the intellectual curriculum (see p. 545). In schools and *collèges* the subject is taught for an hour or two a week, usually just sol-fa exercises and a dash of music appreciation; in *lycées* it is an extra that few pupils take, except for the handful that prepare for the music option in the *bac*. So nearly all active learning of music takes place out of class in the *conservatoires*, which charge fees. In a land that prides itself on its free education, this is socially unfair and can deny children from poor homes the chance to express a musical talent. Today some people argue that the larger *conservatoires* should specialize in professional training, while state schools should take over some of the burden of teaching music to children. But this idea still encounters opposition from the teaching corps who fear (a) a decline in academic standards; (b) change of any kind, as ever; (c) that the music teachers might outshine them in popularity – as indeed they might. Many parents, too, are wary, for their first concern is that their children should pass the *bac*.

Since the early 1980s there has been just a little change. The number of schools with their own choirs or instrumental groups has been slowly rising from a low level: but figures are still far below those of Britain, Germany or the USA. Under Lang, the Ministry of Culture finally persuaded its rival to introduce music as a compulsory subject in the training of primary teachers: so some pupils are at least now being taught their sol-fa properly. Education Ministers since then, of Right and Left, have not shown much interest. Today at last there is talk about putting more funds and effort into teaching music at primary level. But it may yet be some time before French children are able to receive the musical education considered normal in so many civilized countries. If that day comes, let us hope that music does not get pushed into some dry academic mould, as could happen in French schools. That could spoil the exuberant and hedonistic nature of France's great musical revival.

In the world of the visual arts, by contrast, France is still in a state of slump, at least as regards new creative work. Plenty of energy goes into mounting brilliant exhibitions, or building new museums: but in the past thirty years hardly a single new French artist has arisen to make any wide impact, and London's creative scene is now far livelier than that of Paris. The French are not unaware of this bleak situation – 'We have been living through a revolution of mediocrity,' wrote the critic Jacques Michel of *Le Monde* – but no one can quite explain it. Certainly Paris has long ceased to be the world's unrivalled capital of great art: painters no longer flock to live there, and New York, even London and Cologne, have become more important as markets for dealers.

The support that Jack Lang lavished on the visual arts included the setting up of several new bodies, both at national and regional level, with funds for acquiring contemporary works for public museums. This did help a few modern French painters and sculptors, such as Daniel Buren, to become better known. But the funds were later reduced. And Lang had less success in stimulating new creation than arousing popular enthusiasm. He poured money into improving museums, which were often fusty and ill-organized by British or German standards. And the public responded. Even before his day, the French like others in the West were beginning to become far more museum-conscious: the tally of visitors to the thirty-five state-owned museums has risen by over 50 per cent since 1970. City councils have played their part, too: several towns, including Lille, Nantes and St-Étienne, have recently built or renovated important museums. At Nîmes, Sir Norman Foster has designed an exciting new museum next to the Roman Maison Carrée. At Grenoble an impressive and varied art collection was taken out of storage in old buildings and put into the handsome new civic museum.

The French today excel at mounting large-scale imaginative exhibitions, usually retrospectives, and these draw large crowds. Impressionists and post-Impressionists are especially popular. Some 800,000 people visited the big Renoir exhibition in Paris in 1985, and 575,000 went to the Cézanne in 1995 (but this was less than the number visiting this same Cézanne show at London's Tate Gallery in 1996). In Paris, the Centre Pompidou ('Beaubourg': see p. 310) has made a speciality of panoramic surveys of the cultural links between Paris and some other capitals: its popular 'Paris–Berlin' and 'Paris–Moscow' exhibitions fed the new public appetite for cultural nostalgia. Beaubourg has thus done something to help revive the vitality of Paris as a forum where art is displayed and discussed, even if good living artists remain few. The creation of Beaubourg, like the rebirth of the Opéra, was a plank in President Pompidou's policy of trying to restore the cultural prestige of Paris. He saw that the *ville lumière* had been losing too much ground to New York: so he poured money into these and other new projects, such as the Festival d'Automne. Mitterrand later continued the policy. Certainly it has refocused some attention on Paris as a lively generator of the performing arts – if not of individual creativity.

Pompidou and Mitterrand both hoped that more foreign artists, writers and others might again be tempted to live and work in Paris, as in the great days of Joyce and Picasso. And there has in fact been some migration. Peter Brook arrived in 1956. Then some political exiles, notably from Latin America, Vietnam and Eastern Europe, chose Paris rather than elsewhere. The Argentine stage director Jorge Lavelli, and the Polish film-maker Roman Polanski, both settled and took French citizenship. The Czech writer Milan Kundera came, too, and has since preferred not to return to Prague. Leading fashion designers such as Karl Lagerfeld (German) now live and work in Paris; Nureyev was there too for a while. Some French have hailed all this as proof of a splendid rebirth of the old Parisian magnetism: *Le Point* even wrote, 'The idea that Paris captivates, bewitches, is spreading again through the world. A vaguely mystical destination – one embarks for Paris as for the Promised Land.' Frankly, that is romantic nonsense. A few *hirondelles* do not make a summer. Now that days in Clichy are no longer so quiet, many foreign artists and writers find Paris too touristy and hectic. David Hockney lived there for a while in the 1980s, then preferred to move to the United States.

The new expatriates tend to be different from those of the Hemingway/Joyce era, when English-speaking writers and Russian or Spanish artists used Paris merely as a picturesque backdrop for their own way of life. Today the newcomers are more often integrated into the city, and have been put to work for its greater glory – Brook, Strehler and others – while the great new building projects, such as the Louvre pyramid, have been confided to foreign architects (a contrast to British insularity).

Indeed, a dominant feature of the entire Paris cultural scene today is its refreshing cosmopolitanism. Paris has an open-door approach. Despite – perhaps because of? – its own poor creative record in many sectors, it attracts and utilizes good foreign talent. In the sense that there is a lot going on, Paris is a *very* lively place. At dinner parties, the talk is all of the latest operas, concerts, art shows, books, plays, films; and a trendy minority is ever anxious to show that it keeps abreast of these things. And yet, quite often, there seems a tiredness about this desperate Parisian search for novelty. The city has become a brilliant museum, a non-stop smart *vernissage* where the talk deafens. In 1985 the Bulgarian-born New York artist Christo, who specializes in the gaudy wrapping of unlikely large objects, came back to Paris where he began his career, invited this time to gift-wrap the Pont Neuf. He did – and it was magical. And it seemed a metaphor for the entire Paris *bella figura* syndrome. Much of Paris's output today may be second-rate and superficial, in true artistic terms. But she sure knows how to get it all beautifully gift-wrapped.

THEATRE:
BRILLIANT DIRECTORS, PLENTY OF FOREIGN PLAYS – BUT WHERE ARE THE NEW FRENCH ONES?

Theatre, if less so than music, is thoroughly alive in France – hundreds of little troupes are active. But there is one notable absentee: the new French playwright. The decline of creative writing is even more marked than in the novel: no new authors of great substance – save maybe Bernard-Marie Koltès, who died young in 1989 – have emerged to take the place of the Genet/Anouilh generation. And in Paris's fifty or so regular theatres, nearly all the good plays are revivals of classics, or foreign imports (often British), or free-wheeling adaptations.

Yet in its own manner – very different from London's – the theatre is varied, creative and refreshingly international. The dearth of good new French plays has led to a greater stress on foreign ones, sometimes performed in their own languages by guest companies. And in the Paris tradition a large serious public remains open to novelty and experiment, which can lead to odd results. Notably, the past thirty years have seen the ascendancy of a new style of virtuoso director – Antoine Vitez, Patrice Chéreau, Roger Planchon and Ariane Mnouchkine have been the big names – who becomes the real star of the play, more than the actors or author. This is a brilliant theatre of lighting, music and gesture, sometimes more than of the spoken word; and its fondness for reworking classic texts has horrified many critics. Today the trend is on the wane: but it has left its mark indelibly.

In Paris, more than in London, there is a sharp distinction between the bourgeois commercial theatre and the big state-subsidized theatres which attract more highbrow audiences and can afford to experiment. The former, the forty or so *théâtres de boulevard*, used to do a handsome trade by providing the middle classes with their staple entertainment: a 'boulevard comedy' was a clearly defined genre, a safe play that would amuse and gently provoke, without being too difficult. But this audience has fallen by over half since 1960: the rival lure of television has taken its toll, while good new plays have become rarer. A few still manage long runs, but many others flop. To have a real chance of success, a play generally needs a star name, say, Alain Delon or Jean-Paul Belmondo. Today the boulevard struggles on, helped by small subsidies. But only a few of its theatres have a serious artistic policy – notably the Comédie des Champs-Élysées, where in 1994–5 Yasmina Reza's *Art* ran for eighteen months.

Nearly all the best and most enterprising new work comes from the main state-backed theatres, some in central Paris, others in the suburbs and provinces. Their grants are often huge: in 1997 the Comédie-Française received 80 million francs, the Théâtre de l'Odéon 52 million. Each of the national theatres is responsible to the Ministry of Culture, but its state-appointed director has a free artistic hand. And the early post-war theatre revival owes its greatest debt to the late Jean Vilar, who founded and ran the Théâtre National Populaire (TNP) at the Palais de Chaillot in 1951–63. With a low-price policy and a big auditorium, he built up a following of students, intellectuals, even some workers. As well as French classics, he pioneered foreign works and serious modern plays, thus introducing wide new Parisian audiences to Brecht, Chekhov, Osborne, and others. Each summer the company would decamp to the Palais des Papes in Avignon, where Vilar built up one of Europe's foremost annual festivals. This was still going strong, more international than ever, at its fiftieth anniversary in 1996.

After Vilar left it, the TNP did less well; and in 1972 the Ministry of Culture took the unusual step of abolishing it as such in Paris, and transferring its title, attributes and subsidy to the provinces – to Roger Planchon near Lyon. But the TNP's old home at Chaillot is still an informal state theatre, used for popular versions of the classics and lively modern experiments: it was run for some years by Antoine Vitez (see below) and is now in the hands of Jérôme Savary, a devoted populist, who created the famous *Magic Circus* in 1966. A more venerable institution is the Comédie-Française, which dates from the seventeenth century and remains France's leading theatre. It has long regarded itself as the trustee of French classical drama, and of a certain stylized, rhetorical tradition of acting that can be tedious. After a difficult post-war period, it was modernized in the 1970s by its director Pierre Dux, who encouraged new acting styles and built up audiences for a repertoire mixing the French classics with some foreign and modern plays. Thus the theatre staged the French première of Ionesco's *La Soif et la faim*, and managed to shock its traditional dinner-jacket audiences with the scene parodying Christian conversion. Today, under Jean-Pierre Miquel, it ranges from Racine to Genet. It is one of the few major French theatres to have its own full-time repertory company: the others may keep a nucleus of their own actors but will hire others for individual productions.

Another famous state theatre, the Odéon, was in 1960–68 the home of the marvellous Barrault–Renaud company, invited there by Malraux. Jean-Louis Barrault put the stress on foreign classics such as Shakespeare, alongside premières of new French plays by Duras, Billetdoux and others. Then in May '68, when militant students seized the Odéon and used it as an open parliament, Barrault dramatically joined them: 'I am on your side!' For this, Malraux sacked him. But the Barraults bounced back: they took over part of the disused Gare d'Orsay, and used it as an informal circus-like open-stage theatre, where eager crowds attended their plays, concerts and happenings: Madeleine Renaud (Barrault's wife) was notably memorable in Duras's *Des journées entières dans les arbres*. But in 1980 Giscard claimed this old railway station for a museum, so the Barraults, like some circus troupe, had to move yet again, for the eighth time in thirty years. Barrault remained splendidly active up until his death in 1994.

The diverse French theatre scene was given a boost by Jack Lang after

1981. He increased state funding for the five national theatres by 32 per cent in real terms, and for the forty-three regional dramatic centres by 75 per cent, while the number of independent companies receiving subsidy rose from 189 to 464. Right-of-centre Governments later made cutbacks, and today some small troupes have been finding it harder to survive. But total funding in real terms remains higher than before 1981.

Lang also encouraged the Paris theatre's noted cosmopolitan tendency. For some years Giorgio Strehler, of the Piccolo Teatro di Milano, had been presenting seasons of Goldoni, in Italian, at the Odéon. Then from 1983, at Lang's invitation, he started an annual international season there, with plays in their original languages: visiting companies included the Royal Shakespeare. Today, under the brilliant Georges Lavaudant, the Odéon has been continuing this policy, and so has the *maison de la culture* in the drab suburb of Bobigny (see below). They have brought in companies from St Petersburg and Chicago, also London's National Theatre and a German production by Peter Zadek; Deborah Warner did *Elektra* in English, with Fiona Shaw. Foreign plays are shown with surtitles, and are generally popular: 'Our audiences are very curious-minded and open to other cultures,' Lavaudant told me, while at Bobigny one production in four is foreign. The great Peter Brook has also based himself in Paris, since 1956: his multiracial experimental company at the Bouffes du Nord is a vital and respected feature of the Paris scene.

Of the five theatres with 'national' status (the others are the Comédie-Française, TNP, Odéon and one in Strasbourg), the Théâtre de la Colline has the 'mission' of staging modern plays: these are performed in French, but many are foreign – Bernhardt, Heine Müller, Bond, etc. Created in 1954, the theatre was launched in its present role in 1987 by the Argentinian director Jorge Lavelli, and is in working-class eastern Paris, at Ménilmontant. In fact, for some years there has been a striking tendency for top avant-garde directors to settle in the poorer suburbs, in converted halls or in new theatres built for them. Daniel Mesguisch went for a while to St-Denis, Vitez to Ivry, and Chéreau to Nanterre. Bernard Sobel, a serious Communist, has for thirty years been presenting classics and experimental plays at his theatre in the PCF-run suburb of Genevilliers. From May '68 and before, such directors have been trying to activate their Leftist ideals by bringing serious drama to popular audiences (and the rentals and other costs are far lower than in the city centre). But in practice, as Sobel admitted to me, they attract few workers, whereas a great many Parisian intellectuals find it chic to travel out to see some clever new Brecht adaptation amid the dreary HLMs. The showcase today is Bobigny, where Ariel Goldenberg, a brilliant and amusing showman from Argentina (yes, another), uses a huge *maison de la culture*, lavishly funded by the Communist-led local council, to present foreign plays and other lively modern productions: in his 1995–6 season, he had three plays in English and one in Italian (Dario Fo). 'I like being out here,' he told me, 'with the challenge of fighting the black image of *la banlieue rouge*.' But for his premières, the BMWs with Paris number-plates stand thick outside his theatre.

The Paris theatre scene today remains lively, in its own way. Even the café-théâtre vogue of the 1970s is still alive – tiny late-night theatres with cafés or *bistrots* attached, where you can watch a kind of revue, or one-man show, or a modern playlet. But the 'fringe' as a whole is less active than in London. And there remains the mystery of the dearth of good new French playwrights. Is it that the new talent is just not there, or that the new-style directors' theatre does not encourage it?

Take a step back in time, and the new plays were brilliant and plentiful: Genet, Ionesco, Beckett, Adamov, Sartre, Camus, Montherlant, Audiberti, Anouilh – not all of these were French born, but they wrote in French and lived in France, and they made a huge contribution to modern European theatre. But who has emerged since? Marguerite Duras, better known for her novels, wrote some interesting short plays such as *La Musica*. Michel Vinaver is the author of sharp Brechtian satires on the world of big business. And Jean-Claude Grumberg has written some moving and realistic dramas of Jewish life, notably *L'Atelier*. In the past twenty years, the most admired new playwright has been Bernard-Marie Koltès, who died of AIDS in 1989, aged forty-one: his clever philosophical fables were influenced by his travels in Africa and America, and he was much helped by Chéreau, who in 1987 did a memorable production of his *Dans la solitude des champs de coton*. In the 1990s Koltès has been the recent French playwright most often performed abroad. Since his death, one of the very few new plays to have made much impact has been *Art*, by Yasmina Reza, a Parisian. Her witty, perceptive study of male friendship, and of Parisian attitudes to modern art, ran for eighteen months on the boulevard in 1994–5, and was then one of the rare new French plays to have been a success also in London. Its subject is typical of the present trend for slight chamber pieces about personal problems, in contrast to the post-Brechtian plays of social protest and political involvement in the 1970s.

Nearly all young playwrights today find it hard to get a break. Private theatres are wary of taking the risk of presenting a serious play by an unknown author, while the state-backed houses make less effort than in Britain to seek out new talent. 'We do read lots of manuscripts, but they are almost all useless,' claimed one producer. Some leading figures, including Planchon, Lavaudant and Mnouchkine, prefer to devise their own texts as the basis for a dramatic spectacle. And one frequent trend in recent years has been to take a well-known literary text, or maybe a political one, and work it into a kind of play. Vitez did this with the transcript of talks between Mao and Pompidou; he also took a novel by Aragon, *Les Clochers de Bâle*, and with six actors turned it into an ad hoc playlet, with much noisy rhetoric and jumping off tables. Others since then have used the legends of Yeats, or bits of Proust, or Zola's *Germinal*, but not always with great success. In 1997, at Sobel's theatre, I saw a dramatization of Plato's *Symposium*, intercut with bits of the text of Godard's *Le Mépris*: it was effective in parts, but infuriatingly overdirected. Today the public is tiring of this genre, which can seem like just one more attempt to get round the lack of good new plays. So theatres will often prefer to play safe with translated foreign imports. Established English authors are popular (Pinter, Stoppard, etc.), as are Austro-German ones (Botho Strauss, Handke, Bernhardt, etc.). Thus the dearth of new French material does bring one blessing in disguise: it helps to account for the stimulating cosmopolitanism of the French stage. Many producers and actors feel that foreign plays best provide them with meaty subjects, stimulating ideas, and strong acting roles that relate to the real modern world. Many new French plays, by contrast, seem too hermetic.

Yet there may be quite another explanation for the French dearth: this lies in the dominance, at least in the 1970s and '80s, of a coterie of brilliant and fashionable directors who have had a different concept of theatre. They have just not been interested in taking an author's text and then faithfully staging it, like a kind of publisher. To them a living author is a potential nuisance, an impediment to their own creative fancy. So they prefer either to reinterpret the plays of dead authors (who are not there to interfere), or to invent their own texts.

Sometimes a director and cast will take a theme and collectively improvise a play around it during rehearsal. The most talented pioneer of this has been Ariane Mnouchkine, whose famous Théâtre du Soleil has for thirty years performed in a former cartridge factory at Vincennes, in the suburbs. Born of May '68, this idealistic troupe is run as a workers' cooperative, each member drawing the same wage. It recalls Joan Littlewood's former Theatre Workshop: it, too, is militantly Leftist; it, too, as in *Oh, What a Lovely War*, pastes history into a collage for fine dramatic effect. This the troupe did with the French Revolution, relating it to the events of 1968 in their brilliantly original *1789* and *1793*, two productions of the 1970s which caused more stir than anything on the Paris stage for years. Later the troupe did a collage adaptation of Klaus Mann's novel *Mephisto*, about the rise of Nazism; and they tackled the difficult subject of genocide in Kampuchea. Mnouchkine is an activist who sees theatre and politics as closely intertwined, and will hit out at any extremism. In 1995 she took her troupe to the Avignon festival with a *Tartuffe* adaptation that attacked fundamentalism, portraying Molière's hypocrite as a mad mullah! She and some of her troupe then went on hunger strike against Serb atrocities in Bosnia. Her inventions seem to me a valid and exciting form of theatre: but they do push the playwright on to the sidelines.

Several other star directors have applied their creative gifts to reworking the classics. Planchon, Chéreau and the late Antoine Vitez, like Peter Zadek in Germany, have been the high priests of this cult. And in the 1970s and '80s they dominated – some would say, tyrannized – the serious French theatre. This is very much in the French tradition, where fashionable coteries have for a while imposed a 'terrorism of taste' in some sphere: Bocuse and his 'gang' in cuisine, Barthes and Robbe-Grillet in literature. Vitez's work in particular was found exhilarating by some, tiresomely gimmicky by others. He was invited to the Comédie-Française, where in 1975 his version of *Partage du Midi* was seen by some as a splendid rediscovery of Paul Claudel, by others as a massacre. The actors spoke the lines in a Noh-like sing-song voice, which stung Richard Roud to comment in the *Guardian*, 'It made nonsense of Claudel's poetry.' He accused the new directors of deliberately distorting classic texts so as to display their own originality. In 1973 the young Chéreau startled Paris with his Chaillot production of Marivaux's *La Dispute*: with a parade of virtuoso lighting effects and other visual inventions, he managed to spin out this subtle fifty-minute playlet to a full two-and-a-half hours. Some critics felt that Marivaux had been buried out of sight beneath the deluge of tricks – 'this dreadful, crawling horror', wrote Bernard Levin. But another British critic, Gary O'Connor, raved over

Chéreau's ability to expand the images conveyed by Marivaux's words 'into a visual spectacle of epic proportions'. *De gustibus* . . .

These directors also set to work on Racine and Molière. It was argued that at least this helped to liberate these authors from the dead hand of formal classic production imposed on them for so long by the Comédie-Française and others. Whereas British post-war directors managed to present Shakespeare in new, lively ways, in France the classics had remained draped in fusty tradition, and to tamper with them was heresy. So Vitez the heretic set to work – 'The text must be given a modern force, a twentieth-century resonance,' he told me. But he swung from one extreme to another. When he and Planchon staged Racine and Molière in 1980, one critic, Pierre Marcabru, wrote scathingly in *Le Point* of 'Planchon's strip-cartoon tragedy'. In his review headed 'The classics under torture', he wittily analysed these directors' possible motives in rearranging or even rewording the texts: 'In such a director, I sense the jubilant sadistic streak of a failed would-be author who is trying to take it out on a colleague, albeit one dead for three centuries.'

Vitez, a brilliant multilingual intellectual, once told me, 'I do not reject new authors. The kind I look for is a poet and experimentalist. I despise plodding realism, and I despise the modern British theatre. The only good British director is Brook – and it's symptomatic that *he* has chosen to live here.' And Vitez and his friends have had plenty of supporters. One drama critic summed up: 'Our sophisticated new directors are giving us a new vision of theatre. All in all, I'd rather be excited or maddened by a *feu d'artifice* from Chéreau than sit through some worthy comedy of manners *à l'anglaise*.' So the critics and public have been divided. Yet today, in the late 1990s, the vogue for 'mangling the classics' has waned and lost favour. Vitez is dead, Planchon is close to seventy, Chéreau has been turning to cinema; and apart from the brilliant Stanislas Nordey, they have few notable successors. As far as budgets allow, productions may still be visually dazzling and inventive: but the text is less often distorted. Yet another Parisian cultural firework has burned itself out. In cinema, however, the whirling Catherine wheel of the wonderful *nouvelle vague* is still alight.

CINEMA:
LIVELY SUCCESSORS TO THE *NOUVELLE VAGUE*

Not only did the French pioneer cinematography in the 1890s, but since then, in my view, they have produced more great films than any other nation, even the United States. They have pursued the concept of the *film d'auteur*, of cinema as a means of personal artistic expression; and if the novel and the theatre play have declined in recent decades, one reason is that some of the best creative talent has preferred to express itself through cinema – notably in the heyday of the so-called '*nouvelle vague*'.

Today the major figures of this 'new wave' are ageing, and some are dead. Apart from the remarkable Bertrand Tavernier, hardly any 'great' directors have emerged in their wake. So this is no longer a golden age. Yet France's cinema, though beset with economic problems, remains more prolific and lively than any other in Europe. It continues to turn out a number of small-scale personal films that may lack the striking originality or lyric genius of the *nouvelle vague* but are still in the French humanist tradition. Directors benefit from a generous system of state aid, which the Government has struggled to retain in face of American efforts to get it reduced. The French are obsessed as ever with American competition: in a bid to rival Hollywood, they have even turned to producing large-scale historical epics based on literary classics – a venture not always very well judged.

The cinema has never had to struggle, as in Britain, to win acceptance beside theatre or music as a major art form. In the 1920s Cocteau was turning to film as readily as to verse as a medium for his poetry. And writers such as Sartre, Malraux, Duras and Robbe-Grillet have readily collaborated in film-making, or even directed films. In the post-war decades, the passion for cinema among the educated young reached its height: thousands of *ciné-clubs* sprang up across France, where people would gather in a hired hall or flea-pit to watch anything from the latest Godard to an old scratched copy of *Potemkin* and then eagerly discuss it. The craze for these clubs has today waned, under the impact of television and video; and the interest in new personal off-beat movies, from France or abroad, is not what it was, perhaps because there are fewer good new films around. But Paris today still has scores of art-house cinemas, and on any day it offers the public a far wider choice of films of all sorts, old and new, than any other city, even New York. Of course the cinema is also a mass-entertainment industry, in France as anywhere, and it has become harder to reconcile these pressures with the ideals of the *film d'auteur*. But the French still believe that cinema, given the right conditions, can be used as powerfully or subtly as any other art to express a personal artistic vision.

It was from this background that the hundred or so young directors of the *nouvelle vague* emerged with such clamour in the late 1950s. This new generation had taught itself cinema in its teens, in the clubs and art-houses, and it grew up 'speaking cinema' as its elders spoke literature. If they turned foremost to film-making, more than writing, maybe one factor was the difficulty of producing a humanist novel in the literary climate of that time, dominated by the *nouveau roman*.

The 1930s had been the golden age of Clair, Carné and Renoir. The early post-war years were at least a luminous silver age, with such films as Becker's *Casque d'Or*. But soon paralysis grew. Established directors became short of inspiration, save for a few rare figures like Robert Bresson. Subjects were stereotyped: *policiers*, sex dramas or costume pieces, carrying the stale air of the studios. And meanwhile France was changing, a new mood and style of life were emerging that the cinema seemed to ignore, and a new audience began to lose patience with the artificialities offered on the screen. Some producers began desperately to search for novelty.

The new generation then proceeded to force their hand, in one of the most startling revolutions in cinema history. Some tyro directors began trying their hand at self-financed low-budget features, and in the mid-1950s a few unusual films began to slip into the art-houses: Agnès Varda's *La Pointe courte* was one. Then in 1956 a young producer, Raoul Lévy, engaged the very young Roger Vadim to try his hand at a theme today common but in those days seldom attempted – the amorality of modern pleasure-seeking youth. Filmed on location in St-Tropez, *Et Dieu créa la femme* was no great film, but it broke new ground: here at last was youth looking at itself with a raw directness. What is more, the film was a fantastic commercial success, in France and worldwide: so this encouraged producers to look for other new talent and real-life subjects. They did not need to look far. A few slightly older directors had already been working in documentary, and they now took the chance to make their first feature films: thus in 1959 Alain Resnais, aged thirty-six, made

Hiroshima mon amour. A second key source of talent was the young group of critics on the magazine *Cahiers du Cinéma*, led by Godard, Chabrol and Truffaut. Some were from moneyed backgrounds and sank their own capital into modest features. Thus Chabrol made *Le Beau Serge* for a mere 480,000 francs with a legacy inherited by his wife.

It was an exciting time to be in Paris. I remember in 1959 attending previews of Chabrol's first films (*Le Beau Serge* and *Les Cousins*) without having heard of him before, and enjoying the shock of a new cinema language, rather as Londoners had done in the theatre with Osborne's *Look Back in Anger*. Resnais and Truffaut took the leading prizes at Cannes that spring. *L'Express* invented the label 'nouvelle vague', and journalists applied it to any new name, despite the wide differences. Some of the new directors (Godard, Resnais) were cinematic revolutionaries; others (Truffaut, Rohmer, etc.) were applying an up-to-date personal style to more conventional themes and subjects. Yet the *nouvelle* label had some validity, for in several ways the new directors differed from their predecessors. Above all they were devoted to the *film d'auteur*, the concept of film as a unique personal creation. This was not a new idea in France, but the new wave carried it further than before. Many of them, such as Truffaut with *Les 400 Coups*, approached their first film like a first novel. Some directors had studied at the official French film school, but few had worked their way up through the usual tedious channels of technical apprenticeship in big studios. So they gained in freshness what they lost in experience. They arrived with anti-industry ideas on how to make films: no big stars or lavish sets, and thus less need for concessions to alleged popular taste. They were helped by the French system of state financial aid for good scripts: Resnais, Varda and others could thus take risks with commercially doubtful subjects.

A quick survey of the main directors' achievements across forty years could begin with the *Cahiers* group. Here Claude Chabrol has been the archetype of *nouvelle vague* flair-plus-perversity. In his early films, behind the sardonic misanthropy there seemed to lurk a despairing tenderness, an awareness of human isolation. *Le Beau Serge*, shot on location in his childhood village near Limoges, told a story of alcoholism and peasant decadence, and for all its naïvety was drawing on felt personal experience. Its raw intensity excited the critics. Then *Les Cousins*, about a provincial student's corruption by a cynical Parisian milieu, displayed the same nervously urgent camerawork and youthful sincerity. *Les Bonnes Femmes* (1959), another brilliant film, was a bitter if contrived study of naïve

Parisian schoolgirls and their cruel defeat by life. After this, Chabrol developed into a more polished commercial director, less unconventional. He made several stylish psychological thrillers, such as *Que la bête meure*; and he has since continued in this genre, right up to *La Cérémonie* (1995), about two paranoid girls in a Breton household. His work has always been prolific but uneven, and his period adaptations of *Madame Bovary* and Hélias's *Le Cheval d'orgueil* were flat and disappointing. The better films of his mature period are more than thrillers, they are also sharp studies of modern bourgeois life and hypocrisy, and this gives them their edge. But for me he has become too much the craftsman-entertainer, like Hitchcock, his idol. I prefer his earlier, clumsier, more ingenuously personal films.

François Truffaut, like Chabrol, began his career in a blaze of humanism. *Les 400 Coups*, his masterly début aged twenty-seven, was the story of a boy driven to delinquency by loneliness and unhappiness: based partly on his own childhood, it was also a model of implied social criticism. But after this he generally avoided such themes, saying that he was not interested in dealing with social problems. Nor was he a great innovator: his enduring reputation rests largely on his lyrical gifts and his gentle wit and humanism, in the Renoir tradition. These qualities were seen at their best in *Jules et Jim* and in *La Nuit américaine* (*Day for Night*), about people making a film – his own loving serenade to the movie world. As Penelope Houston put it, 'He has the gift of making film-making look wonderfully easy, like a man running down a long sunlit road with a camera in his hand.' He died from cancer at the age of fifty-two.

Éric Rohmer, like Truffaut, has been concerned with private relationships, not social questions. His six *contes moraux* in 1962–71 analysed sexual moral dilemmas: in *Ma nuit chez Maud*, an earnest Catholic re-examines his principles in the light of meetings with two contrasting women; in *Le Genou de Claire* (1970), his finest film, a diplomat by the lake of Annecy finds himself disturbingly attracted by two teenage girls. There is never much plot in Rohmer's films: people talk a great deal, very intelligently, about their thoughts and feelings; a spell is cast. It is literary cinema. In *Le Genou de Claire*, he created exquisite poetry out of wistful minor incidents, girls by a lakeside in summer. These films, about bourgeois people wrapped up in their private worlds, have been called reactionary by the Left: but this is what interests him, and he is being true to himself as an artist. And, though he often repeats himself, he has shown an extraordinary resilience. In his mid-seventies, with such films as *Un Conte d'été* (1995), he was still displaying an unpatronizing intuitive sympathy for his main characters, young enough to be his grandchildren.

Jean-Luc Godard could not be more different from Rohmer in outlook, style and subject-matter: but he, too, has remained true to himself in staying outside the system. Like many of his fans, I do not care much for his later films. But the *oeuvre* of his early period remains one of the most original achievements of post-war world cinema. He was a quintessential child of the 1960s, their mirror and prophet: in its quirky way, his work was full of insights into the France of that time. His first feature, *A bout de souffle* (1959), was filmed in streets and flats with a hand-held camera for a mere 400,000 francs. Not everyone found the subject or characters rewarding (Belmondo's posturing beatnik, Seberg's bewildered American): but it was clear that the wry, semi-improvised *ciné-vérité* style marked a startling début. Godard blithely broke all the cinema's textbook rules simply by ignoring them. Over the next years, by keeping to tiny budgets, he was able to stick to his own terms of style and subject, and would make two or three films a year. Working compulsively by flair or mood, rather like a poet or painter, he rarely prepared a scenario in advance, but wrote the script daily as the film went along, and might change the story halfway through. His admirers (they included Malraux) used the word genius; his many detractors called him childish and woolly-minded.

His critics remarked on the fragmented, pop-art surface of his films, with their sign-symbols and slogans, typical of that 1960s period. Yet although highbrows exploited him as a cult figure, he was never assertive, but shy, meditative, even taciturn. And so he kept a kind of purity. Each new Godard film before 1968, for all the jokes and visual high spirits, struck me as an ever-sharper personal statement of horror at the way he felt modern life was going. Violence and terrorism, loneliness, confusion, the dehumanizing effects of science and affluence came out Goya-like in his anarchic yet strangely topical films. Life, like a bright light, seemed to hurt and bewilder him. When someone asked his ex-wife, Anna Karina, why he always wore dark glasses, she said, 'It's not that his eyes are too weak. His universe is too strong.'

In the brilliant *Alphaville* (1965), he used a tongue-in-cheek science-fiction plot to point at a 1984-ish moral. One artifice was that the portrait of Alphaville, grim city of machines, was edited largely from Paris location shots, filmed in modern buildings and computer centres. The technocrats ruling the city are shown brainwashing their enemies '*dans les HLM, c'est-à-dire, les Hôpitaux de la Longue Maladie*' – and the camera pans up a

Sarcelles skyscraper. To a Paris audience, such typical Godard jests were both funny and frightening. *Weekend* (1968), the most ferocious and pessimistic of his films, then prophesied a French society disintegrating into brigandry and cannibalism: the car, with its ritual mass murders on French roads every weekend, was shown as the chief villain. Godard has always seen himself as a kind of documentarist – 'Each of my films is a report on the state of the nation.' But some of his work has also been highly personal, notably *Pierrot le fou* (1965), perhaps the greatest of his films. Amid images of violence and gangsterism, it shows a young writer (Belmondo) escaping from Paris to an idyll of perfection on an island along with the girl he adores (Karina), who then betrays him. So, in a climax of fierce beauty, he shoots her, paints his face blue, and blows himself up with dynamite, as voices whisper, '*Nous enfin réunis pour l'éternité.*' 'It is a film about France,' said Godard. It was also about himself, his nostalgia for some other, purer life; and it seemed an almost embarrassing hymn of love for Karina, who in real life had just broken their marriage.

Godard's early work was uneven, and intellectually often facile and muddled: but it had its own logic and sensitivity. As Françoise Giroud said in her *Express* review of *Pierrot le fou*, 'Godard, too, is mad. He knows how to talk about the pain of loving. Godard's films, I like them, even the ones I don't.' But in 1968 this sad-funny poetic Godard perished somewhere on the May barricades. That revolt, when he sided with the *gauchistes*, had a shattering effect on him. He became bound up with the Maoists' un-Godardian solemnity, and fell under the influence of a Leftist guru with whom he made some leaden films preaching *gauchiste* sermons. A serious motorbike accident in 1971 (had the scenes in *Weekend* been clairvoyant?) seemed to add to this mood. Later, in the 1980s, Godard returned to something nearer his old style, using well-known players such as Nathalie Baye. With *Je vous salue Marie*, about a nude present-day Virgin Mary, he again displayed his love of provoking and mystifying the bourgeoisie. In his mid-sixties he was still active: *For Ever Mozart* (1995), about attitudes to the Bosnian war, was muddled but interesting. These later films may lack the charm and sharpness of his earlier work, but they remain individual and thoughtful.

The new wave's most influential director after Godard has been Alain Resnais, born in 1922. He, too, has been an innovator, but very different. He is a withdrawn, elusive person, and this enigmatic quality is apparent in his films. Although each is marked with his highly personal style, he prefers not to write his own scripts, and has often collaborated with a well-known writer: thus it is not always easy to tell how much in these strange films comes from him. He can give the impression of being more concerned with style than subject-matter. Yet certain themes have recurred: time and memory, the elusiveness of reality, the erosion of love and loyalties by the chaos of modern life and the passing of the years. Resnais stunned the 1959 Cannes Festival with his first feature *Hiroshima mon amour*, often seen as one of the major landmarks of world cinema. It began as a film about atomic war, then grew into a love story. Some critics found it in bad taste for a minor private tragedy to be thus exalted above a major public one. But Resnais and his writer, Marguerite Duras, were using the sorrow of the girl in wartime France as a paradigm of the far greater sorrow of Hiroshima, within the total madness of war. Yet the film was unique less for its message than its style. By marvellous editing and camerawork, by the creative integration of image, music and language, Resnais transmuted the script into a work of power and subtlety. It was the mature expression of a technique that he had elaborated in his earlier documentaries: the elegiac travelling shots, the incantatory repetition of images and phrases that has been likened to opera, and the use of stream-of-consciousness flashbacks to convey, as in Proust, the texture and feel of memory.

Resnais trod the same path in his next film, *L'Année dernière à Marienbad*, but this time he was let down by his writer, Alain Robbe-Grillet, who produced a typically tricksy scenario (see p. 513). In a baroque luxury hotel, man meets girl and tries to persuade her that they had a love affair the year before: whether they did is immaterial. Resnais's *mise en scène* is mesmeric, but fails to rescue a film that, devoid of real human interest, lapses into boredom. It showed the hazards of his reliance on writers with a strong individuality. After this he returned to a more recognizable everyday world. *La Guerre est finie* is the moving story of an ageing Spanish left-wing agent in France. In *Providence*, made in English with a fine performance by Gielgud, a dying novelist looks back on his life, distorting reality into nightmare in true Resnais fashion. Of his more recent work, often erratic, *Smoking/No Smoking* was admired. Then in 1997, in his mid-seventies, he showed himself as imperishable as Rohmer: *On connaît la chanson*, a typical meditation on reality and illusion, won France's César award for the best French film of the year, and six other prizes. In fact, one remarkable aspect of the *nouvelle vague* has been the staying power of its ageing directors: in 1996–7 five of these veterans made new films, not only Rohmer and Resnais but also Chabrol, Godard and Jacques Rivette.

Resnais's circle of friends includes Agnès Varda, a pioneer among woman directors. Like Resnais, she holds strong left-wing views but has rarely paraded them in her films. *Le Bonheur* (1965), one of the most interesting of all new-wave films, was an ironic attempt to analyse the concept of happiness. Varda chose a prototype of the happy simpleton: a young carpenter, living joyously in a suburban villa with his pretty blonde wife and lovely babies. When he starts an even more joyous affair with another girl, his bliss is multiplied by two, until his wife (whom he still loves) drowns herself. But this proves to be just a passing cloud on the surface of his ecstatic amorality: his domestic idyll goes on as before, save for a new blonde wife in place of the old one. It was a truly shocking film, and was meant to be: the bright colours, soft smiles and Mozart clarinet music made the irony all the sharper. Some audiences were outraged by a film that seemed to serenade middle-class family values only to cock a snook at them. It brilliantly conveyed the cruelty of a certain mindless happiness, while also expressing Varda's ambivalent attitude to a milieu very different from her own intellectual world. In its odd stylized way, *Le Bonheur* was a true critique of contemporary values. Later Varda made *L'une chante, l'autre pas*, an endearing feminist tale of the friendship of two girls. *Sans toit ni loi* (*Vagabonds* in English) won the top prize at Venice in 1985 and is seen as her finest work. It is a bleak but compassionate study of a young middle-class drop-out (Sandrine Bonnaire) who rejects all help and dies of exposure. Varda was again examining the equivocal nature of the search for happiness. She was also making a realistic comment about the plight of those who cannot accept society's values.

Louis Malle, a superb director, was often classed with the *nouvelle vague* but was really a lone figure, different from the others, more cosmopolitan, more eclectic. In his earlier films he would unpredictably hop from subject to subject, even from style to style: some critics thus found him lacking in a defined personal approach. But he enjoyed the versatility. And his work did have two common threads. One was its strong human warmth. The other, his major trademark, was his fondness for focusing intimately on themes provocative or embarrassing at the time, which he treated without moral judgement: they included incest (*Le Souffle au coeur*), child prostitution (*Pretty Baby*), suicide (*Le Feu follet*) and wartime collaboration (*Lacombe Lucien*). He said that he aimed to disturb audiences, so as to force them to reappraise their values and to see that good and evil are often bound up.

The finest of his early works was *Le Feu follet* (1963), adapted from a 1920s novel by Drieu La Rochelle about a young alcoholic's tragic search for a meaning in life. Malle made a very moving film, Bresson-like in its concentration on the hero's inner suffering. But he depressed himself so much in doing it that he leapt off to Mexico to film Bardot and Moreau in their underpants in a period romp (*Viva Maria!*). Then, another abrupt change, he made a powerful documentary series about poverty in India. *Lacombe Lucien* (1974) told of a dim-wit teenage peasant in the Massif Central who by accident comes to work for the Nazis. Malle's aim was to show that not all *collabos* were wicked, some were merely naïve: but a few critics felt that, by focusing on such an imbecile, Malle had sidestepped the true moral dilemmas of the Occupation. Also set in that period, and perhaps his greatest film, was *Au revoir les enfants* (1987), based on an incident in his own schooldays, when a Jewish schoolboy was denounced to the Gestapo. Malle made one film in Britain, *Damage* (cold and trite), and several in America, where he lived for some years: the best was *My Dinner with André*, an unusual *tour de force* that focused on a long discussion between two friends in a New York restaurant. He died of cancer in 1995, aged sixty-three.

The new wave threw up a number of other talents, such as the documentarist Chris Marker, an associate of Resnais, and Jacques Rivette, one of the *Cahiers* group: his affinities with Godard were seen in *Paris nous appartient*, with its disturbing view of modern urban life. Later he made two films about women persecuted by the Church – a version of Diderot's *La Religieuse* (1966), and recently a fine study of Joan of Arc, *Jeanne la pucelle*, with Sandrine Bonnaire. The 1960s also saw a vogue for films of innocent poetic romanticism: the pioneer of this charm school was Varda's then husband, the late Jacques Demy, whose first feature *Lola* (1960), a wistful reverie set in Nantes, beautifully created a private imaginary world. Then came another fantasy, *Les Parapluies de Cherbourg*. In 1966 Claude Lelouch entered the charm school, winning the Cannes Grand Prix with *Un Homme et une femme*, the biggest box-office hit the new wave ever made. It was a banal romantic love story, dressed up with arty soft-focus photography: but it caught a mood in the France of the time.

The *nouvelle vague*'s success in the 1960s was far more cultural than commercial. Many of its first films (*Les Cousins*, for example) easily recouped their slender costs: so producers jumped on this low-budget bandwagon, and for a while any young hopeful with a new idea found a camera thrust in his hands. In 1959–63 more than 170 directors made a first film, a gold rush without parallel in world cinema. But it did not last. Few of the newcomers had the talent of a Truffaut or Resnais. Encouraged to be as 'personal' as they liked – the apparent formula for success – many went outrageously too far, making frivolous, esoteric films about themselves and their friends. So an image formed in the public's mind of the typical new-wave film, full of arty camera shots and in-jokes about other films – imitations of *Les Cousins*. Cinema-goers soon wearied of a realism that had declined into gossip. In fact, a few successes apart, the new wave was never a great money-spinner in France.

Artistically, one achievement was to renew the great lyric traditions of French cinema, springing from Cocteau, Clair and Vigo. Directors were helped by some fine cameramen: Sacha Vierny, Henri Decaë and others. The new wave also renewed a *cinéma d'auteur*: but in exploring their own vision of reality, directors were often criticized for neglecting modern French social issues. Was this fair? Godard, in his own manner, tried to mirror French society as he saw it. Resnais, Varda and others, too, in their oblique and often baffling way, were expressing a mood of the times, possibly at a more subtle and disturbing level than the explicit social comment of some British and American film-makers. The French were less obsessed by problems of community, but more by solitude within community, by the chaos on the fringes of life. Typical was Jean Eustache's cult classic *La Maman et la putain* (1973), exploring the love life of a clever, immature young Parisian. It was overindulgent and inexcusably long (219 minutes), and its anti-hero was infuriatingly pretentious. Yet it had a desperate painful intensity and its non-stop chit-chat was bright as gold and quintessentially Parisian.

There were other reasons why the new wave – like the modern French novel and theatre – neglected a more direct analysis of society. In de Gaulle's day, there was the danger of censorship if a film dealt too boldly with a topic involving official policies. Or producers and backers would claim that the public was not interested in workaday social realism. But many directors themselves, including Rohmer, Truffaut and Chabrol, were not interested either. Most were bourgeois living in Paris, and they said they wanted to stick to what they knew and cared about. Few, Godard apart, explored the striking social changes of the period. In fact,

many of the better new-wave films have been set either in the past, or
abroad, or within the director's own dream world.

A number of other talented directors have emerged since the 1970s,
in the wake of the new wave. They are diverse and they form no school.
They may lack the stylistic genius of the great figures of the new wave.
But theirs is still a *cinéma d'auteur*, and though their films individually
tend to be slight, they give a vivid naturalistic picture of French life.

The major figure is Bertrand Tavernier, whom I would rate among
the world's best directors of recent years. Born in Lyon in 1941, he is a
very serious man whose radical-Leftish views emerge in his realistic films,
but not too polemically: above all he is a gentle humanist in the Renoir
tradition. And though the tone of his work has recently grown sombre,
it remains imbued with his warm sympathy for people. He is not too
'Parisian' but has a gift for conveying the mood of other cities. All this
was evident from his first film, *L'Horloger de Saint-Paul* (1974), set in the
vieille ville of his native Lyon, about a watchmaker (Philippe Noiret,
superb) who is forced to reassess his life and beliefs when his son is
accused of murder. A study in courage, loyalty and melancholy, it
beautifully conveyed the daily local life of Lyon. Next Tavernier filmed
two historical subjects, then *Les Enfants gâtés*, a rare French movie study
of a contemporary social issue – that of tenants versus landlords. Like
Malle, Tavernier enjoys sharp changes of subject, and next he was in
Glasgow, of all places, making a philosophical sci-fi fantasy in English,
La Mort en direct (*Death Watch*), on the theme of the media's ruthless
invasion of privacy. The moody photography of Scotland was fine, but
the film itself was a bit contrived.

'One should stick to one's cultural roots,' said Tavernier, and back in
Lyon he then made his finest film, *Une Semaine de vacances* (1980): slight
in plot but infinitely touching, it lingers in the mind like a melody. A
young teacher (delicately played by Nathalie Baye) is on the edge of a
breakdown, so her doctor prescribes a week off work. She mooches
about, visits her dying father, makes new friends, and gradually finds the
courage and peace of mind to make a new start. Tavernier uses gentle
photography of Lyon and the Beaujolais to counterpoint the moods and
thoughts of his characters, and the message is one of hope: death hovers,
work is tough, happiness is fragile, but for those with the heart to grasp
it, life is marvellously there, flowing on like the Rhône through the heart
of the city. Without artiness, Tavernier uses snatches of poetry, memory
echoes, the wintry townscapes, to forge a synthesis between the people

and their setting. 'For me,' he said, 'Lyon is a character in the film, as Glasgow was earlier. I love these secretive cities that do not easily yield their inner life to the casual eye.' Then *Un Dimanche à la campagne* (1983) was the evocative portrait of an elderly painter and his family, near Paris early this century. The shimmering photography, the quiet humanism, the elegiac mood, all added up to something almost too close to pastiche Renoir (*père et fils*): but the scene where father and daughter talk tenderly at a *bal guinguette* is wonderfully moving. Then came more warm nostalgia in *Round Midnight*, about a friendship in Paris in the 1950s between an ageing American black saxophonist and a young Frenchman. Another film in English, *Daddy nostalgie* (*These Foolish Things*, 1990), with Dirk Bogarde, pursued the familiar Tavernier theme of relationships with elderly parents.

Around this time a darker, more distressed note came to the front in his work. The humanism remained, but the subjects grew more austere – the futility of war, the modern decline of values. Two films explored the aftermath of the 1914–18 war. *La Vie et rien d'autre* (1989) is about an officer returning to the desolation of Verdun; *Le Capitaine Conan* (1996), drawn from a novel by Roger Vercel, examines a little-known episode in 1918–19 when France and her allies sent an army to fight the Bolsheviks in the Balkans and thousands gratuitously died. Tavernier was drawing some parallel with Bosnia in the 1990s. The oddly named *L.627* (1992) was a study of racism and brutality in the Paris police; and *L'Appât* (1994) was a harsh portrait of a group of feckless middle-class youths, knowing no values but those of money and violence. When I met Tavernier again in 1996, I found him changed after fifteen years: in place of the old geniality, he seemed upset and bitter about the state of French society, and he spoke of his worry about the decline of civilized values among young people. And whereas most of his earlier films had made money, *Le Capitaine Conan*, though a fine work, failed to draw the public to this remote and dour subject. 'I film only what interests me,' he said. 'My usual theme is the minor heroism of daily life.' His films reflect his state of mind. Not an élitist cult figure, he is anxious to relate to a wide public, so he wants to entertain. But he also wants to express his own urgent anxieties about the world, and to do both at once is not easy.

Another notable post-new-wave director is Maurice Pialat, whose vision of humanity has always been more dour and misanthropic than Tavernier's. In a low-keyed naturalistic style, his films explore sensitively the world of the humdrum suburbs and what he sees as the mediocrity of daily life, the inadequacy of people. *La Gueule ouverte* (1974) was the study of a woman dying of cancer and the embarrassed reactions of her family and friends. For *Passe ton bac d'abord* he moved to his home ground, a mining town near Lille, where he filmed a portrait of a group of *lycéens* from working-class homes, and showed these high-spirited youngsters settling into menial jobs and drab domesticity as the adult world inexorably closed in. The same sour note persisted in the much-praised *Loulou* (1980): here a well-off middle-class woman (Huppert) leaves her dull husband for a sexy delinquent layabout (Depardieu, superbly cast), and trails around with him and his equally loutish friends in a sleazy district of Paris. Riveting and convincing, the film tackled the theme of class differences, usually avoided in French cinema. Equally gloomy was *A nos amours* (1983), a story of teenage revolt that made a star of Sandrine Bonnaire. Then Pialat's powerful Bernanos adaptation, *Sous le soleil de Satan*, deservedly won the Grand Prix at Cannes in 1987. Of his later films, *Le Garçu* (1995) was another grimly realistic study of family life. His camera consistently focuses with unsparing intensity on his characters, showing them as messy victims not only of life but of their own weaknesses. He passes no judgement, and even mixes compassion with his misanthropy. Like him or not, he is a true *auteur*.

The other talented new directors since the 1970s are a varied bunch. Love and family have been their commonest themes. Claude Sautet, like Pialat, began his career quite late, and made his two best films in his sixties, *Un Coeur en hiver* and *Nelly et Monsieur Arnaud*, both starring Emmanuelle Béart. Both are delicate studies of love unfulfilled – one of a 'wintry heart' that cannot give love, the other of the barrier dividing youth from age. Claude Tacchella's *Cousin Cousine* (1975) was a delightful romantic-comedy-cum-family-satire. André Téchiné's Brechtian family saga *Souvenirs d'en France* was much praised, as was his more recent family study, *Ma Saison préférée*: but *Les Soeurs Brontë*, made on location in Yorkshire, showed once again that French directors are seldom at ease with non-French subjects made in Britain. They can excel with French historical subjects, as witness Alain Corneau's elegiac study of seventeenth-century musicians, *Tous les matins du monde* (1992). The excellent Claude Miller shows the influence of Truffaut in his wryly perceptive portraits of adolescence, notably the successful *L'Effrontée*. Nelly Kaplan, Argentine-born, has made some witty and hard-hitting satires on sexual hypocrisy, *La Fiancée du pirate* and *Néa*. And offbeat social satire has been the forte of that quirky and beguiling film-maker, Patrice Leconte. His

Les Bronzés, made in West Africa, was a zestful send-up of holiday life at Club Med, an easy target. Then came *Monsieur Hire*, a clever thriller, then the delightful *Le Mari de la coiffeuse*, a satire on mindless marital bliss, funnier and less acid than Varda's *Le Bonheur*. In the highly successful *Ridicule* (1996), Leconte poked elegant fun at the court life of Versailles under Louis XVI, and drew an oblique moral parallel with today's society.

These directors have been making civilized films about French life past and present – films with many of the traditional virtues of French cinema, its irony, its eye for human absurdity, its sense of atmosphere. They have not been making 'art movies' on the fringe of the industry, but nor are they integrated into its system: they are something in between, as often in France, and theirs is still a *cinéma d'auteur*. They have regularly made use of the gifted younger generation of French cinema players who sometimes call themselves 'anti-stars'. The ubiquitous Gérard Depardieu is the best known abroad. But he has been overused and not always well cast; and though certainly a serious actor he may not in fact be a better one than some of his contemporaries, such as Daniel Auteuil. Most of the other striking new performers are female – Fanny Ardant, Emmanuelle Béart, Sandrine Bonnaire, Isabelle Huppert and the hypnotic Juliette Binoche.

Lastly, a word about a few younger trendy directors. Luc Besson made a hit with his flashy Parisian thriller *Subway* (1985), then moved into big-budget international cinema (e.g. *The Fifth Element*, a futurist fantasy). Jean-Jacques Annaud likewise turned to big-time expensive movies (e.g. a version of Eco's *The Name of the Rose*), after a promising start with his satire on colonization in Africa, *La Victoire en chantant*. And the talented Jean-Jacques Beineix followed up *Diva*, a showy 'pop' success, with the curious *37°2 le matin* (*Betty Blue*, 1986). This account of an *amour fou* had patches of blatant bad taste but it worked to a fierce emotional climax.

Today in the later 1990s the French cinema is certainly in no golden era: but it is the liveliest in Europe, and very prolific. There have been two main recent developments. First, the arrival of another wave of younger directors, none outstanding but many of them good, with a new youthful outlook. Second, a stress on big-budget historical epics, mostly adapted from literary classics. This is not in the French tradition. But some producers, and official export promoters, had come to feel that France needed this kind of 'big' film to face the growing power of Hollywood on world and domestic French markets. In the old days, French cinema triumphed abroad through its sheer genius and originality: but this kind of *qualité française* has today grown less sure, and newer films tend to lack a worldwide impact. So it was felt that France, for reasons of prestige as well as commerce, should try to rival Hollywood on its own ground of the big popular spectacle – with the added value of a special French 'literary' element.

The trend was set by the huge success in 1990–91 of Jean-Paul Rappeneau's version of Edmond Rostand's verse play *Cyrano de Bergerac*, starring Depardieu with a long nose added. The film was France's most expensive yet (some 120 million francs) but made a profit. Shortly before, Claude Berri's two-part Pagnol adaptation, *Jean de Florette* and *Manon des sources*, less costly to make, had also done well at home and abroad. Berri followed this in 1993 with a version of Zola's saga of the Nord coal mines, *Germinal* (Depardieu *yet again*, this time wrongly cast as a starving miner). The film was worthy but ponderous: yet it made money, more at home than abroad. In fact, most of these costume epics have won a wide enough public to justify the strategy behind them: but a few have flopped. Patrice Chéreau filmed Dumas *père*'s tale of the sixteenth century *La Reine Margot*, with Isabelle Adjani amid lashings of blood and violence: it did only so-so. And in 1990–91 the young Leos Carax made an amazing folly, *Les Amants du Pont-Neuf*, with Juliette Binoche. This film with no literary pedigree was a modest tale of two tramps in Paris: but incredibly its budget topped *Cyrano*'s to become France's biggest ever, largely because the overambitious Carax rebuilt a whole *quartier* of Paris in a disused quarry in the Midi. He lost millions.

It is noticeable that very few of these and other 'big' films have been the work of top-class *auteur* directors (Chéreau apart). And some of the films might have been far better if made in a more subtle and intimate style, on a smaller budget. Witness Rappeneau's bid to repeat the success of *Cyrano* with *Le Hussard sur le toit* (1994), his epic version of Jean Giono's tale of bravery during a cholera epidemic in Provence in 1832. The film was stagey and superficial: cholera suffering, on screen, surely needs Bresson treatment, not Errol Flynn. But such is the usual problem of art versus box office in cinema. Could *Les Enfants du Paradis* have been a masterpiece with ten times the budget?

Alongside this big-budget trend, plenty of new young directors have appeared recently: in the later 1990s some thirty were making their first feature each year, a figure unequalled since the heyday of the *nouvelle vague*. They have been helped by government policies of aid to the cinema (see below). Mostly they make small, relatively low-budget films, very varied; there is no 'school', and no supreme new talent to provide a focus as in new-wave days. But the films are fresh; some of them reflect the mood and preoccupations of a younger generation today; and some touch on topical social questions – such as AIDS, unemployment or *la banlieue*. Notably, Mathieu Kassovitz's *La Haine* caused a stir in 1995. It told of a trio of high-spirited young friends in a dreary Paris suburb, an Arab, a Black and a Jew, who take the mickey out of authority and vent their frustrations about unemployment. It was the first time for years that a French movie had tackled *la banlieue* so directly, and it brought hordes of ordinary young people into the cinemas – 'At last, a film about *us!*' Socially and politically, the film was of value, particularly in featuring interracial youth friendship rather than the more usual topic of racial hostility. But it was not in itself such a good film: it was jokey and stylized, not a serious exploration of its social milieu. Some other recent movies, for instance Jean-François Richet's powerful *État des lieux*, have examined youth in *la banlieue* far more realistically: but they are more austere and demanding, and have done less well at the box office.

Érick Zonca's first feature, *La Vie rêvée des anges* (1998) set in Lille, was a sensitive study of two working-class girls and their struggle to find a meaning in life. It was in the best French realist tradition and won top prizes at Cannes for its two young actresses Élodie Bouchez and Natacha Régnies. Some other new directors have expressed personally their own anguish in today's world. Xavier Beauvois's powerful *N'oublie pas que tu vas mourir* was about a student with AIDS who takes drugs, goes to wartime Bosnia and courts death romantically. And several of the best of the new directors are women. Martine Dugowson's *Mina Tannenbaum* was a sympathetic study of a friendship between two girls in a *lycée*, one of them Jewish. Sandrine Veysset's impressive 1996 début, *Y aura-t-il de la neige à Noël?*, was an austere portrait of family life and hard work on a poor farm in Provence in the 1970s. The film, like some others by the new female directors, focused on the difficult role of women in a male-dominated world. Dourly realistic, based on felt personal experience, it contrasted alike with the cosy Pagnol-inspired view of Provence and with the Paris-centred approach of many of the other bright new cinema talents.

One of these, Arnaud Desplechin, made an extraordinary movie in 1996, *Comment je me suis disputé . . . (ma vie sexuelle)*, about the love lives and personal problems of a group of hyper-articulate young middle-class Parisians, centring round a self-obsessed teacher, wittily played by Mathieu Amalric. Lasting a full three hours, this intensely French film is in some ways absurdly self-indulgent but also inventive and oddly absorbing, and it clearly harks back to Eustache. With its endless intimate chatter, it also recalls Rohmer, while Desplechin admits the influence of Truffaut, too. He is in the true *nouvelle vague* tradition. Cédric Klapisch, somewhat different, has made offbeat comedies with a family or social setting. In *Chacun cherche son chat* (1995), a girl in a mixed quarter of Paris goes looking for her lost cat, and is thus drawn out of her loneliness into warm contact with her neighbours. It is charming and human, if slight. Klapisch told me, 'Yes, today's films *are* slight. There are plenty of good ones, but no "great" ones as in former days. Why? – maybe it's the spirit of the times. People don't want heavy movies that make them think, they want to be entertained. And directors and producers daren't take commercial risks, so they need to please their audience. Hence all the light comedies.' But they can have a tougher edge. Robert Guédiguian's highly praised *Marius et Jeannette* (1997) is a superb evocation of the low life of his native Marseille. Owing less to Pagnol than to Brecht or Renoir, it seems to be making a statement almost political in its optimism about the resilience of ordinary people – a film in the best French humanist tradition.

'Ever since the 1930s,' says Tavernier, 'our cinema industry has lurched from crisis to crisis and producers have moaned and groaned. But here we still are, we survive.' Inevitably, the cinema in France is in economic trouble, as in other countries: but it is showing more resilience than most. After a period of decline in the early 1990s, it is again producing some 100 to 120 full-length features a year, plus others in co-production: this compares with the dire situation in Germany and Italy, where very few good films are now made. And even in Britain, although a few key directors are turning out superb original work, the overall output is heavily dependent on America for finance and leadership. The French cinema has managed to remain largely independent of Hollywood, and most of its co-productions are with other European countries.

Much of the buoyancy is due to help from the TV networks, and to the special state policy of aid to the cinema, more generous than in most countries. Malraux in 1959 set up a system of *primes à la qualité*, whereby a film can receive an advance on earnings, assessed on the basis of the artistic merit of its scenario. Some fifty films a year, including nearly all the more serious ones, benefit from these loans, which often are crucial in helping a young director to start a venture. Much of the funding for this aid comes from a 10-per-cent levy on cinema tickets: so, as American films tend to dominate the box office, Hollywood is indirectly helping to subsidize the French industry. Some other aid goes to distributors and to the small *art et essai* movie houses that show classic or quality films. It remains French official thinking that cinema is an art form worthy of support, like music or theatre, and that it plays an important role in French cultural prestige. Catherine Trautmann is today giving it new special aid.

The Government has been seeking to make cinema and television into allies, not enemies. It tries to protect the movie industry by obliging the TV networks to collaborate in the co-production of some films, and by limiting the networks' own rights to show new movies. As TV accounts for some 97 per cent of all viewing of features, some entente between the two rivals has become crucial: many of the better new French movies today are joint ventures between film producers and the networks, which are obliged to undertake this co-financing. Then they must not show these films on their own screens for the first two years, nor other new films for three years, nor can they show a total of more than some 190 cinema films of any kind per year, per network: the restrictions are lighter for the subscription channel, Canal Plus, which plays a more active role in co-production. Under EU rules decided in 1991 there is also a quota whereby at least 50 per cent of all material shown on television must be European: in practice, in France, the vast majority of it is French. 'This has curbed the massive invasion of our screens by Hollywood product,' I was told by one leading film producer, Daniel Toscan du Plantier. 'And the co-production rules help the cinema hugely.' However, some of the major networks, notably TF1, have recently been falling short of their quotas or failing to give enough help to smaller producers of offbeat films. And they have been developing their own features and series made solely for TV, a genre where hitherto France had lagged behind Britain. The small independent producers today feel threatened by these trends. They, and others, would like to see the Euro-quota extended from TV to cinemas, where at present there are no limits. In the GATT talks the French have taken the lead in trying to protect the European film industry from so-called 'American cultural imperialism' (see p. 707).

While cinema production in France is buoyant, the level of cinema-going has finally stabilized. The belated impact of TV took its heaviest toll between 1957 and 1971, when one cinema in three closed and annual attendances fell from 411 to 177 million. But the collapse in other countries was greater: in Germany from 801 to 124 million between 1957 and 1977. The French figure fell again in the 1980s, due to the opening of new TV networks. However, in the 1990s it has again been stable: it has even risen since 1995 from 129 to 148 million (the figure in Britain is around 120 million). More disturbing has been the fall in exports, notably within Europe. This is due in part to the decline of cinema-going in Germany and Italy, but also quite probably to the fall in the quality and reputation of new French films.

Within France, American movies account for some 50 to 55 per cent of all cinema entries, French ones for about 35 per cent, and the rest of the world for some 10 per cent. British films remain rather popular: but Italian and German ones, today mostly so mediocre, have fallen right back. Although the French may affect to despise American mass culture, the public still flocks to the big Hollywood films. But the national product holds up against them far better than in most of Europe. Yet the biggest French domestic successes are rarely the *films d'auteur* admired by critics and intellectuals, for public mass taste is little loftier than elsewhere. The top earner in France since the war, in real terms, has been *La Grande Vadrouille* ('the great gad-about'), a low comedy that few people abroad will even have heard of. More recently, the biggest successes have been other low comedies such as *Les Visiteurs* (1993), or banal feel-good movies like *Le Bonheur est dans le pré*, or provocative farces such as Josiane Balasko's *Gazon maudit* (*French Dressing*), about lesbians. The French mass public may like to be shocked: but, as Klapisch said, it seldom wants to be made to think.

Stylish entertainments such as *Ridicule* do well, as do some of the costume epics. But of the *nouvelle vague* veterans still at work, Chabrol is the only one still assured of a big public. And of the new young directors, Kassovitz's big success with *La Haine* was something of an exception. Many of the other good new films barely cover their costs. 'Even the more discriminating public has become less interested in the minor offbeat film, whether French or foreign,' said one critic, Michel Simon. And the recent growth of big multi-screen cinemas, whether downtown or in new suburban shopping centres, has been making life harder for the small independent producers. The owners of these multiplexes are seldom interested in their kind of film, and have been pushing some of the smaller individual cinemas out of business.

Compared with Britain or America, the French systems of distribution and production have always been fragmented, with few large-scale cinema circuits and countless small production companies. Even today, the three main distributors, Gaumont, Pathé and the Union Générale Cinématographique, control only about 20 per cent of cinemas. This fluidity has in many ways been helpful for the low-budget personal film: but it leads to high costs and inefficiencies which today can be a burden. So the trend is now to share production costs through deals not only with the TV networks but with foreign companies.

One unfortunate result can be the Euro-pudding – the hybrid de-nationalized film with unauthentic casting. For example, a co-production might have a Franco-Italian cast all playing Germans and improbably talking English. For nations to pool their talent in this way can be artistically disastrous. Happily, many of these Euro-puddings have flopped and the genre now seems past its prime. By all means nations should see each other's films as much as possible: but they should be made with authentic language and casting. And joint financing need not be an obstacle: *Carrington* was no less genuine and realistic an English film for having been made partly with French money. If the subject-matter is genuinely cross-national, as in Tavernier's *Round Midnight*, then more than one language can be used, with subtitling. One shining virtue of French cinema, in good films or in silly ones, is that it has always radiated a genuine Frenchness. This has been a prime reason for its popularity abroad. And today, despite economic hazards, despite the lack of top-level new directors, France still has its own lively authentic cinema. The issue is how to reconcile commercial needs with the tradition of the *film d'auteur*. 'It can be done,' says the commercially minded Toscan du Plantier, 'so long as it is not too esoteric, as too many *nouvelle vague* movies were. There's no reason why a personal film should not reach a good public.' It is a question, as ever, of those rare commodities, talent and originality.

TELEVISION:
FROM THE STATE FRYING-PAN INTO THE
COMMERCIAL FIRE?

France's educated classes have long envied Britain its television. 'In London,' wrote *Le Monde*'s critic, Claude Sarraute, in 1980, 'you press a button and you have the feeling of uncorking a champagne bottle, of being bathed in a cascade of wit, fun and imagination unknown on our side of the Channel.' Since then, that champagne may have gone flat too often, as triviality advances; and French TV, freed from state control, has at least become more frank and lively. Yet the contrast remains striking.

While French Governments have poured money and effort into helping the established arts, they have never properly understood the new medium of television. In Gaullist and pre-Gaullist days, they were scared politically of giving it a freedom that might be abused, so they kept it under close control: this was one aspect of that historic French conflict between Jacobinism and contentious opposition. The state monopoly, especially under de Gaulle, produced a television that was timid and self-censoring: so, unlike the BBC, it never acquired the self-confidence and prestige essential for creating high programme standards and attracting the best talent. Giscard liberalized it a little, reducing government pressures. And Mitterrand later ended the state monopoly: but he also introduced commercial channels of dubious quality – an odd step for so cultured a man. As a result, French television today still lacks prestige. It has long been despised by most educated people – first as a tool of the State, today as a tool of big business. Many talented people are at work in television, and they manage to produce some lively programmes, notably chat shows, at which the French excel. But even their better work still tends to be oddly conformist – in contrast to the French tradition of radical innovation in other cultural fields. Television in France is still struggling to find itself – and today's new rise of countless digital channels seems hardly likely to improve its quality.

Television was slower to make its impact in France than in many countries. One reason was the low priority given by the State to its development: a second network started only in 1964. The conservative French public, too, was slow at first to adapt its habits to watching *la télé*: an educated family might say that it had a set just '*pour la bonne*' or '*pour les gosses*', and would hide it in a back room. In 1963 there were still only 3 million sets, compared with 12 million then in Britain: but the French have since caught up, and 95 per cent of homes now have a set.

Broadcasting was state-controlled from its birth. The Office de la Radio et Télévision Française (ORTF), as it was called, began life as a branch of the Postal Ministry, and in the post-war years it depended directly on the Ministry of Information or the Prime Minister's office. A few liberals made worthy efforts in Parliament for the ORTF to be provided with a real autonomy like the BBC, but no Government would part with so valuable a weapon. Under the Fourth Republic, there was frequent suppression of critical views in broadcasts, or measures against hostile staff journalists. Then the Gaullist regime made matters worse, placing its own loyalists in the key ORTF posts. The charming Gaullist who ran the Brittany station told me, 'With only fifteen minutes of local news a day, do we have time to air local criticisms of official policy? We, the Government, are doing all we can to promote regional progress. The time isn't ripe to let Bretons criticize us on the screen. They're too immature.' I had rarely heard a more candid résumé of Gaullist paternalism. De Gaulle himself, a brilliant screen performer, regarded TV as his fief: 'My opponents have much of the press on their side, so I keep television,' he once said – a common official justification for control of the medium. In his day, almost any programme on an economic or social subject had to be vetted in advance by the relevant ministry.

The brighter side of this coin, in de Gaulle and Malraux's day, was that French TV did try to keep up a certain cultural tone. State monopoly carried this advantage: there was no need to compete with commercial TV for audiences, so the proportion of serious or cultural programming could be kept quite high. The ORTF bought little American pulp material; and though it did show its own banal quizzes and variety shows, these were balanced by long hours devoted to the arts, history, and so on. This was Malraux's influence. Television was didactic in the French pedagogic manner, and took no great account of audience tastes. But these worthy programmes were often sloppily edited and presented. Unlike their BBC counterparts, most of the top ORTF executives were not broadcasters but people brought in from the civil service or industry: few of them had much experience or understanding of creative work, and they failed to set standards.

Morale was low. Many producers, reporters and technicians were on the Left, but they had to toe the line or else . . . Then the events of May '68 gave the staff its cue for a showdown with the Government, whose initial handling of the TV coverage of the Sorbonne rebellion was typical: it refused to let the ORTF screen any account of it, although the press was full of it. So, as Gaullist power seemed to be crumbling, the ORTF staff staged a *putsch* and for a few glorious days reporters said what they liked on the screens. When the Government replied with threats of an army takeover, the staff went on full strike for a month. But when de Gaulle finally restored order in France, there were heavy reprisals: more than sixty journalists on radio and TV were dismissed, and the more critical programmes were axed. The aim was to purge the ORTF of its 'star' personalities, who might try to use their popularity with viewers to combat the regime.

However, the Government was not unanimous. Throughout these years, under de Gaulle and then Pompidou, a protracted battle was going on behind the scenes at top level, between 'liberals' who argued that too much state control could become a vote-loser, and 'diehards', led by Debré and Pompidou, who replied that any relaxation was dangerous. The liberals finally gained ground after 1969, and opposition leaders could at last be interviewed on the screen and their activities covered in bulletins. The liberal-minded premier Jacques Chaban-Delmas even persuaded President Pompidou to let him appoint a well-known radical TV journalist, Pierre Desgraupes, as news editor of the First Network, with a brief to inject some balance and critical comment into its output. The experiment lasted about two years, until Pompidou forced Desgraupes's resignation.

A more durable liberalization, of a kind, then began under Giscard. He hoped to set up an independent commercial channel, maybe on the British model: but he was opposed by his Gaullist allies and by the left-wing unions. So instead he reduced the ORTF's unwieldy bureaucracy by breaking it into seven smaller bodies (three ran the TV networks), in the hope that new competition might improve quality. He also did away with the Gaullist style of direct daily interference in TV: editors now had more freedom and could even cover events such as the Communist Party congress with some objectivity. But the State kept ultimate control, and it appointed the chiefs of the new companies. So TV was still deferential and institutional: it would interview left-wing leaders, but seldom take its cameras into the streets for probing reports. Delicate or controversial topics were still taboo. Nor did Giscard's reforms do much for artistic quality. The networks were still mainly funded by money from the licence fee: but now they took advertising, too, which prompted a battle for ratings. With Malraux gone, the stress on culture declined, and cheap American imports were allowed to flood French screens. In short, under Giscard, television became more lively and open, but also more trivial. As one critic wrote, 'He made a muddled attempt to graft a private-enterprise philosophy on to a public-service bureaucracy.'

The Socialists then came to power with plans for a new deal, as in many other areas of French life. Having denounced for so long the abuses of state control, they were now committed to practising what they had preached. But they were divided about ending the monopoly, for most leaders were ideologically opposed to commercial TV. So at first they simply took a stage further the granting of more BBC-like autonomy to the three existing public networks. They set up a new Haute Autorité to protect the media alike from official and commercial pressures; and they brought in new blood: many staff sacked by earlier Governments were reinstated, but there was no real witch-hunt. The climate in the studios brightened, and bulletins became more newsy, less dully institutional. An official communiqué or a foreign visit by the President was no longer automatically the lead story but had to fight for space on its news merits.

Mitterrand was in favour of truly ending the state monopoly, but the method that he finally chose was most peculiar. First, in 1984, he sanctioned an independent nationwide pay-TV channel, Canal Plus, which has since been highly successful (see below). More controversially, in 1985–6 he gave the green light to two purely commercial channels on the dubious Italian model, financed by advertising and lowbrow in content. One of them was run by two of his business friends, in association with the Italian tycoon Silvio Berlusconi, and it began to show quizzes and imported soap operas, with no news or current affairs; the second, aimed at youth, included lots of pop-music video clips. Mitterrand took these decisions in the teeth of opposition from his advisers, and he had to dissuade Jack Lang from resigning. In a pre-electoral period, this highly cultured President was acting out of political expediency: he wanted to forestall the Right by currying popular votes, and by putting his own allies in charge of the new networks, knowing that commercial TV was bound to come. But his measures seemed a betrayal of the earlier Socialist intentions that the ending of the monopoly should involve neither a sell-out to business interests nor a debasement of quality. Plans by Jack Lang for a publicly run European cultural channel were considered, but rejected: their one sequel has been the highbrow Franco-German evening channel Arte (see below).

The Right, back in power under Chirac in the *cohabitation* of 1986–8, then went further than Mitterrand in dismantling the monopoly. Notably it privatized the main channel, Télévision Française 1 (TF1) – apparently the first time in the world that a state-run network had been sold into private hands. There were raucous debates in Parliament; President Mitterrand was himself hostile, but he could do little. The Government's motives were in part ideological, in line with its 'liberal' stance; they were also political, aiming to make it harder for TF1 to be recuperated by any future left-wing regime. Chirac then staged a 'TV sale of the century' of the three non-state networks. TF1 went to a consortium led by Francis Bouygues, the building industry magnate; Channel 5 ('*la Cinq*') remained with Berlusconi, in alliance with the right-wing press baron Robert Hersant (see p. 504), and later with Hachette; and Channel 6 went to a group led by the mighty Compagnie Luxembourgeoise de Télédiffusion. Anxiety grew that the old tyranny of state domination might simply give place to a new right-wing commercial control by big monopolies. But in the event this has not happened as much as was feared. In fact, in 1992 '*la Cinq*' went bankrupt and no new buyers were found: so the Government took back the network and made it into a public educational channel, shared with Arte. This has marked a modest victory for serious television.

Apart from this, the structure has not changed since 1987. There are still six main networks, three in public hands, three private, plus some tiny local stations and the beginnings of digital TV by satellite. TF1, still owned by the Bouygues group, has the largest audience, averaging 36 per cent of the total. Its two main rivals, publicly owned, are France 2 (formerly Antenne 2), with about 24 per cent, and France 3, partly regional, with some 18 per cent. M6, owned largely by the CLT plus Lyonnaise des Eaux, gets around 10 per cent, with a programme of pop music, variety and films aimed mainly at youth, plus a few good documentaries. Then there is the '*la Cinquième*'/Arte channel, which has small audience figures; and the Canal Plus cable network, partly owned by Havas, which does well.

For more than ten years now, government interference in the media has been slight, and this issue seems resolved. 'The situation is normalized; it's the same as in other countries,' I was assured by Jacques Rigaud, the chairman of Radio Télévision Luxembourg (RTL, part of CLT). 'One factor is the frequent political alternation of recent years, which has made it harder for any Government to keep a grip on the media. Also, the growth of so many networks in competition has made Governments less sensitive about any individual one.' A watchdog body, the Conseil Supérieur de l'Audiovisuel (CSA), a successor to the old Haute Autorité, is appointed by President and Parliament to keep a general eye on standards; this CSA also nominates the chairmen of the public networks, but does not interfere in their programmes. Television may still be a little more respectful of authority than in some countries, such as Britain, but this is more by French tradition than by command. Canal Plus even has a sharp satiric puppet show. Some experts would argue that television has too much influence in France today, since Parliament is rather weak.

The problem now is less that of state influence than of the impact of budget shortages and of ratings battles on the quality of programmes. Nearly all French television has become very commercial. The private channels, TF1 and M6, depend almost entirely on advertising; France 2 and France 3 are allowed to draw up to 51 per cent of their income from this source, while the rest comes from the licence fee. But as this state funding is limited, even the public channels get drawn into a non-stop tussle over ratings. Hence most networks put their stress on easy entertainment programmes. As money has grown short, they have come to rely heavily on cheap foreign products and repeats. Ten episodes of some American soap opera can often be bought for the same sum that is needed to make an hour-long documentary. And Governments, for demagogic reasons, have been reluctant to increase the licence fee, today 735 francs a year. Yet by no means all programmes are bad, and some good French creative work does reach the screen.

TF1, operating from a hefty skyscraper downstream from the Eiffel Tower, moved downmarket for a few years recently, with a banal selection of quizzes, sex shows, vulgar variety, plus the cheap imports. But it went too far, and found that this diet actually lost audiences. Today its programming has become more sober. It is a well-run, profitable company, whereas France 2 has been losing money despite a rise in its audience. The intense rivalry between the networks can be ridiculous. Notably, for many years both have insisted on screening their main evening news bulletin at 8 p.m. This is a social ritual in France, *le sacré de 20 heures*, when a family sits round its table watching a star newscaster. But the public has no other choice of timing. Attempts to persuade either network to change its hour have always failed, for each thinks it would lose out.

France 2, like its rival, screens plenty of light popular programmes and feature films. Yet it also has something of the BBC-like ethos of a public service; and its charter obliges it to present some serious programmes for minorities or special interest groups, for example religious ones. Although its work has a slightly more 'official' flavour than TF1's, it is no longer seen as *la télé de l'État* and is mostly free – sometimes even *too* free. Witness, in 1996, the strange affair of Jean-Pierre Elkabbach, who was president of France-Télévision, the public body that operates France 2 and France 3. This brilliant journalist, perhaps France's best TV interviewer, was an arrogant, ambitious high-flyer who sought to boost France 2's fortunes by hiring a coterie of star presenters and producers, his chums, to whom he gave enormous salaries. There was no one to check him, and he felt above the law. But finally the staff found out and turned against him, and he was forced to resign. It was a big national scandal, but more a matter of imprudent management than corruption. Some observers drew the moral that French television, though now stable, was still immature, and the public channels were thus capable of abusing their new freedom.

No such taint has yet marred France 3, which has recently shown itself the best of the non-cable networks, with a coherent policy and rising audiences. It makes some good fiction films and documentaries, relying little on quizzes or star presenters – and many viewers rally to its relative *sérieux*. Above all, it has a strong regional dimension, with large studios in the main cities (100 journalists are on its staff at Lyon), and its local evening news magazines have a good following. They are reasonably critical and objective, and so can add something to local debate – unlike the days when this channel was simply the Government's voice in the regions. Some of its work is networked nationally, some is purely local. But its studios have no organic links with their region, no boards where local worthies sit *ex officio*. 'In some ways this is a weakness,' said the news director of the Lyon station, 'but it does protect us from many local pressures.' Even so, not always: when Alain Carignon was mayor of nearby Grenoble and also Minister of Communication, he had one of his buddies put in charge of France 3 at Lyon, which as a result kept mum about his scandal for a long time. It was a rare example of such direct official pressure in TV's new liberated age.

After the dizzy changes of the 1980s, French television has now settled down, and the average quality of home-grown output has possibly risen a little in recent years from a low level. By comparison with the best British TV, it can often seem stiff and pedestrian, even clumsy: but it is less parochial, and will sometimes go deeper into a subject. There are a few decent regular current affairs programmes, mostly on France 3 whose weekly *La Marche du siècle* tackles serious social problems, and gets a good audience. Other regulars include *Envoyé spécial* (France 2) and *7 sur 7* (TF1), where a public figure is interviewed in depth. The French generally prefer ideas to facts – maybe a reason why the best current affairs TV tends to be debate, not documentary. A programme where a politician is grilled for two hours by a panel of journalists can win high ratings as a kind of intellectual bull fight. French TV can have the edge over British or American TV in the quality of such debates, for the French are gifted talkers. By our crisp standards, these programmes can seem overextended, even ill-disciplined, with everyone trying to talk at once. But a French public is used to lengthy and excited argument – witness any public meeting in France.

Even the news bulletins can be prolix by British standards. They are also more personalized: a star newsreader will sometimes intersperse the news of some crisis with his own moralizing about it – a cardinal sin in Britain but accepted in France. On TF1, Patrick Poivre d'Arvor, one of France's major celebrities, is editor-in-chief well as newscaster, so he can shape the content of 'his' forty-minute evening bulletin. 'People like me to give my own views,' he assured me; 'I also try to be a bit pedagogic – say, to explain what the EU is all about. They like that, too. The decline in the role and prestige of the political parties has given us in television a huge extra responsibility. We are now France's main opinion formers, and we have to be careful.'

Yet background documentary on modern French subjects remains one of French TV's weaker points. Many of its best documentaries are imported from a variety of countries, which at least makes the pattern less parochial than in Britain. The networks have occasionally made their own historical series, even on such delicate topics as the Dreyfus affair or the First World War mutinies – all very frank, but safely dealing with the past. When it comes to current French issues, searching documentaries are far fewer. There have been some programmes on personal moral matters such as AIDS, homosexuality, even abortion. But on such issues as unemployment or immigration, there is seldom much attempt to explore the state of French society through vox pop inquiries; as for the corruption scandals, investigative reporting is left to the press to initiate, while TV merely summarizes what it says. A section of the public, according to surveys, would welcome more documentaries: but they are expensive. And the networks are still too unsure of their new freedom to want to be too controversial.

In the areas of fiction and culture, the main networks show a large number of old cinema feature films, about forty to fifty a week *in toto*, notably on Canal Plus. Many are routine dross: but a surprising number are serious classics, or art movies from the world over, or new experimental work. Many new French cinema films are co-productions with TV, and the networks are now making more of their own hour-long *téléfilms* or series: some are produced by France 3 in regional studios. But serial adaptations of classic novels rarely reach the quality of the best British work. And there is not much policy of encouraging new TV drama on modern subjects: good new writers are lacking, as in the theatre. Non-fiction cultural programmes, either documentary or spectacle, are also few; and they tend to have poor ratings, curiously. One reason may be that the French intelligentsia are still not geared to television: they expect little of it, and prefer other forms of relaxation such as a long chat over a good meal. Possible exceptions are the literary chat shows, such as *Bouillon de culture*, which have no real British equivalent and do well.

At the lower end of the spectrum, French TV offers plenty of variety shows, quizzes and games shows, seldom of much quality. A few of the quizzes feature half-naked girls and sexy innuendoes – unthinkable in the old days. Until the early 1980s TV had hardly emerged from the ethos of the Hayes Code, and one critic said, 'In a bedroom scene in the cinema, people are naked to the waist or more: on TV they wear dressing-gowns. It's all so genteel – a reflection of a hypocritical society.' Then, following on the reforms of birth control and abortion, the new freer values of society finally reached the screen in the Mitterrand era: today nudity and sexiness are permitted almost as much as in the cinema, and French TV has moved ahead of America. But when it comes to very frank personal analysis of moral issues, it remains more reticent than in Britain.

French TV is technologically advanced in its way. It makes full use of electronic news-gathering techniques, and it deploys split-screen and montage effects with a virtuosity verging on gimmickry. Yet despite the qualities of the film work, the studio continuity and presentation can still be slapdash. One reason may be that the network chiefs are less concerned with setting high professional standards than with securing good ratings and keeping out of political trouble. Recruiting has always been haphazard – people drift to and fro from the press and cinema worlds – and French TV has never bothered itself much with the rigorous training of new staff, as the BBC does. So the networks' plentiful talent has not been fully drilled in TV techniques. It may help to explain the mediocrity of many programmes.

And the reactions of the great French public? They have few illusions, and even today they accept the inadequacies of TV with a shrug. When it first made its impact in the 1960s, it had some disruptive social effects and there were complaints that it was eroding the noble French art of conversation: in cafés or in homes people would sit glued to the screen instead of arguing. But this has now changed a little. The set may be on, but people will often lend it only half an eye or ear. Except for the news or big sporting matches or popular films, television tends to be a background against which they carry on talking or eating. And although the French watch it quite a lot (some twenty-two hours a week on average, against twenty-five in Britain), it is seldom central to their lives, at least in the educated classes. Less than in Britain are the regular programmes eagerly discussed the next day.

Two specialized channels stand out as having rather more quality, and more discriminating audiences, than the others. One is the pay-TV Canal Plus, owned mainly by the giant Havas advertising group and by Générale des Eaux. After a difficult start in 1984 it has since blossomed, with over 4 million subscribers in France who pay 180 francs a month; and it has expanded into Spain, Italy and elsewhere to become Europe's leading pay-TV venture. Its success in France is due above all to its good feature films and sports programmes: it has negotiated exclusive rights to some football matches and other events, and is able to show new French feature films sooner than the main networks, in return for the co-production support it gives to film companies. It also has the money and initiative to make better documentaries, on average, than the open networks. And it leads in political satire: every night it screens, free and unencrypted, a five-minute puppet show, *Les Guignols*, which mercilessly pokes fun at politicians and is very popular. For instance, in 1994 the puppet Balladur was shown thrusting a dagger into the back of his friend Chirac.

The other special channel is the fifth, which during the day is occupied by the state-owned '*la Cinquième*', worthily devoted to education and to programmes about work and finding jobs. From 7 p.m. to midnight, this channel belongs to the Franco-German Arte, which has many excellent serious programmes but alas a very small audience. It was decided on in 1988 by President Mitterrand and Chancellor Kohl as part of their bid for a closer Franco-German entente; Mitterrand may also have had a bad conscience after his lowbrow commercial TV ventures, and wanted to make amends with something more cultural. Publicly owned and funded, with no advertising, Arte is based suitably in Strasbourg, and has just one bilingual programme beamed to both countries, dubbed or subtitled as necessary: the German audience is the larger.

It offers a varied diet of quality feature films (say, a season of Bresson or Fellini), plus documentaries, historical, social or cultural (say, on Siberia, or the novels of García Márquez), mostly bought from outside. This worthy output is much of it interesting and of good quality: but it is austerely presented with few concessions to its audience, and Arte has not managed to make the same impact as Channel 4 in Britain. Its average audience is only 4 to 5 per cent: yet surveys show that a similar programme on a given subject might reach three or four times that figure on TF1 or France 2 or 3. It is not just the content, however, that puts viewers off: many, it is thought, are deterred by Arte's 'German' image (just as some Germans find it too French). So Arte has been trying to broaden its base: by 1997 a Spanish channel was showing some of its programmes, while the Belgians and Poles were also interested. But Britain, typically, has remained aloof; and it has never been found feasible to turn Arte into a full European cultural channel, as Lang originally planned. Many people on the Right, or in the big networks, have been demanding the death of a venture that costs the French taxpayer some 1 billion francs a year. In response Arte has now been trying to widen its range, for example by screening debates on Tarzan or rock 'n' roll. This could lose it some of its credit with French intellectuals, who admire it in theory even if they watch it seldom. For the moment, it is well protected by the Government; and its expected merger in 1999 with '*la Cinquième*' could lend it added security. Arte seems to me a brave, worthwhile venture – a sobering illustration of the problems of trying to feed a wide public with a diet of serious television *plus* pro-German friendship.

The television scene is today again being modified – but not totally transformed – by the advent in France of digital TV by satellite, ahead of Britain. This allows the viewer a choice of some thirty or more extra channels at a fairly modest cost. After much jockeying for position, two main groups were formed in 1995–6, and they went on the air with their rival 'clusters' (*bouquets*), each charging their subscribers about 120 francs per month. The dynamic Canal Plus got ahead first with its CanalSatellite, using its strength and experience in pay-TV to prepare channels heavily geared to sport and old feature films. Then its rival, Télévision Par Satellite (TPS), was created by a large unholy alliance of nearly all the other French networks plus France Télécom and the Lyonnaise des Eaux. Other possible contenders, the Murdochs and Bertelsmanns of this world, were kept at bay. By mid-1998 Canal Plus had 900,000 subscribers and TPS 600,000, and both were growing fast. They had fought over the pickings and shared them out. Thus Canal Plus did an exclusive deal with Warner Brothers, and TPS with Paramount; Canal Plus got the first French football league, so TPS took the second; Canal Plus also bought the French rights to international rugby from Murdoch. TPS was showing the new EuroNews channel, in French. It was also offering a range of foreign networks, including CNN, BBC1, Germany's ZDF and Italy's RAI: but the audience for these programmes not in French is likely to remain tiny.

The big question is what effect this digital revolution will have on the existing hertzian (i.e. non-satellite, non-cable) networks: will the new competition lead to a further downward spiralling of quality? Most experts were still sanguine in 1998: 'I am very optimistic about the future of TF1,' said its deputy chairman, Étienne Mougeotte. As digital TV is quite cheap to operate, the networks are going to it to make extra profits: so it could even improve their funding. Secondly, as nearly all the material except for sport is likely to be recycled, rather than new work, digital TV will not put an extra strain on creative resources. It is thought that the hertzian networks' share of the TV audience could fall to about 70 per cent: but in an expanding market, this could mean no real fall at all. And for some viewers at least, digital may open new windows on the world, beaming BBC or ZDF into French homes.

Yet if digital does not damage the older networks, it is hardly likely to improve their programme quality. And so, to sum up, we are left with this curious situation in France that television remains the weakest link in the entire cultural apparatus. The Government pours money into live theatre, art galleries, music and film-making: but it does very little to help the arts on the TV screen, which is where most average adults today get so much of their cultural exposure (intellectuals apart). This potent vehicle for the spreading of culture has been poorly understood and poorly served by politicians, who in the past confused it too much with politics. Mitterrand may have freed it from state control, but he then failed to take it seriously in cultural terms. Jack Lang, who agonized helplessly over the damage done, expressed to me a common view: 'It is a grave pity that our Socialist reforms of 1985–6 did not look for inspiration to the British model, not only to the BBC but to ITV and its superb Channel 4, which has proved that commercial television, if properly organized, *can* be creatively innovative. But in France the clash of business groups debases cultural content.' And Jacques Rigaud, chairman of RTL, added in 1996, 'Governments and Parliament should have found the political courage to raise the licence fee much higher. Then some channels, made less dependent on advertising, could have set a standard for better programmes, as in Britain.' Late in 1998 Catherine Trautmann presented a modest new law, with the aim of strengthening and protecting television: but whether it would remedy the real problems was far from clear.

One handicap is that educated people in France, not just the so-called 'intellectuals', still have a stronger bias against television than in most countries. Except maybe for the news and a few special programmes, they watch it little, and pay little attention to it. Hence if a serious or cultural programme is shown, they are often unaware of it, or they hardly expect it to be worth seeing. It is one reason why serious material does not get better ratings, and it is a vicious circle. Meanwhile, since the early 1980s French television may have moved from the state frying-pan into the commercial fire. Decisive battles have been won, politically, and TV will never again be as tame as in Gaullist days. But, culturally, one can be left hankering for the high-minded Reithian ethos of the Malraux era.

In the case of radio, the Government in Gaullist days was never able to impose the same monopoly as in television. Since land-based transmitters could reach so far, several popular commercial stations, largely French-owned and backed by French advertising, were able to dodge the monopoly by broadcasting from just outside French soil. They included Radio Luxembourg (RTL), Radio Monte Carlo (RMC) and Europe 1 with its transmitters in the Saar. They needed to keep large studios in

Paris, and the cables to their transmitters belonged to the French Post Office: so the Government could have made their life difficult. But this might have been politically unwise: so instead it cleverly sought to acquire financial control over these *radios périphériques*. A state-owned holding company, Sofirad, had owned most of the shares in RMC since 1945, and in 1959 it won a hold over Europe 1, too, through various intrigues. Even mighty RTL, despite the initial opposition of the Grand Duchy, came under the aegis of a French consortium led by Havas, then state-owned. So in pre-Mitterrand days these 'free' stations were in practice under almost as much surveillance as the state TV and radio networks. Their news programmes were also wary of criticizing officialdom too boldly: when one news director of Europe 1 went too far, he was dismissed. So Governments had little cause to fear these stations. They may have detracted from the state networks' audience, but they were also a useful source of revenue, via Sofirad and Havas. All in all, it was a cynical state of affairs.

Under Mitterrand's new deal for the media, the pressures eased. Havas is now privatized, also Matra/Hachette, which controls Europe 1, and the small Monte Carlo station was finally sold to private owners in 1998. In fact, the issue of the 'free' peripheral stations no longer exists. And French radio today is largely free from interference: the picture is much the same as in television, save for the much larger number of small local stations. The most popular station, as for the last thirty years, is RTL, still broadcasting from Luxembourg but very much part of the French scene. With some 18 per cent of the total audience, it follows an astute policy of monitoring readers' tastes, and it mixes good news bulletins plus some serious debates and phone-ins with a wide range of light entertainment, very professionally done. Its long-time rival, Europe 1, has suffered from a less coherent policy, and its audience, falling for several years, is down to about 9 per cent. Both networks put an accent on lively news magazines around breakfast time, with star interviewers and commentators: at this hour they are far ahead of television in a land where breakfast TV has never caught on as in Britain.

The state-owned sector, today called Radio France, was never supervised as strictly as television; and it now enjoys much the same degree of liberty as France 2 or France 3. It has several networks: France-Inter, equivalent to the BBC's Radio 4, and the non-stop news channel France-Info, each commanding about 11 per cent of the audience. Two cultural networks, France Musique and France Culture, roughly equivalent to BBC Radio 3, do a valuable job, especially for classical music (as I wrote earlier), but have fairly small audiences. The newer commercial pop-music channels, inevitably, reach a wider public. Since Mitterrand's ending of the fictive state monopoly and the advent of the FM band, many new private networks have sprung up, appealing mostly to youth. The light-music channel NRJ wins the largest French audience after RTL; others, with such franglais names as Fun Radio, SkyRock and Nostalgie, also do well.

Even before Mitterrand formally deregulated French radio, the 'monopoly' had been invaded at grassroots level. In the later 1970s over 100 local pirate radio stations sporadically started operations all over France. They were of all kinds, some purely commercial, some militantly left-wing like the CGT's station at Longwy during the Lorraine steel crisis. Others were created by ecologists, like Radio Fessenheim in Alsace, which campaigned against the local nuclear power station. Many just wanted to prove that a need did exist for the kind of local community radio already flourishing in some other countries. Usually run by idealistic volunteers, these stations were one token of the search for new styles of local and informal *vie associative* at that time. But Giscard's Government tried to clamp down on the pirates, many of them clandestine and hard to unearth. The police sometimes seized their equipment and made arrests. Many tiny stations were thus cowed into silence, or stamped out. But others sprang up to take their place.

The Socialists came to power with a pledge to sanction local radio stations, and a law was quickly passed to that effect. During the following years some 2,000 came into being: but many have since perished and the number today is about 1,000. Under economic pressure the Socialists' ideal of a mass of little local community stations has not really worked out. Some today are subsidized by town councils, or associations, while two are run by the Church and some by local ethnic bodies. But others are no more than networked music channels with local antennae giving a little local news. Many struggle to survive. So the hopes of the early idealistic pirates have not really been fulfilled. In fact, the major effort of local radio today comes from Radio France: this, like the BBC, has set up several stations in the regions dealing primarily with local news. State-run radio thus has a stronger role on the local than the national level, where France-Inter and the others have only some 30 per cent of the total audience. It is a regional strength mirrored, in a very different way, by newspapers.

A FREE BUT FRAGILE PRESS:
LE MONDE AND LESSER FRY

The press, unlike television, has rarely suffered from direct state tutelage: newspapers are independently owned, and some have long been fiercely and frequently critical of Governments. But although magazines and weeklies flourish, the daily press in France, and notably in Paris, has for some years suffered from notorious weaknesses, mainly economic, but also editorial. During the 1990s its crisis has deepened.

One of its hazards is that the French by inclination have never been great newspaper readers, and have grown even less so: sales of dailies per 1,000 inhabitants have fallen from 244 in 1914 to 157 today, compared with 598 in Norway (the champion), 580 in Japan, 314 in Britain, 306 in Germany and 209 in the United States. The French figure is the lowest of advanced countries. Moreover, France lacks a national press as we know it in Britain: provincial papers account for over two-thirds of the dailies' total sales of 9 million, while of Paris papers only *Le Monde* has much circulation in the regions, and this is a modest 110,000. The Paris daily press has been wilting. *Le Monde* and *Le Figaro* do quite well, also the sporting *L'Équipe*: but the enterprising centre-Left *Libération* came into serious trouble in the 1990s, and the city's one former big seller, *France-Soir*, has fallen from a peak of 1.4 million to 155,000 copies. Rising costs, a clumsy distribution system, print unions' militancy, falling advertising revenue due to TV rivalry – these and other factors have thrown Paris newspapers into a greater crisis than those of London or New York. Journalists have been dismissed by the score, papers have closed or survive only through mergers. Paris had thirty-one dailies in 1945, and today has eleven: in the 1990s, two new papers were launched there, but both failed. And in terms of quality, whereas the ultra-serious *Le Monde* is one of the world's greatest newspapers, it has no rivals in its league.

These weaknesses are compensated, to an extent, by the rise of the weekly news magazines, led by *L'Express* and *Le Nouvel Observateur*. Especially in hectic Paris, people are today less ready to find the time for reading a daily, so they want weekly news-digest and feature material. Sunday papers have never caught on as in Britain, due partly to failures to create a distribution system for them: but *les news magazines* have done well. Borrowing their formula from *Time* or *Der Spiegel*, they have become more glossy than these, with thick shiny pages full of colour ads. At first glance they might resemble British Sunday 'colour mags', but their content is more newsy. Their circulations are modest by British standards, yet these are prosperous papers thanks to their high cover price (*c.* 15 to 20 francs) and copious advertisements. Of the three main ones, the doyen is *L'Express* (sales 560,000), formerly owned by Sir James Goldsmith and today by the huge Havas media group. Its rival, *Le Point*, puts its accent on analysis and reporting in a vivid, sometimes flippant style. It has lower sales (*c.* 310,000), but a more high-powered readership of senior *cadres* and others, while *L'Express* appeals more to the family. Both papers are very commercial, anxious to seek out what their readers want. Their main rival, '*Le Nouvel Obs*', as it is called (sales 437,000), is pro-Socialist, more wordy and earnest, and has an intellectual following: but it, too, has been popularizing itself, with a new stress on TV coverage. In October 1997 Havas sold *Le Point* to the assertive tycoon François Pinault (he then also bought Christie's in London): but for devious reasons the Government intervened to prevent its proposed sale of *L'Express* to either Dassault or *Le Monde*. It was a rare example today of such direct official intervention in the press.

The success of these papers has prompted the appearance of other weeklies, among them *Le Figaro*'s Saturday supplement, a platform for right-wing views. The TV listings paper *Télérama* has broadened into a lively cultural news weekly (sales 650,000). And in 1997 the polemical left-wing journalist Jean-François Kahn launched *Marianne*, aiming to combine news-digest material with investigative reporting. This paper has been very successful. Even the veteran *Paris-Match*, the biggest seller (807,000), has shifted towards the news-magazine style: it still carries its famous shock photos of celebrities, but it now puts less stress on big photo-stories, where often it is scooped by TV. In 1998 another newcomer was *L'Européen*, with a curious parentage: it was owned one-third by the pro-European *Le Monde* and two-thirds by the Eurosceptic Barclay brothers, British financiers. Its editor was the leading TV journalist Christine Ockrent, also Europhile, and she eagerly tried to stimulate debate on matters European. But sales were very poor, and by the end of 1998 the paper had collapsed and closed, like its London stablemate, the Barclays' *European*.

Some weeklies or monthlies are much more sensational. France has never had a daily tabloid press in the manner of Britain: there is no equivalent of the *Sun* or *Mirror*, and Paris's one big-selling popular morning paper, *Le Parisien* (450,000) is quite respectable. Among weeklies, the picture is different. *France-Dimanche* (582,000) and *Ici-Paris* (477,000), both owned by Hachette, have existed since 1946 and do quite well. They carry scandalous or sentimental stories about showbiz stars and other celebrities, often full of untruths. They now have two newer rivals, the monthly *Gala* (328,000) and the weekly *Voici* (700,000), both German-owned by the Bertelsmanns: these go further on the path of sensationalism, giving intimate details about the lives of royalty, movie stars and others. They had a field day after Princess Diana's death, when *Voici* published a lurid account of her last hours in hospital. *Voici* in particular will often fabricate stories, and several times has been prosecuted by its 'victims' and obliged to pay damages. For this it keeps a special reserve budget, and it considers the risks worth taking, for the lurid details bring in big sales. The damages awarded are usually quite low, even just a symbolic franc; and many celebrities do not bother to sue, for they do not take these papers seriously.

While the laws of libel are no stronger than in Britain, there is a special law on privacy to prevent photographers or others from intruding into private lives. Thus it can be illegal to take a photo of someone who is off duty, without his or her consent. When paparazzi took pictures of a near-naked Duchess of York in the Caribbean, and these were published in a British paper and in *Paris-Match*, Fergie was able to invoke the French law to sue the Paris magazine, but the British paper got away with it. Often this law is used for taking action against *Voici* or *Gala*. It may have had some impact, for the titles of this *presse indiscrète* or so-called *presse* '*peuple*' have all seen their circulations fall in the past two years.

The French press is noted also for its huge number of special-interest magazines, many of them monthlies: it has over 2,500, more per head than any other country in Europe. They are devoted to sport, cuisine, health, DIY, technical or business matters – every kind of subject. For example, *Le Chasseur français* (partly owned by the British group EMAP) was once essentially for huntsmen but is now a more general monthly about rural life, with sales of 570,000. Why do so many of these magazines fare so much better than the Paris dailies? They have modernized with more success, whereas the dailies are still saddled with multiple problems, some inherited from long ago. Since the war they have nearly all depended on a heavy and costly distribution agency, the Nouvelles Messageries, which enjoys a near-monopoly: but its grip cannot easily be broken, owing to the hold of the principal union involved, the Syndicat du

Livre–CGT. Printers also belong to this tough body, which has fought to keep salaries and staffing at high levels, and it waged a long rearguard action against the new technologies.

For these various reasons, French costs of production and distribution are higher than in most comparable countries. Add to this other factors: the vast recent increase in newsprint prices imposed by Swedish and other suppliers; and the fall in advertising revenue, due to rising competition from TV and radio. What is more, many readers are deterred from buying dailies or weeklies by their high retail price: most dailies cost 7 francs, nearly twice the British level. Owners claim that they need to charge a lot as their sales are so low – a familiar vicious circle. Finally, the leisure pattern of the French may discourage newspaper reading. They work long daily hours, leaving little energy for reading, and they like their long meals: then they have unusually long holidays, when they want to forget about the crises reported in the papers. All in all, life is hard for the press. Catherine Trautmann, on coming to power, promised measures to help, but little has yet emerged.

In recent years some papers have given themselves facelifts, maybe changing their lay-out or format almost as often as the '*Indie*' in efforts to make themselves more attractive, or to cut costs. It has not always worked. It used to be suggested that one reason for the dailies' weakness was that they lacked astute professional management. There were no true press barons: many papers were run as sidelines by industrial tycoons whose main interests lay elsewhere: *Le Figaro* and *L'Aurore* belonged to textile kings. But then in the mid-1970s a true professional began to loom very large. This was the controversial Robert Hersant, alleged wartime collaborator, man of the Right, man of mystery, who shunned all personal limelight but powerfully pulled the strings behind the scenes. He quietly built up an empire of provincial dailies and weeklies, and of specialized magazines such as *L'Autojournal*. He would take over some ailing local title, cut its overheads and payroll and bring it into profit – a formula that made him rich and provided his nickname, '*le papivore*' (paper-eater). In 1975 he bought the ailing *Figaro*, then two other tottering dailies, *France-Soir* and *L'Aurore*. The latter he merged with *Le Figaro*, which he managed to revive. This is roughly France's *Daily Telegraph*, equally conservative, and very intelligent, with a gifted editor, Franz-Olivier Giesbert. It even makes money!

Hersant, who died in 1996, was a dynamic businessman, alert to the way the world's newspaper industry was evolving; and by tough talking to the Syndicat du Livre he led the way into the computer-typesetting age. More politically active than Murdoch, he was compared to Randolph Hearst – and Citizen Hersant was not to all tastes. It was said that sometimes he obliged his staff to twist facts in support of his views: some *Figaro* journalists resigned in protest. So the growth of his empire (he came to own thirty titles around France) led inevitably to voices being raised about the dangers of politically inspired press monopolies – especially as Hersant was in clear breach of a 1944 law forbidding any one person to own several dailies. Yet Giscard's Government turned a blind eye (was not Hersant a useful ally?). The Socialists then passed a law in 1984 that limited to 15 per cent the share of national/regional circulation that any one person could hold (Hersant's was more like 38 per cent). But this proved hard to apply, notably as he hid behind his immunity as a member of the European Parliament. However, nemesis of another kind then came as Hersant overreached himself. In 1990 he had his fingers badly burned by the fiasco of his bid to move into television, with Berlusconi and '*la Cinq*'. Then by the mid-1990s, with recession in the industry, Hersant's own group was losing money heavily, and when he died it was in debt to the tune of some 3 billion francs. His successors set about selling off some titles. In sum, *le papivore* had not in the end proved quite the saviour that France's press needed.

The waning of the Hersant hegemony has reduced the fears that the press might, under today's economic pressures, become less varied and independent. For the moment, the Paris dailies may be weak but they are still quite diverse. They include the Catholic *La Croix* (97,000), owned by a community of Augustinians; the Communist *L'Humanité*, which has been flagging (its sales have dropped from 150,000 to 60,000 since the early 1980s); the successful sporting paper *L'Équipe* (335,000); and the economic daily, *Les Échos* (127,000), owned by the Pearson group but far less powerful or profitable than its stablemate, the *Financial Times*. Some of these and other papers lose money. Witness the case of *Libération*, the radical daily created exuberantly in the wake of May 1968, with Jean-Paul Sartre as a founding editor. Owned partly by its own staff, it became a rival to *Le Monde* but more irreverent and hard-hitting, with an influence well in excess of its modest circulation. However, by the early 1990s its sales were falling and its debt was rising: 'Younger people, such a big part of our readership, don't buy papers any more, they watch television,' complained one editor. So its charismatic and much-admired *directeur* (editor-in-chief), Serge July, was obliged to seek outside help; and in 1996 the Chargeurs industrial group took a 65-per-cent stake, reducing the staff's share to 20 per cent. *Libération* remains a lively part of the press scene: but some of its old sparkle and authority are gone, and its sales are still only 170,000.

Its case typifies the problems, essentially economic, of serious papers in France today, whatever their viewpoint. Most of the press is more or less on the Right, or at least conservative: but this has long been balanced by a small but solid body of Left or centre-Left dailies and weeklies. Sometimes, under right-wing regimes, they have come under strong official pressures, as when Giscard in 1980 began to prosecute *Le Monde*: but they have never been muzzled. The press may be weak but it is relatively free. Among weeklies, *Le Canard enchaîné*, that renowned French institution, continues robustly, with sales as high as 420,000. With its lampooning style, it may seem at first a mere court jester, like *Private Eye*: but this left-wing paper is in fact deadly serious about its investigative journalism, which it pioneered many years ago. Frequently, it has come up with scoops, on such topics as Giscard's gift of diamonds from Bokassa. Governments have often been maddened by *Le Canard*'s revelations (once its offices were bugged): but they have never managed to silence it. Under Socialist regimes, the paper's satiric style has been a little gentler. But it was still fearless in seeking to expose the scandals around Mitterrand and his court at the Élysée.

Le Monde has also hit out against Left as well as Right, on occasions. This evening daily still towers above the rest of the French press. It is proud of its independence alike from big business and political parties, and its editorial staff own part of its shares and elect its *directeur*. While the rest of the world changes, *Le Monde* still basically adheres to its austere format, with small print, hardly any photographs, and lengthy articles with elaborate sentences that do not make for easy casual reading: many are sharply or elegantly written, some are turgid or prolix. But this is *the* paper read by the upper professional classes, and a crucial part of the French political scene. For sheer range and depth of reporting, on home or foreign subjects, it has hardly any equals in the world, and it puts to shame papers like *The Times* or the *Independent*: the *FT* may be its peer in political and economic matters, but its range is narrower. The lack of parochialism compared with most British papers, especially in cultural affairs, is refreshing: one typical long article on its arts pages had the headline, '*Pourquoi le nouveau cinéma des Philippines n'est pas très intéressant*'. Indeed *le monde* is its oyster.

Its political stance has sometimes varied. Under Jacques Fauvet as *directeur* in 1969–82, it moved quite far to the Left. Not only did it swing behind the Socialist/Communist alliance, but it showed an outsize anti-imperialist conscience in Third World affairs: this led it imprudently to greet the Pol Pot regime's victory in Kampuchea as a triumph for democracy and to ignore the genocide. But since then it has kept to the moderate centre-Left, notably under the present *directeur*, Jean-Marie Colombani. Its natural habitat is in opposition, and it tends to be critical of the Government of the day: while Fauvet and Giscard developed a fervent mutual hatred, Mitterrand in his turn fell out with the paper on certain issues. Broadly, it is Christian Democrat, very pro-European and pro-liberty, strong against racism and nationalism.

In the booming 1960s and 1970s *Le Monde* tripled its circulation and was selling more than any other Paris daily. It was as if *The Times* outsold the *Sun* – but of course *Le Monde* does not face the same competition from other 'quality' dailies. Then, in the darker early 1990s, it fell back, like so many papers: with rising costs and falling sales, it began to pile up losses. So in 1995 Colombani tried the familiar recipe of changing its formula – but not too much. Readers responded, and since 1995 sales within France have risen by over 10 per cent to 338,000, their highest level since 1981. Today the reporting is less heavily centred on institutions and on 'official' events and viewpoints, but has been widened to include more articles dealing with daily life, on subjects such as *la banlieue*, popular culture, sexual problems, science and sport. During the World Cup it even carried a special eight- to ten-page supplement each day about the games – to the horror of some more purist readers. But the paper's general approach remains serious, not gossipy in the manner of Britain's 'Quality' papers. The presentation has become a little lighter, and there are now photographs on the feature pages – but still no news photos, just lovely quirky cartoons.

The regional press seems at first sight to offer an impressive contrast with the struggling Parisian dailies, at least in terms of circulation. In so centralized a country, this relative strength may seem curious: it stems in part from the Occupation, when the division of France in two, and the limits on transport, destroyed the pre-war provincial circulations of the Parisian press and allowed the local papers to build up positions which they have since held and even extended. Since 1939 sales of provincial dailies have risen from 5.2 to 6 million, while those of Parisian ones have fallen from 6 to 2.8 million. And the French daily with the highest circulation is not a Parisian one but *Ouest-France* (786,000), published in Rennes, with forty editions covering all north-west France. Next, outside Paris, come *Sud-Ouest* of Bordeaux (370,000), *La Voix du Nord* in Lille (328,000) and *Le Progrès de Lyon* and *Le Dauphiné libéré* of Grenoble (both around 300,000). There are sixty-six provincial dailies, and they have successfully resisted efforts by Parisian newspapers to penetrate their areas. In Caen, which is a little further from Paris than Rennes, *Ouest-France* has four times the sales of all the Paris papers together! And many of these larger dailies are solid empires with fine new offices, making some Paris papers look like struggling poor relations.

Their success with their readers is evidence of the strength of local attachments in France. But alas their editorial quality is seldom an inspiring asset for the regionalist cause. Many of them are trite and parochial. Some have built up their strength by killing off smaller rivals, thus creating a near-monopoly in their areas; and they feel that they must therefore appeal widely and not risk alienating readers by flaunting bold opinions. With rare exceptions, they avoid taking a strong editorial line on issues that matter. They deal in a deadpan way with national news, and will dismiss foreign affairs on a page or two of poorly edited agency reports. Yet for most local people, this is their sole written source of news and political comment. The papers put their stress on endless pages of local news; and surveys show that this is what readers turn to first. The multiple editions are so localized that there may be little news of the regional capital in one sold in a town 50 kilometres away. The coverage is thorough and fairly objective and maybe it helps local awareness. But alongside a few articles on public issues are columns of tittle-tattle: flower shows, Rotary dinners and minor accidents – what the French call '*la rubrique des chiens écrasés*'.

The press conflicts in the Lyon/Grenoble area provide an interesting case study. When in the 1960s the commercially aggressive *Dauphiné libéré* staged a battle royal with the staid *Progrès de Lyon* for sales in overlapping areas, the Grenoble paper won by exploiting every kind of trivia. Then the two reached an entente and agreed to divide up readership zones. This lasted until 1979, when *Le Progrès* acquired a radical-minded new owner, Jean-Charles Ligniel, who said he would make it 'one of Europe's great papers, with the courage of the *Washington Post*'. In practice he did little, and was soon losing readers and money. Then in the 1980s both papers and some other local titles were acquired by the dreaded Hersant who thus achieved a near-monopoly in the region. He pulled *Le Progrès* downmarket, made it more lively and increased circulation. But in 1986 *Le Monde* entered the fray, launching a daily Rhône/Alpes edition with two pages of regional news and features. And *Libération* even started a genuine local paper written and printed in Lyon, into which the national edition was inserted. But this lost money, and was stopped in 1992; *Le Monde*, too, later cancelled its local pages. So today this rich and sophisticated region is served by two very mediocre papers, still owned by the Hersant group, and serious readers have to rely on *Le Monde*, which comes the next morning. When the Carignon scandal broke, the Paris papers were full of it while the Grenoble paper kept a cowed silence until the trial began.

Just a few provincial papers do have a real quality and will speak out frankly. *La Voix du Nord*, in Lille, makes money and has proved that to succeed and to win readers, you do not need to appeal to the most trivial tastes or avoid voicing opinions. *Ouest-France*, owned by a local Breton family, is also ready to criticize Governments, to show a social conscience, and even to give decent coverage to foreign news. These and some other larger papers are still financially sound: but some others, and many of the smaller ones, have finally run into trouble after the boom decades as advertising revenues decline and younger readers turn to other media. *La Dépêche du Midi* in Toulouse, once a great radical paper, has fallen into mediocrity. And although the waning of the Hersant empire may have lifted one threat of monopoly, there are other new trends that might endanger the pluralism and variety of the press. *Les Dernières Nouvelles d'Alsace* in Strasbourg has just been sold to a rival paper in Nancy. Hachette, busily building a regional empire, has just merged two well-known papers in Marseille that had been founded by Gaston Defferre. And in 1998 *La Voix du Nord* itself, hitherto locally owned, was due to come under the control of the big Belgian Group Rossel, closely linked to Hersant. All of this seems another threat to diversity. Today, as in Paris, the press of the regions faces uncertain times, and its golden age may be ending.

Until not so long ago, one editorial weakness of the French press as a whole, *Le Monde* included, was the relative lack of the kind of fearless investigative reporting common in America, and to an extent in Britain. Papers were stronger on polemic, or on news digest, than on fully researched factual exposés. Often they were afraid of making powerful enemies – 'A Watergate-style inquiry would be impossible in France,' admitted one editor. *Le Canard* bravely produced its political scoops, but it was a lone voice and it lacked the resources for full-scale research into, for instance, corruption scandals. Then in the late 1970s one or two news weeklies began to grow bolder, and a turning point came in 1985 with *Le Monde*'s series of scoops on the Greenpeace affair (see p. 22). Today this type of investigation has grown much commoner, led by *Le Monde, L'Express* and *Le Point*: all have set up permanent cells of staff reporters who work on these stories full-time. Thus *L'Express* in 1992 unearthed the Socialist leader Charles Hernu's former links with Ceauşescu's Romania, while others have dug into the Crédit Lyonnais débâcle, various recent corruption scandals and some murky doings at the Élysée under Mitterrand. Some of the reasons for the change I looked at in the context of French justice (see pp. 41–59). It has something to do with shifts in public opinion, the decline in the power of politicians, and the new more assertive role of examining magistrates, helped by many journalists. The downside is that sometimes the reporters go too far, damaging the reputations of the innocent.

Some national papers are now fearless in this field. But many others remain more cautious, especially local ones. The press traditionally has always shown deference to the French establishment, and not only in governmental spheres: in a centralized and secretive society, most journalists have relied for their news sources on their personal links with people in positions of influence, be they ministers or civil servants, tycoons or trade union leaders, or mayors or other *notables*. And they have hesitated to jeopardize their sources through embarrassing revelations. So newspapers have prudently tended to publish less than they know, and not just because of the libel laws. Seldom have they followed up such matters as corrupt practices on town councils, or the murkier aspects of business takeovers. This is especially true of local papers, which depend so much on these contacts and often are owned or run by men who are part of the establishment. In the Manufrance crisis (see p. 109), in the Carignon and Médecin affairs, and others, local newsmen often knew what was going on behind the scenes, but could not tell it until later. And if some ruthless colleague arrived from Paris and told the truth, they could be horrified. Today this is changing a little, under the impact of the new-style reporting. But it remains far easier for such investigations to be made by national than by local papers.

Another issue, if a lesser one, relates to the French concern with ideas and style, more than with facts. In Britain's press, too, factual accuracy has much declined: but I think the French are worse. Standards of reporting and sub-editing can be very casual, even on serious papers. In their coverage of foreign stories, for instance, visiting reporters tend – even more than the British – to rely on easy clichés, *a priori* judgements or minor picturesque details, rather than trying to assess the real situation. Few make much effort, for instance, to explain to readers the true nature of the Northern Ireland problem. In the late Thatcher period, before the Charles-and-Diana crisis, a star reporter from a weekly came to London, ordered by his editor to prepare a cover story on how Britain's 'deep malaise' was due to the royal family's problems. We talked, and I said that yes, the British were worried and morose, but the royals had little to do with it. He disregarded me and went ahead, unwilling to spoil a good pre-arranged story. His ensuing article was nonsense.

Régis Debray, in his book *Le Pouvoir intellectuel en France* (see p. 526), pointed his finger at this tendency to disdain detailed factual accuracy in favour of clever ideas and eloquent style: 'The higher French journalism chases two hares at once which collide and come a cropper: the brio of ideas and the substance of events; commentary and reporting.' This could be due to lack of professional rigour, he felt. But it seems also to me that the French deductive methods of teaching are to blame. All pupils are taught first to enunciate a thesis, then to parade facts to support it,: this could have shaped the way that French journalists' minds work, even their mixing of news and comment. Just as they were taught at school, they select facts to prove a chosen viewpoint: they lack humility in the empiric pursuit of truth. It is the reverse of the inductive Anglo-Saxon method (which can produce its own excesses). It is a system full of cerebral merit, but not the ally of objective inquiry. And it colours the whole French intellectual scene.

THE NOVEL:
STYLISTIC INNOVATION IN THE
POST-ROBBE-GRILLET VOID

'When I go to Paris,' a London publisher told me, 'and I ask a French colleague what good new novels he might have for me, he'll say gloomily, "Oh, as usual, nothing much – but what have *you* got for me?"' Today new serious British fiction is doing far better in France than vice versa.

This may be an aspect of the famous British insularity: but, as French critics will admit, it is also a sign of the severe decline of the French novel over the past three decades. In the early post-war years, some important writers were still at work, not only Camus, but Jean Giono, Julien Gracq, Marguerite Yourcenar, and others. Then came the much-contested *nouveau roman*. And since then? I could quote a name or two – Tournier, Perec, Le Clézio. But in literature, more than in the other arts, this seems to be an age of criticism and documentary rather than creativity. The French novel has lost much of the old humanist universality that made it, from Stendhal's day to Proust's, the world's very greatest. Is it still suffering from the terrorism of avant-garde experimentation?

From the mid-'50s to the 1970s, the scene was dominated by the writers loosely known as the 'new novelists', led by Alain Robbe-Grillet, Michel Butor and Nathalie Sarraute. Rejecting plot, narrative and character portrayal, they were bourgeois writers attacking the bourgeois tradition of fiction – and this in itself set them squarely in a French tradition stemming back to Flaubert via Sartre and Proust. While Flaubert used social realism to attack his own bourgeoisie, the 'new novelists' preferred other weapons. Their aim was to write novels that the ordinary bourgeois reader would not enjoy or even understand. So their sales were usually slight: but their influence on other novelists was vast, and not always for the best.

In its heyday, the so-called *nouveau roman* caused more journalistic ink to flow than any other European literary trend of its time. It was never a 'school', for its leading exponents were very different and they often quarrelled. They were lumped together for convenience, and through the smart public-relations work of their self-appointed prophet and president, Robbe-Grillet. Yet they did have some common points. In rejecting normal story-telling, they were broadly in a line traced from Proust and Joyce via Queneau, Genet and others. And they were obsessed with minute physical description, whether of objects or sensations. Their semi-scientific approach had a clear link with structuralism, which came to the fore at much the same time.

It was Robbe-Grillet, now in his late seventies, who took the most extreme position and formulated his theories most sharply. His novels may be dehumanized, yet he himself has always been very human and jolly: you might even think, talking to him, that his whole operation could be a leg-pull at the expense of literature. 'My favourite author is Lewis Carroll,' he told me. Precisely. Talking to him, or reading his books or seeing his films, one can feel like Alice at the Mad Hatter's tea-party. ' "Have some more wine," the March Hare said. "I don't see any wine," remarked Alice. "There isn't any," said the March Hare.' By training an agronomist, Robbe-Grillet won fame in 1955 when *Le Voyeur* took the Prix des Critiques, and from then he waged a vendetta, with panache and impish good humour, against those who dared to write or admire any different kind of novel.

His foremost dogma was that fiction must rid itself of what Ruskin called 'the pathetic fallacy', the tendency of novelists to describe events emotively. Mountains must not be allowed to 'loom' majestically, nor villages to 'nestle', and any attempt to endow the physical world with emotion was a step towards the illicit belief in God. This view, known as *chosisme*, was influenced by Barthes who wrote warmly of Robbe-Grillet's work, with its long painstaking descriptions of such mighty matters as the physiognomy of squashed centipedes (*La Jalousie*) or the shape of a tropical plantation. Yet Robbe-Grillet claimed that Man still held the centre of his stage: 'My descriptions,' he told me, 'are *passionate*, they portray the world through the obsessed eyes of my heroes.' Of his scenario for Resnais's *L'Année dernière à Marienbad*, he said, 'What happens on the screen is the struggle in the girl's mind, so the spectator can never be sure of the level of reality he is seeing. The amount of furniture varies with how she is feeling.' How are we to assess the artistic worth of this? Robbe-Grillet's strength is his sonorous and lyrical prose style, lending a dream-like fascination to many of his descriptions. But the effect is finally gratuitous, as there is no identifiable human impetus behind the images. He first arouses our sympathy, then mockingly plants a booby trap that snuffs it out and leaves us feeling cheated.

Michel Butor is a 'new novelist' less removed from tradition: his earlier books even have characters and plots, of a sort. He is a dedicated Proustian, and his novels, like Proust's, are concerned with time, also with the relativity of time and space: *La Modification* (1957), takes place entirely in the mind of a young man on a train journey from Paris to Rome, while *L'Emploi du temps* uses distortions of chronology to build up a nightmarish picture of Manchester, where Butor once spent a year. He later moved away from fiction towards experimental prose, such as the dream narratives of *Matière de rêves* (1975–81). This mannered writer has sought to explore the time-space relation in an age of jet travel: clocks, timetables, airports fascinate him. Nathalie Sarraute, different again, is a Russian Jewish *émigrée* now in her nineties. Like Robbe-Grillet she has condemned the moralistic novel of explicit narrative or social comment: but her themes and subject-matter are not his. She is concerned with the living tissue of tiny, subtle sensations which she believes make up our lives: admiring Proust and Woolf, she uses a stream-of-consciousness technique not so different from theirs to depict minutely a world of psychological flickering (*tropismes*, she calls them), which for her are the real substance of human contact. Her novels are not easy to read: but within her chosen range, she is a psychological realist and a true poet.

The distinguished Marguerite Duras (1914–96) was often lumped with the *nouveau roman*, as her elliptical techniques of dialogue and narrative seemed so 'experimental'. But in fact she was closer to the *engagé* Sartrean line: note the difference between the two Resnais films, *Hiroshima mon amour* with her script and the never-never-land of *Marienbad*. Duras was a warm-hearted writer with a feeling for real people and problems, something to welcome in the modern French novel. In the best of her stories, such as *Moderato Cantabile*, and the autobiographical *L'Amant*, she showed a rare feeling for atmosphere and place. Also linked with the *nouveau roman* is Claude Simon, though his full-blooded evocations of his youth are a far cry from Robbe-Grillet. In 1985 he won the Nobel Prize for Literature for an *oeuvre* that has included *Le Palace* and *La Route des Flandres*.

These and other writers were nearly all left-wing in their personal sympathies, but rarely did any hint of this enter their pages. Some, such as Claude Mauriac and Philippe Sollers, seemed concerned with writing novels about the problems of writing novels. But this rarefied school found little success with a wider public: their books seldom sold more than 4,000 copies, save for a few *succès d'estime*. By the mid-1970s the trend was expiring. Today it has few imitators among younger writers, and its ageing leaders have stopped producing novels. Students seldom turn to them eagerly as they still do to Camus, Malraux or Giono. So what did the 'new novel' achieve? Some critics feel that it was useful as a language laboratory or testing ground – 'It has done for French what Joyce did for English.' Yes, but Joyce was a far greater genius. And for some years Robbe-Grillet in particular, with the help of Barthes, exerted a kind of tyranny over younger novelists, making them feel unable to write in a humanist mode any more. Only recently has the French novel been cautiously returning towards its older values.

*

There has long been a gulf in France, deeper than in many countries, between the 'literary' novel and the conventional bourgeois novel with its far wider public. And while the 'new novel' for a while stole much of the critical limelight, it did little damage to the fortunes of established writers such as Henri Troyat or Jean Lartéguy who went on topping the bestseller lists, with sales over ten times those of a *nouveau roman*. Partly because public libraries in France are rather weak, a bourgeois public is used to buying new fiction in some quantities, and a successful work of this kind – maybe a tale of history, adventure or family life, or a sensitive story by Françoise Sagan – can easily sell 100,000 copies or more. However, between the two genres there is also the serious novel which is not *too* experimental and has some plot: these are the books that often win the coveted annual literary prizes, the Goncourt, Renaudot, Fémina and others, which make so much difference to sales in this fashion-dominated land. For instance, after winning the Goncourt in 1990, Jean Rouaud's first novel *Les Champs d'honneur* went on to sell 600,000 copies. If you want to show your dinner guests that you're in the swim, then you must parade the new Goncourt on your coffee table within days of publication, even if you do no more than skim through it. But the books that take these prizes are not always the best: the juries are virtually controlled by Gallimard, Le Seuil, Grasset and one or two other leading publishers, who carry off most of the awards.

Today hordes of novels are still published each year – some 1,580 in 1997 – but few are of much distinction. And French publishers readily complain that this is far from a golden age, even a silver one. It has no dominant school (fortunately?), nothing more than a few shadowy trends. Most of the books by new younger writers tend to be slight, even inconsequential, rather as in cinema. Many are semi-autobiographical little tales, or well-crafted jewels that strain, in the French manner, after surreal or poetic effects or a clever style; in either case, they are often introspective or self-indulgent. Only a few writers, mostly women (Annie Ernaux, Sylvie Germain), have the talent and originality to orchestrate this *petite musique* into literature. And few books provide Balzacian insights into modern French society, or even a robust narrative and strong character-drawing. Hence a public wanting a serious good read will turn very often to translated work. Among British writers, William Boyd, Graham Swift, Anita Brookner and others do extremely well; also Julian Barnes who pays the French the compliment of writing about *them*. In reverse, modern French novels fare badly in Britain, and few are even translated – perhaps due less to their own lack of quality than to British lack of interest. The Rouaud smash hit in France sold only 10,000 copies in Britain: but that is a very high figure for a new foreign novel. Significantly, translations of foreign books of all kinds account for only 3 per cent of sales in Britain, against 34 per cent in France.

Of the good novelists to have appeared in the past thirty or so years since the *nouveau roman*, many have set their books in the past, in realistic or mythical mode. The veteran Michel Tournier took the Goncourt in 1971 with *Le Roi des Aulnes*, a powerful Gothic fantasy relating to Nazi Germany. He followed this with some reinterpretations of historic myths, and has been compared to Tolkien. Patrick Modiano, Goncourt winner in 1970 for *Rue des boutiques obscures*, has written evocatively about life under the Occupation and the Paris of former days. Pascal Quignard's speciality is poetic historical studies of musicians (*Tous les matins du monde*, about seventeenth-century viola da gamba players, was made into a beautiful film). More recently, some younger writers have been exploring the impact of the First World War on its survivors. Sébastian Japrisot's clever and original *Un long dimanche de fiançailles* was on this theme, and so was Rouaud's *Les Champs d'honneur*, a poignant study of old age. Among recent novels with a Second World War setting, *Le Livre des nuits*, rather overwritten but scarily powerful, is by one of the most admired of younger women writers, Sylvie Germain.

Some other writers have been concerned with stylistic innovation. Georges Perec, perhaps the most interesting, was influenced by the *nouveau roman* but also included some social criticism, notably in his much-praised first novel *Les Choses* (1965), an ironic portrait of the consumerist vogue of the 1960s. Then he turned to verbal experiment: *La Disparition* was a whole novel written without any 'e's, while *Les Revenentes*, even bolder, used only the vowel 'e'. It begins (in Ian Monk's clever translation): 'The seven green Mercedes Benzes resembled pestered sheep. They descended West End Street, swerved left, entered Temple Street then swept beneath the green vennels' beeches . . .', and so on for fifty-five pages! Jean-Marie Le Clézio has also been concerned with stylistic virtuosity: but his work is more philosophic, more broodingly personal. *Le Déluge* (1966), is a cosmic allegory telling of a young man's nightmare odyssey through the streets of a modern city, haunted by images of death and decay. His later work, much of it set in the Third World or in his home town, Nice, has projected the same vision of disgust at material civilization. More recently, other talented writers who innovate poetically within their private worlds have included Daniel Pennac, Pierre Michon and Jean Échenoz. Marie Darrieussecq's *Truismes* (*Pig Tales*) (1995) was an abrasive feminist fantasy about the piggishness of the human condition. In a more realistic genre, too, it is generally women novelists who have produced the best intimate accounts of the struggles of daily life: Annie Ernaux's slight but sensitive stories are based on her own working-class parentage in Normandy (e.g. *La Place*, 1984). And many of the best recent novels in French are by expatriates in France describing their homelands – North Africans, South Americans and East Europeans such as Andreï Makine whose study of his Russian background, *Le Testament français*, won both the Goncourt and the Médicis prizes in 1995.

Some talented novelists have indeed emerged in recent years: but few of them make much impact, and are concerned to portray the French society around them (an exception is the controversial Michel Houellebecq, see p. 528). I find it a pity, when that society has been moving through so fascinating a period of transition, that the novel has virtually abdicated its classic Balzacian role as its chronicler: nor have cinema or television been very effective in taking its place. There were some exceptions in the 1970s, such as Jean Carrière's 1972 Goncourt winner, *L'Épervier de Maheu*, a study of rural life in the Cévennes; or Victor Pilhes's 1974 Prix Fémina winner, *L'Imprécateur*, a satire on the Paris international business world. And sharp little studies of bourgeois greed and hypocrisy, by bourgeois writers, continue to appear. But there has been little equivalent of the post-war English school of realistic working-class fiction.

When I ingenuously ask a writer or publisher, 'France today needs her Balzac, her Zola: why is no one filling the gap?' the 'new novelists' just laugh. And François Nourrissier, a serious realistic writer, said, 'Recent years have seen a growth of critical forms to the detriment of creative ones; a takeover of the literary heritage by pedagogues, psychoanalysts, linguists . . . and this has stifled the spirit of adventure, the taste for imaginative writing.' Others suggest that highbrow Parisian literary critics would merely scorn a realistic Balzacian study of provincial society and this deters publishers. Nor, it seems, is the average novelist very interested in the daily life of modern France: by choice he stays detached from it, strikingly more so than British writers. If he lives in the provinces, working maybe as a teacher, he seldom integrates into local life. Many others stay in Paris, afflicted by *le parisiannisme*, mixing only with each other in that rarefied milieu: 'I was born in Amiens, but you can't *live there*,' said one. So their raw material is drawn from their childhood family memories, or the current intrigues of their own little world, or from living abroad. 'As a creative artist,' said one, 'I am not concerned with exploring the social tensions or crude consumerism of today's France. I prefer to concentrate on my private world and the refinement of my style. I am not a documentarist – I leave that to the media and to sociology.' A valid stance, maybe – for those with the artistic qualities to justify it. So the novel survives as a pallid creature, cut off from the mainstream of French life as it never was in Flaubert's day. Equally, where today are the great philosophers?

THE LEFT BANK PHILOSOPHERS: IS POST-STRUCTURALISM STILL *MÉDIATIQUE*?

The intellectual has long been a star figure in France, playing a weightier role in public life than in most countries – witness Zola's defence of Dreyfus. But recent years have seen no major new charismatic thinkers to take up the torch from Sartre and Camus. Intellectual life seems in a fallow period, without clear 'schools' or trends; and intellectuals have been losing some of their old influence and reputation. And yet, general interest in philosophical questions has been increasing in an anxious age that grasps for meanings. There is even a mini-vogue for *cafés philosophiques* in Paris and other towns. But it is all very different from another troubled age, that of the Occupation, when the so-called existentialist movement was born.

It was in 1943 that Sartre, already well known for his novel *La Nausée*, brought out his key work *L'Être et le néant*. The Occupation, with its disruption of bourgeois values, tempted many young thinkers besides him towards a disenchanted humanism: so following the Liberation he found an immediately sympathetic audience. For the next years this ugly, tousled, pipe-smoking little man would sit with disciples in the St-Germain-des-Prés cafés discussing problems of moral responsibility. They were hard-working and ascetic, these true existentialists (as opposed to the phoney parasites who followed their trail, wilfully mistaking Sartrean liberty for licence) and they had much influence in academic and left-wing circles. It was a time of high aspiration, when it seemed to some that social revolution might be possible in France; and the early post-war years were full of intellectual fervour and creativity amid political chaos.

Existentialism was at first seized on hopefully as a light to live by. Yet before long many intellectuals felt it to be leading to a moral impasse, at least in its atheistic Sartrean form. Developing the ideas of his German predecessors, Heidegger and Husserl, Sartre taught that man creates himself by his actions, for which he has freedom of choice and responsibility: each choice is 'absurd' because there is no objective moral standard, but (and here Sartre never made himself quite clear) in the act of choosing a man confers value on what he chooses. Many young French agnostics warmed to the courage and humanism of this austere philosophy, which seemed more hopeful than determinism. But to those who searched more closely among the paradoxes of *L'Être et le néant* and *L'Existentialisme est un humanisme*, this humanism began to look suspiciously like solipsism; and not everyone felt able to share Sartre's seemingly gloomy view of the impossibility of human relationships. Existentialism had brought freedom from the bonds of convention – but to what ends?

In the 1950s the movement withered: but it was to leave an indelible mark on French thinking. Its end was hastened by external factors, such as the political failures of the Left under the Fourth Republic and the alluring rise of a new climate of prosperity. It was destroyed also from within: by the failure of its intellectuals to pass from theoretical *engagement* to the effective political action that they claimed to espouse, and by the shifts and ambiguities in Sartre's own pronouncements after about 1950. He began to assert that Marxism was the only great philosophy of the century and existentialism was merely its handmaiden, taking charge of a field of humanist ideas that it had neglected. While his hatred of right-wing oppression was admired, few people, even Marxists, could follow the logic that led him from 'absurdity of choice' to doctrinaire commitment. If man has freedom of choice, by what existentialist right could Sartre insist that Marxism is the only 'valid' choice? He never convincingly answered this question. And like many Marxists he would put forward ingenious arguments for violating democratic principles if the defence of a left-wing cause was at stake. This led him to quarrel and break with many former sympathizers, notably Albert Camus.

Towards the end of his life Sartre appeared a somewhat lonely and tragic figure, despite the warm support of his life-long companion, Simone de Beauvoir. As was often said, his was the tragedy of a man with a deeply religious temperament who had killed God. And he in turn was a god who failed: it was just because his earlier intellectual magnetism had been so hypnotic that he left such disarray. In May 1968 he was quick to side with the militant students: but they did not look to him as a leader. To modern youth he had come to seem irrelevant: they still read his earlier books with interest, but as classics, as they might read Kafka. In the 1970s he espoused various humanitarian causes, campaigning in the streets of Paris against racism and other abuses. This activism won him respect, even if it had little to do with his work as a philosopher. In his final years, before his death in 1980, he gave up supporting Communism-at-any-price and accepted that human rights were a higher priority. He spoke out on behalf of Soviet dissidents and pleaded the cause of the Vietnamese 'boat people'. When he died, there were tributes from all sides – 'I disagree with his answers,' said the right-wing philosopher Alain de Benoist, 'but he was just about the only person to ask the right questions.'

Today existentialism has become part of the air that the French breathe daily, like nineteenth-century rationalism. Few intellectuals any longer dub themselves 'existentialist'; but even the younger ones have been marked by it. As a catalyst, its influence was positive: it was one of the forces that helped to unjam the windows of the stifling pre-war bourgeois world described by de Beauvoir in *Mémoires d'une jeune fille rangée*. Then after the war, in sociology and criticism, in the *nouveau roman* and some films of the *nouvelle vague*, even in the songs of Georges Brassens or Léo Ferré, existentialism with its sceptical voice of disenchantment continued to show its influence.

In the 1960s a new 'ism' of a different kind came into prominence: structuralism. Intellectually very high-powered, it was endlessly talked about but not so often understood. It was not a philosophy but a method, and in no sense a 'school', for its exponents were very diverse in approach and speciality: they included Roland Barthes, literary critic; Claude Lévi-Strauss, who taught ethnology; Jacques Lacan, influential psychoanalyst; and Michel Foucault, philosopher and historian. Structuralism began to have influence among linguists in the 1950s; and in some ways it related to existentialism, with which its leaders shared an atheistic rejection of the bourgeois view of history and morality. But whereas existentialists saw man as the free captain of his conscience, the structuralists tended to regard him as the prisoner of a determined system. Using the language and methods of anthropology, psychoanalysis or linguistic philosophy, they asserted, very broadly, that man's thoughts and actions have been determined throughout history by a network of structures, social and psychological, where free will plays a minimal part; and that history is like a series of geological layers, each created by the pressure of the preceding one. Lévi-Strauss applied these ideas to the study of primitive societies; Barthes used them in semantics or semiology, the study of the set of signs or symbols which he believed to shape our thoughts and actions; and Foucault applied structuralism to philosophy proper. In *Les Mots et les choses* (1966) he argued, 'Man with a capital "M" is an invention. If we study thought as an archaeologist studies buried cities, we can see that Man was born yesterday, and that he soon may die.' This book sent tremors well outside academic circles: it was a bestseller, *the* smart topic of party conversation, whether you had read it or (more probably) not. An educated public reacted with fascinated horror at a new philosopher who made even Sartrean views look humane and optimistic. Sartre had killed God: were the structuralists now killing Man, too?

Their ideas were a symptom of the belated French discovery of anthropology and the other social sciences, which they seized on with a true French extremism and imagination. Critics who were able to follow Barthes's ironic and intricate thought usually found him stimulating and mentally elegant, whether they shared his views or not. His very personal style, full of neologisms, had many imitators and was even parodied in a book, *Le Roland-Barthes sans peine* ('Barthesianism without Tears', 1978), which showed how to turn simple remarks into his code language (' "I" live a "desire-to-know" = "why?" '. ' "This conceptual articulation self-criticizes itself as failing to materialize" = "It's impossible" '). So Barthes's preciosity was also linguistic satire.

The structuralists were frequently criticized for wilful obscurity, arrogance, aridity and much else. Richard Webster in the *Observer* (1 February 1981) attacked their 'habit of reducing human nature to pseudo-mathematical formulae'. Yet by the 1970s their influence was extending far outside France: in Britain they belatedly made more impact in academic circles than ever Sartre had done, while in America numerous theses were written on Barthes and Lacan. However, in France itself, structuralism was by then a waning force. The brilliant young philosopher and critic Jacques Derrida had already in the late 1960s emerged as the leading counter-weight to structuralism, using an approach known as 'decon-structionism', whereby classic or other texts were re-examined in a new way. He and the philosopher Gilles Deleuze came to be called 'post-structuralists', and they attacked Lacan, Foucault and others. Most of these famous names are now gone. The veteran Lévi-Strauss is alive, but turned ninety; Barthes, Lacan and Foucault are all dead, and Deleuze too, who in 1995 threw himself from the window of his Paris flat.

Today structuralism is no longer much talked about as such. As a method it has been assimilated, and it may have left a permanent mark on the way that texts are analysed and ideas approached: after Barthes, as after Leavis, criticism can never be quite the same again. However, the structuralists' particular ideas on mankind and society no longer dominate the social sciences in France as they did thirty years ago. One writer suggested to me, 'In the 1960s it had seemed to many of us that the new social sciences and linguistics, allied to left-wing politics through the work of Foucault and others, might at last explain the world and lead to change. But that hope withered. The social sciences failed to deliver the goods.' Today they are being rehumanized and reinvented by a new generation of intellectuals who believe there is just a hope that Foucault was wrong about the imminent death of Man.★

The structuralists and their successors, notably the post-modernists, still have influence abroad, and critics abroad. In 1997 an American physicist, Alan Sokal, and a Belgian academic, Jean Bricmont, published a book, *Impostures intellectuelles*, which relaunched an old criticism of French intellectuals as deliberately abstruse and convoluted. They wrote, 'If they seem unintelligible, this is for the good reason that they do not want to say anything', and they proceeded to castigate Lacan and others, plus such eminent post-structuralists as Jean Baudrillard and Julia Kristeva. They quoted a morsel of Kristeva: 'The notion of constructibility, which implies the axiom of choice associated with all we have put together for the poetic language, explains the impossibility of establishing a contradiction in the space of the language of poetry.' The French of course hit back. Kristeva spoke of Francophobia, while *Le Nouvel Observateur* devoted pages to the furore, under the headline, 'Are our philosophers impostors?' Sokal and Bricmont may have overstated their case: but the public were left again with the feeling that the post-existentialist thinkers, by retreating without much clarity into abstract, highly specialized areas, had done no great service to humanist intellectual causes.

For some years now, no major new intellectual leaders, nor philosophical movements, have appeared on the French scene. 'Ideological vacuum'

★ See François Dosse's book, *L'Empire du sens: l'humanisation des sciences humaines* (1997).

is the phrase often used. A few very clever thinkers, it is true, such as Alain Finkelkraut, Bernard-Henri Lévy and Emmanuel Todd, parade their ideas frequently on the radio and TV chat shows and keep up a modish intellectual debate. These pundits have become household names: but they do not pretend to be true *maîtres à penser* in the old sense. On the other hand, quite a number of more obscure intellectuals, in universities and research institutes, are seriously active, holding seminars or writing articles in learned reviews; and they, it is claimed, are producing original and fruitful work, though it does not hit the headlines. 'There may be no new schools or trends, yet I'm sure that in its low-keyed way this is a fertile period, with promise for the future,' I was told by Pierre Nora, editor of the leading review *Le Débat*: he had just produced a 250-page issue called *La Philosophie qui vient* on the work of twenty new thinkers. Much of the best new work is in specialized fields, such as the social sciences, pure science, or literary theory; but intellectuals are also debating more general issues, such as the future of democracy in an age when the ideological Left has lost much of its force. Marxist ideas have been on the wane since the early 1980s; and in the newer climate of pragmatism and economic realism, many intellectuals feel ill at ease. Their overall prestige and influence in France have certainly declined.

The traditional French intellectual has long been a clearly recognizable species, highly conscious of his status and responsibilities. At least till recently he has won wider public respect than his counterparts in Britain or America. The breed is to be found all over France, notably in academic circles, but is most heavily focused on the Paris Left Bank. Many intellectuals hold teaching posts, or they combine a living from journalism, part-time jobs in publishing, writing novels or monographs, giving radio talks or doing television. Though nearly all are bourgeois by origin, they have few social contacts except maybe family ones with the despised classic bourgeoisie of business or technocracy. They prefer to cling together, meeting for drinks or the occasional publisher's lunch at some Left Bank haunt such as the Brasserie Lipp or the Dôme: but they no longer frequent the St-Germain-des-Prés cafés so much. It is an intense little world of rival coteries, endless intrigue, much given to self-criticism – 'Yes, I know we are a hermetic society,' said one pundit. 'We constantly review each other's books, so few critics write what they really think.' This may apply to similar circles in London or New York: but in Paris the passionate and polemical French temperament sends the intellectual temperature soaring. The intellectual lives, and is expected to live, more urgently and publicly than in Britain.

Many a visiting intellectual from placid Britain is captivated by the Parisian climate of eager debate, the passion for ideas, the provocations, the curiosity about all that is new. Nicholas Snowman, the British musical expert who worked with Boulez, told me of the latter's public meetings in the 1970s with Barthes, Lacan and others, to explore the possible links between serial music and structuralism: 'We drew big audiences, such as I can't imagine in London for a similar topic. To follow the avant-garde is chic, but also a sign of real intelligence, and Parisians are truly curious to see what happens when you set one top thinker against another in a different field – like a boxing match. Paris may generate a lot of hot air, but at least it's alive.' Others, however, are more sceptical, suggesting that intellectuals tend to show more respect for ideas than for facts: one critic has pointed to their 'lack of interest in reality' and 'contempt for the authenticity of information'. Influenced maybe by the deductive methods instilled into them at school, they have a habit of selecting or even distorting the facts to suit their case – especially this has been true of the Marxists. In its own way this is a conformist world, as much as the bourgeois milieu it denounces. Intellectuals are wary of mixing with those who do not share their basic assumptions: 'If a banker went to one of their parties, he'd be ignored,' said one young woman.

This pattern, it is true, has become less clear-cut in the past ten years. A certain milieu may still be crazy for fashion and novelty: but today, taking a leaf from the banal British book, it is almost as concerned with personalities as ideas. Many intellectuals have even been growing a touch more modest, less sure of themselves, and readier to meet the outside world on its own terms; more of them now go on exchange visits to America or elsewhere, so they have grown less insular. They are settling into a less intense, more reflective mode. Pierre Nora wrote in 1980, 'Paris, obsessed by its own navel, gobbles up an ideology a week, an ontology every month', but he might not write that today. Two typical leaders of Left Bank radical chic in the 1960s and '70s were Philippe Sollers and Jean-Édern Hallier. These young aesthetes founded a well-known monthly review, *Tel Quel*, which championed the Platonic ideal of formal beauty, while also promoting left-wing views. Hallier, from a wealthy Breton family, was a bizarre megalomaniac whom many people thought phoney, but his literary talent was real. Wild-eyed, shock-headed, he received me one day in his trendy flat: 'I'm a *monstre sacré*,' he said affably, 'and the only living Frenchman who fulfils the role of a great writer in the nineteenth-century sense.' John Weightman, reviewing one of his erotic, highly coloured and very personal novels, wrote of

the pathetic bleat of his style and the fashionable mixture of genuine social and aesthetic concern with personal mythomania. We find here, in a concentrated form, a sort of intellectual dottiness, which is present elsewhere on the Paris literary scene in smaller doses, and may indeed be an essential ingredient of cultural ferment.

Hallier is now dead. But Sollers, a more serious and stable figure, is still active.

Then came the so-called '*nouveaux philosophes*' who irrupted noisily on to the scene in 1977–8. This assorted group of young men of the Left, led by two *normaliens*, André Glucksmann and Bernard-Henri Lévy, produced books and articles loudly asserting their loss of faith in Marx, Lenin and their tribe. In a pre-election period, their outbursts had political impact, being portents of the young intelligentsia's disenchantment with the old Leftist ideals, after reading Solzhenitsyn on the Gulag. And for a while these 'new philosophers' caused a furore hard to imagine in Britain, as Lévy's book *La Barbarie à visage humain* and Glucksmann's *Les Maîtres penseurs* became bestsellers – and Deleuze hit back for the Left with a pamphlet denouncing the whole thing as 'a media racket mounted by the Right'. 'This is intellectual street theatre of a kind the world expects from Paris,' commented one British observer.

Before long, the *nouveaux philosophes* trend was forgotten. But Lévy himself, brilliant and charismatic, remains a febrile star on the Paris scene. He was twenty-eight when he won fame with *La Barbarie*, a book rich in romantic pessimism ('Life is a lost cause and happiness an outworn idea'). With his wavy black hair, careful chic and sharp clarity of analysis, he is the ideal of what the French call *médiatique*, a prince of the media: he has made TV documentaries, even a feature film, and is often on the box, pronouncing on some topical issue. Others in this category include the sociologist Alain Finkelkraut, the economist Alain Minc and the demographer Emmanuel Todd (son of Olivier). They have plenty to say and they say it cleverly: but they are not aspiring to be intellectual gurus in the classic sense of a Sartre or Camus, even a Barthes or Lacan. The veteran left-wing sociologist Pierre Bourdieu does fancy himself in that role.

*

The Paris intellectual debate is aided by the nature of the publishing industry in France, where a book is habitually produced in a matter of weeks – as compared with eight to ten months in Britain or America. Pundits can thus exchange their ideas in a steady stream of rapidly written *essais* (monographs) which have little British equivalent. Another channel for debate is provided by the monthly or quarterly reviews. The veterans, the *Nouvelle Revue française*, and *Les Temps modernes*, which Sartre used to edit, still exist but do poorly: they have today been overtaken in importance by Nora's *Le Débat* (centre-Left), *L'Esprit* (Catholic centre-Left, edited by Olivier Mongin), and Jean-Claude Casanova's *Commentaire* (centre-Right). In the old days, most such reviews were bitterly polemical: but today, a sign of the times, they are milder and more open, and Nora, Mongin and Casanova are on friendly terms. Though still more numerous and influential than in Britain, these periodicals have lost ground since the 1970s, in face of the more immediate if superficial outlets offered by the news magazines and the media.

A virtuoso indictment of the *médiatique* trend came in 1979 from the famous Marxist intellectual Régis Debray, the man who had helped Che Guevara. His best-selling and much-discussed book *Le Pouvoir intellectuel en France* alleged that true intellectual debate was being debased and trivialized by the lure of the new media, and that many serious thinkers, maybe against their better judgement, were being prostituted into accepting the easy fame and high fees thus provided:

Why invest ten years of your life in writing a thesis which will make you a PhD, imprisoned in some provincial faculty, when with a mere month's work you can turn out a vitriolic pamphlet on a topical theme ('Destiny and the Gulag') which will put your name in the headlines and allow you a spirited hour on television, thus making you a national hero?

In this open attack on the Lévy phenomenon, Debray suggested that over the past hundred years the main power centre of intellectual persuasion had shifted first from the Church to the universities (their heyday was *c.* 1880–1930), then to the big publishing houses like Gallimard with their reviews (*c.* 1930–68), and now to the mass media.

The trend is by no means solely French: what other Western country does not have its facile TV pundits, dispensing instant wisdom? But in Paris, when American media techniques were copied belatedly in the 1970s, matters were special: the new media's impact on an intellectual world already so prone to polemics and histrionics produced a strange combustion. The media would exploit it as showbiz, and the public would enjoy the spectacle of intellectual jousting: TV channels and magazines would vie for what Debray called '*le scoop idéologique*'. The term '*médiatique*', meaning, roughly, 'playing to the gallery via the media', became a neologism still ubiquitous in France. Today, twenty years after Debray wrote, the scene has settled down a little: intellectuals, at first caught off guard and seduced by the new media, have learned how to handle it. Some refuse to appear at all, others exploit it sensibly. And, within the limits of TV, by no means all the debates of this kind are trivial. French television's three regular books programmes, plus the current affairs ones, often include intellectual discussions of good quality. And authors fight for the privilege of appearing on the literary shows, which have little equivalent in Britain. For some years the Friday-night *Apostrophes*, with up to 6 million viewers, was the high point of the intellectual week; its famous presenter, Bernard Pivot, today has another programme, *Bouillon de Culture*, where he might engage in serious debate with, say, Salman Rushdie or Umberto Eco. Debray saw Pivot as France's baleful mediacrat-in-chief: 'This columnist of the Eternal has transcended History because he amuses himself with *toutes les histoires*' (the word means both 'history' and 'gossip'). This was unfair, for Pivot is an erudite man who has done much good work.

Intellectuals' attitudes to *le pouvoir* have long been equivocal, under de Gaulle and even Mitterrand. In the 1960s the Left Bank found itself challenged by the rise of a go-ahead prosperous society with other ideals, intent on technology and practical reform. And some bona fide intellectuals virtually defected to this camp by working with the reformers. So there was a striking divorce between those who broadly accepted this new France and those – still the majority – who rejected it in the name of their left-wing ideals. Each group charged the other with betrayal. There were famous figures who did not fit into either camp, but the prototypes were blatant: Malraux building his cultural centres versus Sartre crying woe in the wilderness.

When the Left took power in 1981, the picture changed radically. Glad to be rid of Giscard and his technocratic creed, most intellectuals warmed to Mitterrand as a true man of culture, and they welcomed the steps that he and Jack Lang took to help literature. But then they grew suspicious. Lang showered honours on writers, and while some were flattered, others felt they were being exploited for political ends – especially when the none-too-tactful minister denounced as 'reactionaries' those who dared criticize the Government. Some Leftish writers such as Duras remained loyal to Mitterrand; others distanced themselves. A few even felt, somewhat perversely, that writers or artists can suffer from the bear hug of a sympathetic regime and their integrity is best preserved in opposition. Today few on the Left Bank warm to Chirac, who is a cultured man in his way (he loves oriental art and Chinese poetry) but politically has little time for *les intellectuels*. Even Jospin has lost the support of some of them, notably those who oppose European integration: they in some cases are now flirting again with a Communist Party shorn of its Stalinism and grown more respectable. Marxism itself is making a modest comeback, in some circles, under the impulse of capitalism's failure to find an answer to unemployment – 'but it's the true creed of Marx's own youth,' said one disciple, 'not the later Marx, who so often is distorted.'

And the ideological Right? Ever since the defeat of Nazism, to be an intellectual in France had meant being on the Left, or perhaps the tolerant centre, while the intellectual Right hardly dared show its face. Then in 1979 *la nouvelle droite* emerged, and was even taken seriously: but it was an odd animal, not what you might expect. Its chief propagandist was Alain de Benoist, a minor aristocrat. He and his assorted fellow thinkers were unlike the old pre-war intellectual Right, usually militarist and nationalist (witness Maurras) or monarchist. De Benoist preached another creed, a mystical élitism, drawing ideas from Nietzsche, inveighing against American consumerism as well as the Left; he argued that Europe must return to the spiritual fount of its early civilization, Hellenic, Germanic and Celtic, and he stressed the basic inequality of man. This woolly doctrine at first had some appeal. But then the political rise of the Front National (which has no ideas, only prejudices) thoroughly discredited the *nouvelle droite*, which today is little heard of. A handful of intellectuals support the traditionalism of Philippe de Villiers, while the Papon trial has brought out some Vichyist ideas: but if the intellectual Right still has any voice, it is mainly in the context of Catholic integrism (see p. 583).

In 1998 a free-thinking iconoclast blazed across the Parisian sky, causing the biggest intellectual furore for some years. Michel Houellebecq, a mousy computer technician aged forty, was the author of two novels of average literary merit: *Extension du domaine de la lutte* (1997) and *Les Particules élémentaires* (1998), which dared to challenge the *idées reçues* of the progressive intellectual Left. In the former he denounced the corrosive influence of consumerism and computerization – and the Left cheered him for it. But the latter was an attack on the 'liberation' ideology of the '68 generation and its consequences, in particular the sexual super-freedom which corrupted human values – and now the Left howled in fury at him. This 'young fogey' not only wanted more authority and less choice, but he opposed abortion, found hard-line Catholics *sympathiques* and had little time for anti-racist or *écolo* causes. He felt that modern 'liberation' produced its own destructiveness, and dared speak against the conformism of the Left and its 'political correctness'. The publication of his second novel sparked off a huge – and rather healthy – debate on modern values, fuelled by a myriad interviews, articles and TV shows. Philippe Sollers himself, though a target in the book, praised Houellebecq for usefully breaking taboos. And so, after a dry period, the intellectual milieu plunged into a passionate frenzy of debate on ideas – it was all very Parisian.

Since the time of Sartre, indeed since Dreyfus and before, many intellectuals have felt the need, even the duty, to be *engagés* in public affairs and try to influence them. They campaigned with distinction against French army use of torture in Algeria. But more recently some of their actions may have been less well judged. In 1994 a group led by Glucksmann worthily put forward a 'Sarajevo list' for the European Parliament elections, to rally opinion against Serbian brutalities. But it failed to win support and they withdrew it, amid general embarrassment. This provoked a debate as to whether it was the proper role of intellectuals to engage in such public action. This may have even fuelled the decline in their prestige. Add to this, on a lesser level, the desertion of the Left Bank cafés by true serious intellectuals. Tourists come to the Flore or Deux Magots looking for Sartre's successors, and they find each other.

And yet, in quite another sense, philosophy nowadays is *à la mode*. Very curiously, the past few years have given signs of a widening of popular interest in philosophical inquiry among average but educated people. The potential is already there, if only because so many people (unlike in Britain or Germany) have studied the subject perforce at the *lycée*. Today some non-specialist books on philosophy win big sales; and at the mighty École Normale Supérieure, the number of students choosing it has recently more than doubled. The trend may well relate to the new doubts of a troubled era. For many people, neither Leftism nor the Church provides the answers, so they grope for something else. Professor François Jullien, president of the new Collège de Philosophie, and a crusader for widening the subject's impact, told me, 'I hold seminars for the managers of big firms, and they come eagerly. They have lost their old certainties and are asking new questions. They no longer feel that growth and profit are ends in themselves. So they seek some philosophical scheme that can explain and justify their work. This is new.'

One new vogue is for the *café philosophique*, where a group meets publicly in a café to debate questions of metaphysics or ethics, and anyone can turn up. The trend was launched in 1992 by a philosophy teacher, Marc Sautet, who until his death from cancer in 1998 would hold regular Sunday-morning sessions at the Café des Phares, by the Place de la Bastille. His idea caught on, and today there are some twenty-five 'philosophy cafés' in greater Paris, another twenty-five in the provinces, and one at the Institut Français's café in London. In the racially mixed HLM estate of L'Arlequin, at Grenoble, I listened to ninety people discussing 'intolerance'. And at the Bastille I found the Café des Phares packed with some 150 people, paying just the price of a drink to take part in a two-hour debate, animated by Sautet in a black jersey, sitting among them on a stool. The theme was 'What is the use of art?', and aphorisms and rhetorical reflections flowed non-stop. Many speakers expressed their distaste for a market-oriented society that makes art a commodity: but politics were avoided. Most people were middle class, but a few were working class. Many appeared to be forty-ish housewives who had done their *philo* for the *bac* years ago – 'It makes me quite nostalgic, to be debating again like this,' said one of them. I reflected that a session of this kind could not easily happen in Britain (save among students), where people lack the mental training, and all would soon become jokey. At the Phares, the tone was serious, but not earnest – and Sautet kept it light by *tutoie*-ing everyone. Had I stumbled into some intellectual Club Med?

Many academic intellectuals scorn these amateur talk-ins. But who knows if philosophy – like music, gastronomy, or sport – does not need to broaden its grassroots appeal? The revived interest in philosophic questions seems to say something about the mood of France today; and it could perhaps provide some basis for an intellectual renewal. The village or suburban café may be decaying, but here is the city café giving new life, in a way, to an old French tradition that some thought had died with Sartre at St-Germain-des-Prés. Mesdames, Messieurs, take your debating partners, let the Flore show go on!

7

EDUCATIONAL REFORM:
EQUALITY VERSUS ÉLITISM

Today's younger generations do not throw up politically minded Leftist rebels, like those of May '68. They are more reserved, more elusive, and though serious they do not flaunt their ideals. Many have a thirst for education, for gaining the right diplomas that can open doors to jobs, at a time when youth unemployment is around 23 per cent. Hence about four-fifths of the age group stay at school until eighteen or more, and some 50 per cent of it then proceed to higher education – much larger figures than in Britain.

France's vaunted state-run education system, in theory free for all but in some aspects very élitist, has not found it easy to adapt to these broad new pressures. And so a great national debate on the subject has been raging ever since the 1950s, as the highly traditional structure of schools and universities has been constantly under reform. In schools, the aim has been to make opportunity more truly equal, and to lighten the academic grind without spoiling the high intellectual standards that have long been such a feature of French teaching. The accent is still on classroom work, with far less emphasis on the out-of-class activities or 'character-building' that are seen as a big part of education in Britain. In universities, funding and curricula have not kept pace with the vast explosion of student numbers. And there is still a wide gulf between the ordinary faculties, with their low prestige, and the privileged few in the Grandes Écoles. But the Socialists today finally have active plans to modify this élitism, so often criticized.

BACCALAURÉATS FOR BLUE-COLLAR WORKERS

'What! – yet *another* reform? It's crazy' was the reaction of many a teacher when the mighty *baccalauréat* leaving examination was remodelled yet again in the early 1990s. Ever since the war, in no other area of French life has there been such a steady avalanche of piecemeal reform as in school education, where the French struggle, amid endless controversy, to square the circle of modernizing their traditional state-run system without sacrificing its proud and precious qualities.

These are considerable. In the classroom the average level of academic teaching remains higher than in Britain, and children at all levels are given a strong basic grounding of *culture générale*. Under the Jules Ferry laws of 1882, which instituted compulsory education for all, state schooling is still virtually free, and in theory at least it provides equality of opportunity. As many as 85 per cent of small children between two and five are in nursery schools, which are mostly also state-run, and free. And the French take schooling very seriously: some 80 per cent of pupils remain in education until at least eighteen, compared with only 35 per cent in Britain.

Yet for the past forty years the French have been striving intermittently to make this rigorous competitive system less authoritarian, more genuinely equal; to adapt it to new economic needs, new social aspirations, and to a modern educational ethos that will put the stress on developing a child's whole personality, not just his mind. Most French have agreed that change is needed – but how can it be achieved without a severe drop in standards? How can technical education be extended and its low prestige improved, so as to help the less academic child? How can discipline be lightened and humanized without a spread of the violence now affecting many schools of *la banlieue*?

Above all, can equal opportunity be made a reality without a lowering of standards? The *lycées* (state grammar schools) offer mainly free tuition and in theory are open to all: yet social barriers and prejudices have long been such that the more prestigious of them – such as Henri IV in Paris – have in practice been almost as much the preserve of a certain social class as the higher-priced English public schools; and even in the average *lycée*, the working classes have been badly under-represented. Yet the *lycée* prepares for the *baccalauréat* (*bac*), essential gateway to higher education. For some years, a whole new social class has aspired to the *lycée*, and often to university, too; and some major reforms since 1963 have aimed at broadening the *lycée* intake, with some success. But the process was not going fast enough, according to Lionel Jospin, who became Minister of Education in 1988. His stated aim was that the numbers sitting the *bac* should rise to 80 per cent of the age group by the year 2000 – and today this is not far from being achieved. But the result, a doubling of the *lycée* population, has led to severe overcrowding, and in the universities, too, for new funds have not kept pace with the changes.

These have been the central dilemmas of much post-war reform, as in other countries. Does 'more' always mean 'worse'? Can academic teaching be reconciled with vocational needs, and with self-expression?

Eighty-two per cent of French schools are run by the State on a civil service basis (the rest are mostly in the hands of the Church, see p. 549). This centralized state control makes reform easier to decide on paper than in Britain, but often harder to apply in practice, for it has to be imposed from above rather than proceed by groundswell movement. And the left-wing militancy of many teachers is equalled only by their conservatism in face of academic change. Especially, they have tended to oppose reforms emanating from right-wing Governments, even those whose content they approve. So the authorities have found it easier to make structural changes, involving new kinds of school or examination, than to tackle the harder but more crucial task of updating the approach and methods of French teaching.

The classic pattern is still alive, and has its magic. 'In *Andromache*, did Racine respect the rules of the three unities?' – a sixteen-year-old, in tieless shirt and informal jersey, stands up to give the perfect formal answer, the way he's been taught; then the teacher resumes his own brilliant didactic performance, tripping his way through the subtleties of literary analysis as only a Sorbonne *agrégé* can. It could be any classical *lycée* in the French cultural empire, from Tahiti to South Kensington.

Much of the best and the worst in the French national spirit can be imputed to this concept of education as inspired academic pedagogy confined to the classroom walls: its role is to transmit knowledge and to train intellects, not – as in Britain – to develop the full individual. Traditionally, teaching has been deductive, rhetorical, preoccupied with style, and the teacher has had little human contact with pupils outside the class. The *lycées* have provided the bourgeoisie with the loftiest academic discipline in the world; they have moulded a cultural élite where technocrats can turn to any problem with the same clarity they were taught to apply to Racine. Scientists and classicists alike have received a strong dose of the same *culture générale*, with lashings of philosophy. And even children leaving school earlier have been put through sufficiently rigorous mental hoops in junior schools for a foreigner often to be impressed by the French working man's articulateness and grasp of ideas.

Yet after the war the system came under growing criticism for being too severe, too unrelated to modern life. In the Ministry of Education, a few liberal reformists managed to steer some innovations between the Scylla of state parsimony and the Charybdis of teacher conservatism. In the 1960s the school-leaving age was raised from fourteen to sixteen. Other measures sought to lighten the severities of the examination system. Yet today the competitive ethos is by no means abandoned. In junior schools class marks are still awarded monthly. So a child is still under pressure from his teacher, and often from parents, too, to outshine his rivals. Probably this encourages him to work harder: but it can also lead to tensions and snobberies, and can inhibit the less bright child. It has even been held responsible for some of the rivalries and discords in French adult society.

De Gaulle's reformist Government was eager to remedy the inequalities of opportunity. So in 1963, in a bid to democratize the *lycée* intake, it decreed that there would now be only one kind of state school for all children, rich or poor, between eleven and fifteen. Hitherto, though all attended the same primary schools till the age of eleven, the *lycées* then took their own privileged stream, in practice mainly middle class, while the rest went to a secondary school that led straight into a job or at best to a technical college. Under the 1963 reform the two streams were merged into a network of new comprehensives (*collèges*). Selection from these for *lycée* entry at fifteen would be on school record, not by exam. Streaming was thus pushed back four years. Thousands of *collèges* were formed, and working-class intake into the *lycées* gradually increased. But the *collèges* were opposed by some *lycée* staff, fearing a decline in standards, and by many bourgeois parents, fearing that *lycée* entrance would now be less automatic for their children. So under a compromise the *lycées* were allowed to retain direct control of their own junior classes – and some social discrimination continued. But often working-class families excluded themselves: a parent might feel, maybe with reason, that his own child with a different home background would be ill at ease in the *lycée* atmosphere, so he would not even attempt entrance. And as only a *lycée* or private college prepared for the *bac*, universities remained something of a middle-class preserve. Since 1959 the percentage of working-class students has risen from 4 to 13 per cent, but in Britain it is 30 per cent.

In the May '68 uprising *lycéens* rebelled alongside students. When the dust had settled, the Government did not at once embark on a major major programme of change in the schools as in the universities. But soon the reformists were urging that the 1963 reforms needed a follow-up; and Giscard, on coming to power, proclaimed a new deal for education as part of the blueprint for his 'advanced liberal society'. For Minister of Education he made a surprise choice, René Haby, a university rector with a forceful manner and radical views. Haby initiated some badly needed improvements in primary schools, where standards had been falling. Above all, he pushed through Parliament a new masterplan for the *collèges*, whereby children would follow identical courses. His main innovation was mixed-ability classes. Henceforth, he decreed, there would be no more streaming by intelligence, only by age group: future Einstein would sit next to future roadsweeper. For France, it was a sharp break with tradition. One motive of the reform was egalitarian, while another was to help the economy: in the new hi-tech age, so the Government argued, it was no longer enough merely to select and cosset the intelligent. Haby insisted also that the curriculum be made more practical: every pupil of whatever background should now learn some manual skills, such as metalwork or sewing. Some teachers feared a further blow to academic standards, but others were pleased: 'It is good for a mentally precocious child to find out that he can't wield a hammer, it makes him less cocksure,' said one headmaster.

Mixed-ability classes were progressively set up in the *collèges*. But they required some pedagogic dexterity, and many teachers found it hard to cope. So schools tacitly found ways of not applying the reforms too literally: in practice, they kept a degree of streaming in some classes, and were under pressure to do so from parents of abler children. The abrasive Haby was unpopular with the teachers' unions and with parents alike; and in 1978 he was dismissed by Giscard, with his reform only half adopted. Teachers were then instructed not to apply it too rigidly, in a pre-election period. However, the modern and democratic principle of mixed-ability classes was retained by the Socialists after 1981. And today it remains in force, though schools are allowed discretion in how strictly they follow it.

The Socialists were at first entirely preoccupied with the church schools issue (see below). Then in 1984 the brilliant and unusual Jean-Pierre Chevènement was appointed Education Minister. He had come from the Left of his party but was also an *énarque*, and he declared himself appalled at the drop in standards, especially in basic skills such as spelling and arithmetic, at a time when France badly needed well-educated and mentally disciplined young people. He had the backing of Mitterrand, worried at the decline in knowledge of history and literature. So Chevènement issued orders for primary schools to put less accent on the non-academic motivation courses that Haby had promoted, and to lay the stress again on the 'three Rs', and on history, geography and science. So here was a left-wing Socialist turning back to traditional values, after the 'free expression' modernism of Haby under a Government of the Right! Chevènement's aim was partly to restore public faith in the state system after the confusion of the post-May-'68 period. And many parents, in despair at their unruly, badly taught children, reacted warmly. So did some teachers, though many others would rather have kept the Haby approach. Chevènement's measures were more or less applied then continued by the Chirac Government in 1986–8. But latest surveys indicate that, as in other countries, pupils' spelling has declined a lot compared with the old days. Knowledge has suffered, too, but not abilities of analysis or synthesis.

When Jospin became minister in 1988, he switched attention to the senior *lycée* classes. He, too, was a reformer, but in many ways closer to Haby than to Chevènement in his ideas. Having been a university teacher, he knew all about the crisis of the overswollen campuses: even so, as a doctrinaire Socialist he felt it important to give more young people a chance of higher education. So he made *baccalauréat* reform his priority.

In the *lycées* life is still lived in the shadow of this most sacred and imperious of French institutions. Taken at eighteen or so, *le bac* is a more rigorous and brain-searching exam than its English equivalent, A-level GCE. It has been called 'the national obsession of the middle classes'; and although the exams are strictly controlled, there have been some notorious cases of parents paying lavishly to bribe examiners or secure advance copies of papers. As a mental grounding for the more gifted child, one of the *bac*'s virtues has been its emphasis on a high level of *culture générale*, including philosophy, alike in the literary and scientific options. But the syllabus, and the rhetorical and deductive teaching methods, have tended to develop a conformist turn of mind, theoretical, uncreative, schooled to think and verbalize with great clarity along predetermined lines. And although a brilliant pupil can perhaps contribute his own originality, others can get submerged. What is more, the syllabus is so non-vocational (except in the case of the *bac technique* and the new *bac professionnel*, see below), that the *bac* itself is a poor job qualification. Those who fail have few useful skills, but a stigma of inferiority; those who pass feel impelled to then take a degree or specialized diploma.

Reform has therefore been in the air since the 1960s, as measures and counter-measures have flowed from a vacillating ministry, alienating even those teachers pressing for change. In 1965 the options were rearranged and modernized. Economics, sociology and statistics were at last recognized as subjects worthy of a *lycéen*'s study. In the main arts option, French literature no longer stopped at 1900 but reached to Sartre and beyond. But *la culture générale* was not abandoned: today the science option still includes a philosophy paper. As in Britain, there is ongoing debate over early versus late specialization, and the pendulum swings to and fro. But although the latest trend in the 1990s is to move it earlier, the degree of non-specialized *culture générale* remains greater than in Britain. A student sitting the economics and social sciences *bac* has to master a syllabus that takes in two foreign languages, mathematics, history and philosophy. Bravo for true education.

In 1993–4, with François Bayrou as minister under Balladur, the *bac* was again remodelled – this time, with the principal aim of reducing the 'tyranny' of maths and science. Although the *bac* is so intellectual, the prestige of 'option A' (literature and philosophy) had gradually been usurped by 'option C' (maths, science, economics), seen as the royal road of entry into a modern élite career via the Grandes Écoles or ENA. Teachers of humanities complained that many of the brightest pupils felt pressured into following this 'C' option, even if their talents and inclinations lay elsewhere. So the Bayrou reform reshuffled and renamed the options ('A' was now 'L', 'C' was now 'S'); it broadened and strengthened the syllabus of the new 'L', so as to make it more attractive to high-flyers, and it urged the Grandes Écoles to take account of this. Across the seven options, the reform has made the *bac* a little harder intellectually. But examiners have been instructed to counterbalance this by being more indulgent in their marking. This is in line with Jospin's 1989 policy of creating more *bacheliers*.

In 1953 a mere 7 per cent of the age group passed the *bac*. By 1986 the figure had increased to 29 per cent. Jospin's target, set in 1989, was for some 80 per cent of an age group to be sitting the exam by 2000. This was overambitious: yet the level today has climbed to 70 per cent. The failure rate is some 23 per cent: but many pupils try again the next year, and pass. Thus today 61 per cent of the age group obtains the *bac* – a doubling in ten years. But it brings problems. Jospin was no doubt sincere in wanting to democratize: 'France still needs its élites,' said this *énarque*, 'yet without a mass output, too, there can be no satisfactory élite.' But he was also accused of demagoguery in wanting to please his party's electorate. Nor did he back up his reform with adequate new funding for the *lycées*, which doubled in average size in 1986–92 and whose classes grew bigger. 'It may be good in theory for more pupils to have a chance for the *bac*,' said a liberal headmaster I met in Angers, 'but the reform has been done the wrong way. Many of our weaker pupils are unsuited to the exam. Many prolong their education simply to escape the job rat race for a few more years. It is understandable, but not the best motivation.' And a Sorbonne professor added, 'The recent measures have effectively devalued the *bac*. We get more and more weak students, inadequately taught. The *bac* has become a monstrous machine, out of touch with real needs.'

One major issue is: where are the weaker *bacheliers* to go, if not to the classic universities? Another: what are the outlets for all those who fail the *bac* or do not try for it? France still has a shortage of good middle-grade technicians; and long before Jospin the Ministry of Education had begun trying to divert non-academically inclined children away from the classic *lycées* and into a more technical education provided by the newer *lycées techniques*. But these do not have the same prestige. Paradoxically, whereas technological education has supremely high status at the level of the Grandes Écoles, this ends abruptly lower down. Bourgeois parents will be proud for their children to move via the maths *bac* to a Grande École and a career as a engineer: but they will turn up their noses at his going to a *lycée technique* to take the *bac technique*, a more practical workshop exam. At one *lycée*, I visited a class immersed in the final strained weeks of cramming for the *bac*, and their teacher said, 'Most of these kids will end up in clerical jobs or petty commerce. Few have the minds for this high-quality theoretical work: they'd have done better in a technical stream, if only their silly parents had let them.' Then a staff assistant, a woman from a modest family, told me, 'My son went happily to a *lycée technique*, then to an electronics college, and now in his blue-collar job he's doing better than most of these kids ever will.' So the bourgeoisie is caught in its own snooty trap.

This pattern today is slowly changing, as more parents and pupils come to accept that the technical stream may more readily lead to a job. And the Government has made efforts to develop schools for training skilled workers. In the post-*bac* classes of the *lycées techniques*, it offers a two-year course for a higher diploma (*brevet de technicien supérieur*, known as BTS) that in job terms is usually worth more than a university DEUG diploma (see below). But the problem remains of how to make the *bac* itself more useful for a job, and thus limit the Gadarene stampede into high education. In 1985 the ministry created a new *bac professionnel*, very practical, involving a few weeks of *stages* in firms, and this has proved quite popular and is being accepted as a job qualification by many firms in industry, commerce and tourism. It is helping a little to square the circle between the Jospin campaign and the traditional *bac* itself, which is often found worthless for the job market. But what of those who fail the *bac*? You can try it again, but only once, and of those who fail a second time, many are left with a stigma. Some, with well-to-do parents, will take a course in some specialized private college, or they look for a job – though they are often among those with the least chance of finding one. For those not trying for the *bac*, there is the option of a more junior technical qualification, the *brevet d'enseignement professionnel* or the *certificat d'aptitude professionnelle*, taken at seventeen or eighteen, sometimes together with an apprenticeship. A BEP or CAP usually leads directly into the job market, or it can be followed by further study for the *bac*: the system is flexible. In fact, today only 15 per cent of French pupils leave school with no qualification at all, and many of these are the 'social' cases of the troubled suburbs.

Apprenticeship in firms, as a part of formal education, is finally gaining some ground. There used to be lots of apprentices in France, under a tradition dating from the *compagnonnages* (trade guilds) of the Middle Ages. But with the rapid post-war expansion of secondary education, pupils stayed at school longer and fewer became apprentices. The left-wing unions, hating the Patronat, wanted to keep pupils within the pure ambience of school and not have them contaminated by work in firms.

So the divide was much sharper than in most countries between school and working life. But today, with high youth unemployment, teachers' hostility has waned; some are even coming to accept the modern view that education is not solely a matter for school! A law in 1987 provided a new framework for apprenticeship, and some funding; and the number of trainees has since risen from 150,000 to 300,000. 'We have contacts with many local firms, large and small,' I was told by the headmaster of one big *lycée technique* in Toulouse, 'and we send them kids to learn carpentry, metalwork, bricklaying, or cooking or sewing. It is good for academic duds to discover they have some manual talent. Many of my teachers are still wary, but things are improving.'

The system is more developed than in Britain, but far less than in Germany which has some 1.8 million *Azubis*. Apprenticeships there are basically run by the firms, while the trainees also spend time on study in vocational centres. In France, conversely, the trainees remain within the state-school framework, whence they go out into firms on *stages*: the stress on continued study is greater. In fact, many French apprentices are studying for a CAP or BEP, or even the *bac*. The French do not want to copy too closely a German model which they feel is too narrowly vocational (and the Germans themselves are today having doubts about their own system). But there are problems in France over who pays. An apprentice receives a small wage, equal to about half the SMIC. The regional councils and chambers of commerce provide some money, but not much. Most firms remain reluctant to pay, which limits the scheme. And the Education Ministry has too many other obligations. Even so, the steady growth of apprenticeships, and of candidates for the technical *bac* streams, is today slowly shifting the balance away from the old lofty academic *baccalauréat*.

EDUCATION FOR LIFE AND LIVING, OR JUST FOR THE MIND?

Education in France means classroom work: what happens outside class is infinitely less important. Compared with Britain, or America, there is minimal stress on organized leisure activities, on giving responsibility to pupils or on trying to run the school as a warm living community. Some see this as a serious weakness: but it is not in the French tradition. However, there have been some moves since 1968 towards lightening the discipline, making schools more human, giving them a little more autonomy within the harsh centralized system.★

When in May '68 the *lycéens* rebelled so massively, it was above all against the severe atmosphere of the average school, where there was seldom much informal contact between teacher and pupil, and life was governed by a myriad regulations decreed from Paris. The smallest departure from routine, such as an extra half-day holiday, could not be decided without written order from the ministry, which also fixed the precise duties of each member of staff.

Long before May '68, *lycéens* had been growing restive. Then, when the Paris students rebelled, *lycéens* all over France gleefully followed them. Small politically minded groups formed a national action committee; other pupils joined in to air their grievances or just for the hell of it. Amazing scenes took place, hardly believable in this milieu where schoolkids had been seen and not heard. Many *lycées* were 'occupied' by their pupils, like the factories by workers, and red and black flags were hoisted. Teachers no longer dared sit at their rostra, but either fled the classroom or, the more liberal of them, sat for hours beside their striking pupils, discussing school, politics, sex, careers, life. 'I never knew my girls before except as minds: now I know them as people,' said one woman teacher. Parents, invited to take part in the impromptu debates, were often amazed to hear persuasive public orations from their own offspring – how the babes had grown up! Some other parents hit back, even storming into *lycées* to beat their kids up. At one girls' school in Paris, 'liberated' by a male army from a nearby boys' *lycée*, I saw the *directrice*, a tiny, elderly figure, totally bewildered, clutching at the jacket of a wild hippy youth towering above her: '*Mais non, Monsieur, je ne refuse pas le dialogue! Je ne le refuse pas!*' All over France, the revolt did indeed open a new era of dialogue between pupils and many teachers – even if its immediate legacy was also some years of contention and unrest. A few *lycéens* remained aggressively political, calling themselves Maoists

★ One aspect of this centralization, resented by teachers, is that as civil servants they must go where the Education Ministry posts them. This can lead to personal hardship. I heard of a woman living with her husband and child near Pau, where he had got a job, who was refused a transfer from her teaching post in Paris, 900 km away: so much of her salary, and much time and energy, were spent on weekend visits home. However, the personnel office of the ministry has become more humane, to the extent that couples are no longer separated in this way. But a single teacher goes where ordered, like a soldier.

or Guevarists, scrawling angry graffiti on school walls, in some cases rioting. But then the subsequent youth generation proved much less politically minded, as in the universities.

The more permanent legacy of May '68 is that it did lead to a more humane spirit in the *lycées*, and to more contact between their formerly hermetic world and the 'real' world outside. Today a new teacher generation is more open-minded; and there is more discussion, less rigid discipline, even if pressure of work and of pupil numbers makes it hard to continue the euphoric, intimate teacher–pupil dialogues of the May carnival.

In July 1968 de Gaulle gave the Education portfolio to the astute Edgar Faure, a former Prime Minister, ordering him to draw on the lessons of the May revolt. This was mainly at university level. In the schools, Faure tried to institutionalize the new dialogue, with a reform that set up democratic governing boards (*conseils d'établissement*) in all *lycées* and *collèges* – a break with French tradition. Still in force today, these boards are made up one-fifth of parents, one-fifth of senior pupils (elected from their own ranks), and the rest of teachers and other staff, plus a few ministry officials and local *notables*. The board has no powers over syllabus and exams, but can advise the headmaster on a range of decisions concerning the internal running of the school, the use of its budget, teaching methods and discipline. The boards meet once or twice a term, and their success has varied greatly. Under a strong headmaster a board may be little more than a cipher. In some cases cooperation is smooth, but in others there can be chaos or stalemate: some boards have become heavily politicized, as staff pressure groups argue endlessly. The reform was also a bid to give pupils a sense of sharing in the running of their school, but this has not always worked well. However, overall the reform marked a useful attempt to decentralize some powers away from a ministry which hitherto controlled every detail down to the buying of blotters.

More recently, other measures have further reduced the role of the ministry. Under the devolution of the 1980s, the *conseils généraux* and regional councils are now responsible for school buildings and equipment. And under the Jospin reforms of 1989, headmasters have a little more autonomy – still slight by British standards – in such areas as fixing school timetables and spending their budget. But not all make much use of this greater freedom. Many have grown scared, as it carries with it a new legal responsibility, in matters such as safety, that used to be held by the ministry. In 1994 a pupil at a *lycée* near Paris was killed when a rusting basketball post hit him: the *proviseur* was found guilty of manslaughter and given a two-month suspended prison sentence. There have been other such cases. And some of the ablest senior teachers have thus become wary of accepting the post of headmaster, which carries other stresses, too, now that *lycées* have swollen in size.

Despite these problems, the climate in the average class has changed a lot since pre-1968 days. Discipline used to be paramilitary: in junior schools a class would have to line up in order at the end of each lesson before being dismissed. Some teachers might indulge in petty tyranny. Then after May '68 some schools swung at first from an authoritarian extreme to permissiveness. A not illiberal teacher in a girls' *lycée*★ told me in 1972, 'The girls talk and smoke in class, and if you put your foot down, there's a riot or a walk-out. The head does little – she has orders from the ministry to avoid trouble. The positive aspect is that the old prison-like austerity has gone and the girls are happier.' Within a few years a balance was achieved, and *lycéens* today are neither as cowed as in the old days, nor as unruly as after 1968 (save in some 'difficult' areas of *la banlieue*: see below). Pupils can smoke in the courtyard, but smoking in class has become rarer. And teachers, most of them products of May '68 or younger, make more effort to treat their pupils with human concern in class: '*Odile, à quoi penses-tu?*' has replaced '*Dupont, taisez-vous!*' They now put less accent on the *cours magistral*, and more on group work and question-and-answer methods (but less than in Britain). In primary schools especially, the teaching has become more informal, with less learning by rote. These schools have also seen some moves to develop extra-curricular activities, even to promote a sense of community. In 1996 the ministry launched a pilot scheme in several hundred primary schools, whereby classroom lessons would be confined to the morning, and the afternoons until 4 p.m. would be given over to sport and cultural and social activities – quite an innovation.

In the secondary schools, which tend to be larger, change has been less great. Discipline may have eased, but neither teachers nor ministry have made much effort to turn a school into a living focus of loyalty, a fun place to stay around in after lessons are over. That is not the French tradition. A school is a facility for the transmission of knowledge and the passing of exams, nothing more. Small wonder that pupils seldom show

★ Many schools used to be single-sex, but today nearly all are co-educational.

much enthusiasm for their school and its life. 'This place for me is like a supermarket,' said a boy at one smart Paris *lycée*. 'I come for what I need to get from it, the *bac*: but I feel no emotional attachment.' No question of *floreat Etona*. Most schools do have their clubs of sorts, for chess, jazz, sometimes drama, and so on: but they are feeble by Anglo-Saxon standards, and often poorly attended. Generally, they lack funds and suitable premises. The ministry, and many headmasters, pay lip service to the need for more out-of-class activities, but in practice it is often among the lowest of their priorities. Even the libraries of good *lycées* tend to be small and ill-stocked: new books of general interest are mostly acquired through parents' donations or the children's own modest subscriptions. In fact, some teachers are quite glad that there are not too many readable or foreign books around to distract the pupils: better Voltaire or Molière, who are on the syllabus, than Updike or Boyd, who are not.

Lycées also lack the large halls that could help create a sense of community; and overcrowding has not helped. The august Lycée Fermat in Toulouse has graceful old buildings: but its biggest hall holds only 400 whereas numbers have swollen to over 2,000, so that any ceremony such as a prize-giving or school concert, which might induce some communal spirit, is virtually impossible. 'The school has lost all atmosphere; it's just a teaching factory,' one headmaster told me. 'The staff is so large that we hardly know each other.' If out-of-class activities such as clubs are so few in France, one reason is that not many teachers are prepared to stay on after hours to help organize them. A teacher does not see this as part of his job; in fact he probably belongs to a union that militantly opposes this kind of 'unpaid overtime'. Teachers work hard, to be sure, and many spend hours each evening correcting essays. But the average *professeur* regards the school as a kind of office job: he arrives, holds his series of classes, maybe with donnish brilliance, then goes home. Jospin in 1989 proposed a change that would widen the teacher's role, giving him more responsibility for pupils' out-of-class lives: many teachers were in favour, but the reform foundered amid endless wrangles at union level.

Many older teachers still regard out-of-class activities as frivolous and a threat to academic work. Younger teachers are often more flexible. So the activities depend on the goodwill of a minority of *profs*, or on the pupils' own initiatives. But the latter are so transitory a breed, so soon caught up with swotting for the *bac*, that their ventures often do not last.

One *lycée* headmaster told me, 'Sporadic attempts have been made to get a drama group going, or a school newspaper, or a poetry club. But they rarely survive more than a few terms. There's no one to provide continuity: the kids can't, the teachers won't. Also these buildings are so gloomy that the kids understandably prefer to clear off when the bell goes.' And a girl of seventeen in Angers said, 'Real life for us is what we get from travel, friends, family, even television. I love drama, but not inside the school: I've joined a theatre club in town.' This is typical of large *lycées* in cities, where nearly all pupils live at home. At smaller *lycées* in country towns, the picture can be brighter. At one in Lorraine, I found teachers helping the pupils to stage a Molière play, run an orchestra and organize cultural sight-seeing tours.

Within the formal curriculum the role allotted to music and the visual arts has increased a little recently, from a *very* low level. I was always amazed, in a country calling itself *la mère des arts*, how little these subjects were taught – usually about an hour a week, and often not at all in the senior *lycée* classes. As they played hardly any part in the exam syllabus, teachers and parents conspired to believe that they could be ignored. The Ministry of Culture might press for change, but its rival Education Ministry would refuse the funds. Then after 1981, when the influential Jack Lang took the Culture portfolio, he forged an agreement with his colleague at Education, Alain Savary. As a result, pilot classes in some primary schools have been taken on cultural tours of museums, castles, etc.; and professional artists are hired to hold workshops in some *collèges*. But these worthwhile projects are still limited, and prone to budget cuts. In music the number of schools with choirs has increased – quite a step, in this 'nation of talkers, not of singers', as it has been called. But class teaching of music remains very restricted. Each *lycée* has its music room: often it is locked and silent, in contrast to the sounds that echo round schools in Britain or Germany. And the revival of French musical life (see pp. 443–56) has been due less to any effort inside schools than to the *conservatoires*, which charge fees.

At *lycée* level, in the shadow of the *bac*, pupils are still taught little music or art unless they opt for the new arts option of the *bac*. This can include practical work, helped by professional musicians, actors or artists who live locally. But this worthwhile venture is limited to just a few *lycées*, due to lack of funds and suitable staff. In short, France still lags behind many countries in education in the arts other than literature. But it might be wrong to hold this to blame for the recent decline in French creative culture: in the old days of France's cultural prime, the arts were taught even less in schools.

In another important domain, that of sport, there has been some improvement. In the mid-1960s the ministry began to put more emphasis on an aspect of school life previously much neglected. It has stepped up funding, so that most newer schools today do have adequate playing fields and gymnasia. All *lycées* are now supposed to offer five hours' compulsory sport and physical training a week – in practice it tends to be less – while the *bac* itself contains an obligatory gymnastics test. The results vary. Pupils do not care much for '*la gym*', but they enjoy real sports such as football, basketball, tennis, even judo. The problem is a lack of good qualified teachers. At one primary school I was told, 'An instructor comes to give physical training once a week, but the kids treat it as a joke.'

In 1973 the ministry launched a new initiative to introduce extra-curricular variety. Instead of all schools following the same routines, each was now to be allowed to spend 10 per cent of working hours any way it pleased, preferably on non-academic activities. Sometimes the response was remarkable: at a *lycée* in Grenoble, 400 pupils and staff spent a week of term living with farmers in upland villages. In some other schools teachers took their pupils to local factories, or encouraged creative projects such as mounting an exhibition. But as the ministry once again failed to come up with funds, it was parents who had to subsidize the ventures. And most teachers opposed the new scheme for the usual reasons: few were ready to put their hearts into the kind of work accepted as a basic part of the job in Britain or America. 'It's the usual French problem,' said one headmaster: 'teachers complain about state control, but then have no idea how to use freedom when they get it.' Today the '10 per cent' venture has been largely discontinued. Pressure to study and pass exams is now so great that most parents, teachers and pupils see a scheme of this kind as anything but a priority.

A further criticism of the French system concerns the lack of practical training in democracy or leadership – either on American lines, where a school becomes a parliament in embryo, or as in Britain where senior pupils are in charge of discipline. There are some classroom lessons in government and in civics, but as one teacher put it to me, 'We tell them how Parliament and Government work, but give them little chance to try it all out in practice. *We* tell them about *préfets*, *you* make them into prefects. Maybe in Britain your school prefects have too much power: here, children aren't given enough.'

Discipline in class has always been left to the teacher; and outside it to the *censeur*, a kind of school sergeant-major, helped by a team of part-time *surveillants* with the role of keeping the schoolkids out of mischief. Today the *surveillants* have mostly been replaced by *moniteurs*, who are more like moral tutors. Their job is to look after pupils' welfare as well as discipline, and to liaise with parents when a child has personal problems – a small belated step forward. The ministry has also been trying to give more of a role to senior pupils through the system of delegates to school councils. And within each class, the elected leader is expected to keep order when a teacher is not present. But there is no move to establish a school-prefect system: French teenagers remain firmly hostile to imposing discipline on their fellows in the name of the school authority – '*Nous ne sommes pas des flics*,' said one. Parents, too, remain opposed: many a bourgeois father would find it intolerable for his little Pierre to be bossed around at school by the son of a neighbour, perhaps considered socially inferior! Traditionally, it is parents, not school, who are supposed to train character; and if a school were to attempt training in leadership, parents would resent it as an intrusion. Yet maybe this leaves a void in the child's full education. Much of the egotism in France, the lack of civic feeling, the instinctive mistrust of authority, may well stem from attitudes inherited at school.

The only recent reform has been a new emphasis on lessons devoted to civic duty, notably in *collèges*. Weekly classes on civics were introduced by Chevènement in 1985. And the pupils, though unexcited about French institutions, will often eagerly debate topical issues of social justice, freedom and equality. At a time when French adults have grown disaffected with politics, any attempt to stimulate a child's political awareness – even if limited to the classroom – is certainly valuable. The Jospin Government is now laying a further stress on civic training.

If schools are less enclosed than they used to be, they still have little contact with the everyday world outside. In a bid to narrow this gulf a few 'open school' experiments began in the 1970s. Notably, in the Arlequin district of Grenoble (see p. 218), the ministry allowed the *collège* and primary schools to integrate with local daily life. Progressive teachers volunteered to take part in a scheme which bore the influence of Ivan Illich. Groups of pupils were encouraged to devise new reading primers, and to renovate the squalid environment of L'Arlequin. Parents were invited to share in the schools' daily life, including the free-and-easy lessons. This proved popular. But the staff unions objected to a scheme that obliged teachers to spend extra hours on out-of-class activities and to share their pedagogic skills with mere parents. They feared, too, that the children were suffering academically. The results apparently disproved this. Even so, in the early 1990s the ministry abandoned the scheme, partly for budgetary reasons. It seemed all too typical.

The various liberal experiments of the post-1968 period would no longer be so feasible in today's climate. New and more urgent problems have arisen in a time of financial cutbacks, rising unemployment and unrest in some suburbs. Inevitably, the violence and malaise of *la banlieue* have spilled over into some schools, where thefts, punch-ups, racial slanging matches, even knifings, are often reported. The problem is worst in areas of high unemployment, as children become affected by their parents' anger and frustration, and so vent it on the school: 'How can we expect our pupils to behave and work hard, when they find their parents lounging in bed half the day?' said one teacher. 'The duller ones think they'll never get a job, so they regard school as useless, and it makes them rowdy.' In some Muslim families boys can become violent in reaction to being beaten up at home by their fathers. Outside class, there are sometimes brawls between Blacks and Arabs, or between rival mixed gangs. The violence tends to be worst in large schools in 'ghetto' areas, but to build new smaller schools cannot be done overnight.

The Government began to take action in the mid-1980s. It turned about 10 per cent of schools into *zones d'éducation prioritaires* (ZEP), where some of the staff were volunteers and some received special psychological training in dealing with difficult pupils and their parents. At the same time, about 1,000 young conscripts under army control were drafted to act as vigilantes in the ZEPs, thus placed on a kind of war footing. Still in force today, the scheme has proved useful; in 1996, in face of growing violence in *la banlieue*, it was intensified, with 2,200 more conscripts called in. In 1997, in the 'difficult' Bellefontaine district of Toulouse, I called on the headmaster of one big ZEP *collège*: 'We have thirty nationalities here, and 40 per cent of parents are unemployed, which of course affects the school's climate. Several of my staff are volunteers for this area, and some have done special training. They try to help kids who have conflicts at home, and they talk with parents. There's not too much violence, but a lot of racial insults, and thefts of bicycles, cars, etc.' I then found my own car outside, with a window smashed and a coat and typewriter stolen (see p. 215).

*

While these new problems have arisen, some older ones have faded away. One is the vexed issue of state aid for church schools, over which many a Third and Fourth Republic Parliament fought and bled in the days when the power of clericalism provoked such sharp feelings. But already by the 1960s the old tensions were waning, and the two school systems, church and state, moved into easier cohabitation. Today many teachers in church schools are non-Christians, many Catholic families send their children to state schools, and many state *lycées* have Catholic almoners attached to their staff. A *curé* in a country town told me, 'A parent today chooses his school for practical more than confessional reasons. The *école laïque* debate today interests only a few older priests and a hard core of anticlerical teachers. The general public couldn't care less.'

Most non-state schools are run by the Catholic Church; a few others are Protestant, Jewish, and so on. The State pays the staff salaries, and part of the running costs, of any private school that agrees to follow the state education system, as nearly all do. Private schools were far less affected than state ones by May '68 and its unruly aftermath, and they have since tended to remain immune from teachers' strikes and other agitation. So the proportion of children in private schools rose after 1968 from 12 to 17 per cent, as many parents, especially in the middle classes, turned to them in the belief that they offered better discipline and a surer education. Thanks to the state aid, tuition fees in the church *collèges* are seldom more than 4,000 to 6,000 francs a year, so no great sacrifice is required of parents.

Just when the issue seemed buried, crisis erupted after 1981. The anticlericalists among state teachers were still angry that the use of public funds to help private schools was possibly harming the state ones. This lobby dominated the big left-wing union, the Fédération de l'Éducation Nationale (FEN), which persuaded the Socialist Party to write into its election programme a plan to absorb private schools into the state system. Neither Mitterrand nor the moderate Alain Savary, his Education Minister, regarded the matter as a high priority: but 50 per cent of the party's deputies in the National Assembly were teachers, and many of them backed the tough FEN line. So in 1984 Savary put forward a bill for integrating those church schools that wanted to go on receiving aid. Those choosing to remain independent could do so, but their aid would be cut off. This would have put them in the same position as the expensive English prep or public schools: but French parents do not expect to have to pay such sums for educating their children, nor are there the same benefits of social status. So the middle classes rallied to defend their bastion of subsidized private education. In June 1984 in the largest public demonstration Paris had seen since the Liberation, nearly 2 million people marched on the Bastille under the slogan 'Defence of civil liberties!' Although the Church discreetly backed the movement, the issue was less one of religion than of freedom of choice; and surveys showed that the Savary plan was opposed by 75 per cent of the French, i.e. including a majority of those with children in state schools. So the Government backed down and the bill was dropped. Then in 1994 it was the turn of the anticlerical Left to protest massively, when Balladur sought to allow church schools new and greater access to public funding. Again, the Government backed down. But generally, since the Savary affair, the issue of church schools has remained dormant.

In 1996 an official committee headed by Roger Fauroux, a distinguished former minister, made some radical proposals for a reform of the entire educational system. He recommended, *inter alia*, that schools be given more autonomy and be brought closer to the world outside. His report was greeted with howls of protest by the teachers' unions, and was quietly shelved by Juppé's minister, François Bayrou. Jospin then appointed the well-named Claude Allègre, a likeable talkative figure with a sense of public relations: he astutely sent a questionnaire to all *lycéens*, asking what they would like to be taught, and this produced some revealing replies, such as, 'I want to do cooking, theatre and computer work.' Allègre claimed famously that he wanted to '*dégraisser le mammouth*', i.e. somehow slim down the vast, tentacular world of the ministry with its million-plus staff. He was greeted with rumbling strikes among teachers. Then in October 1998 a wave of protests by *lycée* pupils broke out. They demonstrated and boycotted their classes, complaining of decrepit buildings, over-crowding and lack of modern equipment, notably computers. Unlike in 1968, the *lycéens* were not politically motivated; they simply wanted better conditions. And the vast majority of French thought their revolt was fully justified. Allègre's rapid response was an emergency 4.6-billion-franc aid package for extra staffing in schools and the renovation of some school buildings. He also began to speed up reforms which he had promised earlier, for smaller class sizes and closer pupil/teacher contact. But a year later, the *lycéens* demonstrated again, for the reforms had only been applied patchily – due to inadequate funding and lack of cooperation from many teachers, suspicious of Allègre's plans.

Recent events have shown again that teacher conservatism is a prime obstacle to effective change. Despite moves to overhaul their training, teachers are still little versed in modern pedagogic techniques, or in what might be called education for civics and leisure; they are trained to develop a child's mind, and they do not see their role outside this. Over the years, schools have indeed become more liberal, more egalitarian. But there remains an ongoing debate on the priorities: how can France's cherished academic standards be preserved, if schools are also to cater for vocational needs, and even for the wider development of character? How far does training an élite still matter in a mass age? In the universities this debate is even more pertinent.

THE MALAISE OF THE OVERSWOLLEN UNIVERSITIES

'The *lycées* and universities are badly adapted to each other,' said one Paris professor in 1997. 'The *bac* has become a monstrous machine, churning out its thousands – but what are we to do with them?' He was giving voice to the malaise of French universities, shared widely among students and teachers alike, and compounded by several factors. The spread of the *bac* has served to swell the numbers in higher education to over 2 million. But government funding has not kept pace with the growth, which has coincided with rising unemployment. This leaves a hecatomb of jobless graduates, along with anxieties that so many degree courses are poorly geared to the needs of the market. What's more, universities have failed to make good use of the new deal offered them after May '68.

French students are not equal. Nearly all of higher education is in the hands of the State: but within this structure, a gulf separates the privileged few in the Grandes Écoles, with their strictly limited numbers, from the 'student proletariat' in the swollen, amorphous universities. The former are mostly assured of good careers; many of the latter struggle on poor grants to glean their crumbs of learning in crowded lecture rooms, limping along in pursuit of pass degrees of limited practical value after which they may end up as bank clerks or sales touts. Even within the universities there is equally a gulf between this lonely crowd, in the junior years, and the rarefied postgraduate milieu. The faculties, geared in the past to training an academic few, have not proved easily adaptable to the mass needs of a new age. So should courses be made more vocational? Or should the university remain *une finalité culturelle*, unconcerned with practical ends, as the traditionalist professors still insist? Should anyone with the *bac* still be able to enrol? Or should the wary recent attempts to limit numbers be hugely extended?

Matters steadily worsened during the 1960s, fomenting the student grievances that erupted into the May '68 revolt. Overall numbers had risen from 122,000 in 1939 to 612,000 by 1968, and only some 5 per cent of these were in the Grandes Écoles. Students at the Sorbonne numbered at least 160,000 by 1968. But this growth was not adequately matched by the rise in funds or needed reforms. The Government did create seven new provincial universities in the 1960s in a bid to relieve pressure on the Sorbonne, but this solved little. A lecture hall in Paris seating 500 was often filled with twice that number. Students complained also of the impersonal *ex-cathedra* style of teaching, and of the heavily theoretical content of their syllabuses, which limited career outlets, so they felt. The Government did respond with a few new measures: it set up technological institutes at below Grande-École level, and it created a short-term diploma course, intended as an easy option for weaker students. But this did little to stem the growing flood into the faculties. Some voices were raised in favour of imposing selective entry: but this was politically impossible, given the old French tradition that anyone with the *bac* has the right to higher education.

Universities before 1968 suffered also from an absurd centralization and bureaucracy, just like the schools. It was often said, 'There is just one big university in France, with groups of faculties around the provinces, all following identical courses', and if one university outshone the others in some subject (as Lyon in medicine), this was usually the result of some pre-Napoleonic heritage, the prowess of some local professor, or of state policy. A university's faculties, isolated from each other, were each responsible direct to the ministry via the Paris-appointed rector, who was more a kind of *préfet* than an English-style vice-chancellor. Ministerial approval was needed for the smallest change in routine, even for holding a dance in a student hostel. All this added to the students' malaise. Above all, they resented what they saw as their professors' high-handed remoteness. If they wanted to voice their discontent on some issue, instead of being able to stroll across the quad into the dean's study for a chat, as in Britain, they were forced into unionized protest action like metal-workers demanding more pay. It was another of France's famous barriers.

The frustrations came to a head in the 1968 uprising, which began at Nanterre, a bleak new overspill campus in the western suburbs. Here early in 1968 a few 'action groups' of extremist students – mostly in sociology, psychology and philosophy – set about plotting the overthrow of capitalist society. When they broke into open revolt, they were rapidly joined by students all over France: few of these shared their passionate revolutionary ideals, but many seized eagerly on the chance to clamour for an overhaul of the university system. It was a spontaneous outburst, and for a few brief weeks France witnessed amazing scenes. Not to mention the barricades, the burning cars, the brutal police repression, there was also the spectacle of the 'desanctified' Sorbonne like a cathedral in the hands of joyous pagans, with red flags and Maoist slogans stuck all over the venerable statues of the gods of French culture, Molière and others. Throughout France there was the same scenario. Students and the more liberal teachers, who in the past had hardly exchanged a word, sat around in sunlit courtyards discussing future plans, or created assemblies to declare their universities 'free'. Soon the excitement subsided, de Gaulle restored order, everyone cleared off for the long summer holidays, and it grew clear that the extremists had lost *their* revolution. But the revolt did shock the Government into rethinking the universities on a new pattern; and as never before it opened the public's eyes to their problems.

Edgar Faure, appointed minister, consulted a range of professors and student leaders, then rapidly prepared a radical bill, which in the autumn won a 441–0 majority in the National Assembly. This law abolished the twenty-three universities as such: then, as a first stage, it invited teachers and students to form themselves into some 700 *unités d'enseignement et de recherche*. Each UER then elected its own council, and all were allowed to group themselves as they wished into new universities, smaller and more numerous than the old ones, each with some autonomy over teaching, exam methods and spending. For France, all this marked quite a change. Faure was giving the universities a chance to reform themselves from the bottom up. Only the broad framework was imposed: the rest each UER and new university could work out for itself, and the personality and constitution of each could differ. It seemed a step towards the Anglo-Saxon model.

This is more or less the system that survives today, for there has been no further major reform since 1969, only a series of tinkerings. The seventy-six new universities, using the existing buildings, took shape in

1969–71. Larger ones split into two or three. Paris, with today some 300,000 students, now has thirteen: the seven central ones, carved out of what used to be known loosely as '*la Sorbonne*',* are simply called 'Paris I', 'Paris II', etc. These new smaller entities are clearly more manageable than the old dinosaurs. But from the outset, when the UERs came to negotiate for grouping into universities, the Faure reforms ran into trouble – predictably – from the teaching corps, with its penchant for political and academic feuding, and the narrow hostility to change of most professors. Vast intrigues took place as to who should line up with whom. For example, disciplines in Leftist hands such as sociology were often reluctant to join with UERs of law or languages, where the professors were often more Rightist. When huge Aix/Marseille divided into three, the split was made not on rational grounds of geography (the two towns are 30 kilometres apart) but on ideological ones. Such quarrels have led to an irrational waste of resources in some places. Worse, they have hindered the cross-fertilization and multi-disciplinary teaching that was lacking in France and was one of the aims of the Faure reforms. At Toulouse, for instance, today with 100,000 students, the three universities are little more than the old faculties under a new name: law, arts and science. This is because the law professors, mostly right-wing, refused to cohabit with the more Left-inclined ones in other faculties, and vice versa. It is true that within each university, at Toulouse and elsewhere, there has been progress towards inter-disciplinarity: thus a student can combine mathematics with economics, as he could not before 1968, and all science students study foreign languages. But the broad exchange of courses and ideas across disciplines, as found in many British universities, has seldom materialized.

In some ways the universities did abuse their new semi-autonomy. But the Faure reforms, though often regarded today as a failure, did mark some improvements on the old system. Each university now elects its own governing council, where some seats are reserved for students and for junior non-teaching staff. The council then elects its president, usually a senior professor, and he has some power. So although this choice requires ministry approval, France is now closer to the British self-governing system. The council can also co-opt delegates from outside,

---

* Properly speaking, 'la Sorbonne' is merely the name of the building that housed the headquarters of University of Paris. Today it houses parts of some of the new universities, but is not an academic entity in itself.

such as local businessmen or trade unionists, and this has done a little to bridge the famous gulf in France between universities and the rest of public life. And a university has more control over minor details of its day-to-day running. Yet the ministry still keeps reserve powers and holds many strings, both academic and financial: it still decides on, and pays for, major new building and equipment, and it remains in charge of awarding the national degrees and diplomas (e.g. *licence, maîtrise*) and sets their exams. True, a university can now create its own diplomas, too, if it wishes, but these have lower prestige.

However, a university *is* now free to decide its own teaching and exam methods leading to the national degrees, and can vary the syllabus so long as it satisfies the ministry that standards are being kept up. Thus some UFRs (the name has been changed to *unités de formation et de recherche*) have moved towards an American-style system of credits and 'continuous assessment', while others have not. 'This pedagogic freedom is one of our few lasting gains of the Faure reforms,' said one professor. Today there is less emphasis on the old impersonal *cours magistraux*, and more on group work and seminars, if numbers permit. This is still a long way from the British tutorial system: but a lasting legacy of May '68 is to have produced easier contact between students and teachers. 'There's a more informal spirit now,' said one lecturer; 'the younger teachers are readier to chat with students outside class. We even use *tu* a lot, unheard of in the old days.' Many older professors still make no effort to get to know any of their students personally: but they have grown less arrogant. The 1970s saw a mass appointment of new junior lecturers and *assistants*, and this improved matters. Today the growth of student numbers has again worsened the teacher/student ratio. But the new informality still survives.

The students themselves may be much less politically minded than in the 1968 period: but at teacher level universities are still politicized. As in the secondary schools, most are on the Left, and under centre-Right Governments they have carried on non-stop vendettas with the ministry, even over new measures whose content they approve. Some teachers and student delegates have used the university councils as a terrain for their fight against the State, so that such councils have become highly politicized and sensible new projects have been endlessly blocked or contested. A liberal newspaper editor told me, 'I was co-opted on to one council, and at first was glad of the chance to bring in new ideas and help bridge the gulf that isolates the academic world. But our meetings were wasted in such stupid wrangling that I got fed up and resigned.'

Politics can impinge on the appointment of teaching staff, a crucial issue that inevitably stirs up passions: should not a university be able to select its own professors (as in Britain)? Under the Faure reforms the ministry still has the final word, but UFRs and universities can now draw up their own shortlist of candidates. This has led to various conflicts. Conservative professors often accuse the left-wing unions of trying to impose their own selection; and the minister, in turn, has sometimes been charged with appointing too many of his own political faithfuls to the top posts. 'On both sides, this has grown worse,' one teacher lamented to me. 'The right person for a job is no longer chosen on merit. It's all political.'

Since 1969 there has been no major new reform of the university world, though in many respects it still badly needs one. Some attempted reforms were scuppered by teacher opposition or student riots. In 1978, under Giscard, a new post of Minister for Higher Education was given to a formidable lady, Alice Saunier-Seïté, *recteur* of Reims. A confirmed Jacobin, she felt that the universities were getting out of hand, and she made a bid to regain greater control, using her reserve powers under the Faure law. She did not get far. But then, in 1986, Chirac's Minister for Higher Education, Alain Devaquet, proposed a bill to give the universities a more effective freedom and to coax students into taking more useful courses. It was a sensible, moderate reform project. But students interpreted it as a sly attempt to limit their rights. So they staged the biggest and rowdiest mass demonstrations since 1968, not with political motives, but simply with the aim of killing off the bill – and they succeeded, as Devaquet backed down. It seemed ironic that the two major educational reform attempts of the 1980s – by the Left over private schools, and now by the Right – had both been defeated by people power in the streets.

Today over 2 million students, or 50 per cent of the age group, are in higher education. Some are in the Grandes Écoles, or in technical institutes, private colleges or business schools. But 1,460,000 are in the state universities, now totalling eighty-three. Student numbers have nearly doubled since 1980; and this growth, fuelled by the spread of the *bac*, cannot easily be controlled so long as the *bac* gives legal right of entry into a faculty. Yet Governments ever since 1969 have not increased funds adequately to keep pace with the growth. This is the major single cause of malaise today among teachers; and, along with anxiety about jobs, it is a main cause of the student malaise, too. In 1995 the dean of the science faculty at Rouen refused to start the new term in protest against the lack of funds for teaching materials: his students went on strike in support, and some other universities followed. The ministry grudgingly promised more money: but, across the recent years of austerity cutbacks, this kind of spending has never gained a high priority. Anyone visiting an average French university is struck by the dilapidated state of many buildings, and by the general shortage of equipment such as videos and photocopiers, or even of rooms where teachers can hold meetings with each other or with students; often, they have to go home to do so. A geography teacher in Toulouse told me that his UFR could no longer afford to supply the library with new books, or to fund his students' field research.

In their junior years the students are affected mainly by the physical overcrowding, and by the lack of follow-on between their *lycée* studies and university work. All of them supposedly take an initial two-year course leading to a diploma called the DEUG (*diplôme des études universitaires générales*); after this, if they have survived, they stay a third year to sit for their *licence* (equivalent of a BA), then maybe a fourth to try for the *maîtrise*, which opens the gates to research or postgraduate work. During these third- and fourth-year courses, where numbers are fewer, life is generally tolerable. But the DEUG years can be a bewildering nightmare, especially for those many students who are not really suited to university. In their *lycées* their work was closely supervised and it followed prescribed lines: but then they discover that this has not prepared them for working on their own, using their initiative. Many feel bereft of guidance: they are far too numerous for teachers to bother with them individually. And they have to face the fearsome bureaucracy of the faculties, with its many registration forms, long queues, often unhelpful staff. They have to learn how to manipulate this system, and many fail. It is hard especially on weaker students, or those from poorer homes, who comprise a large part of the new student mass. Many come to wonder why on earth they are trying for a degree. So the drop-out rate is high. On average, some 30 per cent of students abandon their studies during the first year, and in some faculties it is up to 60 per cent. A further 10 per cent fall out before the DEUG, or they fail the DEUG. In 1997 Bayrou made a bid to modify the DEUG system so as to reduce the wastage rate, but this has not got very far.

Traditionally, the system does have its admirably liberal side, allowing a flexibility of choice for the more enterprising student. Anyone with the *bac* can enter almost any faculty. He can enrol in several different courses at once, maybe in more than one university in the same town, and thus can test out his aptitudes and interests by sampling a range of lectures before settling into one final study course. But this annoys professors, who often do not know how many 'serious' students they have. 'At the start of the first DEUG year,' one history teacher said to me, 'I may be faced with a roomful of 200 faces. Four months later, fifty are left. Where have they gone? Have they left the campus? Or do they simply not fancy my lectures? This liberal system was fine in the days of small student numbers. Today it is a waste of time and resources.' One reason for the high fall-out is that, although tuition fees are minimal, many students are obliged to earn their keep. About a third get help from parents: but only 18 per cent receive a state grant, and these average a mere 8,000 to 17,000 francs a year. Many students take part-time jobs, if they are lucky enough to find them, maybe as porters, sales assistants, or *moniteurs* in *lycées*. But this, combined with study, imposes a strain, so the weaker ones get discouraged and give up the academic race.

Some students are not serious at all. They enrol as a kind of status symbol, or so as to be eligible for cheap meals in the subsidized canteens. But most others do work hard. Some suffer breakdowns, or go on trying and failing the same exams. Today, if they can afford it, many of them try to delay the end of their studies as long as possible, knowing that the future may be only the dole queue. Many should probably not be at university at all. Some teachers in fact have long argued that more selective entry – either raising the pass mark for the *bac*, or a *numerus clausus* – is the only rational answer to the high drop-out rate and the overcrowded campuses. But nearly all students, although chief victims of the congestion, remain firmly opposed to a *numerus clausus*, which they claim would be undemocratic. Many professors, too, still feel that entry based on the *bac* is the only fair one: any other might lead to the personal bias of selection boards. 'What's more,' said a lecturer I met in Angers, 'it is hard to tell in advance, on the basis of his *bac* results or school report, if a pupil is going to be suitable for university or not. At least the first year's work gives him the chance to *prove to himself* that he's not right for the academic grind, rather than be told in advance by some board.' It's a generous, widely held view: but the results are expensive.

La sélection has long been a hot political issue in France and no minister has dared impose it widely. However, it has now been applied piecemeal and surreptitiously in some places. In face of the growing surplus of doctors (see p. 155) and the high costs of their training, a kind of *numerus clausus* was imposed in medicine in 1971: the students greeted it with a long strike but then acquiesced. Anyone with the right kind of *bac* can still enrol in a medical school, but after his first year he faces a stiff competitive exam which only about one in five passes. The rest must move to another discipline. In some universities other faculties have now followed, maybe applying a *numerus clausus* on a first-come-first-served basis, after setting a limit on the size of classes. This they are entitled to do. So *la sélection* is creeping in by the back door. But if you have the *bac*, and you shop around, you can still be certain of a place somewhere.

Today, as much as ever, the official policy is not to dissuade people from entering higher education, but to channel more of them into new technical and business colleges, whose courses are more directly geared to job needs. The policy has borne modest fruit: according to ministry statistics, the universities' share in the total of higher-education students fell from 72 to 68 per cent between 1980 and 1996. The Instituts Universitaires de Technologie, set up in 1966, initially ran up against the middle-class prejudice against technical education below élite Grande-École level. But this has now waned, as more students have come to realize that an IUT diploma can often open the door to better jobs than a mere DEUG or even *licence*. Operating by selective entry, the ninety-two IUTs offer a good practical two-year course just after the *bac*, and have filled some of the gap in technical education below the Grandes Écoles. Then Jospin in 1992 created a new type of technical college at a higher level than the IUT: the Instituts Universitaires Professionnalisés, with a four-year course. So the alternatives to the *licence/maîtrise* stream have been growing. More students, if they or their parents can afford it, have been turning to private business schools (see below) or to specialized colleges for accountancy, interpreting, catering, and so on. And students no longer have the automatic choice of any university: for example, if they live just outside Paris, they are diverted away from the crowded faculties within the city to the newer campuses further out.

Within the universities, after the dispiriting DEUG years, those who stay may well find the *licence* and *maîtrise* years something of a relief. Classes are smaller, group work and seminars are more possible, contact with teachers is easier; and the average quality of teaching is possibly

higher than in Britain, so the experts say. But there is still the worry
about jobs, still the shortage of facilities. In 1996, at Lyon II, I talked
with two groups of students in history and geography, each in classes of
about twenty-five, preparing the *maîtrise* (as this is the fourth year after
the *bac*, it is known in jargon as '*bac plus quatre*', just as the *licence* year is
'*bac plus trois*', postgraduate years are '*bac plus cinq*', etc.). Nearly all of
them wanted above all to find secure, permanent jobs. Many hoped to
become state teachers, essentially for this reason, but only one claimed
much sense of vocation for it. Several aimed for other branches of the
civil service. 'I'd like to try for journalism or the media,' said one girl,
'but I just daren't take the risk.' One oddball youth aimed to start a
boutique selling war games – I admired his enterprise, if nothing else.
Some of the geography students said they found the course too academic.
'I might have done better to go to an IUT,' said one, 'but the work
there is too utilitarian. I'm here because I really enjoy studying geography
– but where does it lead?' Of the history students, many wanted to
do postgraduate research. 'The market for good jobs has become so
competitive,' said one, 'that we feel the mere *maîtrise* is not enough. To
push ahead of the others, you need extra diplomas, *bac plus cinq, bac plus
six!*' Toujours plus!

An arts degree, in a subject such as history, has never carried the same
broad value in career terms as in Britain. The French are often amazed
that a firm such as ICI will gladly take on an Oxford classics graduate
for an executive post, or that a degree in English can lead to a managerial
traineeship in commerce. 'At the upper level, we're more vocational in
France,' said one student. 'It's the influence of the Grandes Écoles and
the maths option of the *bac*.' Yet in the ivory towers of the universities,
the study courses at *maîtrise* level have been little geared to the needs
of the world outside. Literature graduates have normally had few obvious
career outlets except to be teachers of future students – a hermetic circle.
Even in science faculties, much of the teaching is too theoretical to be
of great use to industrial firms, who prefer to recruit from the Grandes
Écoles or IUTs. And teaching posts have been reduced by austerity cuts
and the delayed-action effects of birth-rate decline. In 1996–7, for the
first time in fifty years, the ministry cut the number of teaching posts in
schools (by 5,000), quoting reduced pupil numbers as the main reason.
For the senior teaching diplomas with their rigid selection, led by the
prized *agrégation*, there are now ten times more applicants than places.
So most graduates must look elsewhere; and on today's harsh labour

market, many are obliged to accept jobs far below their qualifications. Some, with the *licence*, end up working at the check-out in supermarkets, or as motorway toll collectors.

Giscard's Government began urging universities to gear a few *maîtrise* courses more closely to career outlets outside teaching. It even brought industrialists on to ministry boards to advise on the kind of training needed. This was revolutionary – the first time the Patronat had been invited to have a direct say in the doings of the ivory towers – and it raised a storm of protest from teachers and students alike. Strikes broke out. 'We shall be brainwashed to meet the needs of the boss class!' said one militant. But the revolt fizzled out. And since then, various new *maîtrises* have been created in management studies, applied electronics, and so on, with some success. But it has not been easy. The head of one faculty told me, 'When we set up a *maîtrise* in applied modern languages, we had most of the staff against us at first. They thought the course too non-literary, too business-geared. But today our graduates *are* managing to get jobs, for example in export services or with international bodies. We are breaking the vicious circle of teachers training teachers.'

The dispute has raised the whole issue of what a university is for. Professors often complain that the 'purity' of their scholarship is being degraded by the workaday world, that the university is becoming a utilitarian tool. 'As I see it, our role is to provide students with a high level of general culture to last them through life. The issue of career outlets should remain secondary,' said one veteran scholar. Many are more interested in pursuing their own research projects than helping their students; they live in tight little social cliques, having few friends beyond their own colleagues; and some still scorn the milieux of the media, industry or public service. It is true that nowadays many professors are happy to appear on TV programmes, while some even become town councillors or mayors, or they do consultancy work for firms: so change has been coming. But many remain resentful of the reverse trend, that is, of intruders into their own world, however distinguished: when one *polytechnicien* retired from the civil service and broke precedent by giving a course of lectures at the Paris law school, the reaction of some professors was, 'But how can he? He's not a *professeur ès droit*.' Everyone must abide by his *titre*, no one must poach on another's preserve.

The staunchest guardians of this ethos are those who have crossed that fearsome hurdle, the *doctorat d'État*, essential qualification for a full professor's chair. Usually this has involved up to ten or fifteen years' work preparing an encyclopaedic document of about 1,000 pages on a specialized subject, while often doing a teaching job at the same time. It is exhausting, but the final prize is great. A *docteur* with a professorship can do much as he likes for the rest of his life. He gets a salary of maybe 300,000 francs a year for an easy sinecure and does not have to teach more than seventy-five hours a year. Many *docteurs* abuse this freedom. Today a simpler version of the doctorate has been introduced, alongside the classic one. It involves writing a much shorter thesis, taking maybe three or four years: but it can also lead to a full professorship, though with more teaching duties. Many postgraduates now opt for this: but so many become *docteurs* that some fail to find the right posts. And the old diehards complain that the title of *docteur* is being devalued.

Willy-nilly, the university has slowly been moving out of its ghetto. It has become readier to help industry with research (see p. 105). And it is now playing a larger role in adult education and in-service training courses. Here France used to lag: but today all firms are obliged to spend a sum equal to their wage bill on vocational training in the company's time. As a result, many employees have attended courses aimed at creating job enrichment and better promotion prospects. Universities have also developed far more foreign exchanges, both at student and teacher level, many of them within the EU's Erasmus and Socrates schemes. Here France is now even setting a lead: in May 1998 Claude Allègre held a meeting at the Sorbonne with his British, German and Italian counterparts where they signed a joint charter calling for the gradual harmonization of courses and diplomas, and greater mobility for students and teachers, leading to the eventual creation of a 'European university'.

Outside their work, what is the leisure and social life of French students? It is certainly different from that in Britain or America – just as today's French students are different from those who stormed the 1968 barricades. Nowadays protest may flare up over a specific grievance: but gone is much of the old Leftist idealism. Some students are Communists, or still belong to little *gauchiste* groups, while just a few dare to parade Front National sympathies. But the majority share the current French disillusion with ideologies. It helps to explain why there has been so little violent unrest on the campuses recently, despite all the malaise and anxiety. The Devaquet affair of 1986 was followed later by periodic protests over lack of funds or projects to increase selective entry, culminating in the big strikes of 1995. And in 1994 there was a crisis when Balladur's Government proposed to reduce the legal minimum wage (SMIC) for young people. He claimed that this would encourage firms to take on more young workers, at a time of high youth unemployment: but the student unions retorted that it would devalue young people's work and turn them into cheap labour. Students went on the streets, and Balladur dropped his plan – yet another example of student power, and of government fears of provoking a new May '68.

As individuals, French students tend to be hard-working, anxious, serious-minded. Many are worried about the environment, or world issues such as poverty, racism and civil war. But over France and the EU they are sceptical, and they have lost faith in the ability to improve even their own university life, let alone society. Significantly, only 4.5 per cent bother to join a student union; of the two sizeable ones, both are on the Left and one is Communist-led. And it is a setback to the 1969 ideals of participation that few students nowadays vote in university elections or come forward as candidates – so few, in fact, that they often fall short of the quorum and their quotas on councils are underused. One apolitical student suggested to me, 'What's the point of voting, when to fill up the quorum simply benefits the extremes of Left or Right, as no one else can be bothered to stand?' So the students stay quietly in the background, their noses in their textbooks.

Even in their leisure lives many feel isolated, for French universities are not warm club-like communities. Unlike in Britain, the habit is that you go to your local university: some 40 per cent of students therefore live at home (54 per cent in Paris), where they have the comfort of family and a nucleus of existing friends. Others, mostly those whose homes are too far away, stay in rented rooms, or hostels, and here they can be lonely. Many are too reserved to make new friends easily, or they lack the time or money to group together for creating their own social life. Except in the older Grandes Écoles, no collegiate tradition exists to welcome them, and the authorities do little to help. A small minority, children of indulgent well-to-do parents, have a jolly time: you can see them dashing about in sports cars or in the downtown discos, or sometimes in their glad rags, going to some posh event like the law faculty's Bal du Droit. But for the rest, often struggling on low grants, there is no *dolce vita*.

French campuses have no equivalent to the big English union building, a focus for social life. The occasional club centre is usually little more than a few drab rooms with a bar, a ping-pong table, a record-player for dances on Saturday nights, a notice board covered with appeals for digs, part-time work or lifts to Paris. It is true that sport is popular, and proper facilities for it have now been provided; also the students run a few of their own activities such as *ciné* and jazz clubs. But such initiatives have grown rarer, now that they have become so preoccupied with exams and job prospects. The pattern varies. Student orchestras have grown more numerous; and at one Paris faculty I attended a play by Pinter in English, put on by students. But at Angers a teacher said she had failed to interest her students in an English-language theatre club – 'They're too busy swotting' – and some universities have no drama group at all.

'It's a matter of temperament. The French are not club joiners,' said the director of a welfare body. 'I've tried to start discussion groups and the like, but the students won't come. They have their own knot of friends and they sit around in cafés or each other's rooms, but they won't take part in anything organized. As a result, many feel adrift – unless they live at home, or are motivated to join some political or religious group.' A few teachers try to help by getting to know some students personally, as a professor at Montpellier told me, 'I try to be a kind of moral tutor to a few whom I feel need me. Sometimes my wife and I have them to dinner.' But this is still rare, and not in the French tradition: 'Our job is to teach our students, not to offer them *apéritifs*. That would be favourit-ism, very *mal vu*,' said one teacher. Some others complain that when they do try to make contact, the students are evasive. 'I have a kind of weekly "surgery" where they can come to discuss their problems, but few ever do. It's so unlike America,' said a professor in Toulouse. A student with problems can turn to the university's welfare service: but he has no individual 'moral tutor' to keep an eye on him, as in Britain. It is usually only at postgraduate, or maybe *maîtrise*, level that personal links develop.

The building of campuses in the 1960s and '70s did not help. Before then, nearly all universities were downtown, where the students did have some contact with 'real life'. Then, with the growth in numbers, most departments were transferred to big new campuses on the outskirts. Some of these are attractive: but the students became more isolated than ever, especially those living in the hostels. The saga of Grenoble is instructive. Here in the 1960s the university welfare authorities made an imaginative attempt, unusual for France, to tackle the human problems of the new student ghettos. They persuaded a few single teachers to go and live on the campus among them; they also found funds for building a socio-cultural centre, with theatre and library. The students were encouraged to develop a community life, under the guidance of the resident teachers – and they responded. I found drama and debating clubs in progress, and lively cosmopolitan parties. But then came May '68, which left this campus more politicized than most. The Leftist ringleaders decided to stamp out officialdom's attempts to 'direct' their leisure life. So the teachers departed, and the socio-cultural centre fell silent in this neat, spacious and idyllic setting below the Alps.

However, today in the late 1990s this campus has found a new lease of life. It even has one or two shops. It is typical of academe's 'purist' mentality that most universities have never allowed any shop on a campus: so students at Grenoble would have to walk a couple of kilometres to buy even a pen or newspaper. But in 1996 a proper bookstore and general store finally opened. And a new official body, the Pôle Universitaire, has been putting money into culture on the campus, helping the students to run theatre groups, orchestras, film clubs. Those who respond are mostly from the cluster of Grandes Écoles on campus, generally more lively than the lumpen mass from the faculties. Another new factor: in Grenoble and some other towns, the building of a modern transport system has brought campus and city centre closer together. *Le tramway nommé culture*, as it is dubbed, can whisk students between the two in a few minutes; and in Toulouse the new Métro does the same, between the Capitole and the huge, sad campus of Le Mirail. So some students have gone back to living in digs downtown – a wheel has come full circle – and they commute to the campus for their classes. The city, with many student bars and dives, has become more lively. But the campus, apart from sporadic cultural events, is at night a huge, lifeless dormitory, where solitude can sometimes breed suicide in the dreary hostels.

France is not alone in facing a crisis of higher education. In Italy the confusion and paralysis have been worse; Germany faces many similar problems, and even in Britain the bid to raise student numbers has spread doubts about standards. In France nearly everyone agrees on the need for more reform, but not on what reform; and practical proposals are generally rebuffed by students and teachers alike. In 1996 Roger Fauroux's official report put forward sensible ideas for reorganizing the DEUG, giving universities more autonomy, and so on. Most of this was curtly rejected. François Bayrou as minister then produced a timid minor reform that was ill-applied. He is followed today by Claude Allègre, who has no major plans. Yet, sooner or later, real change will have to come. The French are being forced to rethink what a university is for. Can it still fulfil the Renaissance ideal of producing the well-rounded, cultivated man? Or, in an age of the masses that is also an age of specialization, should it become more vocational? There are many who believe that it can and must do both: but the two diverse aims should be clarified. The sprawling universities need a radical new deal, if they are to cease being mere poor relations of the Grandes Écoles.

GRANDES ÉCOLES: ÉLITIST PRIVILEGES FINALLY UNDER THREAT

'Yes, we are the super-élite,' said a tall posh-voiced girl of nineteen, one of a quartet of senior *lycéens* I met at Angers in 1996. Three were children of professors. All were in a special post-*bac* class of their *lycée*, cramming for the entrance exams to HEC or ENS (École Normale Supérieure), two of the most prestigious Grandes Écoles. 'I'm on the Left,' said the girl, 'and I'd like to destroy this whole rotten self-perpetuating super-élitist system.' She added with a smile, 'But not till I've first profited from it myself' – as if echoing St Augustine's views on chastity.

The most distinctive trait of French higher education, and one that profoundly marks French society, is this gulf between the sprawling universities and the exclusive Grandes Écoles, most of them devoted to engineering, applied sciences or management studies. Each has a good deal of freedom; each controls its numbers with its own highly competitive entrance exam, requiring two or three years' special study after the *bac*; and once admitted the lucky student leads a relatively privileged life. He has close contact with his teachers, and he is usually assured of a worthwhile career, especially if he is from one of the more prestigious colleges, led by the École Polytechnique. The Grandes Écoles account for no more than one in twenty of the numbers in higher education, but they turn out a high proportion of France's top engineers and administrators, and on the whole they have served France well (see pp. 96–100). Reformers have thus tended to leave them alone, nor were they much affected by the virus of May '68. Yet the system is constantly under criticism. Is it healthy for a modern society, this divorce between an élitist stream and the universities? And do the Écoles really provide such a wonderful training, or are they living on their reputation?

Since 'Grande École' is a general term, not an official one, it is hard to specify the exact number of these schools: but some 275 lay claim to the title, with an average of 400 students each. They range from provincial business schools to advanced postgraduate colleges, specializing, for example, in aerospace or telecommunications. Some are privately owned, some are run by local chambers of commerce, while most belong to the State. But not all are under the Ministry of Education: Polytechnique, for instance, is responsible to the Defence Ministry.

Competition for the better schools has always been intense, and has grown more so with the decline of the universities' prestige. An abler *lycée* pupil will tend to make a Grande École his first option: but first he must convince his teachers that he is worth a place in one of the *classes préparatoires* that exist only in certain *lycées* and alone prepare for the entry exams. These post-*bac* classes, some known in slang as *hypotaupes* and *hypokhâgnes*, put their pupils through a rigorous two- or three-year course; and competition is such that many work a 70- to 80-hour week, turning into pale swots and driving their parents mad. The work in these *lycée* classes is of far higher standard than in university classes for the DEUG: but for all except the most brilliant, it is an unnerving obstacle race with a large prospect of failure, as the better Écoles have places for only about one candidate in ten. The rest try for a lesser school, or end up at a mere university. And yet, once admitted, the lucky few then find that inside the Grandes Écoles the work is not so exacting, and at *their* passing-out exams the failure rate is almost nil. So the real mind-stretching test is in the *lycée* classes – 'the cram *de la crème*', said a headline in the *Guardian*.

The Écoles do not necessarily provide better teaching than in some senior university classes: but they have the highest prestige and draw the most brilliant pupils, and this essentially is why so many alumni rise to the top posts in the land. Above all, this is true of the École Polytechnique, known as 'X' for short because of its badge of two crossed cannon. By origin this is a military college, founded by Napoleon to train engineers for the armed forces. Today it is still run as a kind of residential officer cadet school, with a serving general at its head: its pupils, *les X*, go on parade four times a year in full-dress uniform with strange curly hats. But the military spirit is now greatly diluted, especially since the school's transfer in 1976 from its old enclosed home near the Panthéon to more open premises at Palaiseau in the suburbs. Formerly, *les X* were confined to barracks most of the week: now they can come and go almost as freely as any other student, though in class they must still wear khaki uniforms. Few today enter a military career: most go into public service or private industry. But this diaspora has not weakened the mystique of their old-boy network. Once an 'X' always an 'X': all alumni high and low call each other *camarade* whether they have met before or not, and the lowliest 'X' can write out of the blue to a famous colleague and be sure of help and sympathy.

Yet is the school's arrogant influence substantiated by the quality of its training? All students used to receive the same encyclopaedic general education at a high level, with plenty of thermodynamics and astrophysics, but their detailed timetables left little scope for initiative. Pétain once said of an 'X', 'That man knows everything, but he knows nothing else.' Since 1969 the syllabus has been updated to include more economics and languages, and second-year students can specialize and work on their own research projects. But there is still a debate as to whether Polytechnique's proper role is to train good research scientists or good managers, and many people believe that it falls between these two stools. The science lobby argues that the system still does too little to encourage the kind of creative thinking required for top-level research. The counter-argument is that graduates in practice tend to move into administrative rather than boffin jobs, yet the courses are inadequately geared to modern management techniques. Partly for these reasons, the school's appeal has recently declined a little. But its directors argue that its role is simply to provide a high-level background education. Only 10 per cent of its graduates go straight into jobs: others move on to further studies, which may be a top American business school, or one of the élite French *écoles d'application* such as the École des Mines or the École des Ponts et Chaussées. One such is the aeronautical college at Toulouse known as 'Sup Aéro', where students live in elegant halls of residence. They lead a separate social life from the despised campus proletariat, and will maybe slip off to Paris at the weekend in aircraft placed at their disposal. 'We've never had student unrest here,' said the director. 'What is there to protest about?'

Of the other Grandes Écoles of all types, each has its own old-boy network and all are rivals in the intricate hierarchy of national influence. Among engineers, the École Centrale comes next after 'X'. A special case is the mighty École Normale Supérieure, near the Panthéon: this concentrates on the humanities as much as science, and its primary role is to prepare university and senior *lycée* teachers via the *agrégation*. Sartre,

Blum and Pompidou were among the *normaliens* nurtured in this citadel of French scholarship. The ENS's influence declined during France's boom years, when the national trend was away from the classic humanities and towards technology. But today it has been rising again, at the expense of Polytechnique.

Other schools now in vogue are those dealing in business studies and *le management*. Here the leader is the École des Hautes Études Commerciales (HEC), founded in 1881; owned by the Paris Chamber of Commerce, it is spaciously housed in a park near Versailles, where 850 students, one-third of them girls, follow a wide-ranging modern business course that includes at least two languages and compulsory *stages* abroad. Employers eagerly offer jobs to HEC leavers, and alumni include the heads of some big banks. But it is not all work and no play in this residential college, where the ambience − at last! − is more like that of Oxbridge or Ivy League than of the average French campus. The students run their own drama, music and debating clubs. And though some bursaries are available on a means test, most parents pay sizeable fees. Over half the students come from Paris, and little more than 10 per cent are from working-class families. On the model of HEC, scores of business colleges have now sprung up across France to meet the economy's new needs. They are uneven in quality, and not all have won the true status of a Grande École: but most offer the kind of vocational training that usually leads to securing a job. Many are international in outlook and have developed exchange links with similar colleges abroad. The total number of schools claiming Grande-École rank has nearly doubled since 1980.

Often accused of encrusted conservatism, the Grandes Écoles have now been modernizing their courses, and have introduced more group work and practical field projects. Clearly, the system has been, and still is, a fertile source of strength for the French economy. But its near-monopoly of the best jobs may have served to perpetuate the barriers in French society, and critics have long argued that ways should be found of bringing the system closer to the university structure. In some cases this has been happening, piecemeal. A few Grandes Écoles now share some facilities and teaching staff with a university. And the Instituts Universitaires Professionnalisés set up by Jospin in 1992 are a bid to provide a high-level practical course that leads to an engineering diploma within the university structure, thus breaking the Grandes Écoles' monopoly in this field.

Claude Allègre, himself no lover of the system, in 1997 set up a commission to look into the future of the Grandes Écoles and of all higher education. It was headed by none other than Jacques Attali, alumnus of both 'X' and ENA, yet very critical of their privileges. In May 1998 he advised that the recruiting system be broadened radically, so as to make it easier for students from technical *lycées*, and others, to enter the Grandes Écoles; also that cooperation with universities be extended, though without any merger of the two streams. The directors of the Grandes Écoles, and business leaders, issued strong warnings that to go too far along this path could lead to a lowering of standards, harmful to the economy. However, some reform does now at last look probable. And if it reduces the old élitist gulf, then it could benefit society as a whole, if not the economy. The Angers *lycéenne* may have her wish granted, after all.

LA JEUNESSE TODAY: SCEPTICAL, SERIOUS AND ELUSIVE

What are they like, the young people of this enigmatic new generation for whom all the educational crusades are fought? Ostensibly, they have been pursuing much the same paths as in other countries: they have their own consumer markets for music and clothes, their own world of discos and rock groups. All, or nearly all, enjoy far more freedom from parents than in the cloistered pre-'68 days, and more sexual licence, too. Yet they are not rebels, at least not in the outgoing sense of wanting to change society. Adults tend to see them as withdrawn, passive, sceptical. They are marked by the fear of unemployment, high in their age group, and many take a gloomy view of the future. Some turn to petty crime, especially in the poorer *banlieues*. Or they take drugs, which are now widespread but mostly the 'softer' ones. The young show little interest in politics, and many are pursuing their own private routes to some kind of happiness and fulfilment. Some are ambitiously careerist, but in a conformist sense: they seek job security within a firm, and are less likely than in Britain to dare to start their own ventures. Nor do they show much idealism for public initiative.

It used not to be so. In the earlier post-war period, many of the most important changes in France were due to a new generation rising against the standards of its elders – from the young farmers of the JAC to the cinema's *nouvelle vague*. In those open, adventurous days, the upheavals of wartime had broken some of the barriers that kept youth in its place, and an idealistic new wave was able to make inroads into the *positions acquises* of the established hierarchy. It happened most strikingly on the farms, but also in industry, commerce and the arts, where many of the leading pioneers were amazingly youthful at the outset. Édouard Leclerc was twenty-three when he began his cut-price campaign (see p. 632); Gourvennec at twenty-four led the Breton farmers' revolution; Planchon founded his Villeurbanne theatre at twenty-one, while Godard, Chabrol and others made their cinema breakthrough in their mid-twenties. Today these pace-setters are elderly established figures. But the generations that followed, born into an age of greater scepticism, seldom showed the same innovating spirit, while today's younger people are lacking in enterprise.

A few much-publicized phenomena gave the image of a youth that was also in philosophical, sexual or personal revolt in those early post-war years. First, there were the young Parisians who flocked around Sartre at St-Germain-des-Prés to denounce their bourgeois background before settling back into it to pursue their careerist lives. Then in 1954 the eighteen-year-old Françoise Sagan published *Bonjour tristesse*. Her smart world of wealth and whisky was far removed from the intellectual milieu of the true existentialists: but her heroine's cool rejection of social morality seemed to borrow something from the ideas of Sartre. In 1956 the young director Roger Vadim took a little-known starlet to a modest Riviera fishing port to make *Et Dieu créa la femme* – and God-knows-who created Bardot and St-Tropez. France and the world were amazed: was this what French youth was like? On the whole, it was not. But the Bardot and St-Tropez myths remained potent at least until May 1968. The media built Bardot into a goddess of sensualist emancipation, and thousands from *une certaine jeunesse* flocked to the Côte to join a cult that seemed to answer a certain youthful need. A Dominican priest at St-Tropez said to me, 'This place is a kind of Lourdes. Young people feel a lack in their lives, they want to be cured of their desolate yearnings, so they come to be touched by magic and reborn. But all they find is each other.'

A wider trend in the 1960s was the pop movement of *les copains* ('chums'), innocent and vaguely charming but vapid, which gave a new brand image to French youth and pushed the precocious cynicism of Sagan on to the sidelines. A new generation, sipping its Coca-Colas, looked less to Bardot the sex kitten than to Sylvie Vartan, chirpy chum and elder sister, or to Françoise Hardy huskily leading all-the-boys-and-girls-of-her-age. The trend was launched by a radio jazz programme, *Salut les copains*, which became an immediate smash hit with teenagers tired of sharing Piaf and Trenet with their elders: they wanted their own modern thing, like the Americans. A curly-haired boy of sixteen with an ugly mouth made his shy début singing rock 'n' roll tunes in French – and young France took up Johnny Halliday as its idol and self-image. It was all very derivative, as some stars took Anglo-American names as well as tunes (Halliday was born Jean-Philippe Smet): but *les copains* did acquire a certain French style of their own, less virile and inventive, more romantic and sentimental, than either Beatledom or US rock. In 1963 one famous open-air live broadcast from the Place de la Nation, Paris, brought 150,000 teenagers surging into the square, twisting and rocking, brushing the police aside. Some worried parents saw it as a political event, comparing it with the mass hysteria of the Nazi rallies. But it was really very innocent.

And today? Halliday, in his suave late fifties, is still active and in 1996 gave a successful concert in Las Vegas. Some of his contemporaries are also still busily singing: Hardy, Vartan, Julien Clerc . . . But few newer figures of any note have emerged in the past twenty years, save maybe for Pascal Obispo, the enigmatic rock singer Alain Bashung, or Sylvain Vanot and Dominique A, influenced by rock or by Jacques Brel. The French pop music scene, and French *chanson*, too, are notoriously in a fallow period: so the young turn rather to *les Anglo-Saxons*, as ever. Hence the fuss in 1994 when the Government tried to protect French pop music by imposing a quota for it on radio (see p. 706). Probably the most creative work has been coming from ethnic singers who have borrowed and adapted American rap and hip hop – notably the rap group IAM from Marseille and the popular poet MC Solaar (see p. 454). His wistful, angry yet humorous songs about the sorrows of *la banlieue*, show a striking talent. It is all a far cry from St-Tropez or *les copains*.

After the *copains*' heyday, the May '68 student revolt then gave the world yet another image of French youth. Beyond initial fury at their conditions of study, students were giving vent to far deeper feelings in that European age of ideologies when a new generation – or part of it – decided that society *could* be changed. Youth burst into action, bubbling with ideas, many absurd, some constructive – *'l'imagination au pouvoir'* was the slogan scrawled on many a wall. When the dust had settled, it was clear that society had not been overthrown and that not all French youth had been turned into revolutionaries – far from it. And yet May

'68 was not without its permanent legacy, notably in the change it wrought in relations between the young and their elders. Within families, as in schools and colleges, the old barriers of authority were broken. During and after May, family crises broke out 'on a scale the nation had not seen since Dreyfus', as one father put it: kids disappeared from home for days on end, or hotly argued with their parents for the first time. It took a while for these wounds to heal, or for parents accustomed to obedience to adjust to a freer and more open relationship. But most of them soon were making greater efforts to understand. And so French youth won its freedom – later, and with more dramatic suddenness, than in Britain.

Today, thirty years on, the young are so different. They now face less of a generation gap, and they generally feel that their parents *do* understand them, maybe worry about them too much. But today's youth in turn does not quite see what May '68 was all about, nor does it mean much. 'What! You could rally those huge crowds just to argue about politics, love and freedom? – I can't believe it,' one girl said to a veteran of the barricades. And many young people accuse the '68 generation, now in power, of getting France into its present mess. In a word, while the idealists of '68 rejected the consumer society, today's youth are eager to join it: but they are desperately worried that it might leave them behind, standing in the dole queues.

In all social classes anxieties about unemployment haunt them. In their age bracket, leaving aside those still studying, some 23 per cent are looking for work. The optimistic gloss on this is that over two-thirds *do* have jobs: yet it is fear of joining the sad minority that has spread insecurity and pessimism across a whole age group. 'I got a good if dull job after college,' said one 24-year-old salesman, 'but my brother has been looking for five months and has found nothing. I can see it making him cynical and apathetic, as his self-confidence drains away.' '*Désenchantée*' and '*angoissée*' are words repeatedly used in the media to describe this generation. One recent poll found 75 per cent of them saying they lacked confidence in the future, either for themselves or for society; and France leads the EU in its youth suicide rate, ahead of Germany and Sweden. But unemployment is not the only factor behind these aspects of the wider French *morosité*. It is reflected in several of the recent French films by young directors, such as Xavier Beauvois's *N'oublie pas que tu vas mourir*, about a drug-addicted student with AIDS.

In this climate, many young people have been turning back to their families as a refuge (see p. 592). The percentage of twenty-year-olds still living with their parents, which had been steadily falling, has now risen again since 1982 from 59 to 72 per cent. To remain in the parental home till marriage had long been commoner in France than Britain: formerly, this was due to the housing shortage, as well as to convention and family pressure. But flatlets or bedsitters then became more plentiful, while May '68 brought new ideas of independence: so more late teenagers began to follow the Anglo-Saxon practice of leaving home, even though so many students attended university in their home town. But now there is a reverse trend, prompted by emotional insecurity as well as unemployment. Some young people return to the family home after a marriage break-up or losing a job. And in a number of liberal-minded families, an unwed young couple will shack up together in the parental home of one of them.

Within the same family, youth can vary so much. Friends of mine in Paris, who are teachers, have one son who is an ambitious lawyer, while his brother is something of a drop-out, unconcerned to find a steady job, yet idealistic. Among the career-minded, the 1980s in France as elsewhere were the golden age of the yuppies, often starting very young. At the prestigious Lycée Buffon in Paris, I found that a few senior pupils had set up a *club d'entreprise*, making contact with firms: many had ambitions to start their own venture, and their idol at the time was the entrepreneur showman Bernard Tapie. These trends were welcomed in business circles as signs of a new 'practical realism' among French youth, after the post-1968 period. Today, however, so many respected business figures – including Tapie himself (see p. 54) – have come under suspicion of sleaze that the ideals of material success and money-making have lost some of their cachet. The yuppie vogue is past its prime. And the hazards of creating a new business in France have reduced the zest for enterprise. In fact, many of the brightest young careerists, when their studies end, will nowadays go off to try their hand in Britain or America, maybe working for some international firm. They often admire the spirit of initiative among Britain's youth. In France many high-flyers will make for safe public-service jobs. Or they simply want to make money quickly in some firm, and then spend lavishly. They are a world away from the post-war pioneering idealists, or from the ideals of 1968.

Some others, at all levels, are less ambitious. They will swot hard to pass exams, but their attitude is utilitarian: their path to self-fulfilment comes via leisure and private life, and not via a career, which they see as a means to an end. Few share the passionate work ethic that drove their elders to build the new France: 'I think papa is crazy to spend his life as he does, working twelve hours a day and most weekends,' said the young son of one top civil servant. Employers find that *cadres* under forty try to make a clean break between their work and leisure lives, unlike the older ones: they are less ready to stay late in the office or bring work home at weekends. Some even prefer to dabble for a few years after ending their studies rather than join the career rat race: they will take a series of easy short-term jobs, interspersed with doing nothing, and are ready to live simply. Some of these semi-drop-outs may turn to drugs. Others are more greedy: Tavernier in his film *L'Appât* painted a harsh picture of a section of middle-class youth, amoral and uncultured, even violent, ready to steal to raise money for instant pleasures – 'I based it realistically on a milieu that I know,' he told me.

Drug-taking has much increased in recent years, and so has heavy drinking by some younger people (see p. 160). Both are related to unemployment and the general malaise – 'We drink or smoke hash to escape and forget our worries' is a common remark. Drugs appeared on the youth scene later than in many countries, and it was not until about 1970 that peddlers began serious efforts to penetrate the *lycées*, newly 'liberated' by May '68. According to surveys, in 1972 still only 3 per cent of *lycéens* admitted to having tried drugs, while by 1985 the figure had risen to 11 per cent and is now around 30 per cent – a sign that today soft drugs are not only commoner but more socially tolerated and talked about. But all are still illegal, and there is plenty of confused debate as to whether it would be better to legalize the soft ones. Nearly all the young stick to these, mainly cannabis and ecstasy: only about one drug-taker in ten goes on to harder drugs such as heroin, whose estimated number of addicts has at last been falling. But these *vieux blancs*, as the hospitals call them, still account for over half the 400 or so drug-related deaths each year, and their thieving to pay for a fix adds to the crime rate. Most heroin cases today are among older people, for the young have become less addicted.

Among cannabis users, however, nearly 80 per cent are reckoned to be under twenty-six. This soft drug is relatively cheap and easy to find. In Paris, as I dined with a professional couple and their student children plus young friends, joints were passed round the table and no one thought twice. The taking of ecstasy has also increased greatly, mostly in discos and at parties. In the *lycées* it is mainly cannabis, starting among fourteen-year-olds: in 1996 an official survey showed that 39 per cent of boys and 22 per cent of girls had taken drugs – and the need to pay for them can lead to thefts from parents. Drugs are as common in the smart *lycées* as in those of *la banlieue*. Most schools long pretended that the issue did not exist, and today they may still turn a blind eye.

The legislation is on paper quite tough, but incoherently applied, and is considered absurd by most serious opinion. In an effort to get it reformed, various celebrities have openly paraded their taking of drugs – especially cocaine, which is far pricier than hash and popular with showbiz people. In 1998 Johnny Halliday admitted to taking it in an interview in *Le Monde*: he was followed by Patrice Chéreau, Marina Vlady and some 200 other artists and intellectuals, who signed a petition saying they had taken drugs, and offered themselves for prosecution. No action was taken. As in other countries, the debate is between (a) those who say that soft drugs are fairly harmless, probably more so than alcohol, and that to legalize them would end a lot of hypocrisy and make it easier to deal with the whole issue, as with alcoholism; and (b) those who regard any drug as evil, or claim that taking soft drugs leads on to hard ones. Jospin, before the elections, said he favoured decriminalizing cannabis: but then, under various pressures, he did nothing. Meanwhile, the police continue their campaign. They concentrate mostly on hard or synthetic drugs and will rarely prosecute for smoking hash: but the penalties for peddling it are heavy, and 39 tons were seized in 1995. The cannabis comes mainly from Morocco, either direct to France or via Holland; the heroin arrives mostly from Holland. 'I used to be against legalizing soft drugs,' said a professor of law and Socialist town councillor whom I met in Montpellier, 'but I've now changed. It would be much easier to fight the excesses if it were all out in the open and not so secret.' Meanwhile, the drugs problem simply adds to young people's vague sense of confusion, guilt and alienation.

Today they have few heroes – maybe one or two figures from the past, like Schweitzer or Gandhi, but hardly any present-day ones. They admire Bernard Kouchner, the humanitarian doctor who was a founder of Médecins sans Frontières (Nobel Peace Prize, 1999), did exceptional work in Bosnia, and in 1997–9 was Minister of Health before becoming chief UN administrator in Kosovo. But the young have little faith in political parties and a contempt for most politicians. Many vote Left, and when Mitterrand was elected in 1981, young people cheered and danced all over France, hoping that his regime might be more sympathetic to their aspirations than Giscard's had been. But then scepticism returned, as youth found it had lost even the comfort of being able to vent its frustrations on an unpopular right-wing regime. After Mitterrand's fall from grace, Chirac was at first vaguely welcomed by some, but then scorned – even though he did put an end to the unpopular military service. Today Jospin's Government is liked for its emphasis on ecology, and for doing more than its predecessors to tackle youth unemployment. But even the Socialists are still eyed suspiciously; their promises are seldom believed, and their ministers are seen as too middle-aged. More than in Britain, the young in France tend to feel that the adult world of politics or business does not understand their problems or give them fair opportunities – however sympathetic individual parents or teachers may be.

Many young people are seeking a greater attachment to local roots, as to family: it may be linked to their search for security. As for patriotism, though they may believe that French lifestyles are best, they have no great feeling for *la France*: old-style emotional jingoism went out with de Gaulle, as far as youth is concerned, and no longer does it stir to the sound of a military band on 14 July – *tout ça, c'est du folklore*. Idealism over a United Europe has also waned. Yet in a more general sense the young feel 'European': they are less insular than British youth, they have little animosity towards Germans (see p. 693), nor any great sense of frontiers – 'We go to Munich or Amsterdam as naturally as to Lyon or Bordeaux,' said one Parisian student. One heartening sign is that French youth as a whole is much less racist than its elders, and some will take pride in showing open solidarity with Beurs and others (see p. 223): but a minority, mostly the poorer unemployed, are getting *more* racist. Some young French feel a humane concern towards the developing world, and thousands each year express this by going to work as teachers or technicians in poorer countries, mainly in ex-French Africa. This government scheme of *la coopération* has provided an attractive alternative to military service for some.

The young today may reject formal institutions, whether political parties, trade unions or the Church. Yet they vaguely feel a desire for collective action of some kind, maybe through associations, or groups of friends. This is not to change society as a whole – that ideal of '68 has gone – but at least to change their own corner of it in some respect. But they are often unsure how to do so. For some, ecology still provides an outlet for their ideals, if less powerfully than in the 1970s. But above all, their sense today is one of isolation. They speak of their feeling of helplessness, their absence of contact with the many others who broadly share their ideas. Society is *les autres*, therefore alien – and so they cling to their own circle of family and friends, rejecting any wider allegiance. 'Community is a fine idea,' said one student, 'but in France it doesn't seem to work. *Enfin, on est toujours seul.*' Among the more intellectual, this can lead to a stoical pessimism, echoing Camus; or else to a self-indulgent narcissism harking back to Baudelaire. Among others, it can simply be a nihilistic *je-m'en-foutisme* ('I don't care a fuck'), leading maybe to the violence of the suburbs.

Perhaps this is too harsh a picture. If they have jobs, friends and love, many young people are not too affected by the malaise. They may be hesitant, vaguely anxious, even introverted, but not really unhappy – at least when they can forget the world outside. Within their own milieux, they are absorbed in seeking their own satisfactions, through sport, music or other interests and relationships. Towards each other, in their own circles, they show great camaraderie and tolerance; the couple, wed or unwed, has assumed huge importance, for mutual support as well as sexuality. The young no longer read so much, and even the more reflective ones have few *maîtres à penser*: but they travel, they go to films and concerts, they seek nourishment through contact with nature or maybe through keep-fit routines. They have little faith in the Church: but many have been turning back to the togetherness of pilgrimages, or to other forms of Christian worship (see p. 585), or even to sects. Today's general French concern with an ethos of personal fulfilment, spiritual, cultural or hedonistic, is especially strong among the young.

It can be foolish to generalize about a world so elusive, so constantly renewing itself, as the youth of a nation. Older people today claim that young people lack vitality and enterprise; young ones say they are not given a chance. Youth has won a new freedom from parents and teachers, but in return has lost its sure moral leadership; it cannot trust the values of a world without certainties, so in the search for its own values it retreats into its shell. But is it really so numbed? Talk to young people and you are aware of some latent strength, a potential not yet harnessed; they are lucid, realistic, alert to past follies and wary of false hopes. Youth is an actor waiting in the wings.

8

PRIVATE AND LEISURE LIFE:
NEW FREEDOMS, NEW HEDONISM

When the euro arrives, will the French adapt to it easily, or not? They are a people ever torn between tradition and modernity: they love novelty, yet can also stay very conservative in their attachment to old habits and rooted ways of thinking. Witness the new franc (100 old francs), introduced back in 1959. For decades, a high percentage of people, many highly educated or born after the change, continued to calculate in old francs, and not for want of arithmetic – 'prête-moi dix mille balles' means 'lend me 100 francs'. Only now is this fading away.

The French love modern trends and inventions but prefer them to be French, like the Minitel or nouvelle cuisine. They have been turning back to some of their old traditions, in regional folklore, weekend rural homes and les produits du terroir. Yet many young ones at least flock also to the mass American imports derided by intellectuals, from Disneyland to le fast-food du McDo. In a muddled way, they have opened out hugely to the world. The same ambivalences apply on a more serious social level, too. They have adapted with eager appetites to many modern lifestyles: but as we have seen in the new suburbs, basic social attitudes can be harder to change. Thus holiday and weekend habits have evolved more radically than class structures; and the French took to hypermarkets more easily than to abortion reform, unsurprisingly. Yet social and psychological change has come, too, especially since 1968 – seen in the greater equality enjoyed by women, greater sexual tolerance, freer parent/child relations, more informality in social contacts, and much else. And as the old formal institutions wane in influence, new, more fluid patterns emerge. Thus the churches are emptying, but other forms of Christian worship have been growing.

CATHOLICS:
RELIGION REVIVES, BUT THE CHURCH DECLINES

The joyous atmosphere mixed religious fervour with the mood of a rock festival. The scene was a racecourse outside Paris in August 1997, where over a million people, mostly young, were attending the Pope's celebration of Mass. And some observers wrote eagerly of a revival of Christianity after the post-war decades of decline. But although today more young people may be turning to spiritual matters, this does not mean that the Church itself is reviving. Except for the Protestant, Jewish, Muslim and other minorities, most French are Catholic by background: but few are still regular church-goers.

The changes in the role of Christianity have been as striking as anywhere in Europe, and they vividly reflect the French shifts in values since the war. In a word, the authority of the Church has crumbled, yet a new-style spirit of religion is much alive and takes diverse forms. On the one hand, regular attendance at Mass is down to 7 or 8 per cent of the population; the priesthood is alarmingly short of new recruits; the parish *curé*'s influence has waned sharply; and though most people, if asked, still more or less believe in God, few of them do much about it. But among true believers there has been a re-examining and sharpening of faith, and a shift of emphasis away from old-style pious liturgy. In the earlier post-war decades, this strikingly took the form of community social action; today it is more a matter of private prayer and fellowship. The Church, from being a central pillar of society, has come more to resemble a network of groups militating within a largely irreligious nation; and priests and laity alike are splintered into various tendencies. Some lay Catholics have formed their own groups, without priests, for worship or social service. Some priests, at least until the 1970s, flirted with Marxism; a few others have returned to dogmas of integrism, insisting on the Mass in Latin. Most are loyal to the Vatican in denouncing the abortion reforms, but some preach greater sexual freedom or urge a more lenient attitude to birth control, especially in a time of AIDS. And many believing Catholics do not follow the Church's teaching on these matters. In face of the diverse challenges to its authority and unity, the French Episcopate, under the cautious Cardinal Lustiger, Archbishop of Paris, has made various attempts to reassert itself, but without great success.

★

The first major change was in the early post-war years, when the Church at all levels – from bishops to laity – began to shift leftwards and concern itself with social issues. In the context of the pre-war history of the Church in France, this was a remarkable departure. Although in 1905 the State became secular and the Church was disestablished, the hierarchy continued to identify itself with the ruling upper-bourgeoisie, and defended the social status quo. In rural areas priest and gentry were natural allies. The Church was ultra-clerical, allowing little scope for lay action: it inspired sharp anticlericalism, and was also anti-temporal, concerned with spiritual, not social welfare. Yet it did dabble in politics. Many bishops collaborated under the Occupation, or at least did nothing to help the Resistance.★ So the strong Catholic element in the *maquis* passed into the hands of lay leaders.

Yet even in the 1930s the Church was not monolithic in its right-wing stance. Forces were at work which formed the Christian trade union, Confédération Française des Travailleurs Chrétiens (CFTC), and founded worker movements, the Jeunesse Ouvrière Chrétienne (JOC) and Jeunesse Agricole Chrétienne (JAC). A new Mission de France became active, whose priests swore to devote their lives to the 're-christianization of the working class', and after 1944 about a hundred of them began the dramatic experiment of the worker-priests: they took factory jobs, sharing the workers' lives and dress. The aim was partly to preach Christian example, partly to discover what the alienated working class was really like and so bridge the gulf of ignorance dividing it from the bourgeois Church. So disturbed were some priests by this experience that they fell under Marxist influence and began to militate in the CGT. The Vatican grew worried, and in 1954 it suspended the worker-priest experiment.

These priests were just a small commando unit within a much wider neo-Catholic movement which gathered strength after 1944 and was to play a big part in the reshaping of post-war France. Much of the impulse came from the laity, who felt that it was time for the Church to share in building a better world. Look at any of the grassroots movements of post-war social reform and in nearly every case you find that some

★ It was not until September 1997, after more than fifty years, that the French Episcopate finally issued a formal declaration of 'repentance' for its failure at the time to speak out against the wartime persecution of French Jews, when 76,000 of them were deported to the Nazi camps (see p. 243).

nucleus of Catholic militants played a central role. The farming revolution led by the JAC was an obvious example (see p. 386); there were others, too, in business, industry and civic life, even in the campaign for birth control. These 'neo-Catholics' were influenced by the theologian Pierre Teilhard de Chardin and his world-loving optimism, and even more by Emmanuel Mounier, founder of the review *Esprit* and one of the boldest early advocates of the need for the Church to engage in improving the world – in those days, quite a novel idea. The neo-Catholics, you could say, were the spiritual leaven in the material modernization of France.

The new militant Christian action took many forms. Michel Debatisse in farming and Édouard Leclerc in commerce were two of its leading pioneers in the 1950s. Neo-Catholics also played a major role in the CFDT union (successor to the CTFC, see p. 171), and in the Centre des Jeunes Patrons, a liberal pressure group within the Patronat. 'We animate a large part of the upper civil service,' one Catholic told me triumphantly, as if announcing the success of some *putsch*. And in 1965 over half the mayors of France were ex-JACists or ex-JOCists. Gradually, more and more priests, even bishops, came to join this laity-led movement: 'We are now working,' said one, 'to build God's kingdom on earth – something that the Church never used to care much about.'

Many of the more radical figures in the movement, priests and laity alike, developed a collaboration with the Marxists. These were the two most dynamic ideological groups in the France of the 1950s and '60s, and they had a weird respect and fascination for each other. I do not mean the old Stalinist diehards in the Communist Party, nor Sartre and his circle, but some of the thousands of other active Marxists in France, trade unionists, teachers, doctors and the like, many of them open-minded and pragmatic. Like the neo-Catholics they were frequently notable for their energy, dedication and urge towards practical social action; and when the two met, they often felt more common ground with each other than either had, respectively, with old-style Catholics or with Stalinists. This kind of field collaboration had begun in the Resistance, and by the 1960s much of the voluntary social work in France was being done by these two groups: in a poor district of Paris in the 1960s I found Catholic and Marxist doctors working together to combat mental disease and alcoholism. Even in the intellectual field, both sides made efforts to exchange ideas, at debates and conferences. One leader was the maverick Communist philosopher Roger Garaudy, admirer of Teilhard de

Chardin, who tried to explore common ground in the debates. Sceptics doubted whether the exchanges really added up to much – 'These people are making a false synthesis of the two ideologies, based on sloppy wishful thinking,' said one critic. Perhaps in rational terms this was true. But if the contacts helped towards better understanding, they had a practical usefulness.

The Episcopate itself, after some years of hesitation, increasingly swung its weight behind the neo-Catholic movement during the 1960s, and was influenced by it. But it was less pleased at the growth after May '68 of a more radical left-wing minority trend, the self-styled *prêtres contestataires*, about 1,000 strong, who dedicated themselves to 'liberating Christianity from the bourgeois Church'. And they provoked a backlash. The big conservative element in the Church, the older pious masses and rank-and-file clergy, had grown alarmed even at neo-Catholicism: 'People don't talk about God any more, but about the housing crisis,' complained one elderly lady, while many aged priests feared that Christ was being overlooked amid the new secular zeal for social progress. Against this background a right-wing reaction developed, as an integrist minority became furious, for example, at changes in the liturgy, with Mass now being celebrated in French, not Latin.

And so an explosion occurred. In 1971 France's leading integrist priest, the elderly Monseigneur Marcel Lefebvre, former Archbishop of Dakar, founded his own seminary in Switzerland, where he set about training young men on integrist lines; and in 1976, against the orders of Pope Paul VI, he ordained thirteen of them as priests. The Pope replied by forbidding Lefebvre to say Mass or administer the sacraments: Lefebvre hit back holding a big integrist rally in Lille, and accusing the Vatican of 'flirting dangerously with Communism' and of 'destroying' itself with its liberal reforms of Council II. The Vatican, though embarrassed, shrank from excommunicating the rebel, for this could have provoked him to set up a 'parallel Church'. So it turned a blind eye to his activities. And today, with Lefebvre now dead, this remains much the picture. His followers continue to say their Mass in Latin each Sunday at their church on the Left Bank (opposite Notre-Dame!), St-Nicolas-du-Chardonnet. They number about 10,000 in France as a whole; and though Rome and the French hierarchy do not recognize their faction, they are tolerated. A rival integrist movement, of about the same size but milder, *les Silencieux de l'Église*, does not openly defy Rome, and is formally recognized. It, too, campaigns for traditional values. Today hard-core integrism remains a small, stable force in France. It is not a serious threat to the modern Church: but since many of its members are young, it may still be many years before it fades away.

Since the Lefebvre affair, an anxious calm has prevailed within the Church, punctuated by occasional excitement or controversy over a papal visit, or over issues such as AIDS. Archbishop Lustiger is himself a tolerant conservative. Some of his bishops are more liberal. And within limits individual priests can each follow their own style, with a certain liberty. As with French society as a whole today, it is a confused, fragmented situation where multiple different tendencies coexist and the old authority has declined.

On the one hand, after its rapid fall in the 1960s and '70s, the influence of the Church as an institution has continued a slow decline. While some 75 per cent of people still call themselves Catholics, most of them neglect church-going except at the crucial moments of marriage, baptism and burial. Nearly all are still given a Christian burial. But the percentage of marriages conducted in church has fallen since the 1950s from 80 to 52 per cent, and many young couples go to the altar just to please their parents. Similarly, the proportion of children baptized has fallen from 90 to 58 per cent, and many parents now prefer to wait till a child is about eight or ten, so that he or she can make a choice. In the middle classes Sunday church-going as a family ritual has virtually ceased. In fact, only 7 to 8 per cent of the Catholic population now goes to Mass 'regularly' (at least once a month): in traditionalist areas like Brittany the figure is much higher, but in industrial towns it can be only 3 or 4 per cent. And if the Church has lost touch with its popular roots, one reason has been the post-war rural exodus: 'The Breton *émigré* loses his religion when he arrives in Paris,' said one observer. What's more, while a majority of older people still believe in God, atheism has been growing among the young: according to one 1997 survey, the number of believers in the 18–24 age group has fallen from 81 to 46 per cent since 1967.

The weakening of clericalism has been followed by a waning of anticlericalism, too – and so one of the sharpest of feuds that used to tear France apart has been fading into history. The old quarrels between *rouges* and *blancs*, where a village was ranged in two camps behind teacher and *curé*, have come to seem as much part of folklore as horse-drawn carriages. Even the old issue of state aid for church schools has been largely solved (see p. 549). However, the issue of *la laïcité* remains dormant: in a country where Church and State are constitutionally so separate, there are always secular watchdogs, mostly Socialist, ready to pounce on any signs of high-level rapprochement – a problem that erupted briefly in 1996 when the Pope came to Reims cathedral to celebrate the 1,500th anniversary of the baptism of Clovis, the first king of France. Chirac, secular President but a practising Catholic, had earlier been to the Vatican and spoken perhaps a little too warmly about its close links with the French State. And there were fears that the Pope at Reims might exploit this, maybe with some reference to 'France, eldest daughter of the Church', an historic description hated by secularists. In the event, canny old Wojtyla was extremely tactful and did nothing to provoke, so the storm passed away.

While the churches have been emptying, new more informal styles of worship have come into vogue – a trend not confined to France. This disturbs traditional priests more than the modern ones. A *curé* in a country town told me, 'I know many young Christians here who hardly ever go to Mass and care little for the sacraments, but they seek to practise their faith in their daily lives, and through private prayer. Religion is no longer a matter of social convention but of conviction, and so it is more sincere.' Another observer said, 'A young person's faith is no longer so "protected" by the environment of family and parish. It has to pass through the ordeal of contact with atheism, and if it survives, it may be more real than in the old days.'

While social action today continues, if less widely than before, another important minority has been turning back to the spiritual sources of Christianity, to the fundamentals of prayer and worship. This has sometimes been due to a feeling that social action had gone too far and Christ was being overlooked. But it may also be, in this anxious age, that many people feel a greater need for spiritual consolation – just as others are showing a new interest in philosophy (see p. 530). New books on Christianity have been doing well: one on Christ sold 300,000 copies. Church services may no longer mean so much: but retreats, prayer groups and lay communities have become more popular – also rallies and pilgrimages among young people who seek the fulfilment of open-air togetherness and shared emotions. The big annual pilgrimages to Chartres and to other holy places have seen their numbers revive. It is a return to traditionalism: but only in a few cases is it linked with integrism.

France, like some other countries, has witnessed the rise of 'charismatic' movements, whereby informal groups meet regularly for prayer and discussion, often in private homes. People of all kinds sit cross-legged on the floor together – say, a middle-aged priest, a scientist, a teacher, immigrants and students. First, they informally celebrate Mass, then pray for an hour or so, read from the Bible, maybe sing modern hymns to a guitar, and give cries of joy and thanksgiving, with waving of hands. Often no priest is present. It is vaguely revivalist, American-influenced. And the prayers are spontaneous, expressed in daily language, a break with the ritual rosary-type Catholic prayers. The Church at first looked warily on these charismatic movements (Emmanuel and Chemin Neuf are two leading ones): then it came to accept and recognize them. But in 1996 a respected publisher, Le Seuil, produced a book, *Les Naufragés de l'Esprit: des sectes dans l'Église catholique*, by three former acolytes, who accused the Church of harbouring harmful 'sects' full of shipwrecked souls. Its attacks were not as harsh as those made in America or Britain against non-Christian sects such as the Scientologists or Moonies. But it similarly made accusations of brainwashing, leadership cults, false mysticism, rejection of the outside world, and so on. It then emerged that the authors had much exaggerated, and were referring to some unfortunate elements in the French charismatic movement which had since been purged. But their book left a sour taste.

A number of new-style residential communities were born of the 1968 period, and some are still active. These are not enclosed centres like the old monasteries, but more informal places where priests and laity feel less constrained by the established dogmas of the Church. A few of these autonomous centres have grown out of hand, such as the Boquen community in Brittany, led by a homosexual priest, Bernard Besret, who encouraged sexual liberty for all: he was finally pushed out, and went to America. Other centres are more sober, such as the two excellent communities both called L'Arche but unconnected. One, near Paris, does social work, mostly with the handicapped. The other, in the Languedoc hills, was founded by a Sicilian nobleman, disciple of Mahatma Gandhi, and preaches pacificism. Here I found a large international group of young people leading the simple communal life amid manifest joy and serenity: they pooled their money, made their own clothes, had no electricity. Buddhism, too, has been growing in appeal. And France does have its small lunatic fringe of new-style sects. These create havoc less often than in America: but there was a nasty incident in 1995, when sixteen members of the Swiss-based Ordre du Temple Solaire were found dead in the Vercors, near Grenoble.

The climate among Catholics has changed since the heyday of social action in the post-war years. On the one hand, various small informal groups are at work locally, maybe helping the homeless or handicapped. But the wider neo-Catholic movement has lost much of its force, and official Church-backed bodies like JOC and JAC (renamed Mouvement Rural des Jeunes Catholiques) are now weaker: after all, there are few young farmers left. This flight from institutions towards more disparate action is typical of France today. Some devout Christians are still active in managerial jobs, or in the CFDT union, and in politics – Jacques Delors was a shining example. But such leaders are less likely to proclaim their faith; they keep a lower profile. And the old dialogue with Marxists has mostly gone, too – after all, Marxism is out of fashion. But this does not mean that priests have been moving back towards the Right. On the contrary, in former right-wing Catholic regions such as Brittany and Lorraine, which have shifted left in recent years, many priests have readily gone along with this trend and now vote Socialist – unthinkable thirty years ago. Surveys suggest that today about half of French priests under forty are pro-Socialist. Clergy and laity have also been developing links with France's 2 per cent Protestants: there are many joint youth activities and church services, and thousands of Catholics go eagerly on visits to the famous oecumenical centre at Taizé, in Burgundy.

Some priests are still actively concerned to make real contact with the working class, long so suspicious of the 'bourgeois' Church. There are few worker-priests nowadays, and the Vatican does not encourage them. But some French bishops welcome and help them, so long as they act discreetly. So the pattern varies from one diocese to another. In Brittany in 1986 I found ordained priests doing manual work in factories and on building sites. But in some parts of France, their relations with the more conservative clergy can be strained. In the town of Montargis, near Orléans, I found a dramatic example of this kind of divorce between two conceptions of the priesthood. The parish church had been taken over by a team of five worker-priests. But that of an adjacent suburb was run by an elderly priest of the old school, Abbé Powet, not integrist but a conservative, who was sticking to the Church's classic role of ministering to the sick, catechizing the young and celebrating Mass. 'Those worker-priests spend so much of their time and energy on their paid jobs,' he said, 'that they have little left over for true spiritual duties.' They in turn accused him of being out of touch with modern needs, of sticking to a small circle of mainly middle-class believers, and of making no effort to go out to conquer new ground in this industrial town. The Montargis bourgeoisie were angry that their own church had fallen to this 'Leftist *putsch*', as one of them put it; and they, if they attended Mass, went to Abbé Powet. Of the worker-priests, two worked in factories, one was a cleaner and one a male nurse (living with his mistress). They formed a little commune in the presbytery, with hardly a crucifix in sight. Their leader, Abbé Gallerand, a full-time priest in a colourful jersey, impressed me with his cheerful alertness, while Powet seemed lonely and embittered, full of gloom about the future of the Church. Gallerand held jazz sessions in his church, and offered a lay wedding service for atheists. He and his team were popular – but had the Christian baby gone out with the bathwater? Ten years later I returned, to find the abbés both dead, the worker-priests gone, and both churches in the hands of decent liberal *curés*, but with tiny congregations.

Abbé Powet had given me some amazing statistics. In his diocese, as many priests were over eighty years old as under forty, and more were in their seventies than their forties. Since then, throughout France, matters have only got worse. Some seminaries have closed for lack of recruits, and today only 100 to 120 priests are ordained each year, against about 1,000 in the 1950s. The average age is now over sixty-five. As a result, many parishes lack a *curé*, and are being regrouped: the church itself, whose upkeep in France is the charge of the commune, is kept locked save for some special occasion. The lack of priests, and of active lay workers, can add to social problems, too: 'If only there were more of us,' said one *curé*, 'we could certainly do more to provide guidance to the despairing, lonely, delinquent youth in the poorer suburbs.' In 1996 in Burgundy I visited a region of seventy communes with only four priests, all over sixty, one Polish and one Vietnamese. They greeted me charmingly, but seemed a little sad and isolated. 'Many people still come to us for marriages and baptisms,' one of them said, 'and above all for funerals. Even people who have lost their faith still want a Christian burial for their loved ones. It's not hypocrisy, but a respect for the dead, an awe in face of the mystery of death.'

The celibacy rule remains the major deterrent to new recruitment. Some priests have abandoned their vocation because they wish to marry. Some have girlfriends, and their bishop knows but is tolerant, so long as they are discreet. According to one survey, some 80 per cent of clergy disapprove of compulsory celibacy. 'Sooner or later, the Church will change,' said one. 'To Vatican Council III, bishops will come with their wives. To Vatican IV, they will come with their husbands!'

In face of these trends, the Episcopate retains a wary prudence. After its post-war swing away from the Right, it has remained progressive on most social issues, yet is loyal to the Vatican on moral and sexual matters. But positions vary, and an individual bishop or priest can, within limits, follow his own line. Some of the most liberal bishops are the older ones, appointed under Pope John XXIII or formed in the neo-Catholic era. Cardinal Lustiger himself, born in 1926, is more conservative, and so are some of the more recent appointments. Even so, the Episcopate has come out strongly in favour of more social equality and against racism, and it backs the Pope's stand on helping the world's poor. But under Vatican influence it has also been taking a firmer line against abortion, pre-marital sex, divorce and (mostly) birth control.

This pleases the integrists and other right-wing Catholics, but it dismays many other believers. Most younger Catholics nowadays practise birth control and some accept abortion; and they do not find this inconsistent with their Christian faith. So they may feel ill at ease in today's Church, and this is a factor behind the decline of church-going. Since the rise of AIDS (see p. 616) occasionally a prelate will openly query the Church's ban on condoms – as the maverick Monseigneur Jacques Gaillot, Bishop of Évreux, did in 1995, and he was promptly removed from his post by the Vatican. Several bishops privately sympathized with him but felt that he had managed the affair tactlessly. Then, a year later, the Episcopate's social commission officially declared that the use of a condom was 'comprehensible' in certain cases (i.e. if there was a serious risk of AIDS). The Church quickly denied that this marked any change in its teaching. But it was hailed by many laymen as a sign that bishops were at last growing more humane and realistic about the subject, readier to put their own gloss on John Paul II's rigid line.

As Pope, he has paid four visits to France since 1980. It had seemed he was growing less popular: according to surveys, those 'severely critical' of his policies rose from 26 to 51 per cent between 1988 and 1996. But then his visit in 1997, when he came for the World Youth Festival was a huge success. Over a million, twice more than expected, attended his outdoor Mass at Longchamps racecourse; earlier, they had formed a 30-kilometre 'chain of brotherhood' around Paris. It was all impressive, and well orchestrated, and it led some Catholic observers to speak excitedly of a 'crucial turning point', even of a 'religious revival'. This could be an exaggeration: the French youth attending this very special event were only a small minority of their age group, and most were from the provincial middle class, with transport arranged by Catholic schools and youth groups. Yet the event did cast a spotlight on a real, deeper feeling among young people, anxiously questioning, seeking leadership. Many who cannot accept the Pope's moral teachings are still drawn by his personal charisma, his evident concern for the poor. Others yearn for a new intellectual leader in the mould of Mounier or Teilhard de Chardin: but there are none around today, any more than in secular philosophy.

One sociologist of religion, Danièle Hervieu-Léger, wrote at the time (*Le Monde*, 17 August 1997):

The mass of French youth may feel unconcerned by this event. But, strikingly, many of them today are interested in spiritual questions and open to all kinds of beliefs. The previous generation had rejected the Church, while today's is simply indifferent; yet it can also feel sympathetic towards the individual religious leaders it may meet, including the Pope. The Church today suffers from youth's overall dislike of institutions, and is no worse placed than the rest.

Others, too, have commented on this renewal of spiritual feeling, related not so much to the Church, or to community action, as to individual expression and fellowship. It may not be easy for the Church itself to draw on this potential. Today's paradox is that while many young people are looking for certainty, firm rules, moral leadership, they also want modern freedom and choice. It leaves them insecure and bewildered. Many are now turning back to the old sure values of family affection and loyalty.

RENEWAL OF FAMILY, DECLINE OF FORMALITY — AND THE MYTH OF FRENCH INHOSPITALITY

The anxious 1990s, with the rise of youth unemployment, have brought a renewed sense of the importance of the family as a trusted value and a personal refuge of security. This follows a long post-war period when the old tight family ties had been steadily loosening, and it marks a striking new change.

Traditionally, daily social relations in France have been more heavily dominated by family ties than in Anglo-Saxon lands. The family has seemed the focus of the individual's loyalty and affection, of his economic interest – even of his legal duty, for the rights and obligations of the family were defined in the still operative Code Napoléon of 1804. Many an older Frenchman has spent his youth in a world where he was expected to regard cousins, uncles and grandmothers as more important to him than friends of his own age, and where the family's needs and demands were put before those of the local community or even of the State: 'I cannot pay my taxes: you see, I've a duty to support Aunt Louise' has been a common attitude.

The main change in the post-war decades was that the focus of loyalty steadily narrowed from what sociologists call 'the extended family' to the 'nuclear family': from the big multi-generational clan to the immediate home cell of parents and children. The trend varied from class to class. In the propertyless lower bourgeoisie the nuclear family had long held more importance than the clan: but in rural areas the patriarchal peasant families lost their influence as the young drifted away. And in the upper bourgeoisie, as property gave way to income, as family managements grew fewer and sons dispersed to new salaried careers in other parts of France, so the tight network of the big family gathering, subject of a thousand bitter novels, became less necessary for the individual's future and security, and also less easy to maintain. Today many couples are likely to prefer pleasure travelling, or a weekend cottage shared with friends, to the traditional family reunions on Sundays and in August.

Within the nuclear family, however, links can remain close. A young teacher of twenty-five told me, 'I had to cancel my holiday in Greece this summer: you see, my grandmother got ill and my mother was worried.' Would her English equivalent display such a sense of duty? Although clan loyalties towards more distant relatives may have waned, an adult's ties with his own parents and even with *their* parents can still be remarkably close. And if many younger people are trying to live more emotionally independent lives, it can often be with a sense of guilt, or an awareness of the pain it causes to parents who cling to a different family tradition. This may be so in any country: it is especially sharp in France.

In all classes couples no longer accept so readily that an elderly widowed parent should live with them: granny or grandpa is expected to live in a flat of his or her own. This has caused some heartache. But officialdom has now come to recognize the more independent status of the elderly: old-age pensions have been raised (see p. 196), thousands of town councils have built hostels for old people. Society has finally accepted that its elderly are no longer solely a family responsibility, and more than 10,000 clubs for the so-called *troisième âge* have been created. Old people themselves have been adapting to the change, and are grouping to build their own social life. You see busloads of middle-class widows going on outings together – an American phenomenon that has belatedly hit France.

After the war the rise in the birth rate, *le bébé boom*, did much to strengthen the social importance of the young nuclear family. Baby-making and baby-rearing came to be seen as a prestige industry, as in the Soviet Union, and the young mother filling her HLM with tots and nappies was saluted as of more value to the nation than the old family patriarch. Stimulated by the large child allowances, the average size of families swelled. These factors, plus a Latin adoration of small children, let to a true *culte de l'enfant*, as the new suburbs pullulated with the kind of images of fecundity that Agnès Varda satirized in her film *Le Bonheur*. But then the birth rate began falling, as in other Western countries (see p. 4). Giscard's and Mitterrand's Governments anxiously responded with larger allowances for families with two or more children, so in official eyes baby-making remained a prestige industry: but in the eyes of the public, the baby cult was over. Sociologists today find that many young couples still seek a first child almost instinctively (*l'enfant biologique*) as a symbol of fertility: but in an uncertain world they will think twice about having even a second child (*l'enfant économique*).

Families may be smaller, yet the past few years have seen a new strengthening of the links that bind the nuclear family, after a tense period of transition. Around 1968 French teenagers kicked over the traces of parental authority more suddenly and sharply than in most Western countries (see p. 573). This was a blow to the nuclear family. But today, having asserted their right to independence, young people have been moving back to closer emotional ties with their parents, on a basis of greater equality than before. So the family is united less by constraint and convention than in the old days, and more by genuine need and affection. In practical terms, a boy or girl of nineteen or twenty is less likely than in the 1960s to be still living at home: but he or she will still keep in close touch with parents, pay frequent visits, and probably confide more readily than in the old days. Now that youth's rebellion is won, the generational conflict has subsided. And whereas the youth of the '60s rejected their parents' values, today's young people have been turning again to family as a bulwark and source of comfort, since they no longer find such solid values in the public world outside. The fears created by the sharp rise in youth unemployment have increased this homing trend: some young people now return to the *foyer* if they cannot find work, while some parents, anxious for their children's welfare, are again trying harder to dissuade them from leaving home. According to opinion surveys, the numbers citing family as 'the most sure of all values' has risen greatly since the early 1980s, and here France is in the lead in Europe, along with Italy and Greece. So the modern-style liberated family regains a new importance as a point of anchorage in an anxious and shifting world.

Since their first loyalty has generally been to family, when it comes to friendship the French tend to be more selective and reticent than the casually gregarious Anglo-Saxons. As their conceptions of friendship can differ from ours, this may cause confusion: though more loquacious, they are also more *socially* reserved. There are three levels here. First, a Frenchman may more readily strike up a chat with a stranger in a train or café: there may be a lively discussion, but it will remain anonymous, personal questions are not asked, and there is no presumption of acquaintanceship. On the second level, the British and Americans seem more open than the French at making new acquaintances, developing them quickly into friends, asking them home, swapping personal details. The French will admit this, knowing they are wary of new friendships in a society still based in part on mistrust (see p. 726), where the initial reaction to a stranger is often one of suspicion, and much chatting-up has to be done for this to be overcome.

Yet the French – like the Germans – consider the Anglo-Saxon style of so-called friendship rather superficial, an undiscriminating chumminess which they see as one aspect of our emotional reserve, a façade to hide the fear of real friendship. They distinguish more sharply between acquaintances and – the third level – *les vrais amis*, few and select, and here they consider they outclass us in terms of emotional depth and subtlety. The French do not make true friendships lightly, and most of them are formed in youth, or slowly over the years among work colleagues. Once made, they tend to be enduring and loyal: but the reserve against breaking the ice with new friends can lead to a stiff atmosphere in office life. Except at senior executive level, office colleagues do not often meet each other socially, and friendship is rare between staff of differing grades. Thus the social ambience of the traditional French office can be less chummy and relaxed than in Britain; and this can make life lonely for anyone arriving to work in a new town, especially Paris, without existing friends. However, this stiff pattern has been weakening in recent years among younger employees, and in new-style offices such as those dealing with the media.

Under the impulse of this generation, there has been a steady easing of the social formality and ceremonial that had hitherto been such a feature of daily human contact in many aspects of French life. True, an Anglo-Saxon may still raise his eyebrows at a respect for hierarchies that can seem almost Teutonic. Any ex-chairman expects to be addressed until his death as '*Monsieur le Président*', and letters may still ask you to agree to the assurance of most distinguished sentiments. Though the French can be stimulatingly outspoken in the voicing of opinions, they can also be oddly conventional about manners and behaving *comme il faut*. In one sense, this is the outward sign of a snobbish society that respects a person's position and diplomas more than what he is ('*Ah, Monsieur est polytechnicien!*'). But in another sense, the formality should not be mistaken for coldness: courtesy may be stylized among older people, yet can still be a channel for expressing warmth. The habitual '*cher Monsieur*' does not mean '*dear Sir*': an older Frenchman will often call his buddies just that, and it can be cordial, like '*mon vieux*'.

Anyway, for some years a younger generation has been showing impatience with the old formal approach and is setting less store by titles and decorum. Today there are fewer ceremonial banquets with speeches, and more informal home entertaining. Among the new *cadres* a new easiness has been emerging which can be seen in leisure and holiday habits such as the Club Méditerranée, and in the trend towards casual clothes, casual décor and what the smart 'ads' call '*une élégance vraiment relax*'. I would even say that today, among their own friends and family, the under-forties are almost as informal as Anglo-Saxons. The use of Christian names has also been increasing: it is now far commoner than in Germany, though not yet as universal as in Britain or America, where the coinage has been debased into virtual meaninglessness. Again, this is a matter of generation. Typically, I have a friend in his sixties who only after several meetings cautiously dropped the 'Monsieur' and called me 'John', whereas his son of thirty did so right away. The use of *tu*, rather than *vous*, used to be largely restricted to male camaraderie and family life, and even today I have many older French friends who call me 'John' but *vous*. But *tutoiement* is now almost universal among students and teenagers, and has been spreading among younger *cadres* and in left-wing circles, where it is a conscious anti-bourgeois gesture. In the upper bourgeoisie, by contrast, you will find some older married couples who even call each other *vous*, by an old tradition. In this class, though a man will now generally call the wife of a male friend by her Christian name, to call her *tu* in public may still give the wrong impression. Women are usually more formal than men, and I know two married couples in their fifties where the men use surnames and *tu* with each other, while the wives still call each other 'Madame'. But between their grown-up children, it is 'Jacques', 'Odile' and *tu*.

The French have a reputation, quite unjustified, of not entertaining in their own homes. Most Anglo-Saxon horror stories about this are based on stays in Paris, where it is true that daily and business life is so hectic that many families prefer to hug their privacy to themselves: but go to other areas and you will find a people as welcoming as almost any in Europe. And even Parisians, when they get round to it, are now entertaining less stiffly than in the old days, except in a small 'fashionable' milieu. Most younger people, freeing themselves from their parents' formal standards, have become more casual in inviting friends to meals, and are thus readier to do so more often. And the deeper you go into country areas, the warmer the welcome may be. Even in big towns, the welcome can be lavish: on a five-week research visit to Toulouse, a city where I had no friends when I first arrived, I was asked home to lunch or dinner by *seventeen* French families, some of them several times. I say this not to boast but to set the record straight, for foreigners often have a false picture. Generally, the welcome was spontaneous and unpretentious, maybe a family meal shared with the children.

My only criticism is that the French have the disconcerting habit of offering you either a slap-up meal or not even a glass of water. Of course, if a friend invites you specifically to *prendre un verre à la maison*, it is different: but in my job I frequently arrange to call on people *chez eux*, where we chat cordially for an hour or so, during which time not even a coffee or juice is offered. They are not being mean: it simply does not occur to them. Then, as I get up to go, my host says, '*Mais vous restez dix minutes prendre l'apéritif?*' – by which time it may be too late, if I have another appointment. It can be trying, at the end of a hot and tiring day.

So my policy is either to get up to leave ten minutes before I need to; or else to arrive flustered, saying, 'I'm *so* thirsty – have you just a glass of water?', which usually prompts them to bring out *le scotch*. In most other countries, a drink of some sort is offered as one enters the door, but not so in France – and the same applies to office meetings, where a visitor is not plied with tea or coffee, and only a few senior executives yet follow the Anglo-American habit of keeping a drinks cabinet in their office. As an example of French behaviour at its most extreme, I remember a day my wife and I spent touring the Burgundy vineyards at harvest-time for the BBC. We called on a number of leading growers and shippers who showed us their *chais*, their cellars and tasting rooms, and were most friendly: wine, wine, everywhere, but not a drop to drink were we given all day. But one grower, a Chevalier du Tastevin, invited us to come as his guests two days later to one of the famous banquets at the Clos de Vougeot, where we were wined and dined royally as rarely in our lives.

Hospitality is often warmest in the provinces, where even a Parisian can be quite different when away from the big-city rat race. I know an English married couple in official jobs in Paris who became friendly with two French civil servants. There were cordial business lunches, and sometimes my friends asked the French to parties and were assured, '*Vous devriez venir dîner à la maison, on vous fera signe*', and then of course nothing happened. But one day the English and both the Frenchmen and their wives found they were all going to spend August in villas in the same part of Auvergne. Holiday addresses were exchanged and the usual promises of hospitality, which my friends took with a pinch of salt. But lo! – in Auvergne the phone rang, dates were fixed, their French hosts plied lavish meal upon lavish meal with grace and warmth. The English had broken through the barrier: they were *des vrais amis* at last. But, back in Paris, the iron curtain descended again. Of course, this is a big-city disease not confined to Paris: the French in London have the same grievances.

At smart 'society' level in Paris, the tradition of formality still powerfully exists. Here dinner-party habits can sometimes include printed invitation cards, white-gloved waiters, rigid conventions about serving the correct food and wines. The notion lingers that, if you are to give a party in your own home, it must be done perfectly or not at all: so it is not done very often. 'I can't have people to dinner this month,' said a leisured housewife; 'you see, my maid has hurt her leg.' However, at the slightly lower social level of lawyers, teachers and the like, entertaining has now become a little less elaborate. A *Parisienne* who has moved back into this world after years in London noted the change: 'People are now readier to give an informal buffet party at a few days' notice. But even in this more casual style, Parisians still expect excellence: you have to provide the best of everything, all elegantly laid out. So of course you don't do it very often. Above all, compared with London, social life is cliquey: there's less gregarious interchange, less sense of overlapping circles.' When people throw a party, they tend to invite their own kind: you are less likely than in London to find all types rubbing shoulders in the same room, go-ahead bankers, left-wing thinkers, way-out artists. Doctors will invite other doctors, and so on: I heard of one big buffet party where two-thirds of the men were *inspecteurs des finances*. But at least there is one important change, in this kind of milieu: more of those élitists are today likely to be women. They have been gaining ground in the professions, and in politics, too.

MORE EQUALITY FOR WOMEN – BUT *VIVE* FRENCH FEMININITY!

In 1997 Lionel Jospin put four women deputies into senior cabinet posts, with Martine Aubry as his deputy premier. Earlier, Édith Cresson had been France's first woman Prime Minister (albeit no great success). These have been new stages in one of the major silent revolutions of the past forty years in France – the progress of women towards fuller emancipation, professional, legal, indeed sexual. Today French women want to remain very feminine, they like to be gallantly courted, and they dislike the brash, anti-sexist kind of feminism: but in working and public life they now want the same opportunities as men.

The movement happened later than in many advanced countries. Only in the 1970s did women begin to make any impact in politics, or was abortion made legal or female contraception widely practised. Only in 1980 did the Académie Française, then bastion of male chauvinism, admit its first woman member, the novelist Marguerite Yourcenar. And until the 1964 Matrimonial Act, a wife still had to obtain her husband's permission to open a bank account, run a shop, or even get a passport, while much joint property was legally the husband's and the divorce courts were obliged to regard a wife's infidelity as more serious than a man's. Only in the 1975–85 period did further laws remove the last remaining inequalities in matters of divorce, property and the right to employment. And even today many women can still find it harder than men to find good jobs with equal pay.

The latent machismo of a Latin society with Catholic traditions may help to explain these delays. It is more curious that French women themselves, whose social role in some other ways has always been so strong, did not show much interest in this kind of legal equality or in sharing a man's privileges, at least until recently. Theirs has been a reticent revolution, save for the work of a small band of feminist pioneers. Even the 1964 Act was not especially popular with women, as one feminist told me: 'Many felt it implied a mistrust of the husband. They seemed less concerned with equality than with using their charms on a man to win their way.' Since then, times have changed: but even today most French women prize femininity above feminism.

Socially, women in France have rarely been segregated or treated as inferior, as in some southern countries. A woman has regarded herself, and been regarded, as the equal of a man★ – *equal, but different*. Given the opportunity to play the same role as a man in public life, she has often shied away in fear of losing her femininity, and men have cheered her for it! Cliché or not, this has been the land of *la petite différence*, not of suffragettes, nor of Anglo-Saxon-style women's clubs. A woman has seen herself in relation to family – where her role is powerful – and to individual men, rather than to other women or the community. So it is no surprise that the modern 'Women's Lib' movement in its more militant form has remained marginal.

Yet in the past generation a milder and different kind of feminism has taken root among younger people, as a result of May '68, and of foreign influences. Maybe Simone de Beauvoir's key feminist text, *Le Deuxième Sexe*, read but disregarded by so many women at the time, has had some belated impact, too. French women today expect equality of rights and career prospects, equal personal freedom (sexual and otherwise), and equality in marriage. But they do not want to become the *same* as men; nor do they hate or shun men, like some militants. They want it both ways – to be flirted with and told they are beautiful, but also to lead an emancipated life. And why not?

★

★ And often living longer: witness Jeanne Calment, who knew Van Gogh and died in Arles in 1997 at the age of 122. She was said to be the oldest woman in Europe, *la doyenne de l'humanité*.

French women were finally given the vote in 1945 by the Liberation Government under de Gaulle (not himself a noted feminist). But although not legally barred since then from any office of State, they have been slow to enter active politics. Initially, 30 women were elected to the National Assembly in 1945, but their numbers dropped to 10 by 1977 (against 26 British women MPs then); and in all the shifting ministries of the 1945–74 period, only three women reached even junior office. This, it seems, was due equally to male bias and to women's own reluctance to come forward: traditionally, they have preferred to wield influence behind the scenes – with Pompadour as their prototype, not Jeanne d'Arc – and I am sure that Madame de Gaulle had more influence on affairs than all the women politicians together, in her time. But then Giscard, a genuine champion of women's causes, brought some able women from outside politics into his Government: Simone Veil, a brilliant and liberal-minded lawyer, became Minister of Health, and was so successful that the polls were soon showing her as the most popular minister ('The best man in our team is a woman,' said Chirac). By 1976 there were five women in the Government: but most had been co-opted, like technocrats. Giscard had given women their chance to be effective ministers: but they were not yet showing themselves able, or willing, to fight their way up inside the party hierarchy, like Thatcher.

The Socialist leaders did make efforts to promote women through party ranks, and this bore modest fruit in the 1981 elections when the total of female deputies rose to 26, 19 of them Socialist. Mitterrand himself was not only a ladies' man (as we know) but a supporter of women in politics. However, some people felt that he had somewhat confused these two roles when in 1991 he startled France by appointing Édith Cresson (a former *amour*, it was whispered) as the nation's first woman Prime Minister. This bouncy feminist had already been Minister of Agriculture. She was lively and talented, but provocative, and she began to make some tactless remarks in public, calling the Japanese 'ants' and claiming that a quarter of Anglo-Saxon men were homosexual. In more serious ways, too, she proved inadequate for her job, and some of her male ministers set about subtly sabotaging her: under public pressure Mitterrand dismissed her after only a year. The episode had done little good to the cause of French women in politics – even though, in the 1993 elections, their tally of deputies in the Assembly did rise to a new peak of 32: but France was still in the lowest position in the EU, behind Greece. Then in 1995 Chirac and Juppé made their own effort to improve the balance: they appointed nine women as members of the Government, nearly 30 per cent of the total; and here France now ranked fourth in the EU. But Juppé later grew dissatisfied with these ladies, and in a reshuffle in 1996 he sacked seven of them. It was one of the clumsiest episodes of his baleful premiership.

Since women were still hesitating to come forward as election candidates, and many selection boards were still biased against them, for some years there had been talk of introducing quotas – and for the 1997 elections the Socialists did just this. They announced a target of 30 per cent of women candidates, and they achieved 27 per cent. Of the 245 Socialists then elected, only 17 per cent were women: but at least the total of women deputies almost doubled, from 32 to 63, of whom 42 were Socialists. In Britain at the same time, the number of women MPs also doubled, from 62 to 120; and France was still in second lowest rank in the EU. But at least there was progress, and Jospin had some powerful women to choose from for his Government. Martine Aubry, Delors's daughter, became deputy Prime Minister in charge of employment, and today is a possible Socialist choice for presidential candidate in 2002. Elisabeth Guigou, an effective Minister for European Affairs under Bérégovoy, was made Minister of Justice. The redoubtable Catherine Trautmann moved from Strasbourg to be government spokesman and Minister of Culture, while the Greens' leader Dominique Voynet took over regional development and, suitably, environment. Five full ministers and three secretaries of State were now women.

Before the elections Jospin and his senior colleagues had not found it easy to impose the 30-per-cent quota on local party activists, many of whom still feared that women could not pull in the votes. Some *phallocratie* (male chauvinism) endured even among Socialists, as Cresson herself had told me bitterly a few years earlier: 'Most men still do all they can to keep us out. The convention persists, above all at local level, that politics is a man's affair. A woman who pushes herself forward is *mal vue*: if she "gets herself talked about", well, that's an innuendo. I can tell you, life is hellish here for a woman in politics, unless she's old and ugly, which has other drawbacks. Mitterrand has been trying to break these phallocratic traditions, but it's not easy. And yet, the party is dead keen on women's rights – it's absurd. Men often tell me, "You're too pretty to be in politics, my dear" – I feel like slapping them in the face.' Since then some progress has been made, especially among Socialists, and in Parisian circles where women are now easily accepted in politics. But in many rural areas and small towns, the old attitudes persist, especially among right-wing voters. In 1997 the advance was mainly among Socialists: the UDF elected only 7 women among its 109 deputies, and the RPR a mere 5 out of 140. But then in 1999 the RPR made a big advance by electing Michèle Alliot-Marie as its new president: it was the first time that a woman had become head of a classic French party. Also in 1999 the Socialists persuaded Parliament to amend the Constitution to include the principle of 'equality of access' to elected posts. A new law then enforcing equal numbers of men and women candidates in local and European elections was due to come into effect in 2001.

In working life outside politics, women have already advanced hugely in the past thirty years; and in education they have in some ways overtaken men. Long gone are the days when a girl of good family was expected to lead an idle life at home before marriage: today she will probably go on to higher studies, then get a job. Fifty years ago, nearly twice as many boys as girls in *lycées* took the *baccalauréat* exam, essential passport to higher education: but today more girls than boys try for the *bac*, and their pass rate is higher. At university, the percentage of female students has risen from 25 in 1930 to 55 today, while the proportion of girls at ENA has increased since 1985 from 15 to 25 per cent. At the École Polytechnique, long a male preserve, some 10 per cent of students are now girls: the first ever to enter, in 1972, came top in the passing-out exam!

In employment progress has been great, but incomplete. In the liberal professions, the percentage of women has risen from 23 to 33 per cent since 1985. There are four female ambassadors, also women prefects, police chiefs, army generals. Some 65 per cent of primary teachers are women – but only 12 per cent of engineers. And they are still sparsely represented in the upper ranks of industry and big business, where a male bias persists against women in directors' chairs: of creators of new firms, only a quarter are women. While in the educated classes far more women are at work than before the war, conversely in the poorer classes, where women, as in Zola's novels, used to go to work to keep a family above the breadline, rising prosperity has made it easier for many of them to stay at home if they wish. Women account for 44 per cent of the workforce, slightly more than in Britain or Germany. But, for various reasons (see p. 177), more women than men are registered as unemployed – the opposite of the situation in Britain or Germany.

The ideal of equal pay for equal work was enshrined in law under Giscard in the 1970s: but it is not always fully applied. Some firms still manage to cheat, paying women less for the same job. And as more women than men do menial jobs (such as charring) or work below their qualifications (e.g. as secretaries), or are not selected for the most senior posts, so it is that a woman's earnings are still on average 27 per cent below a man's. In 1950 the differential was 50 per cent: but the progress is still not enough, say women leaders. However, some other reforms have had more success in recent years. These include, under Giscard: fairer divorce laws; the legalizing of abortion; sixteen weeks' paid maternity leave. The Socialists, with the dynamic Yvette Roudy as Minister for Women's Rights, then outlawed sex discrimination, for example in the wording of job advertisements.

These and other measures took some of the steam out of the small but militant 'Women's Lib' movement which had emerged in the 1970s, stimulated by the events of May '68. This has made some impact when fighting for specific causes, such as helping battered wives. But its aggressive stance denouncing male 'tyranny' has never gone down well with French women as a whole, and today its influence is small. The more moderate French feminists, and they are numerous, have a different and more subtle approach. '*Le droit à la différence*' is one of their slogans, and while demanding full equality of rights and opportunities, they also put the stress on a woman keeping her feminine qualities. In France men and women alike have a fear and contempt for the bossy, masculine type of woman, and Frenchwomen who emerge as champions of their sex are mostly exquisitely feminine. 'Whenever I make a speech about women's rights, I'm always careful to look *soignée* and appealing,' said the journalist Christiane Collange. 'The American shock-haired, bra-burning kind of feminism gives people here the willies.'

French women today are still in a difficult transitional phase, between the old dependence on a man's world and full emancipation. Forty years ago in the bourgeoisie there was still some prejudice against the young housewife, however gifted, who left her small children with a nanny or au pair and continued a full-time job. But in the 1970s a new generation swung to the opposite dilemma, that of the young graduate wife at the kitchen sink, guilty and frustrated at wasting her education. So today they look for jobs. But in practice many young wives find it a strain to combine a career with running a home, especially in Paris where the tempo is fast, office hours are long, bosses are demanding – and a husband expects everything just perfect when he wants to entertain. This can apply at all social levels. So Governments have been urging firms to offer more part-time jobs, which might also help to share out unemployment more fairly. The proportion of working women in part-time jobs has risen since 1982 from 18 to 28 per cent, but remains well below the British figure. Today the French housewife has been hit badly by unemployment, in many ways worse than men. She wants to be able to have a good job, equal to a man's, *and* to run her home well. In the present climate, it is not an easy balance to achieve.

Among younger people, the greatest change of recent decades is one that is hardest to define, for it concerns the nature of the couple and its intimate power balance. Here it is the man who has often been finding adjustment hardest, for his machismo has been in question. Traditionally, in this Latin society, women have exerted their greatest power within the family, or in relation to individual men rather than to the community. To live for one man, to use feminine charm or guile to persuade or please him: this may be a woman's instinct anywhere, but especially it has been so in France. It may have brought joyous rewards, but it has also made French women vulnerable and subject to strain. For French males, those notorious egotists, have exploited their advantage both emotionally and in practical ways, down to refusing to help with the chores because it is unvirile. Both before and after marriage a woman has usually had to fight harder than in many countries to keep her man's interest; and though this may be a reason why older French women often remain so chic and sexually alert, it could also explain those tense, sharp expressions, the hard lines round the mouth. They lack the puddingy relaxedness of English matrons.

This was the traditional pattern, but in the past thirty years new generations of French women have rebelled. Initially, they were influenced by British and American societies via the media; by May '68; by the spread of contraception and other factors. Today if her man behaves with thoughtless machismo, a woman will simply walk out. She expects the same degree of sexual freedom as a man and, conversely, the same fidelity from him. She no longer accepts his peccadilloes as more forgivable than her own. Inside marriage, she demands equality of decision-making, and equal control over shared finances; and she insists that her own leisure interests, her own cultural or other needs, be taken as seriously as his. Males have reacted in various ways to this onslaught. The younger ones generally adapt, so that the boy–girl camaraderie of their student days is carried on into adult partnership, where they are now readier to share the housework and allow their partner to have her own interests.

Younger French women appear to me more relaxed, less brusquely defensive, than their mothers' generation used to be. Yet the change has not been at the price of femininity. The French game of flirtatious badinage continues, enjoyed by both sides. The Frenchwoman, in emancipating, has not lost her *mystère* nor her natural feminine subtlety; she does not brashly assert herself, like some Americans. Yet, while individual relations may now be more equal, in public and working life the spirit of male chauvinism does not die so easily. The recent laws on divorce and employment, giving equality to women, are not always properly applied by an older generation of judges and *patrons*. And many a French boss still tends to treat his secretary as unworthy of his trust or of responsibility (see p. 728). It may take another generation, or more, for male society to forget its old *phallocratie*. Some younger French women novelists, such as Marie Darrieussecq and Marie Redonnet, have sensitively explored these themes.

The sexual attitudes and mores of French women have also changed, if more recently than in many northern countries. As late as the 1960s, there was still plenty of evidence that French unmarried women as a whole, notably in the provinces, were among the most virginal in Europe, outside Italy and Spain. Of course the old idea of France as the land of unfettered *amour* had always been one of the silliest of foreigners' clichés: it sprang largely from the tourist's inability to distinguish between the strict codes of French domestic life (which he usually never saw) and the tradition of public tolerance which has always sanctioned such conspicuous activities as Montmartre night-life or Left Bank free-living bohemia. If you were outside society, on your own, then the guardians of morality would ignore you; and so Paris was a favoured refuge for those wanting freedom and privacy. But if you belonged within one of society's rigid compartments, then you had to obey its often hypocritical rules. Well into the 1960s the old codes of this Catholic society remained in force, at least on the surface. A survey in 1960 found more than half of French mothers still thinking a girl should not be allowed out with a boy till she was nineteen. Only 27 per cent of girls said they approved of pre-marital sex even between fiancés, while 70 per cent of young married women *claimed* to have been still virgins on their wedding night. Maybe not all were telling the truth: yet there is a true story that, in Lyon in 1962, when a dead baby was found in a hostel for working girls, and all

144 inmates agreed to a police examination, to see who could be absolved from suspicion, all but seven were found to be virgins.

Then, in the wake of the Nordic countries, sexual freedom began to spread. Parents became readier to allow their daughters to go out with boys; young people got more leisure and money. In some student circles, relations were quite free by the mid-1960s. Then the 1970s saw a further change among the very young and in parental attitudes. This came in part from the availability of birth control and the steady decline in the influence of the Church. France's best-known sexologist, the liberal-minded Dr Pierre Simon, told me in 1980, 'My major survey in 1972 had shown that twenty-one was the average age at which a French girl first had full sexual intercourse: since then, all has changed. It is now the "done thing" at school to sleep around, and teenage girls and boys treat each other as sex objects in a free market. Most girls think of virginity as something they *ought* to lose. Only 5 per cent of French of either sex are still virgins at twenty-five, and mostly these are the "old maids" who will stay virgins all their lives. France has now reached the same level of sexual freedom as Britain or Germany – and that, for this so-called Catholic land, is quite a transformation.'

However, as all the surveys indicated, the 1980s then marked a swing away from promiscuity, accentuated as in other countries by the spread of AIDS (see p. 616). In 1997 Dr Simon told me, 'Nearly all teenagers still experiment and lose their virginity early, say at sixteen or seventeen. But then they soon settle down with one partner, whom they usually keep. In their promiscuous phase, they seldom link sex with love or even eroticism: it is a means of communication and self-discovery. Real love comes later, after twenty or so, and with it true eroticism.' It might indeed be wrong to infer from the 1970s teenage revolution that adult women have become more *légères*: they remain *sérieuses*, and do not often give themselves except for love, even if marriage itself has declined. And the sexual emancipation of youth is less evident in rural areas than in Paris or other big towns. Working-class families tend to retain a closer watch over their daughters than the middle classes. And gone are the days when a young bourgeois, after sleeping around with *filles légères*, would expect to take a virgin to the altar. There are simply not enough virgins around; and nearly all parents have given up the unequal struggle to keep their daughters so. Female virginity used to be a sacred property in male eyes: but French girls themselves have done battle against that kind of chauvinism, and have won.

The most startling changes have been in cohabitation outside marriage and the decline of marriage itself. According to a 1995 survey by INSEE, as many as 87 per cent of couples today live together before getting married, or they never get married at all. This compares with 44 per cent in 1977, and a mere 15 per cent in 1965. And 33 per cent of children are born outside wedlock. So 'non-legalized' cohabitation, at least for a few years, has become the norm. Not only has the waning of the housing shortage made it far easier for a young couple to find a flatlet of their own away from the parental nest, but parents' attitudes have changed. Forty years ago, in a Catholic family, if a girl of seventeen wanted to have a love affair and her father said no, she would probably yield to his authority; today, if thwarted, she simply leaves home.

In the post-war years couples were marrying younger than before 1939, and marriage was a great ideal. But since the 1970s they have been turning against it. The annual tally of marriages fell from 416,000 in 1972 to 300,000 in 1983, then to 254,000 in 1994 – a fall only partly explained by the drop in the birth rate. France today has the lowest marriage rate per head of any EU country after Sweden. The French have also been getting married later, at an average age of twenty-seven, against twenty-three in 1972; and a recent church-sponsored survey cited 60 per cent of people in their twenties 'thinking it not worth going through any marriage ceremony'. In response to this decline, the Government since the 1970s has recognized the status of *le concubinage*, and many unwed couples sign on for this: it has tax advantages, and allows rights of social welfare – while adding to the disincentive to get married! The Jospin Government in 1998–9 was seeking to extend the system (see p. 618). In 1999 the Government was also preparing a reform of family law: its principal aim would be to give children born outside marriage exactly the same rights (of succession, etc.) as those born legitimately. This change would bring France in line with other modern countries.

The feminist writer Benoîte Groult told me, 'It is just not true any more that a woman is keener than a man to settle into marital bliss. Women are now often the ones who stay out, wanting to keep free of the formal role of "housewife".' And if a couple living *en concubinage* decide to legalize their union, it is often to please their parents. Or they take the step when they start a family, or not even then. This can cause problems. I have friends in the North whose daughter went to live in the Midi: there she fell in love with a fellow student, and they got jobs locally, and had a child. They were devoted to each other, but opposed to marriage on principle. 'It's horribly embarrassing,' the girl's mother told me. 'Alain and I are quite liberal, *we* don't mind. But we can't let Jeannine come here for a visit when there's been no wedding: our own parents and family, and the neighbours, would be scandalized – this is *la province*!' Later, after much persuasion, the couple did get married, and the tiny tot aged two was somehow explained away. This was in the 1980s. Since then attitudes have softened: *la cohabitation* has become more widely accepted. But in many bourgeois milieux it is still not flaunted openly.

Divorce, too, now carries far less stigma than in the days when it was far less prevalent. According to the surveys, if a marriage is on the rocks, religious conviction or fear of scandal or family dishonour are no longer the main factors inhibiting divorce: fear of harming the children or of financial distress or loneliness rank higher. In this secular State, divorce has never been a major political issue as in Ireland or Italy. After a steady post-war rise, it was affecting one marriage in nine by 1970. Then in 1975 an easy form of dissolution by mutual consent was introduced, rather as in Britain, and this now accounts for some 55 per cent of divorces. Today one marriage in three breaks up, a lower rate than in Britain but above the EU average. One sign of the new tolerance is that the unwed mother with a child born out of wedlock has become much less of a social outcast: officially, her title is now *mère célibataire*, she can legally call herself Madame, and there are plenty of state or private agencies to help her with her problems.

Traditionally, in France the pre-marital affair was much less common than the extra-marital one. Under this code the open season would begin after marriage, and to abduct deceitfully thy neighbour's wife would be less shocking than to sleep with his unattached daughter – a topsy-turvy morality, you might think, but fully in line with the high store set on virginity. Times have since changed; and today adultery has probably grown less common, now that so few marriages are 'arranged', divorce is easier, and people have more scope for sowing their wild oats before wedlock, or they do not bother to marry. On the other hand, the growth of travel and secondary homes may have served to encourage some infidelities in the middle classes. According to a survey reported in *Elle* in 1980, of the sample of wives between twenty and fifty, three out of four admitted to adultery, and a third of these said they had done the running, quoting sexual desire as the prime motive. Nearly 25 per cent of these modern Bovarys said they were looking for an adventure out of boredom with their husband.

Despite this behind-the-scenes activity, the French have always tended to be discreet in public about their love affairs; and in some ways this continues, even in an age when unwed cohabitation is now so common. If a couple are having an affair and neither is married, then that is easily accepted: even so they should not advertise their liaison. If the affair is adulterous, there may be private gossip: but it is all treated very discreetly, especially among older people. The adulterers may or may not be criticized by friends, but wider discussion is avoided – *il y a des choses qui se font mais dont on ne parle pas*.

This is strikingly noticeable in French attitudes to their politicians or other public figures – so *very* different from what happens in Britain or America. Ministers or others may have mistresses, *c'est normal*: but a public man's private life is regarded as his own business, so long as he is discreet and does not step outside the law. He can be a homosexual, or even an arch-philanderer, and there may be jokes about it in private, but it will not be held against him in his career, nor will it be reported in the papers. True, there is a law in France protecting privacy, much stronger than in Britain: but it is not only this which deters the press from harrying politicians. Rather, the public are not pruriently fascinated (as in Britain) nor morally outraged (as in America). When in 1975 Giscard's alleged nocturnal doings began to raise eyebrows, even in the press (obliquely), it was mainly because it was thought that his work at the Élysée might be suffering. Mitterrand, too, was well known in the Paris milieu to have mistresses, but it was hardly ever reported openly; only just before his death was it revealed that he had an illegimate child, whom he saw often and loved, and people were little concerned. It was not his sex life that made him so widely unpopular towards the end of his reign. Compare this with the British tabloids' ritual murder of so many political careers, or Americans' shock at the alleged behaviour of their President. The French, you could say, are more adult about these matters, less ready to destroy a gifted and valuable politician because of some irrelevant peccadillo. True, some French people *are* interested, like others, in the private doings of film stars, notably foreign ones, and of foreign royalty, and these will be featured in the popular press. Even so, if many paparazzi in Paris were following one princess one fatal night, it was quite largely to sell her photos outside France (it was the appalling *Bild Zeitung* that printed the picture of her dying in the car). Even the divorce cases of well-known people usually take place privately in France, and are seldom reported in the press (again, royalty and film stars excepted).

Civilized delicacy, yes, even if it includes an element of hypocrisy. But at least the climate of secrecy may help to keep the romantic temperature running high, with the titillation of *fruits défendus*. Even with the new sexual equality and freedom, a woman should not be brash or assertive, or she will not be found attractive; she must use guile to achieve her sexual ends, and what she still treasures above all is male appreciation of her femininity. It could even be said that the French have the ideal balance between old-style female subservience and the American-Nordic downgrading of the prized *petite différence*. Many women at least think so. An English woman who has lived and worked for years in France told me, 'In England, if you work in an office with men, they either treat you as silly, or if you're good at your job, they forget you're a woman. In France, they manage to treat your work seriously *and* flatter you as an attractive woman, and I prefer that.' A mature *Parisienne*, back in Paris after some years in London, said, 'One feels much more a *woman* in France. Men aren't frightened of you, they gently pester you, and that's nice. There's a subtle courtly aspect.' In short, Frenchmen may flirt, but they seldom pinch bottoms like Italians. In 1992, in line with new directives from Brussels, the Socialists dutifully passed a law against sexual harassment in the workplace by either sex. The French were surprised: few had regarded normal flirtation as harassment. Since then, far fewer complaints on the subject have come to court than in most countries: it has simply not been a big issue as in America. *Vive le sexisme!*

The Frenchman's delight in female company gives to relations a romantic tenderness and intimacy not always equalled in countries with an older record of emancipation. He may often be a sexual egotist: but in part to flatter his own vanity, he is sensitively concerned to see that his woman, too, is fulfilled, and *donner le plaisir* can be for him as crucial a part of love-making as his own fulfilment. Hence his reputation as a good lover, apparently justified. But there can be drawbacks to this idyll between the sexes. Men are often less prepared than in Anglo-Saxon countries to treat women just as friends; and some women, unlike those I quoted above, regret this lack of easy-going camaraderie. A close friendship may well not develop without ceasing to be platonic or else giving rise to gossip. A woman who knows both Paris and London told me, 'In London, if a man takes me out to dinner, I know I can then ask him to coffee in my flat out of politeness, and it needn't mean any more. A Frenchman will usually take it as *une invitation*.'

French women today are torn. They may regard a suave pass as rightful *hommage* and prefer this to English stiffness. But in social and work life they also want the advantages of an Anglo–Saxon style of equality. In the workplace, in politics, in the professions, they have progressed: but not all the new laws on equal work are well applied. This is where women's efforts now go, and they have to fight hard. Is mystery and romance to be lost in the process? Dr Simon, expert and optimist, told me he thinks not: 'Teenage girls may have given up chastity for a more male attitude to sex, but when they emerge from it they are still hugely feminine. The roses and moonshine of romance are still potent in the new France, and that gives poetry to life. Sexual freedom does not destroy it.' So the modern French girl wants her own kind of freedom. She detests the penis-envying extremists, she does not want to be an amazon in the Crusades. She still wants to be serenaded by her troubadour, but not kicked around by him – either in the office, or in the bedroom, where other battles for modern freedom have now been won.

FROM ABORTION REFORM TO 'GAY LIB' AND THE FIGHT AGAINST AIDS

Today in the case of AIDS, as yesterday over birth control, the French are reticent about treating sexual matters as public issues. Perhaps it is not surprising, in a country with a strong Catholic tradition. So, amid some hypocrisy, the law and outward opinion often lag behind the reality of what people think and do privately. Yet the changes in recent decades have been remarkable. The legalization of abortion came in 1975, not unduly late for a Catholic country: it was a year ahead of West Germany, and only two years behind 'liberal' Denmark. What is more surprising is that not until 1967 was there repeal of the archaic law of 1920 banning all contraception. Until about 1960 birth control was almost as taboo a subject as in Franco's Spain, and it seemed that nowhere did the Frenchwoman suffer from social pressure so much as in her intimate privacy. Then, finally, the campaign of a few pioneers forced the issue into the open, and a belated revolution followed, amid national controversy.

The aim of the 1920 law was not so much religious as demographic: to repair the human losses of the Great War. It prohibited all publicity for birth control and all sale of contraceptives except for some medical purposes. And it caused endless hardship and frustration, notably to poorer people who could not afford visits to gynaecologists abroad. Decades after the invention of the diaphragm, most couples still resorted to the time-honoured methods of *coitus interruptus*, vaginal douches or periodic abstinence, or they turned to clandestine abortion: deaths from clumsy self-abortion ran to thousands a year. Abortion was legal only when the mother's life was in danger, and most doctors interpreted this severely. A few rich and informed women would avoid these problems by visits to private doctors in London, Morocco or Geneva – '*Elle va en Suisse*' was a stock whispered joke at Paris salons. But millions of working wives, faced with the horrors of raising a large family under French housing conditions, came to regard sex with panic and greeted the menopause with relief. So the sex life of the romantic French was often far from a paradise: but few writers dared say so.

In 1956 a courageous young woman doctor, Marie-Andrée Weill-Hallé, was the first to declare war on the 1920 law by founding the Mouvement Français pour le Planning Familial: its first advisory clinic opened in 1961, and soon there were 200 all over France. They were illegal: but the Government turned a blind eye, not wanting a showdown with liberal opinion that could make it look ridiculous. But the MFPF, in order not to flout the law too openly, had to resort to bizarre subterfuge. When a woman visited a clinic, she was put in touch with one of the 1,500 or so French doctors who agreed to work with the movement, and he would probably fit her with a diaphragm. But the sale or import of these was illegal. So, by an arrangement with the international movement, the woman sent a 10-franc postal order and her prescription to a clinic in London, which then posted her the cap in a plain envelope. Dr Pierre Simon told me, 'Whenever I went to London, I would bring back dozens in a suitcase for my patients. Once it was inspected by the customs at Orly, and they dropped out all over the floor. The women near me giggled in sympathy. Then the officer laughed, too, and told me to clear out quick or he'd get into trouble.' This was civilized France in the 1960s.

Another example of official hypocrisy: male condoms, on the pretext that they limited syphilis, had long been on sale in chemists' shops, and even the pill began to be available on prescription in the mid-1960s, for preventing various obscure diseases. The Ministry of Health would privately encourage the MFPF. Hypocrisy was at least better than repression, and some people argued that so cleverly had the law been turned by usage that it scarcely needed reforming. But this was not so. Not only did the law add to the hesitance of doctors, but the MFPF could not publicize its clinics. It had to rely on the bush telegraph, mainly in bourgeois circles: and class barriers and female reticence to talk about sex were such that most working-class women never knew of their local clinic. The movement was a rare example in France of effective unofficial civic action on a national scale: but it had to rely on unpaid voluntary staff.

Reform had originally been blocked by Catholic opinion. But the 1960s saw a steady change of heart among rank-and-file Catholics, both laity and priests. Some younger ones even began to advise their faithful on how to seek birth-control advice, while many of the MFPF's own leaders were practising Catholics. But the Vatican, and Madame de Gaulle herself, that *éminence grise*, remained firmly against reform, while the rest of Catholic opinion was divided: so the Government remained wary. But by the mid-1960s the outward conspiracy of silence was shattered, as a crescendo of debate about birth control arose in the press, in polemical articles by feminists in magazines such as *Elle*, and even sometimes on state TV. By now demographers were openly voicing doubts as to whether the 1920 law still had any relevance to keeping up the birth rate. And in face of this tide of public opinion, the Government finally caved in, allowing a progressive-minded Gaullist deputy, Lucien Neuwirth, to put forward his own reform bill, which went through Parliament in 1967.

A few ministers then tried to sabotage the reform by refusing their signatures on its decrees: thus the sale of the coil was held up for five years. Most doctors, too, were at first hostile: twice in the mid-1960s the Conseil de l'Ordre des Médecins, the supreme medical body, had voted that contraceptive advice was none of a doctor's business; and only 4 per cent of doctors in this cautious profession had ever helped the MFPF. But after the new law came into force, young doctors at last took the trouble to learn about modern birth control; and today only about 5 per cent of GPs, mostly older Catholics, refuse to collaborate.

More surprising was the initial reluctance of women to take advantage of their new freedom. Old-style anti-sex Catholicism was by now in retreat, but it had left a legacy of semi-conscious guilt and prudery, even among women calling themselves atheist. Dr Weill-Hallé told me, 'If for so long we lagged behind Britain in family planning, the reasons were less legal or moral than psychological. The first task of our staff at the clinics was often to *déculpabiliser* a new client, to rid her of her complexes about coming to see us.' In those days a woman who ventured to try out a clinic, and was pleased, might still be unlikely to recommend it to her friends: it was as if she had discovered some secret opium den, a source of guilty delight. It illustrated, once again, the lack of club-like solidarity among French women, or else reform might have come sooner. The prejudices were slowest to disappear in the working class, in part, it seems, for political reasons: officially, the Communist Party had long been opposed to birth control as a capitalist trick to reduce the numbers of the proletariat. The MFPF, a bourgeois-led venture, was suspected of being some stratagem of the Patronat. But then the PCF, in part for electoral reasons, swung in favour of contraception, as of abortion, and this helped towards a steady change in working-class attitudes.

Over the past thirty years the old reticences have steadily waned. In 1968, just after the Neuwirth law was passed, less than 4 per cent of women aged between fifteen and forty-nine were using the pill, and a mere handful the coil. But the numbers have since climbed, and today 32 per cent of women in this bracket use the pill and 19 per cent the coil, while others prefer the man to use a condom. In fact, if exception is made of the infertile, the abstinent, the pregnant or those trying to become so, surveys show that today only 3 per cent of women use no form of birth control: France is now on the same level here as other advanced countries. Contraception is easily available, and publicity for it is no longer banned. The pill rightly requires a doctor's prescription, but not parental approval even for young teenagers. Most contraceptives can be obtained at little cost on the health service, for married and unmarried alike.

There are still some problems. Many teenagers feel that information about birth control remains inadequate: they blame the health service, the media, their parents and above all their teachers. Sex education in schools was not made compulsory until 1976; and although it has been extended since the rise of AIDS (see below), it is taught mainly during biology classes, and many teachers still shy away from it. A 1993 poll for a teenage magazine indicated that most girls found out about sex from friends or magazines, or from their mothers – and only 20 per cent from their teachers. But although plenty of modern mothers now take their teenagers to the family doctor ('Please put her on the pill before she gets into trouble'), in many families the subject remains taboo between parents and children. Some parents, glad to have contraception for themselves, resent it for having made sex too easy for their very young daughters.

In sum, the birth-control revolution has provided a good example of how the French, after a painful tussle with their own traditions, have finally adjusted to modern reality – in some social and economic areas, if not in all. The drama is typical of how change takes place. First an intolerable situation is allowed to build up, without anyone taking action. Then a handful of pioneers set to work, and progress slowly follows, haphazard, empirical, usually resisted by the strong social forces always at work to protect the harmony of the status quo. Then, finally, legal or structural reform is sanctioned, partly to regularize changes that have already taken place.

Much the same happened later in the case of abortion, where in the early 1970s French legislation was on much the same repressive level as in Germany or Italy. Clandestine abortions were estimated at some 500,000 a year, many clumsily performed: only a minority of women, some 30,000, had the funds or know-how to go to that new Mecca of abortion, Great Britain. As with birth control, the Government for years was scared of legalizing abortion for various reasons: not only was opposition from the bishops and old-style Catholics far stronger in this case, but there was a clear hostile majority among the pro-Government parties in Parliament, and within the Ordre des Médecins.

Public opinion, however, was more advanced, and in 1972 the notorious 'Bobigny affair' helped to mobilize this behind the growing campaign for reform. A girl of sixteen in this Paris suburb was prosecuted for having an abortion as a result of rape. She was brilliantly defended by the well-known radical lawyer Gisèle Halimi, who tiraded in court against the cruelty of the law. Then Giscard, once in power, urged his Health Minister, Simone Veil, to prepare a reform bill with all speed, which she eagerly did. Polls were now showing 73 per cent of the French (and far more women than men) in favour of reform. But there was also an active 'pro-life' lobby, Laissez-les Vivre, which denounced Mme Veil as an 'assassin', while most centre-Right deputies were hostile, too, on religious or demographic grounds (the birth rate was falling). But Giscard was determined to go ahead, even if it meant splitting his coalition – which it did. In November 1974, on a free vote, two-thirds of the Gaullists and Giscardians opposed the reform, which was passed thanks only to the backing of the Socialists and Communists!

This law, virtually unchanged since then, gives married or single women the right to claim an abortion within the first ten weeks of pregnancy; after this, it can take place only if there is judged to be grave risk to the health of the mother or child, verified by two specialists. There are some other restrictions: the woman must be interviewed by a psychiatrist to establish that the abortion is desirable; and minors, under eighteen, must obtain parental consent. Abortions at first were not free: but in 1983 the Socialist Government brought them within the social security system, which now reimburses 70 per cent of the cost.

The application of the law has had its setbacks, inevitably, but mostly it has been effective. Since the mid-1980s the number of legal abortions has been running at about 180,000 a year; some 60 per cent of the women are unmarried. Fewer now go abroad, and the estimated total of illegal (i.e. non-registered) abortions has also dropped sharply: self-abortion was decriminalized in 1993. The spread of contraception has certainly helped to reduce the number of unwanted pregnancies. But there are still problems, due in part to shortages of hospital facilities, and to the fact that many doctors and nurses will not cooperate: they have the right to invoke a conscience clause. A hospital director can forbid abortions on his premises: so, in a few cases, liberal doctors have built small hut-like clinics in the grounds outside – 'like the segregation of lepers in the Middle Ages', the very liberal Dr Simon said to me. The Laissez-les Vivre movement remains active, and sometimes its commandos will try to chain themselves to hospital beds or otherwise prevent abortions: this is illegal, and in a few cases its militants have been prosecuted and given prison sentences. The movement has also taken to the courts its plea that the Veil law is contrary to international conventions on the rights of man and of children: but in 1996 the supreme French tribunal, the Cour de Cassation, rejected this argument. In sum, Laissez-les Vivre is far less large and powerful than its American equivalents, and its campaign has had no great effect on the application of the Veil law.

More damaging to the law, oddly enough, have been attitudes within parts of the health service. Many public hospitals, under pressure from senior Catholic doctors or others, still fail to grant adequate funding or equipment to their abortion clinics, which have to struggle along with small, underpaid staff. Some hospital chiefs claim that they lack the resources for what they see as an unnecessary operation since it does not cure sickness. Some will accept only single teenagers, or mothers aged forty with several children: but this is against the spirit of the law, which gives all women the right. Some doctors find excuses for delaying the abortion beyond the ten-week limit, after which a woman may have to go to Britain where the limit is eighteen weeks. Matters are easiest in Paris or other big cities, where a woman can usually find a state hospital ready to help: but in smaller towns it can be harder. Many women are thus obliged to turn to the expensive private clinics. But despite these drawbacks, matters have been slowly improving. The Ordre des Médecins has given up its formal opposition to abortion, and most younger doctors are now ready to help. In 1997 the new Socialist Government pledged itself to see that the law is better applied. 'The main advance,' Dr Simon told me, 'is that our legislation is now on the same civilized level as in Britain or America.'

In the fight against AIDS, the French at first made a slow start – once again! – but are now as actively vigilant as most Western nations. One of the first world scientists to identify the virus, in 1983, was a Frenchman, Professor Montagnier at the Institut Pasteur (he studied its effects on African monkeys): but then, as so often, France was slow to apply the research. The Ministry of Health and the welfare associations failed to take AIDS very seriously, thinking it was just a matter between gays, and for them to sort out: not until 1987 was the old ban lifted on the advertising of condoms. But then, as the numbers of known sufferers grew rapidly, so the ministry swung into action, and during the 1990s it has staged various publicity campaigns with large posters, some showing explicitly how to have sex safely. In 1996 the French bishops boldly broke rank with Vatican policy, declaring that condoms could be necessary for limiting AIDS; and today some bishops collaborate with the ministry. Catholic-run schools still do not. But many state *lycées* have now installed condom machines, while state schools have increased their teaching on the subject. In 1994, as Minister of Health, Philippe Douste-Blazy launched a campaign for shops, clinics and slot machines to sell condoms for 1 franc each or less – 'We wanted to break the old taboo against them, a hangover from the days of the 1920 law,' I was told.

It is hard to assess the impact of these and other measures. Certainly, the public young and old, gay and hetero, has become more alert to the dangers, while AIDS sufferers are less likely to be treated as guilty pariahs than ten years ago; a few feature films dealing sympathetically with their plight, such as *N'oublie pas que tu vas mourir*, have been successful. At the same time, as in the USA and elsewhere, the incidence of AIDS has decreased recently, due alike to better precautions and the new methods of treatment. AIDS-related deaths, an estimated 35,000 since 1985, fell from 5,035 in 1995 to 3,043 in 1996. Some 110,000 people are reckoned to be HIV-positive, and France here is on an average level in Europe. It has proportionately more AIDS sufferers than northerly countries such as Britain, but fewer than Italy, Spain or Switzerland. Some 25 per cent of victims are reckoned to be drug addicts, while 27 per cent have contracted the disease heterosexually and 40 per cent homosexually.

Public attitudes to homosexuality have been changing, too, as a subject long taboo has come to be discussed more openly. Homosexual practice was never criminalized as in Britain, whose persecution of Oscar Wilde was thought barbaric by the Paris literary world. Gays in France were tolerated, so long as they behaved discreetly; and the issue was simply ignored publicly, rather as with birth control. Several of the greatest writers of this century were homosexual – Proust, Gide, Cocteau, Colette and Genet. This did little harm to their literary reputations: but some of them felt ill at ease in society, and sometimes their writings reflected a sense of guilt. Proust felt the need to transmute his homosexual feelings into heterosexual love in his autobiographical novel: but Gide and especially Genet truly 'came out', and wrote much more directly.

More recently, many other gays have also been coming out, under the impact of May '68, of American trends and of AIDS; and various 'gay lib' movements have been formed. Lesbian and Gay Pride rallies have brought militant crowds into the centres of French cities: in June 1997, amid music, dance and carnival floats, some 300,000 European gays held their annual Europride parade in Paris, and they marched symbolically to the Bastille itself, to demand full equality of rights. Such public activity has provoked some counter-reactions from people whose hatred of homosexuality had stayed dormant in the years when the matter was not aired openly: a poll in 1996 found 46 per cent of the sample 'rather shocked' by the Gay Pride rallies. However, other recent polls show that young people especially have been growing far readier to accept homosexuality: those seeing it as 'just one way of expressing one's sexuality' rose from 29 to 67 per cent between 1979 and 1996. Today homosexual couples can lead much more open lives than even a generation ago. In a commuter village near Paris, I have friends whose neighbours are a charming gay couple, and they are accepted socially even by local Catholics: 'Thirty years ago,' I was told, 'they would not have dared to live together openly; they would have had separate homes and would have met secretly.' There are senior French ambassadors, civil servants, politicians, even teachers, who are known as gay in their own circles, and it does not affect their careers. But they need to be discreet. And more rarely than in Britain or America will well-known figures admit in public to being gay, for instance on television. It is the same concern for privacy that covers other aspects of sex life in France.

Gays who want improved legal rights have been making some progress, but uncertainly. During the 1990s a few town councils, mostly Socialist-led, agreed to deliver a formal 'certificate of *concubinage*' to homosexuals living as a couple. This has no legal validity and carries only minor practical advantages: but it was hailed by gay rights groups as a useful symbolic step. Then in 1997 the new Minister of Justice, Elisabeth Guigou, announced that the Government would propose a special legal statute for unwed couples, homo- or heterosexual, and a bill was prepared. This proposed new '*pacte civil de solidarité*' (PACS) would carry some tax advantages and rights of inheritance; and it would grant official recognition to an unwed couple, for it would be signed in the *mairie*, like marriage. But it would be much easier to annul later on, and contain no commitment to fidelity. 'Today,' said Guigou, 'the union between two people cannot be limited to the sole institution of marriage.' In a legalistic country this was quite a step, and gay rights bodies were pleased.

However, when the PACS came before the National Assembly in October 1998, it ran into heavy trouble and sparked off quite a national crisis. The Right voted against it, while many Socialist deputies voted with their feet by deliberately keeping away from the debate in the chamber – so the bill was defeated. Some of them, who were also mayors, voiced their alarm at having to solemnize a PACS between gays in their own town hall – might it not antagonize many of their electors? Other critics argued that the project would marginalize marriage still further: 'The instability of the modern couple would have become consecrated by law,' said one. So Jospin and Guigou were left to prepare a new text that might be more acceptable within their own ranks, and they planned to present this later in 1999. In October it was finally passed by the National Assembly, though the Right again voted against. The whole affair showed that conservative reticence about homosexuality is still quite strong in France, in all classes – even if public attitudes to sexuality have come a long way since the 1960s, when the simplest contraceptive was still illegal.

SPENDING FOR CONSOLATION — AND *LE WEEKEND* IN A
RURAL DREAM NEST, OR *CHEZ* DISNEY

The giant post-war rise in affluence and living standards has benefited nearly all French people in all classes, save for a minority of the very poor (as we have seen). As in other countries, the consumer revolution first gathered pace in the 1960s, as a new generation acquired a craze for *les objets* and *la civilisation des gadgets* – cleverly satirised in Georges Perec's novel *Les Choses* (1965). 'They possessed, alas, but a single passion, for a higher standard of living, and it exhausted them,' Perec wrote of a young couple seduced by the new consumer boom. In all kinds of ways, higher incomes plus technological advance brought big changes in the traditional leisure and spending habits of the French, as cars, television, seaside holidays and other new 'privileges' altered the lives of working families.

During the past two decades, save for a slight fall in the early 1990s, consumer spending has gone on increasing, if at a slower rate than in the boom years. But sociologists have noted a shift in the pattern, in this new anxious age, towards more of what is described as 'reassurance consumption'. Spending of all kinds on organic and other health foods, on sport and fitness, has increased considerably; also on traditional local goods (e.g. the knives of Laguiole), rustic furniture and artefacts, local quality farm produce and old country dishes. In short, many people are turning nostalgically to the past, and to the *terroir*, for objects that seem to offer some concrete solace in a time of uncertainty; and they are as much concerned about health as hedonistic pleasure – new, for France. Experts say the trends are most marked among older people, while younger ones may seek a kind of escape in the exotic – ethnic foods and restaurants, holidays in odd far-off places. At the same time, there is less ostentatious luxury, less even of that middle-class penchant for status symbols to 'keep up with the Duponts', so prevalent in the boom years. In their new more worried mood, the French are maybe making less effort to impress each other in these ways.

Anyway, most families have now completed the process of equipping themselves with 'basic' goods such as cars, television, household electric appliances, modern bathrooms. The figures in Table 1 (sources EU and INSEE) show the dramatic advances made (and see p. 200 for the belated increase in bathrooms, p. 87 for that of telephones). In Table 2 the figures show strikingly that, except for dishwashers, working-class families today possess almost as much modern equipment as the bourgeoisie.

Table 1

	France				Other countries (1990)		
Percentage of homes equipped with:	1954	1970	1985	1994	UK	W. Germany	Italy
Passenger car	21	56	73	78	66	68	75
Refrigerator	7	79	97	98	98	99	96
Deep-freeze	0	0	35	45	51	?	?
Dishwasher	0	2	23	33	10	28	19
Washing machine	8	55	83	89	88	85	92
TV (any kind)	1	69	92	94	98	106	95
TV (colour)	0	0	69	91	91	87	?

Table 2

	Social categories in France (1994)						
Percentage of homes equipped with:	managers *patrons*	liberal professions senior *cadres*	junior executives	office employees	farmers	manual workers	inactive
Passenger car	95	96	93	80	95	89	59
Refrigerator	99	99	99	99	99	99	98
Deep-freeze	60	44	44	37	84	52	40
Washing machine	95	94	92	87	96	93	84
Dishwasher	58	62	44	32	50	30	22
Television	95	92	91	92	96	96	95
Telephone	97	98	97	96	97	94	94

In the make-up of the average family budget, the most striking change is that today food and drink at home account for only 18 per cent of the total, compared with 21 per cent ten years ago, 38 per cent in 1959 and 50 per cent before the war! To this must be added some 3.5 per cent for eating and drinking in cafés and restaurants: even so, according to the experts, the French now spend the same proportion of their income on food and drink as the British (21.5 per cent), and a higher proportion on housing (28 per cent, against 19 per cent) – a correction to established ideas about the French stress on food, British stress on home. The budget sector described by the statisticians as 'housing', which includes furniture, equipment and mortgages, has been rising steadily and is now higher than in Germany. The 'health and hygiene' sector has increased slightly, too, from 5.9 to 6.3 per cent since 1950; spending on transport, travel and telephones has risen more sharply in the same period, from 5.4 to 12.8 per cent, more than tripling in real value. In other words, the French have become cleaner and far more diet-conscious; they are now spending much more on cars, sport, holidays and culture but less, in relative terms, on restaurants and cafés. So the dry statistics confirm that French spending habits have been drawn closer to the British or American models, first by affluence, now by anxiety and ecological concern. *Le bricolage* (do-it-yourself jobbery), which used to interest the French little, has become a major pastime, linked to the middle-class vogue for weekend secondary homes. Outside many towns you now see big garden centres, doing a busy trade. And in bourgeois suburbs, a husband no longer considers it undignified for the neighbours to see him mowing his lawn or painting his front door at the weekend.

One notable aspect of the new French concern for home and comfort has been the steady growth in the number of domestic pets owned by non-farmers. Here the French are now top in Europe: with 15.7 million dogs and cats, they have pushed ahead even of the British (14 million). This trend surely relates to the new stress on 'reassurance consumption': a pet is a comforting part of an unchanging natural world that does not turn nasty like politicians or employers; and, as psychologists point out, now that adolescents claim their freedom earlier, the pet can become a substitute child, with the added advantage that you don't have to worry about its career, and you can talk to it without quarrelling. It is true that the French peasantry have frequently been cruel to animals, and today in rural areas one still hears sad reports from holiday-home owners of how their beloved dog or cat has been maltreated by some nearby farmer. But most other French, led by Colette, have been full of love for their own pets. Dogs (7.6 million) have now come to be outnumbered by cats (8.1 million, against 6 million ten years ago) which are easier to look after in flats. According to the sociologist François Héran, dogs are preferred by tradesmen, police and soldiers, and cats by artists, teachers and intellectuals (I cannot but cheer, as the honoured London flatmate of two stunning Burmese, and no dogs). Another 9 million pets are caged birds. The French today spend 20 billion francs a year on pet foods, whose production has risen over fifteenfold since 1965; and the number of veterinary clinics in the Paris region has tripled in twenty years. Some child protection agencies complain that too many parents treat their pets better than their children.

Another animal, the horse, also plays a growing role in French leisure life – in a different sense. Betting on horses, known as *le tiercé* (three-horse bet), though less of an obsession than in Britain, has developed greatly to reach a turnover of 26 francs a week per head. The letters 'PMU' outside a café means that it houses one of the 300 branches of the Pari Mutuel Urbain, the semi-public body that controls all betting in France.

In some respects the French seem not quite sure how to deal with their new domestic affluence. Many sophisticated couples with a smart modern flat show a bias against filling it with modern furniture, and go out of their way to install antiques, real or 'repro', sometimes with odd results. They will scour second-hand shops for good country pieces, especially in regions such as Brittany where the old rustic furniture can be of fine quality. Pierre-Jakez Hélias, in his famous account of his Breton childhood, *Le Cheval d'orgueil* (1975), tells of the fate of the old Breton box-beds, two-tier cupboards where several of the family used to sleep together:

Ah, those *lits clos*, what a good buy! I have found some that have been converted into a coat cupboard in the hall, a bookshelf in the study, a buffet or drinks cupboard in the living room, a music-box combining pick-up, radio and television. I have even seen one that functions as a toilet, to the great satisfaction of its users.

Modern designs, readily accepted in office or restaurant, were long regarded by older French people as cold or unfriendly in the home. This bias has now declined, and many well-to-do families have new flats elegantly furnished in a modern manner, often with Scandinavian influences. But many French are still drawn strongly to their classic tradition, to those spindly straight-backed Louis XV chairs and formal settees that decorate so many bourgeois salons. The French have little equivalent of the comfy vulgarity of the English pre-war style: their taste is either for the classic and antique or the ultra-new. In interior décor, trendy designers such as Philippe Starck have been making a mark. Parisian décor is often at its best when using glittering surfaces of glass and metal to achieve dazzling effects of elegance and lightness.

In the important domain of clothes and fashion, affluence has brought an increase in the level of public taste. In the upper bracket of haute couture, Paris in the 1970s was losing out to New York and Milan as a world fashion centre. But since the 1980s it has recovered ground; and although very few new front-rank French designers have yet emerged, Paris is again a focus for foreign talent, a place where you go to make a reputation. Karl Lagerfeld from Hamburg and Kenzo from Japan have long used it as their base: they have now been followed by other Japanese, by leading British designers such as John Galliano (at Dior), and some brilliant Belgians from Antwerp. The city's revival has even been helped by official patronage: Jack Lang as Minister of Culture put money into sponsoring couture and created a Museum of the Arts of Fashion in the Louvre. At a wider public level, many of the new fashions have for years now been quickly copied and mass-produced by the big stores such as Printemps, at prices within the reach of secretaries and factory workers; and since the war magazines such as *Elle* and *Marie-Claire* have been drumming notions of elegance into the heads of ordinary women who never had any special claim to be well dressed. The average woman dresses with more chic than in former days. Could it even be true that since French women, in my view, tend to be less beautiful than, say, Scandinavians or Italians, they try all the harder with clothes and cosmetics, to make up for what nature has failed to provide?

These and a few similar magazines can also take some of the credit for improvements in housekeeping skills and in hygiene. In the old days, the French took baths seldom, even in well-to-do homes, and French women were among northern Europe's dirtiest and smelliest, according to all the evidence. *Marie-Claire* in the 1930s took the lead in a campaign to get them to wash more; then other papers joined in, the public responded, and the post-war rise in the sales of soap, deodorants and toothpaste was phenomenal. If the provision of bathrooms in the new flats has been one factor in the new cleanliness, the women's magazines can claim a share in the triumph. Marcelle Auclair, founder of *Marie-Claire*, told me, 'French girls used to disguise their dirt with powder and make-up. Now they wash and clean their teeth properly. Haven't you noticed how the Métro now stinks less?'

So the French spend more time on washing and hygiene, less time on eating. The leisurely two-hour family lunch, even on weekdays, is one

French tradition that has sharply declined in the past forty years, under the *force majeure* of suburban commuting and economic change. Lunch used to be the main meal of the day, with children coming home from school and husbands from work – and so it still is, in many smaller towns and rural areas. But the cities have seen changes. Until the 1950s even Paris went dead from midday till two: the banks and big stores closed. But then, as the drift to the suburbs grew, Parisians came to accept that the lunch-break must be made more flexible. A growing number of employees faced the invidious choice between a long trek home in defiance of sense, or else a cheap lunch near their work (if they could find one), followed by an hour or so killing time. Some managers, too, with their new American business ethos, came to realize what a drag the long break could be on a modern economy. So a few firms began to introduce a uniform one-hour lunch for junior staff, with earlier evening closing. This was mostly popular: but many firms delayed the change: it was opposed by staff who did live close, and staggering of hours to suit both parties was not feasible. 'The change has upset my family life,' said one saleswoman; 'I used to get home to cook a big hot lunch for my husband and children, who go to school nearby, and we'd have a cold meal at night. Now I have to eat in the canteen, the *femme de ménage* cooks my family their lunch, and I make myself a hot meal at night. Terrible.' But change has finally been accepted, and in greater Paris the percentage of employees going home for lunch has dropped from 60 to 15 since 1958. Most factories and many larger offices have opened canteens. Most central shops remain open, though not all; and only executives now take long business lunches (or use them as an alibi).

In the provinces, too, most larger or newer factories now have short lunch-breaks, canteens and earlier closing, and staff for the most part approve. But in other respects the provinces have moved more slowly than Paris – notably in the Midi, so close to Spain and its siestas. In larger towns only recently have hypermarkets and some banks begun to stay open; in small ones it can still be hard at lunchtime to find a shop or post office open. After all, the long lunch can be very pleasant in one's own life, and I have spent many a boozy time with friends in the sunny Midi, at an hour when Paris is hard back at work: but the practice is irksome when everyone else is doing it, too, and you can't even buy a loaf of bread.

Lunch habits may have been changing, perforce. But even if they get home earlier, the French remain traditional about their dinner hour: in most social classes it is set for 8 p.m. or 8.30★ (hence the crucial timing of the main TV news, see pp. 491–2), and they will seldom shift it earlier so as to spend a full evening doing something else. Events such as club meetings or theatres therefore do not start till about 9 o'clock; and as many people have to get up early for their work, most organized leisure is left for the weekend. All this may help to explain the relative lack of club-type activity in France.

Now that they are better housed, the French spend more of their evening leisure in their homes, and less on the old habit of café-going, whose share of the average leisure budget has fallen from 40 to 10 per cent since the 1950s: the total number of *bistrots*† has dropped amazingly, from 510,000 in 1910 to some 200,000 in 1960 and 70,000 today. Of course, in the centre of Paris and other cities the larger terrace-cafés and brasseries still do a brisk trade at certain hours: but they have lost much of their old importance as centres of social life and gossip. Some cafés have therefore been trying to diversify. Many now serve light lunches for office workers. Some have introduced jukeboxes and pin-tables (known as *le baby-foot*) and so fill themselves with noisy youth, at the risk of driving away staider clients. Others, in parts of the Midi, are venues for games of boules or *pétanque*. Some in poorer areas have installed TV for clients who still lack a set or want to get away from home. Here the men sit hushed all evening in the semi-dark – what a change from the old days of public chatter!

While lunches and evening café-going have declined, *le weekend* has grown in importance. This used not to be a French concept, hence they have no word for it and have borrowed ours. And their whole stress in recent years has been less on securing shorter daily working hours than on longer weekends and holidays. Not only do they take the longest holidays in Europe (see below), but the number of official *jours fériés* (14 July, 1 May, 1 and 11 November, and the rest) accounts for a further ten days a year. And whenever one of these falls on a Thursday or

★ In their meal-times, however, the French are not as extreme as some. Lunch in Spain is often taken later than supper in northern England – what price European unity?

† In English this Russian word, without its final 't', is taken to mean a small French-type restaurant. In France it is more correctly used to mean a little café selling wines and often, but not always, some simple food. Today, with its final 't', it is also sometimes used as in Britain to mean a small trendy restaurant.

Tuesday, many a *cadre* will *faire le pont* by taking the Friday or Monday off as well, to give himself four free days in a row. Yet this does not mean that the French fail to work hard, merely that they work differently. Executives and professional people will often stay in their offices from 9 a.m. till 7 or 8 at night, but take five or six weeks' holiday a year. However, some changes in recent years have affected all social classes. First came the growth of the weekend, with the ending of Saturday work in offices and factories. This was followed by the shortening of the long lunch-break. And today employees and unions have been pressing for a shorter working week. But even if the 35-hour week (see pp. 184–5) is enforced, it may have less impact on the habits of senior *cadres* and self-employed professional people. Maybe they will go on killing themselves with a 60- or 70-hour week.

Le weekend has become a sacred social institution in the past thirty years. Not until 1966 did Paris ministerial offices give up Saturday morning work in favour of longer daily hours: then nearly all factories began to close on Saturday. Today shops remain open all that day, but many close on Monday instead, for the five-day week is now seen as a universal right. The middle classes go away for the weekend far more than they used to, and some workers do so, too. The trend might have started sooner, were it not that the French have long inflicted on themselves the illogicality of state schools staying open on Saturday but closing on Wednesdays. Pedagogic reasons were given (children were said to need a midweek break from study); and many parents were also in favour, maybe glad to have *les gosses* out of the way on their own free Saturday. But recent reforms, while keeping the Wednesday break, have lightened the burden of classwork by allowing junior schools to close all Saturday and *lycées* to end at noon. This has all added to the craze for the weekend getaway.

You have only to stand beside one of the main roads out of Paris at 7 p.m. on a summer Friday, to see its extent. Even back in 1958, at the height of the crisis that brought back de Gaulle, the sight of that army of cars, piled high with suitcases and children, misled a British reporter to write a scare story about the threat of civil war: 'Mass flight from Paris begins' ran his headline. Today, as in 1958, it is not the threat of paratroops from Algiers but the strains of daily city life that incite so many people to make for the weekend quiet of the country; and as likely as not, they will go neither to a hotel nor to friends or relatives, but to their own cottage or villa. The *résidence secondaire* has become something of a cult among middle-class Parisians and other city dwellers. Many are old farmsteads, left empty by the rural exodus and now sold to bourgeois owners who smarten them up. Others are new villas for the well-to-do, or seaside flats. With some 2.5 million of these secondary homes, France holds the world record outside Scandinavia: one family in ten owns one, against one in fifteen in the United States, one in 200 in Britain (but one in five in Norway). In the Yonne *département*, not far from Paris, 20 per cent of all housing is in this class. From Paris, from Lyon and other cities, people will drive hundreds of kilometres each weekend, arriving back late on Sunday, exhausted from crawling through the traffic jams of similar migrants – the price they pay for their dream nest. It ties in with the recent trends of ecological back-to-nature and the hedonistic or spiritual search for privacy. It can also be a shrewd investment. It is true that in the recession of the early 1990s some owners tried to sell and the market slumped: but today prices have recovered, and many a rural ruin may have increased its value tenfold over twenty years.

One popular new form of leisure, for a weekend or other break, is a visit to a theme or leisure park. The United States has 1,800 and France just a few scores, which are often ephemeral. Most have arrived since the mid-1980s: ten are theme parks, the rest are zoos or aquatic centres. One of the most original and successful is Futuroscope, outside Poitiers, which opened in 1987 and now draws about 3 million visitors a year. This large theme park comprises a number of startling futuristic buildings, spaciously sited: one, the Magic Carpet, looks like a titanic church organ with uneven black pipes; another, Omnimax, is a huge glass cube lying on its side; a third, Kinemax, is a curious fantasy of black jagged shapes. The guiding theme is audio-visual: some fifteen cinemas, with giant screens, circular screens or other oddities, show a variety of unusual films, some absorbingly documentary, some dramatically spectactular, even frightening. Some of the more interesting films were spoilt, I felt, by the gimmicky treatment; and the park's three diverse elements of odd-shaped buildings, bizarre screening and unusual film subject-matter do not properly fuse. But children of all ages adore the place. More traditional is Parc Astérix, north of Paris, which opened in 1989 and has 2 million visitors a year. Many of its diverse side-shows and spectacles are based on characters from the Astérix books, and it is aimed foremost at children. Like Futuroscope, it is an entirely French creation – unlike another new theme park near Paris, today by far the largest and best known in Europe.

Parturient montes, nascetur ridiculus mus . . . For this ridiculous Mouse, the mountains in labour were the French Government, a huge Hollywood company, a new town east of Paris, a 14-billion-franc budget, 5,000 construction workers (many Irish), and acres of newspaper hype. For its first park in Europe, Disney had also considered Barcelona, maybe sunnier: but Paris, near to other big cities of north-west Europe, and itself a major tourist draw, was judged to be the better venue for attracting the needed crowds. Mitterrand himself gave the go-ahead in 1985: many people thought it a curious decision for a Socialist Government which in the cultural field, under Jack Lang, had been loudly denouncing American 'imperialism' in France. Yes, but the Socialists were also aware of the new money that would come from foreign tourists and the thousands of new permanent jobs to be created locally. These arguments won the day, even though Lang opposed the project as did many French intellectuals: the theatre director Ariane Mnouchkine called it a 'cultural Chernobyl'. But the millions of French families who today go to visit Mickey, and to revel in their dream picture of a mythical America, have few such qualms. The Disneyland affair sheds fascinating light on confused French cultural reactions to America (see p. 708).

The 2,000-hectare construction site, on a wheat plain just east of Paris, outside the new town of Marne-la-Vallée, was the largest new building project in Europe after the Channel Tunnel and central Berlin. A new RER Métro line was built. But when Euro Disney (as it was then called) finally opened its gates in April 1992, visitors were much fewer than expected; and for three years the venture was in serious trouble, with debts reaching 5.3 billion francs. The 8.8 million visitors in 1994 were less than enough to break even, and at one point Disney thought of closing it down. What had gone wrong? Maybe entry prices were too high; world recession had reduced the tourist flow; and the location under grey Paris skies was perhaps a mistake after all, compared with Disneyland's sunny settings in Florida and California. Some observers even felt that the artificial transplant of a bit of American make-believe was not catching on with French and other European visitors: the culture clash was too blatant. The British press reacted with gleeful *schadenfreude*, speaking of an unholy alliance of American and French 'pride, conceit, greed and overambition' (as the *Independent* put it).

The Walt Disney Company (US) was the main owner of Euro Disney, whose senior staff were mostly French. Its dynamic new chairman and managing director, Philippe Bourguignon, launched an urgent overhaul which in 1995 began to bring results. He reduced entry prices, changed the marketing strategy, built a snazzy new 650-million-franc attraction, the Space Mountain, where visitors in astronauts' rockets were disgorged from a giant cannon. And he changed the park's name to Disneyland Paris. Thanks to all this, and to an upturn in the world economy, the park's visitors rose steadily to 12.6 million by 1997, and the debt fell. Bourguignon then moved off to become the new boss of Club Med (see below), wearing the halo of the man credited with saving Disneyland. And in 1999 the company announced that it planned to open a second leisure park on the same site in 2002. This, like Futuroscope, would be devoted to cinema and television, and would provide some 4,500 new jobs.

Today Walt Disney has reduced its own share of the equity to 39 per cent, while 24 per cent is held by a Saudi prince and the rest by banks and public. Of the visitors, some 40 per cent are French (half from the Paris region), 18 per cent are Benelux, 15 per cent German, 10 per cent British, less than 1 per cent American – and only 30 per cent are children. Of the 10,000 staff from fifty nations, some 60 per cent are French. They are carefully trained to promote the sense of fantasy: if you are dressed as Mickey or Donald Duck and are questioned by a visitor, it is a sackable offence to admit that you are really a human.

One day in 1996 I took the *autoroute* from Paris towards Metz, and nearly missed the poorly marked turning (were the local signposting authorities in league with Lang?). I reached a pretty lake beside six huge Disney-owned hotels, four with 1,000 rooms or more, all with American names (Newport Bay Club, etc.), and all on American themes. In mine, the Hotel New York, very art deco, I was mildly irked by the showcases full of Disney toys and the Seven Dwarfs muzak: but I liked the cosmopolitan crowds of excited kids. Next day, heigh-ho, it's off to reporting I go, as I passed a drab mall of fast-food stalls, then a palatial pink-pinnacled luxury hotel, to reach the park itself and its entry desks where a Dutch girl bade me '*Bonne journée*' then, noticing my accent, added, '*Have a nice day*'. I crossed the central avenue, Main Street USA, with its 1900s small-town shop-fronts and gas-lamps, to reach the park's centrepiece, a towering high-pinnacled fairytale castle, modelled on old pictures of Perrault's *Sleeping Beauty* by those clever Disney 'imagineers' in LA. Within the park I found restaurants of various kinds, some simple French, some burger-ish, one Italian with charming décor, all discreetly done, and none serving alcohol (but you can get it at the bars and hotels just outside). I explored some of the scores of shows and displays – the

Caribbean pirates, the Swiss Family treehouse, the Visionarium circular cinema, and the daily Disney Parade of 200 costumed actors (sorry, animals), headed by Mickey and Minnie in a plane. On this Saturday in February, the crowds were quite large, well behaved, absorbed.

I cannot compare this Disneyland with the ones in America and Japan, which I do not know. But I found it altogether less brash and vulgar, less Americanized, than I had expected, and I know many people who feel the same. Mickey and his troupe are not much in evidence, save for the daily parade and the ubiquitous souvenirs. The whole thing is mindless, yes, not trying to be educative like some outdoor museums or theme parks: but it is friendly fun for the family. The creators have wisely avoided the temptation to build imitations of European historic buildings, as in the Florida Disneyland, since the real ones – Loire châteaux, Bavarian castles, the Tower of London, etc. – are relatively close at hand. And although the mythology is in one sense American, based on the Disney films, these in turn were drawn largely from European stories and folk-tales – from the Grimms, Perrault, Carroll, Barrie, Verne and others. Peter Pan and Captain Cook are much in evidence, ditto Alice, while Snow White is from Grimm, Pinocchio from Italy, and prominence is given to Jules Verne. The Wild West is there, too, and Indiana Jones. But in general Disney has shown some cultural respect for its host nation and continent. Of course, people do not come wanting a Europeanized Disney, but nor do they seek the real America. What they get is the re-creation of some fantasy America, plus a European heritage: Snow White meets Buffalo Bill! For a summer price of 195 francs per adult, and 120 francs per child, it is fair value. The fears of a 'cultural Chernobyl' may have been exaggerated. And yet, it is very sad that the ancient nations which first created these fairytale fantasies have now sold out to modern American commercialism.

A NEW CHALLENGE TO THE HYPERMARKETS:
THE LITTLE SHOPS FIGHT BACK

Shopping, too, shows American influences. Nowhere was the consumer revolution of the 1960s and '70s more evident than in the retail trade, where the French – who often act by extremes – moved in one leap from the little local shop to the biggest hypermarkets in Europe. Today, on the edge of most towns, you can see these vast emporia, brashly seductive with lights and bargain offers, as ready to sell you a motor-mower or off-the-peg suit as a packet of frozen snails or a bottle of malt whisky, and offering a range of fruit and vegetables as fresh and varied as in the street markets. These efficient stores have marked a dramatic change in mentalities, alike among French retailers and shoppers. With their lower profit margins and price-cutting tactics, they were warmly welcomed by Governments and public alike in the post-war decades as allies against inflation. But today ecology and jobs seem higher priorities; and the hypermarkets have come in for endless criticism, for adding to urban sprawl and devitalizing town centres (nearly all are out on the edges); and for maybe reducing employment and spoiling an old gentle way of life by killing off so many small shops. Consumers are torn. In their new nostalgic mood, they hanker for the old shops: yet in practice they still go as much as ever to the huge new stores, where they find nearly everything they need at the best prices. For better or worse, hypermarkets have been key agents of France's modernization.

The small tradesman class emerged from the war with a muddy black-market reputation. '*Les BOF*' (*beurre, oeufs et fromage*), the old generic term for dairy shops, became a phrase of contempt to denote a selfish crypto-collaborationist breed of petty shopkeepers, vividly described by Jean Dutourd in his novel *Au bon beurre* (1952). In 1955 this was the class that provided a hard core of support for the right-wing demagogue Pierre Poujade, in his opposition to the growth of big industry. With competition as their enemy, their aim was to keep prices and profit margins high: few stopped to consider that a reverse policy might yield better results. And for some years they held their ground. France's first supermarket was not born till 1957. But by 1975 there were 3,800 of them and a new spirit of salesmanship had arrived, novel for France.

Government reforms, foreign influences and the growth of the new suburbs all played their part. But the prime catalyst was an inspired young Jesuit ex-seminarist in a small Breton town: Édouard Leclerc. He has been one of the truly amazing figures of post-war France, variously likened to St Vincent de Paul, Danilo Dolci or Rasputin. Had it not been for his crusading, the old order would never have cracked so easily. He was the first to use discount methods, challenging the conspiracy of industry, shops and middlemen to keep prices high. He bought direct from the maker or producer to sell to the public with low profit margins – a system that in Britain or the US might seem obvious or a sales trick.

But in the France of the 1950s it was an innovation, and it steadily influenced other shops to follow suit.

In a land where shops were usually handed down from father to son, Leclerc came from an unlikely background. Son of an army officer, he was destined for the priesthood: but after some years in seminaries he quit, feeling that his true vocation to serve his fellow men was by smashing a 'wicked' system. In 1949, aged twenty-three, he opened his first little barrack-like store in his home town of Landerneau, near Brest, and began by buying biscuits from a local factory and selling them at 25 per cent below usual prices. Soon he was dealing in a wide range of groceries. At first the local tradesmen laughed at this crazy amateur: but the public flocked in, and his turnover shot up. In 1952 the worried Breton shopkeepers made their first united effort to destroy him by persuading many manufacturers and wholesalers to stop supplying him. They were using a *de facto* French system of retail price-fixing, whereby industry set the minimum price of its goods and boycotted any shop that went lower. The system was in theory illegal, but long condoned, and it suited everyone except the consumer. So Leclerc protested to the Ministry of Finance. Officials had barely heard of this odd idealist in far Brittany, but his plight happened to chime in with their own plans for checking inflation. So in 1953 the Laniel Government, in one of its rare moments of effectiveness, signed a decree that firmly reasserted the illegality of fixed prices and of refusal of supply. This, reaffirmed later by the Gaullists, became the key to all post-war progress in retail distribution. Without it Leclerc would have perished and the supermarkets would have found it much harder to get started.

Leclerc then carried his campaign beyond Landerneau. A few like-minded shopkeepers rallied to him, and so the network of Centres E. Leclerc began to spread across Brittany, then to Grenoble, where its success was dramatic, then to Paris: by 1960 there were sixty Leclerc stores. Other rival groups then sprang up, copying Leclerc's methods and prices, and so the modern supermarket developed fast in France. Today Leclerc is still the largest group, with some 600 stores, many of them hypermarkets, and its 'L' logo stands assertively on the edge of nearly every French town. It is not a chain, but an association run on a franchise basis: no member can himself own more than two stores (Leclerc's are at Landerneau and Brest), and each signs a 'moral contract' promising not to raise margins more than necessary. Leclerc at first held the dogma that it was immoral to spend money on showy décor and equipment, then pay for it by raising prices: his supermarket at Brest was of an imposing austerity, a tawdry warehouse piled with packing cases. But later his rivals, such as Carrefour, proved that low prices could be combined with a bright and cheerful décor: customers came to expect it, and Leclerc was obliged to follow suit.

Leclerc today, a wealthy man in his seventies, spends much of his time in the château he has bought near Landerneau. Still titular head of the group, he leaves its daily affairs to his clever and dynamic son, Michel-Édouard, now co-president. Across the years, with a sharp eye for publicity, Leclerc *père* has fought numerous crusades for lower prices: he has battled against the pharmacists' cartel; he was the first to introduce cheaper petrol, in defiance of state price-fixing in that field; he has helped fishermen to fight their middlemen by symbolically setting up cut-price fish stalls outside Métro stations; and he has gone to advise Governments on distribution reform, even in Communist Bulgaria. Still firmly religious, with a mystic visionary touch and ecological passion, he has conducted campaigns in Brittany against soil erosion and pollution. His diverse crusades, though always in earnest, have been laced with schoolboy high spirits, Robin Hood against the wicked barons, and he enjoys mocking the legend he has helped to create of himself. Some of his enemies call him a crank and a windbag, but others still find plenty of sense behind the half-tongue-in-cheek verbiage. With his soft excited voice and disarming Celtic whimsy, he has an oddly personal manner, as if he were letting you into some secret. 'Maybe my work has been close to religion,' he told me. 'I admire Christ for chasing the tradesmen from the Temple.'

Although the supermarket movement arrived late in France, it was the French who had previously invented the modern department store, with the opening of the Bon Marché on the Left Bank in 1852. This was followed by Printemps, Galeries Lafayette and the other Parisian giants still there today. They formed branches in the provinces, and chains for cheaper goods: Printemps started Prisunic and GL began Monoprix. But, compared with their more efficient Anglo-American counterparts, they were long stunted by their high-price policies and ententes against competition. Then, around 1960, self-service stores began to appear, influenced not only by Leclerc but by American techniques – by the famous sales courses of Bernard Trujillo at the National Cash Register Company in Dayton, Ohio. With the aim of selling more of these machines in France, the NCRC invited thousands of French shop executives to Dayton, where they listened in amazement to his gospel of large stores, rapid turnover and loss-leaders. Back home, many of them began to apply it with fervour, as a new breed of shop executive arose.

The result, the sudden growth of large, gaudy stores, was one of the most eye-catching features of the economic modernization of France in the 1960s. And sceptics who believed that the conservative French housewife could never be wooed away from her local shop, with its human contacts, were soon proved wrong. The number of super- and hypermarkets, nil in 1957, rose to over 1,000 by 1969 and today is some 8,800, while their share of the total retail trade has moved from 4 per cent in 1969 to over 50 per cent today, including 70 per cent of main packaged foods. In Britain these stores may be as numerous, but they are seldom as large: in this as in other fields the French in the 1960s followed the American taste for gigantism. Not content with the word *supermarché*, they coined *hypermarché* to denote the giants with over 2,500 square metres of selling space: France has more of these per capita than any other country, and the biggest ones, with up to 22,000 square metres, such as Carrefour's outside Marseille, are claimed to be larger than anything in America. Two chains are suitably called Mammouth and Géant Casino. You can find them, or smaller versions of them, on the periphery of almost any French town, where the land is relatively cheap and there is plenty of room for car-parking. Behind a row of up to seventy check-outs, the lights blaze down on a garish emporium that sells much else as well as food in mind-blowing profusion, while the tannoy blares out details of the latest bargains. Leclerc may have begun with groceries, but in the 1960s he moved also into clothing, where mark-ups in the traditional shops were absurdly high. Others followed, and today many big stores do most of their trade in non-food sectors: furniture, toys, heavy electrical goods, motor-mowers . . . But the food and drink counters, too, might be offering some 100 kinds of fresh cheeses, thirty brands of whisky, acres of vegetables common or exotic, every cut of meat. On Saturdays the family comes to pile its week's supplies on to giant trolleys. And where would the British day tripper be without the Carrefour beside the Eurotunnel exit?

Of the main hypermarket groups today, Intermarché is an association of individual members, rather like Leclerc, while the others are chains. Carrefour, the most dynamic, was founded in 1960 by a shopkeeper from Annecy: at his first *hypermarché*, some of his clients were local tradesmen who found it cheaper than buying from their own wholesalers, partly because they could avoid tax declarations! One café owner would carry away eighty bottles of Pernod a week. The number of *supermarchés* (over 400 square metres) and of *hypermarchés* (over 2,500) has risen steadily: the total of the latter has increased since 1975 from 320 to 1,100. Of these, Leclerc has 387, Auchan 142, Carrefour 115, Casino 112, Intermarché 80 – all locked in ferocious price wars. According to the consumer bodies, the Leclerc centres are still the cheapest, while prices of food and other mass consumer goods are on average 10 to 14 per cent lower in the *grandes surfaces* than in small shops. If some French products still seem expensive by British standards, this is due less to profit margins than to higher VAT and the inefficiency of some processing industries. So the consumer has benefited from France's retail revolution – but what of the environment and quality of life? – and what of the small shops?

During the boom years, while thousands of small groceries and other stores were killed off by the *grandes surfaces*, at the same time the rise in consumer spending produced a crop of new luxury specialized shops, many in multi-boutique 'commercial centres'. This shows how diversely France's small shopkeepers have reacted to the retail revolution. An intelligent minority have seen that they can even benefit: in the shadow of many a new hypermarket, old general stores have been replaced by coiffeurs, or boutiques selling jewellery, designer clothes, quality leather goods or books, and often they do a busy trade. They profit from their big neighbour's proximity and share some of its clients, without competing with its goods. One owner told me, 'I used to sell hardware, now I've switched to antiques. There will always be some things a small shop can do better than a big one.'

The total number of small shopkeepers has halved since 1954. Of course there are still plenty of little general stores that do well for ad hoc purchases: in Paris and other cities, many are now owned by North African or Vietnamese families, prepared to stay open late – like the Asian-run shops in Britain. But the traditional independent French *petit épicier* is a dying breed, especially in older suburbs or in villages hit by the farm exodus. Government policy – as with farming – has long been to try to protect this dying class from too much hardship, while also encouraging the modern sector. But in the 1970s a militant minority of small traders, far from satisfied, turned to violence in their crusade against the *grandes surfaces*. They were led by a young café owner from near Grenoble, Gérard Nicoud, who saw that strong tactics had brought some results in May '68 and so decided to follow suit. He and his supporters raided local tax offices and blocked main roads: when a Carrefour hypermarket went up in flames near Lyon, sabotage was suspected. Nicoud was often compared to Poujade, but he was less the old-style demagogue, more the modern extremist: he saw the need for the little shops to change, but he wanted the State to pay for it.

Pompidou's Government, alarmed at Nicoud, backed its Minister of Commerce, Jean Royer, a notorious reactionary, to push through a vote-catching law in 1973 that made new expansion by the hypermarkets quite difficult: a firm wanting to set up a large new store would have to submit its case to a local committee, and as these were composed largely of tradesmen and their allies, they often said no. For a few years, the big chains found it hard to develop in France. But then the economy picked up, Nicoud slipped out of sight, and the Socialists in power felt little need to pander to the small traders, who were not their electorate. So the Royer law fell into abeyance, and the expansion continued.

In the past few years several of the big groups, foreseeing new trouble, and finding the French market almost saturated, have turned their main attention to investing abroad – in lands not yet touched by the bliss of the *hypermarché*. By 1997 Carrefour had seven of them in Mexico and others in fifteen different countries, while Leclerc had moved into Spain and Poland. Within France firms have been diversifying, sometimes setting up travel agencies, banks or even cultural centres inside their stores – in sectors less likely to face the venom of some new Nicoud. Today *les grandes surfaces* are a brutal competitive world; and although the Leclerc stores still retain the ethos of low profit margins, some of the old idealism has gone out of their operation, inevitably, and they have to be as tough as any. Michel-Édouard is a friend and political ally of Alain Madelin, France's leading economic 'liberal' with Thatcherite ideas. And farmers, sometimes with reason, have bitterly criticized the growing practice of price-dictating by the big groups, who are thus picking up some of the bad habits once denounced by Leclerc. In beef, for example, after the BSE scare of 1996, prices paid to the farmers slumped badly but they stayed quite high in the stores. These, together with the middlemen, were exploiting the scare to their own advantage.

By the mid-1990s, although the public was still visiting hypermarkets as much as ever, it was also becoming more critical. In the days when the fight against inflation was a top priority, the giants had a special value. But times had changed, the priority struggle was now for jobs, and the big stores were seen as adding to net unemployment by killing off so many small ones. They were accused also of adding to the decline of town centres, and of spoiling the environment on the edge of towns. Sensing this new mood, the small traders again became restive, and violent Nicoud-type protests began in several areas. So Chirac, campaigning for office in 1995, came out strongly as champion of the small local shops and the town-centre heritage, and spoke rudely about hypermarkets (yet privately he let it be known that he was doing this mainly for electoral reasons and was not really against the big stores; in fact, he had backed them strongly when premier in 1986–8). Once elected, he and Juppé then had their Minister of Commerce, Jean-Pierre Raffarin, put through a law that imposed a six-month freeze on all new shops above the size of a small supermarket (300 square metres) and also revived and reinforced the 1973 Royer measures. The public was generally sympathetic, for it judged there were quite enough big stores by now. But of course the owners were furious. 'Chirac is a blatant hypocrite,' Leclerc *fils* said to me, in his group's modern Paris headquarters. 'He urges the public to spur growth by buying more, but he stops us from helping them. His limit of 300 square metres prevents the medium-sized stores, not ours, from expanding – do you call that job creation? As for the town-centre argument, it was he as mayor who banned all opening of new *grandes surfaces* inside Paris: we'd love to build some big stores there, but we never get permission. So can you blame us for expanding mainly abroad?' This complex debate was unresolved when the Socialists came to power. Less committed to supporting the small traders, they applied the Raffarin law less strictly, and in 1997–8 many new hypermarkets or extensions were authorized.

As the century ends, it is clear that hypermarkets are in France to stay, even if their golden age is over. Economists today are divided on whether the move from tiny shops to huge ones kills more jobs than it creates or not: maybe it balances out. As for the debate on town centres, it is certainly true that the shift of big commerce to the periphery has impoverished downtown life in many places: but local councils, and not just in Paris, are themselves often to blame in forbidding big new stores near the centre. The French, once again, have swung to extremes. In Kensington, central London, I have a sizeable Safeway and Marks & Spencer within five minutes' walk, which give me nearly all I need, and I feel no urge to go out to Brent to some mammoth. In France it surely might have been wiser to find more room for medium supermarkets near the centre, and to have fewer colossi on the edge, with their brash American-style malls. The French are starting to realize this. But, as often, they want it both ways. In a sense, they still yearn for the little corner shops. Yet they still go in hordes, and gratefully, to the gaudy palaces of the Breton visionary Jesuit and his semi-Thatcherite son. In their new mood, they may think small is beautiful: but they still think big is beautiful, too.

The weakness of the consumer movement was one factor behind the high prices and poor competition of the early post-war years. Amid price-fixing and rapid inflation, it was hard for customers to become price-wise or develop a sense of value for money. And they were handicapped by the scarcity of advice from consumer bodies, in a country where consumer protection made a slower start than in Britain. But all this has changed since the 1970s.

A forerunner of the modern French consumer movement was an inspired venture started in 1954 in the specialized sectors of photography and electrical goods. André Essel, an ex-journalist, founded a body called the Fédération Nationale des Achats des Cadres (FNAC). It began as a discount store in a field where mark-ups were high: by buying wholesale, this Leclerc of the Leicas was able to undercut other shops, and his turnover rose sharply. He also organized regular scientific testing of the goods that he sold and published the results in FNAC's monthly magazine *Contact*, even if sometimes this meant dissuading its readers from buying his own wares. FNAC has since grown into a huge enterprise that has expanded into other fields, notably books, records and video: its bookstores at Montparnasse and Les Halles are among Europe's largest. It has eight provincial branches, and a cultural club. Along with Richard Branson, it has also influenced the recent growth of city-centre megastores in other sectors: for example, the Decathlon chain selling sports equipment.

The success of FNAC encouraged the Government finally to set up the kind of consumer-protection body that in other countries had come from private initiative. The Institut National de la Consommation (UNC), created in 1970, publishes a monthly magazine that gives consumer advice and prints comparative test reports on brand goods. It is now rivalled by an independent body, the Union Fédérale des Consommateurs (UFC), whose monthly paper, *Que Choisir?*, also does well, on the lines of *Which?* Its test reports have infuriated many industries, not used to this kind of scrutiny in France. UFC is above all a grassroots movement, with some 150 local branches whose members voluntarily assist with inquiries into public services or, for example, the behaviour of doctors, house agents or insurance companies. Voluntary civic action of this kind has come late to France: it was influenced by the ideas of '68, the ecology movements of the 1970s, and the Consumers' Association in Britain. So consumer self-defence in France has finally become an organized force to reckon with.

These movements have campaigned against phoney or misleading advertising, and have pushed the Government into tightening the legislation on the lines of Britain's Trades Description Act. The state radio and TV channels have also played some part. Anne Gaillard, a journalist with a dauntingly aggressive manner, had her own remarkable consumer programme on France-Inter for six years. She and her team would go into shops and make clandestine tape-recordings of the often absurd claims made for their goods by the sales staff, then play back the tapes in the studio to the embarrassed manufacturers: 'Monsieur, you've heard this pharmacist telling us that your drug makes people younger – how do you justify this scientifically?' Gaillard was not afraid to quote brand names: Coca-Cola, Nestlé and others fell under her flail. Her daily programme, highly popular, was in the end silenced under subtle pressures from the Patronat. But she had certainly helped to make the public more exacting about the authenticity and quality of products.

There are still a few specialized sectors of the retail or servicing trades where cartels or vested privileges keep prices high, and consumer bodies or discount stores can do little about it. Opticians and watch-repairers each have their price-fixing ententes: these and some other trades have it in common that they demand special expertise, even special diplomas, and can thus dig in their heels if a Government attempts reform. 'They represent the worst aspects of the old medieval guild spirit,' one state official told me. The worst case is pharmaceuticals (see p. 152). Here the vast majority of drugs can still be sold only in authorized chemists' shops, which keeps the prices high. But Leclerc in 1988, after years of lobbying, did finally persuade the Government to allow certain cosmetics, vitamin pills and simple medicines, hitherto the preserve of the pharmacies, to be available in other shops, too, usually at far lower prices.

Leclerc would like to do the same for books. As in Britain, there is an argument in France as to whether new books, like other goods, should be freed from fixed prices and made available at a discount in all kinds of shops. In Britain publishers have moved in that direction, tearing up the Net Book Agreement. But in France the Socialist Government of the 1980s reaffirmed the principle that new books must have a fixed price: 'Books,' said Jack Lang, 'are a special case. They cannot be treated like food or clothes, open to the vagaries of the market, or serious publishers and authors would suffer.' And the literary and academic worlds cheered him for it. The Leclercs, ultra-liberal, want to be able to offer popular books at cut prices in their hypermarkets. But this could drive many small quality bookshops out of business, making it harder for new or serious authors to find a publisher. The French realize this. The Leclercs' free-pricing policy, for them a religion, may have brought great benefits to France over the years, in many sectors. But, in culture, it has its limits. The visionary of Landerneau cannot treat Barthes the way he once treated biscuits.

FROM *NOUVELLE CUISINE* TO GRANNY'S FOOD AND *LE FAST-FOOD*: DECADENCE OR RECOVERY?

La nouvelle cuisine est morte – vive la cuisine de grand-mère! The vogue for a new inventive style of quality cooking, launched thirty years ago by a few star chefs such as Paul Bocuse, did much at the time to revive the flagging tradition of French gastronomy. But it then produced its own excesses and has now gone out of fashion. Yet its influence lives on, for it has paved the way for today's major trend, a reinvention in a lighter style of the old classic country dishes – the so-called '*cuisine de grand-mère*', maybe an aspect of the new 'reassurance spending' in an anxious age. Go to very smart places like the Hôtel Crillon, and you may find *pot-au-feu* or *civet de lièvre*. Those, like myself, who never cared greatly for the *nouvelle cuisine* with its small portions and pretty-pretty decorations, are left rejoicing.

This is the latest of the manifold changes that have come upon traditional good eating in France in recent decades. From prince to peasant, the French used to have great natural taste in food; they ate better than any other nation, and in some ways they still do. But today all is confusion, as conflicting pressures have been pushing cuisine simultaneously towards decline and recovery. On one side, bars in central Paris serving *le fast-food* and *le hot-dog*; long frozen-food counters in the supermarkets; restaurant standards, once so dependable, now more erratic. On the other, among certain people, a new food-crazy concern for seeking out special high-quality products in the shops; talk of a renaissance in cooking; the best restaurants still full, unless they overprice themselves; and leading chefs, even after *nouvelle cuisine*, still enjoying an idolatry equal to that given to film stars or celebrity musicians.

So what has been happening? Answer, a curious polarization of eating habits. At least in the middle classes, the French used to eat serenely well as a matter of course, every day, notably in their homes. But a modern nation in a hurry no longer has such time or concern for serious daily cooking and eating: alike at home and away from it, routine meals have become more utilitarian. And ordinary restaurants, faced with rising costs, have been cutting corners, using processed foods and mass-production techniques, and mostly their clients accept it. In this sense, standards have been slipping, especially in cities. Yet the Frenchman's gastronomic zeal has not died, it has simply taken a new turn. He has been channelling it towards the once- or twice-a-week occasion – the really good restaurant meal with his beloved, the ritual Sunday lunch, the dinner party at home for a few friends. And here he is as exacting as ever. This is a facet of the new hedonism, just as the utility trend was born of the 1960s modernization. So the French in their food habits, as in much else, have been moving closer to other nations. Good eating has become less regular, more special. But the shift is relative. In rural areas, with their rich traditions, the French probably still eat better than any other people; they still talk and think about food to an amazing extent, and some even show a new concern for seeking out fresh foods of quality in the shops. The issue today is whether these traditions can continue to survive the pressures of city living and industrial catering.

In the difficult years before and just after the war, the Frenchman – so it seemed – clung to good eating partly as a compensation and a constant in a shifting world: his cuisine went on tasting the same; it did not turn sour and betray him as so much had done. But then in the boom years he came to feel less need for this kind of solace, as so many other material temptations arrived, too – television, cars, foreign holidays, better homes. In the middle classes far fewer wives now have servants, more have jobs: so the *bourgeoise* will sooner toss a couple of steaks under her grill than spend hours on a *plat mijoté* as her grandmother or grandmother's *bonne* would have done. Or a young wife may feel the need to assert herself by refusing to be a kitchen slave. The food writer Henri Gault told me, 'A wife's preparation of a really good meal used to be a kind of love-making. But a woman no longer feels she needs to show her love in this way, nor does her man expect it. They eat a plate of ham or pasta, and watch TV.'

There was even a period in the '50s and '60s when many younger educated people took a conscious pride in reacting against their parents' self-indulgent gourmandise. This was the intellectual anti-gourmet era, but it ended after '68. Today many younger people have returned to real cuisine, but only for special meals. Day to day, the average middle-class French family probably does not eat much more excitingly at home than in Britain (where standards have risen so much). But it still eats a little differently: the French still show more flair in preparing salads and vegetables, and they still buy more fresh and less frozen food than the British. But the family pot of which you are invited to *prendre la fortune* may well be no more than a conventional roast veal or chicken dish, followed by cheese and fruit: the housewife rarely bothers with compli-cated desserts. When she entertains, she will probably stick to a classic recipe, or maybe try out an 'amusing' foreign dish discovered on summer holidays (moussaka or paella, for instance).

For office workers, snack bars of all kinds have sprung up, while most cafés in towns offer a light lunch with a *plat du jour*. The French still tend to eat more at midday than the British: but except for a few business lunches, it is no longer the *grande bouffe* that it often used to be. And the change to just one heavier meal a day, either lunch or dinner, may be wise: this has long been a nation of overeaters, where the middle-age *crise de foie* was commonplace and every meal was *de rigueur* a full three-or four-course affair. Today, with the nervous speeding up of life, more care is given to diet. The trend has been towards smaller and less complex meals (except on special occasions), with simpler sauces and better-quality ingredients. It was this change in public demand that helped pave the way for the gastronomic revolution of the 1970s.

'*La bande à Bocuse*' ('Bocuse and his gang'), as they were called, were the group of influential chefs who dominated French gastronomy in the 1970s and '80s. Today most of them are still around, still owning and running their very superior restaurants. They may have modified their style of cooking, which they no longer describe as '*nouvelle cuisine*'. But the enormous legacy of this 'new cooking' remains, and so does the new social role of the star chef, which they pioneered.

La nouvelle cuisine française was described, justly, as the first major development in French gastronomy since Escoffier. Bocuse himself was on the cover of *Newsweek*, while a *Time* cover story in 1980 was devoted to Henri Gault and Christian Millau, the all-influential food critics who first coined the phrase '*la nouvelle cuisine*', believed in it passionately and did so much to propagate its vogue. But that vogue has always been limited. The new style, usually expensive, marked a revolution in *haute cuisine* which profoundly affected the top 10 per cent or so of restaurants, but had a lesser influence on the rest, or on home cooking. Basically, it was an inventive approach to cuisine that reduced to a minimum the rich, high-calorie ingredients such as cream, egg-yolk, sugar and brandy which used to deck out many of the great classic dishes. It spurned flour and other starches, and heavy sauces that masked the taste of the meat. Generally served in small portions, neatly arranged on the plate, its lighter, purer style used the best raw materials, cooking them in their own juices. It relied on very fresh ingredients, rapidly cooked almost in the Chinese manner, with flavours daringly blended: thus a purée of mixed spinach and pear kept the fresh taste of both. Above all, it encouraged the chef to deviate from classic recipes and use his flair for invention. Thus Alain Senderens at Lucas Carton in Paris has offered cooked oysters and leeks with foie gras served with cabbage or apple. This kind of cooking required much time and skill, and depended on best-quality produce, for no longer could second-rate meat be disguised by rich sauces. Hence the cost of such a meal.

The initial impetus came from the owner-chefs themselves. A few young ambitious ones felt that classic cuisine was growing as weary as last week's joint, and they wanted to try something new. Their traditional clients were at first suspicious, but some were soon seduced by the dietetic appeal of the new cooking. One of its initiators, Pierre Troisgros, told *Esquire*, 'Our customers do not want to get up from the table feeling as if their bellies were filled with lead . . . Our challenge is to continue to provide the delight and excitement of *haute cuisine* without its excesses of richness and weight.' The true pioneer was Fernand Point of La Pyramide at Vienne, the most inspired French owner-chef of his day. From the 1930s he had experimented with a new lightness of style which he saw as a return to the true pre-Escoffier tradition. Among his fervent local disciples was the young Paul Bocuse, who in 1959 took over his father's modest *auberge* beside the Saône near Lyon, and began to run it as a showplace for the new cooking. Bocuse has never been himself the greatest of the new cooks: but his forceful personality rallied a new generation of chefs to apply and to propagate the philosophy of Papa

Point. He saw that most top restaurants were not in the hands of cooks but of businessmen who often knew little of cuisine; the chef was a mere employee, obliged to cook as he was told. So Bocuse encouraged some of the brightest to open their own restaurants, and gradually they did so. It was a liberation movement, a revolt of the serfs. Today, thanks to this Castro of the cookpots, sixteen of France's twenty-one three-star (in *Michelin*) restaurants are chef-owned, against two or three in the old days. 'Today,' Bocuse told me, 'cooking belongs to the cooks; we're no longer servants. The cook is no longer hidden away in some basement; he goes into the dining room to meet his guests.'

Another success of his was to create a new fraternity and friendship among leading chefs. This little milieu used to seethe with suspicion: jealously hostile to each other, chefs would seldom meet and each guarded the secret of his own recipes. But the jolly *bande à Bocuse* have run some joint businesses, travelled abroad together, and even pooled their creativity. Bocuse's menu has accredited twenty dishes to his friends, e.g. *loup aux algues Michel Guérard*. And so a new-style élitist owner-chef has emerged, sophisticated, much-travelled, often arrogant, an artist who is also a public figure and sees himself as equal to a master architect or star orchestral conductor. After dinner he emerges proudly from his kitchen, high-toqued, sits to take a drink with his guests, and maybe is applauded as if he had just brilliantly rendered *La Traviata*. Most of the top restaurants in France are today run by this fraternity and their successors. Significantly, most are in the provinces.

Bocuse himself is an amazing Rabelaisian figure. Now turned seventy, tall and burly, he is still a whimsical *provocateur* who has outraged some people by using bizarre PR gimmickry to promote the cuisine that he takes seriously but not solemnly. He has travelled the world as ambassador for French cooking, yet can still play schoolboy pranks on his friends, such as importing near-naked striptease girls into a smart Paris party. In the temple of French cooking he is at once high priest and iconoclast and is known as 'the Emperor': but on my visit I found him warm, funny, unpretentious, saying outrageously conceited things with a merry twinkle. His opulent restaurant I found in *nouveau riche* taste: on one wall was a big portrait of the Emperor cutting up an onion. His tireless globe-trotting pluri-activity has been amazing. At one time, he ran gastronomic sea-cruises, part-owned a firm marketing Beaujolais, operated a cookery school in Japan, and would often fly there or to America to cook special banquets for gigantic fees. All this, of course, to promote not modest Paul but the glory of French culture. He came to be seen as a national prestige symbol, like Cantona or Yves Saint-Laurent.

Bocuse and his friends gradually managed to 'impose' their style of cooking on the majority of France's top restaurants. Leading chefs who in the '70s were still serving only classic dishes then 'saw the light' and added *nouvelle* inventions, either to keep up with fashion or because they truly found the new cooking more exciting. In the first category were such mighty Parisian temples of tradition as Maxim's and Le Grand Véfour. In the second, the great Haerberlin brothers at their Auberge de l'Ill, near Strasbourg, would think up such wonders as mousse of frogs: 'Exquisite!' raved the *Gault-Millau* guide. These two arbiters of taste (their famous guide, now in other hands, still bears their name) held it a dogma of faith that the new cooking was always superior to the old, and their nearly top-rated places were classified as *cuisine inventive*. The cautious *Michelin* was slower to react: but by the 1980s some two-thirds of its own top choices were practising *nouvelle cuisine* too.

Some leading chefs took the style a stage further. Michel Guérard invented what he calls *cuisine minceur*, and opened a famous luxury health farm for gourmet slimmers in a Second Empire mansion near Pau. Here he still wins top ratings in the guides. Some of his guests come on a cure, they drink the waters, they eat exquisite food with less than 500 calories per four-course meal; others, more robust, take his *menu gourmand*. When I telephoned, I was told, 'The Master is holding a seminar': he, Bocuse and Co. have indeed seen themselves as *maîtres à penser* of one of the great arts, and have run gastronomic cruises with lecture courses. *Nouvelle cuisine* has always been diverse in its inventions, and was never a full break with tradition. Many of its better dishes have drawn inspiration from Oriental cookery, or from pre-Escoffier French cuisine; some were clever variations on older recipes. 'Gastronomy,' said Bocuse, 'like any art, cannot stand still, it must renew itself.'

This may be so. And yet, as with some modern art or music, one trouble with *nouvelle cuisine* was that its wilder experiments led down a blind alley. In gifted or responsible hands, like those of a Guérard or Troisgros, it could be splendid: but, as with any liberation movement, it led to excesses by the rank and file. Food had become so fashionable that many young people would open a restaurant to follow the new trend, but often without the basic skills. So the licence to invent produced absurdities, such as raw sweetbreads. Gault himself recognized this: 'Young cooks striving for instant fame have been doing horrible things in the name of the new cooking. In this as in other arts, the cult of innovation for its own sake is stupid.' So why did the new style catch on so widely with a moneyed clientele? Because in the right hands it could be brilliant; and because the French so often fall for novelty and trendiness. But they rarely tried out the new cooking in their own kitchens, despite the bulky tomes of recipes produced by Bocuse and others. These were little more than coffee-table books, *très snob*.

For many tastes, mine included, *nouvelle cuisine* tended to be too chichi, too niggardly. Portions were small, the food was arranged prettily on the plate like Japanese flower decorations. Thin strips of meat beside bland purée of chestnut or spinach; minced partridge, wrapped in a lettuce leaf and shaped to form a cake – no, give me a copious time-honoured cassoulet or *coq au vin*. And many gourmets and food critics, even if bored by the old *haute cuisine* and its rich sauces, none the less resented the 'tyranny' of the new chefs abetted by the guides.

By the later 1980s the vogue for experiment was on the wane, as the public began to tire of it and the great chefs turned back to a more classic genre – not to heavy *haute cuisine*, but to old country dishes done in a new way, maybe *boeuf en daube* or *blanquette de veau*. And this *cuisine du terroir*, or *cuisine de grand-mère*, remains the trend today. Yet *nouvelle cuisine*, though now vanishing, has left its strong and positive mark: its accent on fresh ingredients remains, and on seasonal cooking according to the food market, while the old classic dishes are prepared in a new and lighter style, with less use of cream, butter and flour-thickened sauces. You can find these *plats rustiques* in the smartest restaurants – a *coq au vin* at the Crillon, maybe. And many leading chefs have been reviving the old recipes in a new manner: Joël Robuchon was offering a high-styled version of *tête de cochon* with his own delicious brand of mashed potatoes. The *Gault-Millau* guide, accepting and even welcoming these new trends, no longer speaks of *nouvelle cuisine*: but it still gives its preferred red-toque ratings to what it now calls *cuisine d'auteur*, i.e. personal cooking – the kind of distinction made also in French cinema.

You can still find the excesses of *nouvelle cuisine* in some pretentious but second-rank restaurants – especially abroad, in Britain or Germany, where chefs can be a trend or two out of date. Even in France there can still be overdecoration and undersized helpings in some places: but generally it is the better legacy of the new cooking that survives. In its way, it has done a good PR job for France abroad, and has helped Americans and others to become more gastronomy-minded. At home, it gave a needed shot in the arm to a flagging tradition. The film-star exposure of the new chefs has helped to revive public interest in good food, and has made the French more aware of the need to protect their heritage from the hazards of mass-production. Thirty years ago, there was a growing shortage of good young chefs: many a son of an older chef left for office or factory work with its easier hours, rather than follow in papa's rigorous footsteps. But this has changed. In the hotel schools, training to toil in the kitchen used to be lower in prestige than training to be a waiter, the classic royal road to management jobs. But now many of the more ambitious students want to be chefs. They have Bocuse to thank for creating a new brand image.

Today some of the most expensive restaurants are suffering a certain malaise, due not to styles of cooking but to rising costs and to changes in eating-out habits at that social level. No longer do the rich find it so smart to dine in such places, nor senior executives feel it so important to impress their clients there. So Parisian three-star luxury haunts like Taillevent or Lucas Carton, where a meal can cost over 1,000 francs, can be half empty, especially at night: Alain Senderens has complained of being 'strangled' by taxes. Instead, new medium or upper-medium-priced *bistrots* have come strongly into vogue: many of them specialize in *la cuisine de grand-mère*, with a meal at maybe 300 to 600 francs, and very *soigné* décor. Some famous three-star chefs, such as Georges Blanc near Mâcon, have opened a *bistrot* of this kind next to their main luxury restaurant, with great success. In central Paris the enterprising Guy Savoy (two stars) has opened a mini-chain of six such *bistrots*, often packed.

The sociology and ambience of dining-out have gone through various changes. In the old days, most good restaurants popular for dinner were sober and brightly lit, either conventionally elegant (like Fouquet's) or plain and shabby (like some of the greatest *bistrots*). Then in the 1960s, as in Chelsea, an atmospheric modishness crept into the medium-priced places in vogue with the young: many in the Quartier Latin or Ile St-Louis updated their décor in a mock-rustic or arty-crafty style, maybe installing canned music or a guitarist. The cuisine seldom rose above the level of *viandes aux herbes de Provence grillées au feu du bois*, but a '60s *jeunesse dorée* did not care. The vogue was for intimate restaurants with *ambiance*, open late and helped along by dim lights or candles: yet previously the French had thought it barbaric not to see what they were eating. *Marie-Claire* wrote with a touch of hype, 'Dining has dethroned the show-going habit. The restaurant itself is now a show, lasting for hours, with the diner himself in a small walk-on part.' This kind of place still exists. But, with the return to more serious eating, the accent is now on the refurbishing of classic *bistrots* or high-class brasseries; or on pretty restaurants with mirrors in the trendy *style 1900*. Many of them offer the new granny cooking – a double nostalgia. In the smart restaurants of the star chefs, the luxurious décor can be beautiful – and in the provinces, quite daring, too. Michel Trama (two stars), at Puymirol near Toulouse, has wittily inserted striking modern Italian furniture into a thirteenth-century mansion.

Italy's furniture is more highly rated in France than its food. Even so, foreign cuisines have now become a little less despised, and more widespread. The French (who seldom get as far as Peking) were always acutely conscious of other nations' culinary inferiority, and gourmets would seldom accept even the best Italian or Hungarian dishes as much more than quaint or exotic. But then, in the 1960s, exoticism came to be what some people wanted. There have always been some foreign restaurants in Paris, notably those nostalgic little Russian ones that arrived after 1917: but they formed a kind of ghetto, patronized mainly by fellow exiles. Then the Cantonese and Vietnamese eateries arrived: there are now some 2,000 in Paris, and many others in the provinces. Then came the wave of downmarket pizza houses, some with songful Corsican waiters in Neapolitan costume. Then the Spanish, Greeks, Japanese and Moroccans began to infiltrate Paris, while the *pieds-noirs* imported couscous and *merguez* to many menus. And some foreign restaurants, not just the ubiquitous Chinese and Italian, have opened in other towns where these cuisines were hitherto unknown: I found an Indian one in Grenoble. Tourists on their holidays have been finding that Mediterranean or Austro-Hungarian food is not as coarse as they had been told: so, back home, they have sometimes carried these new tastes into their dining-out. All this has added spice and variety to the scene. But of course these foreign restaurants fill a far less crucial need than in Britain, and are infinitely fewer. Nor, with a few exceptions, are they taken very seriously by gastronomes. The chauvinistic *Michelin* rarely awards its prized stars to non-French restaurants: just two Italians, one in Paris, one in Colmar, each get one star.

Some slick quasi-Anglo-Saxon eateries had a brief vogue in the 1960s and '70s, and were at least quite funny. *Les drugstores*, with their glossy décor, offered a Franco-American menu, such as barbecued spare-ribs and *chien chaud dit hot-dog*, to a French public, not just tourists. As for the British, for decades our island cuisine was a topic of mirth in France. But then the Parisian passion for mimicking (inaccurately) all things English scaled new heights. In Paris and other towns, so-called 'pubs' appeared, implausible baroque pastiches of Victoriana, where the French could be seen gobbling *le London Lunch* (*rosbif et Yorkshire pudding*) or *le Toffy cup* (toffee ice-cream), maybe washed down with one of ten recherché blends of tea – just as in an English pub. Finally, the public cottoned on to the absurdities and the awful unauthentic food, and the 'pub' vogue collapsed.

Le fast-food, by contrast, has survived and has gone from strength to strength among young people, as in so many countries. For years the French had resisted Big Mac and tried to do this kind of catering themselves, in their own style: a dynamic tycoon, Jacques Borel, set up hundreds of steak and burger bars in the 1960s. But he and others lacked the right expertise, and French youth wanted the real American thing. So Borel collapsed, McDonald's spread, and today it has some 500 outlets across France (one is inside the Galeries Lafayette!), while its Belgian imitator, Quick, has 270. With its brash red-and-yellow façades in the graceful old streets, MacDo (as the French call it) is not a pretty sight: but it meets a need among younger people who like its cheap, efficient food in bright, clean surroundings, and are amused by the menus' Mcfranglais of McChicken, McCookie . . . The chain has now invaded the breakfast market, with its McMorning specials including big plastic cups of quite good coffee ad lib: these have made a dent in the trade of many cafés, more atmospheric but more stingy. However, the burger bars were hit in 1996–7 by the *vache folle* scare, and their sales of beefburgers dropped. McDonald's responded with a big PR campaign, to stress that all its beef was *d'origine française*; it even launched '*un hamburger au goût français*', served with old-style French mustard. That seemed to be the right recipe: American know-how seasoned with French chauvinism. Many gastronomes have grown alarmed at the likely impact on French youth not only of this fast food but of the decline of daily cooking in so many homes. Are not the new generations losing touch with the great French traditions? Bocuse and some of his friends have even persuaded the Ministry of Education to create some classes in schools, where chefs come to teach the pupils, not how to cook, but about the basics of taste and smell and how to appreciate good food.

The polarization of eating habits can be as evident in the home as in restaurants. A large part of the middle class is not very interested in food;

if it eats well from time to time, it is just by tradition. However, one aspect of the new hedonism is that a minority of young well-to-do people has grown noticeably food-crazy in a new way: the average age of the readers of the *Gault-Millau* monthly magazine is thirty-two. These are the 'food bores', as some might call them, who to prepare a dinner party will spend hours trekking around Paris for the finest produce sold in special shops – 'My dear, where *can* one buy bread except *chez* Poilane?' Often it is the husband who does the most sophisticated cooking, at the weekend or for parties; and though a wife may say, 'Oh, I never have time to cook, these days', in fact when she does it, for some party, she takes huge trouble. As in Britain, sales of cookbooks have soared: one reason is that many French town-dwellers are having to relearn culinary lore for themselves, as their mothers failed to pass it on. One classic, *La Vraie Cuisine de Tante Marie*, has sold 10 million copies. So Granny's sister's cooking indeed lives on.

Sales of quality charcuterie, pâtés, cheeses, breads and pastries have all risen; and although the taste and texture of the ordinary baguette may have declined, due to mass-production and use of inferior flour, there are more special bakeries now selling rye breads and country breads. New *traiteurs* and small speciality shops have arisen to meet the new demand. Even some supermarkets, notably Carrefour, now have large delicatessen counters, which sell these quality foods at relatively high prices, and do well. And some small farmers (see p. 411) are readily responding, knowing that specialization for quality markets may be the only way of surviving. The enterprising Guy Savoy told me in 1996, 'I feared that gastronomy was dying, but now it's coming back – thanks to this new demand by a certain public, allied to the farmers' new efforts to improve quality. Ten years ago, nearly all French apples were those dull goldens: now there are lots of others, with more taste. Ditto chickens: the insipid battery hens are being challenged by farm-bred local poultry from Touraine, Normandy and Bresse. Ditto vegetables: farmers are experimenting with all kinds of delicious, little-known kinds which find a market – just look in Carrefour. Even amid a so-called economic crisis, a discriminating public finds it *is* worth paying that bit extra, for quality and variety.'

It is often in the far rural provinces that the old standards are surviving best, without any need for the new vogues. These are the bastions of sound cuisine, both *paysanne* and *bourgeoise*. Although value for money may have declined at tourist traps along main roads, and even in towns, there are still thousands of small family-run places where you can eat for a mere 80 francs or so. To quote one example, at the Papillon family's delightful little Logis de France in the Cévennes, I sat among local families on their Sunday outing, and for 74 francs *prix fixe* I had rich country salad, a copious *civet de chevreuil*, and a home-made apple pie: most of the fruit and vegetables were from the hotel's garden. Moreover, 'civilized' eating is not an import confined to an educated class, as in Britain: by tradition it belongs also to the working and *petit bourgeois* classes, and here the gulf between standards in the two countries remains enormous – compare a *relais routier* for lorry drivers with a British transport 'caff'. In many factories unions and works committees are more demanding about the quality of the canteen's food than most other aspects of working conditions – once I had a splendid *cassoulet de fruits de mer* as the *plat du jour* at Motorola (American-owned!) in Toulouse. At home, working families now have more money for good fresh food, and a wife, if not working, will still do proper cooking. But on the modern housing estates, where the workers *s'embourgeoisent*, this tradition is waning. And yet, though they may grow negligent about it, the French at every level still have gastronomy in their bones. At Sedan, I once went to a routine dinner at the prefecture for local dignitaries: we had turbot in champagne, stuffed quails, superb cheeses and an orange soufflé.

The French, it has been said, used to treat cookery almost as an extension of foreign policy. From the days of Escoffier, its impact on the great restaurants of the world, and thus on their clientele, was seen as an aspect of diplomatic influence. But today there are some creative American chefs, even Australian ones, who claim to cook as well as the French. And the primacy of French cuisine has possibly declined – despite, or you might say because of, the legacy of the *nouvelle* variety. Across the world, taste is becoming more universal, less national. Even in France, despite the resistance to top-class foreign restaurants, some diners have been developing a taste for spicier foods – and some great chefs have responded by putting oriental herbs and spices into a few of their dishes. This led to a mini-crisis in 1996 when some other chefs, more purist, led by Robuchon and Alain Ducasse, publicly called for a defence of *la cuisine française*, 'threatened by globalization and by frightful mixtures of everything with anything'. Feeling insulted, ten major chefs then resigned from the Chambre Syndicale de la Haute Cuisine Française.

This incident was one symptom of a crisis of transformation in French cuisine today. The threat to good eating may be less serious than it seemed in the 1960s, thanks to the new positive trends: of France's 50,000 or so restaurants, many of the better family-run ones still do well, as do some of the new 'formula' places with short menus that keep up a decent standard. But many others are in economic trouble, hit by rising costs, especially of staff. There are too many restaurants, and in recent years closures have been common. Moreover, with the polarization of personal eating habits, the use of convenience foods has been growing, both in restaurants and at home: the French may still eat less frozen produce than the British or Germans, but they buy five times more than thirty years ago. Add to this the greater standardization of foodstuffs, quid pro quo of the modernization of farming, as fertilizers make fruit and vegetables larger and more handsome but not always more succulent. These trends, it is true, are relative. It remains easier than in Britain to find tasty fresh vegetables in local outdoor markets or even hypermarkets.

There is one other possible answer, today much advocated by the food writers, to the rise of cheap convenience foods and standardization: this is for industrial labour-saving techniques to be made the ally of real cooking, not its enemy. Methods of dehydration, deep-freezing and canning have been fast improving, and a cassoulet pre-cooked in large quantities in this way, under the guidance of a master-chef, can be almost as good as the real thing. For several years now, this trend has been invading the market: go into any good French food-store, and you will find that quite a percentage of its pre-packaged offerings, either deep-frozen or in tins or cartons, consists not of ordinary staples like fish fingers or tomato soup (as you might find in Britain), but of gastronomic dishes bearing the label of a great chef, thus allying science to art and quality. Michel Guérard was one pioneer, joining up with Nestlé to supervise the mass-production of some of his recipes. Bernard Loiseau, of La Côte d'Or at Saulieu (three stars in *Michelin*), has done the same with the French branch of Findus: his vegetable-and-beef soup, sold in a carton and lasting several months, is delicious and unusual. These and other special dishes have had huge success and are not expensive. 'It's a democratization of classic cooking,' I was told by the food writer Gilles Pudlowski. 'In my view, a dish expertly cooked, then properly frozen and defrosted, or canned, is virtually indistinguishable from the same dish freshly cooked, and generally better than average restaurant fare. I see this as a way of the future, and as a gourmet it does not distress me.' So not only the housewife but even the restaurateur, maybe at a cost to his pride, can raise the average quality of his meals *and* cut his expenses by using these methods – and some are now doing so. Some critics believe that one day it may be as usual for a family to prepare a fresh dish of this kind as it is today to buy hand-made clothes or furniture.

Even so, may not something be lost? The greatness of French cuisine has always depended on its daily grassroots tradition: its genius has grown from the marrow of the nation, like music in Germany, art in medieval Italy. What will happen if the art of home cooking is gradually lost and gastronomy is practised just by a few master-chefs and a few amateur devotees? This is not the French tradition. Bocuse and his friends have 'given cooking back to the cooks', but cooking belongs also to the people – to Tante Marie in her farmhouse, preparing her chicken stew, or to the young housewife in a hypermarket, choosing just the right cut for Sunday's garlicky roast lamb. Just as a nation that plays no music will produce few great musicians, so the French will not continue to eat well unless they know the secrets of food and can share its practice. At present, decline and renewal are equally balanced: the inexorable spread of fast and convenience foods versus the revived interest in the cuisine and quality products of *le terroir*. Is gastronomy in France destined to become more of a special interest, and less universal?

HOLIDAY OBSESSIONS:
CLUB MED'S STRAW-HUT MYSTIQUE GETS A FACELIFT

The old French mania for *la cuisine* has now come to be rivalled by a new one, even more widespread: 'We are the first,' said one French sociologist, 'to have made holidays into a national institution, a collective dream. We think about them all year round.' Other nations do so, too: the post-war growth of tourism is not confined to the French. But there are few countries where the annual urge to get away from it all has grown quite so powerful.

Before the war, long holidays were the preserve of the well-to-do. Now French wage-earners have secured for themselves the longest annual paid leave in Europe: in 1936 the Popular Front gave them the legal right to two weeks' *congés payés*; a third week was added in 1956, and a fourth in 1965. Then the Socialists in 1981 added a fifth, whereas in Britain the legal minimum is three. In 1939 only 25 per cent of people took an annual holiday away from home, but today the figure is 62 per cent. And in the middle classes, growing numbers have two main holidays a year – a longish summer break, then a shorter one in winter, maybe skiing, or travelling further to the sun. But there are still plenty who feel excluded: in any year, some 45 per cent of workers' families do not leave home on their paid leave, usually because they think they cannot afford it. And although the proportion of farmers leaving on holiday has more than doubled since the 1960s, it is still less than 30 per cent.

One strong element in the holiday cult seems to relate to the post-war 'back to nature' urges of the French. Previously, city-dwellers would often feel ill at ease in the deep country with its alien peasantry: they preferred urban resorts like Biarritz with casinos and promenades, or else the orderliness of some family villa or château. But then in the 1950s a vogue arose for going native, as millions grew happy to lose themselves amid the mountains or beaches of this large and still largely unspoilt land. Hotels lost ground heavily to the new cheaper craze for *le camping*: its practitioners have risen since 1950 from 1 to 7 million a year, three times the number that stay in a hotel. And although in August it may seem that all have flocked to the Côte d'Azur, there are plenty elsewhere, too. Sailing, cycling and other holiday sports have also increased hugely in popularity, and so has winter skiing. Whereas the British, at a certain social level, often like to re-create their home environment on holiday, in a well-equipped caravan or cosy boarding house, their French equivalents may prefer as complete a change as possible – to wear as little as weather or decency will allow, and to scrabble amid pine needles in a tent. But this vogue may have passed its prime, as more French now look for a degree of comfort in their back-to-nature settings, maybe in bungalows, villas or superior *campings*.

The return to nature, like the ecological trends of the 1970s, seemed to mark a reaction against France's too rapid urbanization, and maybe a subconscious desire to compensate for the desertion of rural traditions. Sociologists have thus been unsure whether this frenetic urge to escape to a different life has been a token of healthy adventurousness or of maladjustment. The sociologist Michel Crozier has blamed the holiday mania on the tensions of French urban society and office life, where 'no one is truly at ease and so the French *need* holidays more than, say, the Americans'. Many people have thus been looking not only for change and relaxation but for a social liberation not always found in their own lives. Some, of course, do still take the long traditional family holiday amid lots of relatives, in Tante Louise's Limousin farmhouse or *grand-mère*'s Normandy château: but this habit has been yielding ground to a vogue for holidays at once more collective and more individual: the camping site, holiday club or big skiing party, where everyone in theory is equal, yet freed from the emotional ties *chez* Tante Louise.

The French, who used to be insular about their holidays, are today travelling abroad far more: this goes with the growth of cheaper air travel and of European motorways, and maybe with a greater curiosity about other lands, a new taste for the exotic. The first big increase came in the 1950s, after the easing of currency restrictions, when tourist spending abroad rose sixfold; and today some 12 per cent of holidays are spent outside France. But this growth is relative: it compares with 27 per cent of British, 62 per cent of Germans and 66 per cent of Dutch, who go abroad. These peoples do have stronger climatic, even scenic, incentives: the French equivalent of the Northern package tourist who seeks the sun on a beach in Benidorm, or Rimini, is more likely to stay inside France; and France's airborne mass package trade is little developed. As for the destinations favoured by the French, some 2.4 million now go annually to Spain, 1 million to Portugal, 970,000 to Italy and 540,000 to Britain and Ireland. A growing minority has been venturing further – to Israel, India, Thailand, the Caribbean and indeed the United States. City weekend breaks have become popular, too, notably to Amsterdam, Barcelona, London and Prague.

While many people who work hard all year simply want quiet and rest, a growing number of others have been seeking out more unusual, varied and active kinds of holiday. For them, the recharging of batteries offered by a good holiday is found by doing something different and enriching: as one writer has put it, 'The old formula of the "three Ss" (sun, sand, sex) has been giving ground to that of the "three As" (activity, apprenticeship, adventure).' These people, mostly young, might opt for a cultural tour of Mexico, or a cruise along Russian rivers, or a student festival in Budapest; nearer home, they might seek out an activity holiday devoted to painting, farming or archaeology. Many firms now offer these specialized holidays. And at all social levels, those who take no holiday away from home may well content themselves with family day trips to one or other of the popular theme parks, nature parks or fun parks, led by Disneyland Paris, and Futuroscope near Poitiers (see p. 627).★

★ Many of those who come to these parks, especially Disneyland, are visitors to France – in a land where foreign tourism earns nearly twice as much (137 billion francs in 1994) as what the French spend on holidays abroad (76 billion). In numbers

All that I have said about French holiday ideals could be summed up in one magic phrase: Club Méditerranée. Its vast success with the French themselves has revealed a good deal about their spirit and how it has been evolving. *Le Club* has also spread around the globe, attracting other nations, thus becoming a mass export of French stylishness, sensuality and fantasy. In the process it has been changing: it has become more conventional and comfortable, and some of the old magic has been lost. In 1997 it acquired a new chairman/director, Philippe Bourguignon, who had just rescued Euro Disney; and some *gentils membres* feared that their beloved Club Med might be Mickeyfied. But he soon made it clear that his aim, on the contrary, was to revive its original spirit. 'We must keep the Club's uniqueness and restore it to its roots, to the nomadic and pirate culture that was ours,' he told me in November 1998. But he also needs to make a profit, in a cut-throat world where tastes have changed. Whether or not he can succeed, Club Med will certainly go into history as one of the most original and creative large-scale holiday ventures that the world has ever seen.

It began in 1950 when Gérard Blitz, a tall athlete from Antwerp, started a small informal holiday camp on Majorca. It was a big success, and it soon turned into a permanent club, which has steadily grown and internationalized: today it provides holidays to some 1.5 million people a year, of whom 31 per cent are from France, and 32 per cent from the rest of Europe. Club Med and its affiliates operate over a hundred 'villages' across the globe (you must never call them 'holiday camps') and it has diversified to suit varying tastes. It still has seven of those famous original straw-hut villages around the sea that lends the Club its name: but it has also moved upmarket, and most of its villages are now more solidly built, in bungalow or hotel style: some are quite luxurious, roughly the equivalent in price of a four-star hotel. Many are open all year, and sixteen are in winter ski resorts. When Blitz retired, the Club was run

---

of visitors, France is the world's leading tourist country, ahead of Spain. In 1995 this total fell below 60 million for the first time in fifteen years: this was due in part to short-term factors such as the low level of the dollar and sterling, but it set the authorities worrying about a possible decline in the quality of the tourist industry – a report by the Conseil Économique et Social claimed that foreign visitors frequently found French hoteliers and restaurateurs to be 'complacent, boastful and not very hospitable'. However, in 1996, with the recovery of the pound and dollar, the total rose again to 62 million, and the self-criticism waned. The British, with nearly 10 million visitors, were in first place.

from 1963 to 1993 by an equally remarkable man, Gilbert Trigano: rather like Édouard Leclerc, he brought a visionary touch to a harsh competitive field.

'The individual has a horror of promiscuity, but he does need community,' Blitz wrote. 'So we give him a flexible holiday context where at any moment he can join in or escape – a strange cocktail of *la vie de château* and *la vie sauvage*.' And Trigano told me, 'Holidays provide a liberation that enriches the rest of the year. The Club has broken down some barriers: it gives serious people the right to be ridiculous, to try anything.' So the villages were developed to satisfy certain French desires: sophistication amid return to nature; individualism amid camaraderie; a blend of sport, hedonism, culture and exotic foreign settings; a once-a-year escape from the barriers and tensions of society into a never-neverland fraternity. Today this remains the ideal – save that, victim of its own success, the Club has inevitably veered from spontaneity to pre-packaged sensuality on an all-inclusive basis.

Borrowing the model of the Polynesian village, Blitz and Trigano built their first colonies in the tracks of another romantic tradition, the Odyssey. The prototype is at Corfu (Corcyra) near Ithaca, others are on Djerba (authentic island of the lotus-eaters), at Foça not far from Troy, at Cefalù beyond the Sicilian straits of Scylla and Charybdis, at Al Hoceima in Morocco near the Pillars of Hercules – as well as, today, in some thirty other countries, even Cuba. The villages vary in style, but the basic formula is the same. Money is banked on arrival, and no cash changes hands, save in the form of either pop-apart beads, or, today, smart cards or tickets, for buying bar drinks. Meals, often outdoors, are lavish buffets, with unlimited free wine; most tables are for eight and conversation is general, club style. In some villages you sleep down by the beach in thatched huts. The staff, known as *gentils organisateurs* (GOs), mix on equal terms with the clients, the *gentils membres* (GMs), sitting with them at meals, dancing with them, maybe calling them *tu* or seeking to imbue them with *la mystique du Club*. Yet (unlike in some holiday camps) they do not try to force individuals to join activities. You can skulk in your room all day, or wander alone into the hinterland, and no one will care or notice. And there is masses to do for those who want it – cabaret and sing-songs, sports from water-skiing to judo and circus trapeze, mostly included in the basic fees. For an extra charge you can go on sight-seeing excursions, so the village can be used as a base for group exploration of, say, classical Greece or the Sahara. There are open-air concerts of classical music, plus in some villages a supply of live culture. The Club's appeal is middle class, so very different from Butlin's.

In its pioneering years the Club was essentially youthful and exuberant, and everyone was on *tu* terms – amazing for France. Some of the more dedicated GOs and GMs went around in a *paréo* (a gaudy Tahitian sarong, uniform of the new utopia), and a few even wore flower garlands. Phoney and embarrassing to some tastes, maybe: but the appeal to a kind of comradely naturalism was real enough. On my first Club holiday, at Cefalù in 1967, I was stunned by the euphoric spirit, the sense of togetherness, and the readiness of GMs to join spontaneously with the GO *animateurs* in the nightly task of getting the party going. This ambience survives today in some straw-hut villages, where the GMs tend to be young in age or spirit. But the Club is now so well known that it has also become popular with many of the kind of people who at first were suspicious of it. It is no longer the mad adventure of a few uninhibited initiates, but attracts also an older or more sedate clientele. Today there are fewer swinging singles and more families with children: the 'Mini-Club' villages that take charge of toddlers are highly popular. The plumbing is better, the organization smoother, the *paréos* far fewer. Most GMs stick to *vous*, and the GOs are under orders to be careful whom they call *tu*, for it can cause offence.

So in becoming a venerable institution the Club has lost something. Yet it remains a unique and fascinating venture, cleverly stage-managed, with a sensual impact – as in 1991 I noted again, on a holiday at Foça, near Izmir. Like most Club villages, its setting was superb – some 350 solid bungalows terraced along a hillside above the beach, amid olive and cypress trees. Most GMs were French or German, but the Club tried to include some Turkish flavour – folk-dancing shows, a *hammam*, kebabs and mezes in the lavish buffet meals. As dusk fell, the scene by the softly floodlit *piscine* and bar was glamorous: a band played Mozart, exotic multicoloured cocktails were piled high. Ajda from Istanbul belly-danced and the GMs dressed up chic for *la grande bouffe* of dinner, where one night we sat with a Parisian TV presenter, a sleek Chinese girl, a civilized couple from Bremen. At the nightly cabaret, I was dragooned into putting on a pink tutu to dance in *Swan Lake* (as Trigano had said, 'The Club gives you the right to be ridiculous'). And so the therapeutically childish fun ended with all of us singing the crazy hand-waving Club songs ('Hands up! – gimme gimme *your* heart!'). Under their Tunisian *chef de village*, the eighty GOs came from twenty nations: a hefty Austrian girl taught me aerobics, a gentle Malaysian failed to teach me windsurfing. Foça was a chance to meet the world – but also to escape from it. No TV or radio in the rooms, no newspapers on sale. When I asked one GO if there was any more dramatic news from Moscow (it was the time of the coup against Gorbachev), he said scornfully, 'Here, we don't know – and we don't *care*.'

Previously, I had visited three contrasting villages in Greece. *Et in Arcadia ego*: just to its north, at Aighion, our GM group from Paris was greeted musically by the assembled seventy GOs, including Pascal, chief *animateur*, a funny-sad clown in a big green hat. My wife and I were allotted a straw hut called Méduse; other GMs had huts with names like Styx and Zorba. We were then given a pep talk on the beach by bearded Mouche, the *chef de village*, looking like a Greek god. He said that the aim of the Club was that we should all be very nice to each other (which the French needed to be told, as they aren't always nice to strangers, but here they seemed to manage it). A typical day would begin with a visit to the communal *lavabos*, where it was unnerving to shave while a blonde in a bikini was cleaning her teeth. The un-French breakfast (nearly everyone in swimsuits) was a long help-yourself buffet laden with yoghurt, melon, feta cheese, halva, smoked fish, honey, fruit. Then we sunbathed by the idyllic *piscine* where most of the girls were topless. The jokey GO head of sports was organizing tugs-of-war. Lunch on the terraced patio under vine-creepers was another lavish buffet, with some Greek dishes. At our table were a shy Dutch woman doctor and a museum curator from La Rochelle (the straw-hut villages have often attracted a more interesting type of GM than the newer, posher ones). After lunch the hypnotic rhythms of *sirtaki* music invaded the air, and some of us went to the open-air dance floor for our daily *sirtaki* lesson from an ebullient Corfiot GO.

At the outdoor bar by the pool we drank ouzo (price: three gold beads, one black one), and amusedly watched a hefty Belgian being rejected by a girl from Nancy. Then, for an inside view on Club life as seen by the GOs, we talked with Andrew from Leeds, chief water-skiing instructor. With his curly blond hair and virility-symbol speed-boat, he was all the rage with the teenage-girl GMs, and I found his boasts about his string of seductions entirely believable. At dinner, we found ourselves sitting with three Parisian *cadres* and their girls, hard-core GMs swapping anecdotes about previous Club holidays like veterans telling campaign stories ('*Moi, j'ai fait Djerba en soixante-seize, c'était sensas!*') but, significantly, saying not a word about France or their lives back home. Later, we all crowded round the amphitheatre for the nightly *animation*. Pascal and the other *animateurs* embarked on carefully rehearsed pranks and led us into jokey games. Some GOs, whatever their daytime job, are required also to be actors in the evening, and tonight they gave us a Western show, cowboys and Indians, miming to recorded music. A few GMs joined the *animation* – notably an ugly little man with cropped hair whom my wife and I dubbed 'the Bank Clerk' (he probably was one). He arrived looking so drab, but now his inner personality had come alive, as he led us in a riotous chain-dance, wearing a comic hat.

We then took a ferry to Corfu for a very different Club experience. This was not the famous straw-hut village of Corfu-Ipsos, but a newer luxury 600-bed hotel, called Hélios, which the Club had rented. Each room even had a bathroom! But the drawback was that this hideous eight-floor block, built for the ordinary hotel trade, worked against the Club's kind of *ambiance*. What's more, the respectable well-heeled GMs, many on their first Club holiday, were on average much older than at Aighion, and older still in spirit. The large contingents of Germans and Italians tended to keep to their national groups, and the language barriers added to the reserve. The GOs had an uphill task creating *la vraie ambiance du Club*. But Hélios had one star asset: its *chef de village*, the amazing 'Tonton Jean', today a legend in the Club. This professional actor/producer was determined to overcome Hélios's handicaps: he ran it as a one-man show, a non-stop spectacle of bravura gimmicks and classy drama. Shaven-headed, often bare-chested, this manic extrovert on an ego-trip was everywhere at once. The GMs adored him, the GOs found him a bit despotic. He and his wife Annie had been on the Paris stage: then he joined the Club as *animateur* and was sent to problem-child Hélios with a big budget for *animation*. 'It's marvellous,' he told me; 'in our little Paris theatre we had a handful of actors and small, uncertain audiences. Here, I have a huge captive audience of 600 GMs each night, plus ninety GOs I can use as actors or extras.' So he could realize his frustrated ambitions with a series of shows of high ingenuity. He did a Feydeau farce (stars: Jean and Annie), *Irma la Douce* (stars: Jean and Annie) and two large-cast spectaculars with echoes of de Mille. The ritual weekly presentation of the GOs, called 'The Gods Descend from Olympus', was a pageant of blazing torches and robed figures, with a jokey commentary and Jean as Zeus. For 'La Légende des Siècles', a 'historico-erotico revue' with clever lighting, the village *coiffeuse* was Joan of Arc, the head of sports ('Naff-Naff') was Cro-Magnon Man, an *hôtesse* from Martinique was a naked Empress Josephine. GOs cascaded across the stage for ninety minutes in a variety of costumes, then Jean took rapturous curtain calls. But pity the GOs who had been up rehearsing till 2 a.m. on top of their usual daily duties.

Tonton's other coup was the stunning method of bidding welcome to each new group of GMs. From the airport, they were brought to Hélios straight across the bay in the Club's motor-yachts; and as they approached the jetty, teams of GO water-skiers weaved in and out of the boats, bearing aloft the group's national flags, while loudspeakers blared the village's jingly signature tune, and there on the jetty were Tonton and topless GO lovelies, flower-garlanded, ready to kiss the newcomers. Bemused after a dawn flight from, say, Munich or Brussels, the GMs were led up the steps amid applause, for an *ouzo d'honneur* with Jean. A dazzling way to start a holiday. Annie would then give a tactful pep talk to each new group (including some matrons in their fifties): 'You must realize, this is *not* a hotel, it's a club. We like everyone to use Christian names, but don't feel you *have* to use *tu* if it makes you uneasy.' Most GMs accepted this *règle du jeu*, but a few reacted badly. They complained at having to share tables of eight with strangers, or at 'the indignity of eating with the servants'! 'What cheek,' said one august lawyer, 'the girl who teaches windsurfing expects to call me Pierre.' And some of the young GOs, after doing their best to create Club *ambiance*, then being rejected by older or snootier GMs, reacted by withdrawing into their own cliques. Such were the perils and problems of the Club's upmarket move.

My wife and I were keen to get back to the world of *les cases* (huts) – for me, the true aristocrats of *le Club*, of all ages, are those who prefer the youthful *mystique* of the straw huts, and look down on those *arrivistes* who make for the mod cons of the hotel-villages. So we left Hélios for the little *village-annexe* on the Greek mainland: Parga the enchanted. Just forty straw huts in an olive grove, a sandy beach in a cove, a few windsurfers and three very young GOs. As we disembarked in the hot sun, we were greeted by Patrick, *chef de village*, clad in the lowest-slung *paréo* I have ever seen, kept up by will-power. Sally, Scottish music graduate, was his Girl Friday – *hôtesse*, accountant, nurse and pianist. Our fellow GMs, a select band of paradise-seekers, included a Parisian orchestra conductor, a Grande École student, an English headmistress. Some of us sailed to a secluded creek where we could bathe nude and display our *gentils membres*. Then as dusk fell the Parga scene was hypnotic. Flowering oleander and mimosa surrounded the sandy patio beside the bar, where ping-pong, boules, impromptu *sirtaki* and much ouzo-drinking were in progress. At dinner we sat with two factory workers from the Midi: there was democracy in paradise. Later, when it grew chilly, we lit a camp fire on the patio. With Sally at the piano, Patrick sang Serge Lama, Jacques from Blois recited his own love poems. This was our own *animation*, a far cry from Tonton Jean. We were all touched by grace; all day the mood had been dreamy, poetic, intimate, lotus-eating . . .

And so we returned to Paris, brainwashed by two Greek weeks of gregarious sensuality. We wandered around Neuilly, suffering from withdrawal symptoms. Why do these people in the street not say '*bonjour*' as we pass? As I wash my car, why do they not come up to help? What is wrong with them? Socially and physically, the Club is a drug from which one adjusts only slowly. Like Meaulnes, we yearn for our lost domain. Of course there is always next year, with honey-dew and the milk of paradise again included ad lib in the basic fees. But in the meantime, how to live?

So this leads to the question: what has been the impact of this never-never-land on French society, over the years? What impact has it had on French social structures and behaviour, back home? This may sound a ponderous query about a summer frolic, but it is relevant. French GMs are mainly middle class, down to clerks and artisans but with few manual workers. In its French context this is not surprising, even though the cheaper villages would not be outside a skilled worker's means. So as a social catalyst the Club has had its limits. Yet, within its range, it probably played some part in the loosening of French rigidities and formalities during the post-war decades. Some sociologists seriously think so.

In one sense, the Club's therapy has always involved some social make-believe. Its staff enjoy telling the story of two men who struck up a friendship over Samos wine and deep-sea diving at Ipsos: only at the end did they swap names and addresses, to discover that one was a director and the other a night watchman in the same factory. But we are not told what then happened back home; and one company director has admitted, 'I got friendly with one of my clerks: it was all right at the Club, where it's all so free and easy, but it made it harder to keep up *les convenances* back in the office.' Noticeably, French GMs more than foreign ones prefer to remain anonymous and not discuss their jobs or backgrounds with each other. They want to forget about France: exchanging visiting cards is not done. Nor has there been pressure from GMs for Butlin-style winter get-togethers in France: the Club's few attempts at these failed because they showed up the social differences that were masked in the villages, and Blitz told me candidly, 'The Club's success is due to its divorce from daily life. We found that trying to hold meetings in Paris lost us the credit we had won in the villages.' Indeed I have often thought of the Club as a kind of compensatory world, almost Jean Genet territory where men and women act out the fantasy roles they cannot manage in their own lives – classless democrats, noble savages, high-spirited friends-to-all-the-world.

But in the past thirty years France has evolved: the French have become less formal and uptight, in entertaining, in using *tu* and Christian names, in office relations and so on. Millions have been GMs at least once, and it could be that some of the Club's informality has rubbed off on their behaviour back home. In any event, French life has patently been catching up with the Club, as Trigano told me: 'In the '50s we were in advance of our age, but today it comes to meet us. In those days the gulf between the Club and the new GMs who joined us was so great that we had to create a shock by insisting on *tu*. But today Monsieur Dupont is himself readier to be "*toi, Jacques*", so we don't need *tu* so much. It is France that has changed, not us.' So maybe the appeal of the Club has diminished now that the rigidities in daily life are less severe. It is ironic that growing French informality has made the Club a bit more formal.

The success of its whole astute operation still depends above all on the GOs. In world tourism, its supreme innovation has been to make it seem that the staff are on holiday along with their clients. Of course, *ars est celare artem*: to do his or her job properly the GO must work hard and skilfully. It is a highly popular job, not too well paid but attracting many thousands of applicants, not surprisingly. Recruits have usually trained or worked already elsewhere, as sports instructors, actors or *animateurs* for youth clubs or town councils; nearly all are in their twenties, and over half are non-French. The Club then gives recruits its own training, and in Trigano's words 'has created a new profession', closer to the classic *animateur* than to the hotel employee. Bronzed, sexy and sporty, this new élite has turned the traditional hotel industry on its head: at the Ritz or Crillon, a maid or waiter may feel or seem humbler than the guests, but at the Club it can be the reverse. Some arrogant GOs fail to hide their contempt for mere GMs.

The Club has often come in for criticism, especially from the Left, for creating a fictitious world, or for promoting an ethos of gluttony and self-indulgence in the setting of poor countries. At Marrakesh the Club is in the heart of the old city, next to the famous Place Djmaa el Fna, teeming with touts and tourists; and to reach its sports and swimming annexe, we were taken out daily by bus through the desolate suburbs. I was made uneasy by this juxtaposition of luxurious Euro-hedonism and Third World reality, where only a gateway separated our temple of greed and licence from the severe traditional Islamic world outside. However, Marrakesh is not typical: the average village is much more remote, secluded within its own spacious campus.

It must also be said for the Club that it is generally (but not always) saved from cheap vulgarity by its French sense of sophistication. Basically, I agree with the view of one veteran GO: 'Only the French could have succeeded with a holiday formula like ours. The British or Germans would have turned it into jolly boyscoutism. The Americans would have made it into Mickey Mouse. But our French individualism saves us.' Despite the growing majority of foreign GMs, Club Med's style remains French. And it has influenced the rest of the holiday industry, as Trigano has said: 'They flatter us by trying to imitate us. They no longer build big classic hotels, they try out the bungalow style, maybe with club-like features. And by mixing the nations on holiday, free from the usual tensions, we have been doing something to spread international amity.' This may be true. Large national groups of GMs may stick to their own cliques, partly for language reasons: but there are rarely conflicts, while the cosmopolitan spirit of the GOs spills over on to the GMs.

'You and I do much the same job,' Gilbert Trigano once told the Pope. This son of a Jewish grocer has been one of the most remarkable of France's post-war innovators and entrepreneurs. Born in 1920, he left school at fifteen, joined the Communist Resistance and worked for *L'Humanité*. He then started a camping-equipment firm, and thus met Blitz and joined the Club in 1954. He broke with the PCF, but retained the ideal of a comradely classless society and still claimed to hate private property: 'The individual's happiness is ensured by the collective use of wealth.' For him, the Club's villages have reflected this principle, though he has added, 'In the tough world of tourism we cannot be philanthropists.' But in being enticed upmarket, rather than staying with a more 'social' kind of tourism, did he not compromise with his ideals? Some people have thought so. The Club has been a public company since

1966, with an 8-billion-franc turnover (1998): many shares belong to the big banks, or to companies such as the Agnelli group. So, in its heady bid for profits, the Club has steadily expanded and claims today to be the world's largest holiday organization.

Notably, Trigano began to aim at an American mass market. The eighteen villages in Mexico and the Caribbean (one is in Florida) are primarily for North Americans and the first language there is English. The Club's formula appealed readily at first to the open American temperament, given some adjustments of comfort (straw huts were not welcome), and by 1985 over 20 per cent of all GMs were American or Canadian. But then the expansion there faltered – due to growing competition, or a bad image of the Club – and today only 14 per cent of GMs are North American (this compares with 31 per cent French, 6.7 Italian, 5.9 Belgian, 4.2 German, 2 British). Instead, in the 1990s, the accent was on growth in eastern Asia and the Pacific, to cater mainly for the huge potential Japanese market (5.3 per cent of all GMs in 1997) and the Australian (2.4 per cent). Villages were opened in Bali, Malaysia, Thailand, etc., and some are planned for China. But by 1998 the financial crisis in eastern Asia was putting a halt to the growth of GM numbers there. The Club has also been expanding in other ways, for example with sea cruises. But not all these ventures have been successful: over-extension has been held partly to blame for the Club's recent difficulties.

The early to mid-1990s were marked by diverse setbacks. Villages in Corsica and Israel suffered terrorist attacks. Worse, in 1992 an aircraft chartered locally by the Club crashed in Senegal, killing thirty GMs aboard. In 1995 the French nuclear tests near Tahiti led to a partial boycott of the two villages there by French and other GMs, notably Australians. And most curiously, during a French divorce case in 1997, a lawyer discovered that the Club had been compiling secret dossiers on some GMs (their financial status, hygiene, private lives, etc.), whom an official described as 'getting Club Med into trouble because they are behaving like naughty boys and girls'!

These varied events did nothing to improve the Club's image. But perhaps more serious for the future was its commercial decline. The Gulf War, then recession, hit the world's tourist industry, and the early 1990s were bad years for the Club. True, its annual total of holidays sold to GMs has continued to rise, from 1 to 1.5 million since 1986. But many GMs now make shorter visits to the Club, often one week instead of two; and the more expensive villages have been doing less well than the

cheaper ones. Add to this the growth of competition, from Germany's
Robinson Club and other new rivals and imitators. All in all, various
factors explain why Club Med made no profits for five years, to reach
an operating loss of 700 million francs for 1997.

This brought the moment of truth. Trigano had retired in 1993, to
be succeeded as chairman and managing director by his son Serge, who
did not have the same qualities. The Club's board grew restive, accusing
him of poor management; and in 1997 they replaced him with Philippe
Bourguignon, who had just done a brilliant job in rescuing Euro Disney.
Club Med's shares on the Bourse shot up. Serge was fobbed off with a
marginal job, and he soon left in a huff, claiming this would become '_un
club Mickey_'. So he and his father severed their links. It was a sad ending
to thirty years of Trigano _père_'s inspired efforts, even if in latter years he had
grown too rigid and autocratic, like many an ageing boss. Bourguignon set
about wielding a new broom, rather brutally. He sacked many directors
and senior GOs in the Paris head office, while others angrily resigned
in loyalty to the Triganos. And he brought in a new team that included
Henri Giscard d'Estaing (son of Valéry) as his right-hand man, plus some
top managers, oddly enough, from hypermarket firms such as Casino.
However, despite his none-too-_gentil_ style, the new super-GO soon
made it clear that he was not planning to Mickeyfy and spoil the Club.
In fact, this impressive character seems in many ways well suited to his
new job – a transatlantic champion solo sailor, a maverick who wears
matelot jerseys at smart parties, a friend and devotee of Richard Branson,
whom he calls his role model. A tough and able manager with a show-off
sense of fun, he disguised himself as a waiter at one big Club party to
open a new village. 'As a younger man, he would have made an ideal
chef de village,' one GO told me.

Bourguignon has set about renovating the Club, tightening its management, improving its finances. He is aiming to broaden its clientele, but
has pledged also to 'maintain its unique values', based on its original
spirit. It will not be easy to do both. Certainly the Club has been evolving
over some years now, as I found during a week at Kamarina, Sicily, in
1998. This was not a smart upmarket village, but all its bungalow rooms
had hairdryers, safes, door locks, while those in its ugly hotel annexe had
marble basins and satellite TV. Newspapers were on sale in its shop.
Some GMs had brought their mobiles to keep in touch with their offices
back home; and though they were friendly and relaxed, very few used
_tu_. It was all rather different from the old euphoric escapist days I had

known also in Sicily, thirty years ago. Many GMs were small children, well behaved, enjoying the Mini-Club, and creating their own Club ambience, unfazed by language differences. Some GOs had the true outgoing Club spirit, such as bouncy little 'Baby', a blonde from Ravenna who took us through our gymnastics and aerobics. But some others seemed sullen, and I learned that the many Italians, locally engaged, were fed up with being paid at low rates. There were no Sicilian folklore events, but lots of lavish GO playback shows, very well danced and mimed, but too Hollywoodian for my taste, such as a big *Grease* soirée. The Club had lost something, I felt, though much remained – the generous buffets, the vast array of sports, the excellent cultural excursions (an Italian GO took us to Syracuse for the day), and the recorded classical concerts above the beach, where Brahms's Double Concerto found a perfect setting as the sun set into sea. Here a tall German girl, at the Club on her own, was looking intense and soulful. But four hours later, she was on stage in the GM show, giggling gleefully as she and the others paraded around squirting water at each other. Then we all went through the noisy hand-waving ritual of 'Hands up! – gimme gimme *your* heart!' Its euphoria had become a bit mechanical, I felt.

Bourguignon started to give the Club a needed facelift. He extended the policy, begun by Serge Trigano, of refurbishing many of the older run-down villages by improving their décor, plumbing and comfort. For this the board gave him a huge loan, which it had refused to Trigano. Bourguignon changed the marketing strategy, and he cut some costs in the villages (simpler buffets, fewer free cocktail parties, etc.). He made a good start, and for 1998 the Club even made a modest profit again. He also sought to widen its range. Notably, he was preparing to open new Club Med leisure centres in a few big cities such as Paris by the end of 1999, with the aim of reaching a new clientele and maybe of spreading a little of its ethos into daily non-holiday life (Trigano *père* had always wanted this, too: 'I'd like all France to become one non-stop Club Med,' he once euphorized to me.)

In November 1998 Bourguignon told me that he would extend new sporting activities, such as circus trapeze and roller-skating lessons. He will 'bring more music into the villages', including more classical concerts and lessons in local folk-dancing (such as the *sirtaki* classes that I attended in Greece). 'The Club offers so much which most people just don't know about,' he said. Above all, he and his new team have been rethinking the system of nightly shows and *animation*, which had tended to become too stereotyped and mechanical. The GOs' miming and dancing is often superb, quite professional: but recently there has seemed to me too much stress on American pop material, too little use of European culture, and too little direct contact with the GMs, as compared with the old days. Bourguignon told me, 'I want the shows to become simpler, more convivial, with more live music, more interaction with the GMs.' For 1999, he said, he plans new spectacles about a Paris hospital and the history of a Paris street, while the one new American number, *Titanic*, will be 'a derisory send-up'. In a new murder thriller show the GMs will be the jury. All to the good: but will today's GMs be prepared to interact? One veteran GO *animateur* lamented to me, 'GMs have become more passive, less ready to participate' (as compared with the days when I myself, ideal GM, danced in a pink tutu and was thrown into the pool).

This leads to the basic dilemma. GMs today are of different kinds: how can Bourguignon, with a eye on profits, appeal to them all? He has said some remarkable things: 'We have to let the villages be a bit crazy, fun and provocative, but manage them properly', and also, 'We must get back to the nomadic and pirate culture that used to be ours. The *chef de village* was once a drop-out in society, but he's become too bourgeois.' This was music to the ears of old-style GMs and GOs. Yet many newer GMs, young or old, are today suspicious of zany, too-personal GOs or of rooms without baths, as Serge Trigano told me: 'They want not only more comfort but less isolation from the real world, and a more conventional kind of holiday.' So he began to install more telephones, TV sets and door locks, and to speed up the move from bead necklaces to bar tickets or smart cards. Some veteran GMs were horrified. Some Club officials today even refer to '*nos clients*' not '*nos gentils membres*', and instead of '*la mystique du Club*' they talk of 'our consumer product'. Is the Club to be less unique? And if all its bedrooms have modern bathrooms, will not Blitz's original baby go out with their bathwater? Bourguignon is aware of this dilemma: but it can be resolved, so he told me. 'A little more modern comfort need not be incompatible with plenty of youthful camaraderie, a return to our "nomadic and pirate culture". I intend to rebuild the GO tradition.'

He struck me as sincere in wanting to get back to basics and to build on the Club's original assets. But in face of commercial pressures, in a changing world with changing public tastes, can he succeed? He will need to diversify the Club, so as to draw in new popular audiences, but without upsetting the old loyalists. There will still be a few sedate luxury villages, plus plenty of others in the middle range for families with small children, or more conventional clients, plus others again more youthful in spirit. 'Because our image had grown jaded, we lost many of our youthful GMs. We now aim to win new young members by going back to our roots. In France and elsewhere, there's a huge potential – masses of people who adore Club Med values without realizing that they exist. So we shall maintain the straw-hut villages, renovating them a little but basically keeping them unchanged. They are still highly popular.' So this is Bourguignon's challenge. The Club may have changed, but there remains a steady clientele for the old-style convivial back-to-nature holiday. In today's anxious France, plenty of French people still seek just that. The dream need not die that first impelled Blitz and his pioneers to seek the Happy Isles.

There are some echoes of the Club's ambience in other resorts and camping sites along France's coastlines. The French have increasingly been drawn to the seaside (some 41 per cent of all holidays in France were spent there in 1994, against 23 per cent in 1958) and also to the mountains (19 against 10 per cent). At the seaside, the 'topless' revolution hit French resorts in the 1960s and '70s, and soon became widely accepted: even staid resorts like Biarritz and Deauville came to sanction bare bosoms on their public beaches, while the few conservative mayors who tried to forbid them saw their town's holiday trade slump. Today most 'serious' resorts try to restrict the practice to the beach itself and the promenade, though in some towns in summer you can see topless girls also in shops and cafés inland. Total nudism, male and female, has been creeping along some remoter beaches, but is still formally illegal outside the nudist camps: these are booming, notably on the Languedoc coast (see p. 377).

One seaside trend has been the post-war rise of popular tourism along the Côte d'Azur, and then today its slight decline – to the profit of Brittany. After the élitist golden age of the Belle Époque, a more democratic tourism on the Côte saw its heyday in the 1960s and 1970s, when St-Tropez came to fame in the wake of Bardot (see p. 571): the blue-and-orange tents of campers filled the pine forests for kilometres, as jukeboxes blared idly in the sun, and pine needles fell into the *soupe de poisson* at a thousand outdoor *bistrots*. But today many people have come to judge the Côte d'Azur too urbanized, too crowded, too expensive, and some of its beaches too polluted: so there has been a small shift towards the coasts of north-west France, notably Brittany. These may be less sunny, and mistier: but the air and water are purer, the beaches are longer, more varied, less crowded, and the natives generally friendlier. Twenty years after the first ecological trends of the 1970s, this belated new one has gathered pace in the 1990s. The Var *département*, in Provence, may still have the largest number of seaside holiday-makers, 1.6 million a year (foreigners included); but it is closely followed by Charente-Maritime, Vendée and Finistère, along the west coast. All these are ahead of Alpes-Maritimes (capital: Nice).

Sea and mountains provide major settings for the tremendous growth of sport in modern France. The number of private sailing boats and motor-yachts has risen since 1960 from 20,000 to over 800,000, and in summer the Côte d'Azur is so jammed with yachts that some ports have created parking discs for them as for cars. Skiing is even more popular: over 4 million go on holiday to the ski slopes each year (excluding day-trippers) and 10 per cent of these are working class. The French Alps are the favourite venue, followed by the Pyrenees, Vosges and parts of the Massif Central, popular for cross-country *ski de fond*. The building of new ski lifts and hotels in smart Alpine resorts such as Megève and Courchevel has meant big business for some developers.

The new ecological and hedonistic trends have brought a big increase in the individual practice of sport for fitness or pleasure. The French are today more *sportif* than the British, or at least more devoted to participation as opposed to spectator sports. True, the annual Tour de France cycle race* is a massive spectator sport, and so are the big car races and league football. But France's sporting clubs claim a total of 14 million *licenciés* or certified active members (five times the 1958 total), while sales of sports and outdoor gear have risen more than twentyfold since 1960. The football clubs come first, with 1.8 million members, while rugby is popular in the south-west. With these exceptions, the French go in less for team sports than for more individual ones, as you might expect. Horse-riding, ideally combining exercise and communion with nature, has seen a boom: membership of riding clubs has increased tenfold since 1972. Among competitive sports, tennis used to be seen as a game of the

---

* The 1998 race was seriously marred by evidence that some of the competitors – Dutch, Belgian, Swiss and Italian, as well as French – had been illegally taking drugs to improve their performance. Several cyclists admitted it, and some arrests were made. The race ended on an acrimonioius note.

rich, but then it spread to become the top French sport after football in terms of club members (1,238,000). Recently, it has fallen back, mainly among the young: 'It is too stressful, not convivial,' one young player told me. 'You play *against* someone, not *with* him. So I've given it up.' Does this suggest that the French, competitive in business life, want something else from their leisure? Golf, less stressful than tennis, has grown in popularity, and scores of new courses have been built: but it remains much less played than in Britain or America.

As for *la chasse*, stressful mainly for non-humans, it has seen varying fortunes. Generally conducted on foot with a rifle, not horse and hounds, it was formerly the preserve of gentry and peasants, as in Renoir's *La Règle du jeu*: but after the war it spread more widely, and so many urban amateurs took to the woods on Sundays that the accident rate soared and tighter licensing laws had to be introduced. As in Britain, gun ownership has now become a public issue, following some random mass murders, and in 1997 it was further restricted under a new law. This, plus other factors, has reduced the total of registered huntsmen from 2.3 to about 1.6 million. Game has become less plentiful, and permits to shoot on private land more expensive; despite opposition from the hunting lobby, the European Commission has managed to impose some new rules to make hunting less cruel; and anti-hunting pressure groups have become stronger and more influential, warmly backed by the new Green Environment Minister, Dominique Voynet. So *la chasse* has retreated a little, becoming more what it used to be, the preserve of the rich and of some farmers. Some *châtelains*, short of money, have turned part of their estate into a hunting reserve for wealthy visitors who pay them vast fees – and many are Germans, Americans and other foreigners. If, as a popular pastime, this archaic sport is now in retreat, I for one will shed no tear.

In international sporting competitions, the French seldom did well in football World Cups before 1998 (see below). In the summer Olympics, too, their record before 1996 was generally disappointing: at Montreal in 1976, for example, they came eighteenth with only one gold medal. But then, for the 1996 Games at Atlanta, the training was more thorough, morale improved, and the French surprised even themselves by coming sixth, with a total of thirty-seven medals, fifteen of them gold (Britain got just one gold). Most of the medals were for the individual sports of fencing, judo, cycling and athletics. Gratifyingly, many of the winners were from poorer immigrant backgrounds in *la banlieue*, such as the runner Marie-Jo Pérec, from Guadeloupe, and the judoist Djamel Bouras, a Beur. Front-rank French sports champions are rare, but when they do emerge they are lauded as national idols – like the swimmer Christine Caron in the 1970s, or Cédric Pioline, who reached the Wimbledon men's finals in 1997. When the yachtsman Éric Tabarly won transatlantic sailing races in the 1970s, he was given heroic ovations by vast crowds on the Champs-Élysées, and his death by drowning in 1998 was a national tragedy. And the French know that the football star Éric Cantona has made more impact on Britain than almost any politician.

For many years public participation in sports was limited by lack of equipment. Then the State and town councils made special efforts to provide public swimming pools, and today nearly every little town has its civic *piscine*. More recently, hundreds of new sports centres have been built, even on poorer *grands ensembles*, often by Socialist mayors. 'I see this as a crucial aspect of our fight against youth crime and social deprivation,' I was told in Montpellier by its mayor Georges Frêche (see p. 371), who had created twenty new football grounds, twenty gymnasiums and ten *piscines* since 1977. In state schools, too, sport is now being taken more seriously. Since the 1970s some poorer children have been on 'snow classes' to the mountains, where they can ski as well as continue their lessons. But funds are short, and a growing number of teachers have become reluctant to take part, fearing accidents where they might be held responsible.

The holiday boom has been unevenly shared. One person in ten in the 18–34 age bracket has never been on holiday. But recent Governments, notably the Socialists after 1981, have at least made efforts to create subsidized holiday villages and hostels in rural areas, and to develop *colonies de vacances* with trained monitors for children whose parents cannot afford holidays *en famille*. More than a million children visit these colonies annually: you see them on beaches in summer, a touching and slightly pathetic sight.

If only the French could be induced to spread their holidays over a longer period of the year, fuller use could be made of these cheaper tourist amenities. Many camps and hostels are oversubscribed for July and August and at Christmas, and fairly empty the rest of the time. Yet many a Frenchman will stay at home rather than change his habits. Holiday-making in July or August is typically one of those rooted French traditions that have proved hard to alter, despite its increasing inconvenience as tourist numbers have swollen. Some 80 per cent of

French summer holidays are taken in July and August, against less than 70 per cent in Britain and 60 per cent in Germany. Industrial production falls by 40 per cent in August, against 10 per cent in Germany, where factory holidays are officially staggered.

Anyone who has lived in Paris knows how the city then goes to sleep. It is the month that tradesmen choose for their annual bolt to the country: you can stroll in pleasantly empty streets, but your favourite *bistrot* may well be closed, and in some districts you might find it hard to get a haircut or have shoes repaired. In the prosperous classes, mothers and children often depart for up to eight weeks at a stretch, leaving bread-winners behind for part of the time, possibly up to no good. The nation's business slows to a crawl. Until recently, in the bourgeoisie it used to be such a sign of failure to stay in Paris in August that spinsters in genteel poverty might spend the month like hermits behind closed shutters, rather than show that they could not afford to leave. Meanwhile, the traffic jams and casualties mount up along the tourist routes, on the way to the overpacked beaches. The Government's *Bison Futé* (wily bison) operation advises motorists on alternative routes and peak hours to avoid, but this only partially limits the jams. If you leave Paris at 3 a.m. and go by secondary roads, you may still find yourself queuing for hours at the approaches to Provence or the Pyrenees. The tourist industry is the main victim: hoteliers find it ever harder to balance their budgets, with the season so short.

For some years the Government has led a campaign for the spreading of holidays. Notably, it has tried to stagger school holidays. The school year has been divided into two long semesters on the German or American pattern, with a two-week break in February. Industrial workers, too, under a recent law, have been encouraged to take at least part of their holiday in February. With the growing popularity of skiing and of winter breaks to the sunny south, this is now happening to some extent: many people are now taking a second holiday in winter, and have shortened their summer one. So a little of the midsummer crush has been diverted – but not to May, June or September, which remain unpopular, even though the weather can then be at its best. Since 1983 the Government has induced some state-owned firms to take their main break in July, not August, and this has had some effect. But although July is now as popular as August, those two months account for about four-fifths of French summer holidays.

In central Paris an increasing number of theatres, shops and restaurants have finally come to realize what lucrative tourist trade they lose by closing all of August: today nearly half the city's theatres remain open then. But in the suburbs, where tourists are few, the shutters stay closed. The main obstacle to staggering holidays nationally is now purely that of habit. According to a poll taken by the Institut Français d'Opinion Publique (IFOP), 49 per cent of families say they would be ready, in theory, to take their holidays in June or September, but not in practice. The French are individualist about nothing so much as the right to share the same herd-like conventions.

They once seemed rather sedentary, but have now become a restless nation. Ring up a businessman, even a fairly junior one, and he is sure to be just back from Lyon, or off to Frankfurt, or on the point of driving his family 500 kilometres for a short weekend. 'Where are you going for Easter?' I asked a Parisian. 'I'll drive to Biarritz,' he said, while forty years ago it might have been Fontainebleau, 'and my dentist is driving to Prague.' The French have one of Europe's highest levels of car ownership (79 per cent of homes today possess one, against 30 per cent in 1960); and the high taxes on petrol do not deter them from driving their cars an average of 13,700 kilometres a year. These individualists use their own cars more and more, rather than local trains and buses, for medium or shorter journeys, despite the official efforts to improve public transport. In short, this is a car-mad country, where men react as emotionally to their cars as to women: '*Une voiture, Monsieur, est comme une femme*,' said my *garagiste* once, when I complained that my Renault was varying oddly from day to day. Foreign cars are 'smart' (if less so than in Britain), and their share of the market has risen since 1980 from 23 to 40 per cent, despite the size of France's own car industry. Jaguars and BMWs are among the prestige cars, more so than Italian sports models. Though Panhard and Renault were among the great pioneers, the French show less interest than the British in veteran cars.

The French are now at last driving more prudently. They always used to like going fast, using their brakes and taking chances, and the price they paid was an accident rate that by 1972 was reaching 16,600 deaths a year, twice the British level. But initial plans to tighten the liberal speed limits, or to increase the penalties for drunken driving, caused such an outcry that they were shelved. Then in 1973–4, with the energy crisis, the need to save petrol gave the Government the cue to introduce new speed limits, and as these were found also to be reducing the accident rate, they were retained: today they are 130 kmph on motorways and 90 on most other country roads. By 1985 the fatal accident rate was down to 10,450 a year. But this was still far too high, and in 1990 Rocard's Government imposed tougher measures, bringing France at last in line with the rest of northern Europe: these included a 50 kmph speed limit in towns, tighter limits on drinking, and a points system on driving licences that could lead to their removal. This certainly induced drivers to be more cautious, and today the annual fatality rate is down to under 8,500, or 341 deaths per million vehicles. Here the French are roughly on the European average, better than the Spanish (486) or Irish (419), but worse than the Germans (250) or even the supposedly reckless Italians (239), and much worse than the British (175), Europe's most prudent drivers.

Many deaths are still due to speeding, and some 40 per cent to drinking. The permitted limit of alcohol was reduced to 0.5 grammes per litre of blood in 1995, a more severe restriction than in Britain or Germany, and breathalyser tests have been stepped up: some 120,000 motorists a year are penalized. So the days are gone when a driver could enjoy half a bottle of wine with a meal and follow it with a cognac: the safe maximum is now two glasses. The French today are more careful, and many fines have to be paid on the spot. But there are still a few crazy speed-hogs, and drivers who get booked give all kinds of excuses, such as: 'My car isn't built for driving slowly. Send the fine to the manufacturers.'

P.S.: 12 July 1998, *le jour de gloire est arrivé!* It was a Frenchman, Jules Rimet, who founded the World Cup in 1930, but after this France never even reached its final – until 1998. The French play football a lot, but as a spectator sport they were never so fanatical about it as, say, the Germans or Italians. Then Mitterrand, in line with his *grands projets* for a French cultural revival, applied for France to host the World Cup, and the splendid new stadium at St-Denis was built. But in the spring of 1998 the tournament got off to a tricky start, as the French made several own goals in its preparations. A major strike by Air France pilots was called off only at the last moment (see p. 134); and several similar interest groups, including railway and Métro workers, seized the chance to hold the Cup to ransom as a way of airing their grievances. Their strikes were narrowly averted, but some French were embarrassed by the publicity abroad: 'Because we don't care about football, it looks as if we don't mind spoiling the Cup for others' was one comment. Earlier there was a crisis over ticket distribution, as the French authorities were accused by other countries of favouring their own fans and not releasing enough tickets for sale abroad – and they narrowly escaped a big EU fine for breaking the free competition rules. The issue was solved. But there remained problems of security and violence. France and its neighbours took the precaution of arresting some eighty known Islamic militants who might try terrorism – but what about the milder yet still real threat of hooliganism, an English speciality? Governments were trying to dissuade fans without tickets, notably English ones, from travelling to France. But then the Tourism Minister, Michelle Demessine, a Communist, broke ranks by inviting 'everyone to come and join the party' at a press conference in London (she was worried that general tourism might suffer). In the event, plenty of English fans with no tickets did turn up, and some rioted wildly in Marseille (see pp. 701–2). Otherwise, the only severe violence was by a well-organized gang of neo-Nazi German thugs, just before a match at Lens, early on, where they badly injured one policeman.

Apart from these initial troubles, the crowds in the ten stadiums behaved well, and the French organization of the games was widely admired: it was smooth, efficient and stylish, in the French manner. The opening match was preceded by a giant official street party in central Paris (see p. 427). Then, just before the final, came the huge fashion parade of 300 models at the stadium. The 1998 World Cup was billed as 'the largest sporting event in history', with thirty-two national teams competing in ten towns, from Lens in the north to Toulouse, and some 500,000 visiting foreign fans. The French team, stronger than usual, and seen from the start as one favourite, beat Italy on penalty kicks in the quarter-final, then Croatia by 2–1 in the semi-final, thanks to two goals by Lilian Thuram from Guadeloupe. Then, as the nation held its breath, they defeated Brazil, the holders and top favourites, by a convincing 3–0 in the final, helped by two goals from Zinedine Zidane, of Algerian parentage. Much of the credit was due to the coach Aimé Jacquet, who had until then been long reviled by the French sporting establishment and press, but was now suddenly idolized for his qualities of inspiring harmony and precision in his multi-racial team.

The nation went wild. Up to 1.5 million people celebrated along the Champs-Élysées, in a rapturous mood that veterans said had not been seen on that scale since the Liberation. Then Chirac fêted the whole team at his annual Quatorze-Juillet garden party, as some of his smart principal guests chanted '*Zidane Président!*' almost in his face. Zidane and others were now national heroes. Amid the fantastic hype it was permissible to doubt whether the whole nation was really born again, after its years of gloom. But immigrants in France, it was felt, might certainly benefit from increased respect. And football, the cause of it all, today seems set to become a greater French passion than hitherto. During the Cup and before, there were plenty of hostile sceptics: anti-football associations were formed, and many intellectuals denounced the whole thing as a capitalist racket. One wrote in *Le Monde* of '*cette vague foot-ballistique qui crétinise encore plus les Français*'. But if it does really help to improve race relations, then it has been anything but cretinous.

9

FRANCE, EUROPE AND THE WORLD

THE PUSH FOR A UNITED EUROPE: FROM JEAN MONNET'S IDEALS TO THE BIRTH OF THE EURO

Europe, in every sense, would be inconceivable without France – and though they may grumble, the French broadly accept that France would now be hard to conceive without Europe. They have benefited hugely, and not just in economic terms, from the adventure today called European Union, of which they were leading pioneers.

It is true that during the 1990s the old enthusiasm for Europe has waned, as in some other countries. This may be a facet of the current French pessimism about politics and society as a whole, and their disaffection from formal institutions: certainly, the new scepticism is directed far more against the bureaucracy of Brussels than against a united Europe in a more general sense, which most people still see as the way of the future. 'I believe in Europe, but not *this* Europe of technocrats who tell us how to make our cheeses' is a common reaction. But it would be wrong to overestimate the new doubts. The French still feel very involved in the whole European process. It was they who pushed hardest for the single currency. And today nearly two in three welcome it – even if they might have preferred it to have a rather more French name, not euro but *écu*.

In the days of Jean Monnet, the French were the prime creators of the move towards a united Europe, and they have always seen it as their special affair. At least until Germany was reunited, they were able to assume the *de facto* leadership of this Europe, and today they are still one of the two undisputed leaders. It might seem strange that a nation so proud of its historical uniqueness, so touchily aware of its interests, should also have become politically so pro-European, so ready to sacrifice certain aspects of sovereignty. But the French came to believe that their country could best retain its world influence by joining a larger unit and seeking to retain a major role within it, through positive cooperation. Successive Governments have been skilful at exploiting the EEC/EU as a channel for promoting French interests. Far more than the British, they have been able to identify national and European interests on many matters and to ensure that what is good for Europe is good for France, or even vice versa (it is what they call '*l'esprit communautaire*'). Where this is not feasible, they will blithely follow their own path or bend the rules: but they do this less than some other keen 'Europeans', such as Italy.

All French Governments have been pro-European in their way, ever since the Fourth Republic foisted the Treaty of Rome on a hesitant Patronat. Even de Gaulle, though wary about loss of sovereignty, had his own vision of *l'Europe des patries*, and his treaty of friendship with Adenauer in 1963 has been a crucial pillar of all European entente ('We have to walk with Germany every hour of every day,' said the General). Since then Governments under Giscard, Mitterrand, even Chirac, have followed the path of closer integration; and all the main non-extremist parties have been pro-European, the RPR a little less so than others. Even the Communists have now modified their opposition to the EU. The Front National remains hostile, but is not unanimous: in a survey in 1997 as many as 27 per cent of its voters said they were in favour of the construction of Europe.

The need to foster a new friendship with the Germans, after three horrifying wars, has always been the driving force behind France's European policies. Clearly, it was undesirable to develop this just bilaterally: so a wider framework was essential. And Kohl and Mitterrand, during the years they shared in high office together, 1982–95, saw firmly eye to eye on the crucial need to bind Germany tightly into this new Europe, so as to avoid any new German adventurism: 'Make no mistake, I am the last pro-European German Chancellor,' Kohl is said to have warned his French colleague when they first met as leaders. Hence Mitterrand's insistence on a policy of integration leading to monetary union and much else. Though somewhat Gaullist on some other issues, he was guided by a genuine belief in a united Europe, and was one of those who saw this as the way for France to retain its influence: in 1994 he said on television, 'Never separate the grandeur of France from the building of Europe. This is our new dimension, and our ambition for the century ahead.' Chirac has since more or less followed on this path, if with less conviction, and so has Jospin. But during the 1990s the Paris–Bonn axis has come under greater strains: the new reunited Germany, fully sovereign at last, larger, more preoccupied with its own internal problems, has become a less amenable partner. Chancellor Kohl was patently devoted to the close entente with France: but when Gerhard Schröder came to power, though he was quick to reaffirm the alliance, he gave signs of preferring to tighten links with Tony Blair's Britain and to play down the Paris–Bonn axis. In fact, ever since the early 1990s, France has no longer been able to call the tune in Europe so easily. This has probably been a factor in the waning of idealism about Europe, and of belief in its ability to serve French interests. In fact the role of French functionaries within the Commission has now become less dominant. Its new president, Romano Prodi from Italy, in 1999 made a big reshuffle which gave more seats to the British and fewer to the French, who, for the first time since 1958, lost the key post of director-general for agriculture. *Libération* denounced Signor Prodi's 'galloping Anglophilia'.

On several occasions, from the outset, France has dragged its heels or vetoed progress – if less vehemently than Britain – when it has felt that some trend was not in its national interest. Full participation in NATO (not of course an EU matter) has been the most obvious case. Then in the 1990s France for a while held up plans to establish a frontier-free Europe – the famous Schengen Agreement. The history is curious. Since Britain under Thatcher refused to allow removal of border controls to feature as formal EEC policy, some other countries decided to go ahead on their own; and in the Luxembourg frontier village of Schengen, symbolically at the point where France, Germany and Benelux meet, they signed in 1985 a convention to abolish all land and air controls between their five countries: other members soon joined, too. The agreement was originally a Franco-German idea: but though the political will was always there, it took a long time to prepare, for technical reasons, and because of the strong reticences among national police and customs forces – as you might expect. All was finally ready in 1993, when Balladur came to power with the tough, nationalistic Charles Pasqua as his Interior Minister: he did not hide his hatred of 'Schengen', and managed to get the project suspended. Officially, doubts about control of drug-trafficking were cited: but Pasqua spoke also of his fears about illegal immigration, and his doubts about the efficiency of the police in other countries, at the common external borders of the 'seven'.

In 1995 a start was at last made by removing passport controls at airports for flights within the Schengen zone. But France insisted on keeping its own far more numerous border controls: the excuse given, fair and genuine, was the regular drug traffic into France via Belgium from Holland with its easy-going attitudes to drugs (see pp. 575–6). Then in July 1995 the terrorist attack in the Paris Métro, killing seven, led France to reimpose airport controls, too – so it was back to square one. But in 1996, after passions had cooled, France did finally agree to apply 'Schengen' fully, except along its land border with Belgium and Luxembourg, because of the drugs problem. Pasqua has been out of power since 1995, and the French police have now reluctantly accepted orders to cooperate: but they are still opposed to allowing foreign police the right to pursue suspects within French borders (as the accord permits). Apart from this, 'Schengen' is today working quite smoothly: nearly all other EU countries have now joined – leaving Britain in splendid isolation as ever. Under 'Schengen', passports in theory need no longer be shown at control posts within the zone, and many frontiers are now completely invisible, with no posts at all (the customs checks have disappeared under the Single Market: see below). What is more, visas are issued or refused communally: thus, for example, a Moroccan obtaining a visa for Spain can use it for travel to other Schengen countries. So a real advance has been made towards (non-British) European unity. But the affair has shown how sensitive the French can still be in some practical matters concerning their sovereignty.

On a very different issue – the European Parliament – France has tacitly united with Britain to block progress. This body is far less useless than its many scornful critics like to suggest: but certainly its powers are limited, and Germany has always taken the lead in urging that they be strengthened, so as to make the EU more democratic. But French deputies, like British MPs, do not want to surrender any of their own powers; and the French Government, like Britain's, has wanted to keep its own control of EU policies through the Council of Ministers without having to face any rival authority – certainly not one that meets on French soil, in Strasbourg. So the Government has made various efforts to see that the Parliament's role remains restricted. In France its mode of election is not on a constituency basis, as in other countries, but through nationwide party lists: so French MEPs have no direct local link, and this reduces their influence. Paris has sometimes objected to the Parliament 'interfering' in French affairs: thus in 1997, when Elisabeth Guigou, then a Socialist MEP, persuaded it to condemn the Juppé

Government's new immigration bill, the Government protested loudly and called for the Parliament's powers to be cut back. The Socialists, now in office, are a little more sympathetic to it, but are not calling for its powers to be increased – even though many on the Left regret the 'democratic deficit' caused by its weakness, and the harm this does to the EU's popular image. In 1998 Lionel Jospin, with Chirac's support, proposed to introduce regional constituencies for the elections, which would have increased the Parliament's credibility in France. But he was opposed by nearly all the parties, each fearing that it would lose out, and he was obliged to drop his plan. Such are the obstacles to democratic Europeanism, in France as in Britain.

On several occasions – witness the Air France subsidy, and in 1999 the affair of British beef – France has fought to obtain derogations on EU policies to suit its own purposes. But it has never sought major opt-outs like Britain; and generally it has applied the rules correctly, once it has signed up to them. This has helped Europe to retain credibility in the eyes of popular opinion, which up until about 1990 remained strongly favourable to the European Community. Businessmen saw the boost it had given to the French economy; even farmers, ever grudging, had to admit they had benefited hugely from the CAP; and ordinary people saw the EEC as a way of preventing wars, standing up to the superpowers, promoting France's role in the world, and aiding prosperity. Among young people, the old notion of frontiers was disappearing. Europe, in all its forms, had come to be taken for granted, and further integration was seen by most people as right and inevitable. One opinion survey in 1989 showed 78 per cent of the sample favouring 'the construction of Europe' (only 7 per cent were opposed): among the under-25s the figure was 89 per cent, and 92 per cent among executives and professional people. Europe in those days was *à la mode*. For example, in a village in Provence, the mayor built a small recreation lake, baptized it 'Lac de l'Europe', and invited the EEC countries' consuls-general in Marseille to its opening ceremony: would that happen in England?

But then, in France as in other countries, a mysterious groundswell of change began, even before the Maastricht summit of December 1991. Fears of recession, plus dislike of the creeping bureaucracy of Brussels, were mixed together in the public mind with fears of a new dominant reunited Germany; and the Maastricht Treaty, which few people understood, was then made the scapegoat for these anxieties. All this happened to coincide with a slump in the popularity of Mitterrand and his Government, prime sponsors of the pro-EEC strategy. He and the other heads of government, meeting in the Dutch town of Maastricht, had prepared a treaty for a new European blueprint, leading to monetary union and much else (it also changed the name of the European Economic Community to the more forceful European Union, with its political overtones). The treaty needed ratification by Parliaments: but Mitterrand went further and decided to put it to a referendum, though constitutionally he need not have done so. And so a great national debate began about Europe, the first on this scale in France. Many doubts, hitherto half-buried, came to the surface as people looked more closely at their quasi-instinctive feelings for Europe and realized that in practice they had qualms. The debate cut across party lines: along with the Communists and Front National, much of the RPR was in the 'no' camp, as were some centrists and Socialists, although nearly all their leaders were campaigning for a 'yes' vote. Jacques Chirac, reluctant alike about Maastricht and backing Mitterrand, jumped off the fence at the last moment and joined the 'yes' camp. This may have been decisive in swinging the final result to yes, by a narrow margin of 51 to 49 per cent, in September 1992. Mitterrand had won his gamble: but it was no triumph.

There were many and complex reasons for the size of the 'no' vote. Many people were seizing the chance to register their opposition to Mitterrand, in a vote that he had rashly allowed to be also a plebiscite on his own rule. 'Seventy per cent of the French are pro-Maastricht, but 70 per cent are anti-Mitterrand, so that might produce a 50–50 result,' said one observer, predicting the outcome with some accuracy. There were other factors more directly linked to the EU, such as fears that the new Europe of open frontiers might add to illegal immigration. And even many staunch pro-Europeans argued simply that Maastricht was the wrong treaty at the wrong time and better ways should have been found of pursuing integration. On the whole it was younger people, the successful, the urban bourgeoisie and business classes who more readily voted 'yes' while the 'no' majorities were among the unemployed, the workers and those in threatened sectors such as small farmers. Some pro-EU analysts thus saw the vote as a divide between a young, progressive, confident France and an older, out-of-date, declining one.

After the referendum period, Euro-scepticism waned for a while. An official 'Eurobarometer' survey in 1995 found 58 per cent of the French sample thinking France's EU membership 'a good thing' and 13 per cent 'a bad thing'. This was close to the EU average: 57 per cent of Germans approved of membership, 79 per cent of Italians, 80 per cent of Irish, 47 per cent of Spanish and 41 per cent of British. But in 1997 a poll question worded differently, 'What do you think of the construction of Europe?', found 49 per cent of the French sample 'enthusiastic' or 'favourable', while 48 per cent were 'sceptical' or 'opposed' – an even closer result than the referendum, and a far cry from the eagerness of 1989. Yet at the same time support for the single currency was rising. Asked in more detail, the French said they thought that the EU was good for France, on balance, in matters of the environment, economic growth and (more surprisingly) culture and international influence, but bad when it came to jobs, individual living standards, internal security and illegal immigration.

The doubts about Europe would seem to be part of the general French *morosité* and pessimism today, and the decline of faith in institutions: the EU is one of several scapegoats, and the feeling is directed more against its official bodies than against Europe in a wider sense. Many people claim to be still pro-European but disappointed with how it has worked out. All this mirrors similar trends in other EU countries. When questioned, people complain that they are ruled by remote technocrats in Brussels who do not consult them properly. Or they say that decisions are taken by political élites: but this is a common complaint in France on various matters, where public debate is perhaps not so well organized as in Britain, due in part to the weakness of Parliament. People claim ignorance about the EU and how it works. This may be partly their own fault: but it is true that in *lycées* and arts faculties, for instance, where the teaching of languages is now excellent, there are very few classes on the history and functioning of the European Community.

Daily gripes about regulations imposed by the Commission are probably less widespread than in Britain: but they have certainly increased, since the coming of the Single Market has led to all kinds of well-intentioned new rules and standards, in matters of health, safety and environment. 'Those autocrats in Brussels, they oppress us,' said a garage owner I met in Burgundy. 'I've had to spend large sums on tools and machines in order to meet their norms – and for the farmers it's worse. Mind you, I'm not against open frontiers and I'm not afraid of Germany. It's just Brussels that I hate. And we French are too honest: the Italians and Greeks don't obey half these rules, but we're expected to.' The Bretons have objected to EU limitations on the culling of shellfish, and the Pyreneans to a ban on the catching of woodcock in nets. And there was an outcry from producers when the Commission, on grounds of hygiene, tried to forbid the use of non-pasteurized milk for making Camembert and similar cheeses. After a long tussle Brussels backed down and granted derogations, accepting that French exports could suffer if pasteurization was found to affect the taste of these proud cheeses. Conversely, the French have often had to admit that EU norms can be valuable, for example in reducing pollution on beaches.

Inevitably, there are some fears of a loss of national identity: but they are less than in Britain, and mainly confined to Front National voters, some Gaullists and others. The French are less worried about political sovereignty than the British: but they are vaguely concerned that regional cultures, local traditions, and so on, could be steam-rollered by the growing uniformity of lifestyles, and some of them see the EU as abetting this. Their main fear is of globalization spreading from the US (see below). They were encouraged by their leaders to see a united Europe as a bulwark against this: but now they are scared that it might really be more like a Trojan horse, with its encouragement of big international mergers, and so on. This ties in with a general feeling for many years voiced on the Left and among younger people that the Community is too concerned with financial matters, and with helping big business, and is not sufficiently 'social'. Any trade unionist will readily argue this case. It is a complex matter, and in fact it is not true that the EU has ignored labour or welfare matters. Jacques Delors, as president of the Commission, was instrumental in creating the Social Chapter, which commits member Governments to improving workers' rights and conditions: it was set up partly to protect workers in the still-fragile democracies of southern Europe, recovering from dictatorship, and France has loyally gone along with the policy. It is true that the Jospin Government, at the time of the Amsterdam summit, had little success in persuading the Germans to agree to employment being made formally a high EU priority. But a new sense of Euro-solidarity among unions seems to be growing, as witness the 'Euro-strikes' that greeted Renault's decision in 1997 to close a factory in Belgium.

It would be entirely wrong to think that the French have turned against the European Union. They may be irritated or disappointed by some aspects: but overall they tend to take 'Europe' for granted, young people especially, and to accept it as the inevitable path of the future. In the countryside farmers today may complain more than usual about the

CAP: but the EU's structural funds, such as the 'Leader' programme, have done much to help some poorer rural areas, as people can see. Local cafés and shops have been helped to keep going, cinemas to reopen, transport to improve. When it comes to the new EU norms, some have been tactlessly imposed, and of course people resent having their habits forcefully changed. But they will grudgingly accept that many of the changes are humane and sensible, especially the environmental ones. Hunting has been made less cruel, air and beaches cleaner: Governments might not have taken these measures on their own, without the impulse of a wider agreement. And the politicians in the regions see the EU as cementing devolution by helping cross-frontier links: 'Europe today is Lyon's great historic chance,' said one councillor there. In sum, Brussels may be out of favour, but Europe in a wider sense is not.

Around the time that the Maastricht Treaty was signed, the European Single Market also came into force, at the end of 1992. This was devised by Jacques Delors, and for once it was a major European step forward that had the support of Margaret Thatcher from the outset: it suited her 'liberal' free-trade ideals, for it involved the gradual removal of all customs barriers and other obstacles to the free movement of goods, money and people within the EU. The French, too, were enthusiastic; they implemented its 137 different measures more fully and rapidly than any other member State except Denmark, and their trade and industry then did fairly well out of this so-called '1992'. Even France's rather staid insurance sector, then still mostly state-owned, managed to adapt and thrive, in face of vigorous new competition from British insurance firms that moved into France.

Once '1992' was settled, then all efforts were concentrated on the far bigger venture of pushing for European Monetary Union, with a central bank and single currency. France was always keener on this than Germany. It saw EMU as a means of controlling German economic hegemony, and of forging real integration without the heavier loss of sovereignty that strong political union would involve. Mitterrand managed to win over a hesitant Kohl, who was worried about the impact of EMU on domestic opinion, so wedded to the D-Mark, and on the mighty Bundesbank. The President had other motives, too, for wanting monetary union, and one was his old fear not only of the D-Mark's hegemony but the dollar's: long before the dawning of EMU, he once wrote, 'The Americans have dominated by their currency the Europe they liberated by their weapons. The Europeans will free themselves if they can create a currency of their own.' The battle for it was to prove Herculean, but against the odds it seems to have succeeded.

Another Frenchman played in many ways an even greater role than Mitterrand, in giving a new dynamism to the adventure of a united Europe and pushing the great projects forward. The amazing Jacques Delors was often called 'the greatest "European" since Jean Monnet', or 'the most powerful man in Western Europe after Helmut Kohl' – and for me he is unashamedly one of my foremost modern heroes. Born in 1925, a self-made man from simple peasant stock in the Massif Central, he joined the Banque de France as a junior executive, became an ardent trade unionist, and later performed brilliantly as Mitterrand's Minister of Finance. In 1984 he agreed to become president of the European Commission, where he was just a civil servant, albeit Europe's top one: but in some ways he had as much real power as his masters, the heads of Government. He managed this through sheer force of personality – plus intellectual rigour, stupendous hard work, and a shining sense of vocation and long-term vision that inspired those who worked with him, even if they could be irritated by his moodiness and flashes of angry temper. He has always been a profoundly committed Catholic, believing in social action – a blend of social democrat and Christian democrat, and something of an oddball in French left-wing politics. The journalist Alain Dauvergne wrote of him shrewdly in *Le Point*: 'He's a man of deep faith in a land where religion is out of fashion, a man of consensus in a nation of quarrellers, a devotee of discipline in a land where disorder is daily practice, a self-made man in the land of élite diplomas, a lover of a modest lifestyle in a nation where money and chic are supreme values.'

It has to be asked why devotion to Europe came to play so large a part in the creed of this passionate idealist. When I lunched with him in Brussels in 1991, he explained to me, 'As a teenager I witnessed the horrors of war, and like many of my generation, my vision of a united Europe was born of the feeling "never again", the necessity for Franco-German entente. Then in the 1960s I became haunted by Europe's economic decline in face of the United States. Today, though I dearly love France, I feel more a European than a Frenchman. In my view, a high degree of supranationality, of transfer of sovereignty to the Community, is essential: first, because past experience has shown that purely voluntary cooperation between States never works; second, because national sovereignty no longer means very much, or has much scope, in the modern world economy. I feel a duty to fulfil the ideals of Jean Monnet, our founding father.'

Delors took over a Community that was in the doldrums, owing to weak leadership and financial disputes. And he vigorously set about reviving it. He launched the Single Market programme, he devised the Social Chapter, and was a prime architect of the EMU project. He badly wanted to increase the role of the European Parliament, too, but was thwarted by Paris. His immense powers of persuasion were typified by his address to the Trades Union Congress at Bournemouth in 1988, when he managed to convert those hardy Europhobes to his vision of a 'social' Europe. 'It was amazing,' said one TUC leader later. 'He convinced us that we could obtain through Europe all that was blocked here by Thatcher. He's won over much of the Labour Party, too; he's changed the face of British politics!' Thatcher, outflanked, was furious. For her Delors was always *the* enemy, personifying the three evils of Socialism, bureaucracy and supranationalism. But with Chancellor Kohl he got on warmly: 'I trust him completely; his views on Europe's future are close to mine,' he told me. 'But there's a danger of the new united Germany becoming, not more aggressive as many had feared, but the reverse, more inward-looking and isolationist. So the answer is to act quickly to complete EMU and the other projects, so as to create an integrated Europe with Germany irreversibly anchored into it – while there's still a German Government committed to this goal.'

As for France's Government, it was certainly committed: but in 1995–7 it had huge difficulty in getting its economy in the right state for EMU, and in coming to terms with German demands on how EMU should be run. Paris even lost out to Bonn on the issue of what the new currency should be called. It favoured '*écu*', the name of a historic French silver coin and of the 'European Currency Unit' that was already in use in the EU for some accounting purposes. But the Germans thought their sceptical public would get confused with the German for 'cow' (*Kuh*): they judged *écu* too mad-cowish and too French. So 'euro' was chosen. But many people today, not only the French, see this as a weak and muddling compromise, in an age when everything is Euro-this and Euro-that and Eurosceptics can have a field day with euro-confusion, worse than *kuh*-confusion.

The Maastricht Treaty had laid down a maximum budget deficit of 3 per cent of GDP as the most important of the 'convergence' criteria for joining EMU. But in 1995 France's deficit was well over 5 per cent, the highest in the EU after Greece's. So the Juppé Government set about cuts in public spending – and was met by the nationwide strikes of December 1995. Sceptics said this showed that the French were not ready to make personal sacrifices for EMU and was thus more evidence of their waning faith in Europe. In fact, there were other motives behind the strikes. But the French, German and other Governments were worried that their austerity measures to meet the EMU criteria might well be associated in public minds with slower growth and loss of jobs, and so add to Euroscepticism. The French deficit was reduced, but was still too high; and for a while it seemed that either France might have to plead for a weakening of the criteria, or else the EMU target date of January 1999 would have to be postponed (not only France was at fault). But then, by autumn 1997, the deficit was found to have fallen to 3.1 per cent. The austerity cuts had played their part, and so had some clever juggling with figures. But above all the new economic boom in Europe, spreading from America, had helped budgets everywhere. France was saved, *in extremis*.

Chirac had called the 1997 elections on the subject of EMU, but then it featured rather little in the campaign, save that the Communists and Front National both attacked it. Of the larger parties, none felt sure of their electors: the RPR/UDF did not think that EMU would win them votes, but nor did the PS think they could gain by attacking it. So they all kept hypocritically quiet on the great issue. But this later left Jospin with a free hand. He had various doubts himself about EMU: but his senior ministers were all in favour, and they – notably the influential Strauss-Kahn, a devoted European – were able to persuade him to stick to the timetable. But the French were worried that the 'stability pact' insisted on by the Germans for policing EMU might give too much uncontrolled power to the new European Central Bank: so they demanded that it be balanced by an economic council ('Euro X') with some political answerability, and this was accepted. The French had also managed to persuade Germany that Italy, despite its shaky finances, should be included among the initial EMU members: this, Paris felt, could help to balance German power.

So France did succeed finally in getting much of what it wanted over EMU. Then came the tussle over who should be president of the new central bank. The French, having conceded that this be located in Frankfurt, home of the Bundesbank, felt that its presidency by rights should be theirs. But most other countries, led by Germany, wanted the esteemed Dutch banker, Wim Duisenberg. Chirac made a mighty fuss about this at the 1998 summit to finalize EMU, and he managed to win a compromise that bent the Maastricht rules: Duisenberg would serve for the first four years, then Jean-Claude Trichet for the next eight. No one doubted that Trichet, head of the Banque de France, was also an excellent banker, with sound monetarist credentials. But the crisis lent a sour note to the launch of EMU. And it showed that the French are likely to remain touchy nationalist partners within the new supranationalist venture. As with so many Euro-matters, they are strongly *communautaires*, so long as they get roughly the kind of Europe they want.

Public opinion was sceptical at first about the single currency, but then it began to shift. A survey in 1996 showed 49 per cent in favour, but by April 1998 this had risen to 58 per cent, with 36 per cent against: this put France again roughly on the average, ahead of Germany (40 per cent in favour) and Britain (29 per cent), but behind Italy (78 per cent). The French often tend to grouse about what they have already but to enjoy novelty, and this may be a psychological reason why they seem to be more keen on the euro than on existing EU activities. A Sofres poll in 1997 showed that 62 per cent of the under-25s are in favour, and 80 per cent of *cadres* and professional people, but only 42 per cent of workers, many of whom express great ignorance. Educated opinion tends to feel that EMU will boost the economy, though some expert economists are worried and many people on the hard Right and hard Left are doctrinally hostile: 'It will lead to civil war,' said one diehard Socialist. Financial leaders, such as Banque de France directors, have campaigned to stress that a single currency will at last make Europe more concrete, less abstract, in the eyes of citizens. And most smaller businesses are now in favour, glad that Italy and Spain are to join, too, even if this makes for a weaker euro: 'The ending of the currency vagaries will help us a lot, and I expect our exports to grow,' said one industrialist I met, echoing a common view. During 1998 firms were frantically getting ready for the euro, making the necessary technical changes and often holding courses for their staff. 'But of course there'll be a lot of last-minute improvisation in the usual French manner,' said one official.

Jean Monnet himself once said that great adventures are the work of minorities, indeed élites, who first take action, and then others follow. This has often been true in France, in his day and more recently. The public debate about a single currency, in Parliament and in the media, has not been as wide or profound as in Britain: it has been somewhat taken for granted. This has prompted some leaders critical of EMU, such as Philippe Séguin of the RPR, to denounce what they call '*la pensée unique*' – the herd-like tendency to accept an agreed line without scrutinizing it deeply. It may be true that money is too serious a matter to be left to monetarists. Or it may be that Monnet is right. At any rate, the euro was launched in January 1999. During its first ten months, it fell some 12 per cent down to virtual parity against the dollar. But, in Paris as in Frankfurt, few pundits saw this as a sign that the project was failing: rather, it was a useful adjustment which has much helped exports. If the euro can finally prove itself a success, then not only will France and Europe be the richer for it, but the old ideal of a united Europe will receive an important new fillip.

GERMAN AND BRITISH FRIENDS ARE WELCOME –
BUT WHAT ABOUT FRANGLAIS AND AMERICAN POP?

What is it about romantic Heidelberg? – or the lovely streets of the *vieille ville* in Montpellier? In the past thirty years, the twinning these two cities has led to over 200 Franco-German marriages, via the numerous visits and exchanges. It seems an extreme symbol of how French and Germans have turned the page since 1945. These two nations may still have their rivalries and wrangles, over EMU and other matters: but these are family quarrels, within a framework of cooperation and personal friendly links. And towards most other Europeans, too, attitudes are far warmer than in the old days, when they were tinged with xenophobia.

The legitimate patriotism of the French has taken on a more modern flavour. Since the 1960s there has been a waning of the old ideal of *la gloire française* upheld by de Gaulle. When the bugles sound on the 14 July, the nation may still, out of old habit, stand to attention with a tear in its eye: but these rituals have been losing their meaning, except for Le Pen and some of his supporters. Most younger people feel little of this kind of jingoism. And if the French are still nationalist, it is more in the cultural field – defending their language, or their films and popular music, from the threat of 'American commercial imperialism'.

Compared with the British, it still seems true that the French are the more chauvinistic, and we the more insular. The French feel sharply competitive towards other nations, sometimes jealous, sometimes scornful, but at least vividly aware of their existence; the British live more in a world of their own. Compare the two attitudes to the EU. In other fields, too, international cultural or sporting events tend to be underreported in the British media; the French give them fuller coverage, but with huge emphasis on the French role. All this marks a change from pre-war days when the French, too, were enclosed behind their frontiers. But today, sometimes arrogantly, or touchily, they are always trying to score points off other nations. They may remain convinced of the virtues of their own way of life, but at least they regard, say, an Italian's or a Swede's as offering some comparison. So they can more easily make contact when they wish.

Before the war, many French regarded nearly all other Europeans with some suspicion, rather as Front National militants still see them today. There were xenophobic outbursts against the many Italians and Poles settled in France, especially in times of recession. Eight Italians were killed in attacks in the Midi in 1893. These peoples were seen as 'impossible to integrate', just as ethnic immigrants are often seen today. But Italians, Poles, Portuguese and others are nowadays as fully integrated as they wish, and well accepted. So are the Spanish in the south-west: many who came as exiles after the Civil War have now returned to Spain, but others have stayed. Visitors or residents from former Communist Europe are generally welcomed, and there is sympathy for their countries' wish to join the EU – save among many farmers, worried about the likely impact on the CAP.

The Irish in France are especially popular, and often found more friendly and amusing than the uptight British. They have close links with fellow Celtic Brittany (see p. 336); and in Paris the Irish colony has grown from about 500 in 1970 to some 8,000 today – proportionately more numerous than the British or Americans. A high percentage are educated young people, who work as teachers or in engineering or computer trades; and they seem able to integrate socially with Parisians, in a city not always known for its warm embrace of outsiders. The number of Irish pubs in Paris has risen since 1985 from nil to about fifteen; and whereas in some countries these serve as refuges for nostalgic Irish exiles, in Paris they are equally full of French, who enjoy their club-like quality. At Finnegan's Wake in the Latin Quarter, I found an American writer holding a literary soirée – as the Joyce/Hemingway tradition flickered on. Today, if any European tourists are resented, it can be the mild and usually discreet Dutch, who are seen as mean spenders. They have colonized parts of the Midi and Massif Central, where they buy tracts of land, build villas or camping sites, but then bring their own provisions with them on holiday, shunning the local shops; and they stick to their own circles, making little effort to mix socially.

The greatest post-war change has been in French attitudes to the Germans. The process began soon after 1945, in shocked reaction against three Franco-German tragedies in eighty years; and it was helped by an even sharper change of mood on the German side. Today anti-German feelings may persist among some elderly people: but with the younger generations, the old classic fear of *les Boches* has faded into history. The British may often be preferred as amusing individuals: but the Germans are admired as the more serious and trustworthy. In one recent poll, in answer to the question, 'Which country do you see as France's best friend?', Germany came easily first with 33 per cent, ahead of the US (22 per cent) and Britain (16 per cent). Official policies have played their part. The Franco-German Treaty of Friendship, signed in 1963, set up an intensive network of youth exchanges which has sent thousands of young French and Germans across the Rhine each year. Town-twinnings were also encouraged, and today they number over 600. So the two nations have got to know each other quite well. The Heidelberg/Montpellier link is very active: each city runs a cultural centre in the other, and some 2,000 Germans live in Montpellier (the British number 700).

Fear or dislike of Germans still exists among many Jewish people; or in parts of rural Alsace where German settlers do not integrate well (see p. 364) or in a few areas where memories of Occupation brutalities remain sharp – notably in the south-west along the path of the notorious SS 'Das Reich' Division, which in June 1944 hanged ninety-nine hostages in public at Tulle, then massacred 642 innocent civilians at Oradour-sur-Glane, near Limoges. Here, a notice, '*Nicht vergessen*', stands by the grim memorial museum, visited by many German tourists. Of course no one should ever forget. Yet the French as a whole today accept that the Germans have changed and must not be held guilty for horrors committed before most of them were born. One academic said, 'We admire them for accepting their guilt and rebuilding their nation.' And an elderly doctor told me, 'I fought in the Resistance and was fiercely anti-Nazi, but now I'm pro-German. The war was so long ago.' So the Germanophobia still common in Britain, bred of nostalgia for wartime heroics, plus sheer ignorance of today's Germany, happily finds little echo in France today.

In daily working relations, there can be frictions due to the divergent temperaments and methods. At the studios in Strasbourg of the Franco-German television channel, Arte (see p. 496), a French producer told me, 'They like to have everything planned in detail in advance; they are hopeless at improvising or changing plans, as has to be done all the time in TV. With us, it's the other way round' – a common experience. Similar problems have arisen in Brussels, and at countless bilateral meetings. But the nations' leaders have tended to get on quite well, especially when of different political colours (oddly enough): first Giscard with Helmut Schmidt, then Mitterrand with Kohl. The symbolic high point of the latters' partnership came in 1987, when they visited the Verdun 1916–18 battlefields and laid a plaque that pledged their nations to undying reconciliation and friendship. It was very moving for those present, as I found it moving to visit the Verdun museum, where next to the rooms filled with agonizing war scenes are happy photos of recent Franco-German youth exchanges.

Just after the Fall of the Berlin Wall in 1989, Mitterrand introduced a more sceptical note by making it clear on a visit to East Berlin that he disliked the idea of unification. He was not being anti-German *per se*: but he was afraid of a change in the status quo that could lead to a stronger Germany and upset France's *de facto* political leadership of Europe. Thatcher expressed similar views, more sharply, and happily both were overruled. But for the next few years, fears persisted in France – if less than in Britain – of a new, larger and more dominant Germany, fully sovereign at last. These fears have now subsided, thanks in part to Kohl's wise policies of European integration, and to Germany's internal problems, which have made it seem less powerful. So the 'threat' has again diminished. Of course, over the years, there have been repeated Franco-German rivalries and disputes over the building of Europe – inevitable, given the two nations' very different histories, needs and attitudes. They came to a head in 1998, in the clash over who should be president of the new central bank. And yet, throughout all the crises, the Franco-German alliance has basically held steadfast.

During this time, relations with Germany have in some ways been closer than with Britain, on human as well as economic levels. The British may sometimes be preferred as individuals, but they remain a mystery. A *lycée* teacher told me, 'The British have more *finesse* and humour than the Germans, but I don't understand them so well. Those yachting types who come to Cherbourg where I live, they're so aloof, they make me uneasy.' A young Parisian said, '*L'Allemand, c'est un con, mais un bon con. Les Anglais, ils sont trop différents de nous*', while a student in Toulouse added, 'Young Germans can be arrogant, but they're outward-going, generous, interested, eager to get to know us: the British are too reserved and self-absorbed; they have less of a gift for deep friendship.' So there is an odd paradox about attitudes to Britain. On the one hand, things English have a certain snob-appeal. The upper classes have long considered it *de bon ton* to import their Savile Row suits, malt whiskies and nursemaids from Britain, or to cultivate English milords, while since the early '60s English pop music, clothes and slang have been in vogue with teenagers. The French, monarchists at heart, remain fascinated by British royalty. Yet this Anglomania remains oddly superficial: seldom does it relate to any deeper curiosity about what British society is really like, or how it has changed or might be relevant to France. (The reverse is equally true: few of the millions of Britons who devour Peter Mayle are seriously interested in the real socio-economic problems of Provence.)

French clichés and false ideas about British life remain even stronger than British ones about France. There is the old Major-Thompson-rolled-umbrellas-fog-and-soggy-veg image, which lingers on, and the newer Beatles-Spice-Girls image, perhaps more valid: but there's not much in between. Britain is quaint, but inexplicable. Yet those French who do go to live there and make true British friends are usually delighted: it is said of diplomats or business people and their spouses, warily accepting a London posting, '*On arrive en pleurant et on part en pleurant.*' What's more, recently, the image in France of Britain's economy, its culture, even its politics, has suddenly improved. This may be superficial, but many things English are now in fashion, more perhaps with the French than with the Germans and others, and it applies across the board – from re-swinging London to Dianamania and *les muffins de chez M&S*, and from *The Full Monty* to the very full Tony.

'*Énergie, frénésie!*' was the banner headline, in 1996, in *Le Monde*'s special supplement on the London 'renaissance'. 'The city is completely abuzz,' enthused this so-serious paper. 'It's a huge Culture Club rediscovering the attitudes and ideals of Swinging London . . . Liberated Londoners are thrusting themselves once more to centre stage . . .' This remarkable salute from proud Paris would not have come ten years earlier: but it chimes in with the experience of many of the young French who have been crowding to London, maybe for the weekend by Eurostar, for its night-life, pubs, theatre, parties, shopping, and much else. Americans, Germans and others are also drawn to this new Mecca, but none so much as the French: in part it may be a reaction against the prevailing *morosité* in France, or a shamed acceptance of the fact that Paris has become a bit dull. It may hurt their pride, but they find a rival city that is more exuberant, open and relaxed, and more vitally creative alike for popular culture and some classic culture. Short-term visitors find this, but so do French who live in London. And until sterling rose so high in 1997, they also found it rather cheap.

The tourists come mainly to London itself. Some visit Bath, Oxford, Edinburgh . . . but they are drawn to the rural provinces far less than the British in France, for obvious reasons. Via the ferries or Tunnel, plenty now make short trips over to Kent, where they will visit the pubs and Canterbury Cathedral: but they do not do the same mass shopping as British trippers to Calais. *Le vrai shopping* is done in London, if at all. Nearly half of the French coming to London are between sixteen and twenty-four, and another quarter are under thirty-five (language courses are one draw). Besides the pubs, music, fringe theatres, and so on, many of them enjoy the ethnic mix, where the Afro-Caribbeans and Asians are patently better integrated into the city's social life than in Paris. And the French to their surprise generally find the food better than they had been taught to believe. True, if they are lodged with an English family, it can be *dégueulasse*: but they love the ethnic variety of the lively, crowded restaurants.

In France itself, too, a few *spécialités anglaises* are now becoming popular with shoppers in the foodstores, thanks to skilful marketing. Marks & Spencer, as ever, has set the trend, selling British biscuits, shortbreads, chutneys, and much else, at its twenty French branches, in Paris and other towns. It also does a brisk trade in such very English foods as houmous and tsatsiki, made in Britain, while one big Paris grocery imports Thai dishes from Scotland and Indian curries from Lancashire. A rival of M&S, the Monoprix chain, has been having success with its *sandwiches anglais*, flown in daily from London. The appeal of such goods may be restricted to a minority, but it has been growing fast.

In the cultural field, a wider vogue is for British movies, which today win far larger audiences than French films in Britain. This may be due largely to Britain's feeble distribution system for foreign-language films, but it also reflects quality: for the first time ever, Britain may well be producing better and more interesting new films than France, where the good ones tend to be slight and conventional (see pp. 481–2). British movies are admired for their quirky humour (*Trainspotting*), or their readiness to tackle difficult subjects (*Regeneration*) or to look sharply at modern society (Ken Loach, Mike Leigh).

Another new trend is for French businesses to move across the Channel. They are attracted by Britain's lower labour costs (see p. 176), its more flexible working practices, lighter taxes and simpler bureaucracy. Many young entrepreneurs feel that 'liberal' Britain offers them a better climate for starting up their own firm, so they have done so. Some banks and financial services, too, have moved part of their operations to London. Altogether, about 1,200 French companies have set up in Britain or acquired British firms, e.g. the buying of Christie's in 1998 by the tycoon François Pinault. Some French firms have even registered their head office in Britain, to the annoyance of the French Government, which in 1998 began to take legal action against them. So, after years of scorning the British economy for its archaic labour relations, declining industrial sector and low productivity, the French are now openly admiring it – for its new sense of enterprise, fairly low unemployment, and much else. But if they look closely outside London, they can see the bad sides, too – the poor living standards in northern towns, the lower levels of training and worker skills, the sluggish transport. 'But you British are so laid back about all this,' said one manager, 'that you don't seem to mind. It would drive us crazy.'

Politically, relations have improved since the departure of Mitterrand and Thatcher, with their rather frosty views of each other's countries. In May 1996 Jacques Chirac's state visit as President was a success: with his excellent English, and his Anglophilia dating from boyhood links, he went down well with the British – as the French observed. And he formed genuinely warm links with John Major. The visit took place just after the furore over French nuclear tests in the Pacific; and Chirac was able to praise Britain's 'elegance' in being alone among France's allies in not condemning them. This pleased those in France who also favoured the tests – just as, conversely, those hostile were gratified that the British public's boycotts had reduced imports of French wines by a third. Two other crises at the time soured relations for a while – French anger at 'mad cow disease', allegedly imported from Britain; and the fury of British truckers and tourists caught up in the French lorry drivers' strikes.

Then in 1999 came the second and worst crisis over British beef imports (see p. 399). The British press, which adores exploiting any Franco-British tiff made a mighty meal of all this.

In May/June 1997, by a pure coincidence of timing, both nations moved to the Left in their elections, ousting their right-wing Governments. And so, for the first time in fifty years, both countries simultaneously had Socialist/Labour Prime Ministers. The victory of New Labour was welcomed by many French pro-Europeans as signalling a more positive approach on EU matters, after the difficult Tory years; and its first steps, such as the signing of the Social Chapter, fulfilled some of these hopes, even if a decision over the single currency was delayed. But above all it was Tony Blair himself who caught the French imagination, more than in many countries. Here at last was a young British leader who spoke good French and was openly Francophile: he had worked as a barman during his student days in Paris, and had recently spent family holidays in France. Most significantly, because of his shift to the centre ground, Blair began to prove more popular in French centre-Right circles than among hard-line Socialists, who viewed him with some suspicion: they were annoyed at comments in the French press which compared Labour's pragmatic 'revolution' with the Socialist Party's more traditional stance. Martine Aubry hit back, claiming – not unreasonably – that it was French Socialists (under her father's impetus) who had moved towards the pragmatic centre in 1982–3, while Labour was still antiquated and anti-European; and that New Labour had stolen conservative ideas while her own party was more truly social-democratic.

In March 1998 Blair, by invitation, addressed the National Assembly. Whereas Churchill and Heath, in their time, had mangled the language embarrassingly whenever they tried to speak it in public, young Tony pleased his audience by talking for forty minutes in almost perfect French: 'Marvellous, brilliant,' commented Jack Lang. But what Blair actually said, extolling his 'third way', failed to find much response in a chamber still ideologically reticent about third ways between Right and Left. When, on a minor issue, he playfully teased his Socialist counterparts, they sat in stony silence while the centre-Right applauded. *L'humour anglais* may be appreciated in France, but not when it comes to breaking serious political taboos. However, *le grand public*, as opposed to Socialist politicians, is more enthusiastic about *le blairisme* and its creator. In a survey for *Le Monde* in December 1997, a remarkable 82 per cent of the sample said they had a 'good' or 'rather good' opinion of Tony Blair.

But of the British sample polled, only 11 per cent felt the same about Jospin and 82 per cent had 'no opinion': perhaps that says more about Britons' knowledge of France than their views on Socialism.

The mass public's interest in Blairism is tiny compared with its ongoing curiosity about the Royal Family; and since 31 August 1997 this has been greater than ever. Some French at first felt shame that *their* paparazzi or *their* drunk driver might have caused the crash in the Alma tunnel. Then the interest in the Paris aspect of the tragedy came to focus mainly on whether there was not some vast police cover-up going on, ordered from on high. Apart from this, France had its inevitable share of Dianamania, as for months the popular press and media produced a spate of material about the troubles of Britain's royalty – for example, in July 1998, a two-hour prime-time programme on the main TV channel, TF1. The French are proud to be republican, and they do not wish back their own monarchy: yet in their bones they retain some perverse nostalgia for it, as witness their fascination with foreign royalty, mainly Britain's. The media tend to exaggerate greatly the importance of the Royal Family in British life, and the public will follow suit: educated French people have often asked me, in effect, 'How can you, a democracy, still allow yourselves to be governed by a monarch in this way?' They cannot believe that the Queen is quite outside politics.

At least they have been getting to know some of her subjects rather better, those who have recently come to live in France. Far more Britons, proportionately, have now settled there than at any time since the Hundred Years War: at least 60,000 own secondary homes. These newcomers have little in common with the arty expatriates in Paris between the wars, or with the rich who used to colonize the Côte d'Azur: they are average middle-class people who have acquired holiday or retirement homes all over rural France, mainly in the south and west. They were drawn by images of the good life in France, and in the later 1980s the vogue gathered pace, as more people realized that rural properties were far cheaper than in Britain, and plentiful: many were abandoned farmsteads, which they bought and converted. And in some areas of rural depopulation, they have been welcomed locally for helping to check the process of decline. About half of the houses have been bought for holidays, and half for permanent retirement. According to one survey, British residents in Limousin rose fivefold in 1980–91, and more than threefold in western Normandy, Brittany, Poitou-Charentes and Midi-Pyrénées.

Most have fared perfectly well. But there has been one less happy outcome. Many people decided to take early retirement, or to sell their house and business in Britain and move to *la belle France*, where they thought they could find enough work to keep going: these were mostly tradesmen, artisans or businessmen. But they found that living full-time in France was not the idyll they had imagined from their holidays there. The winters were cold. Many felt isolated in the deep country. And with unemployment high, it was harder than they had expected to find the work they planned, maybe as builders, decorators, gardeners, traders. The local French preferred to give this work to each other, so the expats had to rely on other foreigners, who were too few. Many Brits did not bother to learn French, or adapt to French ways. The French ignored them, or pitied them. And so the minor human tragedies piled up. Marriages collapsed. There were nervous breakdowns, a few suicides. Many people slunk back home with their tails between their legs to accept a lower living standard, for they had given up their house and job in Britain. Retired people, too, dependent on pensions, were badly hit by the fall in the pound in the early 1990s, and many returned home.

Plenty of other expats fare more happily today and even find solid jobs, in the professions or in business. The Bordeaux area has about 9,000 British residents, some of them working as teachers, lawyers, financial advisers, estate agents, hoteliers, or in the wine trade. One is a sturgeon farmer, producing local caviar. In some other regions, a few farmers from Britain have bought land and started serious farming. This is feasible under EU rules: but it is not always so easy to be accepted in a French farming world habitually suspicious of outsiders (see p. 410). Some of the blow-ins did not take the trouble to adapt to French ways, and have ended up being victimized, *à la* Jean de Florette: there have even been tales of sabotaged crops or herds. But this is rare, and most British newcomers have managed well. Tim Green, from Cheshire, with his wife and three daughters, showed me round his big sheep farm in Normandy: 'If you try to impose British farming methods and think you know best, the locals get angry. So you need to be tactful – and to learn good French. I get on well with my farming neighbours.'

In any *métier*, those who come with a proper skill, and work hard, tend to be liked and accepted; and this is true of the many writers, artists and retired people who have settled. They do best if they adapt and mix, rather than keeping to their own social ghettos. 'My French neighbours have become true loyal friends, so caring,' says an elderly friend of mine from Hampstead, who has settled with her Siamese cat in a village near Cherbourg. As for Peter Mayle, in the Lubéron village of Ménerbes, his genuine feeling for French life shines through his books, and he enjoyed fraternizing with the quirky locals, even if he then satirized them (and his British visitors even more so). Having spent some time in the United States, he now lives in Provence again. *A Year in Provence* was not published in Paris until after he left Ménerbes. It at first failed to find a French publisher, but has since been a bestseller in France, as elsewhere.

Tourism has been growing, in both directions. The annual total of French holiday visits to Britain has now reached some 1.7 million. The British figure has always been the larger, for obvious reasons of climate, cuisine and rural appeal, and has now climbed to over 6 million, excluding day trips. Youth exchanges have been growing, even if officially only one-tenth as much is spent on these as on Franco-German ones. Town-twinnings have grown, too, from 150 in 1972 to some 400 today. These are somewhat hampered, on the British side, by poor local funding: a town council sees few votes in allocating sums for such jaunts, whereas in France they are more readily accepted, like all cultural spending. In fact, the exchanges involve not just mayors and other worthies but schoolkids, football teams, amateur choirs, firemen, and so on – and the ambience can be very jolly. The total numbers taking part may not be large, but the moral is clear: once the British and French do get to know each other, they usually end up friends. The common anti-French prejudices in Britain come mainly from those who have never been to France or met many French people, and they are stronger than the prejudices on the French side. The poll survey in *Le Monde*, about Blair and Jospin, found also that while 50 per cent of French claim to be 'rather sympathetic' to the British, the feeling the other way is only 35 per cent. Personal impressions bear this out: 'You British don't like us much, do you?' said one French student. The British prejudices have been sedulously fostered by the *Sun* and other tabloids, with their 'Hop off you Frogs' and 'Up Yours Delors' campaigns. It sells papers, but does damage to relations, even if at one level it is just a sophisticated joke: the *Sun* editor responsible for these features was a Francophile with a country château in France. Perhaps the French need to be more aware of *l'humour anglais* and its irony.

Their liking for British visitors took a jolt at the time of the World Cup, when English football hooliganism exported itself, yet again. There were bad riots in Marseille after the England versus Tunisia match there:

provoked in part by young Tunisians, some English fans rampaged, and the French police, ill-prepared for trouble on this scale, made thirty-six arrests. Some fans were deported, six were given on-the-spot prison sentences by special courts. One of them, well-known hard-core hooligan James Shayler, a beefy toughie with an English flag tattooed on his belly, admitted throwing missiles at *les flics*. After this, the police took better precautions in the other towns where England played, and there was little trouble. But France heaved a sigh of relief when England was beaten by Argentina and the fans went home. As for the Tartan Army, it was all much happier. They descended on France with their painted faces, tam-o'-shanters, ginger wigs and kilts; and though they drank the bars dry, and caused traffic jams with their crazy frolics, it was all good-humoured and non-violent. After the Scotland match at Bordeaux, some residents took a full-page advertisement in a Glasgow paper, thanking them warmly: 'We will never forget your *joie de vivre*. . . and your sense of fair play. Come back soon.' In short, the auld alliance stood up strong, and the French came to accept that there are fans and fans. Despite the bad image created, it is unlikely that a hideous minority of thugs will have done much lasting damage to Franco-British personal relations.

In their attitudes to speaking other languages, notably English, the French have changed dramatically since the early 1970s. As theirs was formerly the world language of diplomacy and culture, they have naturally resented its being overtaken by English. In Gaullist days the battle for *la défense de la langue française* was intense, and public servants were even forbidden to speak in other languages at international meetings. But after de Gaulle left, it was tacitly decided, 'if you can't lick 'em, join 'em': the French came to accept, if with regret, that in the interest of promoting exports and their world status, they had no choice but to use the world's top language, like everyone else. A turning point came in 1974, when Giscard on the night of his election victory made a speech in his fluent English for the foreign media. Some diehards were shocked, and maybe de Gaulle turned in his grave: but it was official recognition of the fact that speaking English was now not merely allowed but encouraged. After this, Giscard and Helmut Schmidt always spoke English together, while Chirac uses it fluently in public.

Foreign-language classes are now compulsory in all university courses and at most school levels; and over 80 per cent of pupils make English their first choice. The teaching in junior schools, once so dry and pedantic, is now livelier, with plenty of games and acting: but in higher education the teaching has now become less literary and is mostly geared to utilitarian commercial ends. A pity, in many ways. In working life, under a law of 1971, firms have to spend the equivalent of at least 1 per cent of their wage bill on in-service training schemes, and many of these are devoted to language courses for executives and secretaries. As a result, far more educated French speak reasonable English than a generation or so ago – less than in Germany or Scandinavia, but more than in Spain. They may still prefer to speak French when they can, especially inside France. But faced with a foreigner who can only mumble a few words in bad French, they will no longer pretend to know no English.

Politicians, however, remain concerned at the decline in the use of French in many countries where it used to be spoken so widely, such as Greece, Poland and Vietnam; and by the steady eclipse of French by English as the first *lingua franca* of European meetings, not only in Brussels but on French soil in Strasbourg. The French Government has made repeated demands to EU bodies to protect the use of its language, but to little avail. Mitterrand was worried by the trends, and in 1986 he launched the first of what are now regular summit conferences of Francophone nations, notably the French-speaking parts of Belgium and Canada, and France's former African and Far Eastern territories. 'Must we give orders to our computers in English?' he once asked, and in one book he complained of 'the irritating habit of some of our civil servants and even politicians to talk in a language other than their own'. But in practice there has been no attempt to return to the spirit of the Gaullist ban. In London the Institut Français today holds frequent lectures and conferences in English, unthinkable in the old days. And I notice that French diplomats in London, who once spoke just French with me, now quite often seem to prefer to use English (or is it that my French has deteriorated?).

Some French have above all been concerned about the craze for franglais – alleged distortion of their language by a mass incursion of ill-assimilated English terms and phrases. It began in the 1960s, when oddities emerged in the advertisements of the glossy magazines: '*Le temps d'un long drink . . . immeuble de grand standing . . . une star est interviewée . . .*' Whatever was happening to the tongue that Proust and Flaubert spoke? The invasion caused an intellectual outcry, and a Sorbonne professor, Étiemble, wrote a book denouncing it. But the problem was often misunderstood. It was not that ordinary people were voluntarily abandoning their language: rather, they were victims of a commercial conspiracy. Modern techniques of publicity arrived late in France, but then swept through the land with hurricane force, and marketing experts decided that the French could be conditioned to accept a commodity as smart and new if it were given an Anglo-Saxon name. The clothing and cosmetics worlds adopted English as their own, and house agents did so, too. This spilled over on to journalists and others, who picked up the trendy newspeak, often using it facetiously.

The Giscard Government grew alarmed. It supported the bill of a Gaullist deputy, Pierre Bas, which became law, and from 1977 forbade the use of foreign words – if French equivalents could be found to exist – in advertising and official documents. The press reacted with scorn, pointing to the absurdity of trying to put legal curbs on anything as fluid and spontaneous as language; in Britain, the Francophile Bernard Levin denounced in *The Times* 'this cultural crime of a crackpot nation that will impoverish its own tongue through this protectionism'. But the law did have its effect, as each year over 100 companies and individuals were penalized: the Évian mineral water firm, for instance, was fined for advertising a product as '*le fast drink des Alpes*'. So the use of franglais in such cases, and in documents, did greatly diminish. But it was hardly possible to prevent its use in daily spoken practice. In fact, as the French economy has opened to the world, so there has been a permanent incursion of English terms into the vocabulary of business and technology, simply because there are no French equivalents, or they are less neat and snappy. Words like *le marketing*, *le cash-flow*, *le software*, even *le design* and *le fast-food*, have become common currency in business or daily life. When the fax arrived, officialdom dutifully invented '*la télécopie*': it is the correct formal term, but most people say '*le fax*'.

French sensitivity about their proud tongue is understandable. But surely any language will wither if it is not in constant evolution, fertilized from outside – and now it is the turn of the French to import English words, just as English was enriched by countless French terms in the past. The French must accept this: *noblesse oblige*, as we British say. As we have cafés, so they now have *le snack*; as we have maisonettes, so they have *le parking*; as we find things chic, so they now find them *smart*; and so on, as with *le weekend*, *le duty-free*, *le check-up*, *le scoop*. But the process, admittedly, may have gone too fast and too far, and the French sometimes borrow falsely: English eyebrows may be raised at such quaint terms as *un tennisman*, *le footing* (jogging), and *grand standing* (house-agentese for 'upmarket'). Equally ludicrous are some official efforts to squeeze out franglais by fabricating French equivalents. This often flops because the French language is not adequately supple or concise: *le cash-flow* does not convince when turned into *la marge brute d'auto-financement*, nor *e-mail* when it becomes *le courrier électronique*, and who will bother with *un appareil de forage en mer* when he has *un oil rig*? Attempts to gallicize English spellings, as with *le beuledozère*, have fallen equally flat.

Undeterred, the Balladur Government in 1994 decided that the Bas law had not gone far enough nor been properly applied. So the Minister of Culture, Jacques Toubon, produced a new and tougher version, which proposed fines or prison sentences for the use of foreign words in advertising or the media, and in all public announcements: it even forbade French scientists and others, at conferences and seminars, to give papers or take part in discussions in a foreign language. Again, there was mockery in the press and on the Left, plus outrage among academics who feared being ridiculed when they went abroad. 'Excess franglais may be absurd,' said Jack Lang, 'but to ban it is dictatorship and more absurd.' Fortunately, the Constitutional Council stepped in, declaring that the new measures contravened the right to freedom of expression under the 1789 Declaration of the Rights of Man. It spared only the clauses decreeing that works contracts, and instructions on medicine bottles, machinery and suchlike, must either be in French or carry a full translation – and this was generally accepted as sensible consumer protection. So the law was passed in a very weakened form, and Toubon was left looking foolish. One comical feature is that, in advertising, all foreign phrases must include a translation: thus, for example, the heading 'It's nice to meet you', at the top of an ad in *L'Express* for an electronics firm, solemnly carried below it the phrase '*Ravis de vous rencontrer*'. The law's aim, not necessarily chauvinistic or silly, is to prevent misinformation: but some advertisers enjoy sending it up.

The Jospin Government has now sensibly pushed the franglais fracas aside, and is trying to promote English as a working second language, as in other countries. Claude Allègre, who speaks it well, said in 1998 that attempts to stop its spread in France were futile, so it was better to ensure that more people learned it correctly: he ordered the teaching of English in primary schools to be made universal. His rationale is that, if more French speak English fluently as a matter of course, then franglais will cease to have any gimmicky or novelty value in commercial use and will wane. Some English words are now here to stay: but they will be assimilated and forgotten, as we forget that 'restaurant' is a French word.

The major debate today is much more on the issue of how to protect French culture – in popular music, television and cinema – from American mass commercial pressures. This is part of the whole problem of globalization, and it leaves the French confused and equivocal. By 1994–5 some 80 per cent of popular music on French radio stations was American or British in origin. So a second Balladur law imposed a quota of at least 40 per cent of material to be by French artists singing in French, with heavy fines for any failure to comply. The directors of the stations specializing in light music were furious: they pointed out that Anglo-Saxon music was what most of their audience wanted, as France's own pop and rock were today too mediocre (see p. 572): only about six French groups generally made the Top Twenty. But by early 1996 the law was in force and has since been respected, even if some stations find ruses such as bunching their French quota into the less popular hours. The programme director at Fun Radio complained at having to fill so much air time with ageing French rockers such as Johnny Halliday, not popular with the young. The law may have been clumsily applied, and is against today's ethic of giving the public what it wants: but it does at least contain the laudable motive of trying to promote new original work, in face of mass 'industrialized' music.

In television programming, the pattern has been somewhat the same; and here, as in cinema, France has paraded as the defender of all Europe. Aiming to prevent the import of too much American soap, or similar diet, the European Commission in 1989 produced its famous directive, '*Télévision sans Frontières*', which laid down that at least 50 per cent of the material should be European in origin on each network in a member State. France took the lead in pushing for this, in face of reticence from some more 'liberal' countries, notably Britain. The directive has been only vaguely applied by some members, such as Italy. But France went ahead and made it a law, whereby at least 40 per cent of material on its TV screens must be French, with up to 20 per cent coming from other EU countries, to a total minimum ceiling of 60 per cent, while the rest can be *Kojak* or whatever. French film producers, afraid of their own output being pushed off TV screens by Hollywood, have strongly insisted on these quotas. And, generally, the rules have been obeyed, even if TF1, complaining of a lack of good suitable European material, was fined recently for falling short. In 1995 the directive came up for review, and France by lobbying was able to get it reinforced, despite opposition from the British and others. Jacques Toubon, in full cry, denounced America's 'cultural colonialism'.

For cinemas there are no quotas, and they can show what they like. With French movies accounting for almost 40 per cent of entries, France's own film industry stands up better against Hollywood than others in Europe. But it depends heavily on its state subsidies and other aids (see pp. 482–3). And so, in 1993–4, when these seemed threatened by the Uruguay Round of GATT talks, the French Government fought ferociously to have cinema excluded from any new free-trade deal that might limit subsidies. Directors, producers, actors and intellectuals, in France and throughout Europe, rallied readily to its cause. Roger Planchon accused the US of planning a 'great genocide' of national cultures and languages; Depardieu said Europe's cinema was 'in danger of death'; Tavernier added wittily, 'The Americans want to treat us like redskins. We will merely have the right to live in the hills of Dakota, and if we are well behaved, they will give us another little hill.' Behind this and other hype was the serious argument that cinema is not just a commercial product but a major art form that needs special help, like opera, and cannot be left to the icy winds of free trade. In the teeth of the EU's chief negotiator, Sir Leon Brittan, who thought otherwise, the French argued this case and won: cinema was excluded from the GATT deal, to the fury of Hollywood. But today the threat has re-emerged, with a new OECD project for multilateral agreements: in 1998 this was still being fought out, and again it seemed that France would win wide backing for its view that the *exception culturelle* must be kept, both for cinema and television.

The debate is part of a wider issue of globalized commercial culture versus 'real' national culture. It may be absurd to legislate against franglais, or even to impose quotas for pop music, when France's output is today so poor: but with cinema the French are on far stronger ground, and most cultural pundits agree that they are right to protect their industry and its lively creation of new *films d'auteur*. This is more than just protectionist defence of *l'exception française*. Whatever the arguments for or against globalization in other economic fields, in culture the dangers are real. National and regional cultures need to be defended – even if this means protecting the French public against its own bad taste in lapping up a vulgar American prefabricated diet! It is an old democratic dilemma.

French attitudes to America remain equivocal. On the one hand, as in any country, American products are hugely enjoyed, notably by the young: hence the successes of McDonald's, American films and pop music, Disneyland Paris (after a difficult start), teenage baseball caps. But this has little to do with the 'real' America; and adult French today show very little desire to copy America's lifestyles, or to admire its social model. In the post-war decades, anti-Americanism was rabid, especially among intellectuals and dedicated Gaullists. US economic dominance was feared, its wealth resented, its naïve tourists mocked, its foreign policies abhorred, above all during the Vietnam War. Today the French attitude has softened. Now that Europe has narrowed the gap in terms of modernization and economic influence, the old envy-cum-scorn has declined, and individual Americans are accepted more easily. The French may still resent American dominance in NATO: but in the Gulf War they were far readier than would have been possible in de Gaulle's day to see their soldiers fighting under US leadership. A professional élite admires American technical and business prowess, but wants to adapt this to the French model, rather than simply copy it. More French are now visiting the USA as tourists, and are often gratified to find a land that is no glossy futurist utopia but full of ordinary folk muddling through.

Yet among the mass of French, suspicions persist. According to surveys by Sofres in 1988 and 1996 published in *Le Monde*, the proportion of French looking on America 'with sympathy' fell in that period from 54 to 35 per cent, while those viewing it 'with antipathy' rose from 38 to 46 per cent. Asked which key words best evoked for them the United States, the numbers quoting 'violence' rose in that time from 28 to 59 per cent, and 'inequalities' from 25 to 45 per cent, while 'dynamism' fell from 32 to 26 per cent, and 'freedom' from 30 to 18 per cent. Maybe such polls should not be taken too literally. But these figures suggest a curious trend in attitudes, sometimes at odds with practice. Some 70 per cent of the 1996 sample judged American cultural influence in France 'excessive'. That does not deter them from going to big popular US movies in numbers truly titanic.

BRILLIANT EXPORT SUCCESSES — YET A PANIC
ABOUT GLOBALIZATION

Fears of American domination, cultural or economic, lie at the heart of the passionate debate in France today about *la mondialisation*. The French may well be right to worry about the general world impact of this globalization, which carries dangers for any country: but in particular they fear being much less well placed to deal with it, or to gain from it, than *les Anglo-Saxons*. This ties in with the current French identity crisis, the fear that the so-called 'French model' of society, and the famous *exception française*, are under threat from the new world trends – as indeed they may be. The French republican traditions, of social organization and of culture, may well be in danger. Yet in strictly *economic* terms, of world competition and efficiency, do the French have so much to worry about? *Prima facie*, it would seem not. For some years, their trade balance has been amazingly positive, despite high labour costs, the *franc fort* policy, and other seeming handicaps for exports: the surplus rose to a record 173 billion for 1997, and was 138 billion in 1998. France is the world's fourth largest exporter, after the United States, Germany and Japan: it does notably well in agricultural goods and many heavy industrial products, including armaments where sales reached 43 billion for 1997. But its total share of world trade has been falling slightly, from 5.8 to 5.5 per cent since 1980. Few smaller firms are export-geared: the foreign-trade success has depended mainly on some thirty of the larger groups, most of which today are highly efficient and competitive.

Both outward and inward investment have been forging ahead for some years, as the French economy has opened to the world. Industry's outward movement has not yet reached British or German levels, but it has been growing. Thus, for example, L'Oréal, the fourth largest French firm on the Bourse, has forty factories around the world and sells 82 per cent of its goods abroad; Michelin has a big operation in South Carolina; Renault and Peugeot, after setbacks in Africa and China, are expanding strongly in Latin America. The French unions have complained that the trend takes potential new jobs from France: but the Patronat retorts, in effect, 'In this new free world market, if we don't act first our competitors will do so, and the French economy as a whole will lose out.' Some 400 French firms are represented in Singapore, and 200 in Malaysia: but expansion there may now be badly affected by the financial crisis in eastern Asia.

As for foreign investment in France, this has on the whole been encouraged officially – but under certain conditions. The birth of the EEC brought a rush of American firms looking for footholds inside Europe; and in the 1960s France proved a favourite venue for investors attracted by its political stability, well-trained labour force, and so on. But de Gaulle was not too happy about this compliment. He saw threats to national independence, and on several occasions he and then Pompidou vetoed applications by American and other firms: thus Fiat was prevented from trying to take over Citroën. Then under Giscard the policy became more pragmatic and it remained so under Mitterrand and Chirac. Today Germany and the United States are the main investors, followed by the Netherlands and Britain. US firms include Ford, IBM, Motorola and Hewlett-Packard, while the British have made a speciality of buying up luxury hotels such as the Carlton in Cannes. Japanese firms such as Canon and Sony have arrived. And in 1997 the Government was delighted when France narrowly defeated bids from Ireland and Poland to win a new investment by Toyota for its second automobile factory in Europe. This will create some 2,000 jobs at Valenciennes, a depressed industrial town near Lille with high unemployment. In foreign investment, as in so much else, new jobs are the guiding priority.

The creation of a new factory has almost always been welcomed. But for many years, proposed foreign acquisitions of existing French firms were looked at more carefully. Usually, they were allowed, even encouraged, if they seemed likely to bring in new technology or lead to new jobs. Yet a 'French solution' was often preferred where feasible: if an ailing French firm needed to be saved by a takeover, a foreign bid might be rejected if the Government could find a French buyer, even at a lower price. This could be so where national prestige was involved. Thus, when the mighty Château Margaux vineyard came on to the market, the Government ensured its sale to a French grocery chain at a price below the offers made by German and US firms: the reason given was that Margaux was part of the national heritage. However, today this kind of interference is illegal, under the new European rules of the single market: Governments no longer have the right to prevent any foreign takeover. The only exception is in the field of defence and armaments, where the State is still allowed to ensure that France keeps control of its own industries. Thus when in 1997 the Jospin Government set about partly privatizing the Thomson defence electronics group, it was careful to see that a 'French solution' was found. Joint ventures with foreign arms firms are sometimes allowed, but only on a basis of equality.

Today the principal anxiety is about something else, more insidious than overt takeovers: the gradual penetration by foreign shareholders into major French companies of all kinds quoted on the Bourse. Mostly, these moves are made by American and British pension funds, eager to seek new markets. And they are welcomed by the French firms, which need the extra capital and cannot find adequate backing from French shareholders (pension funds of the Anglo-American kind hardly exist in France). As much as 35 per cent of capital on the Bourse is now held by foreign institutional investors of this kind, and many of the major French groups have thus come under part foreign ownership: the figures include 50 per cent of Total, 46 per cent of Elf-Aquitaine, 43 per cent of L'Oréal, 40 per cent of Rhône-Poulenc, 35 per cent of Peugeot, 34 per cent of St-Gobain. It is true that these and other firms have big holdings abroad, so there is a degree of cross-financing. Even so, French industry is becoming increasingly less French-owned, and some politicians have expressed disquiet: 'It is a serious threat. Our big firms are more and more exposed to takeovers,' said Laurent Fabius, president of the National Assembly, in November 1997. But there is little that the Government can do legally to prevent the invasion. Proposals to develop France's own pension funds have fallen foul of the taxation system.

The issue is a major aspect of the whole problem of American-led globalization which so much troubles the French today. In industry and business, the debate is whether France stands to gain or lose from the trend, and views differ. Companies find that their Anglo-Saxon investors are often highly critical of French methods of management: they expect greater profit motivation, greater financial *transparence* (open account-ability), rather than the secretiveness that has been traditional in France, and sometimes they make this a condition of further investment. Guy de Panafieu, director-general of Lyonnaise des Eaux, has said, 'We are usually scrutinized, interrogated by two or three people who know our sector well. Some of their questions are very pertinent, but surprising. It is a tough and abrasive exercise, but enriching.' In other words, French firms may well resent being pushed into adapting to international, i.e. American, business practices: but if there seems no choice, then they must learn. The process comes easiest to those many senior *cadres* who have already been partly educated at, say, the Harvard Business School.

Then there is the fear that the new world mobility of capital makes a firm more vulnerable: a big foreign investor can suddenly turn against a company or a country, and pull out its shares. Above all, the unions and the Left are worried that globalization can depress wages and add to unemployment, in an advanced nation such as France. At a Thomson electronics plant in Burgundy, a unionist told me, 'We make parts for the group's video factory in Singapore, where wages are one-quarter of French levels; and in Thailand they are one-twentieth, in Burma one-hundredth! So of course Thomson knows where to expand, and our staff here has fallen from 1,200 to 400 since the 1970s. It's terrifying. If all employees in the world are in direct competition, then those in higher-wage countries will suffer. And if France is flooded with more cheaply made goods from Asia, then French jobs will go.' It is an old argument, which has now been gathering force. But opinions differ. An OECD report in 1997 claimed that technical progress, not overseas competition, was the principal cause of rising unemployment among lower-skilled workers in Europe – and many French economists back this view, including Raymond Barre, who has written, 'The industrialized countries have much to gain from intensifying their trade with those in development.'

And yet, the French as a whole are today more worried about globalization than any other people in Europe: 'For them it is a nightmare on the way, an inevitable decline,' wrote *Le Monde*'s editor, Jean-Marie Colombani. They fear, rightly or wrongly, that France is not well suited to coping with this American-led trend that will benefit most *les Anglo-Saxons*. They are scared of its likely impact on the 'French model', thus maybe on their welfare society and privileges – and this has been one motive behind several recent strikes, such as those of December 1995. These may have been aimed primarily against EMU, but also against the wider global movement perceived as coming in its wake. One striking change in recent years is that many French, who used to see a united Europe as a protection for France against the world, have now come to see it as a Trojan horse for American domination, a breach in the wall of defence against *la mondialisation*.

In many ways, these fears are irrational and exaggerated. After all, some big French firms are doing as well as American ones in the new global competition (witness the trade surplus). And in opening out to the world, France has revealed some of its weaknesses but also its strengths, and it can do superbly – ironically, the World Cup which France hosted, organized and won so brilliantly was known in France as '*le Mondial*'! Yet globalization will certainly have its negative sides for everyone, and maybe the French are showing more imagination about these than most other countries, such as Britain. The world until now has been dominated mainly by Governments, notably in the Cold War period: but now it will be run more and more by a handful of giant industrial and financial groups, ever larger, over which Governments will probably have less and less control. It is indeed a disturbing prospect.

Yet the right response surely is not an ostrich-like protectionism, but to battle for ways of controlling the titans, and of ensuring that inevitable globalization benefits the global village, France included. The more open-minded French are aware of this, and of how much France can contribute. The sociologist Alain de Vulpian told me in 1997, 'The past years have brought a huge growth in public awareness that we all live on one small planet. Some people react positively: "Yes, I am a citizen of this world, I must help to look after it"; but others are scared, so they respond with a *repli sur soi*. And many feel *both* at the same time.' Many French today accept that globalization could be the best way of achieving economic take-off for the Third World and of helping its very poor. Yet the trend is most heavily attacked in France by the Left and the unions, first because it is too 'liberal' and capitalist-led, and also because it might affect French workers. But what price world solidarity? In his book *La Faute aux élites* (1997), the journalist Jacques Julliard, pro-Socialist but critical of the Left, writes of its betrayal of its internationalist worker-movement role:

The globalization of the economy, like the former industrialization of Western countries, is a hope for the entire world, despite the sufferings it brings. It is good to have moralistic intellectuals to denounce its brutality. The left-wing intellectual is to predatory capitalism what the missionary is to the colonizer. He walks behind, at a respectful distance, to repair the damage of the conquest and, without knowing it, to give it a meaning . . .

But the blanket rejections of the global trend

are short-sighted and full of a parochial egotism. At the end of the day, what is globalization if not the introduction of poor countries into the concert of modern economy. Seen from the Communist Party headquarters, it is an abomination. Seen from the suburbs of Manila, it is the only hope.

And so the French are deeply torn. National pride is involved, for they have difficulty in accepting that France's old 'universal mission' is no longer so valid, and that it must adapt to fit in with a wider effort. This colours the views even of those who accept the positive sides of the new global trend. French culture, the 'French model', must play still useful but less arrogant roles. On the most banal symbolic level, Minitel must now yield to Internet, and *la haute cuisine* must learn to lie down with McWorld. In short, the French are having an identity crisis, a large part of their recent malaise.

CONCLUSION:
LA MOROSITÉ AND BEYOND

'*Une dépression nerveuse collective*' is the term that has endlessly been used, even by serious experts, to describe the sulky French mood since about the early 1990s – '*la morosité ambiante*'. This 'prevailing gloom' has been worse among the Paris chattering classes than in the more easy-going provinces. And it was at its zenith under Juppé in 1995–7. Since then, it has lightened a bit: Jospin's Government is more popular, the economy has improved so that unemployment has fallen, and maybe the World Cup victory has helped. But the gloom is still there, plus the vague feelings of insecurity and pessimism about the future. They seem in some ways excessive, for the French economy is basically strong and the country is stable. And they may have an element of self-fulfilling prophecy, for the more the French analyse and discuss the general malaise, the more pessimistic it can make them. Chirac on television has several times urged these *malades imaginaires* to snap out of it.

France for some years has been in an uneasy state of transition, and has been taking it harder than many countries with similar problems. So the *malaise* is not new: it can be traced back at least to the world economic slow-down of the mid-1970s that followed years of rapid growth. There were more periods of gloom in the Mitterrand era, and later they grew worse. One major official survey, the 'European barometer' of Ipsos in 1997, found 61 per cent of French pessimistic about their economic future, compared with figures of 47 per cent for Italy, 38 for Germany, 33 for Britain. In the same survey, the French were also top of the league for negative views about the future of their country: 46 per cent pessimistic, against figures of 37 per cent for Italians, 32 for the often angst-ridden Germans, a mere 19 for the sunny British.

Of course national temperament plays a part. The French are habitually more demanding than the easy-going British; they are always highly critical of their leaders, and of French society, where they blame it all on *les autres*. So they express their gripes to pollsters. And even if anxious about public matters, they are still able to enjoy life privately – above all in the provinces, with their *douceur de vivre*. In a small town in the Midi, a local businessman with Paris contacts told me, 'There's far less *morosité* here than in Paris. I have my garden, I play sport with the kids, I go fishing, the sun shines, I have warm friends. Life is good. Yet when I think of it, I worry about the future of France.' In fact, the French more than many peoples seem to have lost much of their old post-war faith that economic progress will lead inevitably to social progress: today progress is seen as essentially technical, while other matters may not necessarily get better. What has waned also is a faith in the State or the community to improve things: this is now seen as much more up to the individual, with his family, friends and contacts, his own efforts and values.

Among the obvious causes of the malaise are: (a) the national identity crisis, linked to the rise of globalization; (b) the economic anxieties, linked to high unemployment; and (c) the disillusion with politicians, linked to the corruption cases. All these factors have come together in recent years. Despite the Socialists' other successes, the revelations about Mitterrand's cynical malpractices at the Élysée have left a sour taste, above all on the Left. Then came Chirac's broken promises and Juppé's tactless arrogance, and the series of fraud scandals involving both Left and Right, from Tapie and Dumas to many mayors and *mairies*, including Paris. People came to feel that politicians, and many business leaders and state technocrats, were not to be trusted, or were incompetent. And the public has expressed its dismay through electoral fickleness: in the three presidential and five parliamentary elections since 1981, the voters, swinging confusedly between Right and Left, have kicked out the incumbent leader or majority *seven* times out of the eight. Normal alternation may be healthy – but not to such a point! Today, however, the patent honesty of Jospin and his team is giving a better image. But the centre-Right is still in disarray.

The waning and mellowing of the old Stalinist Communist Party is healthy for France and is welcomed by most democrats on the Left. But it has been balanced by the ominous rise of the Front National, which provides an outlet for the angry despair of some voters, but adds to the malaise of many others, worried about its threat to democracy – so the angst is double-faced. Many French people of all kinds feel aware of a growing gulf between ruled and rulers – not only the politicians but the *énarques* and other so-called élitist technocrats, who are more heartily disliked than ever: 'It is *they* who have got us into this mess; I'd like to see them hanged in public,' said one mild woman doctor I know, while the sociologist Michel Crozier has written a book on 'the powerlessness of the élites to reform themselves'. Jacques Attali has now officially proposed a reform of the Grandes Écoles system: but its impact remains to be seen. And it could not itself remedy another weakness in today's France – the lack of new charismatic leaders coming from the grassroots, in commerce, industry or local affairs. Where are the visionary innovators, to take up the torch from the Triganos and Leclercs, the Dubedouts and Gourvennecs? The age is not propitious for them, and the French feel aware of this need. They cry out for inspiring new leaders – but not Bruno Mégret.

The unemployment crisis since the 1980s has been a major factor behind *la morosité*. It may directly affect only one active adult in eight: but it creates a pervasive climate of insecurity, among *cadres* as well as workers. Many people in a good job are worried that they might lose it and not find another, and they discuss this endlessly. The problem has spread to the educated middle classes, so it has hit home among journalists and politicians, fearful for their own children's future, and is more talked about in the media. In reality, most people do find ways of coping quite well with unemployment, if it comes; and as in America some even welcome the enforced chance to take a break, enjoy the leisure or rethink their career. But though the jobless figures have been falling a little since 1997, the feeling widely persists that this can only be a temporary respite, in a fast-changing world of new technologies and emerging nations. When in 1996 a left-wing critic, Viviane Forrester, published a polemical book, *L'Horreur économique*, warning that heartless global capitalism was bound to destroy for ever old patterns of employment, it was a massive bestseller (350,000 copies), responding to the general mood of apprehension about *la mondialisation* and its effects.

The French today are torn in their attitudes to those two great opposing models, the old state-controlled system and the new 'liberal' world economy. They would like to enjoy the best of both. But they know that to have this *gâteau* and eat it is hard – and it leaves them muddled and disturbed. It seems significant that the word 'liberal', in French or English, has shifted its meaning so strangely. A 'liberal' used to be an advocate of social reform and personal freedoms, in face of the old dictatorship of creeds or institutions, such as Church or State. But today a 'liberal' economist is something quite else: he wants total freedom for the market, which surely could lead to other dictatorships by giant anonymous financial powers, gobbling up smaller human-scale firms. It is happening all the time – and many French have reason to be worried.

Some of them, the more modern-minded, feel fully at ease in this new 'liberal' world: they see the advantages that it can bring to their own business, and maybe to France. They and many others are also glad that the old state control has waned, and they welcome devolution, the decline of *dirigisme*, the privatizations: when in 1996 the State gave up majority control of Renault, its old flagship, few protests were heard. Yet many of these same people are worried at the waning of the 'French model' through deregulation. Or they may fear that the general retreat of the State is leaving a vacuum in public life. Significantly, when in 1996 the 'liberal' UDF party ran an opinion survey asking voters if they wanted more or less state intervention in various fields, economic, social and cultural, the majority replied that they wanted *more* help from the State in every domain, in terms of funding, protection, even guidance. So this dilemma – hatred of nanny, but fear of losing nanny – also lies at the heart of French *morosité* today.

The problem is not new. De Gaulle, who adored *la France* but never thought so highly of the French, said of them in 1966, 'They can't cope without the State, yet they detest it. They don't behave like adults.' How much has changed since then, as this modern nation still agonizes over one of its oldest problems, the mistrust between State and citizen? The ubiquitous role of the State has its roots deep in royalist history and was reinforced by Napoleon. And of course its strong authority brought many advantages: the post-war economy benefited from the intelligent lead of the planners, while state servants imposed a cohesion on a disparate and quarrelsome people. But this bred a complex of dependence. De Gaulle observed that the French grouse constantly at state interference, yet howl as loudly if the State fails to provide; they rely on it too much, and will seldom take the initiative for grouping to solve their own problems. This trait, bred of centuries of centralism, was analysed by Alain Peyrefitte in his famous bestseller *Le Mal français* (1976):

How to break the vicious circle in which France is locked? – a population at once passive and undisciplined, thus justifying *dirigisme*, and a bureaucracy which discourages initiatives, suffocates activity and manages to make the citizens even more passive to the point where, exasperated, they pass in one bound from lethargy to insurrection, while the State moves from pressure to oppression.

And that writer was no left-winger but a Gaullist minister!

Today, in a new age, that vicious circle has begun to unlock a little, as France opens out to the world. In the economy, *dirigisme* has declined and far fewer big firms are now state-owned. In government, the devolution of the 1980s has transferred many decisions from central to local hands. And state technocrats have been instructed to consult local people more carefully, rather than impose their schemes arrogantly. This has borne results. For example, I met a young *châtelain* in the Dordogne who in 1979 had formed an association for improving the environment: he won wide local support, but was thwarted by the prefect and other local state officials, who did not wish his scheme to poach on their preserves. Ten years later, in a new climate, he tried again and won their backing. They could no longer stop him.

Yet all over France there is still a wide resentment of 'them' – the privileged castes from the Grands Corps and the top Grandes Écoles, whose élite diplomas separate them from the rest. Today they may consult more often. But they are still regarded as too arrogant, too out of touch with the needs and views of ordinary people, too ready to take key decisions in the secrecy of Paris offices. Alain Juppé was seen as the archetype. Jacobins, however, will readily state an opposite case: that frequently these derided technocrats have proved *more* go-ahead, liberal and far-sighted than local bodies might be. Look, they will say, at the Languedoc schemes; or the Education Ministry's reformers, who have been more progressive than the teachers; while Juppé himself dared to impose his needed reforms of *la Sécu* on the reactionary doctors. If progress were left to the groundswell of local opinion, the *esprit de clocher* might win the day – or so the centralists argue. But here again is the vicious circle: *étatisme* can breed apathy or opposition, or stunt local initiative. Today the French are in a curious transition. *Étatisme* has grown out of fashion, while local ventures now have more scope and are even encouraged. But while some are launched and succeed, in many others, citizens remain reticent about seeking their own remedies. 'People are still not used to taking responsibility,' said one social worker. 'Too often, they still expect the State to provide. Like a small child, they scream defiance at nanny while clinging to her apron-strings for comfort.'

One major problem, perhaps worse in France than in many countries, is the weight of bureaucracy, with its countless regulations – compounded by the climate of mistrust that can exist between the public and minor bureaucrats. To obtain a permit may well entail not only endless form-filling but a tussle with the official behind the desk, who does not see it as part of his or her duty to be helpful. Since the 1970s Governments have been making efforts to lighten and humanize this machine, with erratic success. Giscard set up a kind of ombudsman to provide a channel for grievances against bureaucratic injustices. And some services have been urging staff to become more customer-friendly. This has brought some results, especially with a change of generation, as sombre old *huissiers* are replaced by uniformed young *hôtesses* with quick smiles, trained in the new schools of public relations. The telephone service in particular has made a real effort to improve its image and be more helpful. And as deregulation brings competition, this trend could develop, in this and other services.

Official attempts at reform have been coming up against two main obstacles. One is that centralized bureaucracy tends to intensify under modern conditions, as life grows more complex and more written regulations – some emanating from Brussels – are churned out to deal with new situations. So the most dynamic of technocrats can be a victim of the monster thus spawned, as one *polytechnicien* told me: 'We feel ever more helpless in face of a machine ever harder to control. I've been puzzling for weeks over the new rules for part-time employment and I fail to understand them – so how can I expect my junior *cadres* to do so?' Private firms may seek to simplify their own rules, perhaps introducing American methods: but they are hampered by the fact that much of their work depends on following official norms. And the paperwork can still be monstrous. Even a simple matter like collecting expenses for a TV assignment once drove me into one of those fits of Francophobia which afflict every Francophile. I had to fill in several long forms with such vital details as my mother's maiden name and my father's place of birth, then I was obliged to stand in queues at cash desks and go across Paris to another office, and only when a tolerant clerk deftly fiddled the rigid rules was I able to collect the money. Governments, aware of such problems, have been making a few efforts to simplify: for example, changes in the archi-complex fiscal system have led to a reduction by half of the number of separate categories of tax exemption.

A second obstacle: well-meant reform has often been subtly obstructed by the bureaucrats themselves. The senior ones are anxious to hold on to their power, or they genuinely believe that the old system is fairest and best; the junior ones are too hidebound or afraid. In several public offices, bold technocratic initiative has foundered on the inability or refusal of *petits fonctionnaires* to adapt to the changes. They block reforms through incompetence, bloody-mindedness – or mistrust. In any office, every post or grade has its defined duties and rights; and every employee may fear that *he* will be the one to suffer from changes: so he digs his heels in. One solution could be to improve the quality of practical civil-service training at the lower levels, or to reduce numbers and increase computerization: this has been done, but it provokes rearguard action from the unions. In the present employment climate, no Government dares do much to reduce chronic overstaffing in the civil service.

Reform of bureaucracy has made slightly more progress since Chirac came to power with promises to 'narrow the gap between rulers and ruled' and fight 'blockages by *fonctionnaires*'. Inspired in part by John Major's 'citizens' charter', Juppé embarked on a programme which Jospin is broadly continuing. It is hardly radical, but better than nothing. Thus the list of thousands of local activities requiring official authorization has been pruned by some 300: so you can now hold a dog show, or open a village tourist office, without getting advance permission. Citizens' advice bureaux have been set up in some suburbs. And public offices have been instructed to speed up replies to letters: any request not answered within two months is now deemed to have been agreed to, whereas hitherto any letter not answered within four months was deemed to have got the reply 'no' – quite a major shift. Most important, following up reforms begun years ago, the devolution of official decision-making from Paris ministries to local prefectures and their services is being much increased. Thus, for example, a hotelier wanting a licence to sell alcohol can now acquire it locally, whereas previously his application went up to the Ministry of Tourism, then to the Ministry of Health, in Paris: the change is expected to reduce the time needed from six months to two. The aim is for more decisions to be handled by people in touch with local realities, rather than by distant bureaucrats. Yet the move is being resisted by the Paris administrations, unwilling to lose any of their power – and even by some citizens who might stand to benefit. Thus many musical and theatre people fear that the regional officials of the Culture Ministry might find themselves under too much pressure from local *notables* or others, whereas Paris can take a broader and more generous view. It is the familiar debate about the pros and cons of paternalistic state centralism.

★

And so today the great argument continues over what should be the proper role of the State, and how to distinguish between 'good' and 'bad' *étatisme*. In the economy, it is widely agreed that a weakening of the old heavy state control was necessary, and this has now been largely achieved. In bureaucracy, there is still much to be done. But what of the 'French model' of the public services? How are its nobler qualities to be preserved in the face of the new gods of European competition and efficiency? And more widely, what is the role of patriotism today? In an age that has seen the break-up of so many old values, is the citizen's sense of service to State and nation still a worthwhile ideal?

The issue emerged recently during the debate on the ending of compulsory military service. This was created by Napoleon III; and ever since, in peace as in war, every young able-bodied French male, at least in theory, has gone through his year or two of duty under the flag, from square-bashing to learning some military craft. Traditionally, the aim was to provide the armed forces with a cadre of trained reservists, for use in time of war; also, to instil a sense of patriotic public service, which is seldom well taught in schools. Recently, the service had been reduced to about ten months, and many conscripts were exempted on medical or family grounds, while the few conscientious objectors were given non-military duties: but over two-thirds of each age group did their service. However, in the 1990s, with the ending of the Cold War, the sentiment grew that the system was no longer so necessary: it was not very expensive, but its abolition could well contribute to the defence budget cuts under the 'peace dividend'. Spain, Belgium and the Netherlands have all now ended conscription, and Italy is preparing to do so. Germany retains the system: but this is because of official fears that the nation's strong anti-military feelings would make it hard to recruit an adequate purely professional army, and this could become dominated by belligerent neo-Nazi elements.

De Gaulle himself, that great patriot, had argued before the war for a skilled professional army without conscripts (in his book, *Vers l'armée de métier*, 1934). And Chirac, loyal to the General's ideas on many matters, then took this up, as President: so his Defence Minister, Charles Millon, began to prepare the change. The parties of the Left were against ending military service. But Jospin, on coming to power, felt unable to oppose Chirac on this: defence is one of the few sectors where the President, constitutionally, has a deciding voice. So the Socialists went ahead with the plan, and in 1997 the National Assembly voted for it (with the

Communists, those staunch 'republicans', abstaining). Conscription is to be steadily phased out by 2002. The Government scrapped Millon's interesting proposal for a so-called '*rendez-vous citoyen*', whereby each teenager, boy or girl, would take a week's crash course of induction into military and civic duties. But Jospin has kept the central features of Chirac's plan: the professional armies will be strengthened, and conscription will be replaced by a system of short voluntary service, either in these forces or in new civil aid units, partly humanitarian, at home or abroad.

The majority of senior military staff were even more opposed than the Left to ending conscription: many officers felt angrily that Chirac had foisted it on them without due consultation. As well as arguments about training reservists and patriotic duty, they came up with other practical reasons for retaining the status quo. Some warned of Britain's experience: had she not failed to recruit enough professional servicemen of high calibre? Or they stressed the usefulness of graduate conscripts who brought their skills and know-how, especially in the medical field. Some officers even argued that a citizen conscript leaven could be a safeguard against possible fascist pressures within the army – and they pointed to Algeria in 1958 and 1962, when the presence of *appelés* helped twice to prevent an army *putsch* against Paris: but surely this thinking, though valid then, hardly applies today. As for the young people themselves, they are divided. Many see conscription as a waste of time, or as a career disruption that can lose them a good job. Others, conversely, look on it as a way of staving off the dole for a year, or of learning a new craft, or of seeing the world – some go to join French units in Africa or the Pacific, or they can volunteer to take part in UN peace-keeping missions. About 40 per cent of the 7,300 French troops in Bosnia in 1995 were conscripts.

Talking to a group of *appelés* in 1997, at an air force base near Marseille, I found these views well represented. Two of them had studied mechanical sciences, and thought their work on the base would be useful for their careers: but others saw it as just time-serving. All agreed that a conscript's life is today quite cushy: his wage is tiny but he works mainly office hours, can go home at weekends, and is usually posted within his own part of France. The army still does square-bashing, but there is little of this in the air force. One law student, aiming to join the military police, gave me a view common among serving officers: 'The army makes up for the faults of school education. Some conscripts are semi-illiterate, and it teaches them to read and write properly. What's more, in France we do not have a proper civic education system like you in Britain: so the army trains men in group responsibility, shared living, respect for others, which they have missed at school. It is good for the character.'

This sturdily traditional view may have much to be said for it (we all know that France lost the battle of Waterloo on the playing fields of Eton). But it hardly makes a case for retaining conscription: so it might be better to reform the educational system. Meantime, the Jospin Government is preparing Chirac's *volontariat* scheme: young men and women alike, aged eighteen to twenty-five, will be urged to volunteer for a year or two's service, either in the armed forces or police, or in some new civil corps to be geared towards social or humanitarian service, or in similar work abroad, mostly in poorer countries. This last has already existed, in one form, for some years: under a scheme called '*la coopération*', some 5,000 conscripts each year have been able to do their service either in technical or aid work, say in France's former African colonies, or in some other foreign posting: for example, the literary attaché at the embassy in London is usually some *normalien* doing a conscript job far removed from square-bashing.

Today the *volontariat* idea is generally welcomed. But some questions remain. Will the professional armed forces, some 300,000 strong, become more effective, or less so, when shorn of their annual intake of some 200,000-plus conscripts? Will the end of national service add to unemployment? Will there be enough volunteers for the new schemes to succeed? And can they help to promote ideals of public service?

French society has evolved remarkably since the war, and not only in its prosperity and lifestyles. Human relations have been changing, too. This book has attempted to trace the pattern: the greater freedom for women and young people, the rise of social informality, the less strict climate in education and working life, the sporadic signs of a new spirit of community self-help. Together with this has come a decline in some of France's old sectarian feuds. Catholics and anticlericals are much less at each other's throats. The old ideological dog fights have waned, and so has the militant far Left.

All this might have led, you would think, to a waning of the old French traits built around mistrust and defence of *positions acquises*, and to the rise of a more open society. And in some ways it has. Why, then, do so many respected French pundits, by no means all on the Left, still wring their hands at what they see as the stubborn persistence of the national failings that create the so-called '*société bloquée*'? Maybe they exaggerate, focusing on French faults that are simply part of the human condition: other nations too, Britain included, have their full share of vested interests, clumsy bureaucrats and class divisions. In a confused situation today, French society seems to have evolved much more in some ways than in others. Personal attitudes and lifestyles have changed; there is more informality and freedom. But, despite reform, many out-of-date regulations and routines persist; and so do the closely guarded privileges of a stratified society. Some closed shops, such as those of the printers' union, are breaking down under the impact of technical change: but others, like those of chemists and Paris taxi drivers, stay in place. Society is still too corporatist, as each body protects itself from its rivals: thus teachers still have little contact with the world outside their own. And in the public utilities now affected by deregulation, staff are fighting with some success to keep their special status. Change of these structures is coming, slowly, but it lags behind economic change.

In certain public bodies and large firms, the *droits acquis* are still very strong. These are the corporate privileges that employees have steadily acquired and cling to doggedly.* They may include special pension or holiday rights, or rigid salary grades and rights of promotion based on length of service. Notably, this is so in the big savings banks, and in the state electricity and railways. And it can make it harder for a firm to modernize: thus computerization plans were badly delayed in some banks, as the new specialist staff required were refused by the unions. Some of these problems have gradually been solved, under the impact of technical change. But even today, in certain state sectors, staff will go on strike if they feel that their *droits acquis* are threatened by reform: hence the recent sharp strikes by airline pilots, railwaymen, postal workers and others. Remarkably, these privileged rebels will often win considerable sympathy from the public – from people who are happy to see a hated Government contested (as under Juppé), or who may simply feel, 'It could be our turn next, so let's show solidarity.' When in 1996 the state-owned Crédit Foncier bank, losing money, threatened major job losses, and the staff in protest held their own managing director hostage, the public cheered them for it.

Over the centuries the French built up a framework where each class,

---

* As François de Closets described in his famous book *Toujours plus!* (1982).

each interest group, had its own position and privileges, many of them defined by written rules or at least by accepted custom. In a nation prone to disorder, this was found to be the best way of avoiding conflict. And it brought a degree of harmony and stability, although the defensive rigidity made change and progress more difficult. The role of the State was to guarantee and defend the interests of each group, even if this meant propping up archaism. Throughout public life, stress was put on juridical texts and defined prerogatives, so that everyone knew what was expected of him: the Code Napoléon, for instance, laid down rules even for the details of family life. The system gave the individual much security; and paradoxically it left him with much freedom, so long as he toed the line. Society had discovered how to steer French creative individualism away from anarchy, without having to draw the reins too tight.

But the system was based also on the mutual mistrust of groups. A Frenchman grew up to look on his neighbour as potentially a selfish and hostile rival who might try to do him down; and laws and privileges existed to protect him. Though he would join vigorously in association with other members of his own trade or social group, this was more for self-defence than out of sentiment or civic duty. There were few organic loyalty groupings between the crucial unit of the family and that of the State. And even towards the State his attitudes were ambivalent. Its agents, the public authorities, were to be evaded or hoodwinked. The rational fear of the hostility of other sections of society was extended, less rationally, to the assumption that the public administration, too, was some malignant rival force, operating on behalf of *les autres*. And from a child's early years, these attitudes were enhanced by an educational system that offered him little practical training in group responsibility.

This climate of mistrust may have been waning under modern conditions. But it remains quite strong, especially in cities, where it has served to inhibit community life in the new suburbs. A stranger still tends to be treated warily as a potential enemy until proved a friend (just as the law gets distorted into treating you as guilty till proved innocent). So it is endlessly necessary to chat people up, so as to overcome their instinctive initial suspicion – a tedious process. One example: in Britain, if an acquaintance has changed his address and you do not know the new one, you ring up and probably the new tenant or owner will help. In France, he is more likely to say, 'I'm sorry, I don't know his new number.' Probably, the previous resident has been wary of giving such details to a stranger. Happily, this spirit of suspicion is now less evident among younger people.

A new generation has also been growing impatient with the French legalistic spirit, which is rooted deep in history and pervades so much of life. Not only are the laws complex, but the French, if less than the Germans, are conditioned to thinking in their terms. For example, a famous law of 1901 sanctions privately formed clubs and associations as being *de l'utilité publique* (non-profit-making); and if he wants to start, say, a sports club, a Frenchman will not feel easy until it has been thus regularized. Today the French still feel a need for this framework, yet also a desire to break out of it. Their lives are spent devising ingenious rules, then finding equally cunning ways of evading them – it is the notorious *système D*, a cardinal feature of French life. That is, everyone including officials accepts that red tape can be tacitly ignored from time to time, especially when it is done between pals over a friendly *verre*. A friend of mine with a villa in the Midi applied for electricity to be installed, and was told that it would take years of delay and form-filling – 'But,' said the village mayor, 'there's some old wiring in the vaults of the *mairie*, and my electrician might fix you up if you ask, but keep it quiet.' *Le système D* brings human proportion into inhuman official procedures – but is it the way to run a modern nation in a hi-tech age?

In business terms, the French will not regard a deal as valid unless it has been drawn up in meticulous legal detail. They have little understanding of the British 'gentleman's agreement', since each party to a deal fears, as one manager put it, 'that the other will slyly introduce a fatal comma'. But having codified their agreement, their attitude to it is then very ambivalent. They will continually refer back to these written texts: but they will also feel the need to keep on questioning them, or finding ways round them. The British are content with a much simpler set of rules, which they then stick to without worrying: it is all the difference between a nation with a strict written constitution and one with none at all. So in France there are always two sets of rules, the written ones and the real ones. It is a system that works in practice and is not nearly as dishonest as it may sound. However, it is today contested by the new generations, especially those who have trained in America. Some try to introduce American techniques into their offices. But it can drive them mad, for although attitudes may have changed, the official regulations that govern working life have not been properly updated.

One trait that changes only slowly is the old French dislike of delegation of power, coupled with their fear of informal relations between superiors and subordinates. Work routines and chains of command are thus formalized, to avoid favouritism; and so it becomes hard for anyone in a junior position to act officially on his own initiative, for this means breaking the codes. Michel Crozier has pointed out that the desire to avoid awkward face-to-face confrontations is a common facet of French society and its work relations. This hierarchical pattern, he feels, may have served France in the past: but nowadays it can lead to strain, or make it harder to introduce modern methods, or to put younger people of initiative at middle level, where they are needed. The revolt of May '68 was in part a bid to create a more informal system in offices. It may have eased the old authoritarianism. But, except in a few cases, it has not brought much new sense of team responsibility. The head of an office is still likely to keep the key work and decisions in his own hands, rather than share the load.

This dislike of delegation can extend even to relations between a boss and his secretary. Executives tend to make inadequate use of their secretaries, and will merely offload typing chores, rather than treat them confidentially and give them responsibility. Some will even insist on opening their own mail. Once I sent a crucial express letter to an editor and got no reply: a week later, calling at his office, I found him on holiday and all his letters lying unopened on his desk, including mine: he had ordered his secretary not to touch them. Such habits can help to explain why the French secretary often seems unhelpful to outsiders. If you ring up and the boss is not there, she may well not know his movements. And she will probably be unable to fix an appointment for you, even if you tell her that you know he wants to see you. She behaves, in short, as if her role was to protect him from you. But if she is sourly unhelpful, it is more likely to be her boss's fault: he has simply not given her a chance. Here again, it is true that the pattern is now changing in many modern firms with younger executives.

The old tendency to centralize operates not just at the level of the nation, but even within a firm or office: here it can tend to create a gulf between the dynamic few at the top, who take the decisions, and the frustrated time-serving junior levels. It is strikingly true in ministries and public offices, and in some private companies, too. This hierarchical system has been widely criticized, and sporadic efforts have been made to spread the responsibility. But as Crozier observed to me, the decline in the prestige of authority since 1968 has led in some institutions to a kind of power vacuum: people fail to work well because there is no one to lead them, and they have little tradition of organizing their own group leadership. This is less of a problem in the larger modern firms: but it can be serious in smaller ones or in the public sector.

My book has been full of examples of the energetic pioneers, outside party politics, who pulled France forward in the post-war decades. And constantly I have been struck by the contrast between such individuals, creative and far-sighted, and clumsy officialdom. If they are in public service, then the very weight of the system can act as a stimulating challenge. But most have been in the private sector – either in a commercial field, like Édouard Leclerc or Gilbert Trigano; or in labour relations like Fernand Carayon; or in civic affairs like Hubert Dubedout; or in cultural or social projects like Marie-Andrée Weill-Hallé, champion of birth-control reform. A few have been great civil servants, like Paul Delouvrier. These have been the heroes of my book, and much progress in France has depended on them. But perhaps it has been *too* dependent on this kind of rare individual leader, rather than on wider group effort: if he or she goes, then often the project collapses. And in recent years, few new pioneers of this kind have emerged. Their breed seems to be dying, and they are sorely missed.

French society today is in an uneasy state of transition, full of disparate trends. On the one hand, as many observers note, the French in the past three decades have been growing disenchanted with the old institutions which had long dominated their lives. And not only the political parties suffer: the Church, the army, the trade unions and universities, have all seen their prestige decline, as churches empty and union membership falls. Even *mairies* and local councils are involved, despite the excellent work of some mayors. This general disaffection could be harmful if carried too far. But it does have a positive side. The French may have been retreating into privacy: but they have also been moving sporadically towards the Anglo-American model of voluntary citizen-led ventures. The so-called '*vie associative*', so much talked about, has become more active. And while most of these clubs and societies are for pleasure and recreation – for culture, sport and hobbies – some are for neighbourhood self-help or humanitarian causes. Thus the big national associations, such as *mutuelles*, are losing ground to more local, informal ones. In Marseille I found that some well-to-do families had formed a group to raise money for helping local poorer people and their children, including immigrants.

Parallel to this, however, has come the rise of new kinds of individualism, more autarkic and self-centred, wary alike of institutions and of wider community. Much commented on today by sociologists, this trend is not unique to France: but it seems typically strong among a people noted for their individualism, and it clearly relates to current feelings of insecurity and economic fears. People have been turning back to family, to trusted groups of friends; and they have been creating new personal networks, often scattered, not based on the neighbourhood. A positive aspect of this *repli sur soi* can be the search for personal fulfilment, through a richer private life, love, culture, travel, maybe religion. But there is also the danger that these new groupings can become enclosed, scornful of society, intolerant towards *les autres* and those who are 'different' (the Front National breeds on this trend). The sociologist Pierre Rosanvallon spoke to me of 'the decomposition of society due to technological changes which leave the individual feeling isolated, so he turns to building these new *réseaux*'. Another, Bernard Cathelat, said, 'We are seeing the rise of a new society of clans and tribes – archaic in some ways, very modern in others, kind and loyal to their own members, but suspicious of outsiders. But new neighbourly self-help activities are developing, too, and new forms of community action. The two trends are in parallel – which will win? Both of them reject the old institutions, so society has changed, utterly.' The reliance on personal groupings is in the old French tradition. But if these are no longer balanced by State and institutions, what other community are they to find?

Recent years have seen growing signs that private citizens, with the right lead, have become readier to initiate non-official community projects. It happened in farming soon after the war; and in the 1970s an independent consumer-protection movement took off nationally. Today, in many a suburb or small town, there are new local associations, maybe humanitarian or environmental, aimed at serving the community, and thus balancing the autarkic trend of the 'clans'. It is all very diverse, hard to assess. But one clear advance is that local ventures are no longer so likely to be sabotaged by political infighting, as happened too often in the aftermath of May '68, during the 1970s and early '80s. Citizens would embark on some non-partisan initiative in good faith, for the general good; then some faction, generally of the far Left, would seek to gain control of it, or exploit it politically, or sabotage it for their own reasons.

I have given examples in the environmental crusades of the 1970s, and in Sarcelles and other suburbs. In one, a team of moderate, mainly pro-Socialist doctors embarked on a laudable project for a cooperative health centre. But the Communist-led town council, jealous, managed to kill it: they did not want their rival party to succeed with it and take the credit. In other instances, an arts club or youth centre would be taken over by *gauchistes* and yoked to the cause of *la lutte des classes*. This constant dragging of politics into the non-political would deter many non-partisan people of good will, who either withdrew or were squeezed out, or were forced to take sides and lose credit. Practical local issues were constantly being debated in political terms, rather than on their merits.

During the 1990s this has waned. First, the Communists are now weaker, more diverse and moderate, less geared to this kind of crusade. The *gauchiste* factions, too, are smaller, and keep a lower profile. And the Greens, now in government, are more respectable, and have won wider consensus for many of their causes such as pollution. It is true that the Front National can cause severe local disruption on certain issues: but mostly they run their own ventures and are excluded from joint ones. In general, the French have grown much less politicized – and though this may carry dangers for democratic government, in practical local matters it can often be an asset. The younger generation are today more open-minded, tolerant and pragmatic, compared with those who stormed the barricades thirty years ago.

In sum, I am less pessimistic than many French about the state of France today. The nation has come a long way. It is more modern, and better equipped to face the new challenges, than it often realizes. And it may have done better than it thinks in adapting to modern change while keeping the best of its traditions. Thirty years ago, in the flush of material modernization, there were many who feared that France was growing too Americanized in its styles and habits (witness the franglais craze): 'Are we becoming Americans?' was the theme of many an article. But the worst has not happened. When a nation modernizes, it cannot help copying the Americans to an extent, for they got there first; and much of France's hectic 'Americanization' was just that. Of course some anxious voices are still raised, notably over culture: Jack Lang made a famous speech in Mexico in 1982, when he called for a worldwide 'crusade' against 'American financial and intellectual terrorism that no longer grabs territory, but grabs consciousness, ways of thinking, of living'. He and others were worried about the invasion of cheap American commercial culture in the media, and he was one of those most doubtful about the Disneyland project. But since then the French have taken stronger steps to protect and subsidize their heritage: and this is right, for culture is not a commodity to be left to the savage laws of the market. Of course French cultural chauvinism can also be unattractive. But the French today seem to have struck a balance: in the serious performing arts, the scene is far more international and outward-looking than it once was.

On a material level, the French have in many respects modernized successfully. They have adjusted to new lifestyles while adding a French flavour; or they have taken foreign concepts and transmuted them, as often in their history. True, the process is uneven. *MacDo* on the Champs-Élysées is not a happy sight: but for its cousin *le drugstore*, the French borrowed an American term and American formula of multi-purpose boutiques, and turned them into a novelty, half vulgar, half chic, that owed more to Paris than to any Main Street chemist's. From Japan they have now adapted the utility motel, very cheap and basic but super-efficient: e.g. the new Formule 1 and FastHotel chains (*c.* 130 to 150 francs per double room). So, travelling around France, you can find a country that is very modern but in its own style, a blend of the native and imported, the new and traditional. Of course a motorway or skyscraper is much the same in any land: but with the help of foreign architects, the French have now produced some striking and ambitious new buildings, in central Paris and elsewhere, from the Pompidou Centre to the Stade de France. The La Villette complex especially, with its centres for music and science, typifies the continued French ability to innovate imaginatively. And so, in a different field, does Club Med.

Inevitably, France has lost some of its old picturesqueness – what modern country has not? But the environment is now being protected more effectively. And the French can still show a flair for giving a phoenix-like rebirth to the picturesque in a bright new dress. A bizarre but apt example is the *pissotière* (its official name, *la vespasienne*, came from its invention by the emperor Vespasian). For a century these rough male toilets, mostly iron shacks, adorned the pavements and squares of Paris and other towns. Conservationists found them quaintly French, mild stench and all: others tried repeatedly to get them removed, as unworthy of the new France. Finally, Mayor Chirac decreed death to

Paris's 300 surviving ones, and in their place have come super-hygienic unisex contraptions, *les sanisettes*. Special water music plays as you do nature's duty, then all is flushed clean by automated machines. A genuine French invention, apparently.

So the new France can reinvent the lavatory: but it has shown less success at reinventing the novel, the play or great painting. For some years now, individual creative culture has been at a low ebb – disturbing to those who believe in France as '*la mère des arts*'. The theatre turns to clever gimmicks; intellectual life is dazzle more than substance; there are no important new philosophers. Britain today may be more fertile: but what of Germany or Italy? Maybe the French cultural staleness is part of a general staleness of the West in this age of mass media and technology; and maybe it seems most severe in France in contrast to her past brilliance. This is an epoch that favours individual creative power less than the spreading of culture to new audiences – and here France is full of impressive activity.

Social and private life have evolved radically over the past thirty years, towards more informality, more freedom: the old stifling rigidities of family life, described by Mauriac or de Beauvoir, have been losing their grip. Yet the family remains important as a sure value. And many of the major traits in the French personality survive, for better or worse. The French are still argumentative, hedonistic, highly competitive, full of energy, also often egotistical, and some are downright bigoted. But they keep their immense wit and style, their sense of quality, their enthusiasm for new ideas and projects (witness their attitude to the Channel Tunnel as compared with Britain's). And they still combine a love of novelty with a love of tradition (just as, in politics, they are conservatives with a cult of revolution). Recently, they have been turning back to their own traditions: hence the return to rural roots, the revival of interest in cuisine, the renewal of folk cultures, the eager new concern for local history. A book such as *Montaillou*, Le Roy Ladurie's scholarly account of medieval life in a Cathar village, sold well over a million copies.

For this kind of nostalgia to go too far could be harmful: it could even draw France back towards the decadent pre-war mood. It is clearly an aspect of the *repli sur soi* that has been a theme of this book, as the worried French turn to security and personal enrichment. Their *morosité* may have real causes: but it is probably exaggerated, nor is it new. Theodore Zeldin wrote in *Time* magazine (15 June 1988):

After listening to what the French say about themselves, it is hard to decide whether this is a country moving towards suicide, or a country very successfully managing change behind a smokescreen of complaints. I, for one, think the patient has nothing more than a headache and a case of amnesia . . . Everyone repeats that France is in crisis, several different crises. But they seem to forget that this has always been true, or that France's identity has always been contradictory: at once generous and cruel, brilliant and sordid, disputatious, undefinable.

Today there are several main question marks over the future. First, can the faith of the French in their politicians and other leaders be adequately restored, after a dour period? If not, democracy could suffer – and the Front National has already brought strains. The French have always been critical of their leaders, as de Gaulle found: this is not in itself unhealthy, but recently it has got out of hand. Much now will depend on whether Jospin and his team continue to present an image of competence and honesty, after the cynical Mitterrand years; also on whether the new Alliance can revive the centre-Right; and on whether the examining magistrates' exposure of corruption will have taught politicians and business leaders an effective lesson. France is basically very stable, politically. It has benefited recently from the decline of archaic Stalinism in the PCF, plus the success of normal alternation of power. Between classic Right and Left the old destructive polarization has waned, and a degree of consensus has grown. But today far-Right extremism is a greater threat than the old extremism of the far Left. And maybe only a more effective leadership on the centre-Right, plus more effective social policies, can woo a minority of sickened, frustrated French voters away from the lure of the Front.

Secondly, will the flight from institutions, and from established patterns of society, lead to greater egotism and conflict, or to the growth of new forms of positive community action? It is a complex issue. On the one side, French individualism seems to have been reasserting itself as people turn to private fulfilments. In many ways this is positive. But what if the so-called 'ghetto' mentality grows, too, based on intolerance towards *les autres*? – The rise of youth gangs and Front-led racism are the most ferocious examples of a trend of social 'parcellization', noted by sociologists. On the other hand, will there be an increase in civic self-help initiatives, and non-sectarian community associations? The trend is visible, in the new *vie associative* of the suburbs and some environmental projects. But to the French, with their *étatiste* traditions, it does not always come easily.

Thirdly, in the new global village that is our planet, can the French succeed in doing what they would really like best, to find some middle way between their old safe state-led 'model' and the open world market, with all its risks yet advantages? The issue of deregulation versus public services lies at the heart of this dilemma, which also goes wider and is basic to the question of French identity. The French way of doing things and seeing things – the French model, if you like – has many strengths which the world has admired, even copied: can these be adapted, so that the best in them is kept? Among scores of examples, I could mention three. In farming, large-scale industrial agriculture has arrived, and it has its value: but alongside it, can there still be a place for that crucial feature of France, the old human-scale family farm? So long as it adapts to new specialized quality production, maybe it can survive. In culture, are the French not right to insist on public patronage, even some protectionism, rather than leave all exposed to the cruel winds of free trade? And as for the role of women: while the American-led trend in the West today is against so-called sexism, the French still uphold a different model, which French women themselves seem to cherish. The late Jean-Marie Domenach, a respected intellectual, wrote in his *Regarder la France: essais sur le malaise français* (1996):

If the masculinization of women wins the day, the keystone of French civilization will have gone . . . It is in the loving practice of sexuality that the model and the test of difference . . . lie . . . that elegance of body and mind which is the mark of what has received in France the name of civilization.

Vive, then, not only *la petite différence* but the entire *exception française*?

The French have been talking much recently about this *exception française*, and whether it is under threat. Yet, for all their special qualities, they have no right to think of themselves as unique. De Gaulle used to see *la France* as some mystical chosen land: since then, like him, her politicians have stubbornly pursued national interests when it suits them, but perhaps less than the British. Mostly, the French are very ready to cooperate internationally, and to adapt – more so than their neighbour with its *exception britannique*. Witness the 'Schengen' open frontiers: France, after doubt and delay, has adapted to the scheme, except along the Belgian border, whereas Britain still refuses to join at all. Today the French, like other peoples, want to preserve their traditions as much as possible: they have been managing quite well, with the needed compromises, and only a few want to close frontiers. The talk about *l'exception française* is often ironical: it is like speaking of 'true British grit'.

And the French have so much to contribute. In Europe they are strongly placed. Some practical doubts may have been felt: but the vast majority accept that their future is in a united Europe, from which they have gained a lot and still have much to gain. Some pundits may worry about *l'identité nationale*, but this is more a theme of debate than a real public anxiety (save maybe for Front supporters). Most French are concerned above all to enjoy a good and secure life, to see an easing of social problems, in a France open to the world. The nation is agreeably international and outward-looking, yet still delightfully French. More than most peoples in Europe, it brings a vast heritage of wisdom, taste and humanism to the task of preserving the best of the past so as to marry it with the future. The French may have reason, like us all, to worry about that future. Yet their recent self-doubts about their own society have been excessive. They have so many assets. To misquote de Gaulle, France in the 1990s lost a few battles, with its social and political problems and its self-esteem. It has not lost any war, for its own destiny or for Europe's.

BIBLIOGRAPHY

GENERAL AND POLITICAL

Michel Crozier, *The Bureaucratic Phenomenon*, Tavistock Press, 1964

Michel Crozier, *La Crise de l'intelligence*, InterÉditions, 1995

Michel Crozier, *On ne change pas la société par décret*, Grasset, 1979

Patrick Devedjian, *Le Temps des juges*, Flammarion, 1996

Jean-Marie Domenach, *Regarder la France: essais sur le malaise français*, Perrin, 1996

J.-B. Duroselle, François Goguel, Stanley Hoffmann, Charles Kindleberger, Jesse Pitts, Laurence Wylie, *France: Change and Tradition*, Harvard University Press, 1963

Pierre Favier, Michel Martin-Roland, *La Décennie Mitterrand*, Le Seuil, 1990

Robert Gildea, *France since 1945*, Oxford University Press, 1996

R. W. Johnson, *The Long March of the French Left*, Macmillan, 1981

Jacques Julliard, *La Faute aux élites*, Gallimard, 1997

Serge July, *Les Années Mitterrand*, Grasset, 1986

Herbert Lüthy, *The State of France*, Secker and Warburg, 1953

Gérard Mermet, *Francoscopie*, Larousse, 1997, 1998

Alain Minc, *Au nom de la loi*, Gallimard, 1998

Henri Nallet, *Tempête sur la justice*, Plon, 1992

Catherine Nay, *Les Sept Mitterrand*, Grasset, 1988

Alain Peyrefitte, *Le Mal français*, Plon, 1976

Robert Picht, Jacques Leenhardt (editors), *Au jardin des malentendus: le commerce franco-allemand des idées*, Babel, 1997

Guy Sorman, *Le Bonheur français*, Fayard, 1996

Alain Touraine, *Le Mouvement de mai ou le communisme utopique*, Le Seuil, 1968

Pierre Viannson-Ponté, *Histoire de la République gaullienne*, 2 vols, Fayard, 1970–71

Theodore Zeldin, *The French*, Collins, 1983

ECONOMY AND INDUSTRY

François de Closets, *Toujours plus!*, Grasset, 1982
Jean-Paul Fitoussi, Pierre Rosanvallon, *Le Nouvel Âge des inégalités*, Le Seuil, 1996
Viviane Forrester, *L'Horreur économique*, Fayard, 1996
J.-A. Kosciusko-Morizet, *La 'Mafia' polytechnicienne*, Le Seuil, 1973
Alain Minc, *La France de l'an 2000*, Odile Jacob, 1994
Jean-Jacques Servan-Schreiber, *The American Challenge*, Hamish Hamilton, 1968
Christian Stoffaës, *Services publics, question d'avenir*, Odile Jacob, 1995
INSEE, *Tableaux de l'économie française, 1997–8*

SOCIETY AND URBAN LIFE

Gérard Alezard and others, *Faut-il réinventer le syndicalisme?*, L'Archipel, 1995
Marc Bernard, *Sarcellopolis*, Flammarion, 1964
Jean Boissonnat, *Le Travail dans vingt ans*, Odile Jacob, 1995
Bernard Cathelat and others, *Le Retour des clans*, Denoël, 1997
Alec Hargreaves, *Immigration, 'Race' and Ethnicity in Contemporary France*, Routledge, 1995
Béatrice Majnoni d'Intignano, *La Protection sociale*, Le Livre de Poche, 1993
Henri Mendras, *La Seconde Révolution française*, Gallimard, 1994
Alain Minc, *La Machine égalitaire*, Grasset, 1987

REGIONS AND PARIS

Antony Beevor and Artemis Cooper, *Paris after the Liberation*, Hamish Hamilton, 1994
Pierre Frappat, *Grenoble, le mythe blessé*, Alain Moreau, 1979
J.-F. Gravier, *Paris et le désert français en 1972*, Flammarion, 1972
Pierre-Jakez Hélias, *The Horse of Pride*, Yale University Press, 1980
Jérôme Monod, *Transformation d'un pays*, Fayard, 1974
Edgar Morin, *Plodémet*, Allen Lane, 1971

AGRICULTURE AND RURAL LIFE

John Ardagh, *Rural France*, Century, 1983
Michel Debatisse, *La Révolution silencieuse*, Calmann-Lévy, 1963

Bertrand Hervieu, *Les Champs du futur*, Julliard, 1994

Raymond Lacombe, *Un combat pour la terre*, Rouergue, 1992

Danièle Léger and Bertrand Hervieu, *Le Retour à la nature*, Le Seuil, 1979

Peter Mayle, *A Year in Provence*, Hamish Hamilton, 1989

Gillian Tindall, *Célestine*, Sinclair-Stevenson, 1995

Gordon Wright, *Rural Revolution in France*, Oxford, 1964

Laurence Wylie, *Village in the Vaucluse*, Harrap, 1961

PRIVATE AND LEISURE LIFE

Simone de Beauvoir, *The Second Sex*, Cape, 1953; Penguin, 1974

Étiemble, *Parlez-vous franglais?*, Gallimard, 1964

Robert Rochefort, *La Société des consommateurs*, Odile Jacob, 1995

Dr Pierre Simon, *Rapport sur le comportement sexuel des Français*, Julliard, 1972

Philip Thody and Howard Evans, *Faux Amis and Key Words*, Athlone, 1985

Service des droits des femmes, *Les Femmes*, INSEE, 1995

ARTS AND INTELLECTUALS

Roland Barthes, *Critique et vérité*, Le Seuil, 1966

Régis Debray, *Le Pouvoir intellectuel en France*, Ramsay, 1979

François Dosse, *L'Empire du sens*, La Découverte, 1997

Michel Foucault, *Le Mots et les choses*, Gallimard, 1966; *The Order of Things*, Tavistock, 1970

André Glucksmann, *Les Maîtres penseurs*, 1977

Michel Houellebecq, *Whatever (Extension du domaine de la lutte)*, Serpent's Tail, 1999

Michel Houellebecq, *Les Particules élémentaires*, Flammarion, 1998

Bernard-Henri Lévy, *La Barbarie à visage humain*, 1977

Olivier Mongin, *Face au scepticisme*, La Découverte, 1994

Pascal Ory, Jean-François Sirinelli, *Les Intellectuels en France, de l'affaire Dreyfus à nos jours*, Armand Colin, 1987

Jean-François Revel, *La Cabale des dévôts*, Julliard, 1962

Georges Suffert, *Les Intellectuels en chaise longue*, Plon, 1974

ACKNOWLEDGEMENTS

For this book and for its predecessors, many hundreds of people gave up their time to help me with my field research. In many cases they were generously hospitable. I cannot mention them all by name. But I should like first to mention some friends who were especially kind and helpful: *In Paris*: Robert and Judith Cottave and family, Yves and Ghislaine Gonssard, Brigitte Marger, Claire and Jean-Baptiste Touchard. *In the provinces*: Christine Brooke-Rose, Henry and Alice Delisle, Henri Nallet, Catherine and Pierre-Yves Péchoux, Morley and Shula Troman.

My special thanks go also to:

Politics and general: Jacques Chirac; the late François Mitterrand and his staff at the Élysée in 1981–95, notably Jean-Louis Bianco; Valéry Giscard d'Estaing and his staff at the Élysée in 1974–81; Alain Lamassoure, Vincent Labouret; Martine Aubry, Pierre Mauroy, Michel Rocard, Dominique Strauss-Kahn, Elisabeth Guigou; Pierre Blotin, Pierre Juquin, Lucien Sève; Antoine Marger; Michel Crozier, René Rémond, Henri Mendras, Pierre Rosanvallon, Alain de Vulpian, Bernard Cathelat.

Economy: Michel Albert, Jean Wahl, Bernard Cazes, Alain Madelin, Jacques Dondoux, Christian Stoffaës, Jean Cottave; Denis Kessler, Emmanuel Julien, Jérôme Monod; Patrick Bessy and his colleagues at Renault; Paul Busquet de Caumont; Jean-Paul Constantin, Jean-Pierre Salzmann of INSEAD; François de Closets, Peter Ricketts, Robert Fitchett, David Andrews, Antoine Cuvelier; Bernard McCoy, Peter Mills, John D. Noulton.

Society: Gérard Alezard, Jean-Claude Mailly, Matilda Hartwell, Hubert Martin; Jean-Pierre Duport and his staff at Bobigny; Éric Raoult; Michèle Tribala, Philippe Bernard, Jean-Marie Delarue, Alec Hargreaves.

Regions: Raymond-Max Aubert, Denis Cauchois and their colleagues at DATAR, Jacques Voisard, Catherine Gremion, François Grossrichard.

Agriculture: Édith Cresson, Edgar Pisani, Jean-Claude Pichon, Bertrand Hervieu, Jean-Claude Trunel; Raymond Lacombe, André Valadier, Daniel Crozes; François and Jeannine Brager, Philippe and Catherine Galzin, Jean-Pierre Le Verge.

Arts and intellectuals: Jack Lang, Claude Mollard, Yves Mabin, Gilles Chouraqui, Jean-Pierre Angrémy; Tristan Lecoq; Hugues Gall, Ariel Goldenberg, Georges Lavaudant, Ariane Mnouchkine, Frédéric Ferney; Bertrand Tavernier, Daniel Toscan du Plantier, Arnaud Desplechin, Cédric Klapisch, Florence Moncorgé, Michel Simon; Jacques Rigaud, Patrick Poivre d'Arvor, Michèle Cotta, Jean-Pierre Elkabbach; Luc de La Barre de Nanteuil, Olivier Chevrillon, Georges Suffert, Jean Schmitt, Alain Dauvergne and others of my former colleagues at *Le Point*; Denis Jeambar; Bernard Brigouleix, Michel Roland-Martin; Pierre Nora, Olivier Mongin, François Jullien. David Ricks and his colleagues at the British Council.

Education: François Crouzet, Mireille and Henri Quéré, René Haby, Claude Thélot, Hélène Mathieu.

Private and leisure life: Jacques Duquesne, Robert Rochefort, Henry Dougier; Dr Pierre Simon; Philippe Ravanas and others of Disneyland Paris; Michel-Édouard Leclerc; Henri Gault, Paul Levy, Gilles Pudlowksi, Guy Savoy; Gilbert Trigano, Serge Trigano, Philippe Bourguignon, Constance Perrin, Isabelle Desmet; the staff of INSEE.

In the regions:

Paris: Jean-Yves Autexier, Georges Sarre, Georges Mesmin, Claude Comiti, Fouad Awada, M. Berteaux.

Brittany: Édouard and Marianne Leclerc; Edmond Hervé, Pierre Méhaignerie, Claude Champaud, Antoine de Tarlé; Alexis Gourvennec, Christian Michaelini; the Pilpré and Bousquet families, Yvonne Le Goaziou.

Normandy: Frédéric and Diana Delouche, Jean Lepetit, René Garrec.

Nantes: Jean-Marc Ayrault and his staff at the *mairie*; Paul Chevilliet; *Angers:* Jean-François Dreyfus.

Alsace, Strasbourg: Catherine Trautmann and her former colleagues in the *mairie*; Adrien Zeller, Daniel Hoeffel; Yvan Blot; Vincent Froelicher, Luc Gwiazdzinki, Gilbert Hadey; Sabine Rollberg, Dominique Bromberger and their colleages at Arte; Roger Beetham. *Burgundy:* Jean-Michel Bossard, Jean Durup, Gérard Arnouts, Francis Chouville, Abbé Gailledrat. *Loiret:* Jacques and Dominique Goût, Jacques Denis-Le-Sève.

Grenoble: the late Hubert Dubedout; Michel Destot and his colleagues

at the *mairie*, notably Maude Cottave; Louis Ratel, Guy Saez, Pierre Frappat, André and Chantal Veyrat; Alain Carignon.
Lyon: André Soulier, Maurice Charrier, Régis Neyret, Xavier Ellie, Bruno Caussé, Bernard Villeneuve; Brian Pullen; Paul Bocuse; Yan Le Bohec, Jacques Bonnet.
Languedoc: Georges Frêche, Raymond Dugrand, Marie-France Dewaest, Daniel Parent and their colleagues at the *mairie* of Montpellier; Jean Joubert, Magnus Hutchins; Jean-Philippe Granier, Peter Prowse.
Provence: Fernand Carayon, Marc Leduc, Bruno Anthony.
Toulouse and South-West: Dominique Baudis, Michel Valdiguié and their colleagues at the *mairie*; Michel Plasson, Denis Milhau, Stéphane Thépot, Roger Virnuls. *La Rochelle, Poitou:* Michel Crépeau and his staff at the *mairie*; Robert Kalbach; Hélène and François Levieux.

Europe and the world: Jacques Delors; Christopher Mallaby, Michael Jay and their colleagues at the Embassy in Paris, notably Michael Arthur, Vincent Fean, Tim Livesey; Robert Picht and his colleagues in Stuttgart; Jacques Viot, Jean-Marie Le Breton, Christopher Johnson, Peter Petrie, Ann Kenrick and their colleagues on the Franco-British Council; Dominique David.

In Paris, friends I should like to thank include: Jean-Philippe and Martine Atger, Claude and Christine Benoît, John Calder, Jean-Michel Catala, Guy and Chantal Carron de la Carrière, Diana Geddes, Michelle and René Lapautre, André and Sibylle Zavriew.

In London: Jean Guéguinou and his colleagues at the French Embassy, notably Charles Fries, Gabriel Keller; Olivier Poivre d'Arvor, René Lacombe, Geraldine di Amico and their colleagues; Angela Lambert, Gerald Clark, John Sidgwick, Vivienne Menkès-Ivry, Munro Price, Nicholas Snowman; Gillian Green and others at the French Government Tourist Office; Toby Oliver and others at Brittany Ferries; Patrice de Beer; Bernard Lebrun, Joëlle Gee and others at France 2 television; Anne and Graham Corbett, Jean-Pierre Perier, Marie-Hélène Gastineau; the staff of the Kensington and Chelsea Borough Library.

Above all, my thanks must go to *Le Monde*'s Editor, Jean-Marie Colombani, and many of his colleagues, who gave up their time, and whose articles in that great newspaper have provided me with endless background information and insights. I should also thank my editors Peter Carson, Juliet Annan and Hannah Robson and others at Penguin Books; also Perrine Simon-Nahum of Flammarion. And my wife Katinka, who gave continual help and encouragement.

INDEX

Principal references appear in italics.